John Updike

Recent Titles in
Bibliographies and Indexes in American Literature

Bibliography of the Little Golden Books
Dolores B. Jones, compiler

A Chronological Outline of American Literature
Samuel J. Rogal, compiler

Humor of the Old Southwest: An Annotated Bibliography
of Primary and Secondary Sources
Nancy Snell Griffith, compiler

Images of Poe's Works: A Comprehensive Descriptive Catalogue
of Illustrations
Burton R. Pollin, compiler

Through the Pale Door: A Guide to and through the
American Gothic
Frederick S. Frank

The Robert Lowell Papers at the Houghton Library,
Harvard University
Patrick K. Miehe, compiler

Bernard Malamud: A Descriptive Bibliography
Rita N. Kosofsky

A Tale Type and Motif Index of Early U.S. Almanacs
J. Michael Stitt and Robert K. Dodge

Jerzy Kosinski: An Annotated Bibliography
Gloria L. Cronin and Blaine H. Hall

James Fenimore Cooper: An Annotated Bibliography of Criticism
Alan Frank Dyer, compiler

Ralph Waldo Emerson: An Annotated Bibliography of Criticism,
1980–1991
Robert E. Burkholder and Joel Myerson, compilers

John Updike
A Bibliography, 1967–1993

Compiled by
Jack De Bellis

Foreword by John Updike

Bibliographies and Indexes in American Literature, Number 17

Greenwood Press
Westport, Connecticut • London

Library of Congress Cataloging-in-Publication Data

De Bellis, Jack.
　　John Updike : a bibliography, 1967–1993 / compiled by Jack De Bellis ; foreword by John Updike.
　　　　p.　cm.—(Bibliographies and indexes in American Literature, ISSN 0742–6860 ; no. 17)
　　Includes index.
　　ISBN 0–313–28861–5 (alk. paper)
　　1. Updike, John—Bibliography.　I. Title.　II. Series.
Z8913.85.D4　1994
[PS3571.P4]
016.813'54—dc20　　　　93–28538

British Library Cataloguing in Publication Data is available.

Copyright © 1994 by Jack De Bellis

All rights reserved. No portion of this book may be reproduced, by any process or technique, without the express written consent of the publisher.

Library of Congress Catalog Card Number: 93-28538
ISBN: 0–313–28861–5
ISSN: 0742–6860

First published in 1994

Greenwood Press, 88 Post Road West, Westport, CT 06881
An imprint of Greenwood Publishing Group, Inc.

Printed in the United States of America

∞™

The paper used in this book complies with the Permanent Paper Standard issued by the National Information Standards Organization (Z39.48—1984).

10 9 8 7 6 5 4 3 2

For Patty, who knows how to conjugate the verb to be.

Contents

Foreword by John Updike	ix
Preface	xi
Acknowledgments	xv
I. Works by Updike	
1. *Books*	1
2. *Plays*	29
3. *Short Fiction*	31
4. *Poetry*	45
5. *Articles and Essays*	65
6. *Reviews*	87
7. *Interviews*	113
8. *Letters, Manuscripts*	121
9. *Translations by Updike*	125
10. *Graphics and Readings*	127
II. Works about Updike	
1. *General Commentary*	135
2. *Criticism of Individual Works*	169
3. *Other Media*	231
4. *Dissertations and Theses*	237
5. *Parodies and Caricatures*	249
Appendix I. *Translations of Updike's Work*	253
Appendix II. *Periodicals in Which Updike Has Published*	271
Index	275

Foreword
by John Updike

    Bibliographer De Bellis's invitation to add to the already bulky front matter of his giant scholarly work meets in me a certain skepticism. Must I orate at my own funeral? I seem to have reached in my career a terminal phase of tidying-up; in my recent *Collected Poems* I did much dating and alphabetizing, with the usual anal satisfactions that the conscientious researcher and accountant feel. Bibliography, though--especially the listing of reviews and interviews, most of which I would prefer to forget--I have happily left to others, and must from a distance marvel at their zeal and method, which in Mr. De Bellis's case has taken him into the maze of *The New Yorker*'s archives, to ferret out anonymous material he could have compiled from my own tearsheets, had I thought it wise to admit so fierce a researcher to my fragile castle keep. Surely a writer should properly face forward, to the words he has not yet written, rather than backwards, to those he has put behind him. Of course, his old words continue to echo in his ears, as he reads them from academic platforms, confronts them in critical reprises, and seeks to eliminate thirty-year-old typos from new editions. Among the mysterious utilizers of Professor De Bellis's mighty work I expect to number myself, as occasion arises, and for this I thank him, as well as for the very generous interest he has taken over the years in my work.

    What a solemn if not quite ghastly sensation it is, glancing into such a compilation and finding that not even my few published drawings and the announcement of my wedding in my home-town paper have escaped the bibliographer's eagle eye! Are no secrets to be left me at all? Since privacy and secrets are the author's base of operations and his lode of treasure, it is alarming to see my life's loot here so systematically paraded. Yet even the omnivorous De Bellis has missed, I believe, my one formal contribution to my own bibliography, a published letter to the *Bulletin of Bibliography* (Westport, Connecticut) which I hereby in conclusion include:

December 17, 1989

Dear Gentlemen:

    I was entertained, four years ago, by Stuart Wright's bibliography of my Shillington High School *Chatterbox* contributions from 1945 to 1950. In those same years, however, I was sending out contributions to magazines whose addresses I culled either from the local newsstands or a book of periodicals' addresses in my mother's possession. I had small success, but my mother's recent death returned to me a file in which all (I believe) of my acceptances were retained, and for some reason I feel compelled, before these antique magazines again pass out of my possession, to make a bibliographical note of them. C. Clarke Taylor's *John Updike: A Bibliography* (The Kent State University Press, 1968) mentions a few of them, but most eluded his research. All the pieces are poems, light verse mostly, and I believe that, except for five or ten dollars for the poem in *National Parent-Teacher*, my only reward was seeing them in print, such as it was in these modestly budgeted publications.

Reflections, Vol. XV, no. 11-12, November-December, 1948. Poem, "It Might Be Verse," p. 10.

The American Courier, Vol. 10, no. 7, issue 134, July 1st, 1949. Poem, "I Want a Lamp," p. 11.

National Parent-Teacher: The P.T.A. Magazine, Vol. XLIV, February 1950. Poem, "The Boy Who Makes the Blackboard Squeak," p. 39.

Reflections, Vol. XVII, no. 3, March-April 1950, 1948. Poem, "To a Bottle of Serutan." p. 9.

The American Courier, Vol. 11, no. 10, issue 149, October 1st, 1950. Poem "Evangelist, p. 36.

Florida Magazine of Verse, Vol. XI, no. 1, November, 1950. Poems [under "Light Verse"] "Move Over, Dodo" and "The Last Word."

Reflections, Vol. XVII, no. 5, Holiday Issue. Poem, "Microphone." p. 4.

Different, Vol. 6, no. 5, November-December 1950. Poem, "The Lonely One," p. 7.

American Weave, Vol. XIX, no. 1, [no date, but copyright 1954]. Poem, "Astronomer, in Love," p. 22.

Preface

Compiling a list of works by and about John Updike is a sobering task. Updike's writing is so prolific, his sources of publication so numerous, his special printings so many and various, and the commentary of reviewers and scholars in newspapers and learned journals so copious as to defy the most intrepid bibliographer. Moreover, Updike's passion for accuracy is well-known, and it sets a very high standard against which any work about him, particularly a bibliography, is inevitably judged.

So one must be humble to embark on a bibliography of John Updike; if humility is not brought in advance, it arrives eventually, along with the excitement of discovery. The humility and the joy are provided by two points which inform all Updike bibliographies: his career-long contributions to *The New Yorker* since he began writing for it in 1954; and his very personal guardianship of his published work seen in his assiduous revising and reprinting of essays, reviews, poems, stories and novels.

The New Yorker's policy of printing unsigned "Talk of the Town" items and brief reviews— "Casuals" and "Brieflies" in *New Yorker* parlance— creates detective problems for the seeker of Updike contributions. Although Updike has given approximate dates for some of the short pieces included in his four collections of essays and reviews, the magazine does not file them under Updike's name, a problem that persists in the 1991 "anatomy" of *The New Yorker* on computer disk. Discovering his authorship can thus require exploration of old payment invoices, among other things. For most "Casuals" I have used the titles adopted by Updike in his collections, but for uncollected items I have used the first words of the piece or a catchword to facilitate the reader's identification of them.

The second and more complex problem for bibliographers resides in Updike's tireless revising of his work. Some dazzled readers acquainted with what he refers to as his "oeuvre" tend to imagine that Updike is rather like Mozart, that his pristine hard copy goes unaltered from his mind to his publishers. In fact, like other writers, Updike has known moments of such Mozartean composition, as his remarks on the composition of "Seagulls" reveal, some of his works go unretouched from their inception, like ice cubes that "slide on their own melting," as he once quoted Robert Frost. But examination of his manuscripts, typescripts, and proofs— many of which are listed here— mix wonder at his achievement with awe at his tenacity, for Updike continues rewriting, revising and reviewing his work even after appearance between hard covers. *The Collected Poems* (1993) shows that even poems already collected were adjusted for punctuation, rhythm and diction. Furthermore, he updates and footnotes his essays and reviews in *Odd Jobs* (1991) while supplying stylistic alterations. He adjusts his stories for greater precision when transferring them to collections like *Trust Me*, or special editions, like the Metacom Press printing of "Brother Grasshopper." No doubt many of these stories will be further changed when he collects his short fiction in the near future. When he finds a story "has legs," as he puts it, a short piece like "Couples" becomes his celebrated novel of that name. His zeal for accuracy has led him to acknowledge minor factual errors in *The Poorhouse Fair* and *Rabbit Is Rich*. He has even observed that he needs to restrain himself from making revisions in his paperback editions, alarmed by any imperfections like typos which may be eliminated in future printing. Naturally, the enthusiasm of Updike collectors (and, in a few cases, pirating publishers) may have contributed to the creation of some special editions, but, clearly, Updike simply refuses to permit his work to go forward without using his blue pencil once more, as shown here in his addition of a phrase in the *Bulletin of Bibliography* letter he included in his "Foreword" to this book.

Such reprintings deserve special bibliographic consideration, as Updike himself shows in his "Autobibliographical" foreword to *Sixteen Poems* and in his generous indications of the dates of the composition of his poems in an appendix to *Collected Poems*. I have indicated textual changes from one printing to another, and such comparison of texts offers a clear opportunity for critics interested in establishing patterns in Updike's creative process. For such study, the various manuscript repositories in this list will be indispensable. Certainly, those with linguistic facility could carry such analysis into Updike's translations and the translations of his work into a great many languages. My list of translations of Updike's books includes reprintings since these may contain variations unknown to me. I have sought to list Updike's work, as it has been reprinted in anthologies, though a gathering of all such books would make a formidable library, as aggressive collectors like Dr. Jack Hagstrom well appreciate.

This bibliography includes all primary and secondary material which has appeared since 1967, and some items before that date. I have chosen 1967 because that is the last year in which C. Clarke Taylor included material for *John Updike: A Bibliography*. Taylor's work is the last substantial Updike bibliography, though it was followed, naturally, by others. The plan of the bibliography follows Taylor's. Under Part I: "A" I list all works by Updike arranged chronologically in ten chapters, and in Part II: "B" I list in five chapters all items of critical interest, segregating general commentary from work specifically concerned with individual books. Those in group I are listed in the bibliography and in the index as "A" and those in group II as "B." The index is thoroughly cross-referenced by author, title and selected subjects. I have listed (in Appendix I) Updike's work in translation, and in Appendix II I have provided a list of periodicals publishing his work. This appendix is effectively an index to his work published in periodicals since it contains entry numbers from the bibliography. Items not personally inspected are marked with an asterisk (*). Unavoidably, errors have been entombed in this volume, awaiting correction by some future investigator of this vast and imposing terrain of Updikeana.

Taylor was justly praised for listing items from Updike's high school and college years, but he neglected much, inevitably, and made understandable errors. Therefore, I have included items earlier than 1967 that were incorrectly listed or not cited by Taylor, while repeating items he listed which prompted post-1967 reprintings— poems assembled in poetry volumes, stories gathered into various collections and unsigned articles bound into *Talk from the Fifties*, for example. I have listed reviews of films and of audio and video tapes because of the gathering critical concern for Updike's interest in the popular arts, but I have not included reviews of books anthologizing only one or two of his works. I have included Updike's graphic interests— he once aspired to work for Disney as a cartoonist— which may prompt critics to investigate the inter-relation of Updike's visual and verbal arts, perhaps in relation to semiology and structuralism, about which Updike has written. I have incorporated many works in translation, master's and doctoral theses and important newspaper material from the *Reading* (Pa.) *Eagle* and *Times* since Updike and his parents lived near Reading, and he worked for the *Eagle* in the summers of 1950, 1951, and 1952. Since his career was carefully tracked by these newspapers, such items will be useful to biographers responding to Updike's recent decisions to record his history, notably in *Self-Consciousness*. Like the cartoons and drawings Updike produced, the video interviews provide a personal sense of the man who created this world of words.

For both primary and secondary collections I have provided analytical descriptions of the contents of collections and anthologies. I have listed reprints of items by Updike as well as scholarly commentary, since such reprintings may well be useful to those tracing the impact upon the academic community. "A & P" and "Ex-Basketball Player" are routinely used in high schools and colleges, his essays in courses in Freshman Composition, and his reviews of Borges and Nabokov as ancillary reading in courses in modern literature. His inclusions in academic anthologies will help to track his reputation as Updike becomes increasingly consolidated in the American literary canon, a winner of prestigious awards and honors, and a candidate, to many, for the Nobel prize.

Risking redundancy in the cause of greater utility, I have occasionally listed items twice: if a book by Updike contains his foreword it is listed as a book and the "Foreword" is listed under "Articles and Essays." Although I have indicated repositories of Updike's mother's work (Linda Grace Hoyer Updike) which will surely be of concern to future biographers, I have excluded primary and secondary material relating to her fiction and that of Updike's son David, also a professional writer.

I have listed in bold all poems in collections reprinted from Updike's other books, providing some sense of the history of a given text, assisting (in a small way) Updike, who wrote in *Collected Poems*: "My poems are my oeuvre's beloved waifs, and I feared that if I did not perform the elementary bibliographical decencies for them no one would." I hope that my bibliography will prove a decent home for these and other "beloved waifs."

Acknowledgments

If a proverb is the wisdom of many and the wit of one, a bibliography may be the good will of many and the persistence of one. Therefore, I am pleased to acknowledge the generous help I have received from so many kind persons sharing my passion for Updike's writing. The Lehigh University Office of Research provided considerate support for research and indexing; Ms. Ann Cassar proved to be a valedictorian indexer. The Lehigh libraries extended generous aid: Inter-Library Loan of the Fairchild-Martindale Library procured documents, and Philip Metzger, director of Lehigh's Special Collections of Linderman Library, offered a great many kind services and facilitated my inspection of Amherst College's imposing Updike collection, where Mr. John Lancaster of the Frost Library, despite "the blizzard of the century," kindly assisted me. Mrs. June M. Courtney and Mrs. Pam Hehr of the Reading Public Library courteously allowed me to see material Updike had given to his parents. Mr. Charles Gallagher, editor-in-chief of the *Reading Eagle* and *Reading Times*, permitted me to examine the newspapers' private archives, while Professor Paul Schlueter allowed me to rummage in his private files. CNBC generously supplied a tape of an interview, and Updike scholars, Professors Robert Detweiler and Donald Greiner, offered sympathetic collegiality. In its early stages, I received timely help from a talented research assistant, Edyta Oczkowicz, as well as valuable suggestions from editors of *Modern Fiction Studies*, where a selection of this work was first published. Formatting the bibliography for publication would have been impossible without Douglas Reese, a computer sorcerer to whom I played apprentice. Mr. Reese and Mr. Metzger were instrumental in my effort to understand desk-top publishing intricacies that gave me the opportunity to produce an attractive camera-ready book. They enabled me to transfer each chapter from Leading Edge Word Processing to WordPerfect, keyboarding each chapter to WP 5.1 and the index to WP 6.0, select Garamond Antiqua font, and then print the book with the high-resolution HP LaserJet 4. Mr. Updike gave plentiful responses to my enquiries about translations, and of course kindly consented to write the "Foreword" to this book. His generous letter of introduction to *The New Yorker* enabled me to gain the inventive aid of Ms. Truax and Ms. Frisch. To all phases of this project, my wife Patty lent her ready eye and cheerful heart.

I. Works by Updike

1. Books

A1	*Hoping for a Hoopoe.* London: Gollancz, 1959. (Contains a note by Updike not in the American edition.)
A2	*The Poorhouse Fair.* London: Gollancz, 1959.
A3	*Rabbit, Run.* London: Deutsch, 1961.
A4	*The Magic Flute.* N.Y.: Knopf, 1962. (Adaptation.)
A5	*Pigeon Feathers.* London: Deutsch, 1962.
A6	*Rabbit, Run.* Greenwich, Conn.: Fawcett, 1962.
A7	*The Same Door.* London: Deutsch, 1962.
A8	*The Centaur.* London: Deutsch, 1963. (Excerpted in *Montage: Investigations in Language.* Ed. William Sparke and Clark McKowen. N.Y.: Macmillan, 1970. 405-06.)
A9	*Pigeon Feathers.* Greenwich, Conn.: Fawcett, 1963.
A10	*Telephone Poles and Other Poems.* London: Deutsch, 1963.
A11	*Telephone Poles and Other Poems.* N.Y.: Knopf, 1963.
A12	*The Centaur.* Greenwich, Conn.: Fawcett, 1964.
A13	*The Magic Flute.* London: Deutsch, 1964. (Adapted by Updike.)
A14	*The Poorhouse Fair.* Greenwich, Conn.: Fawcett, 1964.
A15	*Rabbit, Run.* Harmondsworth, Middlesex: Penguin, 1964. (The spelling has been Anglicized for this first revised edition.)

A16   *The Ring*. N.Y.: Knopf, 1964.

A17   *The Same Door*. Greenwich, Conn.: Fawcett, 1964.

A18   *Assorted Prose*. London: Deutsch, 1965.

A19   *Assorted Prose*. N.Y.: Knopf, 1965.

A20   *Assorted Prose*. N.Y.: Knopf, 1965. (With an extra signed, tipped-in leaf.)

A21   *A Child's Calendar*. N.Y.: Knopf, 1965. Illustrated by Ekholm Burkert.

A22   *Dog's Death*. Cambridge, Mass.: Adams House and Lowell House, 1965. (Rpt. in *The John Updike Newsletter* 2 Spring 1977: 4. [Signed, limited edition]; in *Midpoint*, N.Y.: Knopf, 1969. 52; in *Poetspeak*. Ed. Paul Janeczko. Brandbury P, 1983. 184; and in *Collected Poems: 1953-1993*. N.Y.: Knopf, 1993. 51.)

A23   *Of the Farm*. London: Deutsch, 1965.

A24   *Pigeon Feathers*. Harmondsworth, Middlesex: Penguin, 1965.

A25   *The Poorhouse Fair* (fourth printing, revised) and *Rabbit, Run*. (fifth edition, revised). N.Y.: Modern Library, 1965, with an unpaginated "Foreword" by Updike.

A26   *Verse*. Greenwich, Conn.: Fawcett Premier, 1965. (Rpt. from *The Carpentered Hen And Other Tame Creatures*. N.Y.: Harper's, 1958, with revision of "Vacuum Cleaner." Poems reprinted are: **"Duet, with Muffled Brake Drums," "Ex-Basketball Player," "Player Piano" "Shipbored," "An Ode," "The Clan," "Why the Telephone Wires Dip and the Poles Are Cracked and Crooked,"** "The Population of Argentina," "Even Egrets Err," "Scenic," "Tune, in American Type," "Lament, for Cocoa," "Recitative for Punished Products," "V. B. Nimble, V. B. Quick," "Song of the Open Fireplace," "March: A Birthday Poem," "Sunflower," "Poetess," "Pooem," "Capacity," "An Imaginable Conference," "The Story of My Life," "The Newlyweds," "Humanities Course," "English Train Compartment," "Time's Fool," "Philological," "To an Usherette," "Sunglasses," "Cloud Shadows," "A Modest Mound of Bones," "Youth's Progress," "Dilemma in the Delta," "A Wooden Darning Egg," "Mr. High-Mind," "The One-Year-Old," "Superman," "Publius Vergilius Maro, the Madison Avenue Hick," "In Memoriam," "Planting a Mail Box," "Tsokadze O Altitudo," "Little Poems,"; "Tao in Yankee Stadium Bleachers," "Due Respect," "Tax-Free Encounter," "Room 28," "The Sensualist," "Snapshots," "Mountain Impasse," "A Bitter Life," "Glasses," "A Rack of Paperbacks," "Popular Revivals, 1956," "Ode II.ii: Horace," and "A Cheerful Alphabet of Pleasant Objects." Poems reprinted from *Telephone Poles and Other Poems*. N.Y.: Knopf, 1963, include: **"Bendix," "Reel," "Cosmic Gall," "In Praise of $(C_{10}H_9O_5)x$," "The Descent of**

Mr. Aldez," "Caligula's Dream," "White Dwarf," "Toothache Man," "Deities and Beasts," "Sonic Boom," "Party Knee," "Thoughts While Driving Home," "Idyll," "A Song of Paternal Care," "Marriage Counsel," "Recital," "Tropical Beetles," "B. W. W.," "Exposure," "Comp. Religion," "Bestiary," "The High-Hearts," "The Menagerie at Versailles in 1775," "Upon Learning that a Bird Exists Called the Turnstone," "Upon Learning that a Town Exists in Virginia Called Upperville," "Zulus Live in Land without a Square," "Pop Smash, Out of Echo Chamber," "The Moderate," "Kenneths," "Tome-Thoughts, from the Times," "I Missed His Book, But I Read His Name," "Agatha Christie and Beatrix Potter," "Meditation on a News Item," "Telephone Poles," "Wash," "The Short Days," "Suburban Madrigal," "Mosquito," "Earthworm," "Calendar," "Seagulls," "Maples in a Spruce Forest," "Vermont," "Hoeing," "How to Be Uncle Sam," "February 22," "Shillington," "Movie House," "Old-Fashioned Lightning Rod," "The Stunt Flier," "The Fritillary," "Mobile of Birds," "Les Saints Nouveaux," "Die Neuen Heiligen," "Trees Eat Sunshine," "Fever," "Seven Stanzas at Easter," "Vibration," "Modigliani's Death Mask," "Summer: West Side," "3 A. M.," "Erotic Epigrams," "Flirt," "The Blessing," "The Great Scarf of Birds," and "Winter Ocean." Poems in bold are reprinted in *Collected Poems, 1953-1993*. N.Y.: Knopf, 1993.)

A27   *Assorted Prose*. Greenwich, Conn.: Fawcett, 1966.

A28   *The Centaur*. Harmondsworth, Middlesex: Penguin, 1966.

A29   *The Music School*. N.Y.: Knopf, 1966. (First edition has lines 15 and 16 transposed in "The Madman." 46.)

A30   *The Music School*. N.Y.: Knopf, 1966. (The error on 46 was corrected on a tipped-in page.)

A31   *The Music School*. N.Y.: Knopf, 1966. (The third state of this first edition has a corrected page bound in.)

A32   *The Music School*. Greenwich, Conn.: Fawcett, 1967.

A33   *The Music School*. London: Deutsch, 1967. (Contains the same error as first American edition.)

A34   *Of the Farm*. Greenwich, Conn.: Fawcett, 1967.

*A35   *Verse*. London: Deutsch, 1967.

A36   *The Angels*. Pensacola, Fla.: King & Queen P, 1968. (Signed, limited edition, of 150 copies. Rpt. from *The New Yorker* 27 January 1968: 34; in *Midpoint and Other Poems*. N.Y.: Knopf, 1969. 56; and in *Collected Poems: 1953-1993*. N.Y.: Knopf, 1993. 58.)

A37	*Assorted Prose*. Harmondsworth, Middlesex: Penguin, 1968.
A38	*Bath After Sailing*. Stevenson, Connecticut: Country Squires Books, 1968. (Edition limited to 125 signed copies. Rpt. in *Tossing and Turning*. N.Y.: Knopf, 1977. 17-19; and in *Collected Poems: 1953-1993*. N.Y.: Knopf, 1993. 59)
A39	*Couples*. London: The Book Society, 1968.
A40	*Couples*. London: Deutsch, 1968.
A41	*Couples*. N.Y.: Knopf, 1968.
A42	*Couples*. Taipei: Chen I Shu Yuan, 1968. (Taiwanese piracy with Chinese text on verso of title page and on last page.)
A43	*December*. N.Y.: Edward Naumburg, Jr., 1968. (Printed card. Rpt. from *A Child's Calendar*. N.Y.: Knopf, 1965. Unpaginated. Rpt. in *Family Circle*.)
A44	*Of the Farm*. Harmondsworth, Middlesex: Penguin, 1968.
A45	*On Meeting Authors*. Newburyport, Mass.: Wickford P, 1968. (Signed, limited edition of 250 copies.)
A46	*The Poorhouse Fair*. Harmondsworth, Middlesex: Penguin 1968. (Includes the "Foreword" from the Modern Library edition.)
A47	*The Same Door*. Harmondsworth, Middlesex: Penguin: 1968.
A48	*Three Texts from Early Ipswich: A Pageant*. Ipswich, Mass: 17th Century Day Committee: 17th Century Day 1968. (Signed, limited edition of 26 lettered copies. Updike notes that the pageant used *Ipswich in the Mass. Bay Colony*, Volume I by Thomas Franklin Waters; *History of Ipswich, Essex and Hamilton*, by Joseph B. Felt; *The Simple Cobbler of Aggawamm in America*; and Anne Bradstreet's poems from *The American Puritans*, ed. Perry Miller.)
A49	*Assorted Prose*. Greenwich, Conn.: Fawcett, 1969.
A50	*Bottom's Dream*: Adapted from William Shakespeare's *A Midsummer Night's Dream*. With music by Felix Mendelssohn and illustrated by Warren Chappell. N.Y.: Knopf, 1969. Signed, limited edition.
A51	*Couples*. Greenwich, Conn: Fawcett, 1969.
A52	*The Dance of the Solids*. N.Y.: Scientific American, Inc., 1969. (Rpt. from *Scientific American* 220 [Jan. 1969]: 130-131. Rpt. in *Midpoint and Other Poems*. N.Y.: Knopf, 1969; and in *Collected Poems, 1953-1993*. N.Y.: Knopf, 1993. 78-81. Jack W. C. Hagstrom notes in *The John Updike*

Newsletter Fall, 1977, that this December reprint was a Christmas card, issued with a "separate printing of W. H. Auden's 'A New Year Greeting.' The total printing of each separate was 6,200 copies. Of these 5,000 were issued together with a white card sleeve on which was printed in red 'seasons greetings/from/SCIENTIFIC/AMERICAN' and 1,200 were issued together with a wrapper [sleeve] on which was printed 'seasons greetings/from'. The sleeve was in turn enclosed in a printed white card mailing carton.")

A53   *Midpoint and Other Poems.* London: Deutsch, 1969.

A54   *Midpoint and Other Poems.* N.Y.: Knopf, 1969.   (Includes: **Midpoint**: I. Introduction; II. The Photographs; III. The Dance of the Solids; IV. The Play of Memory; V. Conclusion. *Poems*, "Fireworks," "Lamplight," "Home Movies," "The Origin of Laughter," "Topsfield Fair," "Dog's Death," "Decor," "Camera," "Dream Objects," "The Angels," "Sunshine on Sandstone," "Pompeii," "Roman Portrait Busts," "Amoeba," "Seal in Nature" and "The Average Egyptian Faces Death." *Love Poems*, "Nuda Natens," "Love Sonnet," "Chloe's Poem," "Report of Health," "My Children at the Dump," "Washington," "Fellatio," "Subway Love," and "Minority Report." *Light Verse*: "Some Frenchmen," "Farewell to the Shopping District of Antibes," "Exposé," "The Amish," "Air Show," "Postcards from Soviet Cities: Moscow, Leningrad, Kiev, Tillsi and Yerevan." "Poem for a Far Land," "Antigua," "Azores," "Vow," "Miss Moore at Assembly," "Sea Knell," "Omega," "In Extremis," "On the Inclusion of Miniature Dinosaurs in Breakfast Cereal Boxes" and "The Naked Ape." Poems in bold were reprinted in *Collected Poems, 1953-1993.* N.Y.: Knopf, 1993.)

A55   *Midpoint and Other Poems.* NY: Knopf, 1969. (Signed, limited edition of 350 copies.)

*A56   *Die Neuen Heiligen, Übertragen von Uwe Johnson zum Jahreswechsel 1969-1970.* Biberach an der Riss: Dr. Karl Thomae GmbH Chemisch-pharmazeutische Fabrik. [1969-1970]. (Facsimile of a holograph poem with German translation. Rpt. from *Harper's* 25 [Aug. 1962: 550.] Rpt.in *Telephone Poles.* N.Y.: Knopf, 1963. 69; and in *Collected Poems, 1953-1993.* N.Y.: Knopf, 1993. 322.)

A57   *Bech: A Book.* Greenwich, Conn.: Fawcett, 1970.

A58   *Bech: A Book.* London: Deutsch, 1970.

A59   *Bech: A Book.* N.Y.: Knopf, 1970. (Signed, limited edition of 500 boxed, numbered, signed copies. Includes: "Foreword," "Rich in Russia," "Bech in Rumania," "The Bulgarian Poetess," "Bech Takes Pot Luck," "Bech Panics," "Bech Swings?" "Bech Enters Heaven," "Appendix A," and "Appendix B.")

A60	*Bech: A Book.* N.Y.: Knopf, Book Club Edition, 1970.
A61	*Bech: A Book.* N.Y.: Knopf, 1970. (Taiwanese piracy. Chinese characters on the copyright page.)
A62	*Couples.* Harmondsworth, Middlesex: Penguin, 1970.
A63	*Midpoint and Other Poems.* Greenwich, Conn.: Fawcett, 1970.
A64	*The Music School.* Harmondsworth, Middlesex: Penguin, 1970.
A65	*Rabbit, Run.* N.Y.: Knopf, 1970.
A66	*Seventy Poems.* London: Deutsch, 1970. (Includes selections from *Telephone Poles* and *Midpoint*.)
A67	*Bech: A Book.* Harmondsworth, Middlesex: Penguin 1971.
A68	*The Indian.* Marvin, S.D.: Blue Cloud Abbey, 1971. (Rpt. from "The Indian." *The Blue Cloud Quarterly* XVII, No. 1. Also printed in *The New Yorker* 17 Aug. 1963: 24-26; and in *The Music School*. N.Y.: Knopf, 1966. 9-17.)
A69	*Pigeon Feathers and Other Stories.* Boston: G. K. Hall, 1971. (Large Print edition.)
A70	*Rabbit Redux.* N.Y.: Knopf, 1971.
A71	*Rabbit Redux.* N.Y.: Knopf, 1971. (Book-of-the-Month Club edition.)
A72	*Rabbit Redux.* N.Y.: Knopf, 1971. (Signed, limited edition of 350 copies, slipcased.)
A73	*Rabbit Redux.* "N.Y.: Knopf, 1971." (Taiwanese piracy with Chinese text on verso of title page.)
A74	*Rabbit, Run.* N.Y.: Knopf, 1971.
*A75	*Bech: A Book.* Harmondsworth, Middlesex: Penguin, 1972.
A76	*The Centaur.* Ipswich edition. London: Deutsch, 1972.
*A77	*The Centaur.* N.Y.: Knopf, 1972.
*A78	*Minutes of the Last Meeting. Audience.* 2(July-Aug. 1972), 34-36. (Rpt. in *Problems and Other Stories.* N.Y.: Knopf, 1977. 12-17.)
A79	*Museums and Women and Other Stories.* N.Y.: Knopf, 1972. Includes: "Museums and Women," "The Hillies," "The Day of the Dying Rabbit," "The Deacon," "I Will Not Let Thee Go, Except Thou Bless Me," "The

Corner," "The Witnesses," "Solitaire," "The Orphaned Swiming Pool," "When Everyone Was Pregnant," "Man and Daughter in the Cold," "I Am Dying, Egypt, Dying," "The Carol Sing," "Plumbing"; *Other Modes* "The Sea's Green Sameness," "The Slump," "The Pro," "One of My Generation," "God Speaks," "Under the Microscope," "During the Jurassic," "The Baluchitherium," "The Invention of the Horse Collar," "Jesus on Honshu." *The Maples* "Marching Through Boston," "The Taste of Metal," "Your Lover Just Called," "Eros Rampant," and "Sublimating.")

*A80   *Museums and Women and Other Stories.* N.Y.: Knopf, 1972. Edition limited to 350 boxed, numbered, signed copies.

A81   *Rabbit Redux.* London: Deutsch, 1972.

A82   *Rabbit, Run.* Ipswich Edition. London: Deutsch, 1972.

A83   *Seventy Poems.* Harmondsworth, Middlesex: Penguin, 1972. (Includes selections from *Telephone Poles* and *Midpoint*. Caricature on cover.)

*A84   *Stories from Museums and Women.* Edited with notes by Nobuo Kjima and Kiyohiro Miura. Tokyo: Nan-un-do's Contemporary Library, 1972.

A85   *A Good Place: Being a Personal Account of Ipswich, Mass. written on the occasion of its Seventeenth-Century Day, 1972, by a Resident, John Updike.* N.Y.: Aloe Editions, 1973. (Signed, limited edition.)

A86   *Museums and Women and Other Stories.* Greenwich, Conn.: Fawcett, 1973.

A87   *Museums and Women and Other Stories.* London: Deutsch, 1973.

A88   *The Music School.* Ipswich Edition. London: Deutsch, 1973.

A89   *Of The Farm.* Ipswich edition. London: Deutsch, 1973.

A90   *Of The Farm.* N.Y.: Knopf, 1973.

A91   *Phi Beta Kappa Poem, Harvard, 1973.* Cambridge, Mass.: Harvard University News Office, 1973. (Signed, limited edition.)

A92   *Pigeon Feathers.* N.Y.: Knopf, 1973.

A93   *Rabbit Redux.* Harmondsworth, Middlesex: Penguin, 1973.

*A94   *Rabbit, Run.* N.Y.: Knopf, 1973.

A95   *Six Poems.* N.Y.: Aloe Editions, 1973. (Poems include: "Upon Shaving Off One's Beard." Rpt. in *Tossing and Turning*. New York: Knopf, 1977.

45. "À L'Ecole Berlitz." Rpt. in *Tossing and Turning*. New York: Knopf, 1977. 36; and in *Collected Poems, 1953-1993*. N.Y.: Knopf, 1993. 105. "South of the Alps." Rpt. in *Tossing and Turning*. New York: Knopf, 1977. 37-39; and in *Collected Poems, 1953-1993*. N.Y.: Knopf, 1993. 106. "Tossing and Turning." Rpt. from *Tossing and Turning*. New York: Knopf, 1977. 67; and in *Collected Poems, 1953-1993*. N.Y.: Knopf, 1993. 109. "On an Island." Rpt. in *Tossing and Turning*. New York: Knopf, 1977. 20-21; and in *Collected Poems, 1953-1993*. N.Y.: Knopf, 1993. 110. "Phenomena." Rpt. in *Tossing and Turning*. New York: Knopf, 1977. 84-85; and in *Collected Poems, 1953-1993*. N.Y.: Knopf, 1993. 231.)

A96   *Warm Wine*. N.Y.: Albondocani, 1973. (Signed, limited edition of 250 copies.)

A97   *Cunts (Upon Receiving the Swingers Life Club Membership Solicitation)*. New York: Frank Hallman, 1974. (Edition of 250 numbered, 26 signed copies. Note by Roberts [*American Book Collector*, 1: 12: "Printed in different form in *The New York Quarterly*, Sum. 1973, Number 15, copies of this journal were issued in 1978 as a 'special signed edition' of 457 numbered copies and 26 lettered copies. The notice of limitation and signature appear on page 65. This is not a primary first edition, but a recycled periodical appearance." Rpt. in *Playboy* Jan. 1984: 162-3; *Tossing and Turning*. N.Y.: Knopf, 1977. 75; and in *Collected Poems, 1953-1993*. N.Y.: Knopf, 1993. 116-20.)

A98   *Query*. N.Y.: Albondocani, 1974. (Signed, limited edition. The first edition, first printing was suppressed because of a misprinted cover illustration; Rpt. in *Tossing and Turning*. N.Y.: Knopf, 1977. 13; and in *Collected Poems, 1953-1993*. N.Y.: Knopf, 1993. 127-28.)

A99   *Flirt*. Pittsburgh: International Poetry Forum, 1975. (Signed, limited edition.) Rpt. from *Commonweal*. 77 [30 Nov. 1962]: 253. Rpt.in *Telephone Poles and Other Poems*. N.Y.: Knopf, 1963. 80; and in *Collected Poems, 1953-1993*. N.Y.: Knopf, 1993. 28.)

A100   *A Month of Sundays*. London: Deutsch, 1975. (Retains the printing error of the American edition, "sermon" for "semon.")

A101   *A Month of Sundays*. N.Y.: Knopf, 1975.

A102   *A Month of Sundays*. N.Y.: Knopf, 1975. (Book of the Month Club.)

A103   *A Month of Sundays*. N.Y.: Knopf, 1975. (Signed edition limited to 450 copies in slipcases.)

*A104 *A Month of Sundays*. Taipei, Lin Jou Book, Sound & Gift Co.: Imperial Books and Records Co, 1975. (Possibly a pirated edition. See *The John Updike Newsletter* 8 [Fall 1978]: 3.)

A105   *Museums and Women*. Harmondsworth, Middlesex: Penguin, 1975.

*A106	*Of The Farm*. N.Y.: Knopf, 1975. (Contains "Foreword to the Czech Edition.")
A107	*Picked-Up Pieces*. Greenwich, Conn.: Fawcett, 1975.
A108	*Picked-Up Pieces*. N.Y.: Knopf, 1975.
A109	*Picked-Up Pieces*. N.Y.: Knopf, 1975. (Edition of 250 numbered, signed copies, boxed.)
A110	*Picked-Up Pieces*. N.Y.: Knopf, 1975. (Quality Paperback Book Club printing.)
*A111	*Sixty Photographs to Celebrate the Sixtieth Anniversary of Alfred Knopf, Publisher*. Alfred A. Knopf. N.Y.: Knopf, 1975. (Picture of Updike with "wistful comments." 60.)
A112	*Sunday in Boston*. Derry, Pa.: Rook P, 1975. (First published as part of a series of broadsides sold as a package, then detached and sold in "deluxe edition" of 100 signed, illustrated numbered copies, then 130 numbered, signed. Rpt. in *Tossing and Turning*. N.Y.: Knopf, 1977. 28; in *The John Updike Newsletter* Spring, 1978: 7; and in *Collected Poems, 1953-1993*. N.Y.: Knopf, 1993. 135.)
A113	*Couples: A Short Story*. Cambridge, Mass.: Halty Ferguson, 1976. (Signed, limited edition of 276 copies, 250 numbered, 26 lettered.)
A114	*Marry Me: A Romance*. Franklin Center, Pa.: Franklin Library, 1976. (Signed, First Edition Society limited edition, leather bound. Illustrated by Barbara Fox.)
A115	*Marry Me: A Romance*. N.Y.: Knopf, 1976. (Updike notes: "Chapter I has been previously published as a booklet by the Albondocani P [N.Y.; 1973]. Chapter II appeared, in a somewhat different form in *The New Yorker*," as "The Wait." *The New Yorker* 43 [17 Feb. 1968]: 34-40, 42, 45-46, 48, 51-52, 54, 57-58, 60, 65-66, 68, 70, 72, 77-78, 80, 83-84, 86, 89-90, 92, 95-96.)
A116	*Marry Me: A Romance*. N.Y.: Knopf, 1976. (Book Club edition.)
A117	*Marry Me: A Romance*. N.Y.: Knopf, 1976. (Limited, signed edition, of 300, boxed and numbered.)
A118	*A Month of Sundays*. Greenwich, Conn.: Fawcett, 1976.
*A119	*A Month of Sundays*. Harmondsworth, Middlesex: Penguin, 1976.
A120	*Picked-Up Pieces*. London: Deutsch, 1976.

A121 *Scenic.* San Francisco: Roxburghe Club, 1976. (Signed, limited edition of 150 copies. Rpt. from *The New Yorker.* 33 [9 Mar. 1957]: 37. Rpt. in *The Carpentered Hen and Other Tame Creatures.* N.Y.: Harper and Row, 1958. 13; in *The John Updike Newsletter* 5 [Sept. 1978]: unnumbered 4; and in *Collected Poems, 1953-1993.* N.Y.: Knopf, 1993. 283.)

A122 *Superman.* Playing-card size format with poem on one side and sepia-tone portrait of Updike on the reverse. n.d. but post-1976. (Rpt. from *The Carpentered Hen.* N.Y.: Harper and Brothers, 1958. 47; and in *Collected Poems, 1953-1993.* N.Y.: Knopf, 1993. 270-71.)

A123 *Buchanan Dying.* Readers Theatre adaptation by Robert McCoy. San Diego: San Diego State U, 1977.

A124 *Hub Fans Bid Kid Adieu.* Northridge, Calif.: Lord John P, 1977. Edition limited to 300 copies. "Preface." ix-xii. (Rpt. from *The New Yorker* 36 [22 Oct. 1960]: 109-31. Rpt. in *Assorted Prose.* N.Y.: Knopf, 1965. 127-47 with notes 128-32, 134-38, 143; in *Sports in Literature.* Ed. Henry B. Chapin. N.Y.: McKay, 1976. 289-305; in *The Lexington Reader.* Ed. Lynn Z. Bloom. Lexington, Mass.: Heath, 1987. 470-83; and in *The Norton Book of Sports.* Ed. George Plimpton. N.Y.: W. W. Norton 1992. 355-67.)

A125 *Marry Me: A Romance.* Greenwich, Conn.: Fawcett, 1977.

A126 *Marry Me: A Romance.* London: Deutsch, 1977.

A127 *The Poorhouse Fair.* First edition, sixth printing, revised, with "Introduction to the 1977 Edition" by Updike. N.Y.: Knopf, 1977.

A128 *Rabbit, Run.* Franklin Center, Pa.: Franklin Library, 1977. The First Edition Society. (Signed, limited edition, with "A special message for subscribers from John Updike.")

A129 *Raining at Magens Bay.* Issued as a broadside of 200 copies with *The John Updike Newsletter* 2 (Spring 1977): 5. (Rpt. from *Transatlantic Review* 55/56 [Fall 1976]: 55-56; Rpt. in *Tossing and Turning.* N.Y.: Knopf, 1977. 24-25, retitled "Raining in Magens Bay"; and in *Collected Poems, 1953-1993.* N.Y.: Knopf, 1993. 135-36.)

A130 *Tossing and Turning.* London: Deutsch, 1977.

A131 *Tossing and Turning.* N.Y.: Knopf, 1977. (Includes: *I* "Dream and Reality," "The Solitary Pond," "Leaving Church Early," "The House Growing," "Query," "Late January," "Touch of Spring," "Melting," "Bath After Sailing," "On an Island," "Wind," "Poisoned in Nassau," "Raining in Magens Bay," "Sleepless in Scarsdale," "Sunday in Boston," "Apologies to Harvard," "Commencement, Pingree School," "A L'Ecole Berlitz," "South of the Alps," "Calder's Hands." *II* "The Cars in Caracas," "Los Carros En Caracas," "Business Acquaintances," "Upon Shaving Off One's Beard," "Insomnia the Gem of the

Ocean," "To a Waterbed," "Courtesy Call," "The Jolly Greene Giant," "Authors' Residences," "Painted Wives," "Milady Reflects," "Seven New Ways of Looking at the Moon," "Skyey Developments," "News from the Underworld," "Sin City, D. C.." *III* "A Bicycle Chain," "The Melancholy of Storm Windows," "The Grief of Cafeterias," "Rats," "Sand Dollar," "Tossing and Turning," "Living with a Wife: At the Piano, In the Tub, Under the Sunlamp, During Menstruation, All the While," "Marching Through a Novel," "Night Flight, Over Ocean," "Golfers," "Pale Bliss," "Cunts," "Pussy," "Sunday," "Sunday Rain," "Phenomena," "Boil," "Mime," "Note to the Previous Tenants," "Dutch Cleanser," and "Heading for Nandi." Poems in bold were reprinted in *Collected Poems, 1953-1993*. N.Y.: Knopf, 1993.)

A132   *The Coup.* Greenwich, Conn.: Fawcett, 1978.

A133   *The Coup.* N.Y.: Knopf, 1978.

A134   *The Coup.* N.Y.: Knopf, Book-of-the-Month Club edition, 1978.

A135   *The Coup.* N.Y.: Knopf, 1978. (Limited and signed edition.)

A136   *The Coup.* N.Y.: Knopf, Quality Book Club. 1978.

A137   *The Coup.* Taipei: Chen I Shu Yuan, 1978. (Taiwanese piracy with Chinese text on verso of title page and on last page. A pirated edition.)

A138   *From the Journal of a Leper.* Northridge, Calif.: Lord John P, 1978. (Signed, limited edition. Rpt. from "From the Journal of a Leper." *The New Yorker* 52 [19 July 1976]: 28-33. Rpt. in *Problems*. N.Y.: Knopf, 1979. 181-96. Excerpted in *Self-Consciousness*. N.Y.: Knopf, 1989. 76n.)

A139   *The Lovelorn Astronomer.* Boston: G. K. Hall, 1978. (Signed, limited edition used as Christmas card.)

A140   *Assorted Prose.* N.Y.: Knopf, 1979. Third edition.

A141   *The Coup.* Harmondsworth, Middlesex: Penguin, 1979.

A142   *The Coup.* London: Deutsch, 1979.

A143   *The Coup.* Saint Lucia: University of Queensland P, 1979.

A144   *Earthworm.* Princeton, New Jersey: Ontario Rev P, 1979. (Signed, limited edition postcard with two states: a first printing with an error in the third stanza, "God bless" for "God blesses"; the second printing corrects the error. Rpt. from *The New Yorker* 38 [12 May 1962]: 145. Rpt. in *Telephone Poles and Other Poems*. N.Y.: Knopf, 1963. 48; and in *Collected Poems, 1953-1993*. N.Y.: Knopf, 1993. 29.)

A145   *An Oddly Lovely Day Alone.* Richmond, Va.: Waves P, 1979. (Signed, limited edition of 250 copies. Rpt. in *Facing Nature*, N.Y.: Knopf, 1985. 44-45.)

A146   *Pigeon Feathers.* Logan, Iowa.: Perfection Form Co., 1979. (School text with exercises.)

A147   *Problems and Other Stories.* N.Y.: Knopf, 1979. (Includes: "Commercial," "Minutes of the Last Meeting," "Believers," "The Gun Shop," "How To Love America and Leave It at the Same Time," "Nevada," "Son," "Daughter, Last Glimpses of," "Ethiopia," "Transaction," "Separating," "Augustine's Concubine," "The Man Who Loved Extinct Mammals," "Problems," "Domestic Life in America," "Love Song, for a Moog Synthesizer," "From the Journal of a Leper," "Here Come the Maples," "The Fairy Godfathers," "The Faint," "The Egg Race," "Guilt-Gems," and "Atlantises.")

A148   *Problems and Other Stories.* N.Y.: Knopf, 1979. (Signed edition limited to 350 copies.)

A149   *Sixteen Sonnets.* Cambridge, Mass.: Halty Ferguson, 1979. "Autobibliographical Note." Limited edition of 250 copies. (Considerably revised, these sonnets first appeared in *The New Yorker* except for "Mass. Mental Health," written for this volume. Rpt. in *Facing Nature*. N.Y.: Knopf, 1985. 3-24. The note is reprinted in *Hugging the Shore*, N.Y.: Knopf, 1983. 866-67. Poems included are: "To Ed Sissman," [3 sonnets], "Waiting Rooms" [two sonnets: "Boston Lying-In" and "Mass. Mental Health"], "Shaving Mirror: A Double Sonnet," "Ohio" [2 sonnets], "Spain" [8 sonnets].)

A150   *Talk from the Fifties.* Northridge, Calif.: Lord John P, 1979. (Signed, limited edition of 300 copies. Includes: "Introduction." "Green," "Emergency," "Building Décor," "Speech on Spool," "Adequate Wiring," "Swifts and Stuffers," "Rockefeller Center Ho!" "Pre-Expulsion Yellow," "Glance," "Outdoor Art," "Tritylodonts," "Said Yonkers to Gloversville," "Convincing," "Bird Census," "Resemblances," "Green Grow the Yesses, O!," "Physiologist's Holiday," "Our Own Baedeker," "Auction," and "Oasis".)

A151   *Three Illuminations in the Life of an American Author.* N.Y.: Targ Editions, 1979. (Signed, limited edition of 350 copies. Rpt. from "Three Illuminations in the Life of an American Author." *The New Yorker* 54 [21 Aug. 1978]: 24-32. Rpt. in *Bech Is Back.* N.Y.: Knopf, 1982. 3-27.)

A152   *Too Far To Go: The Maples Stories.* Greenwich, Conn.: Fawcett, 1979. (Includes: "Foreword," "Snowing in Greenwich Village," "Wife-wooing," "Giving Blood," "Twin Beds in Rome," "Marching Through Boston," "The Taste of Metal," "Your Lover Just Called," "Waiting Up," "Eros Rampant," "Plumbing," "The Red-Herring Theory," "Sublimating,"

"Nakedness," "Separating," "Gesturing," "Divorcing: A Fragment," "Here Come the Maples.")

*A153 *The Visions of Mackenzie King.* Northridge, Calif.: Lord John P, 1979. (Rpt. from *The New Republic* 180 [8 Apr. 1979]: 28. Rpt. in *The John Updike Newsletter*, Number 12, Fall, 1979; in *Facing Nature*. N.Y.: Knopf, 1985. 108-10; in *Five Poems*. Cleveland: Bits P, 1980, unpaginated; and in *Collected Poems, 1953-1993*. N.Y.: Knopf, 1993. 344-46.)

*A154 *Your Lover Just Called: Stories of Joan and Richard Maple.* London: Deutsch, 1979. (Signed, limited edition. Rpt. from *Harper's* 234 [Jan. 1967]: 48-51. Rpt. in *Museums and Women*. N.Y.: Knopf, 1972. 242-51.)

A155 *Bech: A Book.* N.Y.: Vintage Books, 1980.

A156 *The Chaste Planet.* Worcester, Mass: Metacom, 1980 (Limited edition of 326 signed copies. Rpt. from "The Chaste Planet." *The New Yorker* 51 [10 Nov. 1975]: 43-44. Rpt. in *SF:75*; and in *Hugging the Shore*. N.Y.: Knopf, 1983. 35-39.)

A157 *Ego and Art in Walt Whitman.* N.Y.: Targ, 1980 (Signed, limited edition of 350 copies. Originally given as a talk at the Morgan library in N.Y. October 4, 1977. Rpt. in "Walt Whitman: Ego and Art." *The New York Review of Books* 25 [9 Feb. 1978]: 33-36; and in *Hugging the Shore*. N.Y.: Knopf, 1983. 106-17 with a note 106 and the title changed to "Whitman's Egotheism.")

A158 *Five Poems.* Cleveland: Bits P, 1980, unpaginated, with an Updike drawing. (Includes: "Energy: A Villanelle," "Self-Service," "The Visions of Mackenzie King." "On the Way to Delphi," and "Taste." Rpt. in *Facing Nature*. N.Y.: Knopf, 1985; and in *Collected Poems, 1953-1993*. N.Y.: Knopf, 1993.)

A159 *Iowa.* Portland Oregon: John Laursen at P-22, 1980. (Signed broadside limited to 250 copies. Rpt. in *Facing Nature*. N.Y.: Knopf, 1985. 16; and in *Collected Poems, 1953-1993*. N.Y.: Knopf, 1993. 154.)

*A160 *The Music School.* N.Y.: Vintage Books, 1980.

A161 *People One Knows: Interviews with Insufficiently Famous Americans.* Northridge, Calif.: Lord John P, 1980. (Signed, limited edition of 100 copies. Includes: "The Pal," "One's Neighbor's Wife," "The Running Mate," "The Counsellor," "The Golf Course Owner," "The Child Bride," "The Mailman," "The Widow," "The Undertaker," and "The Bankrupt Man." Rpt. in *Hugging the Shore*, N.Y.: Knopf, 1983. 3-21)

A162 *Problems and Other Stories.* London: Deutsch, 1980.

A163 *A Sense of Shelter.* Logan, Iowa: Perfection Form Co., 1980. (School text, with exercises.)

A164   *Your Lover Just Called: Stories of Joan and Richard Maple* Harmondsworth, Middlesex: Penguin, 1980. (British edition of *Too Far to Go*.).

*A165   *Couples*. Harmondsworth, Middlesex: Penguin, 1981.

A166   *Hawthorne's Creed*. N.Y.: Targ Editions, 1981. (Signed, limited edition of 250 copies. Rpt. from "Hawthorne's Religious Language." *Proceedings of the American Academy and Institute of Arts and Letters* 30 [1979]: 21-27. Revised as "Hawthorne's Creed," *The New York Review of Books* 28 [19 Mar. 1981]: 41-42; Rpt. in *Hugging the Shore*, N.Y.: Knopf, 1983, 73-80, with a note 73.)

A167   *Hugging The Shore*. N.Y.: Knopf, 1981. (Includes: "Foreword," **Persons and Places** "Interviews with Insufficiently Famous Americans: The Pal, One's Neighbor's Wife, The Running Mate, The Counsellor, The Golf Course Owner, The Child Bride, The Mailman, The Widow, The Undertaker, The Bankrupt Man." "The Tarbox Police," "Venezuela for Visitors." "The Chaste Planet." "Invasion of the Book Envelopes." "Golf Dreams." "Thirteen Ways of Looking at the Masters." "New England: The First Kiss, Out There, Going Barefoot, Common Land, New England Churches," and "A Mild 'Complaint'." **Other People's Books: Three Talks on American Masters:** "Hawthorne's Creed," "Melville's Withdrawal," and "Whitman's Egotheism." **Letters** "The Bear Who Hated Life," "Simple-Minded Jim," "Advancing Over Water," "Nothing Is Easy," "An Armful of Field Flowers," "Hem Battles the Pack; Wins, Loses," "The Doctor's Son," and "The Shining Note." **Wilson and Nabokov**: "Edmund Wilson's Fiction: A Personal Account," "An Earlier Day," "The Cuckoo and the Rooster," "An Introduction to Nabokov's Lectures," "The Fancy-Forger Takes the Lectern," "Proud Happiness," and "Vale, VN." **Bellow, Vonnegut, Tyler, Le Guin, Cheever:** "Draping Radiance with a Worn Veil," "Toppling Towers Seen By a Whirling Soul," "All's Well in Skyscraper National Park," "Family Ways," "Loosened Roots," "Imagining Things," and "On Such A Beautiful Green Little Planet." **Some British:** "Jack and Lolly Opt Out," "Indestructible Elena," "An Introduction to Three Novels by Henry Green," "Green Green," and "Through The Mid-Life Crisis with James Boswell, Esq." **Spark, Murdoch, Trevor, Drabble**: "Topnotch Witcheries," "Worlds and Worlds," "Drabbling in the Mud," "Of Heresy and Loot," "Coming into Her Own." **Some Irish:** "Small Cheer from the Old Sod," "Flann Again," and "An Old-Fashioned Novel." **Jarry, Queneau, Céline, Pinget**: "Human Capacities," "Thirty-four Years Late, Twice," "The Strange Case of Dr. Destouches and M. Céline," and "Robert Pinget." **Northern Europeans**: "A Primal Modern," "Saddled with the World," "Scherazade," "Brecht's Dicta," "Discontent in Deutsch," and "Disaffection in Deutsch." **Calvino, Grass, Böll:** "Metropolises of the Mind," "Card Tricks," "Readers and Writers," "Fish Story," and "The Squeeze Is On." **Eastern Europeans** "Polish Metamorphoses," "Czarist Shadows, Soviet Lilacs," and "Czech Angels." **Lem and Pym, Stead and Jones:** "Lem and Pym," "Selda, Lilia, Ursa,

Great Gram, and Other Ladies in Distress," and "Eva and Eleanor and Everywoman." **Some Nachtmusik, From All Over**: "No Death of Death," "Dark Smile, Devilish Saints," "Layers of Ambiguity," "Stalled Starters," and "Frontiersmen." **Barthes, Berlin, Cioran**: "Roland Barthes," "Texts and Men," "The Last of Barthes," and "A Monk Manqué." **Poets**: "The Heaven of an Old Home," "Alone but Not Aloof," "Owlish and Fisby," "Sissman's Poetry," "Three Poems on Being a Poet, by Yevgeny Yevtushenko," and "Stand Fast I Must." **Tales**: "Magic Mirrors," "Fiabe Italiane," "A Feast of Reason," and "Happy on Nono Despite Odosba." **The World Called Third**: "African Accents" "Mixed Reports from the Interior," "Journeyers," "Raman and Daisy and Olivia and the Nawab," and "India Going On." **The Far East**: "Spent Arrows and First Buddings," "From Fumie to Sony," "The Giant Who Isn't There," and "The Long and Reluctant Stasis of Wan-li." **Art and Act**: "Gaiety in the Galleries," "Tote That Quill," "Wright on Writing," "Borges Warmed Over," "Pinter's Unproduced Proust Printed," "Suzie Creamcheese Speaks," and "Female Pilgrims." **Long Views**: "A Cloud of Witnesses," "Who Wants to Know?" and "To the Tram Halt Together." Appendix: "On One's Own Oeuvre.")

A168   *Invasion of the Book Envelopes.* Concord, N.H.: William B. Ewert, 1981. (Signed, limited edition of 125 copies. The earlier first printing of the first edition was suppressed because of a misprint. Rpt. from "Invasion of the Book Envelopes." *The New Yorker* 57 [20 July 1981]: 33. Rpt. in *Hugging the Shore*, N.Y.: Knopf, 1983. 40-42.)

*A169   *Museums and Women.* N.Y.: Vintage, 1981.

A170   *Pigeon Feathers and Other Stories.* Franklin Center, Pa.: Franklin Library, 1981. (Issued "for subscribers to the Collected Stories of the World's Greatest Writers.")

A171   *Problems and Other Stories.* Greenwich, Conn.: Fawcett, 1981.

A172   *Rabbit Is Rich.* N.Y.: Knopf, 1981. (An excerpt was reprinted as "Il Court, Il Court." *Nouvelle Revue Françaaise* 62 No. 366 [July-Aug. 1983] N366: 13-22. Translated by Maurice Rambaud. See **Appendix I. 196.**)

A173   *Rabbit Is Rich.* N.Y.: Knopf, 1981. (Limited, signed edition of 350 copies in slipcases.)

A174   *Rabbit Is Rich.* N.Y.: Knopf, 1981. (Book-of-the-Month Club edition.)

A175   *Rabbit Is Rich.* N.Y.: Knopf, 1981. (Limited, signed edition for "The First Edition Circle.")

A176   *Rabbit Is Rich/Rabbit Redux/Rabbit, Run.* N.Y.: Quality Book Club, 1981.

A177   *Rabbit Redux*. Franklin Center, Pa.: Franklin Library, 1981. (Signed, with "A special message to subscribers from John Updike .")

A178   *The Same Door*. N.Y.: Vintage, 1981.

A179   *Bech Is Back*. N.Y.: Knopf: 1982. (Includes: "Three Illuminations in the Life of an American Author." Rpt. from *The New Yorker* 54 [21 Aug. 1978]: 24-32. Rpt. as *Three Illuminations in the Life of an American Author*. N.Y.: Targ Editions, 1979. "Bech Third-Worlds It," "Australia and Canada," "The Holy Land," "Macbech," "Bech Wed," and "White on White.")

A180   *Bech Is Back*. N.Y.: Knopf: 1982. (Limited and signed edition of 500 copies in slip cases.)

A181   *The Beloved*. Northridge, Calif.: Lord John P, 1982. Limited edition of 300 copies. (Rpt. from *The New Yorker* 47 [6 Nov. 1971]: 46-47, in "slightly different form," as "Love: First Lessons," and as "The Beloved" in *The Transatlantic Review* 50 [Autumn 1974]: 19.)

A182   *The Carpentered Hen And Other Tame Creatures*. N.Y.: Knopf: 1982. (Rpt. from *The Carpentered Hen And Other Tame Creatures*. N.Y.: Harper's, 1958; and *Verse*. Greenwich, Conn.: Fawcett Premier, 1965. With a new "Foreword." The poems are printed in a slightly different order and with changes in the following poems, "Player Piano"; "The Population of Argentina"; "Cloud Shadows"; "Dilemma in the Delta"; "Mr. High-Mind"; "The One-Year-Old"; "In Memoriam"; "Little Poems"; "Tao in Yankee Stadium Bleachers"; "Room 28"; "Letter Slot"; "Pendulum" [format]; "Quilt" [a footnote deleted]; "Umbrella"; and "Vacuum Cleaner." Poems in bold in *Verse* were reprinted in *Collected Poems, 1953-1993*. N.Y.: Knopf, 1993.)

A183   *Couples*. N.Y.: Ballantine, 1982.

A184   *A Month of Sundays*. N.Y.: Ballantine, 1982.

A185   *Museums and Women and Other Stories*. N.Y.: Knopf, 1982.

A186   *Rabbit Is Rich*. Harmondswroth: Penguin, 1982.

A187   *Rabbit Is Rich*. London: Deutsch, 1982.

A188   *Rabbit Is Rich*. N.Y.: Ballantine, 1982.

A189   *Rabbit, Run*. N.Y.: Ballantine, 1982.

A190   *Small City People*. Northridge, Calif.: Lord John P, 1982. (Signed, limited edition of 126 copies.)

A191	*Spring Trio*. Winston-Salem, N.C.: Palaemon, P, 1982. (Signed, limited edition of 150 copies.)
*A192	*Styles of Bloom*. Winston-Salem, N.C.: Palaemon P, 1982. (Signed, limited edition.)
A193	*Too Far To Go: The Maples Stories*. N.Y.: Ballantine, 1982.
A194	*Bech Is Back*. Harmondsworth, Middlesex: Penguin, 1983.
A195	*Bech Is Back*. London: Deutsch, 1983.
A196	*Bech Is Back*. N.Y.: Ballantine, 1983.
A197	*The Centaur*. N.Y.: Ballantine, 1983.
A198	*Two Sonnets Whose Titles Came to Me Simultaneously*. Winston-Salem, N.C.: Palaemon P, 1983. (Signed, limited edition broadside in the portfolio *Northern Lights*. Contains "Oxford Thirty Years After" and "Somewhere Else." *Collected Poems, 1953-1993*. N.Y.: Knopf, 1993. 208-209, "Somewhere Else" is retitled as "Somewhere.")
*A199	*Bech: A Book*. Harmondsworth, Middlesex: Penguin, 1984. (For overseas distribution only, not for publication in the U. K.)
*A200	*Bech: A Book*. Penguin: Harmondsworth, Middlesex: 1984. (First publication in the U. K.)
A201	*Confessions of a Wild Bore*. Newton, Iowa: Tamazunchale P, 1984. (Signed, miniature, limited edition of 250 copies. Rpt. from *The New Yorker* 6 Feb. 1960: 34-35. Rpt. in *Assorted Prose*. N.Y.: Knopf, 1965. 31-36.)
A202	*Emersonianism*. Cleveland, Ohio: Bits P, 1984. (Signed, limited edition of 203 copies. Updike's note: "This talk was given at the Davis campus of the University of California on October 25, 1983, and then, somewhat revised, at the 1644th stated meeting of the American Academy of Arts and Sciences in Cambridge, Massachusetts on November 9, 1983. Again revised, it appeared in *The New Yorker* of 4 June, 1984. This present version reverts to the form of a spoken address, while keeping a number of details and quotations added for the magazine publication. The quotations from Emerson follow, in their sometimes curious-seeming spelling and punctuation, the text as last proofread by the author himself, as presented in *Ralph Waldo Emerson: Essays and Lectures*, edited by Joel Porte [Library of America, 1983]. For the biographical facts, I depended most heavily upon *Waldo Emerson*, by Gay Wilson Allen [Viking P, 1981]. A number of correspondents have enriched my understanding and refined some of my allegations; I perhaps underestimated the number and passion of living Emersonians." Rpt. in *Odd Jobs: Essays and Criticism*. N.Y.: Knopf, 1991. 148-68 with notes 148

[in which Upddike reprints the above information of the first two sentences], 156, 157, 159 and 164.)

A203 *Hugging the Shore: Essays and Criticism.* London: Deutsch, 1984.

A204 *Hugging the Shore: Essays and Criticism.* N.Y.: Vintage Books, 1984.

A205 *Jester's Dozen.* Northridge, Calif.: Lord John P, 1984. Signed, limited edition of 100 copies. ("Foreword" and poems from the Harvard *Lampoon* 1951-1954, with illustrations by Updike: "Overheard in Widener," "How to Watch a Crew Race," "Professor Harlow Shapley Warbles the Praises of Natural Sciences 115," "Untitled," "Lines," "The Summer Reader," Lines on the Passing of the *Jackolantern*," "Reverie," "I Like to Sing Also," "Ballade for Subway Sitters," Untitled; and Untitled.)

A206 *The Poorhouse Fair.* N.Y.: Ballantine, 1984.

A207 *The Poorhouse Fair.* N.Y.: Knopf, 1984. Second Printing.

A208 *The Witches of Eastwick.* Franklin Center, Pa.: Franklin Library, 1984.

A209 *The Witches of Eastwick.* London: Deutsch, 1984.

A210 *The Witches of Eastwick.* N.Y.; Knopf, 1984.

A211 *The Witches of Eastwick.* N.Y.; Knopf, 1984. (Book Club edition.)

A212 *The Witches of Eastwick.* N.Y.; Knopf, 1984. (Signed, limited edition of 350 copies.)

A213 *Facing Nature.* N.Y.: Knopf, 1985. (Includes: *Sonnets* "To Ed Sissman (3)," "Waiting Rooms: I. Boston Lying-In; II. Mass. Mental Health." "Two Sonnets Whose Titles Came to Me Simultaneously: I. The Dying Phobiac Takes His Fears With Him; II. No More Access to her Underpants," "Upon the Last Day of His Forty-Ninth Year," "Long Shadow," "L.A.," "Richmond," "Ohio (2)," "Iowa," "Spanish Sonnets (8)." *Poems* "Spring Song," "Styles of Bloom," "Natural Question," "Accumulation," "Plow Cemetery," "Nature," "Planting Trees," "Penumbrae," "The Code," "Revelation," "Sleeping with You," "An Oddly Lovely Day Alone," "Small-City People," "The Fleckings," "Two Hoppers," "Gradations of Black," "Head of a Girl, At the Met," "The Furniture," "Pain," "Taste," "Another Dog's Death," "Crab Crack," "Aerie," "The Shuttle," "East Hampton-Boston by Air," "On the Way to Delphi," "Island Sun," "The Moons of Jupiter." *Seven Odes to Seven Natural Processes* "Ode to Rot," "To Evaporation," "Ode to Growth," "To Fragmentation," "Ode to Entropy," "To Crystallization," "Ode to Healing." *Light Verse* "The Rockettes," "Dea Ex Machina," "Young Matrons Dancing," "Shaving Mirror,"

"Food," "Self-Service," "Energy: A Villanelle," "Typical Optical," "On the Recently Minted Hundred-Cent Piece," "Light-Headed in Sweden," "The Lament of Abrashka Tertz," and **"The Visions of Mackenzie King."** Poems in bold were reprinted in *Collected Poems, 1953-1993.* N.Y.: Knopf, 1993.)

A214 *Impressions.* Los Angeles, Calif.: Sylvester & Orphanos, 1985. (Includes: "Author's Foreword," "A City Frieze," "Little Lightnings," "The Apple's Fresh Weight," "Working Space," "Moving Along," "A Case of Overestimation," "The Hand of Saint Saens," "Some Rectangles of Blue," "American Children," "An Outdoor Vermeer," and "Violence at the Windows." All rpt. in *Just Looking.* N.Y.: Knopf, 1989.)

*A215 *The Moons of Jupiter.* Music by Randall Snyder. Lincoln, Nebr., 1985. (Signed, limited edition.
Rpt. from *American Scholar* 52 [Autumn, 1982]: 83-86. Rpt. in *Facing Nature.* N.Y.: Knopf, 1985. 71-74; and in *Collected Poems, 1953-1993.* N.Y.: Knopf, 1993. 165-68.)

A216 *The Witches of Eastwick.* N.Y.: Ballantine, 1985.

A217 *A & P. Lust in the Aisles.* Redpath P, 1986.

*A218 *Facing Nature.* London: Deutsch, 1986.

*A219 *Getting Older,* Helsinki, Finland: Eurographica, 1986. (Signed, limited edition of 350 copies.)

A220 *A Pear Like a Potato.* Northridge, Calif.: CSUP, 1986. (Broadside limited to 126 copies, 26 signed. Rpt. from *The New Yorker* 61 [20 Jan. 1986]: 26. Rpt. in *A Pear Like a Potato.* Northridge, Calif.: CSUP, 1986; in *Recent Poems 1986-1990.* Helsinki: Eurographica, 1989; used in the song "A Pear Like a Potato" by Roy Hinkle. Premier, 6 Dec. 1992; and in *Collected Poems, 1953-1993.* N.Y.: Knopf, 1993. 205-06.)

A221 *Roger's Version.* Franklin Center, Pa: Franklin Library: 1986. (Special limited, signed edition.)

A222 *Roger's Version.* Greenwich, Conn.: Fawcett, 1986.

A223 *Roger's Version.* London: Deutsch, 1986.

A224 *Roger's Version.* N.Y.: Knopf, 1986.

A225 *Roger's Version.* N.Y.: Knopf, 1986. Quality Paperback Book Club.

*A226 *Roger's Version.* South Yarmouth, Mass.: J. Curley, 1986.

*A227 *Seven Gothic Tales: a New Introduction by John Updike.* N.Y.: Book-of-the-Month Club, 1986.

A228   *A Soft Spring Night in Shillington*. Northridge, Calif.: Lord John P, 1986. Limited edition of 250 copies. (Rpt. in a "slightly different form" from *The New Yorker* 60 [24 Dec. 1984]: 37-40, 43-44, 48-50, 52-54, 56-57.)

A229   *The Afterlife*. Leamington Spa, Warwickshire: Sixth Chamber P, 1987. (Edition limited to 175 signed, numbered copies. Rpt. from "The Afterlife," *The New Yorker* 62 [15 Sept. 1986]: 34-41.)

A230   *Forty Stories*. Harmondsworth, Middlesex: Penguin, 1987. (Includes ten stories from each of the first four collections (*The Same Door*, *Pigeon Feathers*, *The Music School*, and *Museums and Women*) placed in three sections, which Updike says dimly echo "the shape of my life." **Section 1, Olinger Stories**, includes: "You'll Never Know, Dear, How Much I Love You," "The Alligators," "Pigeon Feathers," "Friends from Philadelphia," "Flight," "A Sense of Shelter," "The Happiest I've Been," "The Persistence of Desire," "The Blessed Man of Boston, My Grandmother's Thimble, and Fanning Island," "Packed Dirt, Churchgoing, a Dying Cat, a Traded Car," "In Football Season;" **Section 2, Out in the World**, includes: "Ace in the Hole," "The Christian Roommates," "Still Life," "Dentistry and Doubt," "A Madman," "Who Made Yellow Roses Yellow?" "Toward Evening," "Sunday Teasing," "Incest," "A Gift from the City," "The Stare," "The Orphaned Swimming Pool," "The Witnesses," "The Day of the Dying Rabbit," "The Family Meadow," "At a Bar in Charlotte Amalie," "Under the Microscope," "During the Jurassic;" and **Section 3, Tarbox Tales**, includes: "The Indian," "The Hillies," "A & P," "Lifeguard," "The Deacon," "The Carol Sing," "The Music School," "Leaves," "Four Sides of One Story," "I Will Not Let Thee Go, Except Thou Bless Me," and "The Corner.")

A231   *Howells as Anti-Novelist*. Kittery Point, Maine: W. D. Howells Memorial Committee, 1987. (Signed, limited edition. Reprinting of "Howells as Anti-Novelist," *The New Yorker* 63 [13 July 1987]: 78-88. Updike's Note: "Given on May 1, 1987, at Harvard University, in Emerson Hall, as part of a two-day birthday party for Howells." Reviews four early novels in the "Library of America" series commenting on the canon. Rpt. in *Odd Jobs*. N.Y.: Knopf, 1991, 168-89 with notes 171, 178, 186 and 189.)

A232   *More Stately Mansions*. Jackson, Miss.: Nouveau P, 1987. (Signed, limited edition of 300 copies, with a woodcut engraving by Updike. Rpt. from "More Stately Mansions." *Esquire* 98 [Oct. 1982]: 142-46, 148, 151, 153-57. Rpt. in *Trust Me*. N.Y.: Knopf, 1987. 93-120.)

A233   *Trust Me*, N.Y.: Knopf, 1987. (Includes: "Trust Me," "Killing," "Still of Some Use," "The City," "The Lovely Troubled Daughters of Our Old Crowd," "Unstuck," "A Constellation of Events," "Deaths of Distant Friends," "Pygmalion," "More Stately Mansions," "Learn a Trade," "The Ideal Village," "One More Interview," "The Other," "Slippage," "Poker Night," "Made in Heaven," "Getting Into the Set," "The Wallet," "Leaf Season," "Beautiful Husbands," and "The Other Woman.")

A234	*Getting the Words Out*. Northridge, Calif.: Lord John P, 1988. (Signed edition limited to 250 copies. Rpt. from "Five Days in Finland at the Age of Fifty-Five." The *New Yorker* 63 [28 Sept. 1987]: 86-88, 91-93. Rpt. in *More Dirt: The New American Fiction*. Cambridge, England: Granta, 1986; in *Going Abroad*, Helsinki, Finland: Eurographica, 1988; and in *Odd Jobs*. N.Y.: Knopf, 1991. 3-12.)
A235	*Of the Farm*. London: Deutsch, 1988. (First English paperback edition.)
A236	*On the Move*. Cleveland, Ohio: Bits P, 1988. (Contains "Munich." Rpt. from *The New Republic* 194 [21 Apr. 1986]: 38.)
A237	*S*. Greenwich, Conn.: Fawcett Ballantine, 1988.
A238	*S*. London: Deutsch, 1988.
*A239	*S*. London: Deutsch, 1988. (Edition limited to 12 signed roman numeral copies.)
A240	*S*. N.Y.: Knopf, 1988.
A241	*S*. N.Y.: Knopf, 1988. (Book Club edition.)
A242	*S*. N.Y.: Knopf, 1988. (Quality Paperback Book Club edition.)
A243	*Trust Me*, N.Y.: Ballantine, 1988.
A244	*In Memoriam Felis Felis. A Poem*. With Pictures by R. B. Kitaj. Leamington Spa, Warwickshire: Sixth Chamber P, 1989. (Limited edition of 12 signed copies. Rpt. in *Recent Poems 1986-1990*. Helsinki: Eurographica, 1990; and in *Collected Poems, 1953-1993*. N.Y.: Knopf, 1993. 220-21.)
A245	*Just Looking*. London: Deutsch, 1989.
A246	*Just Looking*. N.Y.: Knopf, 1989. (Includes: "What MOMA Done Tole Me," "A City Frieze," "An Outdoor Vermeer," "The Apple's Fresh Weight," "A Case of Overestimation," "The Child Within," "American Children," "Something Missing," "Field's Luminous Folk," "A Case of Solicitude," "Is Art Worth It?" "A Mischievous Monet," "Reluctant Butterfly," "Some Rectangles of Blue," "Violence at the Windows," "Moving Along," "A Case of Melancholia," "The Hand of Saint Saens," "The Vital Push," "Little Lightnings," "Heavily Hyped Helga," "Working Space," and "Writers and Artists.")
A247	*Just Looking*. N.Y.: Knopf, 1989. (Signed edition limited to 350 copies.)
A248	*Just Looking*. London: Deutsch, 1989.

A249 *Recent Poems, 1986-1990.* Helsinki: Eurographica, 1989. (Poems published since *Facing Nature*, with three earlier uncollected poems ("A Pear Like a Potato," "In Memoriam Felis Felis," and "Kiss Sixteen.") The book includes: **Travel Sonnets: "Munich," "Switzerland," "Sonnet to Man-Made Grandeur," "Oxford Thirty Years After,"** "Somewhere Else," **"Airport," "Second Skin," "Charleston," "Tulsa," "Fargo," "Seattle Uplift," "Generic College."** Places and Creatures: **"Goodbye, Göteborg," "Washington: Tourist View," "Condo Moon," "Klimt and Schiele Confront the Cunt," "Returning Native,"** "In Memoriam Felis Felis," **"The Millipede," "Tick," "Mites," "To a Box Turtle," "Squirrels Mating," "Each Summer's Swallows," "Frost."** Personal Weather: **"Back Bay," "Conversation," "Enemies of a House," "Hot Water,"** "A Pear Like a Potato, " **"Fall," "Perfection Wasted," "Sails on All-Saints' Day," "Pillow," "The Beautiful Bowel Movement," "Orthodontia," "Snowdrops 1987," "Working Outdoors in Winter."** Light Verse: **"The Sometime Sportsman Greets the Spring," "Solitaire," "Déjà, Indeed," "Sexy Quatrains," "Rock Video," "An Open Letter to Voyager II,"** "Kiss Sixteen: Translation of 'Basium XVI by Iohannes Secundus.'" Poems in bold were reprinted in *Collected Poems, 1953-1993.* N.Y.: Knopf, 1993, with "Somewhere Else" retitled "Somewhere," and many minor revisions.)

A250 *S.* Harmondsworth, Middlesex: Penguin, 1989.

A251 *Self-Consciousness.* N.Y.: Knopf, 1989. (Includes: i. "A Soft Spring Night in Shillington." ii. "At War with My Skin." iii "Getting the Words Out." iv. "On Not Being a Dove." v. "A Letter to My Grandsons." vi. "On Being a Self Forever.")

A252 *Brother Grasshopper.* Worcester, Mass.: Metacom, 1990. (Short story, substantially revised for this limited edition from "Brother Grasshopper." *The New Yorker* 63 [14 Dec. 1987]: 40-46.)

*A253 *Full Forty Years Have Flown, No Less....* [Pa.]: privately printed, 1990. (Signed broadside.)

A254 *Just Looking.* London: Penguin, 1990.

A255 *Rabbit at Rest.* Greenwich, Conn.: Fawcett, 1990.

A256 *Rabbit at Rest.* London: Deutsch, 1990.

A257 *Rabbit at Rest.* N.Y.: Knopf, 1990.

A258 *Rabbit at Rest.* N.Y.: Knopf, 1990. (Large print edition.)

A259 *Rabbit at Rest.* N.Y.: Knopf, 1990. (Quality Paperback Book Club.)

A260 *A Rabbit Omnibus.* London: Andre Deutsch, 1990. (Includes *Rabbit, Run, Rabbit Redux* and *Rabbit Is Rich*.)

*A261 *Recent Poems 1986-1990*. Helsinki: Eurographica, 1990. (Limited to 350 signed copies.)

*A262 *Self-Consciousness*. London: Penguin, 1990.

A263 *Self-Consciousness*. N.Y.: Ballantine Books, 1990.

A264 *Odd Jobs: Essays and Criticism*. N.Y.: Knopf, 1991. (Book Club edition.)

A265 *Odd Jobs: Essays and Criticism*. N.Y.: Knopf, 1991. (Includes: **Preface**; **Fairly Personal**: "Five Days in Finland at the Age of Fifty-Five," "The Parade," "First Wives and Trolley Cars," "Your Lover Just Called: A Playlet." **Media**: "Being on TV-I," "Being on TV-II," "Books into Film", "A Nameless Rose," "Overboard on Overboard." **Environs**: "Fictional Houses," "Can Architecture be Criticized?" "Is New York City Inhabitable?" "A Sense of Transparency," "A Short and Happy Ride." **Essays on Assigned Topics**: "Women," "Mother," "The Female Body," "Beauty," "Spirituality," "The Fourth of July," "Our National Monuments," "The Importance of Fiction," "High Art Versus Popular Culture," "Popular Music," "The Boston Red Sox, as of 1986," and "Ted Williams, as of 1986." **Mostly Literary: Tributes**: "Edmund Wilson," "Mr. Volente," "Mr. Palomar," " John Cheever— I," "John Cheever— II," "John Cheever— III," "John Cheever— IV." **Speeches**: "How Does the State Imagine?" "How Does the Writer Imagine?" "Should Writers Give Lectures?" "Emersonianism," "Howells as Anti-Novelist." **Introductions**: To *Indian Summer* by William Dean Howells, *Nature's Diary* by Mikhail Prishvin, *The Complete Stories* by Franz Kafka, *Seven Gothic Tales* by Isak Dinesen, *Appointment in Samarra* by John O'Hara, *The Power and the Glory* by Graham Greene, *Wolfgang Amadeus Mozart* by Karl Barth. **Moralists**: "The Gospel According to St. Matthew," "Many Bens," "The Ugly Duckling," "The Heartless Man," "The Virtues of Playing Cricket on the Village Green." **Americans**: "Twisted Apples," "The Sinister Sex," "Cohn's Doom," "Summonses, Indictments, Extenuating Circumstances," "Back in Midland City," "Last Blague," "What You Deserve Is What You Get," "Beattieniks," "Leaving Home," "No More Mr. Knightleys," "Louise in the New World, Alice on the Magic Molehill," "Back to Nature." **Philip Roth**: "Doing His Thing," "Yahweh over Dionysus, in Disputed Decision," "Bound to Please," "Wrestling to Be Born," "And Nothing But." **Frenchmen**: "Art and Artillery," "Between Pinget's Ears," "Illuminating Reversals," "Michel Tournier," "Small Packages." **Iris Murdoch, Paired with Others**: "Baggy Monsters," "Expeditions to Gilead and Seegard," "Back to the Classics." **Britishers**: "Genius Without a Cause," "Among the Masters," "To the Arctic," "Lost Among the Romantics," "A Romp with Job," "Spark but No Spark," "Bad Neighbors," "The Jones Boys," "Seeking Connections in an Insecure Country." **The Other Americans**: "Living Death," "Latin Strategies," "The Great Paraguayan Novel and Other Hardships," "Resisting the Big Boys." **The Evil Empire**: "How the Other Half Lives," "Out of the Evil Empire," "Russian Delinquents," "Visiting the Land of the Free," "Doubt and Difficulty in Leningrad and Moscow."

Other Countries Heard From: "Chronicles and Processions," "Satan's World and Silted Cisterns," "Three Tales from Nigeria," "Chinese Disharmonies," "In Love with the West," "Far-Fetched," "As Others See Us," "Studies in Post-Hitlerian Self-Condemnation in Austria and West Germany," "Rational Faith," "Mutability and Gloire," "Dutchmen and Turks, " "Levels and Levels." **Odd Couples**: "A Pair of Parrots," "Memory Palaces," "In Dispraise of the Powers That Be," "Ungreat Lives," "Old World Wickedness," "VN Again and Again," "Nice Tries." **Hyperreality**: "The Flaming Chalice," "Ecolalia," "In Borges's Wake," "Modernist, Postmodernist, What Will They Think of Next?" "States of Mind," "Final Fragments," "Slogging Sammy," "Still Stirring," "Still Staring," "Writer-Consciousness," "A Materialist Look at Eros." **Landscapes and Characters**: "A Long Way Home," "The Local View," "Hymn to Tilth," "Damp and Dull," "Empire's End," "Schulz's Charred Scraps." **Biographies**: "The Process and the Lock," "Eliot Without Words," "Goody Sergeant; the Powerful Katrinka; K. S. W.," "Witty Dotty," "Was B. B. a Crook?" "The Bimbo on the Barge." **Hard Facts**: "Something Substantial and Useful About It," "Bull in a Type Shop," "Art's Dawn," "Computer Heaven," "Evolution Be Praised," "Deep Time and Computer Time." **Appendix: Literarily Personal.**

A266   *Thanatopses.* Cleveland: Bits P, 1991. (Contains previously published poems, "Perfection Wasted," "The Millipede," "Thin Air" and "Granite.")

A267   *Food.* Washington: Folger's Poetry Salon, 5 Apr., 1992. (Rpt. from "Food." *Light Year '86.* Ed. Robert Wallace. Cleveland: Bits P, 1985. 44; in *Facing Nature.* N.Y.: Knopf, 1985. 100; and in *Collected Poems, 1953-1993.* N.Y.: Knopf, 1993. 349.)

A268   *Memories of The Ford Administration.* N.Y.: Knopf, 1992. (A segment of the novel was rpt. as "A Short and Scary Walk with Andrew Jackson." *American Heritage* 43 [Oct. 1992]: 74-78, 80, 82.)

A269   *Memories of The Ford Administration.* N.Y.: Knopf, 1992. (Book Club edition.)

A270   *Odd Jobs: Essays and Criticism.* London: Deutsch, 1992.

A271   *Collected Poems, 1953-1993.* N.Y.: Knopf, 1993. (Includes: "Preface" and the following Poems, "Why the Telephone Wires Dip and the Poles are Cracked and Crooked," "Cloud Shadows," "Ex-Basketball Player," "A Modest Mound of Bones," "Sunflower," "March: A Brithday Poem," "Burning Trash," "English Train Compartment," "Tao in the Yankee Stadium Bleachers," "How to Be Uncle Sam," "3 A.M.," "Mobile of Birds," "Shillington," "Suburban Madrigal," "Telephone Poles," "Mosquito," "Trees Eat Sunshine," "Winter Ocean," "Modigliani's Death Mask," "Seagulls," "Seven Stanzas at Easter," "B. W. I.," "February 22," "Summer: West Side," "Wash," "Maples in a Spruce Forest," "Vermont," "The Solitary Pond," "Flirt," "Fever," "Earthworm," "Old-Fashioned

Lightning Rod," "Sunshine on Sandstone," "The Stunt Flier," "Calendar," "The Short Days," "Boil," "Widener Library, Reading Room," "Movie House," "Vibration," "The Blessing," "My Children at the Dump," "The Great Scarf of Birds," "Azores," "Erotic Epigrams," "Hoeing," "Report of Health," "Fireworks," "Lamplight," "Nuda Natens," "Postcards from Soviet Cities: Moscow, Leningrad, Kiev, Tbilisi, Yerevan," "Camera," "Roman Portrait Busts," "Fellatio," "Decor," "Poem for a Far Land," "Late January," "Dog's Death," "Home Movies," "Antigua," "Amoeba," "Elm," "Daughter," "Eurydice," "Seal in Nature," "Air Show," "Omega," "The Angels," "Bath After Sailing," "Topsfield Fair," "Pompeii," "Sand Dollar," "Washington," "Dream Objects," "Midpoint: I. Introduction, II. The Photographs, III. The Dance of the Solids, IV. The Play of Memory, V. Conclusion," "Chloë's Poem," "Minority Report," "Living with a Wife: At the Piano, In the Tub, Under the Sunlamp, During Menstruation, All the While," "A L'Ecole Berlitz," "South of the Alps," "A Bicycle Chain," "Tossing and Turning," "On an Island," "Sunday Rain," "Marching Through a Novel," "Night Flight, over Ocean," "Phenomena," "Wind," "Sunday," "Touch of Spring," "The House Growing," "Cunts," "Apologies to Harvard," "Commencement, Pingree Schoool," "Conversation," "Melting," "Query," "Heading for Nandi," "Sleepless in Scarsdale," "Note to the Previous Tenants," "Pale Bliss," "Mime," "Golfers," "Poisoned in Nassau," "You Who Swim," "Sunday in Boston," "Raining in Magens Bay," "Leaving Church Early," "Another Dog's Death," "Dream and Reality," "Dutch Cleanser," "Rats," "The Melancholy of Storm Windows," "Calder's Hands," "The Grief of Cafeterias," "Spanish Sonnets," "To Ed Sissman," "Ohio," "Iowa," "Waiting Rooms: Boston Lying-In, Mass. Mental Health," "On the Way to Delphi," "An Oddly Lovely Day Alone," "Taste," "Penumbrae," "Revelation," "The Shuttle," "Crab Crack," "Nature," "The Moons of Jupiter," "Upon the Last Day of His Forty-Ninth Year," "Planting Trees," "The Fleckings," "East Hampton-Boston by Air," "Small-City People," "L. A.," "Plow Cemetery," "Spring Song," "Accumulation," "Styles of Bloom," "Natural Question," "Two Hoppers," "Two Sonnets Whose Titles Came to Me Simultaneously: The Dying Phobiac Takes His Fears with Him," "No More Access to Her Underpants," "Long Shadow," "Aerie," "The Code," "Island Sun," "Pain," "Sleeping with You," "Richmond," "Gradations of Black," "The Furniture," **Seven Odes to Seven Natural Processes**: "Ode to Rot," "To Evaporation," "Ode to Growth," "To Fragmentaiton," "Ode to Entropy," "To Cyrstallization," "Ode to Healing." "Switzerland," "Munich," "A Pear Like a Potato," "Airport," "From Above," "Oxford, Thirty Years After," "Somewhere," "Sonnet to Man-Made Grandeur," "Klimt and Schiele Confront the Cunt," "Returning Native," "Snowdrops 1987," "Goodbye, Göteborg," "Hot Water," "Squirrels Mating," "Sails on All Saints' Day," "Tulsa," "Washington: Tourist View," "Back Bay," "In Memoriam Felis Felis," "Enemies of a Hosue," "Orthodontia," "Condo Moon," "Pillow," "Seattle Uplift," "The Beautiful Bowel Movement," "Charleston," "Frost," "To a Box Turtle," "Each Summer's Swallows," "Fargo," "Fall," "The Millipede," "Generic College," "Perfection Wasted," "Working

Outdoors in Winter," "Indianapolis," "Zoo Bats," "Landing in the Rain at La Guardia," "Mouse Sex," "Granite," "Relatives," "Thin Air," "November," "Light Switches," "Miami," "Fly," "Flurry," "Bindweed," "July," "To a Dead Flame," "Back from Vacation," "Literary Dublin," "Elderly Sex," "Celery," "Sao Paulo," "Rio de Janeiro," "Brazil," "Upon Looking into Sylvia Plath's *Letters Home*," "At the End of the Rainbow," "Academy," **Light Verse** "Mountain Impasse," "Solitaire," "Duet, with Muffled Brake Drums," "Player Piano," "Snapshots," "An Imaginable Conference," "Dilemma in the Delta," "Shipboard," "Song of the Open Fireplace," "The Clan," "Youth's Progress," "Humanities Course," "V. B. Nimble, V. B. Quick," "Lament, for Cocoa," "Pop Smash, Out of Echo Chamber," "Sunglasses," "Pooem," "To an Usherette," "Time's Fool," "Superman," "An Ode," "The Newlyweds," "The Story of My Life," "A Bitter Life," "A Wooden Darning Egg," "Publius Vergilius Maro, the Madison Avenue Hick," "Tsokadze O Altitudo," "The One-Year-Old," "Room 28," "Philological," "Mr. High-Mind," "Tax-Free Encounter," "Scenic," "Capacity," "Little Poems," "Popular Revivals 1956," "Tune, in American Type," "Due Respect," "A Rack of Paperbacks," "Even Egrets Err," "Glasses," "The Sensualist," "In Memoriam," "Planting a Mailbox," "ZULUS LIVE IN LAND WITHOUT A SQUARE," "Caligula's Dream," "Bendix," "The Menagerie at Versailles in 1775," "Reel," "Kenneths," "Upon Learning That a Bird Exists Called the Turnstone," "In Extremis," "Blked," "Toothache Man," "Party Knee," "The Moderate," "Deities and Beasts," "Within a Quad," "In Praise of $(C_{10}H_9O_5)x$," "Milady Reflects," "The Fritillary," "Thoughts While Driving Home," "Sonic Boom," "Tome-Thoughts, from the *Times*," "A Song of Paternal Care," "Tropical Beetles," "Agatha Christie and Beatrix Potter," "Young Matrons Dancing," "Comp. Religion," "Meditation on a News Item," "Cosmic Gall," "A Vision," "Les Saints Nouveaux," "The Descent of Mr. Aldez," "Upon Learning That a Town Exists in Virginia Called Upperville," "Recital," "I Missed His Book, but I Read His Name," "On the Inclusion of Miniature Dinosaurs in Breakfast Cereal Boxes," "The High-Hearts," "Marriage Counsel," "The Handkerchiefs of Khaibar Khan," "Dea ex Machina," "Die Neuen Heiligen," "Miss Moore at Assembly," "White Dwarf," "Exposure," "Exposé," "Farewell to the Shopping District of Antibes," "Some Frenchmen," "Sea Knell," "Vow," "The Amish," "The Naked Ape," "The Origin of Laughter," "The Average Egyptian Faces Death," "Painted Wives," "Skyey Developments," "Courtesy Call," "Business Acquaintances," "Seven New Ways of Looking at the Moon," "Upon Shaving Off One's Beard," "The Cars in Caracas," "Insomnia the Gem of the Ocean," "To a Waterbed," "The Jolly Greene Giant," "News from the Underworld," "Authors' Residences," "Sin City, D. C.," "Shaving Mirror," "Self-Service," "The Visions of Mackenzie King," "Energy: A Villanelle," "On the Recently Minted Hundred-Cent Piece," "Typical Optical," "The Rockettes," "Food," "The Sometime Sportsman Greets the Spring," "ZIP Code Ode," "Déjà, Indeed," "Two Limericks for the Elderly," "Mites," "An Open Letter to Voyager II," "Classical Optical," "Neoteny." Appendix A: Poems in Previous Collections

Omitted. Appendix B: Poems Published in *The New Yorker* **Omitted. Index of Titles.**

2. Plays

A272 "The Plastic Menagerie." *The Harvard Lampoon Centennial Celebration, 1876-1973*. Martin Kaplan, ed. Boston: Atlantic-Little, Brown, 1973. Unpaginated.

A273 "The Fisherman and His Wife, A Tale from the Brothers Grimm, The Libretto of a Children's Opera." *Texas Arts Journal* Sum. 1977: 14-38. (An adaptation of the Grimm fairy tale, the libretto was set to music by Gunther Schuller.)

A274 "Your Lover Just Called: A Playlet." ("Adapted from the Short Story of the Same Name for an Evening of Fifteen-Minute Plays at the Blackburn Theatre, in Gloucester, Massachusetts, on April 10, 1989." Rpt. in *Odd Jobs: Essays and Criticism*. N.Y.: Knopf, 1991. 26-30.)

3. Short Fiction

A275   "The Different One." *Harvard Lampoon* 140 (May 1951): 12. (Rpt. in *The Harvard Lampoon Centennial Celebration, 1876-1973*. Ed. Martin Kaplan. Boston, Mass.: Atlantic-Little, 1973. Unpaginated.)

A276   "Skylark Story." *Harvard Lampoon* 140 (Nov. 1951): 22. (Rpt. in *The Harvard Lampoon Centennial Celebration, 1876-1973*. Ed. Martin Kaplan. Boston, Mass.: Atlantic-Little, 1973. Unpaginated. Erroneously titled "Skylard Story" and placed with poetry by C. Clarke Taylor, *John Updike: A Bibliography*. Kent: Kent State U P, 1968. 7.)

A277   "The Enormous Package." *Harvard Lampoon* 141 (Dec. 1952): 18-21. (Signed "John H. Updike." Rpt. in *Max Shulman's Guided Tour of Campus Humor: The Best Stories, Articles, Poems, Jokes and Nonsense from Over Sixty-Five College Humor Magazines*. Ed. Max Shulman. Garden City, N.Y.: Hanover House, 1955. 156-59.)

A278   "Ace in the Hole." *The New Yorker* 31 (9 Apr. 1955): 92-99. (Rpt. in *The Same Door*. N.Y.: Knopf, 1959. 14-26; and in *The Sporting Spirit*. Ed. Robert J. Higgs and Neil D. Issacs. N.Y.: Harcourt, 1977. 45-52.)

A279   "Snowing in Greenwich Village." *The New Yorker* 31 (21 Jan. 1956): 30-33. (Rpt. in *Too Far To Go: The Maples Stories*. N.Y.: Fawcett, 1979. 13-28; and in *Modern American Love Stories*. Japan: New Currents International, 1970.)

A280   "Incest." *The New Yorker* 31 (29 June 1957): 22-27. (Rpt. in *The Same Door*. N.Y.: Knopf, 1959. 144-162; in *Too Far To Go: The Maples Stories*. N.Y.: Fawcett, 1979. 13-28; and in *How We Live*. Ed. Penny Chapin and L. Rust Hills. N.Y., 1968. 271-81.)

A281   "The Alligators." *The New Yorker* 34 (22 Mar. 1958): 28-31. (Rpt. in *Parents' Magazine* 40 (Sept. 1965): 62-63; in *The Same Door*. N.Y.: Knopf, 1959. 210-219; in *Olinger Stories*. N.Y.: Vintage, 1964. 10-18; in *Great*

Short Stories of the World. Pleasantville, N.Y.: Reader's Digest Association, 1972. 469-76; in *Selections from Reader's Digest Condensed Books and Other Digest Publications*. Pleasantville, N.Y.: Reader's Digest Fund for the Blind, 1983; and in **Junior Great Books, A Program of Interpretive Reading and Discussion*. Chicago: The Great Books Foundation, 1984.)

A282   "A Gift from the City." *The New Yorker* 34 (12 Apr. 1958): 45-64. (Rpt. in *The Best American Short Stories 1959*. Ed. Martha Foley and David Burnett. Boston: Houghton Mifflin, 1959. 340-58.)

A283   "The Happiest I've Been." *The New Yorker* 34 (3 Jan. 1959): 24-31. (Rpt. in *The Norton Anthology of American Literature*. 2nd ed. Vol. 2. Ed. Nina Baym, Ronald Gottesman, Laurence B. Holland, Francis Murphy, Hershel Parker, William H. Pritchard, and David Kalstone. N.Y.: Norton, 1985. 2166-80; and in **Hansen, You Don't Know What Love Is: Contemporary American Stories*. Ontario, 1987.)

A284   "Should Wizard Hit Mommy?" *The New Yorker* 35 (13 June 1959): 38-40. (Rpt. in *A Reading Apprenticeship*. Ed. Norman A. Brittin. N.Y.: Holt, 1971. 152-57; and in *The Green Man Revisited: Classic English Short Stories*. Ed. Roger Sharrock. N.Y.: Oxford U P, 1988. 260-66.)

A285   "Flight." *The New Yorker* 35 (22 Aug. 1959): 30-37. (Rpt. in *The Abnormal Personality in Literature*. Ed. Allan Stone and Sue Smart Stone. Englewood Cliffs, N.J.: Prentice, 1966. 217-18 [excerpt]; and in *The Story and Its Writer*. 3rd ed. Ed. Ann Charter. Boston, Mass.: St. Martin's P, 1991.)

A286   "The Sea's Green Sameness." *New World Writing* No. 17 (1960): 54-59. (Rpt. in *Museums and Women and Other Stories*. N.Y.: Knopf. 159-64.)

A287   "A Sense of Shelter." *The New Yorker* 35 (16 Jan. 1960): 28-34. (Rpt. in **On Writing, By Writers*. Ed. William W. West. Boston: Ginn, 1966; in **All for Love: Stories for the Human Heart*. Logan, Iowa: Perfection Form, 1979; and in *A Sense of Shelter*. Logan, Iowa: Perfection Form, 1980.)

A288   "Wife-wooing." *The New Yorker* 36 (12 Mar. 1960): 49- 51. (Rpt. in **Prize Stories 1961: The O. Henry Awards*. Garden City, N.Y.: Doubleday, 1961; in *Pigeon Feathers and Other Stories*. N.Y.: Knopf, 1962. 109-16; in *Relevants*. Ed. Edward Quinn and Paul J. Dolan. N.Y.: The Free P, 1970. 323-27, and "Instructor's Manual." 32; in *Montage: Investigations in Language*. Ed. William Sparke and Clark McKowen. N.Y.: Macmillan, 1970. 45-48, the accompanying *Teacher's Manual*, 38; in *Short Story International. Number Six*. Ed. Sylvia Tankel. International Cultural Exchange. II [Feb. 1978]: 167-71; in *Too Far To Go: The Maples Stories*. N.Y.: Fawcett, 1979. 29-36; in *The Experience of the American Woman*. Ed. Barbara H. Solomon. N.Y.: New American Library, 1978.

Short Fiction 33

348-52; in *Lives Through Literature*. Ed. Walter Levy and Helane Levine Keating. N.Y.: Macmillan, 1991. 880-83; and in *Major Writers of Short Fiction*. Ed. Ann Charters. N.Y.: St. Martin's P, 1992: 1268-71.)

A289 "The Doctor's Wife." *The New Yorker* 36 (11 Feb. 1961): 35-38. (Rpt. in *Prize Stories 1962: The O. Henry Awards*. Ed. Richard Poirier. N.Y.: Crest, 1962. 242-50; and in *Charming American Stories*. Tokyo: Kinseido, 1964. Text in English and Japanese, with notes.)

A290 "Lifeguard." *The New Yorker* 37 (17 June 1961): 28-31. (Rpt. in *How We Live*. Ed. Penny and L. Rust Hills, 1968. 968-73; and in *Literature: An Introduction to Fiction, Poetry and Drama*. Ed. X. J. Kennedy. Boston: Little Brown, 1976. 439-44, and Instructor's Manual. 55-57.)

A291 "A & P." *The New Yorker* 37 (22 July 1961): 22-24. (Rpt. in *Here and Now*. Ed. Fred Morgan. N.Y.: Harcourt, 1968. 139-44; in *The Small Town in American Literature*. Ed. David M. Cook and Craig Swauger. N.Y.: Dodd Mead, 1969: 240-45; in *An Introduction to Literature*. 5th ed. Ed. Sylvan Barnet, Morton Berman and William Burto. Boston: Little, 1973. 297-302, and in the accompanying *Manual*, 21; in *The Valentine Generation and Other Stories*. Ed. Margery Morris. Harlow: Longman, 1980. 9-13, a simplified version of Updike's story; in *Fiction: An Anthology of 100 Short Stories*. Ed. James H. Pickering. N.Y.: Macmillan, 1982. 3rd ed. 1030-34; in *Literature*. 2nd ed. Ed. James H. Pickering and Jeffrey D. Hoeper. N.Y.: Macmillan, 1983. 481-85, and in the accompanying *Instructor's Manual* 45-46; in *A & P: Lust in the Aisles*. Toronto: Redpath P, 1986; in **Literature: Art and Artifact*. Ed. William A. Heffernan, Mark Johnston and Frank Hodgins. N.Y.: Harcourt, Brace, Jovanovich, 1987; in **Fictions*. Ed. Trimmer and Jennings. 2nd Edition. N.Y.: Harcourt, Brace, Jovanovich, 1989; and in **The Situation of the Story*. Ed. Diana Young. Lavelette, N.J.: St. Martin's P, 1992.)

A292 "Pigeon Feathers." *The New Yorker* 37 (19 Aug. 1961): 23-24. (Rpt. in *The Best American Short Stories 1962*. Ed. Martha Foley and David Burnett. Boston: Houghton, 1962. 400-19; in *The Abnormal Personality in Literature*. Ed. Allan Stone and Sue Smart Stone. Englewood Cliffs, N.J.: Prentice, 1966. 191-93; and in *An Anthology of Literature*. Logan, Iowa: Perfection Form Co., 1979. 1-38, with notes 39-48.)

A293 "Packed Dirt, Churchgoing, A Dying Cat, A Traded Car." *The New Yorker* 37 (16 Dec. 1961): 59-62. (Rpt. in *Pigeon Feathers*. N.Y.: Knopf, 1961. 246-79; in *Olinger Stories*. N.Y.: Vintage, 1964. 154-85; and in *This Is My Best*. Ed. Whit Burnett. N.Y.: Doubleday, 1970. 4-25.)

A294 "The Blessed Man of Boston, My Grandmother's Thimble, and Fanning Island." *The New Yorker* 37 (13 Jan. 1962): 28-33. (Rpt. in *Prose models: An Approach to Writing*. Ed. Gerald Levin. N.Y.: Harcourt, 1970. 112-13. Updike notes his poem "Shipbored" is alluded to in this story, in *Collected Poems: 1953-1993*. N.Y.: Knopf, 1993. 369.)

A295   "Unstuck." *The New Yorker* 37 (3 Feb. 1962): 24-27 (Rpt. in *Trust Me*. N.Y.: Knopf, 1987. 61-70.)

A296   "Giving Blood." *The New Yorker* 39 (6 Apr. 1963): 36-41. (Rpt. in *Too Far to Go: The Maples Stories*. N.Y.: Fawcett, 1979. 37-58.)

A297   "At a Bar in Charlotte Amalie." *The New Yorker* 39 (11 Jan. 1964): 26-32. (Excerpted in *Self-Consciousness*. N.Y.: Knopf, 1989. 71n.)

A298   "Twin Beds in Rome." *The New Yorker* 39 (8 Feb. 1964): 32-35. (Rpt. in *Too Far to Go: The Maples Stories*. N.Y.: Fawcett, 1979. 59-72.)

A299   "The Lucid Eye in Silver Town." *Saturday Evening Post* 237 (23 May 1964): 54-55. (Rpt. in *50 Great American Short Stories*. Ed. Milton Crane. N.Y.: Bantam, 1986. 487-96.)

A300   "The Bulgarian Poetess." *The New Yorker* 41 (13 Mar. 1965): 44-51. (Rpt. in *The Music School*. N.Y.: Knopf, 1966. 211-31; in *Prize Stories 1966: The O. Henry Awards*. Ed. Richard Poirier and William Abrahams. Garden City, N.Y.: Doubleday, 1966; in *The American Tradition in Literature*. 3rd ed. Shorter ed. Ed. Sculley Bradley, Richmond Croom Beatty, E. Hudson Long. N.Y.: Norton, 1967. 1878-91; in *Bech: A Book*. N.Y.: Knopf, 1970. 49-70; in *The American Tradition in Literature*. 3rd ed. Vol. 2. Ed. Sculley Bradley, Richmond Croom Beatty, E. Hudson Long and George Perkins. N.Y.: Grosset, 1974. 1801-15; and in *A Treasury of American Short Stories*. Ed. Nancy S. Sullivan. N.Y.: Doubleday, 1981. 646-58.)

A301   "Family Meadow." *The New Yorker* 41 (24 July 1965): 41-43. (Rpt. in *How We Live*. Ed. Penny and L. Rust Hills. 1968. 125-29.)

A302   "During the Jurassic." *Transatlantic Review* No. 21 (1966): 47. (Rpt. in *Museums and Women and Other Stories*. N.Y.: Knopf, 1972. 194-201; and in *SF 12*. Ed. Judith Merrill. N.Y.: Delacorte P, 1968. 89-93.)

A303   "Marching Through Boston." *The New Yorker* 41 (22 Jan. 1966): 34-38. (Rpt. in *Museums and Women and Other Stories*. N.Y.: Knopf, 1972. 221-34; and in *Too Far to Go: The Maples Stories*. N.Y.: Fawcett, 1979. 73-90.)

A304   "The Witnesses." *The New Yorker* 42 (13 Aug. 1966): 46-48. (Rpt. in *Museums and Women and Other Stories*. N.Y.: Knopf, 1972. 70-77.)

A305   "The Pro." *The New Yorker* 42 (17 Sept. 1966): 53-54. (Rpt. in *Museums and Women and Other Stories*. N.Y.: Knopf, 1972. 169-74; in *Forbes (Personal Affairs Supplement* 144 [23 Oct. 1989]: 38; and in *The Norton Book of Sports*. Ed. George Plimpton. N.Y.: W. W. Norton, 1992. 157-61.)

Short Fiction 35

A306 "Bech in Romania." *The New Yorker* 42 (8 Oct. 1966): 54-63. (Rpt. in *Bech: A Book*. N.Y.: Knopf, 1970. 22-48; and in *Penguin Modern Stories 2*. Ed. Judith Burnley. Harmondsworth, Middlesex: Penguin, 1969. 60-80.)

A307 "Your Lover Just Called." *Harper's* 234 (Jan. 1967): 48-51. (Rpt. in *Prize Stories 1968: The O. Henry Awards*. Ed. William Abrahams. Garden City, N.Y.: Doubleday, 1968. 259-66; and in *Too Far to Go: The Maples Stories*. N.Y.: Fawcett, 1979. 101-14.)

A308 "The Taste of Metal." *The New Yorker* 43 (11 Mar. 1967): 49-51. (Rpt. in *Too Far to Go: The Maples Stories*. N.Y.: Fawcett, 1979. 91-100.)

A309 "Museums and Women." *The New Yorker* 43 (18 Nov. 1967): 57-61. (Rpt. in *Museums and Women and Other Stories*. N.Y.: Knopf, 1972. 3-17.)

A310 "Under the Microscope." *Transatlantic Review* No. 28 (1968): 5. (Rpt. in *Museums and Women and Other Stories*. N.Y.: Knopf, 1972. 189-93.)

A311 "The Wait." *The New Yorker* 43 (17 Feb. 1968): 34-40, 42, 45-46, 48, 51-52, 54, 57-58, 60, 65-66, 68, 70, 72, 77-78, 80, 83-84, 86, 89-90, 92, 95-96. (Rpt. in *Marry Me: A Romance*. N.Y.: Fawcett, 1976. [Updike's note: "Chapter II appeared, in a somewhat different form, in *The New Yorker*."]; and in *Penguin Modern Stories 2*. Ed. Judith Burnley. Harmondsworth, Middlesex: Penguin, 1969. 9-59.)

A312 "Man and Daughter in the Cold." *The New Yorker* 44 (9 Mar. 1968): 98-107. (Rpt. in *Museums and Women and Other Stories*. N.Y.: Knopf, 1972. 26-40; and in *Penguin Modern Stories 2*. Ed. Judith Burnley. Harmondsworth, Middlesex: Penguin, 1969. 81-90.)

A313 "Eros Rampant." *Harper's* 237 (June 1968): 59-64. (Rpt. in *Museums and Women and Other Stories*. N.Y.: Knopf, 1972. 252-67; and in *Too Far to Go: The Maples Stories*. N.Y.: Fawcett, 1979. 123-43.)

A314 "The Slump." *Esquire* 70 (July 1968): 104-05. (Rpt. in *Museums and Women and Other Stories*. N.Y.: Knopf, 1972. 165-68; excerpted in *Diamonds Are Forever*. Ed. Peter Gordon, Paul Weinman and Sydney Waller. San Francisco: Chronicle Books, 1987. 67.)

A315 "Bech Takes Pot Luck." *The New Yorker* 44 (7 Sept. 1968): 28-36. (Rpt. in *Prize Stories 1970: The O. Henry Awards*. Ed. William Abrahams. Garden City, N.Y.: Doubleday, 1970; and in *Bech: A Book*. N.Y.: Knopf, 1970. 71-98.)

A316 "Corner." *The New Yorker* 45 (24 May 1969): 38-41. (Rpt. in *Museums and Women and Other Stories*. N.Y.: Knopf, 1972. 59-69.)

A317   "I am Dying, Egypt, Dying." *Playboy* 16 (Sept. 1969): 118, 120, 250, 252-60. (Rpt. in *Museums and Women and Other Stories*. N.Y.: Knopf, 1972. 108-41.)

A318   "Day of the Dying Rabbit." *The New Yorker* 45 (30 Aug. 1969): 22-26. (Rpt. in *Museums and Women and Other Stories*. N.Y.: Knopf, 1972. 26-40.)

A319   "I Will Not Let Thee Go, Except Thou Bless Me." *The New Yorker* 45 (11 Oct. 1969): 50-53. (Rpt. in *Museums and Women and Other Stories*. N.Y.: Knopf, 1972. 49-58.)

A320   "One of My Generation." *The New Yorker* 45 (15 Nov. 1969): 57-58. (Rpt. in *Museums and Women and Other Stories*. N.Y.: Knopf, 1972. 175-80.)

A321   "The Hillies." *The New Yorker* 45 (20 Dec. 1969): 33-35. (Rpt. in *Museums and Women and Other Stories*. N.Y.: Knopf, 1972. 18-25.)

A322   "Rich in Russia." *The New Yorker* 45 (31 Jan. 1970): 31-36. (Rpt. in *Bech: A Book*. N.Y.: Knopf, 1970. 3-21.)

A323   "The Deacon." *The New Yorker* 46 (21 Feb. 1970): 38- 41. (Rpt. in *Museums and Women and Other Stories*. N.Y.: Knopf, 1972. 41-48.)

A324   "Bech Swings?" *The New Yorker* 46 (28 Mar. 1970): 33-42. (Rpt. in *Bech: A Book*. N.Y.: Knopf, 1970. 133-69.)

A325   "The Orphaned Swimming Pool." *The New Yorker* 46 (27 June 1970): 30-32. (Rpt. in *Museums and Women and Other Stories*. N.Y.: Knopf, 1972. 85-90.)

A326   "The Carol Sing." *The New Yorker* 46 (19 Dec. 1970): 36-37. (Rpt. in *Museums and Women and Other Stories*. N.Y.: Knopf, 1972. 142-47.)

A327   "Plumbing." *The New Yorker* 47 (20 Feb. 1971): 34-37.(Rpt. in *Museums and Women and Other Stories*. N.Y.: Knopf, 1972. 148-55;. and in *Too Far to Go: The Maples Stories*. N.Y.: Fawcett, 1979. 144-54.)

A328   "Pop/Mom/Moon." *Atlantic* 228 (Aug. 1971): 48-51, 54-63. (Published in slightly different form in *Rabbit Redux*. N.Y.: Knopf, 1971 as the first section.)

A329   "The Baluchitherium." *The New Yorker* 47 (14 Aug. 1971): 39. (Rpt. in *Museums and Women and Other Stories*. N.Y.: Knopf, 1972. 202-06.)

A330   "Rabbit's Evening Out." *Esquire* 76 (Sept. 1971): 109-112, 191-92, 194, 196. (Rpt. in *Rabbit Redux*. N.Y.: Knopf, 1971, as part of Chapter I.)

Short Fiction   37

A331   "Sublimating." *Harper's* 243 (Sept. 1971): 82-85. (Rpt. in *Museums and Women and Other Stories*. N.Y.: Knopf, 1972. 268-78; and in *Too Far to Go: The Maples Stories*. N.Y.: Fawcett, 1979. 165-79.)

A332   "Love: First Lessons." *The New Yorker* 47 (6 Nov. 1971): 46-47. (Rpt. in "slightly different form" as *The Beloved*. Northridge, Calif., Lord John P, 1982. See also "The Beloved." *Transatlantic Review* 50 [Autumn-Wint. 1974]: 19-29.)

A333   "When Everybody Was Pregnant." *Audience* 6 (Nov.-Dec. 1971): 35-36. (Rpt. in *Museums and Women and Other Stories*. N.Y.: Knopf, 1972. 91-97, retitled, "When Everyone Was Pregnant"; and in *America in Literature*. II. Ed. Alan Trachtenberg and Benjamin DeMott. N.Y.: Wiley, 1978. 1147-53.)

A334   "Jesus on Honshu." *The New Yorker* 47 (25 Dec. 1971): 29-30. (Rpt. in *Museums and Women and Other Stories*. N.Y.: Knopf, 1972. 213-217.)

A335   "The Invention of the Horse Collar." *Transatlantic Review* No. 48/49 (1972): 51. (Rpt. in *Museums and Women and Other Stories*. N.Y.: Knopf, 1972. 207-12.)

A336   "Solitaire." *The New Yorker* 47 (22 Jan. 1972): 26-27. (Rpt. in *Museums and Women and Other Stories*. N.Y.: Knopf, 1972. 78-84.)

A337   "Commercial." *The New Yorker* 48 (10 June 1972): 30-32. (Rpt. in *Problems and Other Stories*. N.Y.: Knopf, 1979. 3-11.)

A338   "Believers." *Harper's* 245 (July 1972): 86-87. (Rpt. in *Problems and Other Stories*. N.Y.: Knopf, 1979. 18-23.)

A339   "The Gun Shop." *The New Yorker* 48 (25 Nov. 1972): 42-47. (Rpt. in *Problems and Other Stories*. N.Y.: Knopf, 1979. 24-39.)

A340   "Ride." *The New Yorker* 48 (2 Dec. 1972): 51.

A341   "Son." *The New Yorker* 49 (21 Apr. 1973): 33-35. (Rpt. in *Problems and Other Stories*. N.Y.: Knopf, 1979. 61-67; and in *The Best American Short Stories 1974, the Yearbook of the American Short Story*. Ed. Martha Foley. Boston: Houghton Mifflin, 1974. 306-31.)

A342   "Deus Dixit." *Esquire* 80 (Oct. 1973): 301-02, 494. (Rpt. as "God Speaks" in *Museums and Women and Other Stories*. N.Y.: Knopf, 1972. 181-88.)

A343   "Daughter, Last Glimpses of." *The New Yorker* 49 (5 Nov. 1973): 50-53. (Rpt. in *Problems and Other Stories*. N.Y.: Knopf, 1979. 68-76.)

A344   "Nevada." *Playboy* 21 (Jan. 1974): 167-68, 240, 242.(Rpt. in *Problems and Other Stories*. N.Y.: Knopf, 1979. 47-60.)

A345   "Ethiopia." *The New Yorker* 49 (14 Jan. 1974): 28-32.(Rpt. in *Problems and Other Stories*. N.Y.: Knopf, 1979. 77-87.)

A346   "Nakedness." *Atlantic* 234 (Aug. 1974): 33-36. (Rpt. in *Too Far to Go: The Maples Stories*. N.Y.: Fawcett, 1979. 180-191; and in *Prize Stories 1975: The O. Henry Awards*. Ed. William Abrahams. Garden City: Doubleday, 1975. 316-23.)

A347   "The Beloved." *Transatlantic Review* 50 (Autumn-Wint. 1974): 19-29. (Rpt. in "slightly different form" as *The Beloved*. Northridge, Calif., Lord John P, 1982. Limited edition of 300 copies. See also "Love: First Lessons." *The New Yorker* 47 [6 Nov. 1971]: 46-47.)

A348   "A Month of Sundays." *Playboy* 22 (Jan. 1975): 82-84, 86, 92, 241-42, 244-48, 250. (Rpt. in *A Month of Sundays*. N.Y.: Knopf, 1975.)

A349   "Augustine's Concubine." *Atlantic* 235 (Apr. 1975): 54-56. (Rpt. in *Problems and Other Stories*. N.Y.: Knopf, 1979. 123-140; and in *119 Years of the Atlantic*. Ed. Louise Desauliniers. Boston: Atlantic-Little, 1977.)

A350   "Australia and Canada." *Playboy* 22 (May 1975): 118-20, 126, 176-78. (Rpt. in *Bech Is Back*. N.Y.: Knopf, 1982. 47-65.)

A351   "The Red-Herring Theory." *The New York Times Magazine* 1 June 1975: 95. (Rpt. in *Too Far to Go: The Maples Stories*. N.Y.: Fawcett, 1979. 155-64.)

A352   "Red-herring Theory: Part 2." *The New York Times Magazine* 8 June 1975: 103. (Rpt. in *Too Far to Go: The Maples Stories*. N.Y.: Fawcett, 1979. 155-64.)

A353   "Separating." *The New Yorker* 51 (23 June 1975): 36-41. (Rpt. in: *Too Far To Go: The Maples Stories*. N.Y.: Fawcett, 1979. 192-211; in *Problems and Other Stories*. N.Y.: Knopf, 1979. 116-31; *Prize Stories, 1976 The O'Henry Awards*, with Updike given a special award for continuing achievement; in *Familiar Faces: Best Contemporary American Short Stories*. N.Y.: Fawcett, 1979. 299-312; in *The Norton Anthology of American Literature*. 2nd ed. Vol. 2. Ed. Nina Baym, Ronald Gottesman, Laurence B. Holland, Francis Murphy, Hershel Parker, William H. Pritchard, and David Kalstone. N.Y.: Norton, 1985. 2180-89, and in the "Shorter Edition" by the same Ed., 2404-2425; in *The Heath Introduction to Fiction*. Ed. Clayton. N.Y.: Heath, 1988; in *Fiction 100*. Ed. Pickering. N.Y.: Macmillan, 1988; in *Wives and Husbands: 20 Short Stories About Marriage*. Ed. Michael Nagler and William Swanson. N.Y.: New American Library, 1989. 30-34; and *Major Writers of Short Fiction*. Ed. Ann Charters. N.Y.: St. Martin's P, 1992: 1260-68.)

A354   "Man Who Loved Extinct Mammals." *The New Yorker* 51 (21 July 1975): 24-26. (Rpt. in *The Best American Short Stories 1976, and the Yearbook of*

Short Fiction 39

the *American Short Story.* Ed. Foley. Boston: Houghton, 1976; and in *Problems and Other Stories.* N.Y.: Knopf, 1979. 141-49.)

A355   "Bech Third-Worlds It." *Playboy* 22 (Aug. 1975): 104-06, 144-47. (Rpt. in *Bech Is Back.* N.Y.: Knopf, 1982. 28-46.)

A356   "Problems." *The New Yorker* 51 (3 Nov. 1975): 39. Rpt. in *Problems and Other Stories.* N.Y.: Knopf, 1979. 150-53.)

A357   "Love Song, for a Moog Synthesizer." *The New Yorker* 52 (14 June 1976): 29-31. (Rpt. in *Problems and Other Stories.* N.Y.: Knopf, 1979. 174-81.)

A358   "From the Journal of a Leper." *The New Yorker* 52 (19 July 1976): 28-33. (Rpt. in *Problems and Other Stories.* N.Y.: Knopf, 1979. 181-196; in *From the Journal of a Leper.* Northridge, California: Lord John P, 1978; and excerpted in *Self-Consciousness.* N.Y.: Knopf, 1989. 76n.)

A359   "Here Come the Maples." *The New Yorker* 52 (11 Oct. 1976): 38-43. (Rpt. in *Problems and Other Stories.* N.Y.: Knopf, 1979. 197-212; in *Too Far to Go: The Maples Stories.* N.Y.: Fawcett, 1979. 180-91; in *Great American Love Stories.* Ed. Lucy Rosenthal. N.Y.: Little, 1988. 371-82; and in *The Granta Book of the American Short Story.* Ed. Richard Ford. N.Y.: Viking, 1992. 423-33.)

A360   "The Bankrupt Man." *Esquire* 86 (Nov. 1976): 72-73. (Rpt. in *Hugging the Shore.* N.Y.: Knopf, 1983. 22-24; and *The Oxford Book of Essays.* Ed. John Gross. N.Y.: OUP, 1991. 660-62.)

A361   "The Fairy Godfathers." *The New Yorker* 52 (8 Nov. 1976): 40-42. (Rpt. in *Problems and Other Stories.* N.Y.: Knopf, 1979. 213-21.)

*A362   "The Running Mate." *Esquire* 86 (Dec. 1976): 122.

A363   "Domestic Life in America." *The New Yorker* 52 (13 Dec. 1976): 43-49. (Rpt. in *Problems and Other Stories.* N.Y.: Knopf, 1979. 154-73.)

A364   "The Egg Race." *The New Yorker* 53 (13 June 1977): 36- 40. (Rpt. in *Problems and Other Stories.* N.Y.: Knopf, 1979. 231-44.)

A365   "Minutes of the Last Meeting." *Audience* 2 (July-Aug. 1977): 34-36. (Rpt. in *Problems and Other Stories.* N.Y.: Knopf, 1979. 12-17; and in *Look Ma, I Am Kool! and Other Casuals.* Ed. Burton Bernstein. Englewood Cliffs, N.J.: Prentice, 1977.)

A366   "Guilt-Gems." *The New Yorker* 53 (19 Sept. 1977): 39-41. (Rpt. in *Problems and Other Stories.* N.Y.: Knopf, 1979. 245-52.)

A367   "The Faint." *Playboy* 25 (May 1978): 118-120, 187, 189. (Rpt. in *Problems and Other Stories*. N.Y.: Knopf, 1979. 222-30; and in *Playboy*: Collector's Edition: 35th Anniversary Issue. 35 [Jan. 1989]: 206-08, 276-77.)

A368   "Three Illuminations in the Life of an American Author." *The New Yorker* 54 (21 Aug. 1978): 24-32. (Rpt. in *Three Illuminations in the Life of an American Author*. N.Y.: Targ Editions, 1979; and in *Bech Is Back*. N.Y.: Knopf, 1982. 3-27.)

A369   "Atlantises." *The New Yorker* 54 (13 Nov. 1978): 44-46. (Rpt. in *Problems and Other Stories*. N.Y.: Knopf, 1979. 253-60.)

A370   "Divorcing: A Fragment." *Too Far to Go: The Maples Stories*. N.Y.: Fawcett, 1979. 232-35.

A371   "Gesturing." *Playboy* 26 (Jan. 1979): 231-234, 238, 379-80, 382. (Rpt. in *Too Far to Go: The Maples Stories*. N.Y.: Fawcett, 1979. 212-31; in *The Best American Short Stories 1980*. Ed. Stanley Elkin and Shannon Ravenel. Boston: Houghton Mifflin, 1980. 409-19; and in *How We Live Now*. Ed. John Repp. Boston: St.Martin's P, 1990. 767-75.)

A372   "Trust Me." *The New Yorker* 55 (16 July 1979): 28-31. (Rpt. in *Trust Me*. N.Y.: Knopf, 1987. 3-12; and excerpted in *Self-Consciousness*. N.Y.: Knopf, 1989. 88n.)

A373   "The Golf Course Owner" *Ontario Review* Fall 1979: 31-32.

A374   "Morocco." *Atlantic* 244 (Nov. 1979): 45-48, 52.

A375   "The Holy Land." *Playboy* 26 (Dec. 1979): 168-70, 172, 360, 362-65. (Rpt. in *Bech Is Back*. N.Y.: Knopf, 1982. 66-89.)

A376   "An Encounter Left Out of *Rabbit Redux*." *Pieces* 2 (Jan. 1980): [1-5] unpaginated.

A377   "Still of Some Use." *The New Yorker* 56 (6 Oct. 1980): 52-54. (Rpt. in *Eastern Review* (The Eastern Airlines In-Flight Magazine) July 1987: 41-45; in *Trust Me*. N.Y.: Knopf, 1987. 27-33; in *The Best American Short Stories 1981*. Ed. Hortense Calisher. Boston: Houghton Mifflin, 1981. 312-18; and in *American Families: 28 Short Stories*. Ed. Barbara H. Solomon, N.Y.: New American Library, 1990.)

A378   "The Lovely Troubled Daughters of Our Old Crowd." *The New Yorker* 57 (6 Apr. 1981): 38-39. (Rpt. in *Trust Me*. N.Y.: Knopf, 1987. 54-60; and in *Ourselves Among Others*. Ed. Carol J. Verburg. Boston: St. Martin's P, 1991. 119-25.)

A379   "Pygmalion." *Atlantic* 248 (June 1981): 27. (Rpt. in *Trust Me*. N.Y.: Knopf, 1987. 90-92.)

Short Fiction 41

A380   "Rabbit Is Rich." *Playboy* 28 (Sept. 1981): 110-111, 114, 136, 190, 192, 194, 196, 198, 200-01, 204-06, 208-09. (These segments of the first chapter of the novel were rpt. in *Book Digest* Dec. 1981: 66-67, 69-79, 81.)

A381   "The City." *The New Yorker* 57 (16 Nov. 1981): 53-62. (Rpt. in *Prize Stories 1983*. Ed. William Abrahams. Garden City, N.Y.: Doubleday, 1983. 141-56; and in *Trust Me*. N.Y.: Knopf, 1987. 34-53.)

A382   "Learn a Trade." *The New Yorker* 57 (28 Dec. 1981): 42-44. (Rpt. in *Trust Me*. N.Y.: Knopf, 1987. 121-28.)

A383   "Killing." *Playboy* 29 (Jan. 1982): 102-04, 222, 224, 226. (Rpt. in *Trust Me*. N.Y.: Knopf, 1987. 13-26.)

A384   "Deaths of Distant Friends," *The New Yorker* 58 (7 June 1982): 34-36. (Rpt. in *The Best American Short Stories 1983*. Ed. Anne Tyler and Shannon Ravenel. Boston: Houghton Mifflin, 1983. 249-54; and in *Trust Me*. N.Y.: Knopf, 1987. 83-89.)

A385   "More Stately Mansions." *Esquire* 98 (Oct. 1982) 142-46, 148, 151, 153-57. (Rpt. in *Great Esquire Fiction: the Stories from the First Fifty Years*. Ed. L. Rust Hills. N.Y.: Penguin, 1983. 537-56; in *Trust Me*. N.Y.: Knopf, 1987. 93-120; and in *More Stately Mansions*. Jackson, Miss.: Nouveau P, 1987.)

A386   "First Wives and Trolley Cars." *The New Yorker* 58 (27 Dec. 1982): 36-39. (Rpt. in *Odd Jobs: Essays and Criticism*. N.Y.: Knopf, 1991. 18-25.)

A387   "One More Interview." *The New Yorker* 58 (4 July 1983): 36-40. (Rpt. in *Trust Me*. N.Y.: Knopf, 1987. 137-49.)

A388   "Il Court, Il Court." Translated by Maurice Rambaud. *Nouvelle Revue Française* 62 No. 366 (July-Aug. 1983): 13-22. (Rpt. from *Rabbit Is Rich*. N.Y.: Knopf, 1981. See **Appendix I. 196**.)

A389   "The Other." *The New Yorker* 59 (15 Aug. 1983): 30-39. (Rpt. in *Trust Me*. N.Y.: Knopf, 1987. 150-70; and *The Norton Anthology of Contemporary Fiction*. Ed. R. V. Cassill. N.Y.: Norton, 1988. 480-93.)

A390   "During the Jurassic." *Omni* Oct. 1983: 134, 136, 138.

A391   "Slippage." *The New Yorker* 59 (20 Feb. 1984): 48-51. (Rpt. in *Trust Me*. N.Y.: Knopf, 1987. 171-81.)

A392   "A Little Phone Magic." *Vogue* 174 (May 1984): 340-41, 410-11. (A segment from *The Witches of Eastwick*. N.Y.: Knopf, 1984.)

A393   "The Witches of Eastwick." *Playboy* 31 (May 1984): 92- 94, 174, 176, 178, 180, 184, 186. (Excerpt from *The Witches of Eastwick* N.Y.: Knopf, 1984.)

A394   "Poker Night." *Esquire* 102 (Aug. 1984) 40-43. (Rpt. in *Trust Me*. N.Y.: Knopf, 1987. 182-89; and in *Contemporary Esquire Stories*, Volume I. Albuquerque, N.M.: Newman Communications.)

A395   "The Witches of Eastwick" *Cosmopolitan* Aug. 1984: 266-68, 271-72, 274. (Excerpt from *The Witches of Eastwick* N.Y.: Knopf, 1984.)

A396   "Getting Into the Set." *Vanity Fair* Oct. 1984: 70-71, 122-25. (Rpt. in *Trust Me*. N.Y.: Knopf, 1987. 208-21.)

A397   "A Constellation of Events," *The New Yorker* 61 (25 Feb. 1985) 30-34. (Rpt. in *Trust Me*. N.Y.: Knopf, 1987. 71-82.)

A398   "Made in Heaven." *Atlantic* 255 (Apr. 1985): 48-51, 54, 56. (Rpt. in *Trust Me*. N.Y.: Knopf, 1987. 190-207.)

A399   "The Parade." *The Ontario Review* 22 (Spring-Sum. 1985): 34-48. (Rpt. in *Odd Jobs*. N.Y.: Knopf, 1991. 13-17.)

A400   "The Wallet." *Yankee* Sept. 1985: 114-17, 184-89. (Rpt. in *Trust Me*. N.Y.: Knopf, 1987. 222-37.)

A401   "The Other Woman," *The New Yorker* 61 (23 Dec. 1985): 32-40, 45-46, 51. (Rpt. in *Trust Me*. N.Y.: Knopf, 1987. 277-302.)

A402   "The Afterlife." *The New Yorker* 62 (15 Sept. 1986): 34-41. (Rpt. *The Afterlife*. Leamington Spa, Warwickshire: Sixth Chamber P, 1987; and in *The Best American Short Stories 1987*. Ed. Ann Beattie with Shannon Ravenel. Boston: Houghton Mifflin, 1987. 20-33.)

A403   "Leaf Season." *The New Yorker* 62 (13 Oct. 1986): 47-52, 57-58, 61-72. (Rpt. in *Trust Me*. N.Y.: Knopf, 1987. 238-68; and in *Prize Stories of 1988: The O. Henry Awards*. Ed. William Abrahams. Garden City, N.Y.: Doubleday, 1988. 336-60.)

A404   "Beautiful Husbands." *Playboy* 34 (Jan. 1987): 130-32, 186. (Rpt. in *Trust Me*. N.Y.: Knopf, 1987. 269-76.)

A405   "Bech in Czech." *The New Yorker* 63 (20 Apr. 1987): 32-42, 44-46, 48-49.

A406   "Conjunction." *The New Yorker* 63 (27 July, 1987): 29-32.

A407   "Brother Grasshopper." *The New Yorker* 63 (14 Dec. 1987) 40-46. (Rpt. with substantial revisions: *Brother Grasshopper*. Worcester, Mass.: Metacom, 1990.)

A408   "The Journey to the Dead," *The New Yorker* 64 (23 May 1988): 26-34.

Short Fiction 43

A409 "The Man Who Became a Soprano." *The New Yorker* 64 (26 Dec. 1988): 28-35.

A410 "Part of the Process." *Special Report* Feb.-Apr. 1989: 15-16, 18, 20.

A411 "'Spat' An Architectural Fiction." *Architectural Digest* 46 (Mar. 1989): 26, 28, 30.

A412 "Short Easter." *The New Yorker* 65 (27 Mar. 1989): 38-42.

A413 "The Lens Factory." *Granta* Fall 1989: 263.

A414 "The Virgins' Ornament." *The New York Times Book Review* 3 Dec. 1989: 16.

A415 "Queen's Jewels." *The New York Times Book Review* 9 Dec. 1989: 16.

A416 "A Sandstone Farmhouse." *The New Yorker* 66 (11 June 1990): 36-48. (Rpt. in *The Best American Short Stories 1991*. Ed. Alice Adams and Katrina Kenison. Boston: Houghton Mifflin, 1991. 367-82; 408-09.)

A417 "Rabbit at Rest." *Playboy* 37 (Sept. 1990) 76-78, 155-158, 160.

A418 Excerpt from *Rabbit At Rest*. *New York* 23 (10 Sept. 1990): 104.

A419 "Tristan and Iseult." *The New Yorker* 66 (3 Dec. 1990): 42-43.

A420 "Aperto e Chiuso." *Playboy* 38 (Jan. 1991): 82-84, 178-80, 182.

A421 "Farrell's Caddie." *The New Yorker* 67 (25 Feb. 1991): 33-35. (Rpt. in *The Twentieth Century Book of Sports*. Ed. Al and Brian Silverman. N.Y.: Viking, 1992. 704-710.)

A422 "Falling Asleep up North." *The New Yorker* 67 (6 May 1991): 36-39.

A423 "The Rumor." *Esquire* 115 (June 1991): 121-24.

A424 "The Other Side of the Street." *The New Yorker* 67 (28 Oct. 1991): 34-38.

A425 "His Mother Inside Him." *The New Yorker* 68 (20 Apr. 1992): 34-36.

A426 "The Brown Chest." *Atlantic* 209 (May 1992): 100-02.

A427 "Baby's First Step." *The New Yorker* 68 (27 July 1992): 24-27.

A428 "Playing with Dynamite." *The New Yorker* 68 (5 Oct. 1992): 136-39.

A429 "A Short and Scary Walk with Andrew Jackson." *American Heritage* 43 (Oct. 1992): 75-78, 80, 82.

4. Poetry

A430   "Conception and Reproduction by the Amalgamated Fools of 1951, Inc." *The Harvard Lampoon Centennial Celebration, 1876-1973*. Ed. Martin Kaplan. Boston: Little, 1973. Unpaginated. (Probably published originally in *Harvard Lampoon* in 1951.)

A431   "Poor Chap..." *The Harvard Lampoon Centennial Celebration, 1876-1973*. Ed. Martin Kaplan. Boston: Little, 1973. Unpaginated. (Probably published originally in *Harvard Lampoon* in 1951.)

A432   "While Awaiting Service in a Shoe Store." *Harvard Lampoon* 140 (May 1951): 19. (Rpt. in *The Harvard Lampoon Centennial Celebration, 1876-1973*. Ed. Martin Kaplan. Boston: Little, 1973. Unpaginated.)

A433   "How to Watch a Crew Race." *Harvard Lampoon* 141 (May 1951): 7. (Rpt. in *Jester's Dozen*. Northridge, Calif.: Lord John P, 1984. Unpaginated.)

A434   "Timestyle" *Harvard Lampoon* 140 (June 1951): 11. (Rpt. in *The Harvard Lampoon Centennial Celebration, 1876-1973*. Ed. Martin Kaplan. Boston: Little, 1973. Unpaginated.)

A435   "Modern Americans-I." *Harvard Lampoon* 140 (Sept. 1951): 3. (Signed "John H. Updike.") (Rpt. in *Max Shulman's Guided Tour of Campus Humor: The Best Stories, Articles, Poems, Jokes and Nonsense from Over Sixty-Five College Humor Magazines*. Ed. Max Shulman. N.Y.: Hanover House, 1955. 211-12.)

A436   "Overheard in Widener." *Harvard Lampoon* 140 (Sept. 1951): 12. (Rpt. in *Jester's Dozen*. Northridge, Calif.: Lord John P, 1984. Unpaginated.)

A437   "Lingual Jingle, or Don, Don, The Criterion." *Harvard Lampoon* 140 (Nov. 1951): 3. (Rpt. in *The Harvard Lampoon Centennial Celebration, 1876-1973*. Ed. Martin Kaplan. Boston: Little, 1973. Unpaginated.)

A438 "Professor Harlow Shapley Warbles the Praises of Natural Sciences 115." *Harvard Lampoon* 141 (Oct. 1952): 19. (Rpt. in *Jester's Dozen*. Northridge, Calif.: Lord John P, 1984. Unpaginated.)

A439 Untitled. *Harvard Lampoon* 141 (Dec. 1952): 7. (Rpt. in *Jester's Dozen*. Northridge, Calif.: Lord John P, 1984. Unpaginated.)

A440 "Lines." *Harvard Lampoon* 142 (May 1953): 24. (Rpt. in *Jester's Dozen*. Northridge, Calif.: Lord John P, 1984. Unpaginated.)

A441 "The Summer Reader." *Harvard Lampoon* 142 (Sept. 1953): 7. (Rpt. in *Jester's Dozen*. Northridge, Calif.: Lord John P, 1984. Unpaginated.)

A442 "Lines on the Passing of the *Jackolantern*." *Harvard Lampoon* 142 (Oct. 1953): 9. (Rpt. in *Jester's Dozen*. Northridge, Calif.: Lord John P, 1984. Unpaginated.)

A443 "This Isn't a Chain I'm Smoking." *Harvard Lampoon* 142 (Oct. 1953): 24. (Rpt. in *The Harvard Lampoon Centennial Celebration, 1876-1973*. Ed. Martin Kaplan. Boston: Little, 1973. Unpaginated.)

A444 "Call Him Mister." *Harvard Lampoon* 142 (Dec. 1953): 17. (Signed "John H. Updike.") (Rpt. in *Max Shulman's Guided Tour of Campus Humor: The Best Stories, Articles, Poems, Jokes and Nonsense from Over Sixty-Five College Humor Magazines*. Ed. Max Shulman. N.Y.: Hanover House, 1955. 210-11.)

A445 "Reverie." *Harvard Lampoon* 142 (Dec. 1953): 2-3. (Rpt. in *Jester's Dozen*. Northridge, Calif.: Lord John P, 1984. Unpaginated.)

A446 "Ballade for Subway Sitters." *Harvard Lampoon* 143 (Feb. 1954): 23. (Rpt. in *Jester's Dozen*. Northridge, Calif.: Lord John P, 1984. Unpaginated.)

A447 "I Like to Sing Also." *Harvard Lampoon* 143 (Feb. 1954): 3. (Signed "John H. Updike." Rpt. in *Max Shulman's Guided Tour of Campus Humor: The Best Stories, Articles, Poems, Jokes and Nonsense from Over Sixty-Five College Humor Magazines*. Ed. Max Shulman. N.Y.: Hanover House, 1955. 226-27; and in *Jester's Dozen*. Northridge, Calif.: Lord John P, 1984.)

A448 Untitled. *Harvard Lampoon* 143 (Apr. 1954): 9. (Rpt. in *Jester's Dozen*. Northridge, Calif.: Lord John P, 1984. Unpaginated.)

A449 Untitled. *Harvard Lampoon* 143 (June 1954): 7. (Rpt. in *Jester's Dozen*. Northridge, Calif.: Lord John P, 1984. Unpaginated.)

A450 "Player Piano." *The New Yorker* 30 (4 Dec. 1954): 169. (Rpt. in *The Carpentered Hen*. N.Y.: Harper, 1958. 4; in *A Reading Apprenticeship*. Ed.

Norman A. Brittin. N.Y.: Holt, 1971. 319-320; in *Western Wind*. Ed. John Frederick Nims. N.Y.: Random, 1983. 187; and in *Collected Poems, 1953-1993*. N.Y.: Knopf, 1993. 259.)

A451 "March." *The New Yorker* 30 (12 Feb. 1955): 38. (Rpt. as "March: A Birthday Poem" in *The Carpentered Hen*. N.Y.: Harper, 1958. 19-20; and in *Collected Poems, 1953-1993*. N.Y.: Knopf, 1993. 7-8.)

A452 "Youth's Progress." *The New Yorker* 31 (26 Feb. 1955): 28. (Rpt. in *An Introduction to Literature*. 5th ed. Ed. Sylvan Barnet, Morton Berman and William Burto. Boston: Little, 1973. 377-78; and in *Collected Poems, 1953-1993*. N.Y.: Knopf, 1993. 264.)

A453 "Humanities Course." *The New Yorker* 31 (4 June 1955): 100. (Rpt. in *The Carpentered Hen*. N.Y.: Harper, 1958. 28 [rev. ed., 30]; and in *Collected Poems, 1953-1993*. N.Y.: Knopf, 1993. 265 with a change of "'beauty'" to "'splendor.'")

A454 "Sunglasses." *The New Yorker* 31 (16 July 1955): 65. (Rpt. in *The Carpentered Hen*. N.Y.: Harper, 1958. 33; in *Summer*. Ed. Alice Gordon and Vincent Virga. Reading, Mass.: Addison-Wesley, 1990. 153; and in *Collected Poems, 1953-1993*. N.Y.: Knopf, 1993. 268.)

A455 "Sunflower." *The New Yorker* 31 (10 Sept. 1955): 136. (Rpt. in *The Carpentered Hen*. N.Y.: Harper, 1958. 21; and in *Collected Poems, 1953-1993*. N.Y.: Knopf, 1993. 6-7.)

A456 "Superman." *The New Yorker* 31 (12 Nov. 1955): 56. (Rpt. in *The Carpentered Hen and Other Tame Creatures*. N.Y.: Harper, 1958. 45; in playing-card size format with poem on one side and sepia-tone portrait of Updike on the reverse. n.d but post-1976; in *The Sporting Spirit*. Ed. Robert J. Higgs and Neil D. Issacs. N.Y.: Harcourt, 1977. 44-45; and in *Collected Poems, 1953-1993*. N.Y.: Knopf, 1993. 270-71.)

A457 "Tao in the Yankee Stadium Bleachers." *The New Yorker* 31 (18 Aug. 1956): 28. (Rpt. in *The Carpentered Hen*. N.Y.: Harper, 1958. 52-53; in *Sports Poems*. Ed. R. R. Knudson and P. K. Ebert. N.Y.: Dell, 1971. 35; in *Sports in Literature*. Ed. Henry B. Chapin. N.Y.: McKay, 1976. 78-79; and in *Collected Poems, 1953-1993*. N.Y.: Knopf, 1993. 16-17.)

A458 "The Amish." *Saturday Review* 22 Oct. 1956: 4. (Rpt. in *The Oxford Book of American Light Verse*. Ed. William Harmon. N.Y.: OUP, 1979. 518; and in *Collected Poems, 1953-1993*. N.Y.: Knopf, 1993. 330.)

A459 "Scenic." *The New Yorker* 33 (9 Mar. 1957): 37. (Rpt. in *The Carpentered Hen and Other Tame Creatures*. N.Y.: Harper, 1958. 13; in *Scenic*. San Francisco: Roxburghe Club, 1976; in *The John Updike Newsletter* 5 (Sept. 1978): unnumbered p. 4; and in *Collected Poems, 1953-1993*. N.Y.: Knopf, 1993. 283.)

A460 "Ex-Basketball Player." *The New Yorker* 33 (6 July 1957): 62. (Rpt. in *Here and Now*. Ed. Fred Morgan. N.Y.: Harcourt, 1968. 79; in *Sports Poems*. Ed. R. R. Knudson and P. K. Ebert. N.Y.: Dell, 1971. 80-81; in *Poetry: Sight and Insight*. Ed. James W. Kirkland and F. David Sanders. N.Y.: Random, 1982. 164-65; in *Literature*. 2nd ed. Ed. James H. Pickering and Jeffrey D. Hoeper. N.Y.: Macmillan, 1983. 963; and in the accompanying *Instructor's Manual* 157; and in *Collected Poems, 1953-1993*. N.Y.: Knopf, 1993. 4-5. Updike remarks her on 359: "My only oft-anthologized poem.")

A461 "The Old Tobacconist." *75 Aromatic Years of Leavitt & Peirce in the Recollections of 31 Harvard Men*. Compiled by Richard A. Ehrlich and William Ehrlich. Cambridge: Leavitt and Peirce, 1958. 27.

A462 "Why the Telephone Wires Dip and the Poles Are Cracked and Crooked." (Rpt. from *The Carpentered Hen*. N.Y.: Harper, 1958. 9; Rpt. in *Collected Poems, 1953-1993*. N.Y.: Knopf, 1993. 3.)

A463 "Cosmic Gall." *The New Yorker* 36 (17 Dec. 1960): 36. (Rpt. in *A Stress Analysis of a Strapless Evening Gown and Other Essays for a Scientific Age*. Ed. Robert A. Baker. Englewood Cliffs, N.J.: Prentice, 1963; and in *Collected Poems, 1953-1993*. N.Y.: Knopf, 1993. 313.)

A464 "Telephone Poles." *The New Yorker* 36 (21 Jan. 1961): 36. (Rpt. in *Poetspeak*. Ed. Paul Janeczko. N.Y.: Brandbury P, 1983. 155-56; and in *Collected Poems, 1953-1993*. N.Y.: Knopf, 1993. 16-17.)

A465 "Seven Stanzas at Easter." *Christian Century* 78 (22 Feb. 1961): 236. (Rpt. in *United Church Herald* 23 Mar. 1961: 21; and in *Collected Poems, 1953-1993*. N.Y.: Knopf, 1993. 20-21.)

A466 "Recital." *The New Yorker* 37 (10 June 1961): 29. (Rpt. in *The Oxford Book of American Light Verse*. Ed. William Harmon. N.Y.: OUP, 1979. 519; and in *Collected Poems, 1953-1993*. N.Y.: Knopf, 1993. 317.)

A467 "I Missed His Book, But I Read His Name." *The New Yorker* 37 (4 Nov. 1961): 142. (Rpt. in *The Oxford Book of American Light Verse*. Ed. William Harmon. N.Y.: OUP, 1979. 518-19; and in *Collected Poems, 1953-1993*. N.Y.: Knopf, 1993. 317-18.)

A468 "Earthworm." *The New Yorker* 37 (12 May 1962): 142. (Rpt. in: *Telephone Poles*. N.Y.: Knopf, 1963. 48; includes a final stanza rejected by *The New Yorker*; and in *Collected Poems, 1953-1993*. N.Y.: Knopf, 1993. 29; see Updike's note in *Collected Poems, 1953-1993*: 361.)

A469 "Seagulls." *The New Yorker* 38 (25 Aug. 1962): 28. (Rpt. in *Telephone Poles*. N.Y.: Knopf, 1966. 43; in *Hugging the Shore*, N.Y.: Knopf, 1983. 865-66; in *Poetspeak*. Ed. Paul Janeczko. N.Y.: Brandbury P, 1983.

140-41, including a "Comment" on the poem, 141-42; and in *Collected Poems, 1953-1993*. N.Y.: Knopf, 1993. 19-20.)

A470 "Farewell to the Shopping District of Antibes." *The New Yorker* 39 (20 Apr. 1963): 50. (Rpt. in *Midpoint and Other Poems*. N.Y.: Knopf, 1969. 80; and in *Collected Poems, 1953-1993*. N.Y.: Knopf, 1993. 326.)

A471 "Exposé." *The New Yorker* 39 (25 May 1963): 40. (Rpt. in *Midpoint and Other Poems*. N.Y.: Knopf, 1969. 81; and in *Collected Poems, 1953-1993*. N.Y.: Knopf, 1993. 325.)

A472 "My Children at the Dump at Ipswich." *The Transatlantic Review* 14 (Autumn, 1963): 70. (Rpt. as "My Children at the Dump" in *Midpoint and Other Poems*. N.Y.: Knopf, 1969. 70; and in *Collected Poems, 1953-1993*. N.Y.: Knopf, 1993. 35-36.)

A473 "Some Frenchmen." *The New Yorker* 39 (9 Nov. 1963): 54. (Rpt. in *Midpoint and Other Poems*. N.Y.: Knopf, 1969. 79; in *The Norton Anthology of Light Verse*. Ed. Russell Baker. N.Y.: Norton, 1986. 161; and in *Collected Poems, 1953-1993*. N.Y.: Knopf, 1993. 327.)

A474 "Azores." *Harper's* 228 (Jan. 1964): 37. (Rpt. in *Midpoint and Other Poems*. N.Y.: Knopf, 1969. 89 with a correction; and in *Collected Poems, 1953-1993*. N.Y.: Knopf, 1993. 38-39.)

A475 "Lamplight." *The New Republic* 150 (29 Feb. 1964): 22. (Rpt. in *Midpoint and Other Poems*. N.Y.: Knopf, 1969. 48; and in *Collected Poems, 1953-1993*. N.Y.: Knopf, 1993. 43-44.)

A476 "Sea Knell." *The New Yorker* 40 (28 Mar. 1964): 44. (Rpt. in *Midpoint and Other Poems*. N.Y.: Knopf, 1969. 94; and in *Collected Poems, 1953-1993*. N.Y.: Knopf, 1993. 328.)

A477 "Vow." *The New Yorker* 40 (23 May 1964): 48. (Rpt. in *Midpoint and Other Poems*. N.Y.: Knopf, 1969. 92; and in *Collected Poems, 1953-1993*. N.Y.: Knopf, 1993. 329.)

A478 "Fireworks." *The New Yorker* 40 (4 July 1964): 28. (Rpt. in *Midpoint and Other Poems*. N.Y.: Knopf, 1969. 47; and in *Collected Poems, 1953-1993*. N.Y.: Knopf, 1993. 42-43.)

A479 "Roman Portrait Busts." *The New Republic* 152 (6 Feb. 1965): 21. (Rpt. in *Midpoint and Other Poems*. N.Y.: Knopf, 1969. 59; and in *Collected Poems, 1953-1993*. N.Y.: Knopf, 1993. 49.)

A480 "Poem for a Far Land." *The New Republic* 152 (13 Mar. 1965): 17. (Rpt. in *Midpoint and Other Poems*. N.Y.: Knopf, 1969. 88; and in *Collected Poems, 1953-1993*. N.Y.: Knopf, 1993. 50-51.)

A481 "Sunshine on Sandstone." *The New Republic* 152 (17 Apr. 1965): 26. (Rpt. in *Midpoint and Other Poems*. N.Y.: Knopf, 1969. 57; and in *Collected Poems, 1953-1993*. N.Y.: Knopf, 1993. 30.)

A482 "Postcards from Soviet Cities: Moscow, Kiev, Leningrad, Yerevan." *The New Yorker* 41 (29 May 1965): 34. (Rpt. in *Midpoint and Other Poems*. New York: Knopf, 1969. 84-87; and in *Collected Poems, 1953-1993*. N.Y.: Knopf, 1993. 45-48.)

A483 "Décor." *American Scholar* 34 (Sum. 1965): 412. (Rpt. in *Midpoint and Other Poems*. N.Y.: Knopf, 1969. 53; and in *Collected Poems, 1953-1993*. N.Y.: Knopf, 1993. 50.)

A484 "Home Movies." *The New Republic* 154 (8 Jan. 1966): 23. (Rpt. in *Midpoint and Other Poems*. N.Y.: Knopf, 1969. 49; and in *Collected Poems, 1953-1993*. N.Y.: Knopf, 1993. 52.)

A485 "The Amoeba." *The New Republic* 154 (25 June 1966): 23. (Rpt. in *Midpoint and Other Poems*. N.Y.): Knopf, 1969. 60; and in *Collected Poems*, 1953-1993. N.Y.: Knopf, 193. 53-54.)

A486 "Antigua." *The New Yorker* 42 (11 Feb. 1967): 46. (Rpt. in *Midpoint and Other Poems*. N.Y.: Knopf, 1969. 88; and in *Collected Poems, 1953-1993*. N.Y.: Knopf, 1993. 53.)

A487 "Subway Love." *The New Republic* 156 (20 May 1967): 26. (Rpt. in *Midpoint and Other Poems*. N.Y.: Knopf, 1969. 4; and in *Literature and Liberalism: An Anthology of Sixty Years of the New Republic*. Ed. Edward Zwick. Washington, D. C.: The New Republic Book Co., 1976. 160-61.)

A488 "Memories of Anguilla, 1960." *The New Republic* 157 (11 Nov. 1967): 21. (Rpt. in *Tossing and Turning*. N.Y.: Knopf, 1977. 67-68; and in *Collected Poems, 1953-1993*. N.Y.: Knopf, 1993. 109-10.)

A489 "The Angels." *The New Yorker* 43 (27 Jan. 1968): 34. (Rpt. in *The Angels*. Pensacola, Fla.: King & Queen P, 1968. Signed, limited edition; in *Midpoint and Other Poems*. N.Y.: Knopf, 1969. 56; and in *Collected Poems, 1953-1993*. N.Y.: Knopf, 1993. 58.)

A490 "The Naked Ape." *The New Republic* 155 (3 Feb. 1968): 28. (Rpt. in *Midpoint and Other Poems*. N.Y.: Knopf, 1969. 98; and in *Collected Poems, 1953-1993*. N.Y.: Knopf, 1993. 330-32.)

A491 "The Origin of Laughter (After Desmond Morris)." *Atlantic* 221 (June 1968): 105. (Rpt. in *Midpoint and Other Poems*. N.Y.: Knopf, 1969. 50; and in *Collected Poems, 1953-1993*. N.Y.: Knopf, 1993. 332.)

A492   "Average Egyptian Faces Death." *The New Republic* 159 (6 July 1968): 38. (Rpt. in *Midpoint and Other Poems*. N.Y.: Knopf, 1969. 62; and in *Collected Poems, 1953-1993*. N.Y.: Knopf, 1993. 333.)

A493   "Topsfield Fair." *American Scholar* 37 (Sum. 1968): 419. (Rpt. in *Midpoint and Other Poems*. N.Y.: Knopf, 1969. 51; and in *Collected Poems, 1953-1993*. N.Y.: Knopf, 1993. 61.)

A494   "Dream Objects." *The New Yorker* 44 (26 Oct. 1968): 54. (Rpt. in *Midpoint and Other Poems*. N.Y.: Knopf, 1969. 55; and in *Collected Poems, 1953-1993*. N.Y.: Knopf, 1993. 63-64.)

A495   "The Dance of the Solids." *Scientific American* 220 (Jan. 1969): 130-31. (Rpt. in *Midpoint and Other Poems*. N.Y.: Knopf, 1969. 18-21; as a Christmas card for 1969 by *Scientific American*; in *Alchemy and Academe: A Collection of Original Stories Concerning Themselves with Transmutations, Mental and Elemental, Alchemical and Academic*. Ed. Anne McCaffrey, N.Y.: Ballantine, 1980. 1-4; and in *Collected Poems, 1953- 1993*. N.Y.: Knopf, 1993. 78-81.)

A496   "Post-Impressionist Wives." *Saturday Review* 8 Feb. 1969: 5. (Rpt. as "Painted Wives" in *Tossing and Turning*. N.Y.: Knopf, 1977. 51; and in *Collected Poems, 1953-1993*. N.Y.: Knopf, 1993. 334.)

A497   "Report of Health." *The New Yorker* 45 (22 Feb. 1969): 40. (Rpt.in *Midpoint and Other Poems*. N.Y.: Knopf, 1969. 89; and in *Collected Poems, 1953-1993*. N.Y.: Knopf, 1993. 41-42.)

A498   "Skyey Developments." *The New Republic* 160 (8 Mar. 1969): 28. (Rpt. in *Tossing and Turning*. N.Y.: Knopf, 1977. 56; and in *Collected Poems, 1953-1993*. N.Y.: Knopf, 1993. 334-35.)

A499   "A L'Ecole Berlitz." *The New Republic* 161 (6 & 13 Sept. 1969): A33. (Rpt. in *Tossing and Turning*. N.Y.: Knopf, 1977. 36; in *Six Poems*. N.Y.: Aloe, 1973; and in *Collected Poems, 1953-1993*. N.Y.: Knopf, 1993. 105-06.)

A500   "Business Acquaintances." *The New Republic* 161 (4 Oct. 1969): 28. (Rpt. in *Tossing and Turning*. N.Y.: Knopf, 1977. 44; and in *Collected Poems, 1953-1993*. N.Y.: Knopf, 1993. 336.)

A501   "South of the Alps." *Commonweal* 88 (17 Oct. 1969): 72. (Rpt. in *Tossing and Turning*. N.Y.: Knopf, 1977. 37-39, correcting "our" to "ours," changing "interstice" to "interval," "sun" to "sunlight" and "virgin" to "faded," and using a dash for a comma, while adding the line "a quattrocento paradise"; and in *Collected Poems, 1953-1993*. N.Y.: Knopf, 1993. 106-08.)

*A502   "Rubble of Ruined Temples." Beverly, Mass. *Times* 12 Jan. 1970.

A503   "Upon Shaving off One's Beard." *The New Yorker* 46 (16 May 1970): 37. (Rpt. in *Poetry Brief: An Anthology of Short Poems*. Ed. William Cole. N.Y.: Macmillan, 1971. 149; in *Six Poems*. N.Y.: Aloe, 1973; in *Tossing and Turning*. N.Y.: Knopf, 1977. 45; and in *Collected Poems, 1953-1993*. N.Y.: Knopf, 1993. 338.)

A504   "On an Island." *Saturday Review* 53 (7 Nov. 1970): 29. (Rpt. in *Six Poems*. N.Y.: Aloe, 1973; in *Tossing and Turning*. N.Y.: Knopf, 1977. 20-21; and in *Collected Poems, 1953-1993*. N.Y.: Knopf, 1993. 110-11.)

A505   "Sunday Rain." *Saturday Review* 54 (17 Apr. 1971): 59. (Rpt. in *Tossing and Turning*. N.Y.: Knopf, 1977. 36; and in *Collected Poems, 1953-1993*. N.Y.: Knopf, 1993. 111.)

A506   "Marching Through a Novel." *Saturday Review* 54 (3 July 1971): 24. (Rpt. in *Tossing and Turning*. N.Y.: Knopf, 1977. 71; and in *Collected Poems, 1953-1993*. N.Y.: Knopf, 1993. 111-12.)

A507   "Love: First Lessons." *The New Yorker* 47 (6 Nov. 1971): 46-47, (Rpt. in "slightly different form" as "The Beloved." *The Beloved*. Northridge, Calif., Lord John P, 1982; and in *The Transatlantic Review* 50 [Autumn 1974]: 19.)

A508   "Wind." *Commonweal* 21 Jan. 1972: 373. (Rpt. in *Commonweal* 16 Nov. 1973: 175; in *Tossing and Turning*. N.Y.: Knopf, 1977. 22; and in *Collected Poems, 1953-1993*. N.Y.: Knopf, 1993. 114.)

A509   "Young Matrons Dancing." *Saturday Review* 55 (29 Jan. 1972): 6. (Rpt. in *Facing Nature*. N.Y.: Knopf, 1985. 97; and in *Collected Poems, 1953-1993*. N.Y.: Knopf, 1993. 309.)

A510   "Sand Dollar." *Atlantic* 229 (Mar. 1972): 43. (Rpt. in *Tossing and Turning*. N.Y.: Knopf, 1977. 66; and in *Collected Poems, 1953-1993*. N.Y.: Knopf, 1993. 62-63.)

A511   "A Bicycle Chain." *The New Yorker* 48 (15 Apr. 1972): 48. (Rpt. in *Tossing and Turning*. N.Y.: Knopf, 1977. 61; and in *Collected Poems, 1953-1993*. N.Y.: Knopf, 1993. 108-09.)

A512   "Sunday." *American Scholar* 41 (Sum. 1972): 389. (Rpt. in *Tossing and Turning*. N.Y.: Knopf,1977. 82; and in *Collected Poems, 1953-1993*. N.Y.: Knopf, 1993. 115.)

A513   "Insomnia the Gem of the Ocean." *The New Yorker* 48 (16 Sept. 1972): 40. (Rpt. in *Tossing and Turning*. N.Y.: Knopf, 1977. 46; in *The Norton*

Poetry 53

A514 "To a Waterbed." *Harper's* 245 (Dec. 1972): 66. (Rpt. in *Tossing and Turning*. N.Y.: Knopf, 1977. 47; and in *Collected Poems, 1953-1993*. N.Y.: Knopf, 1993. 339.)

(Continued from previous: *Anthology of Light Verse*. Ed. Russell Baker. N.Y.: Norton, 1986. 48; and in *Collected Poems, 1953-1993*. N.Y.: Knopf, 1993. 339.)

A515 "The Cars in Caracas." *The New Yorker* 48 (30 Dec. 1972): 27. (Rpt. in *Tossing and Turning*. N.Y.: Knopf, 1977. 43; and in *Collected Poems, 1953-1993*. N.Y.: Knopf, 1993. 338.)

A516 "Cunts: Upon Receiving the Swingers Life Club Membership Solicitation." *New York Quarterly* 15 (1973): 63-65. (Rpt. in *Cunts [Upon Receiving the Swingers Life Club Membership Solicitation]*. N.Y.: Frank. Hallman, 1974; and in *New York Quarterly* 20 [1978]; in *Tossing and Turning*. N.Y.: Knopf, 1977. 76-79; in *Playboy* 31 [Jan. 1984]: 162-63, with some additions; and in *Collected Poems, 1953-1993*. N.Y.: Knopf, 1993. 116-20. Roberts comments: "Printed in different form in *The New York Quarterly*, Summer, 1973, Number 15, copies of this journal were issued in 1978 as a 'special signed edition' of 457 numbered copies and 26 lettered copies. The notice of limitation and signature appear on page 65. This is not a primary first edition, but a recycled periodical appearance." *American Book Collector*, 1: 12.)

A517 "Phenomena." *The New Yorker* 49 (24 Feb. 1973): 38. (Rpt. in *Six Poems*. N.Y.: Aloe, 1973; in *Tossing and Turning*. N.Y.: Knopf, 1977. 84-85; and in *Collected Poems, 1953-1993*. N.Y.: Knopf, 1993. 113-14.)

A518 "The House Growing." *The New Yorker* 49 (23 July 1973): 34. (Rpt. in *The John Updike Newsletter* No. 2 (Sum. 1977): 4. [Manuscript page with Updike's revisions.]; in *Tossing and Turning*. N.Y.: Knopf, 1977. 12; and in *Collected Poems, 1953-1993*. N.Y.: Knopf, 1993. 116.)

A519 "Commencement: Pingree School." *The New Republic* 169 (28 July & 4 Aug. 1973): 28. (Rpt. in *Tossing and Turning*. N.Y.: Knopf, 1977. 35; and in *Collected Poems, 1953-1993*. N.Y.: Knopf, 1993. 125.)

A520 "Ethiopia." *The New Yorker* 49 (14 Jan. 1974): 28-32.

A521 "The Jolly Greene Giant." *The Critic* Mar.-Apr. 1974: 67. (Rpt. in *Punch; in Tossing and Turning*. N.Y.: Knopf, 1977. 49; and in *Collected Poems, 1953-1993*. N.Y.: Knopf, 1993. 340.)

A522 "Note to the Previous Tenants." *The New Republic* 171 (30 Nov. 1974): 20. (Rpt. in *Tossing and Turning*. N.Y.: Knopf, 1977. 88; and in *Collected Poems, 1953-1993*. N.Y.: Knopf, 1993. 130-31.)

A523 "Melting." *Transatlantic Review* 50 (Autumn-Wint. 1974): (Rpt. in *Tossing and Turning*. N.Y.: Knopf, 1977. 16; and in *Collected Poems, 1953-1993*. N.Y.: Knopf, 1993. 127.)

A524 "Heading for Nandi." *The New Yorker* 50 (16 Dec. 1974): 4 (Rpt. in *Tossing and Turning*. N.Y.: Knopf, 1977. 90-91; and in *Collected Poems, 1953-1993*. N.Y.: Knopf, 1993. 128-29.)

A525 "Poisoned in Nassau." *Boston University Journal* 23 (1975): 48. (Rpt. from *Tossing and Turning*. N.Y.: Knopf, 1977. 23. Rpt. in *Boston University Journal* 26 (1980): 96; and in *Collected Poems, 1953-1993*. N.Y.: Knopf, 1993. 133-34.)

A526 "Mime." *The New Yorker* 51 (3 Mar. 1975): 42. (Rpt. in *Tossing and Turning*. N.Y.: Knopf, 1977. 87; and in *Collected Poems, 1953-1993*. N.Y.: Knopf, 1993. 132.)

A527 "Golfers." *The New Republic* 172 (5 Apr. 1975): 30. (Rpt. in *Tossing and Turning*. N.Y.: Knopf, 1977. 73; and in *Collected Poems, 1953-1993*. N.Y.: Knopf, 1993. 133.)

A528 "News from the Underworld." *The American Scholar* 44 (Autumn 1975): 584. (Rpt. in *Tossing and Turning*. N.Y.: Knopf, 1977. 57; and in *Collected Poems, 1953-1993*. N.Y.: Knopf, 1993. 341.)

A529 "Author's Residences: After Visiting Hartford." *Harper's* 251 (Dec. 1975): 64. (Rpt. in *Tossing and Turning*. N.Y.: Knopf, 1977. 50; and in *Collected Poems*, 1953-1993. N.Y.: Knopf, 1993. 341-42.)

A530 "Bliss Blanc." *Bits* 3 (Jan. 1976): 6. (Rpt. in *The John Updike Newsletter* No. 2 [Spring 1977]: 4; as "Pale Bliss" in *Tossing and Turning*. N.Y.: Knopf, 1977. 74; and in *Collected Poems, 1953-1993*. N.Y.: Knopf, 1993. 131.)

A531 "You Who Swim." *The American Scholar* 45 (Sum. 1976): 374. (Rpt. in *Tossing and Turning*. N.Y.: Knopf, 1977. 3; and in *Collected Poems, 1953-1993*. N.Y.: Knopf, 1993. 134.)

A532 "Raining at Magens Bay." *Transatlantic Review* 55/56 (Fall 1976): 55-56. (Rpt. in *The John Updike Newsletter* No. 2 (Spring 1977): 5 [a broadside]; as "Raining in Magens Bay" in *Tossing and Turning*. N.Y.: Knopf, 1977. 24-25; and in *Collected Poems, 1953-1993*. N.Y.: Knopf, 1993. 135-36.)

A533 "Calder's Hands." *The New Yorker* 52 (6 Dec. 1976): 45. (Rpt. in *Tossing and Turning*. N.Y.: Knopf, 1977. 40; and in *Collected Poems, 1953-1993*. N.Y.: Knopf, 1993. 146.)

A534	"Dutch Cleanser." *Paris Review* 68 (Wint. 1976): 57. (Rpt. in *Tossing and Turning*. N.Y.: Knopf, 1977. 89; and in *Collected Poems, 1953-1993*. N.Y.: Knopf, 1993. 143-44.)
A535	"Leaving Church Early." *Ontario Review* 5 (Fall-Wint. 1976-77): 14-17. (Rpt. in *Tossing and Turning*. N.Y.: Knopf. 1977. 7-11; and in *Collected Poems, 1953-1993*. N.Y.: Knopf, 1993. 137-41, with many altered words.)
A536	"The Melancholy of Storm Windows." *The Boston University Journal* 25 (1977): 30. (Rpt. in *Tossing and Turning*. N.Y.: Knopf, 1977. 62-63; and in *Collected Poems, 1953-1993*. N.Y.: Knopf, 1993. 145-46.)
A537	"Dream and Reality." *The New Yorker* 52 (24 Jan. 1977): 34. (Rpt. in *Tossing and Turning*. N.Y.: Knopf, 1977. 4-5; and in *Collected Poems, 1953-1993*. N.Y.: Knopf, 1993. 142-43.)
A538	"Rats." *Atlantic* 239 (Feb. 1977): 34. (Rpt. in *Half Serious: An Anthology of Short, Short Poems*. Ed. William Cole. London: Eyre Methuen, 1973; in *Tossing and Turning*. N.Y.: Knopf, 1977. 65; and in *Collected Poems, 1953-1993*. N.Y.: Knopf, 1993. 144.)
A539	"Boil." *Bits* 2 (Spring 1977): 4. (Rpt. in *Tossing and Turning*. N.Y.: Knopf, 1977. 86; and in *Collected Poems, 1953-1993*. N.Y.: Knopf, 1993. 33.)
A540	"Dog's Death." *The John Updike Newsletter* No. 2 (Spring 1977): 4. (Rpt. from *Dog's Death*. Cambridge, Mass.: Adams House and Lowell House, 1965; in *Midpoint and Other Poems*. N.Y.: Knopf, 1969. 52; in *Poetspeak*. Ed. Paul Janeczko. N.Y.: Brandbury P, 1983. 184; in *The Norton Anthology of American Literature*. 2nd ed. Vol. 2. Ed. Nina Baym, Ronald Gottesman, Laurence B. Holland, Francis Murphy, Hershel Parker, William H. Pritchard, and David Kalstone. N.Y.: Norton, 1985. 2189; and in *Collected Poems, 1953-1993*. N.Y.: Knopf, 1993. 51-52.)
A541	"A Vision." *The John Updike Newsletter* No. 2 (Spring 1977): [2].
A542	"Shaving Mirror." *Bennington Review* 1 (Apr. 1978): 37. (Rpt. in *Facing Nature*. N.Y.: Knopf, 1985. 98; and in *Collected Poems, 1953-1993*. N.Y.: Knopf, 1993. 343.)
A543	"Ohio." *American Scholar* 47 (Sum. 1978): 325. (Rpt. in *Anthology of Magazine Verse and Yearbook of American Poetry, 1980 Edition*. Ed. Peter Alan. Beverly Hills: Monitor Book Co., 1980. 415-16; in *Facing Nature*. N.Y.: Knopf, 1985. 10; and in *Collected Poems, 1953-1993*. N.Y.: Knopf, 1993. 153-54.)
A544	"Travel Tips." *Bits* 8 (June 1978): 23. (Rpt. in *The John Updike Newsletter* No. 7 (Sum. 1978): [2]; in *Five Poems*. Cleveland: Bits P, 1980,

unpaginated; and in *Light Year '84*. Ed. Robert Wallace. Cleveland: Bits P, 1983. 98.)

A545 "Spanish Sonnets." *The New Yorker* 54 (24 July 1978): 25. (Rpt. in *Sixteen Sonnets*. Cambridge, Mass.: Halty Ferguson, 1979; in *Facing Nature*. N.Y.: Knopf, 1985. 17-24; and in *Collected Poems, 1953-1993*. N.Y.: Knopf, 1993. 147-51.)

A546 "Mass. Mental Health." *Sixteen Sonnets*. Cambridge, Mass.: Halty Ferguson, 1979. (Rpt. in *Collected Poems, 1953-1993*. N.Y.: Knopf, 1993. 155-56.)

*A547 "To Ed Sissman." *Ontario Review* 1979. (Rpt. in *Facing Nature*. N.Y.: Knopf, 1985. 10; in *Sixteen Sonnets*. Cambridge, Mass.: Halty Ferguson, 1979; in *Pushcart Prize: 4*. N.Y.: Pushcart P, 1979. 311-12; and in *Collected Poems, 1953-1993*. N.Y.: Knopf, 1993. 151-53 with "gave" changed to "lent.")

A548 "The Visions of Mackenzie King." *The New Republic* 180 (8 Apr. 1979): 28. (Rpt. in *The John Updike Newsletter*, no. 12, Fall 1979; in *Facing Nature*. N.Y.: Knopf, 1985. 108-10; in *Five Poems*. Cleveland: Bits P, 1980; and in *Collected Poems, 1953-1993*. N.Y.: Knopf, 1993. 344-46.)

A549 "Living with a Wife." *The New York Times Book Review* 10 Apr. 1979: 28. (Rpt. from *Crazy Horse* 10 (Mar. 1972): 37-39. Rpt. in *Tossing and Turning*. N.Y.: Knopf, 1977. 68-70; and in *Collected Poems, 1953-1993*. N.Y.: Knopf, 1993. 103-05 .)

A550 "Energy: A Villanelle." *The New Yorker* 55 (4 June 1979): 44. (Rpt. in *Light Year '84*. Ed. Robert Wallace. Cleveland: Bits P, 1983. 139; in *Facing Nature* N.Y.: Knopf, 1985. 102; and in *Collected Poems, 1953-1993*. N.Y.: Knopf, 1993. 347.)

A551 "Self-Service." *Atlantic* 244 (Oct. 1979): 82. (Rpt. in *Light Year '84*. Ed. Robert Wallace. Cleveland: Bits P, 1983. 29; in *Facing Nature*. N.Y.: Knopf, 1985. 101; and in *Collected Poems, 1953-1993*. N.Y.: Knopf, 1993. 344.)

A552 "Typical Optical." *The New York Times Book Review* 25 Nov. 1979: 15. (The poem [25 Nov. 1979] and drawing [2 Dec. 1979, see **A1304**] for "Typical Optical" should have been printed together here as they were when reprinted in *The John Updike Newsletter* No. 13 (1980):[4]; in *Light Year '85*. Ed. Robert Wallace. Cleveland: Bits P, 1984. 162; in *Facing Nature*. N.Y.: Knopf, 1985. 103; and in *Collected Poems, 1953-1993*. N.Y.: Knopf, 1993. 348.)

A553 "Melancholy of Storm Windows." *Boston University Journal* 26 (1980): 95. (For reprint information, see **A536**.)

Poetry 57

A554 "Sleepless in Scarsdale." *Boston University Journal* 26 (1980): 97. (Rpt. from *Tossing and Turning*. N.Y.: Knopf, 1977. 26-27; in *Literature*. 2nd ed. Ed. James H. Pickering and Jeffrey D. Hoeper. N.Y.: Macmillan, 1983. 963-64, and in the accompanying *Instructor's Manual* 157; and in *Collected Poems, 1953-1993*. N.Y.: Knopf, 1993. 129-30.)

A555 "Worldly Monk's Song." *Bits* 11 (Jan. 1980): 9. (Rpt. from *Tossing and Turning*. N.Y.: Knopf, 1977; in *The John Updike Newsletter* No. 13 [1980], which changed "O" to "Oh"; and in *Light Year '84*. Ed. Robert Wallace. Cleveland: Bits P, 1983. 44.)

A556 "Taste." *American Poetry Review* 9 (Jan.-Feb. 1980): 20. (Rpt. in *The John Updike Newsletter*. No. 13 (1980); in *Facing Nature*. N.Y.: Knopf, 1985. 55; and in *Collected Poems, 1953-1993*. N.Y.: Knopf, 1993. 158-59.)

A557 "13 Ways of Looking at the Masters." *Golf Magazine* Apr. 1980: 62-69. (Listed incorrectly. See **A788**.)

A558 "Upon the Last Day of His Forty-Eighth Year." *The New Republic* 184 (16 May 1981): 30. (Rpt. in *Facing Nature*. N.Y.: Knopf, 1985. 10; and in *Collected Poems, 1953-1993*. .N.Y.: Knopf, 1993. 169.)

A559 "Crab Crack." *Harper's* 263 (July 1981): 80. (Rpt. in *Facing Nature*. N.Y.: Knopf, 1985. 58-59; and in *Collected Poems, 1953-1993*. N.Y.: Knopf, 1993. 163-64.)

A560 "Penumbrae." *The New Yorker* 57 (14 Sept. 1981): 54. Rpt. in *Facing Nature*. N.Y.: Knopf, 1985. 38-39; and in *Collected Poems, 1953-1993*. N.Y.: Knopf, 1993. 160-61.)

A561 "East Hampton-Boston By Air." *American Poetry Review* 7.iv (1982): 10. (Rpt. in *Facing Nature*. N.Y.: Knopf, 1985. 64-67; and in *Collected Poems, 1953-1993*. N.Y.: Knopf, 1993. 171-74.)

A562 "The Fleckings." *The New Republic* 187 (20 Jan. 1982): 36. (Rpt. in *Facing Nature*. N.Y.: Knopf, 1985. 48; and in *Collected Poems, 1953-1993*. N.Y.: Knopf, 1993. 170.)

A563 "The Moons of Jupiter." *American Scholar* 52 (Autumn, 1982): 483-86. (Rpt. in *Facing Nature*. N.Y.: Knopf, 1985. 71-74; and in *Collected Poems, 1953-1993*. N.Y.: Knopf, 1993. 165-68.)

A564 "INVALID.KEYSTROKE." *Light Year '84*. Ed. Robert Wallace. Cleveland: Bits P, 1983. 110.)

A565 "Plow Cemetery." *Antaeus* N47 (1983): 95-96. (Rpt. in *Facing Nature*. N.Y.: Knopf, 1985. 32-34; and in *Collected Poems, 1953-1993*. N.Y.: Knopf, 1993. 176-77.)

A566	"Two Hoppers on Display at the National Gallery." *The New Republic* 188 (31 Jan. 1983): 35. (Rpt. in *Facing Nature*. N.Y.: Knopf, 1985. 49, retitled "Two Hoppers"; and in *Collected Poems, 1953-1993*. N.Y.: Knopf, 1993. 181.) Also listed incorrectly as **A810**.
A567	"L.A." *The New Yorker* 59 (18 Apr. 1983): 48. (Rpt. in *Facing Nature*. N.Y.: Knopf, 1985. 12; and in *Collected Poems, 1953-1993*. N.Y.: Knopf, 1993. 175.)
A568	"The Rockettes." *The New Yorker* 59 (5 Sept. 1983): 42. (Rpt. in *Light Year '85*. Ed. Robert Wallace. Cleveland: Bits P, 1984. 42; in *Facing Nature*. N.Y.: Knopf, 1985. 95; and in *Collected Poems, 1953-1993*. N.Y.: Knopf, 1993. 348-49.)
A569	"Long Shadow." *Parabola: The Magazine of Myth & Tradition* 8 (1 Nov. 1983): 50-51. (Rpt. in *Facing Nature*. N.Y.: Knopf, 1985. 11; and in *Collected Poems, 1953-1993*. N.Y.: Knopf, 1993. 183.)
A570	"Pain." *The New Republic* 26 Dec. 1983: 34. (Rpt. in *Facing Nature*. N.Y.: Knopf, 1985. 54; and in *Collected Poems, 1953-1993*. N.Y.: Knopf, 1993. 187.)
A571	"Island Sun." *The Sophisticated Traveler. Winter: Love it or Leave it*. Ed. A. M. Rosenthal and Arthur Gelb, N.Y.: Villard Books, 1984. xv. (Rpt. in *Facing Nature*. N.Y.: Knopf, 1985. 69-70; and in *Collected Poems, 1953-1993*. N.Y.: Knopf, 1993. 186-87.)
A572	"The Code." *The Ontario Review* 20 (Spring-Sum. 1984): 34. (Rpt. in *Facing Nature*. N.Y.: Knopf, 1985. 40; and in *Collected Poems, 1953-1993*. N.Y.: Knopf, 1993. 185.)
A573	"Gradations of Black." *The New Yorker* 60 (13 Aug. 1984): 30. (Rpt. in *Facing Nature*. N.Y.: Knopf, 1985. 50; and in *Collected Poems, 1953-1993*. N.Y.: Knopf, 1993. 189-90.)
A574	"Ode to Growth." *Michigan Quarterly Review* 23 (Fall 1984): 485-86. (Rpt. in *Facing Nature*. N.Y.: Knopf, 1985. 82-83; and in *Collected Poems, 1953-1993*. N.Y.: Knopf, 1993. 195-97.)
A575	"Ode to Healing." *Michigan Quarterly Review* 23 (Fall 1984): 483-84. (Rpt. in *Facing Nature*. N.Y.: Knopf, 1985. 90-92; and in *Collected Poems, 1953-1993*. N.Y.: Knopf, 1993. 202-04.)
A576	"The Furniture." The *New Yorker* 60 (1 Oct. 1984): 36. (Rpt. in *Facing Nature*. N.Y.: Knopf, 1985. 53; and in *Collected Poems, 1953-1993*. N.Y.: Knopf, 1993. 190-91.)

A577	"Aerie." *The New Yorker* 60 (26 Nov. 1984): 46. (Rpt. in *Facing Nature*. N.Y.: Knopf, 1985. 60-61; and in *Collected Poems, 1953-1993*. N.Y.: Knopf, 1993. 183.)
A578	"Ode to Evaporation." *The New Yorker* 60 (31 Dec. 1984): 30. (Rpt. in *Facing Nature*. N.Y.: Knopf, 1985. 79-81, retitled, "To Evaporation"; and in *Collected Poems, 1953-1993*. N.Y.: Knopf, 1993. 193-95.)
A579	"A Different Ending." *Light Year '86*. Ed. Robert Wallace. Cleveland: Bits P, 1985. 125-26.
A580	"Pastoral." *Light Year '86*. Ed. Robert Wallace. Cleveland: Bits P, 1985. 273.
A581	"Tick." *Light Year '86*. Ed. Robert Wallace. Cleveland: Bits P, 1985. 110-11.
A582	"Ode to Rot." *Atlantic* 255 (Jan. 1985): 83. (Rpt. in *Facing Nature*. N.Y.: Knopf, 1985. 77-78; and in *Collected Poems, 1953-1993*. N.Y.: Knopf, 1993. 191-93.)
A583	"Ode to Crystallization." *The New Yorker* 60 (21 Jan. 1985): 30-31. (Rpt. in *Facing Nature*. N.Y.: Knopf, 1985. 88-89, retitled, "To Crystallization"; and in *Collected Poems, 1953-1993*. N.Y.: Knopf, 1993. 200-02.)
A584	"Ode to Entropy." *Michigan Quarterly Review* 24 (Spring 1985): 328-29. (Rpt. in *Facing Nature*. N.Y.: Knopf, 1985. 86-87; and in *Collected Poems, 1953-1993*. N.Y.: Knopf, 1993. 199-200, with a punctuation change.)
A585	"Sleeping with You." *Bennington Review* 17 (Spring 1985): 86. (Rpt. in *Facing Nature*. N.Y.: Knopf, 1985. 42-43; and in *Collected Poems, 1953-1993*. N.Y.: Knopf, 1993. 188-89.)
A586	"Poetry's Nouvelle Cuisine." *The New York Times Book Review* 8 Sept. 1985: 43. (Rpt. as "Food." *Light Year '86*. Ed. Robert Wallace. Cleveland: Bits P, 1985. 44; in *Food*. Washington: Folger's Poetry Salon, 5 Apr. 1992; in *Facing Nature*. N.Y.: Knopf, 1985. 100; and in *Collected Poems, 1953-1993*. N.Y.: Knopf, 1993. 349.)
A587	"The Sometime Sportsman Greets the Spring." *Light Year '87*. Ed. Robert Wallace. Cleveland: Bits P, 1986. 30. (Rpt. in *Collected Poems, 1953-1993*. N.Y.: Knopf, 1993. 350.)
A588	"A Pear Like a Potato." *The New Yorker* 61 (20 Jan. 1986) 26. (Reprinted in *A Pear Like a Potato*. Northridge, Calif.: CSUP, 1986; in *Recent Poems 1986-1990*. Helsinki: Eurographica, 1989; used in the song "A Pear Like a Potato" by Roy Hinkle. Premier, 6 Dec. 1992. See **A1568**; and in *Collected Poems, 1953-1993*. N.Y.: Knopf, 1993. 205-06.)

A589 "Munich." *The New Republic* 194 (21 Apr. 1986): 38. (Rpt. in *Collected Poems, 1953-1993*. N.Y.: Knopf, 1993. 205.)

A590 "Oxford, Thirty Years After." *The New Yorker* 62 (21 July 1986): 32. (Rpt. in *Two Sonnets Whose Titles Came to Me Simultaneously*. Winston-Salem, N.C.: Palaemon P, 1983; and in *Collected Poems, 1953-1993*. N.Y.: Knopf, 1993. 208.)

A591 "Airport." *The Ontario Review* 25 (Fall-Wint. 1986-87): 23. (Rpt. in *Collected Poems, 1953-1993*. N.Y.: Knopf, 1993. 207.)

A592 "From Above." *The Ontario Review* 25 (Fall-Wint. 1986-87): 24. (Rpt. in *Collected Poems, 1953-1993*. N.Y.: Knopf, 1993. 207-08.)

A593 "Goodbye, Göteborg." *The New Yorker* 63 (26 Oct. 1987): 42. (Rpt. in *Collected Poems, 1953-1993*. N.Y.: Knopf, 1993. 213.)

A594 "Snowdrops 1987." *The Ontario Review* 27 (Fall-Wint. 1987-88): 20. (Rpt. in *Collected Poems, 1953-1993*. N.Y.: Knopf, 1993. 212-13.)

A595 "Déjà, Indeed." *Sometime the Cow...: Light Year '88/89*. Ed. Robert Wallace. Cleveland: Bits P, 1988. 84. (Rpt. in *Collected Poems, 1953-1993*. N.Y.: Knopf, 1993. 351. Updike offers another second line and an earlier version on 373-74.)

A596 "Hymn to These Newly Abbreviated States." *Sometime the Cow...*: Light Year '88/89. Ed. Robert Wallace. Cleveland: Bits P, 1988. 150. (Note correction in line 9 from "UNBORN" in *Harper's* to "Newborn" with footnote couplet.)

A597 "Solitaire." *Sometime the Cow...: Light Year '88/89*. Ed. Robert Wallace. Cleveland: Bits P, 1988. 64. (Rpt. in *Collected Poems, 1953-1993*. N.Y.: Knopf, 1993. 257-58.)

A598 "Sonnet to Human Grandeur." *Lord John Ten: A Celebration*. Northridge, Calif.: Lord John P, 1988. 123.

A599 "Two Limericks After Lear." *Sometime the Cow...: Light Year '88/89*. Ed. Robert Wallace. Cleveland: Bits P, 1988. 170. (Rpt. as "Two Limericks for the Elderiy." in *Collected Poems, 1953-1993*. N.Y.: Knopf, 1993. 352.)

A600 "Klimt and Schiele Confront the Cunt." *Paris Review* 106 (Spring 1988): 203-04. (Rpt. in *Collected Poems, 1953-1993*. N.Y.: Knopf, 1993. 210.)

A601 "Mites." *The New Yorker* 64 (18 July 1988): 30. (Rpt. in *Collected Poems, 1953-1993*. N.Y.: Knopf, 1993. 352-53.)

Poetry   61

A602   "Condo Moon." *The New Yorker* 64 (28 Nov. 1988): 44. (Rpt. in *Collected Poems, 1953-1993*. N.Y.: Knopf, 1993. 223.)

A603   "On the Recently Minted Hundred-Cent Piece." *Et cetera* [sic] 45 (Sum. 1988): 155. (Rpt. in *Facing Nature*. N.Y.: Knopf, 1985. 104; and in *Collected Poems, 1953-1993*. N.Y.: Knopf, 1993. 347.)

A604   "Tulsa." *The Ontario Review* 29 (Fall-Wint. 1988-89): 18. (Rpt. in *Collected Poems, 1953-1993*. N.Y.: Knopf, 1993. 216.)

A605   "Video." *The Ontario Review* 29 (Fall-Wint. 1988-89): 18.

A606   "Washington: Tourist View." *The Ontario Review* 29 (Fall-Wint. 1988-89): 16-17. (Rpt. in *Collected Poems, 1953-1993*. N.Y.: Knopf, 1993. 216-17.)

A607   "Orthodontia." *The New Republic* 200 (13 Feb. 1989): 35. (Rpt. in *Collected Poems, 1953-1993*. N.Y.: Knopf, 1993. 222.)

A608   "Squirrels Mating." *Atlantic* 263 (July 1989): 60. (Rpt. in *Collected Poems, 1953-1993*. N.Y.: Knopf, 1993. 214-15.)

A609   "To a Box Turtle." *The New Yorker* 65 (11 Sept. 1989): 38. (Rpt. in *Collected Poems, 1953-1993*. N.Y.: Knopf, 1993. 226-27.)

*A610   "The Lens Factory." *Granta* Fall 1989: 263.

A611   "An Open Letter to Voyager 2." *Life* 12 (Nov. 1989): 115. (Rpt. in *Collected Poems, 1953-1993*. N.Y.: Knopf, 1993. 353-55.)

A612   "Frost." *The Ontario Review* 31 (Fall-Wint. 1989-90): 47. (Rpt. in *Collected Poems, 1953-1993*. N.Y.: Knopf, 1993. 225-26.)

A613   "Charleston." *The Ontario Review* 31 (Fall-Wint. 1989-90): 48. (Rpt. in *Collected Poems, 1953-1993*. N.Y.: Knopf, 1993. 225.)

A614   "Perfection Wasted." *The New Yorker* 66 (7 May 1990): 42. (Rpt. in *Thanatopses*. Cleveland: Bits P, 1991; and in *Collected Poems, 1953-1993*. N.Y.: Knopf, 1993. 231.)

A615   "Granite." *The New Yorker* 66 (5 Nov. 1990): 48. (Rpt. in *Thanatopses*. Cleveland: Bits P, 1991; and in *Collected Poems, 1953-1993*. N.Y.: Knopf, 1993. 238-39.)

A616   "Generic College." *The Ontario Review* 33 (Fall-Wint. 1990-91): 77. (Rpt. in *Collected Poems, 1953-1993*. N.Y.: Knopf, 1993. 231.)

A617   "Indianapolis." *The Ontario Review* 33 (Fall-Wint. 1990-91): 78. (Rpt. in *Collected Poems, 1953-1993*. N.Y.: Knopf, 1993. 233.)

A618 "Fly." *The Paris Review* 33 (Fall 1991): 41. (Rpt. in *Collected Poems, 1953-1993*. N.Y.: Knopf, 1993. 243-44.)

A619 "Light Switches." *The Paris Review* 33 (Fall 1991): 40. (Rpt. in *Collected Poems, 1953-1993*. N.Y.: Knopf, 1993. 241-42.)

A620 "Bindweed." *The New Yorker* 67 (26 Aug. 1991): 28. (Rpt. in *Collected Poems, 1953-1993*. N.Y.: Knopf, 1993. 245.)

A621 "Thin Air." *The Ontario Review* 35 (Fall-Wint. 1991-92): 28. (Rpt. in *Collected Poems, 1953-1993*. N.Y.: Knopf, 1993. 240.)

A622 "Flurry." *The Ontario Review* 35 (Fall-Wint. 1991-92): 28. (Rpt. in *Collected Poems, 1953-1993*. N.Y.: Knopf, 1993. 244.)

*A623 "Mouse Trappings." *The Observer Magazine* 16 Feb. 1992: 44.

A624 "Literary Dublin." *Light* No. 1 (Spring 1992): 20. (Rpt. in *Collected Poems, 1953-1993*. N.Y.: Knopf, 1993. 248-49.)

A625 "Fall." *American Poetry Review* Mar.-Apr. 1992: 35. (Rpt. in *Collected Poems, 1953-1993*. N.Y.: Knopf, 1993. 229.)

A626 "Working Outdoors in Winter." *American Poetry Review* Mar.-Apr. 1992: 35. (Rpt. in *Collected Poems, 1953-1993*. N.Y.: Knopf, 1993. 232.)

A627 "Ancient Optics." *The New Republic* 206 (18 May 1992): 42.

A628 "July." *The New Yorker* 68 (20 July 1992): 30. (Rpt. in *Collected Poems, 1953-1993*. N.Y.: Knopf, 1993. 245-246.)

A629 "Back From Vacation." *Poetry* 160 (July 1992): 202. (Rpt. in *Collected Poems*, 1953-1993. N.Y.: Knopf, 1993. 248.)

A630 "Elderly Sex." *Poetry* 160 (July 1992): 203. (Rpt. in *Collected Poems, 1953-1993*. N.Y.: Knopf, 1993. 249.)

A631 "To a Former Mistress, Now Dead." *Poetry* 160 (July 1992): 201.

A632 "Rio De Janeiro." *The New Yorker* 68 (12 Oct. 1992): 68. (Rpt. in *Collected Poems, 1953-1993*. N.Y.: Knopf, 1993. 251-52.)

A633 "Burning Trash." *The New Yorker* 68 (7 Dec. 1992): 92.
(Rpt. in *Collected Poems, 1953-1993*. N.Y.: Knopf, 1993. 9.)

A634 "Neoteny." *Ontario Review* 37 (Fall-Wint. 1992-1993): 100-01. (Rpt. in *Collected Poems, 1953-1993*. N.Y.: Knopf, 1993. 356-57.)

A635 "Untitled." *Collected Poems, 1953-1993*. N.Y.: Knopf, 1993. 373.

A636	"Academy." *Ontario Review* 38 (Spring-Sum. 1993): 46. (Rpt. in *Collected Poems, 1953-1993*. N.Y.: Knopf, 1993. 254.)
A637	"At the End of the Rainbow." *Ontario Review* 38 (Spring-Sum. 1993): 45. (Rpt. in *Collected Poems, 1953-1993*. N.Y.: Knopf, 1993. 253-54.)
A638	"Montes Veneris." *The New Yorker* 69 (31 May 1993): 46.

5. Articles and Essays

A639   "The Fading of the Fad." *Harvard Lampoon* 142 (Oct. 1953): 10-11. (Unsigned. Rpt. in *The Harvard Lampoon Centennial Celebration, 1876-1973* Martin Kaplan. Boston: Atlantic-Little, 1973. Unpaginated.)

A640   ["Notes and Comment"] "Green." *The New Yorker* 31 (10 Sept. 1955): 31-32. (Unsigned. Rpt. in *Talk from the Fifties*. Northridge, Calif.: Lord John P, 1979. 1-3.)

A641   ["Notes and Comment"] "Emergency." *The New Yorker* 31 (24 Sept. 1955): 38-39. (Unsigned. Rpt. in *Talk from the Fifties*. Northridge, Calif.: Lord John P, 1979. 4-6.)

A642   ["Notes and Comment"] "Building Décor." *The New Yorker* 31 (1 Oct. 1955): 27-28. (Unsigned. Rpt. in *Talk from the Fifties*. Northridge, Calif.: Lord John P, 1979. 7-9.)

A643   ["Notes and Comment"] "Speech on Spool." *The New Yorker* 31 (22 Oct. 1955): 37. (Unsigned. Rpt. in *Talk from the Fifties*. Northridge, Calif.: Lord John P, 1979. 10-12.)

A644   ["Notes and Comment"] "Adequate Wiring." *The New Yorker* 31 (29 Oct. 1955): 23-24. (Unsigned. Rpt. in *Talk from the Fifties*. Northridge, Calif.: Lord John P, 1979. 13-15.)

A645   ["Notes and Comment"] "Swifts and Stuffers." *The New Yorker* 31 (17 Dec. 1955): 25-26. (Unsigned. Rpt. in *Talk from the Fifties*. Northridge, Calif.: Lord John P, 1979. 16-18.)

A646   ["Notes and Comment"] "Rockefeller Center Ho!" *The New Yorker* 31 (11 Feb. 1956): 26-27. (Unsigned. Rpt. in *Talk from the Fifties*. Northridge, Calif.: Lord John P, 1979. 19-21.)

A647   ["Notes and Comment"] "Pre-Expulsion Yellow." *The New Yorker* 32 (24 Mar. 1956): 20-23. (Unsigned. Rpt. in *Talk from the Fifties*. Northridge, Calif.: Lord John P, 1979. 22-24.)

A648   ["Notes and Comment"] "Central Park." *The New Yorker* 32 (31 Mar. 1956): 23. (Unsigned. Rpt. in *Assorted Prose*. N.Y.: Knopf, 1965. 51-53; and in *Detail and Pattern*. Ed. Robert Baylor. N.Y.: McGraw, 1972. 15-18.)

A649   ["Notes and Comment"] "Our Own Baedeker." *The New Yorker* 32 (31 Mar. 1956): 25-26. (Unsigned. Rpt. in *Assorted Prose*. N.Y.: Knopf, 1965. 60-64, with minor changes and a note 62.)

A650   ["Notes and Comment"] "Voices in the Biltmore." *The New Yorker* 32 (14 Apr. 1956): 32-33. (Unsigned. Rpt. in *Assorted Prose*. N.Y.: Knopf, 1965. 57-60.)

A651   ["Notes and Comment"] "Glance." *The New Yorker* 32 (26 May 1956): 26-27. (Unsigned. Rpt. in *Talk from the Fifties*. Northridge, Calif.: Lord John P, 1979. 25-28.)

A652   ["Notes and Comment"] "Outdoor Art." *The New Yorker* 32 (23 June 1956): 19-20. (Unsigned. Rpt. in *Talk from the Fifties*. Northridge, Calif.: Lord John P, 1979. 29-31.)

A653   ["Notes and Comment"] "Tritylodonts." *The New Yorker* 32 (21 July 1956): 13-14. (Unsigned. Rpt. in *Talk from the Fifties*. Northridge, Calif.: Lord John P, 1979. 32-34.)

A654   ["Notes and Comment"] "Said Yonkers to Gloversville." *The New Yorker* 32 (15 Sept. 1956): 36-37. (Unsigned. Rpt. in *Talk from the Fifties*. Northridge, Calif.: Lord John P, 1979. 35-37.)

A655   ["Notes and Comment"] "Postal Complaints." *The New Yorker* 32 (6 Oct. 1956): 33. (Unsigned. Rpt. in *Assorted Prose*. N.Y.: Knopf, 1965. 64-66.)

A656   ["Notes and Comment"] "Convincing." *The New Yorker* 32 (10 Nov. 1956): 44. (Unsigned. Rpt. in *Talk from the Fifties*. Northridge, Calif.: Lord John P, 1979. 38-40.)

A657   ["Notes and Comment"] "No Dodo." *The New Yorker* 32 (26 Nov. 1956): 43-45. (Unsigned. Rpt. in *Assorted Prose*. N.Y.: Knopf, 1965. 53-57.)

A658   ["Notes and Comment"] "Bird Census." *The New Yorker* 32 (5 Jan. 1957): 20-21. (Unsigned. Rpt. in *Talk from the Fifties*. Northridge, Calif.: Lord John P, 1979. 41-43.)

Articles and Essays   67

A659   ["Notes and Comment"] "Resemblances." *The New Yorker* 32 (2 Feb. 1957): 26. (Unsigned. Rpt. in *Talk from the Fifties*. Northridge, Calif.: Lord John P, 1979. 44-45.)

A660   ["Notes and Comment"] "Green Grow the Yesses, O!" *The New Yorker* 33 (23 Mar. 1957): 23-24. (Unsigned. Rpt. in *Talk from the Fifties*. Northridge, Calif.: Lord John P, 1979. 46-50.)

A661   ["Notes and Comment"] "Old and Precious." *The New Yorker* 33 (30 Mar. 1957): 26-27. (Unsigned. Rpt. in *Assorted Prose*. N.Y.: Knopf, 1965. 67-70.)

A662   ["Notes and Comment"] "Physiologist's Holiday." *The New Yorker* 33 (20 Apr. 1957): 24-26. (Unsigned. Rpt. in *Talk from the Fifties*. Northridge, Calif.: Lord John P, 1979. 51-53.)

A663   ["Notes and Comment"] "Spatial Remarks." *The New Yorker* 33 (16 Nov. 1957): 41. (Unsigned. Rpt. in *Assorted Prose*. N.Y.: Knopf, 1965. 70-74.)

A664   ["Notes and Comment"] "Our Own Baedeker." *The New Yorker* 33 (23 Nov. 1957): 43-45. (Unsigned. Rpt. in *Talk from the Fifties*. Northridge, Calif.: Lord John P, 1979. 54-57.)

A665   ["Notes and Comment"] "Postal Complaints." *The New Yorker* 33 (15 Mar. 1958): 31. (Unsigned. Rpt. in *Assorted Prose*. N.Y.: Knopf, 1965. 66-67.)

A666   ["Notes and Comment"] "Auction." *The New Yorker* 34 (12 Apr. 1958): 36-37. (Unsigned. Rpt. in *Talk from the Fifties*. Northridge, Calif.: Lord John P, 1979. 58-60.)

A667   ["Notes and Comment"] "Dinosaur Egg." *The New Yorker* 34 (19 Apr. 1958): 31-32. (Unsigned. Rpt. in *Assorted Prose*. N.Y.: Knopf, 1965. 74-76.)

A668   ["Notes and Comment"] "Upright Carpentry." *The New Yorker* 34 (10 May 1958): 29. (Unsigned. Rpt. in *Assorted Prose*. N.Y.: Knopf, 1965. 77.)

A669   ["Notes and Comment"] "Crush vs. Whip." *The New Yorker* 34 (21 June 1958): 21. (Unsigned. Rpt. in *Assorted Prose*. N.Y.: Knopf, 1965. 77-80, with a note 78.)

A670   ["Notes and Comment"] "Metro Gate." *The New Yorker* 34 (24 Jan. 1959): 28. (Unsigned. Rpt. in *Assorted Prose*. N.Y.: Knopf, 1965. 80-82.)

A671   "On the Sidewalk (After Reading, at Long Last, *On the Road*, by Jack Kerouac.)" *The New Yorker* 35 (21 Feb. 1959): 32. (Rpt. in *Twentieth Century Parody: American and British*. Ed. Burling Lowrey. N.Y.:

Harcourt, 1960. 114-16; in *Parodies: An Anthology from Chaucer to Beerbohm-- and After*. Ed. Dwight Macdonald. N.Y.: Random House, 1960. 270-73; and in *Open to Language*. Ed. Patrick Hartwell and Robert H. Bentley. N.Y.: OUP, 1982. 259-60 [excerpt].)

A672 ["Notes and Comment"] "Cancelled." *The New Yorker* 35 (25 July 1959): 21-23. (Unsigned. Rpt. in *Assorted Prose*. N.Y.: Knopf, 1965. 82-86.)

A673 ["Notes and Comment"] "Oasis." *The New Yorker* 35 (8 Aug. 1959): 22-23. (Unsigned. Rpt. in *Talk from the Fifties*. Northridge, Calif.: Lord John P, 1979. 61-63.)

A674 ["Notes and Comment"] "Morality Play." *The New Yorker* 35 (24 Oct. 1959): 33-34. (Unsigned. Rpt. in *Assorted Prose*. N.Y.: Knopf, 1965. 86-90.)

A675 ["Notes and Comment"] "Engadine......" *The New Yorker* 35 (28 Nov. 1959): 41. (Unsigned.)

A676 "Confessions of a Wild Bore." *The New Yorker* 35 (6 Feb. 1960): 34-35. (Rpt. in *Assorted Prose*. N.Y.: Knopf, 1965. 31-36; and in *Confessions of a Wild Bore*. Newton, Iowa: Tamazunchale P, 1984.)

A677 "In These Books Lived Great Friends of My Childhood: A Symposium." *The New York Times Book Review* 8 May 1960: 2, 33. (Unsigned. Excerpted in *The John Updike Newsletter* Fall 1978: 3.)

A678 ["Notes and Comment"] "Bryant Park." *The New Yorker* 36 (16 July 1960): 23-24. (Unsigned. Rpt. in *Assorted Prose*. N.Y.: Knopf, 1965. 92-94.)

A679 ["Notes and Comment"] "Obfuscating Coverage." *The New Yorker* 36 (30 July 1960): 15. (Unsigned. Rpt. in *Assorted Prose*. N.Y.: Knopf, 1965. 90-92.)

A680 ["Notes and Comment"] "John Marquand." *The New Yorker* 36 (6 Aug. 1960): 20. (Unsigned. Rpt. in *Assorted Prose*. N.Y.: Knopf, 1965. 95-96.)

A681 "Hub Fans Bid Kid Adieu." *The New Yorker* 36 (22 Oct. 1960): 109-31. (Rpt. in *Assorted Prose*. N.Y.: Knopf, 1965. 127-147 with notes 128-32, 134-138, 143; in *Sports in Literature*. Ed. Henry B. Chapin. N.Y.: McKay, 1976. 289-305; in *Hub Fans Bid Kid Adieu*. Northridge, Calif.: Lord John P, 1977, with a "Preface" by Updike; in *The Lexington Reader*. Ed. Lynn Z. Bloom. Lexington, Mass.: Heath, 1987. 470-83; and in *The Norton Book of Sports*. Ed. George Plimpton. N.Y.: W. W. Norton, 1992. 355-67.)

Articles and Essays 69

A682 ["Notes and Comment"] "Two Heroes." *The New Yorker* 36 (10 Dec. 1960): 43. (Unsigned. Rpt. in *Assorted Prose*. N.Y.: Knopf, 1965. 96-97, with a note 97.)

A683 ["Notes and Comment"] "Doomsday, Mass." *The New Yorker* 37 (2 Dec. 1961): 51. (Unsigned. Rpt. in *Assorted Prose*. N.Y.: Knopf, 1965. 98-101.)

A684 ["Notes and Comment"] "Grandma Moses." *The New Yorker* 37 (23 Dec. 1961): 17. (Unsigned. Rpt. in *Assorted Prose*. N.Y.: Knopf, 1965. 101-02.)

A685 "Foreword for Young Readers." *The Young King and Other Fairy Tales by Oscar Wilde*. N.Y.: Macmillan, 1962. iii-v.

A686 ["Notes and Comment"] "Spring Rain." *The New Yorker* 38 (21 Apr. 1962): 31-32. (Unsigned. Rpt. in *Assorted Prose*. N.Y.: Knopf, 1965. 102-105; in *The Everlasting Universe: Readings in the Ecological Revolution*. Ed. Lorne Forstner and John Todd. Lexington, Mass.: Heath, 1971. 91-93; and in *The Norton Book of Nature Writing*. Ed. Robert Finch and John Elder. N.Y.: Norton, 1990. 759-61.)

A687 ["Notes and Comment"] "Eisenhower's Eloquence." *The New Yorker* 38 (19 May 1962): 31. (Unsigned. Rpt. in *Assorted Prose*. N.Y.: Knopf, 1965. 105-07.)

A688 ["Notes and Comment"] "Central Park..." *The New Yorker* 38 (16 June 1962): 23. (Unsigned.)

A689 ["Notes and Comment"] "Six persons...." *The New Yorker* 38 (11 Aug. 1962): 15. (Unsigned.)

A690 "No Use Talking." *The New Republic* 148 (13 Aug. 1962): 23-24. (Rpt. in *The Faces of Five Decades: Selections from Fifty Years of The New Republic, 1914-1964*. Ed. Robert B. Luce. N.Y.: Simon, 1964. 447-50.)

A691 ["Notes and Comment"] "Mostly Glass." *The New Yorker* 38 (13 Oct. 1962): 41. (Unsigned. Rpt. in *Assorted Prose*. N.Y.: Knopf, 1965. 107-09.)

A692 ["Notes and Comment"] "Science takes away...." *The New Yorker* 39 (9 Mar. 1963): 31.(Unsigned.)

A693 ["Notes and Comment"] "Baseball, that national...." *The New Yorker* 39 (16 Mar. 1963): 41. (Unsigned.)

A694 ["Notes and Comment"] "Three Documents." *The New Yorker* 39 (1 June 1963): 23-24. (Unsigned. Rpt. in *Assorted Prose*. N.Y.: Knopf, 1965. 109-13, with a note 113.)

A695 ["Notes and Comment"] "Free Bee-hours." *The New Yorker* 39 (19 Oct. 1963): 43. (Unsigned. Rpt. in *Assorted Prose*. N.Y.: Knopf, 1965. 113-15.)

A696   ["Notes and Comment"] "The Assassination." *The New Yorker* 39 (7 Dec. 1963): 45. (Unsigned. Rpt. in *Assorted Prose*. N.Y.: Knopf, 1965. 118-19.)

A697   ["Notes and Comment"] "The Assassination." *The New Yorker* 39 (21 Dec. 1963): 21-22. (Unsigned. Rpt. in *Assorted Prose*. N.Y.: Knopf, 1965. 119-22.)

A698   "An *Arion* Questionnaire: 'The Classics and the Man of Letters.'" *Arion* 13 (Wint. 1964): 5-100. (Pages 88-89 concern Updike.)

A699   ["Notes and Comment"] "Beer Can." *The New Yorker* 39 (18 Jan. 1964): 23. (Unsigned. Rpt. in *Assorted Prose*. N.Y.: Knopf, 1965. 115.)

A700   ["Notes and Comment"] "Modern Art." *The New Yorker* 40 (11 Apr. 1964): 31-32. (Unsigned. Rpt. in *Assorted Prose*. N.Y.: Knopf, 1965. 116-118.)

A701   ["Notes and Comment"] "Whenever we return...." *The New Yorker* 40 (30 May 1964): 23. (Unsigned.)

A702   ["Notes and Comment"] "We are in receipt..." *The New Yorker* 40 (27 June 1964): 40. (Unsigned.)

A703   ["Notes and Comment"] "We looked forward..." *The New Yorker* 40 (22 Aug. 1964): 23. (Unsigned.)

A704   "Foreword." To *The Poorhouse Fair* (4th edition, revised) and *Rabbit, Run* (5th edition, revised). N.Y.: Modern Library, 1965. one page, unpaginated.

A705   "Today's Youth Looks at AAK." In *Portrait of a Publisher, 1915/1965: Volume II: Alfred A. Knopf and the Borzoi Imprint: Recollections and Aspirations*. N.Y.: The Typophiles, 1965. 241-44.

A706   ["Notes and Comment"] "Eclipse." *The New Yorker* 40 (2 Jan. 1965): 22-24. (Unsigned. Rpt. in *Assorted Prose*. N.Y.: Knopf, 1965. 222-24; in *You*. Ed. Joseph Frank. N.Y.: Harcourt, 1972. 253-55; in *Short Essays*. 4th ed. Ed. Gerald Levin. N.Y.: Harcourt, 1986. 373-376; and in *The Norton Book of Nature Writing*. Ed. Robert Finch and John Elder. N.Y.: Norton, 1990. 762.)

A707   ["Notes and Comment"] "T. S. Eliot." *The New Yorker* 40 (9 Jan. 1965): 26. (Unsigned. Rpt. in *Assorted Prose*. N.Y.: Knopf, 1965. 122-23.)

A708   ["Notes and Comment"] "We confess ourself..." *The New Yorker* 41 (5 June 1965): 31. (Unsigned.)

Articles and Essays 71

A709   ["Notes and Comment"] "Why is it, we asked ourself...." *The New Yorker* 41 (6 Nov. 1965): 43. (Unsigned.)

A710   ["Notes and Comment"] "A group of young men and women...." *The New Yorker* 41 (22 Jan. 1966): 23. (Unsigned.)

A711   ["Notes and Comment"] "We have had occasion...." *The New Yorker* 41 (5 Feb. 1966): 29. (Unsigned.)

A712   "Precise Language." *Commonweal* 84 (22 Apr. 1966): 160-161. (Unsigned reply to Anthony Burgess.)

A713   ["Notes and Comment"] "There are years..." *The New Yorker* 42 (2 July 1966): 66. (Unsigned.)

A714   An untitled statement. In *Authors Take Sides on Vietnam: Two Questions on the War in Vietnam Answered by the Authors of Several Nations*. Ed. Cecil Woolf and John Bagguley. London: Peter Owen, 1967. 50-51.

A715   ["Notes and Comment"] "We have found new life...." *The New Yorker* 43 (8 Apr. 1967): 31. (Unsigned.)

A716   ["Notes and Comment"] "We discover that the question. ..." *The New Yorker* 43 (10 June 1967): 29. (Unsigned.)

A717   "Voznesensky Met." *The New Yorker* 43 (26 Aug. 1967): 19-20. (Unsigned. Rpt. in *Picked-Up Pieces*. N.Y.: Knopf, 1975. 7-9, with a note 7 and some deletions.)

A718   ["Notes and Comment"] "We used to think...." *The New Yorker* 43 (9 Dec. 1967): 51. (Unsigned.)

A719   "Introduction" to the Czech Edition of *Of the Farm. O Farme*. Trans. Igor Hajek, 1968. (Rpt. in *Picked-Up Pieces*. N.Y.: Knopf, 1975. 82-83; and in *Dictionary of Literary Biography: Documentary Series*. Volume III. Ed. Mary Bruccolli. Detroit, Gale, 1983. 272-73.) See **Appendix I**: 79.

A720   "Note" in *Three Texts from Early Ipswich*. Ipswich, Mass: 17th Century Day Committee: 17th Century Day Committee, 1968. (Updike records the pageant's use of texts from *Ipswich in the Massachusetts Bay Colony*, Volume I by Thomas Franklin Waters; *History of Ipswich, Essex and Hamilton*, by Joseph B. Felt; *The Simple Cobbler of Aggawamm in America*; and Anne Bradstreet's poems from *The American Puritans*, edited by Perry Miller.)

A721   ["Notes and Comment"] "A United Press dispatch..." *The New Yorker* 44 (30 Mar. 1968): 25. (Unsigned.)

A722   ["Notes and Comment"] "The fine hairs...." *The New Yorker* 44 (6 Apr. 1968): 33. (Unsigned.)

A723   "Letter from Anguilla." *The New Yorker* 44 (22 June 1968): 70-80. (Rpt. in *Picked-Up Pieces*. N.Y.: Knopf, 1975. 63-77, including "P. S., September 1974," and a poem.)

A724   "Writers I Have Met." *The New York Times Book Review* 11 Aug. 1968: 2, 23. (Rpt. in *Picked-Up Pieces*. N.Y.: Knopf, 1975. 3-7.)

A725   "On Creativity." *Playboy* 15 (Dec. 1968): 139.

A726   "Introduction." *Pens and Needles: Literary Caricatures,* by David Levine. Boston: Dorset P, 1969. [v.-.viii]. (Updike made the selections. A limited edition of 300 signed copies also exists. Caricature of Updike by Levine appears on 44 and on the dust jacket's rear cover. Rpt. in *Picked-Up Pieces*. N.Y.: Knopf, 1975. 80-82.)

A727   "An American in London." *The Listener* 81 (23 Jan. 1969): 97-99. (Rpt. in *Picked-Up Pieces*. N.Y.: Knopf, 1975. 40-49, with a note 43, and titled "Notes of a Temporary Resident.")

A728   "Amor Vincit Omnia ad Nauseam (After Awakening from *Bruno's Dream*, by Iris Murdoch, and Falling Into the Nursery)." *The New Yorker* 45 (5 Apr. 1969): 33. (Rpt. in *Picked-Up Pieces*. N.Y.: Knopf, 1975. 52-55.)

A729   "Views." *The Listener* 81 (12 June 1969): 817-18.

A730   "Cemeteries." *Transatlantic Review* 32 (Sum. 1969): 5-10. (Rpt. in *Picked-Up Pieces*. N.Y.: Knopf, 1975. 56-62.)

A731   ["Notes and Comment"] "The obituaries of Judy Garland...." *The New Yorker* 44 (5 July 1969): 19. (Unsigned.)

A732   ["Notes and Comment"] "Americans watching television...." *The New Yorker* 44 (16 Aug. 1969): 23. (Unsigned.)

A733   ["Notes and Comment"] "Some months ago Mr. Kingsley. ..." *The New Yorker* 44 (13 Sept. 1969): 35. (Unsigned.)

A734   ["Notes and Comment"] "We live in the midst of flux...." *The New Yorker* 45 (13 Dec. 1969): 45. (Unsigned.)

A735   "As we read...." *The New Yorker* 45 (3 Jan. 1970): 19. (Unsigned.)

A736   ["Notes and Comment"] "A vacationing correspondent..." *The New Yorker* 46 (5 Sept. 1970): 25. (Unsigned.)

A737	["Notes and Comment"] "This Fair Land...." *The New Yorker* 46 (3 Oct. 1970): 37. (Unsigned.)
A738	"Tribute." *Tri-Quarterly* 17 (Wint. 1970): 342-343. (Rpt. in *Picked-Up Pieces*. N.Y.: Knopf, 1975. 220-22, with a note 221; and in *Nabokov: Criticism, Reminiscences, Translations and Tributes*. Ed. Alfred Apell Jr. and Charles Newman. Evanston, Ill.: Northwestern U P, 1980. 342-43.)
A739	An untitled reply to "Which book or books were your favorites or influenced you most as a teenager and why?" *Attacks of Taste*. Compiled and edited by Evelyn B. Byrne and Otto M. Penzler. N.Y.: Gotham Book Mart, 1971. 44-45.
A740	"Søren Kierkegaard." In *Atlantic Brief Lives: A Biographical Companion to the Arts*. Ed. Louis Kronenberger. Boston: Atlantic-Little, 1971. 429-31.
A741	"Black Suicide." *Atlantic* 227 (Feb. 1971): 108-12.
A742	"The First Lunar Invitational." *The New Yorker* 47 (27 Feb. 1971): 35-36. (Rpt. in *Picked-Up Pieces*. N.Y.: Knopf, 1975. 92-94 with a note 94.)
A743	"Introduction." *Soundings in Satanism*. Ed. F. J. Sheed, N.Y.: Sheed and Ward, 1972. vii-xii. (Rpt. in part in *Time* 102 (23 July 1973): 69; and in *Picked-Up Pieces*. N.Y.: Knopf, 1975. 87-91.)
A744	["Notes and Comment"] "We found...." *The New Yorker* 42 (15 Jan. 1972): 19. (Unsigned.)
A745	"Dawn of the Possible Dream." *Sports Illustrated* 36 (21 Feb. 1972): 38-45.
A746	"Tarbox Police." *Esquire* 77 (Mar. 1972): 85-86. (Rpt. in *Hugging the Shore*. N.Y.: Knopf, 1983. 25-30.)
*A747	"Three Texts from Early Ipswich: A Pageant." *Audience* 2 (Mar.-Apr. 1972). Fifty numbered and signed copies.
*A748	"Why Robert Frost Should Receive the Nobel Prize." *Audience* 7 (Sum. 1972): 45-46.
A749	"Is There Life After Golf?" *The New Yorker* 48 (29 July 1972): 76-78.
A750	"The Dilemma of Ipswich." *Ford Times* 65 (Autumn 1972): 8-15. (Rpt. in *The Best of The Times*. Michigan: Ford Motor Co., 1977.)
A751	"Foreword." *The Harvard Lampoon Centennial Celebration, 1876-1973*. Ed. Martin Kaplan. Boston: Atlantic-Little, 1973. Two unnumbered pages. (Rpt. in *Picked-Up Pieces*. N.Y.: Knopf, 1975. 84-86.)

A752	"Addendum: Excerpts from the Symposium, 'Reality and the Novel in Africa and America.'" U of Lagos, 16 Jan. 1973. Ed. Dr. Theophilus Vincent. United States Information Service. (Rpt. in *Picked-Up Pieces*. N.Y.: Knopf, 1975. 339-42. The Symposium was edited by Updike but does not include his remarks.)
A753	"Golf." *The New York Times Book Review* 10 June 1973: 3, 20.
A754	"Broad Spectrum of Writers Attacks Obscenity Ruling." *The New York Times* 21 Aug. 1973: 38. (Partly Rpt. in *The John Updike Newsletter* Spring 1978: 3.)
A755	"Introduction" to "Leaves." *Writer's Choice*. Ed. Rust Hills. N.Y.: McKay, 1974. 391-92. (Rpt. in *Dictionary of Literary Biography: Documentary Series*. Volume III. Ed. Mary Bruccolli. Detroit: Gale, 1983. 299.)
A756	"Accuracy." *Picked-Up Pieces*. N.Y.: Knopf, 1975. 16-17. (Rpt. *Dictionary of Literary Biography: Documentary Series*. Volume III. Ed. Mary Bruccolli. Detroit: Gale, 1983. 264-65.)
A757	"A Citation Composed for the Awarding of the 1968 National Book Award for Fiction to *The Eighth Day*, by Thornton Wilder." *Picked-Up Pieces*. N.Y.: Knopf, 1975. 437, with a note.
A758	"Foreword." *Picked-Up Pieces*. N.Y.: Knopf, 1975. xv-xx.
A759	"The Future of the Novel." (Rpt. in *Picked-Up Pieces*. N.Y.: Knopf, 1975. 17-23; and in *Dictionary of Literary Biography: Documentary Series*. Volume III. Ed. Mary Bruccolli. Detroit: Gale, 1983. 275-77. Speech given Feb. 1969, in Bristol, England.)
A760	"An Interesting Emendation in the Text of *Mr. Sammler's Planet*, by Saul Bellow." *Picked-Up Pieces*. N.Y.: Knopf, 1975. 438-44.
A761	"Introduction." *Innocent Bystander: The Scene from the 70's*. By L. E. Sissman. N.Y.: The Vanguard P, Inc., 1975. xvi-xviii. (Rpt. in *Hugging the Shore*. N.Y.: Knopf, 1983. 627-30.)
A762	"Remarks on the Occasion of E. B. White's Receiving the 1971 National Medal for Literature on December 2, 1971." *Picked-Up Pieces*. N.Y.: Knopf, 1975. 434-37.
A763	"The Chaste Planet." *The New Yorker* 51 (10 Nov. 1975): 43-44. (Rpt. in *The Chaste Planet*. Worcester, Mass: Metacom, 1980; and in *Hugging the Shore*. N.Y., Knopf, 1983. 35-39.)

A764	"Introduction." In Starr Ockenga, *Mirror After Mirror: Reflections on Woman*. Garden City: N.Y. American Photographic Book Co., Inc., 1976. Four unnumbered pages.
A765	"Reconsideration." *The New Republic* 174 (17 Jan. 1976): 40-41. (Updike notes: "First written, in 1975, as one of *The New Republic*'s series of 'Reconsiderations,' about *Memoirs of Hecate County*. Expanded to include the other fiction for *An Edmund Wilson Celebration*, edited by John Wain [Phaidon, 1978]. Then trimmed back and thriftily reused as an afterword for Nonpareil Books' paperback reissue of *Hecate County* in 1980. This version is the wrap-up, full of footnotes." Rpt. in "Wilson's Fiction: A Personal Account." Ed. John Wain. *Edmund Wilson: The Man and His Work: A Celebration*. N.Y.: NYUP, 1978. 163-73, with a footnote. 166; in "Afterword," in *Edmund Wilson, Memories of Hecate County* [N.Y.: Non Pareil, 1980]; and in *Hugging the Shore*. N.Y.: Knopf, 1983. 196-206, with notes 196, 199, 203, 205.)
A766	"Introduction." *The Poorhouse Fair*. 1st ed, 6th printing, revised. N.Y.: Knopf, 1977. vii-xx.
A767	"People One Knows." *Transatlantic Review* No. 60 (1977): 107-110.
A768	"Preface," to *Hub Fans Bid Kid Adieu*. Northridge, Calif.: Lord John P, 1977. Edition limited to 300 copies. ix-xii.
A769	"'A Special Message' to Purchasers of the Franklin Library limited edition, in 1977, of *Rabbit, Run*." Franklin Center: The Franklin Library, 1977. Two unnumbered pages. (Rpt. in *Hugging the Shore*. N.Y.: Knopf, 1983. 849-51.)
A770	"Vladimir Nabokov." *The New Yorker* 53 (18 July 1977): 21-22. (Rpt. as "In Memoriam." *In Memoriam Vladimir Nabokov, 1899-1977*. N.Y.: McGraw, 1977. 27-38. Adds readings from "An Evening of Russian Poetry" and *Lolita*.)
A771	"The Cultural Situation of the American Writer." *American Studies International* 15 (Spring 1977): 19-28. (Rpt. from another version "The Cultural Situation of the American Writer" in *International Exchange News*. Rpt. in *Abstract of "'The Plight of the American Writer.'" American Enterprize Institute in Washington, D. C. *Change* Dec. 1977: 37-41; and in *Hugging the Shore*. N.Y.: Knopf, 1983. 870.)
A772	"Introduction." Henry Green. *Loving, Living, Party Going: Three Novels by Henry Green*. London: Picador P, 1978. 7-15. (Rpt. in *Hugging the Shore*. N.Y.: Knopf, 1983. 311-20, with two notes 319.)
A773	"Walt Whitman: Ego and Art." *The New York Review of Books* 25 (9 Feb. 1978): 33-36. (Talk originally given at the Morgan Library, N.Y., Oct. 4, 1977. Rpt. as *Ego and Art in Walt Whitman*. N.Y.: Targ, 1980;

and in *Hugging the Shore*. N.Y.: Knopf, 1983. 106-117 with a note 106 and the title changed to "Whitman's Egotheism.")

A774 "From Guidelines to Censorship? One Writer's Testimony." *The National Review* 30 (26 May 1978): 641. (Rpt. in *The John Updike Newsletter* Sum. 1978: 7; and in *Hugging the Shore*. N.Y.: Knopf, 1983. 35-39.)

A775 Comment on John Gardner's *On Moral Fiction*. *The New York Times Sunday Magazine* 6 July 1978: 12-15, 34, 36-39.

A776 "Autobibliographical Note." *Sixteen Sonnets*. Cambridge, Mass.: Halty Ferguson, 1979. (Rpt. in *Hugging the Shore*. N.Y.: Knopf, 1983. 866-67.)

A777 "Foreword." *Too Far To Go: The Maples Stories*. N.Y.: Fawcett, 1979. 9-10.

A778 "Hawthorne's Religious Language." *Proceedings of the American Academy and Institute of Arts and Letters* 30 (1979): 21-27. (Rpt. and revised as "On Hawthorne's Mind." *The New York Review of Books* [19 Mar. 1981]; in *Hawthorne's Creed*. N.Y.: Targ Editions, 1981; and in *Hugging the Shore*. N.Y.: Knopf, 1983. 73-80, with a note 73, and minor revisions.)

A779 "Introduction." In Bruno Schulz, *Sanatorium Under the Sign of the Hourglass*. Trans. Ceilina Wieniewska. Harmondsworth and N.Y.: Penguin, 1979. xiii-xix. (Rpt. in *Hugging the Shore*. N.Y.: Knopf, 1983. 491-97.)

A780 "Introduction." *Talk from the Fifties*. Northridge, Calif.: Lord John P, 1979. ix-xii. (Signed, limited edition. Rpt. in *Hugging the Shore*. N.Y.: Knopf, 1983. 845-849.)

A781 "Golf Dreams." *The New Yorker* 55 (19 Feb. 1979): 35. (Rpt. in *Hugging the Shore*. N.Y.: Knopf, 1983. 42-43.)

A782 "The Updike Report." *The New York Times* 6 June 1979: C-15. (Rpt. in *Harvard Class of 1954, 25th Anniversary Report*. Cambridge: Harvard U Printing Office, 1979: 984-85.)

A783 "The Books That Made Writers." *The New York Times Book Review* 25 Nov. 1979: 80. (Updike responds to the question, "What book made you decide to become a writer?")

A784 "Afterword." In *Memoirs of Hecate County* by Edmund Wilson. Boston: Nonpareil, 1980. 449-59.

A785 "Foreword." *The Chaste Planet*. Worcester, Mass.: Metacom, 1980.

Articles and Essays

A786 "Going Barefoot." *On the Vineyard*. Peter Simon, photographer. N.Y.: Doubleday, 1980. 11-12. (Rpt. in **Eastern Review* June 1980: 52-55; in *The New York Times Book Review* 15 June 1980: 29-30; and in *Hugging the Shore*. N.Y.: Knopf, 1983. 61-63, with a note 61.)

A787 "Introduction." In *Lectures on Literature* by Vladimir Nabokov. Ed. Fredson Bowers. N.Y.: Harcourt, 1980. xvii-xxvii. (Rpt. as "Professor Nabokov." *The New York Review of Books* 27 [25 Sept. 1980]: 12, 14, 16, 18, and 20. Rpt. in *Hugging the Shore*. N.Y.: Knopf, 1983. 223-36, with notes 223, 231, and 234.)

A788 "13 Ways of Looking at the Masters." *Golf Magazine* Apr. 1980. 62-69. (Rpt. in *Hugging the Shore*. N.Y.: Knopf, 1983. 44-55.)

A789 "Going Barefoot." *The New York Times Book Review* 15 June 1980: 29-30. (Rpt. *On the Vineyard*. Peter Simon, photographer. N.Y.: Doubleday, 1980. 11-12; in **Eastern Review* June, 1980: 52-55; and in *Hugging the Shore*. N.Y.: Knopf, 1983. 61-63, with a note 61.)

A790 "Jorge Luis Borges." *Borges y la crítica: antología*. Buenos Aires: Centro Editor de América Latina, 1981. (Spanish translation of "The Author as Librarian." *The New Yorker* 41 (30 Oct. 1965): 223-24, 226-28, 231-36, 238, 241-46.)

A791 "The Hand of Saint Saens." *Réalités* Mar.-Apr. 1981: 43-44.

A792 "Venezuela for Visitors." *The New Yorker* 57 (11 May 1981): 34-35. (Rpt. in *Hugging the Shore*. N.Y.: Knopf, 1983. 31-34.)

A793 "Invasion of the Book Envelopes." *The New Yorker* 57 (20 July 1981): 33. (Rpt. in *Invasion of the Book Envelopes*. Concord, N. H.: William B. Ewert, 1981; and in *Hugging the Shore*. N.Y.: Knopf, 1983. 40-42.)

*A794 "John Updike/1981 Medalist." *Colony Newsletter* 11 (Fall 1981): 3.

A795 "Updike on Updike." *The New York Times Book Review* 27 Sept. 1981: 1, 34-35.

A796 "Blue Nights and Happy Days." *Playboy* 28 (Nov. 1981): 216.

A797 "Lasting Impressions." *Esquire* Dec. 1981: 60.

A798 "Foreword to the 1982 Edition." *The Carpentered Hen*. N.Y.: Knopf, 1982. xiii-xvii.

A799 "Foreword." *Great New England Churches [:] 65 Houses of Worship That Changed our Lives*. By Robert Mutrux. Chester, Conn.: Globe Pequot P, 1982.

A800   ["John McEnroe."] *World Tennis* Jan. 1982: 40.

A801   "An Acceptance of the National Book Critics Circle Award for Fiction." Speech given at the N.Y. Public Library, 28 Jan. 1982. (Rpt. in *Hugging the Shore*. N.Y.: Knopf, 1983. 875-76, with a note 875.)

A802   "A Mild 'Complaint.'" *The New Yorker* 58 (19 Apr. 1982): 39 (Rpt. in *Hugging the Shore*. N.Y.: Knopf, 1983. 68-69.)

A803   "Melville's Withdrawal." *The New Yorker* 58 (10 May 1982): 120-22, 124-26, 128, 130, 132, 134-42, 145-47. (Originally given as the third annual Harold Hacker Lecture in Rochester N.Y., Oct. 23, 1981. Rpt. in *Hugging the Shore*. N.Y.: Knopf, 1983. 80-106, with notes 80, 91, 94, 99, 101 and 104.)

A804   "Books That Gave Me Pleasure." *The New York Times Book Review* 5 Dec. 1982: 9.

A805   "An Acceptance of the American Book Award for Fiction." Speech given at Carnegie Hall, Apr. 27, 1982. *Hugging the Shore*. N.Y.: Knopf, 1983. 876-78, with a note 875.)

A806   "Comment on 'Seagulls.'" *Poetspeak*. Ed. Paul Janeczko. Brandbury P, 1983. 140-41. (Rpt. in *Hugging the Shore*. N.Y.: Knopf, 1983. 865-66.)

A807   "Foreword." *The Complete Lyrics of Cole Porter*. Ed. Robert Kimball. N.Y.: Knopf, 1983.

A808   "Foreword." *Hugging The Shore*. N.Y.: Knopf, 1983. xv-xx.

A809   "Why Write?" *First Person Singular: Writers on Their Craft*. Ed. Joyce Carol Oates. Princeton: *Ontario Review* P, 1983. 1-9. (Originally given as a speech in Adelaide, South Australia, Mar. 1964, on accepting the National Book Award for *The Centaur*. Rpt. in *Major Writers of Short Fiction*. Ed. Ann Charters. N.Y.: St. Martin's P, 1992: 1271-79.)

A810   "Two Hoppers on Display at the National Gallery." *The New Republic* 188 (31 Jan. 1983): 35. (Rpt. in *Collected Poems, 1953-1993*. N.Y.: Knopf, 1993. 181, as "Two Hoppers.") Incorrectly listed. See **A566**.

A811   "The World of Fairfield Porter: Nice People, Nice Places, Pleasantly Redolent of Affection and Money." *The New Republic* 188 (28 Feb. 1983): 24-25.

A812   "The Revenge Symposium." *Esquire* May 1983: 87.

A813   "Kafka's Short Stories." *The New Yorker* 59 (9 May 1983): 121-26, 129-33. (Rpt. from "Foreword." *Franz Kafka: The Complete Stories of Franz Kafka*. Ed. Nahum N. Glatzer. N.Y.: Schocken, 1983. ix-xxi; excerpted

Articles and Essays 79

as "John Updike on Franz Kafka and *The Metamorphosis*," in *The Story and Its Writer*. Ed. Ann Charters. N.Y.: St. Martin's P, 1987. 1270-73; and in *Odd Jobs*. N.Y.: Knopf, 1991. 200-10 with notes 201.)

A814   "Edmund Wilson and the Landscape of Literature." *Esquire* 100 (Dec. 1983): 428-430, 432. (Rpt. in *Odd Jobs*. N.Y.: Knopf, 1991. 101-106.)

A815   "Foreword." *Jester's Dozen*. Northridge, Calif.: Lord John P, 1984. Two pages, unpaginated. Limited edition. (Rpt. in *Odd Jobs*. N.Y.: Knopf, 1991. 842-43.)

A816   "Introduction." *The Best American Short Stories 1984*. Ed. John Updike and Shannon Ravenel. Boston: Houghton, 1984. xi-xxii.

A817   "Introduction to the 1977 Edition." *The Poorhouse Fair*. 1st ed. 6th printing, rev.. N.Y.: Knopf, 1984. vii-xx.

A818   "A Special Message for the First Edition from John Updike." *The Witches of Eastwick*. Franklin Center, Pa.: Franklin Library, 1984. 7-9. (Rpt. in *Odd Jobs*. N.Y.: Knopf, 1991, 853-56, with a note, 853-54.)

A819   "Twisted Apples." *Harper's* 268 (Mar. 1984): 95-97. (Rpt. in *Odd Jobs*. N.Y.: Knopf, 1991. 302-07, note 304.)

A820   "The Golden Age of the 30-second Spot." *Harper's* 268 (June 1984): 17. (Acceptance speech to the National Arts Club on receiving the Medal of Honor for Literature.)

A821   "Emersonianism." *The New Yorker* 60 (4 June 1984): 112, 115-32. (Updike notes: "This talk was given at the Davis campus of the University of California on October 25, 1983, and then, somewhat revised, at the 1644th stated meeting of the American Academy of Arts and Sciences in Cambridge, Massachusetts on November 9, 1983. Again revised, it appeared in *The New Yorker* of 4 June 1984. This present version reverts to the form of a spoken address, while keeping a number of details and quotations added for the magazine publication. The quotations from Emerson follow, in their sometimes curious-seeming spelling and punctuation, the text as last proofread by the author himself, as presented in *Ralph Waldo Emerson: Essays and Lectures*, edited by Joel Porte [Library of America, 1983]." Rpt. in *Emersonianism*. Cleveland, Ohio: Bits P, 1984; and in *Odd Jobs*. N.Y.: Knopf, 1991. 148-68 with notes 148 [in which Updike repeats the information of the first two sentences above], 156, 157, 159 and 164.)

A822   "The Most Unforgettable Character I've Met." *Vogue* 174 (Nov. 1984): 441. (Rpt. in *Odd Jobs*. N.Y.: Knopf, 1991. 67-69, with title changed to "The Most Unforgettable Mother I've Met." and minor revisions.)

A823 "Personal History: A Soft Spring Night in Shillington." *The New Yorker* 60 (24 Dec. 1984): 7-40, 43-44, 48-50, 52-54, 56-57. (Rpt. in *Self-Consciousness*. N.Y.: Knopf, 1989. 3-41, with notes 10, 11, 18, 20, 21, 37, some verbal and organizational changes and titled, "A Soft Spring Night in Shillington." Contains an illustration by Updike.)

A824 "Fictional Houses." *Architectural Digest* 41 (Jan. 1985): 24, 28, 30, 34 and 36. (Rpt. in *Odd Jobs*. N.Y.: Knopf, 1991. 46-50.)

A825 "The Artist and His Audience." *The New York Review of Books* 32 (18 July 1985): 14-18.

A826 "The Importance of Fiction." *Esquire* Aug. 1985: 61- 62. (Rpt. in *Odd Jobs*. N.Y.: Knopf, 1991. 84-87.)

A827 "Personal History: At War with my Skin." *The New Yorker* 61 (2 Sept. 1985): 39-40, 43-44, 46-57. (Rpt. with some verbal and organizational changes in *Self-Consciousness*. N.Y.: Knopf, 1989. 42-78, titled, "At War with My Skin," notes on 49, 50, 58, 71, 76; and in *Inquiry*. Ed. Lynn Z. Bloom and Edward M. White. Englewood Cliffs, N.J.: Prentice, 1993. 50-55, with *Instructor's Manual*, 5.)

A828 "Italo Calvino." *Granta* 17 (Autumn 1985): 242-43.

A829 "An Appreciation of Women." *Cosmopolitan* Nov. 1985: 394, 401. (Rpt. in *Odd Jobs*. N.Y.: Knopf, 1991. 64-67.)

A830 "Is Art Worth It? Renoir at the Mercy of the Megashow." *The New Republic* 193 (4 Nov. 1985): 25, 30-32. (Rpt. in *Just Looking*. N.Y.: Knopf, 1989. 79-91.)

*A831 "Being on TV Is Like Being Alive, Only More So." *TV Guide*. 23 Nov. 1985.

A832 "The Illustrative Itch." *The New York Review of Books* 33 (10 Apr. 1986): 35-6. (Rpt. as "Foreword." *Doubly Gifted*. Ed. Kathleen Hjerter. N.Y.: Abrams, 1986. 7-8 and 148-49; and in *Just Looking*. N.Y.: Knopf, 1989. 191-200.)

A833 "Introduction." *Writers at Work: The Paris Review Interviews, Seventh Series*. George Plimpton, editor. N.Y.: Viking, 1986. xi-xx.

A834 "Getting the Words Out." *More Dirt: The New American Fiction*. *Granta* 19 (Fall 1986): 151-170. (Rpt. from *Criterion* and *Boston Review*. Rpt. in *Getting the Words Out*. Northridge: Lord John P, 1988. and in *Self-Consciousness*. N.Y.: Knopf, 1989. 79-111.)

A835 "Afterword." In *Expelled*. By John Cheever. Los Angeles: Sylvester & Orphanos, 1987. 60-70.

A836	"Preface to a Partial Catalogue of My Own Leavings." Ed. Elizabeth A. Falsey. *The Art of Adding and the Art of Taking Away.* Cambridge, Mass.: The Harvard College Library, 1987. 3.
*A837	"Bookbuilder." The Bookbuilders of Boston. Jan./Feb., 1987.
A838	"Writers as Progenitors and Offspring." *Poets & Writers Magazine* Jan.-Feb. 1987: 13-14. (Rpt. in *Odd Jobs.* N.Y.: Knopf, 1991. 833-35, with a note, 834.)
A839	"The Burglar Alarm," *The New Yorker* 63 (9 Mar. 1987): 30-31.
A840	"Notes and Comment." *The New Yorker* 63 (23 Mar. 1987): 25-26. (Unsigned. Rpt. in *Odd Jobs.* N.Y.: Knopf, 1991. 859-62.)
A841	"Tuning out the Inner Critic." *The New York Times Book Review* 21 June 1987: 29.
A842	"Howells as Anti-Novelist." *The New Yorker* 63 (13 July 1987): 78-88. (Updike's note: "Given on May 1, 1987, at Harvard University, in Emerson Hall, as part of a two-day birthday party for Howells." Reviews four early Howells novels in the "Library of America" series, commenting on his canon. Rpt. in *Howells as Anti-Novelist.* Kittery Point, Maine: W. D. Howells Memorial Committee, 1987; and in *Odd Jobs.* N.Y.: Knopf, 1991. 168-89 with notes 171, 178, 186 and 189.)
A843	"Five Days in Finland at the Age of Fifty-Five." *The New Yorker* 63 (28 Sept. 1987): 86-88, 91-93. (Rpt. in *Odd Jobs.* N.Y.: Knopf, 1991. 3-12; and in *Going Abroad*, Helsinki, Finland: Eurographica, 1988.)
A844	"Thirty Wise Men: Eleven Literary Lights Reveal Their Modern Magi." *Esquire* 108 (Dec. 1987): 291.
A845	"Introduction." *Appointment in Samarra.* By John O'Hara. N.Y.: Book-of-the-Month Club, 1988. (Rpt. in *Odd Jobs.* N.Y.: Knopf, 1991. 216-22, with notes 219, 21.)
A846	"Introduction." *Writers at Work: The Paris Review Interviews.* Seventh Series. Ed. George Plimpton. London: Penguin, 1988. xi-xx.
A847	"Loving the Sox." *Lord John Ten: A Celebration.* Northridge, Calif.: Lord John P, 1988. 117-122. (Rpt. from *The Boston Globe*; and in *Odd Jobs.* N.Y.: Knopf, 1991. 91-96, with a footnote 95 and title changed to "The Boston Red Sox, as of 1986.")
A848	"Préface à l'Edition Française." *La Condition Naturelle (Facing Nature.)* Trans. Alain Suied. Paris: Gallimard, 1988.

A849   "A Symposium on Contemporary American Fiction: 34 Authors Comment on Their Craft and on the Contemporary Literary Scene." *Michigan Quarterly Review* 37 (Wint. 1988): 126.

A850   "Many Bens." *The New Yorker* 64 (22 Feb. 1988): 105-08, 111-13, 115-16. (Rpt. in *Odd Jobs*. N.Y.: Knopf, 1991. 240-261, with notes 252, 253, 256.)

A851   "Reconsideration: *Appointment in Samarra*[:] O'Hara's Messy Masterpiece." *The New Republic* 198 (2 May 1988): 38-41.

A852   "The Writer Lectures." *The New York Review of Books* 35 (16 June 1988): 23-26.

A853   Letter concerning "The Scandal of *Ulysses*: An Exchange." *The New York Review of Books* 35 (18 Aug. 1988): 63. (Concerns the critical and synoptic edition of Joyce's novel by Hans Walter Gabler.)

A854   "What MOMA Done Tole Me." *Art and Antiques* Oct. 1988: 83-84, 86, 88, 138-39. (Rpt. in *Just Looking*. N.Y.: Knopf, 1989. 3-20.)

A855   "John Updike: From Blocks to Books." *Boston Review* 13 (Oct. 1988): 7-8. (Rpt. as: "A Writer's Blocks." *Harper's* 278 [Jan. 1989]: 36, 38-39, 42; and in *Self-Consciousness*. N.Y.: Knopf, 1989. 104-08.)

A856   "An Exile's Impressions." *Architectural Digest* 45 (Nov. 1988): 35, 38, 42.

A857   "Reluctant Butterfly: The Fierce Development of Edgar Degas." *The New Republic* 199 (14 Nov. 1988): 30. (Rpt. in *Just Looking*. N.Y.: Knopf, 1989. 97-112.)

A858   "Foreword." *The Complete Book of Covers from The New Yorker 1925-1989*. Knopf: N.Y., 1989. v-vii.

A859   "A Writer's Blocks." *Harper's* 278 (Jan. 1989): 36, 38- 39, and 42. (Rpt. from "John Updike: From Blocks to Books." *Boston Review* 13 (Oct. 1988): 7-8.)

A860   "Here I Am." *The New Yorker* 65 (23 Jan. 1989): 34-37. (Rpt. in *Self-Consciousness*. N.Y.: Knopf, 1989. 234-43.)

A861   "A Case of Melancholia." *The New Yorker* 65 (20 Feb. 1989): 112-20. (Rpt. in *Just Looking*. N.Y.: Knopf, 1989. 130-53.)

A862   "Fast Art: The Sweatless Creations of Andy Warhol." *The New Republic* 200 (27 Mar. 1989): 26-28.

A863   "Sacred Places." *Popular Mechanics* 166 (May 1989): 27-30. (Rpt. in *Odd Jobs*. N.Y.: Knopf, 1991. 77-84.)

A864	"Modern Art: Always Offensive to Orthodoxy." *Wall Street Journal* 10 Aug. 1989: A-14.
A865	"Making the Spiritual Connection." *Lear's* Dec. 1989: 70. (Rpt. in *Odd Jobs*. N.Y.: Knopf, 1991. 73.)
A866	"Foreword: The Ant and the So-Called Grasshopper." *Brother Grasshopper*. Worcester, Mass: Metacom, 1990. 9-12.
A867	"The 'Original Ending' of *Self-Consciousness*." *Literary Outtakes*. Ed. Larry Dark. N.Y.: Fawcett Columbine: 1990. 328-29.
A868	"A State of Ecstasy: The Erotics of a Chance Moment, Snapped and Seen." *Art and Antiques* 7 (1 Jan. 1990): 74. (Comments on a photograph by Leonard McCombe.)
A869	"Poetry Poorly Served." *Boston Globe* 11 Jan. 1990: Sec. 14: 6. (Updike attacks the careless publication of Robert Lowell's "For the Union Dead.")
A870	"Put-Ons and Take-Offs: Contemporary Furniture that Parodies or Pays Homage to the Classics." *Art and Antiques* 7 (Feb. 1990): 70-75, 104.
A871	"Good, Bad and Beyond— It's Where You Stand at the Time." *The Boston Globe* 4 Mar. 1990: B-33, B-35.
A872	"Monet Isn't Everything: An Orgy of Impressionism in Boston." *The New Republic* 202 (19 Mar. 1990): 28-31.
A873	"The Houses of Ipswich." *Architectural Digest* 47 (June 1990): 26, 32.
A874	"The Fourth of July." *Philip Morris Magazine* 5 (July-Aug. 1990): 8-11. (Rpt. in *Summer*. Ed. Alice Gordon and Vincent Virga. Reading, Mass.: Addison-Wesley, 1990. 75-77; and in *Odd Jobs*. N.Y.: Knopf, 1991. 74-77.)
A875	"Why Rabbit Had to Go." *The New York Times Book Review* 8 Aug. 1990: 1, 24-25.
A876	"Venus and Others." *The Michigan Quarterly Review* 29 (Fall 1990): 494. (Rpt. with revisions as "The Female Body" in *Odd Jobs*. N.Y.: Knopf, 1991. 70-72; and in *The Best American Essays, 1991*. Ed. Joyce Carol Oates. N.Y.: Ticknor & Fields, 1991. 13-16.)
A877	"A Bookish Boy." *Life* 13 (Oct. 1990): 101.
*A878	"Why Rabbit Finally Ran to Ground." *Guardian* 25 Oct. 1990: 23.

A879	"An Act of Seeing: Looking Back Through the Window of His Magazine Covers to Norman Rockwell's Silver Age." *Art and Antiques* 7 (1 Dec. 1990): 92-99.
A880	"Foreword." *My Well-Balanced Life on a Wooden Leg*. Al Capp. Santa Barbara: John Daniel, 1991. 7-12.
A881	"The Gospel According to Saint Matthew." Ed. Alfred Corn. Incarnation: Contemporary Writers on the New Testament. N.Y.: Penguin, 1991. 1-11. (Rpt. in *Odd Jobs*. N.Y.: Knopf, 1991. 228-30 with notes 232 and 235.)
A882	"Introduction." *The Art of Mickey Mouse*. Craig Yoe and Janet Morra-Yoe. N.Y.: Hyperion, 1991. 8 unnumbered pages. (Rpt. "The Mystery of Mickey Mouse." *Art and Antiques* 8 [Nov. 1991]: 60-66.)
A883	"Introduction." *Heroes and Anti-Heroes*. N.Y.: Random, 1991. 10-23.
A884	"I Was a Teen-Age Library User." *Bookends: Journal of the Friends of the Reading-Berks Public Libraries* 6 (Apr. 1988): 1, 3. (Rpt. in *Odd Jobs*. N.Y.: Knopf, 1991. 836-38.)
A885	"Preface." *Odd Jobs*. N.Y.: Knopf, 1991. xvii-xxii.
A886	"Where Money and Energy Gather: A Writer's View of a Computer Laboratory." *Research Directions in Computer Science: An MIT Perspective*. Ed. Albert R. Meyer, et al. Cambridge, Mass.: MIT P, 1991. 8 unnumbered pages. (Originally given as a speech at the Project MAC 25th anniversay Celebration Banquet, Oct. 26, 1988.)
A887	"Safe in the Bosom of Ursinus." *Ursinus Bulletin* 84 (Spring 1991): 10.
*A888	"Formal Vision." *Mirabella* 2 (1 May 1991): 64-89.
A889	"Welcome to New York's Most Endearing Small Museum." *Mirabella* 2 (1 Aug. 1991): 44-47.
A890	"The Mystery of Mickey Mouse." *Art and Antiques* 8 (Nov. 1991): 60-66. (Rpt. in *The Best American Essays: 1991*. Ed. Susan Sontag. N.Y.: Ticknor and Fields, 1992. 306-13.)
A891	"Is Life Too Short for Golf?" *Golf Digest* 42 (1 Dec. 1991): 92-94.
*A892	"Has Anyone Seen Michelangelo, Seen His Marvelous Frescoes the Way We Can Here?" *Mirabella* 3 (8 Dec. 1991): 39.
A893	"Women We Love: Dolly Parton." *Esquire* 118 (Aug. 1992): 83.

A894	"Where Is the Space to Chase Rainbows?" *Forbes* 150 (14 Sept. 1992): 72-74, 78, 80 and 84.
A895	"The Endearing Truth." *The New Republic* 206 (2 Nov. 1992): 25-29.
A896	"Hostile Haircuts." *The New Yorker* 68 (2 Nov. 1992): 120.
A897	"The Twelve Terrors of Christmas." *The New Yorker* 68 (21 Dec. 1992): 136.
A898	"Remembering Mr. Shawn." *The New Yorker* 68 (28 Dec. 1992-4 Jan. 1993): 141.
A899	"Glad Rags." *The New Yorker* 69 (1 Mar. 1993): 55-56.

6. Reviews

A900 "Poetry from Downtroddendom." *The New Republic* 142 (9 May 1960): 11-12. (Rev. of *The Loneliness of the Long-Distance Runner*, by Alan Sillitoe. Rpt. in *Assorted Prose*. N.Y.: Knopf. 227-30; and in *The Critic as Artist: Essays on Books, 1920-1970, With Some Preliminary Ruminations by H. L. Mencken*. Ed. Gilbert A. Harrison. N.Y.: Liveright, 1972. 321-39, and retitled, "The Loneliness of the Long-Distance Runner.")

A901 *Deliverance to the Captives*, by Karl Barth. *The New Yorker* 41 (9 Sept. 1961): 155. (Unsigned. Rpt. in *Picked-Up Pieces*. N.Y.: Knopf, 1975. 125.)

A902 "Anxious Days for the Glass Family." *The New York Times Book Review* 17 Sept. 1961: 1, 52. (Rpt. in *Salinger: A Critical and Personal Portrait*. Ed. Henry Anatole Grunwald. N.Y.: Harper, 1962: 53-56.)

A903 "The Classics of Realism." *The American Scholar* 32 (Autumn 1963): 660-64. (Review of *The Gates of Horn: A Study of Five French Realists*, by Harry Levin. Rpt. in *Assorted Prose*. N.Y.: Knopf, 1965. 269-72.)

A904 "Grandmaster Nabokov." *The New Republic* 152 (26 Sept. 1964): 15-18. (Rev. of *The Defense*, by Vladimir Nabokov. Rpt. in *The Critic as Artist: Essays on Books, 1920-1970, With Some Preliminary Ruminations by H. L. Mencken*. Ed. Gilbert A. Harrison. N.Y.: Liveright, 1972. 325-32, retitled, "The Defense.")

A905 "Death's Heads." *The New Yorker* 41 (2 Oct. 1965): 216-17, 219-23, 225-28. (Rev. of *The Fire Within*, by Pierre Drieu La Rochelle; and *Selected Works* of Alfred Jarry, Ed. Roger Shattuck and Simon Watson Taylor. Rpt. in *Picked-Up Pieces*. N.Y.: Knopf, 1975. 260-69.)

A906 "The Author as Librarian." *The New Yorker* 41 (30 Oct. 1965): 223-24, 226-28, 231-36, 238, 241-46. (Rev. of *Other Inquisitions, 1937-1952* and *Dreamtigers*, by Jorge Luis Borges; and *Borges the Labyrinth Maker*, by Ana Maria Barrenechea. Rpt. in *Picked-Up Pieces*. N.Y.: Knopf, 1975.

169-88, with a note 169. Translated into Spanish: "Jorge Luis Borges." *Borges y la crítica: antología*. Buenos Aires: Centro Editor de America Latina, 1981.)

A907 "The Fork." *The New Yorker* 42 (26 Feb. 1966): 115-23, 125-28. (Rev. of *The Last Years: Journals, 1853-1855*, by Soren Kierkegaard. Ed. and trans. Ronald Gregor Smith. Rpt. in *Picked-Up Pieces*. N.Y.: Knopf, 1975. 107-24.)

A908 *On the Boundary*, by Paul Tillich. *The New Yorker* 42 (9 July 1966): 91-92. (Unsigned. Rpt. in *Picked-Up Pieces*. N.Y.: Knopf, 1975. 123-24.)

A909 *Discourse on Thinking*, by Martin Heidegger. *The New Yorker* 42 (20 Aug. 1966): 135-36. (Unsigned. Rpt. in *Picked-Up Pieces*. N.Y.: Knopf, 1975. 126.)

A910 "Promising." *The New Yorker* 42 (29 Oct. 1966): 236, 238, 241-42, 244-45. (Rev. of *A Voice Through a Cloud*, by Denton Welch; and *Pursuit*, by Berry Morgan. The Welch review was reprinted in *Picked-Up Pieces*. N.Y.: Knopf, 1975. 223-227, with the title changed to "A Short Life.")

A911 *How I Changed My Mind*, by Karl Barth. *The New Yorker* 42 (26 Nov. 1966): 247. (Unsigned. Rpt. in *Picked-Up Pieces*. N.Y.: Knopf, 1975. 125-26.)

A912 *The Heart Prepared: Grace and Conversion in Puritan Spiritual Life*, by Norman Pettit. *The New Yorker* 42 (10 Dec. 1966): 127. (Unsigned. Rpt. in *Picked-Up Pieces*. N.Y.: Knopf, 1975. 127.)

A913 "Two Points on a Descending Curve." *The New Yorker* 42 (7 Jan. 1967): 91-94. (Rev. of *Mouchette*, by Georges Bernanos; and *Two Views*, by Uwe Johnson. Rpt. in *Picked-Up Pieces*. N.Y.: Knopf, 1975. 288-93, with a note 289 and some minor changes.)

A914 "Nabokov's Look Back: A National Loss." *Life* 61 (13 Jan. 1967): 9, 15. (Rev. of *Speak, Memory*, by Vladimir Nabokov.)

A915 "Behold Gombrowicz." *The New Yorker* 43 (23 Sept. 1967): 169-70, 173-76. (Rev. of *Ferdydurke*; and *Pornografia*, by Witold Gombrowicz. Rpt. in *Picked-Up Pieces*. N.Y.: Knopf, 1975. 303-09, with a note 303 and some changes, including changing the title to "Witold Who?")

A916 "Grove Is My Press, and Avant My Garde." *The New Yorker* 43 (4 Nov. 1967): 223-24, 227-30, 233-34, 236-38. (Rev. of *La Maison de Rendez-Vous*, by Alain Robbe-Grillet; *The Miracle of the Rose*, by Jean Genet; and *The Inquisitor*, by Robert Pinget. Rpt. in *Picked-Up Pieces*. N.Y.: Knopf, 1975. 352-65.)

A917 "'My Mind Was Without a Shadow.'" *The New Yorker* 43 (2 Dec. 1967): 223-24, 227, 230, 232. (Rev. of *Hunger*, by Knut Hamsun. Rpt. in *Picked-Up Pieces*. N.Y.: Knopf, 1975. 141-47.)

A918 "Questions Concerning Giacomo." *The New Yorker* 44 (6 Apr. 1968): 167-68, 171-74. (Rev. of *Giacomo Joyce*, by James Joyce. Rpt. in *Picked-Up Pieces*. N.Y.: Knopf, 1975. 154-61, with a note 159.)

A919 "Indifference." *The New Yorker* 44 (2 Nov. 1968): 197-201. (Rev. of *Morning, Noon and Night*, by James Gould Cousins. Rpt. in *Picked-Up Pieces*. N.Y.: Knopf, 1975. 416-22.)

A920 "Albertine Disparue." *The New Yorker* 45 (15 Mar. 1969): 174, 177-80. (Rev. of *The Runaway* and *Astragal*, by Albertine Sarrazin. 1967. Rpt. in *Picked-Up Pieces*. N.Y.: Knopf, 1975. 269-74.)

A921 "Love as a Standoff." *The New Yorker* 45 (28 June 1969): 90, 93-95. (Rev. of *Victoria*, by Knut Hamsun. Rpt. in *Picked-Up Pieces*. N.Y.: Knopf, 1975. 148-53, with a note 152.)

A922 "Van Loves Ada, Ada Loves Van." *The New Yorker* 45 (2 Aug. 1969): 67-75. (Rev. of *Ada*, by Vladimir Nabokov. Rpt. in *Picked-Up Pieces*. N.Y.: Knopf, 1975. 199-211, with a note 208.)

A923 "Talk of a Sad Town." *Atlantic* 224 (Oct. 1969): 124-28. (Rev. of *The Long-Winded Lady: Notes from The New Yorker*, by Maeve Brennan. Rpt. in *Picked-Up Pieces*. N.Y.: Knopf, 1975. 429-31, with a note 429, and retitled, "Talk of a Tired Town.")

A924 *My Travel Diary*, by Paul Tillich. *The New Yorker* 46 (11 July 1970): 80. (Unsigned. Rpt. in *Picked-Up Pieces*. N.Y.: Knopf, 1975. 124-25.)

A925 "Fool's Gold." *The New Yorker* 46 (8 Aug. 1970): 72-76. (Rev. of *The Loss of El Dorado*, by V. S. Naipaul. Rpt. in *Picked-Up Pieces*. N.Y. Knopf, 1975. 457-63, with minor changes.)

A926 "Papa's Sad Testament." *New Statesman* 80 (16 Oct. 1970): 489. (Rev. of *Islands in the Stream*, by Ernest Hemingway. Rpt. in *Picked-Up Pieces*. N.Y.: Knopf, 1975. 422-28, with notes 423, 428.)

A927 *Mary*, by Vladimir Nabokov. *The New Yorker* 46 (7 Nov. 1970): 181. (Unsigned. Rpt. in *Picked-Up Pieces*. N.Y.: Knopf, 1975. 193.)

A928 "If at First You Do Succeed, Try, Try, Again." *The New Yorker* 47 (10 Apr. 1971): 143-44, 147-48, 150, 153. (Rev. of *Dance the Eagle to Sleep*, by Marge Piercy; and *Single File*, by Norman Fruchter. Rpt. in *Picked-Up Pieces*. N.Y.: Knopf, 1975. 394-402.)

A929 "Bombs Made out of Leftovers." *The New Yorker* 47 (25 Sept. 1971): 131-34, 137-39. (Rev. of *Bad News*, by Paul Spike; *Being There*, by Jerzy

Kosinski; and *The Bark Tree*, by Raymond Queneau. Rpt. in *Picked-Up Pieces*. N.Y.: Knopf, 1975. 379-87, with minor deletions.)

A930 *Mysteries*, by Knut Hamsun. *The New Yorker* 47 (9 Oct. 1971): 169-70. (Unsigned. Rpt. in *Picked-Up Pieces* N.Y.: Knopf, 1975. 147-48.)

A931 "Phantom Life." *The New Yorker* 47 (23 Oct. 1971): 176-79. (Rev. of *West of the Rockies*, by Daniel Fuchs. Rpt. in *Picked-Up Pieces*. N.Y.: Knopf, 1975. 444-48; and as *"Afterword" in *West of the Rockies*. N.Y.: Popular Library, 1972.)

A932 "Out of the Glum Continent." *The New Yorker* 47 (13 Nov. 1971): 187-88, 190-94, 197-98. (Rev. of *Bound to Violence*, by Yambo Ouologuem; *This Earth, My Brother...*, by Kofi Awoonor; and *The Wanderers*, by Ezekiel Mphahlele. Rpt. in *Picked-Up Pieces*. N.Y.: Knopf, 1975. 317-27, with an added sentence about Yambo Ouologuem.)

A933 "Infante Terrible." *The New Yorker* 47 (29 Jan. 1972): 91-94. (Rev. of *Three Trapped Tigers*, by G. Cabrera Infante. Rpt. in *Picked-Up Pieces*. N.Y.: Knopf, 1975. 365-69, with changes. Contains remarks on *One Hundred Years of Solitude*, by Gabriel García Márquez excerpted in "From *Picked-Up Pieces*." *Latin American Literary Review* 13 [25 Nov. 1985]: 147.)

A934 "The Crunch of Happiness." *The New Yorker* 48 (26 Feb. 1972): 96-98, 101. (Rev. of *Glory*, by Vladimir Nabokov. Rpt. in *Picked-Up Pieces*. N.Y.: Knopf, 1975. 194-98.)

A935 "Satire without Serifs." *The New Yorker* 48 (13 May 1972): 135-38, 141-44. (Rev. of *Patriotism, Inc. and Other Tales*, by Paul van Ostaijen; and *The Adventures of Mao on the Long March*, by Frederic Tuten. Rpt. in *Picked-Up Pieces*. N.Y.: Knopf, 1975. 369-79.)

A936 "Is There Life After Golf?" *The New Yorker* 48 (29 July 1972): 76-78. (Rev. of *Golf in the Kingdom*, by Michael Murphy. Rpt. in *Picked-Up Pieces*. N.Y.: Knopf, 1975. 98-103.)

A937 "From Dyna Domes to Turkey-Pressing." *The New Yorker* 48 (9 Sept. 1972): 115-16, 118, 121-24. (Rev. of *Divine Right's Trip*, by Gurney Norman; and *Geronimo Rex*, by Barry Hannah. Rpt. in *Picked-Up Pieces*. N.Y.: Knopf, 1975. 403-10, with a note 407 and minor changes.)

A938 "Remembrance of Things Past." *Horizon* 14 (Autumn 1972): 102-05. (Rev. of *Remembrance of Things Past*, by Marcel Proust. Rpt. in *Picked-Up Pieces*. N.Y.: Knopf, 1975. 162-68, with note 166 and titled, "Remembrance of Things Past Remembered.")

A939 "In Praise of the Blind, Black God." *The New Yorker* 48 (21 Oct. 1972): 157-58, 161, 163-67. (Rev. of *A Happy Death*, by Albert Camus. Rpt. in *Picked-Up Pieces*. N.Y.: Knopf, 1975. 279-87.)

A940	"The Translucing of Hugh Person." *The New Yorker* 48 (18 Nov. 1972): 242-45. (Rev. of *Transparent Things*, by Vladimir Nabokov. Rpt. in *Picked-Up Pieces*. N.Y.: Knopf, 1975. 211-15, with a note 213, and minor changes.)
A941	"Polina and Aleksei and Anna and Losnitsky." *The New Yorker* 49 (14 Apr. 1973): 145-46, 149-54. (Rev. of *The Gambler*, by Fyodor Dostoevski, with Polina Suslova's Diary. Rpt. in *Picked-Up Pieces*. N.Y.: Knopf, 1975. 132-40.)
A942	"Ayrton Fecit." *The New Yorker* 49 (5 May 1973): 147-49. (Rev. of *Fabrications*, by Michael Ayrton. Rpt. in *Picked-Up Pieces*. N.Y.: Knopf, 1975. 227-30, with minor changes.)
A943	"A Sere Life; or, Sprigge's Ivy." *The New Yorker* 49 (2 June 1973): 119-22. (Rev. of *The Life of Ivy Compton-Burnett*, by Elizabeth Sprigge. Rpt. in *Picked-Up Pieces*. N.Y.: Knopf, 1975. 236-42.)
A944	"Milton Adapts Genesis; Collier Adapts Milton." *The New Yorker* 49 (20 Aug. 1973): 84, 86, 89. (Rev. of *Milton's Paradise Lost: Screenplay for Cinema of the Mind*, by John Collier. Rpt. in *Picked-Up Pieces*. N.Y.: Knopf, 1975. 242-48.)
A945	"Snail on the Stump." *The New Yorker* 49 (15 Oct. 1973): 182-85. (Rev. of *From The Diary of a Snail*, by Günther Grass. Rpt. in *Picked-Up Pieces*. N.Y.: Knopf, 1975. 298-302.)
A946	"Coffee Table Books for High Coffee Tables." *The New York Times Book Review* 28 Oct. 1973: 4-6. (Rev. of *Erotic Art of the East*, by Philip Rawson; *Primitive Erotic Art*, Ed. Philip Rawson; and *Erotic Art of the West*, by Robert Melville. Rpt. in *Picked-Up Pieces*. N.Y.: Knopf, 1975. 469-74, with verbal changes.)
A947	"Jong Love." *The New Yorker* 49 (17 Dec. 1973): 149-50, 153. (Rev. of *Fear of Flying*, by Erica Jong. Rpt. in *Picked-Up Pieces*. N.Y.: Knopf, 1975. 411-15.)
A948	"Shades of Black." *The New Yorker* 49 (21 Jan. 1974): 84-86, 89-94. (Rev. of *The Great Ponds*, by Elechi Amadi; *In the Fog of the Season's End*; by Alex La Guma; and *Agatha Moudio's Son*, by Francis Bebey. Rpt. in *Picked-Up Pieces*. N.Y.: Knopf, 1975. 327-39, with a note 329 and an added sentence.)
A949	"Mortal Games." *The New Yorker* 50 (25 Feb. 1974): 122- 26. (Rev. of *Flight of Icarus*, by Raymond Queneau; and *All Fires the Fire and Other Stories*, by Julio Cortázar. Rpt. in *Picked-Up Pieces*. N.Y.: Knopf, 1975. 387-93.)

A950 "Inward and Onward." *The New Yorker* 50 (25 Mar. 1974): 133-34, 137-40. (Rev. of *The Inward Turn of Narrative*, by Erich Kahler. Rpt. in *Picked-Up Pieces*. N.Y.: Knopf, 1975. 309-16.)

A951 "A Messed-Up Life." *The New Yorker* 50 (8 Apr. 1974): 137-40. (Rev. of *Great Tom: Notes Towards the Definition of T. S. Eliot*, by T. S. Matthews. Rpt. in *Picked-Up Pieces*. N.Y.: Knopf, 1975. 255-59.)

A952 "Sons of Slaves." *The New Yorker* 50 (6 May 1974): 138-142. (Rev. of *The Sultans*, by Noel Barber; and *The Sultan: The Life of Abdul Hamid II*, by Joan Haslip. Rpt. in *Picked-Up Pieces*. N.Y.: Knopf, 1975. 464-69, with a note 466.)

A953 "A New Meliorism." *The New Yorker* 50 (15 July 1974): 83-86. (Rev. of *The Lives of a Cell: Notes of a Biology Watcher*, by Dr. Lewis Thomas. Rpt. in *Picked-Up Pieces*. N.Y.: Knopf, 1975. 481-85.)

A954 "Saganland and the Back of Beyond." *The New Yorker* 50 (12 Aug. 1974): 95-98. (Rev. of *Scars of the Soul*, by Françoise Sagan; and *The Bridge of Beyond*, by Simone Schwarz-Bart. Rpt. in *Picked-Up Pieces*. N.Y.: Knopf, 1975. 275-79.)

A955 "Alive and Free from Employment." *The New Yorker* 50 (2 Sept. 1974): 80-82. (Rev. of *My Days*, by R. K. Narayan. Rpt. in *Picked-Up Pieces*. N.Y.: Knopf, 1975. 485-89.)

A956 "Before the Sky Collapses." *The New Yorker* 50 (16 Sept. 1974): 140-42, 145-47. (Rev. of *Xingu: The Indians, Their Myths*, by Orlando Villas Boas and Claudio Villas Boas. Rpt. in *Picked-Up Pieces*. N.Y.: Knopf, 1975. 474-80.)

A957 "Motlier Than Ever." *The New Yorker* 50 (11 Nov. 1974): 209-11. (Rev. of *Look at the Harlequins!* by Vladimir Nabokov. Rpt. in *Picked-Up Pieces*. N.Y.: Knopf, 1975. 215-20, with the title changed to "Motley But True.")

A958 "Topnotch Witcheries." *The New Yorker* 50 (6 Jan. 1975): 76-81. (Rev. of *The Abbess of Crewe: A Modern Morality Tale*, by Muriel Spark; and *The Sacred and Profane Love Machine*, by Iris Murdoch. Rpt. in *Hugging the Shore*. N.Y.: Knopf, 1983. 341-50, with a note 348.)

A959 "Metropolises of the Mind." *The New Yorker* 51 (24 Feb. 1975): 137-40. (Rev. of *Invisible Cities*, by Italo Calvino. Rpt. in *Hugging the Shore*. N.Y.: Knopf, 1983. 457-62.)

A960 "Through a Continent, Darkly." *The New Yorker* 51 (24 Mar. 1975): 109-15. (Rev. of *Which Tribe Do You Belong To?* by Alberto Moravia; *By the Evidence*, by Louis S. B. Leaky; and *Alphabetical Africa*, by Walter Abish. Rpt. in *Picked-Up Pieces*. N.Y.: Knopf, 1975. 343-51.)

A961 "Wright on Writing." *The New Yorker* 51 (14 Apr. 1975): 124-27. (Rev. of *About Fiction*, by Wright Morris. Rpt. in *Hugging the Shore*. N.Y.: Knopf, 1983. 773-77.)

A962 "A Monk Manqué." *The New Yorker* 51 (12 May 1975): 138- 41. (Rev. of *The New Gods*, by E. M. Cioran. Rpt. in *Hugging the Shore*. N.Y.: Knopf, 1983. 597-602.)

A963 "Selda, Lilia, Ursa, Great Gram, and Other Ladies in Distress." *The New Yorker* 51 (18 Aug. 1975): 79-83. (Rev. of *The Little Hotel*, by Christina Stead; and *Corregidora*, by Gayl Jones. Rpt. in *Hugging the Shore*. N.Y.: Knopf, 1983. 526-32, with changes.)

A964 "Small Cheer from the Old Sod." *The New Yorker* 51 (1 Sept. 1975): 62-66. (Rev. of *Mercier and Camier*, by Samuel Beckett; and *The Poor Mouth*, by Flann O'Brien. Rpt. in *Hugging the Shore*. N.Y.: Knopf, 1983. 375-83, with minor changes.)

A965 "Draping Radiance with a Worn Veil." *The New Yorker* 51 (15 Sept. 1975): 122, 125-130. (Rev. of *Humboldt's Gift*, by Saul Bellow. Rpt. in *Hugging the Shore*. N.Y.: Knopf, 1983. 247-54.)

A966 "Alone but not Aloof." *The New Yorker* 51 (6 Oct. 1975): 159-64. (Rev. of *W. H. Auden— A Tribute*, by Stephen Spender. Rpt. in *Hugging the Shore*. N.Y.: Knopf, 1983. 616-27, with notes 620, 623, and a few minor changes.)

A967 "Roland Barthes." *The New Yorker* 51 (24 Nov. 1975): 189-94. (Rev. of *S/Z* and *The Pleasure of the Text*, by Roland Barthes. Rpt. in *Hugging the Shore*. N.Y.: Knopf, 1983. 576-83.)

A968 "Drabbling in the Mud." *The New Yorker* 51 (12 Jan. 1976): 88-90. (Rev. of *The Realms of Gold*, by Margaret Drabble. Rpt. in *Hugging the Shore*. N.Y.: Knopf, 1983. 360-64.)

A969 "Suzie Creamcheese Speaks." *The New Yorker* 52 (23 Feb. 1976): 109-14. (Rev. of *Doris Day: Her Own Story*, by A. E. Hotchner. Rpt. in *Hugging the Shore*. N.Y.: Knopf, 1983. 791-801, with minor changes. *The John Updike Newsletter* [2.1: 3] erroneously cites pages 102-14.)

A970 "Simple-Minded Jim." *The New Yorker* 52 (1 Mar. 1976): 93-94, 97-100. (Rev. of *Selected Letters of James Joyce*, Ed. by Richard Ellmann. Rpt. in *Hugging the Shore*. N.Y.: Knopf, 1983. 129-39.)

A971 "Family Ways." *The New Yorker* 52 (29 Mar. 1976): 110-12. (Rev. of *Searching for Caleb*, by Anne Tyler. Rpt. in *Hugging the Shore*. N.Y.: Knopf, 1983. 273-78; and in *Critical Essays on Anne Tyler*. Ed. Alice Hall Perty. Boston: Hall, 1992. 75-79.)

A972 "A Primal Modern." *The New Yorker* 52 (31 May 1976): 116-18. (Rev. of *The Wanderer*, by Knut Hamsun. Rpt. in *Hugging the Shore*. N.Y.: Knopf, 1983. 424-29.)

A973 *Proud Happiness: Details of a Sunset and Other Stories*, by Vladimir Nabokov. *The New Yorker* 52 (14 June 1976): 111-12. (Unsigned. Rpt. in *Hugging The Shore*. N.Y.: Knopf, 1983. 243-44.)

A974 "Flann Again." *The New Yorker* 52 (21 June 1976): 116-18. (Rev. of *Stories and Plays*, by Flann O'Brien. Rpt. in *Hugging the Shore*. N.Y.: Knopf, 1983. 383-88, with notes 384, 385.)

A975 "Raman and Daisy and Olivia and the Nawab." *The New Yorker* 52 (5 July 1976): 81-84. (Rev. of *The Painter of Signs*, by R. K. Narayan. Rpt. in *Hugging the Shore*. N.Y.: Knopf, 1983. 710-16.)

A976 "Eva and Eleanor and Everywoman." *The New Yorker* 52 (9 Aug. 1976): 74-77. (Rev. of *Eva's Man*, by Gayl Jones; and *Miss Herbert*, by Christina Stead. Rpt. in *Hugging the Shore*. N.Y.: Knopf, 1983. 532-38.)

A977 "The Strange Case of Dr. Destouches and M. Céline." *The New Yorker* 52 (13 Sept. 1976): 154, 157-161. (Rev. of *Céline*, by Patrick McCarthy. Rpt. in *Hugging the Shore*. N.Y.: Knopf, 1983. 409-16, with verbal changes.)

A978 "Texts and Men." *The New Yorker* 52 (4 Oct. 1976): 148-150, 153-56. (Rev. of *Sade/Fourier/Loyola*, by Roland Barthes; and *Vico and Herder*, by Isaiah Berlin. Rpt. in *Hugging the Shore*. N.Y.: Knopf, 1983. 583-91, with minor changes.)

A979 "All's Well in Skyscraper National Park." *The New Yorker* 52 (25 Oct. 1976): 182, 185-90. (Rev. of *Slapstick, or Lonesome No More!* by Kurt Vonnegut.)

A980 "Seeresses." *The New Yorker* 52 (29 Nov. 1976): 164, 166, 169-70, 172, 174. (Rev. of *Chilly Scenes of Winter*, by Ann Beattie; and *The Takeover*, by Muriel Spark. Rpt. of Spark review retitled, "Of Heresy and Loot" in *Hugging the Shore*. N.Y.: Knopf, 1983. 364-68, with a note 366 and many deletions. Rpt. of Beattie review retitled, "Stalled Starters," in *Hugging the Shore*. N.Y.: Knopf, 1983. 564-68.)

A981 "Of Beauty and Consternation." *The New Yorker* 52 (27 Dec. 1976): 64-68. (Rev. of *Letters of E. B. White*, Ed. Dorothy Lobrano Guth. Rpt. in *Hugging the Shore*. N.Y.: Knopf, 1983. 187-95, with minor revisions and titled, "The Shining Note.")

A982 "Gaiety in the Galleries." *The New Yorker* 53 (21 Feb. 1977): 121-25. (Rev. of *Art and Act*, by Peter Gay. Rpt. in *Hugging the Shore*. N.Y.: Knopf, 1983. 759-66, with the deletion of a sentence about Gropius.)

A983	"The Heaven of an Old Home." *The New Yorker* 53 (21 Mar. 1977): 128-30, 133-38. (Rev. of *Souvenirs and Prophecies: The Young Wallace Stevens*, by Holly Stevens. Rpt. in *Hugging the Shore*. N.Y.: Knopf, 1983. 603-16, with notes 604, 608, and 613-14, with minor word changes.)
A984	"Card Tricks." *The New Yorker* 53 (18 Apr. 1977): 149-50, 153-56. (Rev. of *The Castle of Crossed Destinies*, by Italo Calvino. Rpt. in *Hugging the Shore*. N.Y.: Knopf, 1983. 463-70.)
A985	"African Accents." *The New Yorker* 53 (16 May 1977): 141-42, 145-48. (Rev. of *Xala*, by Sembene Ousmane. Rpt. in *Hugging the Shore*. N.Y.: Knopf, 1983. 676-86, with a note 683.)
A986	"Loosened Roots." *The New Yorker* 53 (6 June 1977): 130, 133-34. (Rev. of *Earthly Possessions*, by Anne Tyler. Rpt. in *Odd Jobs: Essays and Criticism*. N.Y.: Knopf, 1991. 278-83; and in *Critical Essays on Anne Tyler*. Ed. Alice Hall Petry. Boston: Hall, 1992. 88-91.)
A987	"Who Wants to Know?" *The New Yorker* 53 (22 Aug. 1977): 87-90. (Rev. of *The Dragons of Eden: Speculations on the Evolution of Human Intelligence*, by Carl Sagan. Rpt. in *Hugging the Shore*. N.Y.: Knopf, 1983. 819-25, with some deletions.)
A988	"Discontent in Deutsch." *The New Yorker* 53 (26 Sept. 1977): 136, 138, 141-44. (Rev. of *A Moment of True Feeling*, by Peter Handke; and *The Wonderful Years*, by Reiner Kunze. Rpt. in *Hugging the Shore*. N.Y.: Knopf, 1983. 442-48, with slight changes.)
A989	"Human Capacities." *The New Yorker* 53 (10 Oct. 1977): 179-80, 183-84, 186. (Rev. of *The Supermale*, by Alfred Jarry; and *The Sunday of Life*, by Raymond Queneau. Rpt. in *Hugging the Shore*. N.Y.: Knopf, 1983. 394-401 with minor changes.)
A990	"The Giant Who Isn't There." *The New Yorker* 53 (24 Oct. 1977): 177-82. (Rev. of *Chinese Shadows*, by Simon Leys. Rpt. in *Hugging the Shore*. N.Y.: Knopf, 1983. 742-50, with minor changes, some deletions, and the author's pseudonymous name once appears in quotes.)
A991	"Sheherazade." *The New Yorker* 53 (5 Dec. 1977): 231-32, 234, 236, 238. (Rev. of *Carnival: Entertainments and Posthumous Tales*, by Isak Dinesen. Rpt. in *Hugging the Shore*. N.Y.: Knopf, 1983. 434-41.)
A992	"Through the Mid-Life Crisis with James Boswell, Esq." *The New Yorker* 53 (6 Feb. 1978): 102, 104, 105-10. (Rev. of *Boswell, Laird of Auchinleck, 1778-1782*, Ed. Joseph W. Reed and Frederick A. Pottle. Rpt. in *Hugging the Shore*. N.Y.: Knopf, 1983. 329-40, with a note 335.)
A993	"Pinter's Unproduced Proust Printed." *The New Yorker* 54 (20 Feb. 1978): 129-30, 132-33. (Rev. of *The Proust Screenplay*, by Harold Pinter. Rpt. in *Hugging the Shore*. N.Y.: Knopf, 1983. 784-91.)

A994 "Layers of Ambiguity." *The New Yorker.* 54 (27 Mar. 1978): 127-30, 133. (Rev. of *Players* by Don De Lillo and *Going After Cacciato* by Tim O'Brien. Rpt. in *Hugging the Shore.* N.Y.: Knopf, 1983. 557-64, with minor changes.)

***A995** "Saint of the Mundane." *The New York Times Book Review* 25 (18 May 1978): 3-6. (Rev. of *Hello, Darkness: The Collected Poems of L. E. Sissman.* Ed. Peter Davison. 1978. Rpt. in *Hugging the Shore.* N.Y.: Knopf, 1983. 631-34.)

A996 "Advancing Over Water." *The New Yorker* 54 (31 July 1978): 72-74, 77-78. (Rev. of *Letters to Friends, Family, and Editors*, by Franz Kafka. Rpt. in *Hugging the Shore.* N.Y.: Knopf, 1983. 139-49.)

A997 "Tote That Quill." *The New Yorker* 54 (14 Aug. 1978): 94-98. (Rev. of *200 Years of American Illustration*. Text by Henry C. Pitz. Rpt. in *Hugging the Shore.* N.Y.: Knopf, 1983. 766-73.)

A998 "Czarist Shadows, Soviet Lilacs." *The New Yorker* 54 (11 Sept. 1978): 147-50, 153-56, 158. (Rev. of *Petersburg*, by Andrei Bely; and *The Long Goodbye*, by Yury Trifonov. Rpt. in *Hugging the Shore.* N.Y.: Knopf, 1983. 497-509, with a note 509 and a few verbal changes.)

A999 "Saddled with the World." *The New Yorker* 54 (23 Oct. 1978): 176, 179-180, 182. (Rev. of *The Women at the Pump*, by Knut Hamsun. Rpt. in "Saddled with the World." *Scandinavian Review* 67 (1979): 68-71; and in *Hugging the Shore.* N.Y.: Knopf, 1983. 429-41, with many revisions.)

A1000 "The Doctor's Son." *The New Yorker* 54 (6 Nov. 1978): 200, 202-04, 207-08, 210, 213-14. (Rev. of *Selected Letters of John O'Hara*, Ed. Matthew J. Bruccoli. Rpt. in *Hugging the Shore.* N.Y.: Knopf, 1983. 176-86, with a note 181.)

A1001 "Fish Story." *The New Yorker* 54 (27 November 1978): 203-04, 206. (Rev. of *The Flounder* by Günter Grass. Rpt. in *Hugging the Shore.* N.Y.: Knopf, 1983. 477-82.)

A1002 "Hawthorne's Religious Language." *Proceedings of the American Academy and Institute of Arts and Letters* 30 (1979): 21-27. (Rpt. as "On Hawthorne's Mind." *New York Review of Books* 28 [19 Mar. 1981]: 41-42; and in *Hugging the Shore.* N.Y.: Knopf, 1983. 73-80, with a note 73.)

A1003 "Green Green." *The New Yorker* 54 (1 Jan. 1979): 58-64. (Rev. of *Blindness* by Henry Green. Rpt. in *Hugging the Shore.* N.Y.: Knopf, 1983. 321-29, with a note 321.)

A1004 "Lem and Pym." *The New Yorker* 55 (26 Feb. 1979): 115-21. (Rev. of *The Chain of Chance*, by Stanislaw Lem; and *Excellent Women* and *Quartet in Autumn*, by Barbara Pym. Rpt. in *Hugging the Shore.* N.Y.: Knopf, 1983. 516-25.)

A1005 "To the Tram Halt Together." *The New Yorker* 55 (12 Mar. 1979): 135-38, 141-44. (Rev. of *Karl Barth: His Life from Letters and Autobiographical Texts*, by Eberhard Busch; and *Paul Tillich: His Life and Thought (Volume I: Life)*, by Wilhelm and Marion Pauck. Rpt. in *Hugging the Shore*. N.Y.: Knopf, 1983. 825-36, with a note 829.)

A1006 "Un Pe' Pourrie." *The New Yorker* 55 (21 May 1979): 141-44. (Rev. of *A Bend in the River*, by V. S. Naipaul. Rpt. in *Hugging the Shore*. N.Y.: Knopf, 1983. 686-91, with a note 691 and many changes.)

A1007 "The Cuckoo and the Rooster." *The New Yorker* 55 (11 June 1979): 156-58, 161. (Rev. of *The Nabokov-Wilson Letters: Correspondence Between Vladimir Nabokov and Edmund Wilson, 1940-1971*. Ed. Simon Karlinsky. Rpt. in *Hugging the Shore*. N.Y.: Knopf, 1983. 216-22.)

A1008 *The Myth Makers*, by V. S. Pritchett. *The New Yorker* 55 (11 June 1979): 162-63. (Unsigned. Rpt. in *Odd Jobs*. N.Y.: Knopf, 1991. 450.)

A1009 "Mixed Reports from the Interior." *The New Yorker* 55 (2 July 1979): 89-94. (Rev. of *North of South: An African Journey*, by Shiva Naipaul; *The Joys of Motherhood*, by Buchi Emecheta; and *Petals of Blood*, by Ngugi Wa Thiong'o. (Rpt. in *Hugging the Shore*. N.Y.: Knopf, 1983. 686-701, with notes 691, 692, and many other changes; includes a Rev. of *A Bend in the River* by V. S. Naipaul. 686-691, published first as "Un Pe' Pourrie." *The New Yorker* 55 [21 May 1979]: 141-44.) See **A1006**.

A1010 *Brecht's Dicta: Diaries, 1920-1922*, by Bertolt Brecht. *The New Yorker* 55 (16 July 1979): 107-08. (Unsigned. Rpt. in *Hugging The Shore*. N.Y.: Knopf, 1983. 441.)

A1011 "A Feast of Reason." *The New Yorker* 55 (30 July 1979): 85-88. (Rev. of *The Origin of Table Manners*, by Claude Lévi-Strauss. Rpt. in *Hugging the Shore*. N.Y.: Knopf, 1983. 662-69.)

A1012 "Jake and Lolly Opt Out." *The New Yorker* 55 (20 Aug. 1979): 97-102. (Rev. of *Jake's Thing*, by Kingsley Amis; and *Lolly Willowes; or, The Loving Huntsman*, by Sylvia Townsend Warner. Rpt. in *Hugging the Shore*. N.Y.: Knopf, 1983. 300-07 with notes. 305, 306.)

A1013 "Bruno Schulz, Hidden Genius." *The New York Times Book Review* 9 Sept. 1979: 1, 36-37. (Rev. of *Sanitorium Under the Sign of the Hourglass*, by Bruno Schulz. Rpt. as "Introduction" to *Sanitorium Under the Sign of the Hourglass*. 1979; and in *Hugging the Shore*. N.Y.: Knopf, 1983. 491-97 with note, 491.)

A1014 "Pinget." *The New Yorker* 55 (17 Sept. 1979): 165-69. (Rev. of *The Libera Me Domine* and *Passacaglia*, by Robert Pinget. Rpt. in *Hugging the Shore*. N.Y.: Knopf, 1983. 417-23 with a new title "Robert Pinget.")

A1015 "An Old-Fashioned Novel." *The New Yorker* 55 (24 Dec. 1979): 95-98. (Rev. of *The Pornographer* by John McGahern. Rpt. in *Hugging the Shore*. N.Y.: Knopf, 1983. 388-93.)

A1016 "From Fumie to Sony." *The New Yorker* 55 (14 Jan. 1980): 94, 97-102. (Rev. of *When I Whistle* and *Silence*, by Shusaku Endo; and *Secret Rendezvous*, by Kobo Abe. Rpt. in *Hugging the Shore*. N.Y.: Knopf, 1983. 734-42 with a few word changes.)

A1017 "The Bear Who Hated Life." *The New Yorker* 56 (25 Feb. 1980): 127-128, 131-34. (Rev. of *The Letters of Gustave Flaubert 1830-1857*, Ed. and trans. Francis Steegmuller. Rpt. in *Hugging the Shore*. N.Y.: Knopf, 1983. 118-29, and a note 122.)

A1018 "Journeyers." *The New Yorker* 56 (10 Mar. 1980): 150, 153-59. (Rev. of *African Calliope: A Journey to the Sudan*, by Edward Hoagland; and *Arabia: A Journey Through the Labyrinth*, by Jonathan Raban. Rpt. in *Hugging the Shore*. N.Y.: Knopf, 1983. 701-10, with deletions and additons.)

A1019 "A Cloud of Witnesses." *The New Yorker* 56 (7 Apr. 1980): 143, 146, 149. (Rev. of *The View in Winter* by Ronald Blythe. Rpt. in *Hugging the Shore*. N.Y.: Knopf, 1983. 812-18, with a sentence by Tolstoy deleted.)

A1020 "Disaffection in Deutsch." *The New Yorker* 56 (21 Apr. 1980): 130, 133-34, 136, 139-140, 142. (Rev. of *Approximation* by Hans Joachim Schädlich; and *Winterreise* by Gerhard Roth. Rpt. in *Hugging the Shore*. N.Y.: Knopf, 1983. 448-56.)

A1021 "Imagining Things." *The New Yorker* 56 (23 June 1980): 94, 96, 98-102. (Rev. of *The Beginning Place*, by Ursula K. LeGuin; and *Morgan's Passing*, by Anne Tyler. Rpt. in *Hugging the Shore*. N.Y.: Knopf, 1983. 283-92, with a note 291; the Tyler piece was reprinted in *Critical Essays on Anne Tyler*. Ed. Alice Hall Perty. Boston: Hall, 1992. 126-31.)

A1022 "Dark Smile, Devilish Saints." *The New Yorker* 56 (11 Aug. 1980): 82, 85-89. (Rev. of *Smile Please: An Unfinished Autobiography*, by Jean Rhys; *Short Lives*, by Katinka Matson; and *Port of Saints*, by William S. Burroughs. Rpt. in *Hugging the Shore*. N.Y.: Knopf, 1983. 547-56.)

A1023 "The Last of Barthes." *The New Yorker* 56 (22 Sept. 1980): 151-54, 157. (Rev. of *New Critical Essays*, by Roland Barthes. Rpt. in *Hugging the Shore*. N.Y.: Knopf, 1983. 591-96, with verbal changes, among them the last line "Though Barthes left behind disciples, there can be no replacing him; his brilliance had a wave length all to itself.")

A1024 "The Most Original Book." *The New York Times Book Review* 30 Nov. 1980: 7, 74-76. (Rev. of *The Book of Laughter and Forgetting*, by Milan Kundera. Rpt. in *Hugging the Shore*. N.Y.: Knopf, 1983. 509-15, with title changed to "Czech Angels.")

A1025 "An Earlier Day." *The New Yorker* 56 (15 Dec. 1980): 162-64, 167-68, 170. (Rev. of *The Thirties*, by Edmund Wilson. Rpt. in *Hugging the Shore*. N.Y.: Knopf, 1983. 206-16.)

A1026 "An Armful of Field Flowers." *The New Yorker* 56 (29 Dec. 1980): 69-72. (Rev. of *Letters from Colette*. Ed. and trans. Robert Phelps. Rpt. in *Hugging the Shore*. N.Y.: Knopf, 1983. 150-57.)

A1027 "Fiabe Italiane." *The New Yorker* 57 (23 Feb. 1981): 120, 123-26. (Rev. of *Italian Folk Tales*, by Italo Calvino. Rpt. in *Hugging the Shore*. N.Y.: Knopf, 1983. 655-62 with minor additions.)

A1028 "On Hawthorne's Mind." *New York Review of Books* 28 (19 Mar. 1981): 41-42. (A revision of "Hawthorne's Religious Language." *Proceedings of the American Academy and Institute of Arts and Letters* 30 (1979): 21-27. Rpt. in *Hugging the Shore*. N.Y.: Knopf, 1983. 73-80, with a note 73.)

A1029 "Worlds and Worlds." *The New Yorker* 57 (23 Mar. 1981): 148-50, 153-57. (Rev. of *Nuns and Soldiers*, by Iris Murdoch; and *Other People's Worlds*, by William Trevor. Rpt. in *Hugging the Shore*. N.Y.: Knopf, 1983. 350-60.)

A1030 "Fresh from the Forties." *The New Yorker* 57 (8 June 1981): 148-50, 153-56. (Rev. of *Loitering with Intent*, by Muriel Spark; and *Exercises in Style*, by Raymond Queneau. Rpt. in *Hugging the Shore*. N.Y.: Knopf, 1983. 401-09, with a note 409. The Queneau piece was retitled, "Thirty-four Years Late, Twice" and was linked to the review of *We Always Treat Women Too Well* [originally published as "Two Late Arrivals, Featuring Resilient Females" *The New Yorker* 57 (14 Dec. 1981): 200, 203-04, 206, 209.])

A1031 "Happy on Nono Despite Odosha." *The New Yorker* 57 (29 June 1981): 98-100. (Rev. of *Watunna: An Orinoco Creation Cycle*, by Marc de Civrieux. Ed. and Trans. David M. Guss. Rpt. in *Hugging the Shore*. N.Y.: Knopf, 1983. 669-75.)

A1032 "Hem Battles the Pack; Wins, Loses." *The New Yorker* 57 (13 July 1981): 96-106. (Rev. of *Selected Letters 1917-1961*, by Ernest Hemingway. Ed. Carlos Baker. Rpt. in *Hugging the Shore*. N.Y.: Knopf, 1983. 158-76, with a note, 175.)

A1033 "Readers and Writers." *The New Yorker* 57 (3 Aug. 1981): 90-93. (Rev. of *If on a Winter's Night a Traveler*, by Italo Calvino; and *The Meeting at Telgte*, by Günther Grass. Rpt. in *Hugging the Shore*. N.Y.: Knopf, 1983. 470-77, with minor changes.)

A1034 "1587, A Year of No Significance." *The New Yorker* 57 (5 Oct. 1981): 182, 184, 187-91. (Rev. of *The Ming Dynasty in Decline*; and *The Long and Reluctant Stasis of Wan-Li*, by Ray Huang. Reprints only the review of the first book in *Hugging the Shore*. N.Y.: Knopf, 1983. 750-58, with a note 754.)

A1035 "The Fancy-Forger Takes the Lectern." *The New Yorker* 57 (2 Nov. 1981): 183-88. (Rev. of *Lectures on Russian Literature*, by Vladimir Nabokov. Rpt. in *Hugging the Shore*. N.Y.: Knopf, 1983. 237-43.)

A1036 "Two Late Arrivals, Featuring Resilient Females." *The New Yorker* 57 (14 Dec. 1981): 200, 203-04, 206, 209. (Rev. of *We Always Treat Women Too Well* by Raymond Queneau; and *The Flute-Player*, by D. M. Thomas. Rpt. the Thomas review separately as "Indestructible Elena" in *Hugging the Shore*. N.Y.: Knopf, 1983. 311-20 with notes 307, 310 which correct the number of Thomas's novels. For the Queneau rpt. see **A1030**.)

A1037 "No Dearth of Death." *The New Yorker* 57 (11 Jan. 1982): 92-95. Rev. of *The Death of a Beekeeper*, by Lars Gustafsson; and *Death Sentence*, by Maurice Blanchot. Rpt. in *Hugging the Shore*. N.Y.: Knopf, 1983. 539-47, with notes 540, 543.)

A1038 "Nothing is Easy." *The New Yorker* 57 (1 Feb. 1982): 132. (Rev.of *Letters to Ottla and the Family*, by Franz Kafka. Ed. N. N. Glatzer. Unsigned. Rpt. in *Hugging The Shore*. N.Y.: Knopf, 1983. 149-50.)

A1039 "Toppling Towers Seen by a Whirling Soul," *The New Yorker* 58 (22 Feb. 1982): 120-26. (Rev. of *The Dean's December*, by Saul Bellow. Rpt. in *Hugging the Shore*. N.Y.: Knopf, 1983. 255-63.)

A1040 "On Such a Beautiful Green Little Planet", *The New Yorker* 58 (5 Apr. 1982) 189-90, 193-97. (Rev. of John Cheever, *Oh What a Paradise It Seems*; Ann Tyler, *Dinner at the Homesick Restaurant*. Rpt. in *Hugging the Shore*. N.Y.: Knopf, 1983. 292-99; the Tyler review was reprinted in *Critical Essays on Anne Tyler*. Ed. Alice Hall Perty. Boston: Hall, 1992. 107-110.)

A1041 "Gathering of the Poets of Faith." *The New York Times Book Review* 11 Apr. 1982: 1. (Rev. of *The New Oxford Book of Christian Verse*. Ed. Donald Davie. Rpt. in *Hugging the Shore*. N.Y.: Knopf, 1983. 644-49.)

A1042 "Borges Warmed Over," *The New Yorker* 58 (24 May 1982): 126, 129-33. (Rev. of *Borges: A Reader*. Ed. Emir Moenegal and Alastair Reid. Rpt. in *Hugging the Shore*. N.Y.: Knopf, 1983. 778-84, with a note 783.)

A1043 "The Squeeze Is On." *The New Yorker* 58 (14 June 1982): 129-34. (Rev. of *Headbirths, or The Germans Are Dying Out*, by Günter Grass; and *The Safety Net*, by Heinrich Böll. Rpt. in *Hugging the Shore*. N.Y.: Knopf, 1983. 482-90, with minor changes.)

A1044 "India Going On." *The New Yorker* 58 (2 Aug. 1982): 84-86. (Rev. of *Malgudi Days*, by R. K. Narayan. Rpt. in *Hugging the Shore*. N.Y.: Knopf, 1983. 716-22, with two notes 722.)

A1045 "Female Pilgrims." *The New Yorker* 58 (16 Aug. 1982): 84-89. (Rev. of *Lulu in Hollywood*, by Louise Brooks; and *As They Were*, by M. F. K. Fisher. Rpt. in *Hugging the Shore*. N.Y.: Knopf, 1983. 801-11.)

A1046 "Cohn's Doom." *The New Yorker* 58 (8 Nov. 1982): 167-70. (Rev. of *God's Grace*, by Bernard Malamud. Rpt. in *Odd Jobs*. N.Y.: Knopf, 1991. 316-20.)

A1047 "Spent Arrows and First Buddings." *The New Yorker* 58 (3 Jan. 1983): 66-70. (Rev. of *I Am a Cat* and *Mon*, by Natsume Soseki; and *The Secret History of the Lord of Musashi* and *Arrowroot*, by Junichiro Tanizaki. Rpt. in *Hugging the Shore*. N.Y.: Knopf, 1983. 723-33, with a linguistic note 724.)

A1048 "The Dawn of Art." *The New Yorker* 58 (31 Jan. 1983): 120-23. (Rev. of *The Creative Explosion: An Inquiry Into the Origins of Art and Religion*, by John E. Pfeiffer.)

A1049 "How the Other Half Lives." *The New Yorker* 59 (21 Feb. 1983): 126, 129-32. (Rev. of *Moscow Circles*, by Benedict Erofeev; *The Joke*, by Milan Kundera; and *The Polish Complex* by Tadeusz Konwicki. Rpt. in *Odd Jobs*. N.Y.: Knopf, 1991. 511-519, with a note 511 and minor verbal alterations.)

A1050 "The Jones Boys." *The New Yorker* 59 (21 Mar. 1983): 126-30. (Rev. of *On the Black Hill*, by Bruce Chatwin. Rpt. in *Odd Jobs*. N.Y.: Knopf, 1991. 464-68.)

A1051 "A Long Way Home." *The New Yorker* 59 (2 May 1983): 121-26. (Rev. of *Blue Highways: A Journey Into America*, by William Least Heat Moon. Rpt. in *Odd Jobs*. N.Y.: Knopf, 1991. 727-33.)

A1052 "Kafka's Short Stories." *The New Yorker* 59 (9 May 1983): 121-26, 129-33. (Rpt. as "Foreword" to *Franz Kafka: The Complete Stories of Franz Kafka*. N.Y.: Schocken, 1983. ix-xxi. Rpt. in part as "John Updike on Franz Kafka and *The Metamorphosis*" in Ann Charters, *The Story and Its Writer*. N.Y.: St. Martin's P, 1987. 1270-73.)

A1053 "Empire's End." *The New Yorker* 59 (16 May 1983): 122-26, 129-33. (Rev. of *The Emperor: Downfall of an Autocrat*, by Ryszard Kapuscinski. Rpt. in *Odd Jobs*. N.Y.: Knopf, 1991. 742-51, with a note 748.)

A1054 *The Letters of Karl Barth and Carl Zuchmayer*. *The New Yorker*. 59 (4 July 1983): 132. (Unsigned. Rpt. in *Odd Jobs*. N.Y.: Knopf, 1991. 617 and retitlted, "Rational Faith.")

A1055 "Between Pinget's Ears." *The New Yorker* 59 (11 July 1983): 96-99. (Rev. of *Between Fantoine and Agapa* and *That Voice*, by Robert Pinget. Rpt. in *Odd Jobs*. N.Y.: Knopf, 1991. 389-95, with notes 389, 393.)

A1056   "Louise in the New World, Alice on the Magic Molehill." *The New Yorker* 59 (1 Aug. 1983): 85-90. (Rev. of *In Search of Love and Beauty*, by Ruth Prawer Jhabvala; and *Alice in Bed*, by Cathleen Schine. Rpt. in *Odd Jobs*. N.Y.: Knopf, 1991, 351-57.)

A1057   "Yahweh Over Dionysus, in Disputed Decision." *The New Yorker* 59 (7 Nov. 1983): 174-76, 179-180, 182. (Rev. of *The Anatomy Lesson*, by Philip Roth. Rpt. in *Odd Jobs*. N.Y.: Knopf, 1991. 366-72 with note 31.)

A1058   "Baggy Monsters." *The New Yorker* 59 (14 Nov. 1983): 188, 190, 193-200, 203-05. (Rev. of *The Name of the Rose*, by Umberto Eco; and *The Philosopher's Pupil*, by Iris Murdoch. Rpt. in *Odd Jobs*. N.Y.: Knopf, 1991. 412-25, with a note 414.)

A1059   "First Impressions, Lasting Effects." *The New York Times Book Review* 4 Dec. 1983: 7, 78. (Rev. of *A Treasury of Great Children's Book Illustrators*, by Susan E. Meyer. Rpt. in *Just Looking*. N.Y.: Knopf, 1989. 33-41.)

A1060   "As Others See Us." *The New Yorker* 59 (2 Jan. 1984): 87-90. (Rev. of *The Tennis Players*, by Lars Gustafsson; *Masks* by Fumiko Enchi; and *A Minor Apocalypse*, by Tadeusz Konwicki. Rpt. in *Odd Jobs*. N.Y.: Knopf, 1991. 601-08, with a note which corrects the height of the library tower from which Charles Whitman shot and the number of persons he killed, 602.)

A1061   "The Local View." *The New Yorker* 60 (27 Feb. 1984): 129-132. (Rev. of *Characters and Their Landscapes*, by Ronald Blythe. Rpt. in *Odd Jobs*. N.Y.: Knopf, 1991. 733-738, with a note 717.)

A1062   "Three Tales from Nigeria." *The New Yorker* 60 (23 Apr. 1984): 119-127. (Rev. of *Forest of a Thousand Daemons*, by D. O. Fagunwa; *The Witch-Herbalist of the Remote Town*, by Amos Tutuola; and *Double Yoke*, by Buchi Emecheta. Rpt. in *Odd Jobs*. N.Y.: Knopf, 1991. 571-79.)

A1063   "The Process and the Lock." *The New Yorker* 60 (18 June 1984): 108, 111-113. (Rev. of *The Nightmare of Reason: A Life of Franz Kafka*, by Ernest Pawel. Rpt. in *Odd Jobs*. N.Y.: Knopf, 1991. 757-762.)

A1064   "Art and Artillery." *The New Yorker* 60 (9 July 1984): 89-93. (Rev. of *The Poet Assassinated*, by Guillaume Apollinaire. Rpt. in *Odd Jobs*. N.Y.: Knopf, 1991. 380-389, with a note, 389.)

A1065   "A Romp with Job." *The New Yorker* 60 (23 July 1984): 104-107. (Review of *The Only Problem*, by Muriel Spark. Rpt. in *Odd Jobs*. N.Y.:Knopf, 1991. 452-456, with a note 456.)

A1066   "Genius Without a Cause." *The New Yorker* 60 (3 Sept. 1984): 88, 91-94. (Rev. of *Cyril Connolly: Journal and Memoir*. Ed. David Pryce-Jones; and

The Selected Essays of Cyril Connolly. Ed. Peter Quennell. Rpt. in *Odd Jobs*. N.Y.: Knopf, 1991. 442-50, with a note 443.)

A1067 "Modernist, Postmodernist, What Will They Think of Next?" *The New Yorker* 60 (10 Sept. 1984): 136-37, 140, 142. (Rev. of *Marcovaldo, or, The Seasons in the City*, by Italo Calvino; and *Fancy Goods/Open All Night*, by Paul Morand. Rpt. in *Odd Jobs*. N.Y.: Knopf, 1991. 694-702, with a note 695.)

A1068 "No More Mr. Knightleys." *The New Yorker* 60 (5 Nov. 1984): 160, 162-64, 167-68, 170. (Rev. of *Superior Women*, by Alice Adams. Rpt. in *Odd Jobs*. N.Y.: Knopf, 1991. 345-49, with a note 350.)

A1069 "Hear the Roaring of the Buds." *The New York Times Book Review* 2 Dec. 1984: 9. (Rev. of *The Gardener's Year*, by Karel Capek. Rpt. in *Odd Jobs*. N.Y.: Knopf, 1991. 738-41, with a new title, "Hymn to Tilth," with minor changes and a note 741.)

A1070 "Ungreat Lives." *The New Yorker* 60 (4 Feb. 1985): 94, 97-101. (Rev. of *Voices from the Moon*, by Andre Dubus; and *Concrete*, by Thomas Bernhard. Rpt. in *Odd Jobs*. N.Y.: Knopf, 1991. 649-56, with a few additions and deletions.)

A1071 "Eliot Without Words." *The New Yorker* 61 (25 Mar. 1985): 120, 123-30. (Rev. of *T. S. Eliot: A Life*, by Peter Ackroyd. Rpt. in *Odd Jobs*. N.Y.: Knopf, 1991. 762-70, with notes 763, 767, which cause the deletion of the final paragraph.)

A1072 "Back in the U. S. S. R." *The New Yorker* 61 (15 Apr. 1985): 110, 112, 115-18, 121-22, 124-26. (Rev. of *Another Life* and *The House on the Embankment*, by Yuri Trifonov; *Russian Women: Two Stories*, by I. Grekova; *The Island of Crimea*, by Vassily Aksyonov; and *Wild Berries*, by Yevgeny Yevtushenko. Rpt. in *Odd Jobs*. N.Y.: Knopf, 1991. 519-34 with minor revisions in the first paragraph and rettitled, "Out of the Evil Empire.")

A1073 "Living Death." *The New Yorker* 61 (20 May 1985): 118, 121-25. (Rev. of *Collected Stories*, by Gabriel García Márquez. Rpt. in *Odd Jobs*. N.Y.: Knopf, 1991. 476-84, with notes 479-80, 483.)

A1074 "Memory Palaces." *The New Yorker* 61 (17 June 1985): 120-126. (Rev. of *Seven Nights*, by Jorge Luis Borges; and *The Memory Palace of Matteo Ricci*, by Jonathan D. Spence. Rpt. in *Odd Jobs*. N.Y.: Knopf, 1991. 636-42, with minor alterations.)

A1075 "A Pair of Parrots." *The New Yorker* 61 (22 July 1985): 86-90. (Rev. of *Flaubert's Parrot*, by Julian Barnes; and *Parrot's Perch*, by Michel Rio. Rpt. in *Odd Jobs*. N.Y.: Knopf, 1991. 629-35, with the addition of a few sentences.)

A1076   "Beattieniks." *The New Yorker* 61 (5 Aug. 1985): 80-82. (Rev. of *Love Always*, by Ann Beattie. Rpt. in *Odd Jobs*. N.Y.: Knopf, 1991. 335-39.)

A1077   "Bad Neighbors." *The New Yorker* 61 (21 Oct. 1985): 145-46, 148-49. (Rev. of *The Handyman*, by Penelope Mortimer; and *Nothing Happens in Carmincross*, by Benedict Kiely. Rpt. in *Odd Jobs*. N.Y.: Knopf, 1991. 457-64.)

A1078   "Leaving Home." *The New Yorker* 61 (28 Oct. 1985): 106-08, 110-12. (Rev. of *The Accidental Tourist*, by Anne Tyler. Rpt. in *Odd Jobs*. N.Y.: Knopf, 1991. 339-45, with a note 340; and in *Critical Essays on Anne Tyler*. Ed. Alice Hall Perty. Boston: Hall, 1992. 126-31.)

A1079   "States of Mind." *The New Yorker* 61 (18 Nov. 1985): 167-68, 171-72, 174. (Rev. of *Mr. Palomar*, by Italo Calvino; and *Naomi*, by Junichiro Tanizaki. Rpt. in *Odd Jobs*. N.Y.: Knopf, 1991. The Calvino piece appears on 702-07, and the Tanizaki on 588-91. Rpt. in *Granta* 17 (Autumn 1985): 239-45.)

A1080   "Evolution Be Praised." *The New Yorker* 61 (30 Dec. 1985): 76-79. (Rev. of *The Flamingo's Smile: Reflections in Natural History*, by Stephen Jay Gould. Rpt. in *Odd Jobs*. N.Y.: Knopf, 1991. 817-24, with verbal revisions.)

A1081   "Dutchmen and Turks." *The New Yorker* 61 (6 Jan. 1986): 83-85. (Rev. of *The Assault*, by Harry Mulisch; and *The Sea-Crossed Fisherman*, by Yashar Kemal. Rpt. in *Odd Jobs*. N.Y.: Knopf, 1991. 619-24 with minor verbal additions.)

A1082   "*Seven Gothic Tales*: The Divine Swank of Isak Dinesen." *The New York Times Book Review* 23 Feb. 1986: V: 3, 37. (Adapted from the Book-of-the-Month Club edition of *Seven Gothic Tales*. Rpt. in *Odd Jobs*. N.Y.: Knopf, 1991. 210-16.)

A1083   "Latin Strategies." *The New Yorker* 62 (24 Feb. 1986): 98, 101-04. (Rev. of *The Real Life of Alejandro Mayta*, by Mario Llosa; and *The Old Gringo*, by Carlos Fuentes. Rpt. in *Odd Jobs*. N.Y.: Knopf, 1991. 484-91, with note 488 and minor verbal alterations.)

A1084   "Russian Delinquents." *The New Yorker* 62 (28 April 1986): 117-22. (Rev. of *Novel with Cocaine*, by M. Ageyev; and *Kangaroo*, by Yuz Aleshkovsky. Rpt. in *Odd Jobs*. N.Y.: Knopf, 1991. 534-40.)

A1085   "Expeditions to Gilead and Seegard." *The New Yorker* 62 (12 May 1986): 118, 121-26. (Rev. of *The Handmaid's Tale*, by Margaret Atwood; and *The Good Apprentice*, by Iris Murdoch. Rpt. in *Odd Jobs*. N.Y.: Knopf, 1991. 425-36, with notes 430-31.)

A1086 "The Sinister Sex." *The New Yorker* 62 (30 June 1986): 85-88. (Rev. of *The Garden of Eden*, by Ernest Hemingway. Rpt. in *Odd Jobs*. N.Y.: Knopf, 1991. 308-16 with notes 310 and 315-16.)

A1087 "Ecolalia." *The New Yorker* 62 (18 Aug. 1986): 70-72. (Rev. of *Travels in Hyperreality*, by Umberto Eco. Rpt. in *Odd Jobs*. N.Y.: Knopf, 1991. 680-85, with deletions and additions, and a note 685.)

A1088 "The Great Paraguayan Novel and Other Hardships." *The New Yorker* 62 (22 Sept. 1986): 104-08, 111-16. (Rev. of *Story of a Shipwrecked Sailor*, by Gabriel García Márquez; *I the Supreme*, by Augusto Roa Bastos; *A Funny Dirty Little War*, by Osvaldo Soriano; *The Long Night of Francisco Sanctis*, by Humberto Costantini; and *The Invention of Morel and Other Stories*, by Adolfo Bioy Casares. Rpt. in *Odd Jobs*. N.Y.: Knopf, 1991. 491-510, with a note based on an interview in *Leviatan*, 495, and minor deletions and additions.)

A1089 "Prishvin's Nature." *The New Yorker* 62 (29 Sept. 1986): 130, 132-135. (Rev. of *Nature's Diary*, by Mikhail Prishvin. Rpt. in *Odd Jobs*. N.Y.: Knopf, 1991. 196-200.)

A1090 "The Ugly Duckling." *The New Yorker* 62 (20 Oct. 1986): 116, 119-20, 122, 125-30. (Rev. of *Tolstoy's Diaries*, by Leo Tolstoy. Ed. R. F. Christian. Rpt. in *Odd Jobs*. N.Y.: Knopf, 1991. 261-75 with notes 273, 274.)

A1091 "Summonses, Indictments, Extenuating Circumstances." *The New Yorker* 62 (3 Nov. 1986): 158, 161-65. (Rev. of *A Summons to Memphis*, by Peter Taylor. Rpt. in *Odd Jobs*. N.Y.: Knopf, 1991. 320-27.)

A1092 "Old World Wickedness." *The New Yorker* 62 (15 Dec. 1986): 124-28. (Rev. of *Perfume: The Story of a Murderer*, by Patrick Süskind; and *The Enchanter*, by Vladimir Nabokov. Rpt. in *Odd Jobs*. N.Y.: Knopf, 1991. 656-62.)

A1093 "Visiting the Land of the Free." *The New Yorker* 62 (19 Jan. 1987): 88-91. (Rev. of *Alone Together*, by Elena Bonner Sakharov. Rpt. in *Odd Jobs*. N.Y.: Knopf, 1991. 540-48, with a note 544-45.)

A1094 "Wrestling to Be Born," *The New Yorker* 63 (2 Mar. 1987): 107-09. (Rev. of *The Counterlife*, by Philip Roth. Rpt. in *Odd Jobs*. N.Y.: Knopf, 1991. 373-380, with notes 375, 377.)

A1095 "How to Milk a Millionaire." *The New York Times Book Review* 29 Mar. 1987: 1, 35-37. (Rev. of *Artful Partners: Bernard Berenson and Joseph Duveen*, by Colin Simpson; and *Bernard Berenson: The Making of a Legend*, by Ernest Samuels and Jayne Newcomer Samuels. Rpt. in *Odd Jobs*. N.Y.: Knopf, 1991. 786-95, with a note 791 and retitled, "Was B. B. a Crook?")

A1096	"Back to Nature." *The New Yorker* 63 (30 March 1987): 120-124. (Rev. of *Seven Rivers West*, by Edward Hoagland; *Reindeer Moon*, by Elizabeth Marshall Thomas. Rpt. in *Odd Jobs*. N.Y.:Knopf, 1991. 357-64, with a note on 360.)
A1097	"Back to the Classics." *The New Yorker* 63 (18 May 1987): 110, 113-15. (Rev. of *The Apocrypha*, by Robert Pinget; and *Acastos*, by Iris Murdoch. Rpt. in *Odd Jobs*. N.Y.: Knopf, 1991. 436-41, with a note 441.)
A1098	"Goody Sergeant; the Powerful Katrinka; K. S. W." *The New Yorker* 63 (10 Aug. 1987): 74-78. (Rev. of *Onward and Upward: A Biography of Katharine S. White*, by Linda H. Davis, Rpt. in *Odd Jobs*. N.Y.: Knopf, 1991. 771-78, with notes 776 and 777.)
A1099	"Resisting the Big Guys." *The New Yorker* 63 (24 Aug. 1987): 83-86. (Rev. of *Who Killed Palomino Molero?* by Mario Vargas Llosa; *Of Love and Shadows*, by Isabel Allende; and *Clandestine in Chile: The Adventures of Miguel Littin*, by Gabriel García Márquez. Rpt. in *Odd Jobs*. N.Y.: Knopf, 1991. 503-10 with notes 503, 506-07 based on Allende's "A Few Words About Latin America.")
A1100	"Deep Time and Computer Time." *The New Yorker* 63 (7 Sept. 1987): 105-111. (Rev. of *Time's Arrow, Time's Cycle: Myth and Metaphor in the Discovery of Geological Time,* by Stephen Jay Gould, and *Time Wars: The Primary Conflict in Human History*, by Jeremy Rifkin. Rpt. in *Odd Jobs*. N.Y.: Knopf, 1991. 824-30, with a note 826.)
A1101	"Seeking Connections in an Insecure Country." *The New Yorker* 63 (16 Nov. 1987): 153-59. (Rev. of *The Radiant Way*, by Margaret Drabble. Rpt. in *Odd Jobs*. N.Y.:Knopf, 1991. 469-75, with a P. S. 475.)
A1102	"What You Deserve Is What You Get." *The New Yorker* 63 (28 Dec. 1987): 119-123. (Rev. of *You Must Remember This*, by Joyce Carol Oates. Rpt. in *Odd Jobs*. N.Y.:Knopf, 1991. 329-35 with a note 334-35.)
A1103	"Chronicles and Processions." *The New Yorker* 64 (14 Mar. 1988): 112-15. (Rev. of *Chronicle in Stone*, by Ismail Kadare; and *Baltasar and Blimunda*, by Jóse Saramago. Rpt. in *Odd Jobs*. N.Y.: Knopf, 1991. 557-63, and a note 557.)
A1104	"Witty Dotty," *The New Yorker* 64 (25 Apr. 1988): 109-112. (Rev. of *Dorothy Parker: What Fresh Hell Is This?* by Marion Meade. Rpt. in *Odd Jobs*. N.Y.: Knopf, 1991. 778-85.)
A1105	"In Dispraise of the Powers That Be." *The New Yorker* 64 (13 June 1988): 112-14, 116. (Rev. of *Curfew*, by José Donoso; and *Anthills of the Savannah*, by Chinua Achebe. Rpt. in *Odd Jobs*. N.Y.: Knopf, 1991. 642-49.)

A1106 "Small Packages." *The New Yorker* 64 (4 July 1988): 81-84. (Rev. of *Pierrot Mon Ami*, by Raymond Queneau; *The Mustache*, by Emmanuel Carrère; and *The Pigeon*, by Patrick Süskind. Rpt. in *Odd Jobs*. N.Y.: Knopf, 1991. 404-12.)

A1107 *"A Far Cry from Kensington*, by Muriel Spark." *The New Yorker* 64 (15 Aug. 1988): 82. (Unsigned. Rpt. in *Odd Jobs*. N.Y.: Knopf, 1991. 457, retitled "Spark but No Spark.")

A1108 "Doubt and Difficulty in Leningrad and Moscow." *The New Yorker* 64 (12 Sept. 1988): 108-10, 112-14. (Rev. of *Pushkin House*, by Andrei Bitov; and *Children of the Arbat*, by Anatoli Rybakov. Rpt. in *Odd Jobs*. N.Y.: Knopf, 1991. 548-56.)

A1109 "Satan's Work and Silted Cisterns." *The New Yorker* 64 (17 Oct. 1988): 117-121. (Rev. of *Arabesques*, by Anton Shammas; and *Cities of Salt*, by Abdelrahman Munif. Rpt. in *Odd Jobs*. N.Y.: Knopf, 1991. 563-70, with a note 560 and minor verbal changes.)

A1110 "The Visionary of Drohobycz." *The New York Times Book Review* 30 Oct. 1988: 3, 47 (Rev. of *Letters and Drawings of Bruno Schulz*, Ed. Walter Arndt, Victoria Nelson and Jerzy Ficowski. Rpt. in *Odd Jobs*. N.Y.: Knopf, 1991. 751-56, with a title change, "Schulz's Charred Scraps" and a note 754.)

A1111 *"Chekhov: A Spirit Set Free*, by V. S. Pritchett." *The New Yorker* 64 (31 Oct. 1988): 105. (Unsigned. Rpt. in *Odd Jobs*. New York: Knopf, 1991, 451.)

A1112 "Reluctant Butterfly: The Fierce Development of Edgar Degas." *The New Republic* 199 (14 Nov. 1988): 30-33. (Rpt. in *Just Looking*. N.Y.: Knopf, 1989. 97-112.)

A1113 *"Six Fragments and Under the Jaguar Sun*, by Italo Calvino." *The New Yorker* 64 (5 Dec. 1988): 157. (Unsigned. Rpt. in *Odd Jobs*. N.Y.: Knopf, 1991. 707-08.)

A1114 "The Heartless Man." *The New Yorker* 64 (2 Jan. 1989): 62-68. (Rev. of *Bernard Shaw: Collected Letters, Vol. 1: 1855-1898, The Search for Love*, Ed. Michael Holroyd; and *Bernard Shaw: Collected Letters, Vol. 2: 1926-1950*, Ed. Dan H. Laurence. Rpt. in *Odd Jobs*. N.Y.: Knopf, 1991. 276-90, with notes 288-89.)

A1115 "Chinese Disharmonies." *The New Yorker* 65 (3 Apr. 1989): 109-15. (Rev. of *The Question of Hu*, by Jonathan D. Spence; and *Half of Man Is Woman*, by Zhang Xianliang. Rpt. in *Odd Jobs*. N.Y.: Knopf, 1991. 579-88.)

A1116	"Nice Tries." *The New Yorker* 65 (1 May 1989): 111-14. (Rev. of *Latecomers*, by Anita Brookner; and *A Theft*, by Saul Bellow. Rpt. in *Odd Jobs*. N.Y.: Knopf, 1991. 664-71.)
A1117	*"Stirrings Still*, by Samuel Beckett." *The New Yorker* 65 (26 June 1989): 91. (Unsigned. Rpt. in *Odd Jobs*. N.Y.: Knopf, 1991. 708-09.)
A1118	"Michel Tournier." *The New Yorker* 65 (10 July 1989): 92-96. (Rev. of *The Wind Spirit, Giles & Jeanne* and *The Golden Droplet* by Michel Tournier. Rpt. in *Odd Jobs*. N.Y.: Knopf, 1991. 396-404.)
A1119	"Last Call." *The New Yorker* 65 (24 July 1989): 87-88. (Rev. of *Last Call*, by Harry Mulisch. Rpt. in *Odd Jobs*. N.Y.: Knopf, 1991. 625-28.)
A1120	"Studies in Post-Hitlerian Self-Condemnation in Austria and Germany." *The New Yorker* 65 (9 Oct. 1989): 132-36. (Rev. of *Wittgenstein's Nephew*, by Thomas Bernhard; and *No Man's Land*, by Martin Walser. Rpt. in *Odd Jobs*. N.Y.: Knopf, 1991. 609-17, with a note 615 and retitled "Studies in Post-Hitlerian Self-Condemnation in Austria and West Germany.")
A1121	*"Selected Letters, 1940-1977*, by Vladimir Nabokov." *The New Yorker* 65 (13 Nov. 1989): 147-48. (Unsigned. Rpt. in *Odd Jobs*. N.Y.: Knopf, 1991. 663-64 and retitled "V.N. Again and Again.")
A1122	"Writer-Consciousness." *The New Yorker* 65 (25 Dec. 1989): 103-108. (Rev. of *The Writing Life*, by Annie Dillard; *The Short Stories of F. Scott Fitzgerald*, by F. Scott Fitzgerald; *The Afternoon of a Writer*, by Peter Handke; and *The Storyteller*, by Mario Vargas Llosa. Rpt. in *Odd Jobs*. N.Y.: Knopf, 1991. 710-21, with a note 711.)
A1123	"Rereading 'Indian Summer.'" *The New York Review of Books* 37 (1 Feb. 1990): 13-14. (Rev. of *Indian Summer*, by W. D. Howells. Rpt. as the "Introduction" to Howells's novel for Vintage Books N.Y.: Random House, 1990; and in *Odd Jobs*. N.Y.: Knopf, 1991. 190-95.)
A1124	"In Borges' Wake," *The New Yorker* 65 (5 Feb. 1990): 116-120. (Rev. of *The Adventures of a Photographer in La Plata*, by Adolfo Bioy Casares; and *Foucault's Pendulum*, by Umberto Eco. Rpt. in *Odd Jobs*. N.Y.: Knopf, 1991. 685-694, with a note 690-691, and title changed to "In Borges's Wake.")
A1125	"The Flaming Chalice." *The New Yorker* 66 (26 Feb. 1990): 126-130. (Rev. of *The World Treasury of Science Fiction*, by David G. Hartwell. Rpt. in *Odd Jobs*. N.Y.: Knopf, 1991. 672-80.)
A1126	"Something Substantial and Useful About It." *The New Yorker* 66 (4 June 1990): 99-102. (Rev. of *The Pencil*, by Henry Petroski. Rpt. in *Odd Jobs*. N.Y.: Knopf, 1991. 800-06, with a note 801.)

A1127	"Died 30 B. C., Still Going Strong." *The New York Times Book Review* 10 June 1990: 9, 40. (Rev. of *Cleopatra: Histories, Dreams and Distortions*, by Lucy Hughes-Hallet. Rpt. in *Odd Jobs*. N.Y.: Knopf, 1991. retitled, "The Bimbo on the Barge." 795-99.)
A1128	"A Sort of Intimate Whirlwind." *The New York Review of Books* 37 (28 June 1990): 6, 8. (Rev. of *The Intimate Interiors of Edouard Vuillard* [an exhibition at the Brooklyn Museum] and *The Intimate Interiors of Edouard Vuillard* [catalog of the exhibition] by Elizabeth Wynne Easton.)
A1129	"*The King*, by Donald Barthelme." *The New Yorker* 66 (9 July 1990): 92. (Unsigned. Rpt. in *Odd Jobs*. N.Y.: Knopf, 1991. 328 and retitled, "Last Blague.")
A1130	"The Virtues of Playing Cricket on the Village Green." *The New Yorker* 66 (30 July 1990): 85-89. (Rev. of, *The American Novel and Reflections on the European Novel*, by Q. D. Leavis. Rpt. in *Odd Jobs*. N.Y.: Knopf, 1991. 291-301.)
A1131	"The Passion of Graham Greene." *The New York Review of Books* 37 (16 Aug. 1990): 16-17.
A1132	"A Materialist Looks at Eros." *The New Yorker* 66 (1 Oct. 1990): 107-110. (Rev. of *In Praise of the Stepmother*, by Mario Vargas Llosa. Rpt. in *Odd Jobs*. N.Y.: Knopf, 1991. 721-26.)
A1133	"Better Than Nature." *The New York Review of Books* 37 (8 Nov. 1990): 17-18. (Rev. of *The Art of Albert Pinkham Ryder* (exhibition); *Albert Pinkham Ryder*, by Elizabeth Broun; and *Albert Pinkham Ryder*, by William Innes Homer.)
A1134	"A Bull in the Typography Shop." *The New York Times Book Review* 16 Dec. 1990: 10. (Rev. of *Frederic Goudy*, by D. J. R. Bruckner. Rpt. in *Odd Jobs*. N.Y.: Knopf, 1991. 806-808, and retitled, "Bull in a Type Shop.")
A1135	"Still Staring." (Rev. of *Staring at the Sun*, by Julian Barnes. Though commissioned by *The New Yorker*, this piece was never published. *Odd Jobs*. N.Y.: Knopf, 1991. 709.)
A1136	"Not Quite Adult." *The New Yorker* 66 (14 Jan. 1991): 89-92. (Rev. of *Theodore Dreiser: An American Journey, 1908-1945*, by Richard Lingeman.)
A1137	"Innerlichkeit and Eigentümlichkeit." *The New York Review of Books* 38 (7 Mar. 1991): 10-11. (Rev. of: *The Romantic Vision of Caspar David Friedrich: Paintings and Drawings from the USSR*, an exhibition at the Metropolitan Museum of Art, N.Y., Jan. 23-March 31-1991; *The Romantic Vision of Caspar David Friedrich: Paintings and Drawings from*

the USSR, catalog of the exhibtion by Robert Rosenblum and Boris I. Asvarishch. Ed. by Sabine Rewald; and *Caspar David Friedrich and the Subject of Lanscape*, by Joseph Leo Koerner.)

A1138 "Farfetched." *The New Yorker* 67 (18 Mar. 1991): 102-106. (Rev. of *Yucatan*, by Andrea De Carlo; *The Signore: Shogun of the Warring States*, by Kuno Tsuji; and *Dogeaters*, by Jessica Hagedorn. Rpt. in *Odd Jobs*. N.Y.: Knopf, 1991. 591-601 and retitled "Far-Fetched".)

A1139 "Glasnost, Home, and Conquistadores." *The New Yorker* 67 (29 April 1991): 100-04. (Rev. of *No Return*, by Alexander Kabakov; *The Key*, by Junichiro Tanizaki; and *Sea of Lentils*, by Antonio Benitez-Rojo.)

A1140 *U and I: A True Story*, by Nicholson Baker. *The New Yorker* 67 (13 May 1991): 111-12. (Unsigned.)

A1141 "At the Hairy Edge of the Possible." *The New Yorker* 67 (3 June 1991): 104-08. (Rev. of *Origins: The Lives and Worlds of Modern Cosmologists*. Ed. Alan Lightman and Roberta Brawer.)

A1142 "Inspired Marketeer." *The New Yorker* 67 (1 July 1991): 84, 86-88. (Rev. of *An Artful Life: A Biography of D. H. Kahnweiler, 1884-1979*, by Pierre Assouline.)

A1143 "Vagueness on Wheels, Dust on a Skirt." *The New Yorker* 67 (2 Sept. 1991): 102, 104-05. (Rev. of *The White Castle*, by Orhan Pamuk; and *Love and Garbage*, by Ivan Klima.)

A1144 "First Things First." *Art and Antiques* Oct. 1991: 56-61. (Rev. of *The First Picture Book: Everyday Things for Babies*, by Mary Steichen Calderone and Edward Steichen. Rpt. in the "Afterword" to this book.)

A1145 "A Woman's Continent." *The New Yorker* 67 (21 Oct. 1991): 129-34. (Rev. of *Mating*, by Norman Rush; and *Brazzaville Beach*, by William Boyd.)

A1146 "The Waspshot Chronicle." [sic] *The New Republic* 205 (2 Dec. 1991): 36-39. (Rev. of *The Journals of John Cheever*, Ed. Robert Gottlieb.)

A1147 "Laughter from the Yokels." *The New Yorker* 68 (24 Feb. 1992): 98-101. (Rev. of *The Impossible H. L. Mencken: A Selection of His Best Newspaper Stories*, by Marion Elizabeth Rodgers.)

A1148 "Nobody Gets Away with Everything." *The New Yorker* 68 (25 May 1992): 84-88. (Rev. of *Tropical Night Falling*, by Manuel Puig; and *Time's Arrow*, by Martin Amis.)

A1149 "Facing Death." *American Heritage* 43 (May-June 1992): 98-105. (Rev. of *Sleeping Beauty: Memorial Photography in America*, Ed. Stanley B. Burns.)

A1150 "Mandarins." *The New Yorker* 68 (13 July 1992): 84-87. (Rev. of *Watermark*, by Joseph Brodsky; and *That Mighty Sculptor, Time*, by Marguerite Yourcenar.)

A1151 "*Complete Collected Essays* by V. S. Pritchett." *The New Yorker* 68 (27 July 1992): 72. (Unsigned. Rev. of *Complete Collected Essays*, by V. S. Pritchett.)

A1152 "Man of Secrets." *The New Yorker* 68 (28 Sept. 1992): 114-16, 118-19. (Rev. of *Nathaniel Hawthorne in His Times*, by James R. Mellow; and *Salem Is My Dwelling Place: A Life of Nathaniel Hawthorne*, by Edwin Haviland Miller.)

A1153 "She's Got Personality." *The New Yorker* 68 (19 Oct. 1992): 116-21. (Rev. of *Sex, Art, and American Culture*, by Camille Paglia.)

A1154 "Of Sickened Times." *The New Yorker* 68 (16 Nov. 1992): 134-42. (Rev. of *On Clowns: The Dictator and the Artist* and *Eight O'Clock*, by Norman Manea.)

A1155 "Pilgrim's Progress." *The New York Review of Books* 39 (3 Dec. 1992): 3-4. (Rev. of *The Discovery of America*, by Saul Steinberg.)

A1156 "Things, Things." *The New Yorker* 68 (18 Jan. 1993): 104-06. (Rev. of *The Evolution of Useful Things*, by Henry Petroski.)

A1157 "Recruiting Raw Nerves." *The New Yorker* 69 (15 Mar. 1993): 109-12. (Rev. of *Operation Shylock: A Confession*, by Philip Roth.)

A1158 "Exile on Main Street." *The New Yorker* 69 (17 May 1993): 91-97. (Rev. of "The Library of America" edition of *Main Street* and *Babbitt*, by Sinclair Lewis.)

7. Interviews

Print Media:

A1159   "Airmail Interview." *The Scop* 15 (Jan. 1964): 26-27.

A1160   Howard, Jane. "Can a Nice Novelist Finish First?" *Life* 61 (4 Nov. 1966): 74-74A, 74C, 74D, 76, 79-82. (Rpt. in *Salinger and Updike*. N.Y.: Life, 1966. [Life Educational Reprint Series no. 8.])

A1161   Nichols, Lewis. "Talk with John Updike." *The New York Times Book Review* 7 Apr. 1968: 34-35. (Rpt. in *Dictionary of Literary Biography: Documentary Series*. Vol. 3. Ed. Mary Bruccolli. Detroit: Gale, 1983. 269-72, with pages given as "37-38.")

A1162   Samuels, Charles Thomas. "The Art of Fiction XLIII: John Updike," *Paris Review* 12 (Winter 1968): 84-117. (Rpt. in *Writers at Work: The Paris Review Interviews*. Vol. VI. Ed. George Plimpton. N.Y.: Viking, 1976; in part in "One Big Interview," *Picked-Up Pieces*. N.Y.: Knopf, 1975. 493-518; in Ann Charters, *The Story and Its Writer*. N.Y.: St. Martin's P, 2nd ed. 1987; in *Writers at Work: The Paris Review Interviews*. London: Penguin, 1988; and in Spanish, **Conversaciones con los escritores*. Barcelona: Editorial Kairos, 1980.)

A1163   Rhode, Eric. "John Updike Talks to Eric Rhode About the Shapes and Subjects of His Fiction." *The Listener* 81 (19 June 1969): 862-64. (A transcription of a BBC Third Programme interview. Rpt. in part in "Grabbing the Dilemmas: John Updike Talks about God, Love, and the American Identity." *Vogue* 147 [Feb. 1971]: 157, 184-85; in *Dictionary of Literary Biography: Documentary Series*. Vol. 3. Ed. Mary Bruccolli. Detroit: Gale, 1983. 278-84; and in "One Big Interview." *Picked-Up Pieces*. N.Y.: Knopf, 1975. 493-518.)

A1164   "The Professional Viewpoint." *Twentieth Century Studies* 2 (Nov. 1969): 109-30. (Page 128 concerns Updike.)

A1165   [Bech, Henry] "Henry Bech Redux." *The New York Times Book Review* 14 Nov. 1971: 3. (Rpt. in *The York Times Reviews John Updike: The Author and His Works*. N.Y. Fawcett, 1971. 12-14; in *Picked-Up Pieces*. N.Y.: Knopf, 1975. 10-14, with the title "Bech Meets Me: *The New York Times Book Review* Persuades Henry Bech, Literary Man for All Thin Seasons, to Conduct an Interview"; and in *Dictionary of Literary Biography: Documentary Series*. Vol. 3. Ed. Mary Bruccolli. Detroit: Gale, 1983. 291-94.)

A1166   Gado, Frank. "John Updike." *First Person: Conversations on Writers and Writing*. Ed. Frank Gado. Schenectady, N.Y.: Union College P, 1971. 80-109. (Rpt. in *A Conversation with John Updike*. Ed. Frank Gado. Schenectady: Union College, 1971; and in "A Conversation with John Updike." Ed. Frank Gado. *The Idol* LXVII [Spring 1971]: 3-32.)

*A1167 Sragow, Michael. Harvard *Crimson* 2 Feb. 1972. (Rpt. in "One Big Interview." *Picked-Up Pieces*. N.Y.: Knopf, 1975. 493-518.)

*A1168 Ogle, Jane. 18 Dec. 1972. (Rpt. in "One Big Interview." *Picked-Up Pieces*. N.Y.: Knopf, 1975. 493-518.)

A1169   Kaplan, Martin. "Reminiscence." *The Harvard Lampoon Centennial Celebration, 1876-1973*. Boston: Atlantic-Little, 1973, unpaginated. (Rpt. in *Hugging the Shore*. N.Y.: Knopf, 1983. 843-45, with an error in the book's title.)

A1170   Hills, Rust, ed. *Writer's Choice*. N.Y.: David McKay, 1974. 390-391. (Rpt. in *Hugging the Shore*. N.Y.: Knopf, 1983. 852-53.)

A1171   Rubins, Josh. "The Industrious Drifter in Room Two." *Harvard Magazine* 76 (1974): 42-45, 51.

A1172   Updike, John. "One Big Interview." *Picked-Up Pieces*. N.Y.: Knopf, 1975. 493-518, with a note 503. (This is a composite interview drawn from interviews by Buckingham, Gado, Howard, Ogle, Rhode, Samuels, and Sragow. [See various entries above.])

A1173   Wohlfert, Lee. *Picked-Up Pieces*. N.Y.: Knopf, 1975. 510.

A1174   Campbell, Jeff. "Interview with John Updike Conducted by Jeff Campbell, Georgetown, Massachusetts, 9 Aug. 1976." This is the Appendix to his *John Updike's Novels: Thorns Spell a Word*. Wichita Falls, Tex.: Midwestern State U P, 1987. 277-304.

A1175   *The New York Times Book Review* 29 Aug. 1976: 7.

A1176   Vendler, Helen. "John Updike on Poetry." *The New York Times Book Review* 10 Apr. 1977: 3, 28. (Rpt. in *Dictionary of Literary Biography: Documentary Series: An Illustrated Chronicle*. Vol. 3. Ed. Mary Bruccolli. Detroit: Gale, 1983. 306-08; in part in *The John Updike Newsletter* 3

Interviews 115

(1977): 2; and in *Hugging the Shore*. N.Y.: Knopf, 1983. 862-65, with notes 862, 863.)

A1177 MacDonald, Craig. "A Chat with John Updike." *Writer's Digest* Sept. 1977: 5.

A1178 Burgin, Richard. "A Conversation with John Updike." *The New York Arts Journal* Issues 9, 11 (1978). (Rpt. in *The John Updike Newsletter* Nos. 10-11 [Spring-Sum. 1979]: 10 unnumbered pages.)

A1179 Nesvisky, Matthew. *Jerusalem Post* 10 Nov. 1978. (Excerpted in *Self-Consciousness*. N.Y.: Knopf, 1989. 79n.)

A1180 Reilly, Charlie. "Talking with John Updike." *Inquiry Magazine* 11 (Dec. 1978): 14-17.

A1181 Atlas, James. "John Updike Breaks Out of Suburbia." *The New York Times Magazine* 10 Dec. 1978. 60, 64, 68-70, 73-74, 78.

A1182 McCullough, David. *McCullough's Brief Lives: Selected 'Eye on Books' Interviews*. N.Y.: Book-of-the-Month Club, 1980. 159-64.

A1183 Reilly, Charlie. "A Conversation with John Updike." *Canto* 3 (Aug. 1980): 148-78.

A1184 McCullough, David W. "People Books & Book People." N.Y.: Harmony Books, 1981. 168-71.

A1185 Seib, Philip. "A Lovely Way Through Life: An Interview with John Updike." *Southwest Review* 66 (Autumn 1981): 341-50.

A1186 [Bech, Henry.] "Updike on Updike." *The New York Times Book Review* 27 Sept. 1981: 1, 34, 38. (Rpt. in *Hugging the Shore*. N.Y.: Knopf, 1983. 870-75, with notes 872 and 875. Of course, the interview was written by Updike.)

A1187 Kakutani, Michiko. "Turning Sex and Guilt Into an American Epic." *Saturday Review* Oct. 1981: 14-22.

A1188 Boyers, Robert, Bharati Mukherjee Blaise, and Robert Bud Foulke. "An Evening with John Updike." *Salmagundi* 57 (1982): 42-56.

A1189 Updike, John. "On One's Own Oeuvre." *Hugging the Shore*. N.Y.: Knopf, 1983. 839-78. (This is a composite interview drawn from various sources, as well as forewords and introductions to many editions of his work. Notes 743, 848, 855, 856, 859, 861, 862, 863, 872, 875, and 878.)

A1190 Christy, George. "How Hollywood Influenced Me." *Hugging the Shore*. N.Y.: Knopf, 1983. 842-43, with a note 843.)

A1191   Morgan, Darla J. *Hugging the Shore*. N.Y.: Knopf, 1983. 840-42.

A1192   Updike, John. "The Book That I'm Writing." *The New York Times Book Review* 88 (12 June 1983): 12-13, 40. (Page 40 pertains to *Hugging The Shore*.)

A1193   "What Makes Rabbit Run? A Profile of John Updike." *People* 27 June 1983: 11.

A1194   Findlay, William. "Interview with John Updike." *Cencrastus* 15 (1984): 34.

A1195   Cantwell, Mary. "Updike's Witchy Women." *Vogue* 174 (May 1984): 339, 405.

*A1196   *Magazine Littéraire*. Paris: Magazine Littéraire, 1986.

A1197   "Night Table Reading: Who Reads What Between the Sheets." *Vanity Fair* 49 (May 1986): 126. (Updike reads *Royal Highness*, by Thomas Mann; *The Brass Bed*, by Alexandra Marshall; and the French comic book *Mickey Triomphe*.)

A1198   Salgas, Jean-Pierre. "Hawthorne, Melville, Whitman et l'expérience américaine." *La Quinzaine Littéraire* 462 (15 mai 1986): 11-12.

A1199   Mitgang, Herbert. "'Life Interrupts Me Occasionally.'" *The New York Times Book Review* 31 Aug. 1986: 15.

A1200   Greiner, Donald J. "Updike on Hawthorne." *The Nathaniel Hawthorne Review* 13 (Spring 1987): 1-4.

A1201   McDowell, Edwin. "Fine-Tuning a Collection." *The New York Times Book Review* 32 (26 Apr. 1987): 44. (Updike comments on *Trust Me*.)

A1202   *Eastern Review* (Eastern Airlines in-Flight Magazine) July 1987: 45-47.

A1203   Amis, Martin. "Updike: Life Under a Microscope." *Reading* (Pa.) *Eagle* 4 Oct. 1987: E-18.

A1204   McNally, T. M. and Dean Stover. "An Interview with John Updike." *Hayden's Ferry Review* 3 (1988): 102-16.

A1205   Tothstein, Mervyn. "In *S*. Updike Tries the Woman's Viewpoint." *The New York Times* 137 (2 Mar. 1988): C-21.

A1206   Gross, Terry. "John Updike." *Applause Magazine* June 1988, 11-13.

A1207   Mallon, Thomas. "One Small Shelf for Literature." *The New York Times Book Review* 16 July 1989: 1, 26-28.

A1208	Updike, John. "A State of Ecstasy." *Art and Antiques* Jan. 1990: 75.
A1209	Miller, Roger. "Updike Says This Year's Will Be the Last Rabbit Tale--but No Promises." *Milwaukee Journal* 1 July 1990: E-6.
A1210	Kaplan, James. "Requiem for Rabbit." *Vanity Fair* Oct. 1990: 112, 114, 116, 118.
A1211	"Why Rabbit Finally Ran to Ground." *Guardian* 25 Oct. 1990, Sec. 23:1.
A1212	Italie, Hillel. "Last Rabbit Not Easy to Write." *The Reading* (Pa.) *Eagle* 11 Nov. 1990: F-2.
A1213	Updike, John. "Literarily Personal." *Odd Jobs*. N.Y.: Knopf 1991. 833-72. (This composite interview from various periodicals, introductions, forewords and "special messages" from Updike's reprints, "Notes and Comments," etc. contains notes 834, 853-54, 858, and 867.)
A1214	Schiff, James A. "An Interview with John Updike." In his *Updike's Version: Rewriting* The Scarlet Letter. Columbia: U of Mo. P, 1992. 131-32.
A1215	*Poets and Writers* July-Aug. 1992: 25
A1216	"Personally Speaking." *Vogue* Sept. 1992: 554-55, 618.
A1217	Farney, Dennis. "Novelist Updike Sees a Nation Frustrated by its Own Dreams." *The Wall Street Journal* 220 (16 Sept. 1992): A-1, 8.
A1218	Nunley, Jan. "Thoughts of Faith Infuse Prolific Updike's Novels." *Episcopal Life* May 1993: 1, 4.

Other Media:

A1219	"John Updike Comments on His Work and the Role of the Novelist Today." N.Y.: National Education Television, Sept. 1966. One film reel, 32 minutes. Produced by Jack Sommers for his "USA Writers" series.
*A1220	"The Non-Traditional Novelist." Tucson, Arizona: Motivations Programming Corp., 1970. One sound cassette, 28 minutes.
A1221	Raymont, Henry. "John Updike Completes a Sequel to 'Rabbit, Run.'" *The New York Times* 27 July 1971: 22
A1222	Cavett, Dick. "The Dick Cavett Show." Public Broadcasting Service. Daphne Productions. 14 Dec. 1978. (With John Cheever.)
A1223	Cavett, Dick. "The Dick Cavett Show." Public Broadcasting Service.

Daphne Productions. 15 Dec. 1978. (With John Cheever.)

A1224   Cavett, Dick. "The Dick Cavett Show." Public Broadcasting Service. WNET. Daphne Productions. Dec. 1978. One videocassette, 28 minutes, 3/4 inch.

*A1225 [Interview.] Columbia, Mo: American Audio Prose Library, 1980. One sound cassette.

*A1226 "A Conversation with John Updike." Dallas, Tex. WFAA, 1980. One videocassette, VHS, 24 minutes, 1/2 inch.

A1227   Cavett, Dick. "The Dick Cavett Show." Public Broadcasting Service. Daphne Productions. 9 Nov. 1981.

A1228   Cavett, Dick. "The Dick Cavett Show." Public Broadcasting Service. Daphne Productions. 10 Nov. 1981.

A1229   Calloway, John. "John Calloway Interviews John Updike." Washington, D. C. Public Broadcasting System Video, 1981. One videocassette, VHS, 59 minutes, 1/2 inch.

*A1230 Interview. ARTS. 19 Oct. 1982.

A1231   "What Makes Rabbit Run? A Profile of John Updike." Public Broadcasting Service: WGBH. CS Associates. 28 June 1985. One videoscassette, 30 minutes, VHS, 1/2 inch tape. (Also presented on British Broadcasting Corporation. Released as a video, "John Updike: What Makes Rabbit Run?" Live-Action Video: Center for the Humanities, 1982. WGBH (Boston).

*A1232 "John Updike in Conversation." Northbrook, Ill.: The Roland Collection, 1986. One videocassette, VHS, 52 minutes 1/2 inch tape.

A1233   Interview following "The Roommate." Public Broadcasting System. 27 Jan. 1986. VHS videotape.

A1234   Tomalin, Claire. "Writers in Conversation." London: Institute of Contemporary Arts, 1986. One videocassette, VHS, 52 minutes, 1/2 inch tape.

*A1235 [John Updike.] 1987. One Videocassette, VHS. (A 1987 lecture given at Arizona State University.)

*A1236 "Conversational Highlights." London: Calif. Video, 1988. One videocassette, PAL, VHS, 25 minutes, 1/2 inch.

A1237   Pauley, Jane. "Interview about *S.*" Today Show. NBC- TV 1988.

*A1238 "Rabbit" quartet subject of British TV program shown Autumn 1990.

Weekend Television, Ltd.

A1239 Interview about *Rabbit at Rest*, National Public Radio, 20 Oct. 1990.

A1240 Gumble, Bryant. "Interview about *Rabbit at Rest*." *Today*. NBC-TV. 21 Oct. 1990.

A1241 Gibson, Charles. "Good Morning America." ABC. 27 Oct. 1992. (Concerns *Memories of the Ford Administration*.)

A1242 Cavett, Dick. "The Dick Cavett Show." CNBC. 9 Nov. 1992. (Concerns *Memories of the Ford Administration*.)

A1243 "*Collected Poems*." "Good Morning America." 19 May 1993. 15 minutes.

8. Letters, Manuscripts

Letters:

A1244   "Precise Language." Letter. *Commonweal* 84 (22 Apr. 1966): 160-61. (Reply to Anthony Burgess's "Language, Myth and Mr. Updike.")

A1245   "Updike 'Flatly Denies' That Tarbox Is Ipswich." Letter. *The Ipswich Chronicle*. 25 Apr. 1968. (Rpt. in *The John Updike Newsletter* No. 2 [Spring 1977]: 3.)

A1246   An untitled letter. *America's 85 Greatest Living Authors Present This Is My Best in the Third Quarter of the Century*. Ed.. Whit Burnett. Garden City, N.Y.: Doubleday, 1970. 3-4. (Concerns the inclusion in this book of "Packed Dirt, Churchgoing, A Dying Cat, A Traded Car." Rpt. in *Hugging the Shore*, N.Y.: Knopf, 1983. 851-852.)

A1247   To Samuel Beckoff. Hunt, George W., S. J. *John Updike and the Three Great Secret Things: Sex, Religion, and Art*. Grand Rapids, Mich.: Eerdmans, 1980. 173.

A1248   To George Hunt. Hunt, George W., S. J. *John Updike and the Three Great Secret Things: Sex, Religion, and Art*. Grand Rapids, Mich.: Eerdmans, 1980. 171.

A1249   To George Hunt. Hunt, George W., S. J. *John Updike and the Three Great Secret Things: Sex, Religion, and Art*. Grand Rapids, Mich.: Eerdmans, 1980. 212.

A1250   To Bill Morgan. *Kanreki: A Tribute to Allen Ginsberg*. Part 2. N.Y.: Lospecchio P, 1986. (Signed, lettered and numbered edition. A four-line letter.)

A1251   "Poetry Poorly Served." Letter. Boston *Globe* 11 Jan. 1990. Sec. 14: 6.

A1252   To Karl Barth. Quoted in John McTavish. "John Updike and the Funny Theologian." *Theology Today* 48 (Jan. 1992): 413-25. See also **A611, A712** and **A853**.

Work Sheets:

A1253   Handwritten draft of the first two pages of *The Coup*, dated Jan. 28, 1977. *The John Updike Newsletter* Spring-Sum. 1979, unnumbered pages 12-13.

A1254   Typescript and editorial corrections of the poem "The House Growing." *The John Updike Newsletter* Sum. 1977, unnumbered page 2. (Rpt. in *The New Yorker* 23 July 1973: 34; and *Tossing and Turning*. N.Y.: Knopf, 1977. 12.)

A1255   Typescript of first page of *The Coup*. *The John Updike Newsletter* Spring-Sum. 1979, unnumbered page 11.

A1256   Various manuscripts, typescripts, galleys, etc in *Dictionary of Literary Biography: Documentary Series*. Vol. 3. Ed. Mary Bruccolli. Detroit: Gale, 1983. 251-320. (Typescripts include: "Notes and Comments" 255; of *The Poorhouse Fair*, 257; "Foreword" to the Modern Library ed. of *The Poorhouse Fair*; 258, revised typescript and corrected galley proof for *Rabbit, Run*, 260-261; rev. galley proof of "Walter Briggs," 263; ms. for "The Blessing," 265; note about *Couples*, 270; typescript for "Bech Swings," 285; typescript for *Rabbit Redux*, 287; working draft for a translation of a Borges's poem 303; ms. for *The Coup*, 310; typescript for "Introduction" to Vladimir Nabokov's *Lectures on Literature*, 314; and ms. and revised typescript of *Rabbit Is Rich*, 316-317.)

A1257   Falsey, Elizabeth A. *The Art of Adding and the Art of Taking Away*. Cambridge, Mass.: The Harvard College Library, 1987. (Contains typescripts, manuscripts, galleys and notes for poems, stories and novels.)

A1258   Photocopies of two typescript pages of reminiscence with holograph corrections by Updike. *The Harvard Lampoon Centennial Celebration, 1876-1973*. Ed. Martin Kaplan. Boston: Atlantic-Little, Brown, 1973. Unpaginated.

A1259   Typescript and editorial corrections of *The Poorhouse Fair*. Greiner, Donald J. "John Updike." *Broadening Views, 1968-88: Concise Dictionary of American Literature Biography*. Detroit: Gale, 1989. 282.

Manuscripts and Book Repositories:

*****A1260**   Carter-Danforth Family Papers. 1722. Manuscript. (Contains items about Providence, R.I. concerning Updike.)

A1261   Harmon, William. "Papers." 1971. (260 items in the Southern Historical Collection, University of N. C. at Chapel Hill [#4568]).

A1262   *A Baker's Dozen: Being a Selection of Books and Manuscripts by one English and Thirteen American authors from the library of Keith H. Baker of Oshkosh, Wisconsin.* Bloomington, Ind.: The Lilly Library, 1984.

A1263   "The Jack W. C. Hagstrom Collection." Amherst College Library. Amherst, Mass., 1985. (The collection includes a vast array of first, fine and translated editions of Updike's books, first publications in periodicals, and criticism about Updike in books and periodicals. Also includes tapes and records of Updike reading, booksellers' catalogues, transcripts of television interviews, blurbs and memorabilia.)

A1264   University of Texas, U Park, Tex. M. D. Anderson Library. (See: Bozeman, Pat. *John Updike: An Exhibition*. M. D. Anderson Library: U Park, Tex.: 1985.)

A1265   Harvard University, the Houghton Library. See the partial listing of the collection in Elizabeth A. Falsey, *The Art of Adding and the Art of Taking Away*. Cambridge, Mass.: The Harvard College Library, 1987. Also consult her "Introduction: Making and Changing the Text," 4-6 and Updike's, "Preface to a Partial Catalogue of My Own Leavings," 3.

A1266   "The Linda Grace Hoyer Updike Papers Collection." Ursinus College, the Myrin Library. Collegeville, Pa. A collection of books and papers pertaining to Updike's mother, Linda Grace Hoyer Updike, and letters to and from Updike. [1990].

A1267   Reading Public Library, Reading, Pa.. A collection of 61 first editions each inscribed to Updike's parents. Also two scrapbooks of clippings of his early work. Also includes book by the author's son David. [1990]

A1268   *The New Yorker*. The magazine's private archives contain clippings of Updike's work.

Exhibits:

A1269   "Two Exhibitions in the Library of Mary Washington College." Fredericksburg, Va.: Mary Washington College Library, 1970. (Contains the Sidney H. Mitchell library of John Updike material.)

A1270   "Visual Poetry." Curated by Jack De Bellis. Lehigh University. Bethlehem, Pa. May 10-June 10, 1976.

A1271   "John Updike, a Collection." Cambridge, Mass.: The Bookseller, 1980.

A1272   Falsey, Elizabeth A. *The Art of Adding and the Art of Taking Away.* Cambridge, Mass.: The Harvard College Library, 1987. (An exhibit of typescripts, manuscripts, galleys and notes for poems, stories and novels.)

Autograph:

A1273   *Lord John Signatures.* Northridge, Calif.: Lord John P, 1991. "Introduction," by Stephen King. (A deluxe issue, limited to 150 numbered copies. Also signed by John Barth, R. Bloch, T. C Boyle, J. Blalock, R. Campbell, Harry Crews, J Gilchrist, Jim Harrison, T. Hillerman, Stephen King, Wiliam Kennedy, J. L'Hereux, Ursula LeGuin, E. Leonard, Tom McGuane, Norman Mailer, R. Matheson, B. Moore, J Mugnaini, Joyce Carol Oates, E. O'Brien, R. Parker, Reynolds Price, T. Powers, James Purdy, D. Simmons, P. Straub, R. Thomas, Anne Tyler and Eudora Welty.)

Appearances on Television Programs:

A1274   "Baseball" Entertainment and Sports Network. Mar. 1991.

A1275   "Doris Day: A Sentimental Journey" Public Broadcasting System, WTTW. 15 Nov. 1991. (Updike offers incidental remarks.)

9. Translations by Updike

From Bulgarian:

A1276   Dimitrova, Blaga. "Pain." Ed. William Meredith. *Poets of Bulgaria.* Greensboro, N. C.: Unicorn P, 1986. 20.

A1277   Dimitrova, Blaga. "The Road." Ed. William Meredith. *Poets of Bulgaria.* Greensboro, N. C.: Unicorn P, 1986. 17; version 2: 18.

A1278   Dimitrova, Blaga. "Travelling Alone." Ed. William Meredith. *Poets of Bulgaria.* Greensboro, N. C.: Unicorn P, 1986. 19.

A1279   Karaangov, Peter. "Winter." Ed. William Meredith. *Poets of Bulgaria.* Greensboro, N. C.: Unicorn P, 1986. 51. (Adapted by Updike.)

From Russian:

A1280   Evtushenko, Evgenil. "Ballad About Nuggets." *Life* 62 (17 Feb. 1967): 38.

A1281   Evtushenko, Evgenil. "Restaurant for Two." *Life* 62 (17 Feb. 1967): 33. (Rpt. in *Poets on Street Corners: Portraits of Fifteen Russian Poets.* Ed. Olga Carlisle. N.Y.: Random House, 1968.)

A1282   Yevtushenko, Yevgeny. (Here spelled "Evgenil Evtushenko.") "America and I Sat Down Together." *Holiday* 44 (Nov. 1968): 38, 40-42. (Trans. with Albert C. Todd: "In a Steelworker's Home," "Monologue of a Polar Fox on an Alaskan Fur Farm," "Monologue of an American Poet," "Monologue of a Broadway Actress," "Smog," "Cemetery of Whales," and "New York Elegy.")

A1283   Yevtushenko, Yevgeny. "Stolen Apples." From "Four New Poems." *Playboy* 18 (Oct. 1971): 153. (Rpt. in *Stolen Apples. Poetry by Yevgeny Yevtushenko.* Garden City, N.Y.: Doubleday, 1971.)

From Spanish:

A1284   Borges, Jorge Luis. "The Labyrinth." *Atlantic* 233 (Apr. 1969): 72.

10. Graphics and Readings

Graphics

Illustrations:

A1285   *Rabbit, Run.* N.Y.: Knopf, 1960. (Took part in designing the jacket.)

A1286   *Telephone Poles.* N.Y.: Knopf, 1965. (Took part in designing the jacket.)

A1287   *Midpoint.* N.Y.: Knopf, 1967. (Took part in designing the jacket.)

A1288   *Couples.* N.Y.: Knopf, 1968. (Took part in designing the jacket.)

A1289   *Rabbit Redux.* N.Y.: Knopf, 1971. (Took part in designing the jacket.)

A1290   *Problems and Other Stories.* N.Y.: Knopf, 1979. (Took part in designing the jacket.)

A1291   *Five Poems.* Cleveland: Bits Press, 1980. (The cover design forms a rebus with a caricature of Poe, five fingers aloft and multiple letters M.)

A1292   *Rabbit Is Rich.* N.Y.: Knopf, 1981. (Took part in designing the jacket.)

A1293   *S.* N.Y.: Knopf: 1988. (Took part in designing the jacket.)

A1294   *Rabbit at Rest.* N.Y.: Knopf, 1990. (Took part in designing the jacket.)

Photographs:

A1295   *Museums and Women.* N.Y.: Knopf, 1972. Updike's photo of a museum room and a woman appears on the cover.

A1296   *Something to Preserve.* Ipswich Historical Commission, 1975. (Updike did the photography layout.)

Self-Portraits:

A1297   Plimpton, George. *Writers at Work: The Paris Review Interviews.* "Art of Fiction XLIII." *Paris Review* 45 (Wint. 1968): 85. (Reprinted on the cover of *John Updike: An Exhibition.* U of Texas, M. D. Anderson Library. U Park, Texas. 1985.)

A1298   Kaplan, Martin. *The Harvard Lampoon Centennial Celebration, 1876-1973.* N.Y.: Little, 1973.

A1299   *Self-Portrait: Book People Picture Themselves.* Collected by Burt Britton. N.Y.: Random House, 1976. 8. (Signed. Updike contributed a drawing of himself, drawn with a felt-tip pen. Rpt. on cover of *Impressions.* Los Angeles, Calif.: Sylvester & Orphanos, 1985. See **A214**.)

A1300   Mary Bruccolli, Ed. *Dictionary of Literary Biography: Documentary Series.* Volume III. Detroit, Gale, 1983. 267.

Painting:

A1301   [Still life.] *Ursinus Bulletin* 84 (Spring 1991): 12.

Woodcut:

A1302   *More Stately Mansions.* Jackson, Miss.: Nouveau P, 1987.

Drawings:

A1303   "Letter from Anguilla." *The New Yorker* 44 (22 June 1968): 70. (Rpt. in *Picked-Up Pieces.* N.Y.: Knopf, 1975. 63.)

A1304   "Typical Optical." *The New York Times Book Review* 2 Dec. 1979. The drawing should have been printed in this magazine with the poem Nov. 25. They were so printed in *The John Updike Newsletter* 13 (1980): [4]. See **A552**.

A1305   *Five Poems.* Cleveland: Bits P, 1980, unpaginated.

A1306   Bruccolli, Mary, Ed. *Dictionary of Literary Biography: Documentary Series.* Volume III. Detroit: Gale, 1983. 253.

A1307   "Personal History: A Soft Spring Night in Shillington." *The New Yorker* 60 (24 Dec. 1984): 37.

A1308	"Personal History: At War with my Skin." *The New Yorker* 61 (2 Sept. 1985): 39.
A1309	Hjerter, Kathleen. *Doubly Gifted: The Author as Visual Artist*. N.Y.: Abrams, 1985. 148-49.
A1310	*Jester's Dozen*. Northridge, Calif.: Lord John P, 1984. (Drawings are distributed throughout.)
A1311	*Just Looking*. N.Y.: Knopf, 1989. 198-99.

Cartoons:

A1312	Gado, Frank. "A Conversation with John Updike." *The Idol* 67 (Spring 1971): 3-32. (two cartoons)
A1313	Kaplan, Martin. *The Harvard Lampoon Centennial Celebration, 1876-1973*. Boston: Little, 1973. Unpaginated. Five cartoons.
A1314	Included in McCoy, Robert. "John Updike's Literary Apprenticeship on The *Harvard Lampoon*." *Modern Fiction Studies* 20 (Spring 1974): 3-12.
A1315	Celebrity drowning in cement at Grauman's Chinese Theater. *Los Angeles Times* 3 Dec 1978. (Rpt. *John Updike Newsletter* Wint. 1979. unnumbered p. 4.)
A1316	"Typical Optical." *The John Updike Newsletter* No. 13 (1980): [4].
A1317	*Collected Poems*. N.Y.: Knopf, 1993. 363. ("The Hill of Life.")

Readings

Video Cassettes:

*A1318	"The Dick Cavett Show." Public Broadcasting Service. WNET. Dec. 1978. One video cassette.)
A1319	John Updike with Claire Tomalin. London: IC Video, 1980. One videocassette (PAL) VHS. 4 minutes, 1/2 inch.

Audio Tapes and Records:

*A1320	"John Updike Reading from his Works." N.Y.: CMS Records, Inc. no date. CMS 523. (Includes excerpts from *The Centaur*, "Lifeguard" and poems from *Telephone Poles*.)
*A1321	"The Prose and Poetry of John Updike." N.Y.: McGraw, 1960. One reel, 3/4 ips, 2-track, mono.

*A1322	"The Prose and Poetry of John Updike." YM-YWHA Poetry Center Series. Jeffrey Norton Publishers, 1967. 47 mins.
*A1323	"John Updike Reads from *Couples* and *Pigeon Feathers*." Caedmon TC1276, 1969. One disk. 55 minutes. 33 1/3 rpm.
*A1324	"The Non-Traditional Novelist." North Hollywood: The Center for Cassette Studies, 1970. One cassette, 2-track.
*A1325	*The Spoken Arts Treasury of 100 American Poets*. Volume 18. SA 1057. 12 inch disc. (Updike reads: "To an Usherette," "The Sensualist," "February 22nd," "The Stunt Flier," "Les Saints Nouveaux," "Die Neuen Heiligen," "Summer: West Side," and "Time's Fool.")
*A1326	"Contemporary American Authors Reading Their Own Works." N.Y.; Caedmon, 1972. 1 7/8 ips, 2 track, mono. Reads from *Couples* and *Pigeon Feathers*.
*A1327	*Couples*. Audio Prose Library, Inc.
*A1328	"Responding Records Sequence." Lexington, Mass.: Ginn, 1973. Two discs, 33 1/3 rpm, mono.
*A1329	"John Updike." Washington, D. C.: Tapes for Readers, 1978. One cassette, 2-track mono.
*A1330	Cavett, Dick. "Sex in Literature." 1981. One sound tape 7 1/2 ips mono. 1/4' tape.
*A1331	Lecture. Arizona State U: Associated Students and the Creative Writing Student Association. 1987. One videocassette 1/2 inch, VHS. (Updike reads his poetry and prose and answers questions.)
A1332	"Updike Reads Selected Stories." Audio Prose Library. Random, 1987. Two cassettes. (Reads: "A & P," "Pigeon Feathers," "The Family Meadow," "The Witnesses," "The Alligators," and "Separating.")
A1333	Reads from *Trust Me*. Audio Prose Library. Random, 1988. Two cassettes.(Reads: "Trust Me," "Deaths of Distant Friends," "Pygmalion," "The Lovely Troubled Daughters of Our Old Crowd," "Still of Some Use," "Poker Night," "The City," "Getting Into the Set," and "Learn a Trade.")
A1334	"Reads from his Memoir *Self-Consciousness* and Talks About the Things That Have Embarrassed Him over a Lifetime." Columbia, Mo.: Audio Prose Library, Inc., 1990. One sound disc, 30 minutes. 1 7/8 ips, mono.
A1335	"Reading from *Rabbit at Rest*." Audio Prose Library. Random. M2R811. Two cassettes. 1990.

A1336 "Voices in Time." New York: Harper Audio, 1992. (Reads from *Couples* and from *Pigeon Feathers*: "The Persistence of Desire," and "The Blessed Man of Boston, My Grandmother's Thimble, and Fanning Island.")

II. Works about Updike

1. General Commentary

B1	"Updike Named to Head Board of Lampoon." *Reading* (Pa.) *Eagle* 16 Dec. 1952.
B2	"Updike-Pennington." *Reading* (Pa.) *Eagle* 26 June 1953.
B3	"John H. Updike." *Reading* (Pa.) *Eagle* 30 May 1954.
B4	"Updike Wins Fellowship at Oxford." *Reading* (Pa.) *Eagle* 21 Jun 1954.
B5	"Updike Attends Shillington Class Reunion." *Reading* (Pa.) *Eagle* 5 Sept. 1955.
B6	[Magazine Notes.] *Reading* (Pa.) *Times* 19 May 1960.
B7	Reed, Virginia. "Mrs. Wesley R. Updike Sees Son Become Novelist of High Stature." *Reading* (Pa.) *Eagle* 3 July 1960.
B8	Taggert, Edward A. "Mother Shows Writing Runs in the Family." *Reading* (Pa.) *Times* 7 Apr. 1961.
B9	Geller, Evelyn. "WLB Biography: John Updike." *Wilson Library Bulletin* 36 (Sept. 1961): 67.
B10	Murphy, Richard W. "In Print: John Updike." *Horizon* 4.4 (Mar. 1962): 84-85.
B11	Cimatti, Pietro. "Burroughs e Updyke [sic]." *La Fiera Letteraria* 38 (29 Apr. 1962): 3-4.
B12	Ward, J. A. "John Updike's Fiction." *Critique* 5 (Spring-Sum. 1962): 27-41.

B13 Fisher, Richard E. "John Updike: Theme and Form in the Garden of Epiphanies." *Moderna Språk* 56 (Fall 1962): 255-60.

B14 Detweiler, Robert. "John Updike and the Indictment of Culture-Protestantism." *Four Spiritual Crises in Mid-Century American Fiction*. Gainesville: U of Fla. P, 1963. 14-24.

B15 "The Sustaining Stream." *Time* 81 (1 Feb. 1963): 82-84. (Page 83 concerns Updike.)

*B16 Brodin, Pierre. "John Updike." *Liberté* 5 (May-June 1963): 259-264.

B17 Adams, Mildred. "El Escritor John Updike ?Cuento o Novela?" *Revista de Occidente* 1 (Aug. 1963): 198-202.

B18 Logu, Pietro. "La Narrativa di John Updike." *Studi Americani* 10 (1964): 343-368.

B19 Rotkirch, Kristina. "Den Otillfredsstallde." *Nya Argus* 57 (1964): 142-144.

B20 "National Book Awards." *Wilson Library Bulletin* 38 (Jan. 1964): 374.

B21 "National Book Awards Judges Announce Leading Contenders." *Library Journal* 89 (2 Feb. 1964): 820.

B22 "Updike Elected to Institute." *Reading* (Pa.) *Eagle* 17 Feb. 1964.

B23 Driscoll, Edward A., Jr. "Updike Is Uneasy About Literary Prizes." *Boston Globe* 1 Mar. 1964.

B24 "National Book Awards." *Library Journal* 89 (3 Mar. 1964): 126.

B25 Doyle, Paul A. "The Fiction of John Updike." *The Nassau Review* 1 (Spring 1964): 9-19.

B26 "Updike to Receive Degree from Ursinus." *Reading* (Pa.) *Eagle* 14 May 1964.

B27 "Updike to Receive Honorary Degree." *Reading* (Pa.) *Times* 15 May 1964.

B28 Kappler, Frank. "Existentialism." *Life* 57 (6 Nov. 1964): 86-96, 98, 101, 103-04, 106-08, 110. (Page 94 pertains to Updike.)

B29 Finkelstein, Sidney. "Acceptance of Alienation: John Updike and James Purdy." *Existentialism and Alienation in American Literature*. N.Y.: International P, 1965. 243-52. (Pages 243-47 concern Updike.)

B30 Straumann, Heinrich. *American Literature in the Twentieth Century*. 3rd rev. ed. N.Y.: Harper, 1965. 127-28.

B31	Yates, Norris W. "The Doubt and Faith of John Updike." *College English* 26 (Mar. 1965): 469-74.
B32	Muradian, Thaddeus. "The World of Updike." *English Journal* 54.7 (Oct. 1965): 577-84.
B33	Enright, D. J. "Updike's Ups and Downs." *Holiday* 38 (Nov. 1965): 162, 164-65. (Rpt. in "The Inadequate American: John Updike's Fiction." In his *Conspirators and Poets*. London: Chatto and Windus, 1966. 134-40.)
B34	Le Vot, André. "Updike Poète, ou le Mythe d'Antée." *Les Langues Modernes* 59 (nov.-déc. 1965): 50-55.
B35	Aldridge, John. "The Private Vice of John Updike." In his *Time to Murder and Create: The Contemporary Novel in Crisis*. N.Y.: McKay, 1966. 164-71.
B36	Moritz, Charles, ed. "John Updike." *Current Biographical Yearbook*, 1966 edition. N.Y.: Wilson, 1966. 412-15.
B37	Burgess, Anthony. "Language, Myth, and Mr. Updike." *Commonweal* 83 (11 Feb. 1966): 557-59.
B38	[Correction.] *New Republic* 154 (26 Mar. 1966): 40.
B39	Arnavon, Cyrille. "Les Romans de John Updike." *Europe* 54 (June 1966): 193-213.
B40	Sams, H W. "Updike to Win." *Journal of General Education* 18 (July 1966): 146-49.
B41	Toebasch, Wim. "Regionalistische Literatuur." *Vlaamse Gids* 50 (Dec. 1966): 676-77
B42	Hamilton, Alice and Kenneth. *John Updike: A Critical Essay*. Contemporary Writers in Christian Perspective. Ed. Roderick Jellema. Grand Rapids, Michigan: Eerdmans, 1967.
B43	Matson, Elizabeth. "A Chinese Paradox, But Not Much of One: John Updike in His Poetry." *Minnesota Review*. 7 (1967): 157-67.
B44	Stafford, William T. "Fiction: 1930 to the Present." *American Literary Scholarship: An Annual/1965*. Ed. James Woodress. Durham: Duke UP, 1967. 183, 185, 201.
B45	Walker, Warren S. *Twentieth-Century Short Story Explication: Interpretations, 1900-1966 of Short Fiction Since 1800*. 2nd ed. Hamden, Conn.: The Shoe String P, 1967. 644.

B46   Hainsworth, J. D. "John Updike." *Hibbert Journal* 65 (Spring 1967): 115-16.

B47   "Updike: No Encore Merited." *Reading* (Pa.) *Eagle* 11 Apr. 1967.

B48   Farrell, James T. "Literary Note." *American Book Collector* 17 (May 1967): 9.

B49   Wyatt, Bryant. "John Updike: The Psychological Novel in Search of Structure." *Twentieth Century Literature* 13 (July 1967): 89-96.

B50   Brewer, Joseph E. "The Anti-Hero in Contemporary Literature." *Iowa English Yearbook* 12 (Fall 1967): 55-60.

B51   "Updike to Receive Literary Degree." *Reading* (Pa.) *Times* 11 Oct. 1967.

B52   Rupp, Richard H. "John Updike: Style in Search of a Center." *Sewanee Review* 75 (Autumn 1967): 693-709. (Rpt. in his *Celebration in Postwar American Fiction 1945-1967*. Coral Gables, Fla.: U of Miami P, 1970. 41-57, 215-16.)

*B53   Bruning, Eberhard. "Tendenzen der Personlichkeitsgestaltung im amerikanischen egenwartsroman." *Zeitschrift für Anglistik un Amerikanistik* 16 (1968): 390-401.

B54   Caskey, Jefferson D. *Index to Poetry in Popular Periodicals, 1960-1964*. Westport, Conn.: Greenwood P, 1968. 201.

B55   Stafford, William T. "Fiction: The 1930s to the Present."*American Literary Scholarship: An Annual/1966*. Ed. James Woodress. Durham: Duke UP, 1968. 168, 181-82.

B56   Taylor, C. Clarke. *John Updike: A Bibliography*. Kent, Ohio: Kent State UP, 1968.

*B57   Killinger, John. "The Death of God in American Literature." *Southern Humanities Review* 2 (Spring 1968): 149-72.

B58   "Story Examines Updike's Career." *Reading* (Pa.) *Times* 24 Apr. 1968.

B59   "View from the Catacombs." *Time* 91 (26 Apr. 1968): 66-68, 73-75.

B60   "Updike Visits School." *Reading* (Pa.) *Times* 24 June 1968.

B61   Zuckerman, Jerome. *"Desperate Faith." Studies In Short Fiction* 50 (Sum. 1968): 387-88.

B62   Watkins, Stanley J. "John Updike Reminisces in 'Olinger'." *Reading* (Pa.) *Eagle* 24 June 1968.

B63   Gasca, Eduardo. *Literatura de la tierra baldía: John Updike*. Caracas, Venezuela: Ediciones de la Biblioteca Universidad Central de Venezuela, 1969.

B64   Samuels, Charles T. *John Updike*. U of Minnesota Pamphlets on American Writers, No. 79. Minn: U of Minn. P, 1969.

B65   "Film Company to Start Shooting 'Rabbit, Run' in Berks June 16." *Reading* (Pa.) *Eagle* 16 Mar. 1969.

B66   Petter [sic], Henri. "John Updike's Metaphoric Novels." *English Studies* 50 (Apr. 1969): 197-206.

B67   "'Rabbit, Run' Auditions to Begin Here." *Reading* (Pa.) *Eagle* 17 May 1969.

B68   Zaffiro, Vincent. "'Rabbit, Run' Role Runs Into a Warren." *Reading* (Pa.) *Eagle* 19 May 1969.

B69   Baldeshwiler, Eileen. "The Lyric Short Story: The Sketch of a History." *Studies in Short Fiction* 6 (Sum. 1969): 443-53. (Page 453 pertains to Updike.)

B70   "Newsmakers." *Newsweek* 74 (14 July 1969): 44. (Extract from "Minority Report" from *Midpoint*.)

B71   Reber, Carole. "'Rabbit, Run' Author Blending of Parents, Says *Eagle* Writer after Meeting Updikes." *Reading* (Pa.) *Eagle* 27 July 1969: 35, 44.

B72   "Film Aids Our Economy." *Reading* (Pa.) *Eagle* 31 July 1969: 1-2.

B73   "Ipswich Play Penned by Updike." *Reading* (Pa.) *Eagle* 5 Aug. 1969.

*B74   Hill, John S. "Quest for Belief: Theme in the Novels of John Updike." *Southern Humanities Review* 3 (Sept. 1969): 166-75.

B75   Gratton, Margaret. "The Use of Rhythm in Three Novels by John Updike." *University of Portland Review* 21 (Fall 1969): 3-12.

B76   Petillon, Pierre-Yves. "Le Désespoir de John Updike." *Critique* (Paris) 25 (Nov. 1969): 972-79. (Reviews French translations of *Rabbit, Run*, *The Centaur*, *Couples*, *Pigeon Feathers and Other Stories*, and *Of the Farm*.)

B77   Le Vot, André. "Le Petit Monde de John Updike." *Les Langues Modernes* 63 (Nov.-Dec. 1969): 66-73.

B78   Fiedler, Leslie. *Waiting for the End*. N.Y.: Stein and Day, 1970. 164.

B79	Gerstenberger, Donna and George Hendrick. *The American Novel: A Checklist of Criticism of Novels Written Since 1789. Volume II: Criticism Written 1960-68*. Swallow P, 1970. 349-51.
B80	Hamilton, Alice and Kenneth. *The Elements of John Updike*. Grand Rapids: Eerdmans, 1970.
B81	Hicks, Granville. "John Updike." In his *Literary Horizons: A Quarter Century of American Fiction*. New York UP, 1970. 107-33. (Reprinting for the *Saturday Review* of eight reviews from *The Poorhouse Fair* [17 Jan. 1959] to *Couples* [6 Apr. 1968] with an "Afterword," 132-33.)
B82	Justus, James H. "Fiction: The 1930s to the Present." *American Literary Scholarship: An Annual/1968*. Ed. James Woodress. Durham, N.C.: Duke UP, 1970. 220-21.
B83	Kort, Wesley. "John Updike's Fiction: Cross and Grace in *Beruf*." *Anglican Theological Review* 52 (1970): 151-67.
B84	Walker, Warren S. *Twentieth-Century Short Story Explication: Supplement I to Second Edition, 1967-1969*. The Shoe String P, 1970. 242-43.
B85	Vormweg, Heinrich. "John Updike: Verfall eines Realisten." *Merkur* 24 (Apr. 1970): 394-97.
B86	Aldridge, John. "An Askew Halo for John Updike." *Saturday Review* 53 (27 June 1970): 25-27, 35. (Includes a review of *Bech: A Book*. Rpt. as "John Updike and the Higher Theology" in his *The Devil in the Fire: Retrospective Essays in American Literature and Culture, 1951-1971*. N.Y.: Harper's Magazine P, 1972. 195-201.)
B87	Murray, Michele. "Profile of a Literary Hustler." *National Catholic Reporter* 24 July 1970: 13. (Concerns *Bech: A Book*.)
B88	"John Updike's First Film." *Ipswich Today* 28 Aug. 1970: 4-5.
B89	Richardson, Jack. "Keeping Up with Updike." *The New York Review of Books* 15 (22 Oct. 1970): 46-48.
B90	Gallagher, Charles M. "Characters Narrowed as 'Rabbit, Run' Unreels." *Reading* (Pa.) *Eagle* 29 Oct. 1970.
B91	Morgan, Roy J. "Updike Talks Reluctantly." *Reading* (Pa.) *Times* 27 Nov. 1970.
B92	"Updike Talks of his Work, and Film." Reading (Pa.) *Eagle* 29 Nov. 1970.
B93	Wolff, Geoffrey. "Critic's Choice 1970." *Newsweek* 76 (21 Dec. 1970): 94. (Selects *Bech: A Book*.)

B94 Burchard, Rachael C. *John Updike: Yea Sayings.* Carbondale: Southern Ill. UP, 1971.

B95 Detweiler, Robert. "*The Elements of John Updike*: Another Appraisal." *Newsletter of the Conference on Christianity and Literature* 20 (1971): 24-27. See **B109**.

B96 Gindin, James. "Megalotopia and the Wasp Backlash: The Fiction of Mailer and Updike." *Centennial Review* 15 (1971): 38-52. (Pages 43-51 concern Updike.)

B97 Perosa, Sergio. "Incontri Americani." *Studi Americani* 17 (1971): 379-438. (Pages 395-402 concern Updike.)

B98 Sokoloff, B. A. and David E. Arnason. *John Updike: A Comprehensive Bibliography.* Folcroft, Pa.: Folcroft P, 1971.

B99 Tanner, Tony. "A Compromised Environment." *City of Words: American Fiction, 1950-1970.* N.Y.: Harper 1971. 273-94.

B100 Taylor, Larry E. *Pastoral and Anti-Pastoral Patterns in John Updike's Fiction.* Carbondale: Southern Ill. UP, 1971.

B101 Zulaf, Sandor. With Irwin Weiser. *Index to American Periodical Verse.* Metuchen, N.J.: The Scarecrow P, 1971. 338.

B102 Hill, John S. "Updike: Story to Novel." *CEA Critic* 33 (Jan. 1971): 29. (Reviews Alice and Kenneth Hamilton's *The Elements of John Updike*.)

B103 "Newsmakers." *Newsweek* 77 (15 Feb. 1971): 49. (Includes Updike's comments on publication of his mother's *Enchantment*.)

B104 Duffy, Martha. "Locked in a Star." *Time* 98 (8 Mar. 1971): 80-81.

B105 Meyer, Arlin G. "The Theology of John Updike." *The Cresset* 34 (Oct. 1971): 23-25. (Reviews *John Updike: Yea Sayings* by Rachael Burchard, *The Elements of John Updike*, by Alice and Kenneth Hamilton, *Pastoral and Anti-Pastoral in the Fiction of John Updike*, by Larry Taylor and *John Updike: An Annotated Checklist*, by Michael Olivas.)

B106 Kattan, Naim. "L'éclatement du mythe." *Quinzaine Littéraire* No. 126 (1-15 Oct. 1971): 12.

B107 [Bech, Henry] "Henry Bech Redux." *The New York Times Book Review* 14 Nov. 1971: 3. See **A1165**.

B108 Ricks, Christopher. "Flopsy Bunny." *The New York Review of Books* 17 (16 Dec. 1971): 7-9.

B109 Detweiler, Robert. "*The Elements of John Updike*: Another Appraisal." *Newsletter of the Conference on Christianity and Literature* 20 (Wint. 1971): 24-27.

B110 Adelman, Irving and Rita Dworkin. *The Contemporary Novel: A Checklist of Critical Literature on the British and American Novel Since 1945*. Metuchen, N. J.: The Scarecrow P, 1972. 520-25.

B111 Detweiler, Robert. *John Updike*. N.Y.: Twayne, 1972.

B112 Finkelstein, Sidney. "The Anti-Hero of Updike, Bellow and Malamud." *American Dialog* 7 (1972): 12-14, 30.

B113 Holmes, Charles S. *The Clocks of Columbus: The Literary Career of James Thurber*. N.Y.: Atheneum, 1972. 307.

B114 Lyons, Eugene. "John Updike: The Beginning and the End." *Critique* 14 no. 2 (1972): 44-59.

B115 Stafford, William T. "The Curious Greased Grace of John Updike, Some of his Critics, and the American Tradition." *Journal of Modern Literature* II (1972): 569-75.

B116 Zulaf, Sandor, with Irwin Weiser. *Index to American Periodical Verse*. Metuchen, N. J.: The Scarecrow P, 1972. 375.

B117 "Updike Lauds National Medalist E. B. White." *Wilson Library Bulletin* XLVI (Feb. 1972): 489.

B118 Raymont, Henry. "102 Vie for 10 National Book Awards." *The New York Times* 27 Mar. 1972: 42.

B119 "Updike Named to Post." *Reading* (Pa.) *Eagle* 31 Mar. 1972.

B120 Richardson, Nicholas. "Nicholas Richardson on John Updike." *Spectator* 228 (8 Apr. 1972): 553.

B121 Sudderman, Elmer. *Carleton Miscellany* XII (Spring-Sum. 1972): 156-61.

B122 Bellman, Samuel Irving. "*John Updike: Yea Sayings* and *Pastoral and Anti-Pastoral in the Fiction of John Updike*." *Studies in Short Fiction* 9 (Sum. 1972): 293-96. (Reviews *John Updike: Yea Sayings* by Rachael Burchard and *Pastoral and Anti-Pastoral in the Fiction of John Updike*, by Larry Taylor.)

B123 Hamilton, Alice and Kenneth. "John Updike's Prescription for Survival." *The Christian Century* 89 (5 July 1972): 740-44.

B124 Tree, Christina. "Ipswich Brings Past to Life." *Boston Globe* 16 July 1972: 24B.

B125	Gallego, Candido Pérez. "La Novelística de John Updike." *Arbor* 82 (July/Aug. 1972) 73-84 (355-66).
B126	Todd, Richard. "Updike and Barthelme: Disengagement." *Atlantic* 230 (Dec. 1972): 126-132.
B127	Larsen, Richard B. "John Updike: The Story as Lyrical Meditation." *Thoth* 13 (1972-1973): 33-39. (Discusses "Wife-Wooing," "Harv is Plowing Now" and "Lifeguard.")
B128	Kazin, Alfred. "Professional Observers: Cozzens to Updike." *Bright Book of Life: American Novelists and Storytellers from Hemingway to Mailer.* Boston: Little, 1973. 95-124 (Pages 119-124 pertain to Updike.)
B129	Markle, Joyce B. *Fighters and Lovers: Theme in the Novels of John Updike.* N.Y.: NYUP, 1973.
B130	Nabokov, Vladimir. *Strong Opinions.* N.Y.: McGraw, 1973. 298.
B131	Vargo, Edward P. *Rainstorms and Fire.* Port Washington, N.Y.: Kennikat P, 1973.
B132	Walker, Warren S. *Twentieth-Century Short Story Explication: Supplement II to Second Edition.* The Shoe String P, 1973. 148-50.
B133	Zylstra, S. A. "John Updike and the Parabolic Nature of the World." *Soundings* 56 (1973): 323-37.
B134	Waite, Robert. "Updikes Visit Black Africa, Strangers in a Strange Land." *Hamilton Wenham Chronicle* 8 Mar. 1973: 1-9b.
B135	Hills, Rust. "Fiction." *Esquire* 79 (Apr. 1973): 30, 34, 38, 40.
B136	Hamilton, Alice and Kenneth. "Mythic Dimensions in Updike's Fiction." *North Dakota Quarterly* 41 no. 3 (Sum. 1973): 54-66.
B137	"Devil's Advocate." *Time* 102 (23 July 1973): 69. (Comments on Updike's Introduction to *Soundings in Satanism*.)
B138	Galloway, David D. "The Absurd Man as Saint: The Novels of John Updike." *The Absurd Hero in American Fiction: Updike, Styron, Bellow, Salinger.* Rev. ed. Austin: U of Tex. P, 1974. 21-50, 184-208.
B139	Samuels, Charles T. "John Updike." *American Writers: A Collection of Literary Biographies.* IV. N.Y.: Scribner's, 1974. 214-35.
*B140	Nemioanu, Virgil. "Povestiri de John Updike." *Romania Literaria* 31 (Jan. 1974): 28.

B141   Gingher, Robert S. "Has John Updike Anything to Say?" *Modern Fiction Studies* 20 (Spring 1974): 97-105.

B142   McCoy, Robert. "John Updike's Literary Apprenticeship on *The National Lampoon*." *Modern Fiction Studies* 20 (Spring 1974): 3-12.

B143   Meyer, Arlin G. and Michael A. Olivas. "Criticism of John Updike: A Selected Checklist." *Modern Fiction Studies* 20 (Spring 1974): 121-33.

B144   Stafford, William T., ed. *Modern Fiction Studies (John Updike Number)* 20 (Spring 1974). (Includes: Robert McCoy, "John Updike's Literary Apprenticeship on *The Harvard Lampoon*"; Joseph Waldmeir, "It's the Going That's Important, Not the Getting There: Rabbit's Questing Non Quest"; John B. Vickery, "*The Centaur*: Myth, History and Narrative"; Paula and Nick Backscheider, "Updike's *Couples*: Squeak in the Night"; Alan T. McKenzie, "'A Craftsman's Intimate Satisfactions': The Parlor Games in *Couples*"; Wayne Falke, "*Rabbit Redux*: Time/Order/God"; Robert Alton Regan, "Updike's Symbol of the Center"; Robert S. Gingher, "Has John Updike Anything to Say?"; Alfred F. Rosa, "The Psycholinguistics of Updike's 'Museums and Women'"; Albert J. Griffith, "Updike's Artist's Dilemma: 'Should Wizard Hit Mommy?'"; William T. Stafford, "Updike FourFiveSix, 'Just Like That': An Essay Review"; and Arlin G. Meyer and Michael A. Olivas, "Criticism of John Updike: A Selected Checklist." The last item was rpt. as Olivas, Michael A. *An Annotated Bibliography of John Updike Criticism, 1967-1973, and a Checklist of His Works*. N.Y.: Garland, 1975.)

B145   Regan, Robert A. "Updike's Symbol of the Center." *Modern Fiction Studies* 20 (Spring 1974): 77-96.

B146   McCullough, David. "Eye on Book." *Book-of-the-Month Club News* July 1974.

*B147   Gediman, Helen. "Reflections on Romanticism, Narcissism, and Creativity." *Journal of the American Psychoanalytic Association* 23 (1975): 407-23.

B148   Justus, James H. "Fiction: The 1930s to the Present." *American Literary Scholarship: An Annual/1973* Ed. James Woodress. Durham, N.C.: Duke UP, 1975. 171, 264, 265, and 297-98.

B149   Kunkel, Francis L. "John Updike: Between Heaven and Earth." In his *Passion and the Passion: Sex and Religion in Modern Literature*. Philadelphia: Westminster P, 1975. 75-98, 170-71.

B150   Olivas, Michael A. *An Annotated Bibliography of John Updike Criticism, 1967-1973, and a Checklist of His Works*. N.Y.: Garland, 1975. (Rpt. from Arlin G. Meyer and Michael A. Olivas, "Criticism of John Updike: A Selected Checklist." *Modern Fiction Studies* 20 [Spring 1974]: 121-33.)

B151 Peden, William. "Metropolis, Village, and Suburbia: The Short Fiction of Manners." *The American Short Story*. 2nd ed. Boston: Houghton, 1975. 30-68. (Pages 47-53 pertain to Updike.)

B152 Umphlett, Wiley Lee. "The Agony of Rabbit Angstrom: The Search for a Secure Self." In his *The Sporting Myth and the American Experience*. Lewisburg, Pa.: Bucknell UP, 1975. 145-56.

B153 Wakeman, John, ed. "John Updike." *World Authors 1950-1970*. N.Y.: The H. W. Wilson, 1975. 1464-67.

B154 Hendrikson, Paul. "Updike Run: At 42, Still Making 'Em Look Easy." *National Observer* (1 Mar. 1975): 7.

B155 "John Updike Reappointed to Library." *Reading* (Pa.) *Eagle* 1 May 1975.

B156 Oates, Joyce Carol. "Updike's American Comedies." *Modern Fiction Studies* 21 (Autumn 1975): 459-72. (Rpt. in *John Updike: A Collection of Critical Essays*. Ed. David Thorburn and Howard Eiland. Englewood Cliffs: Prentice, 1979. 53-68; and in *Modern Critical Views: John Updike*. Ed. Harold Bloom. N. Y.: Chelsea House, 1987. 57-68.)

B157 Allen, Mary. "John Updike's Love of 'Dull Bovine Beauty.'" *The Necessary Blankness: Women in Major American Fiction of the Nineteen Sixties*. Urbana: U of Illinois P, 1976. 97-132. (Rpt. in *Modern Critical Views: John Updike*. Ed. Harold Bloom. N.Y.: Chelsea House, 1987. 69-96.)

B158 Hamilton, Alice and Kenneth. "The Validation of Religious Faith in the Writings of John Updike." *Studies in Religion/Sciences Religieuses* 5 (1976): 275-85.

B159 Justus, James H. "Fiction: The 1950s to the Present." *American Literary Scholarship: An Annual/1974*. Ed. James Woodress. Durham, N.C.: Duke UP, 1976. 284, 288-92, 443, 447, 449, and 453.

B160 Lepper, Gary M. *A Bibliographical Introduction to Seventy-Five Modern American Authors*. Berkeley: Serendipity Books, 1976. 397-402.

B161 Nyren, Dorothy, Maurice Kramer, and Elaine Kramer. "John Updike." *A Library of Literary Criticism: Modern American Literature*. IV, Supplement to 4th edition. N.Y.: Ungar, 1976. 487-90.

B162 White, E. B. *Letters of E. B. White*. N.Y.: Harper, 1976. 469, 472-473, 507, 630-32.

B163 "Academy Elects Updike." *Reading* (Pa.) *Eagle* 3 Dec. 1976.

B164 "John Updike Raps Schools." *Reading* (Pa.) *Eagle* 9 Dec. 1976.

B165   Alter, Robert. "Updike, Malamud, and the Fire This Time." In Robert Alter, *Defenses of the Imagination: Jewish Writers and Modern Historical Crisis*. Philadelphia: Jewish Publication Society of America, 1977. 233-48. (Pages 241-48 concern the "Rabbit" trilogy.)

B166   Dickstein, Morris. *Gates of Eden*. N.Y.: Basic Books, 1977. 93-94.

B167   Harper, H. M. "John Updike: The Intrinsic Problem of Human Existence." In his *Desperate Faith: A Study of Bellow, Salinger, Mailer, Baldwin and Updike*. Chapel Hill, N. C.: U of N.C. P, 1977. 162-90.

B168   Justus, James H. "Fiction: The 1930s to the Present." *American Literary Scholarship: An Annual/1975*. Ed. James Woodress. Durham: Duke UP, 1977. 348, and 350.

B169   Steiner, Dorothea. "John Updike: From *Rabbit, Run* to *Marry Me*." In Erwin A. Sturzl. *Essays in Honour of Professor Tyrus Hillway*. Salzburg: Salzburg Institut für Englische Sprache und Literatur, 1977. 477-506.

B170   Walsh, John F. "Can John Updike Win a Nobel?" *Reading* (Pa.) *Eagle* 16 Jan. 1977.

B171   Park, Edwards. "Around the Mall and Beyond." *Smithsonian* 7 (Feb. 1977): 32-40. (Pages 38-40 concern Updike.)

B172   "Updike Involved in Suit." *Reading* (Pa.) *Eagle* 4 Feb. 1977.

B173   Clemons, Walter. "Cheever's Triumph." *Newsweek* 79 (14 Mar. 1977): 61-73. (Page 67 concerns Updike.)

B174   Zissa, Robert F. "Updike Discusses Reading." *Reading* (Pa.) *Eagle* 3 Apr. 1977.

B175   Borgman, Paul. "Beyond Survival: Leisure, Stalemate and Redemption in the Later Fiction of John Updike and Walker Percy." *Reformed Journal* 27 (Sept. 1977): 18-23.

*B176   Gardner, Peter. "Happy Moments at the Mailbox." *Bookviews* 1 (Sept. 1977): 10-13.

B177   Johnson, Robert K. "John Updike's Theological World." *The Christian Century* 94 (16 Nov. 1977): 1061-66.

B178   Donald, Miles. "The Fate of the Traditional Novel." *The American Novel in the Twentieth Century*. N.Y.: Barnes, 1978. 73-107. (Pages 90-107 concern Updike.)

B179   Gardner, John. *On Moral Fiction*. N.Y.: Basic Books, 1978. 98-100.

B180	Gearhart, Elizabeth A. *John Updike: A Comprehensive Bibliography with Selected Annotations.* Norwood, Pa.: Norwood, 1978.
B181	Hendin, Josephine. *Vulnerable People: A View of American Fiction Since 1945.* N.Y.: Oxford UP, 1978. 88-99.
B182	Hunt, George. "Updike's Pilgrims in a World of Nothingness." *Thought* 53 (1978): 384-400.
B183	Justus, James H. "Fiction: The 1950s to the Present." *American Literary Scholarship: An Annual/1976.* Ed. J. Albert Robbins. Durham: Duke UP, 1978. 308.
B184	Klinkowitz, Jerome. "John Updike." *American Novelists Since World War 2.* Ed. Jeffrey Helterman and Richard Layman. Detroit: Gale, 1978. 484-92.
B185	Meyer, Nicholas. "American Authors Assess Hollywood." *The Reporter 1978 49th Anniversary Issue* 1978: 68-78. (Page 78 concerns John Updike.)
B186	Seigel, Gary. "Rabbit Runs Down." *The Modern American Novel and the Movies.* Ed. Gerald Peary and Roger Shatzkin. N.Y.: Ungar, 1978. 247-55.
B187	Stevick, Philip. "Prolegomena to the Study of Fictional *Dreck*." *Comic Relief.* Ed. Sarah Cohend. Urbana: U of Ill. P, 1978. 263-80.
B188	Johnson, Robert K. "The 'Wisdom' of John Updike." *Duke Divinity School Review* 43 (Spring 1978): 112-27.
*B189	Campbell, Jeff H. "Updike's Honky Apocalypse: *Rabbit Redux*." *New Mexico Humanities Review* May 1978: 53-60. (Rpt. in significantly different form in his *Updike's Novels: Thorns Spell a Word.* Wichita Falls: Midwestern State UP, 1987. 97-158.)
B190	"Notes on People." *The New York Times* 3 May 1978: C-2.
B191	Lingeman, Richard R. "$1,250 for the Updike." *The New York Times Book Review* 21 May 1978: 55.
B192	"The Politics of Art." *The New York Times* 29 May 1978: A12.
B193	Cousins, Norman. "When American and Soviet Writers Meet." *Saturday Evening Post* 61 (24 June 1978): 42-45. (Page 42 pertains to Updike.).
B194	Fripp, Bill. "Everybody's Castle." *Boston Sunday Globe* 29 July 1978: 6.
B195	"The Signet Society Medal for Achievement in the Arts Awarded to John Updike, Class of 1954." *The John Updike Newsletter* No. 8 (Fall 1978): [p. 4].

B196   Atlas, James. "John Updike Breaks Out of Suburbia." *The New York Times Sunday Magazine* 10 Dec. 1978: 60-61, 63-64, 68-70, 72, 74, 76.

*B197   Buckley, William F., Jr. *New York* 11 (18 Dec. 1978): 93.

B198   Schopen, Bernard A. "Faith, Morality, and the Novels of John Updike." *Twentieth Century Literature* 24 (Wint. 1978): 523-35. (Rpt. in *Critical Essays on John Updike*. Ed. William R. Macnaughton, Boston: Hall, 1982. 195-206.)

B199   Bjorksten, Ingmar. *Leopardvackning: Tio Forfattare och dan utsatta borgerligheten*. Stockholm: Raben & Sjogren, 1979. 107-40. (In Swedish.)

B200   Justus, James H. "Fiction: The 1950s to the Present." *American Literary Scholarship: An Annual/1977*. Ed. James Woodress. Durham: Duke UP, 1979. 304, 326-27, and 507-08.

*B201   Mesher, David R. "Three Men on the Moon: Friedman, Updike, Bellow and Apollo Eleven." *Research Studies* 47 (1979): 67-75.

B202   Thorburn, David. *John Updike: A Collection of Critical Essays*. Ed. David Thorburn and Howard Eiland. Englewood Cliffs: Prentice, 1979. (Includes: David Thorburn, "Introduction: 'Alive in a Place and Time'"; Richard Gilman, "An Image of Precarious Life"; Dean Doner, "Rabbit Angstrom's Unseen World"; Richard Locke, "Rabbit's Progress"; Robert Alter, "Updike, Malamud, and the Fire This Time"; Joyce Carol Oates, "Updike's American Comedies"; Howard Eiland, "Play in *Couples*"; David Lodge, "Post-Pill Paradise Lost: *Couples*"; George Steiner, "*A Month of Sundays*: Scarlet Letters"; Josephine Hendin, "Updike as Matchmaker: *Marry Me*"; Joyce Markle, "*The Poorhouse Fair*: A Fragile Vision of Specialness"; Larry E. Taylor, "*The Centaur*: Epic Paean and Pastoral Lament"; Martin Price, "A Note on Character in *The Centaur*"; Edward P. Vargo, "Shrine and Sanctuary: *Of the Farm*"; Charles Thomas Samuels, "Family Quarrels in *Of the Farm*"; Robert Towers, "Updike in Africa"; Deborah McGill, "Boy's Life"; Robert Detweiler, "*The Same Door*: Unexpected Gifts"; Arthur Mizener, "Memory in *Pigeon Feathers*"; Michael Novak, "Updike's Search for Liturgy"; Charles Thomas Samuels, "*The Music School*: A Place of Resonance"; Jack Richardson,"Keeping Up with Updike: *Bech: A Book*"; Rosemary Dinnage, "At the Flashpoint: *Museums and Women*"; Richard Todd, "Disengagement in *Museums and Women*"; "Chronology"; and "Selected Bibliography." The articles by Lodge and Oates were rpt. in *Modern Critical Views: John Updike*. Ed. Harold Bloom. N.Y.: Chelsea House, 1987.)

B203   Thorburn, David. "Introduction: 'Alive in a Place and Time.'" *John Updike: A Collection of Critical Essays*. Ed. David Thorburn and Howard Eiland. Englewood Cliffs: Prentice, 1979. 1-9.

B204	Doody, Terrence. "Updike's Idea of Reification." *Contemporary Literature* 20 (Spring 1979): 204-20.
B205	"American Arts Academy in Annual Honors to 63." *The New York Times* 24 May 1979: C20.
*B206	Isenberg, Barbara. "Lord John: Publishing on the Press of Immortality." *Los Angeles Times* 22 July 1979.
B207	Asselineau, Roger. *The Transcendental Constant in American Literature.* N.Y.: NYUP, 1980. 3.
B208	Detweiler, Robert. "Updike's Sermons." *Americana-Austriaca V: Beritrage zur Amerikakunde.* Ed. Klaus Lanzinger. Vienna: Wilhelm Braumiller, 1980. 11-26. (Revised as "John Updike's Sermons" in Robert Detweiler, *Breaking the Fall: Religious Readings of Contemporary Fiction.* N.Y.: Harper, 1987. 91-121.)
B209	Greiner, Donald J. "John Updike." *American Poets Since World War 2.* Detroit: Gale, 1980. 327-34.
B210	Hunt, George. *John Updike and the Three Great Secret Things: Sex, Religion, and Art.* Grand Rapids: Eerdmans, 1980.
B211	Justus, James H. "Fiction: The 1950s to the Present." Ed. J. Albert Robbins. *American Literary Scholarship: An Annual/1978.* Durham, N.C.: Duke UP, 1980. 285, 289, 302-03, 440.
*B212	Klinkowitz, Jerome. *"John Updike: A Comprehensive Bibliography with Selected Annotations* by E. Gearhart." *Resources for American Literary Study.* 10, no. 1 (1980): 96-97.
B213	———."John Updike since *Midpoint." The Practice of Fiction in America: Writers from Hawthorne to the Present.* Ames: Iowa State UP, 1980. 85-97.
*B214	Markovitz, Irving. "John Updike's Africa." *Canadian Journal of African Studies* 14 (1980): 536-45.
B215	Somer, John and Barbara Eck Cooper. *American and British Literature 1945-1975; An Annotated Bibliography of Contemporary Scholarship.* Lawrence, Kans.: The Regents P, 1980.
B216	Uphaus, Suzanne Henning. *John Updike.* N.Y.: Ungar, 1980.
B217	Vinson, James and D. L. Kirkpatrick. *American Writers Since 1900.* Chicago: St. James P, 1980. 589-92.

B218   Roberts, Ray A. "John Updike: A Bibliographical Checklist: Section A--Primary Publications." *American Book Collector* 1, new series (Jan.-Feb. 1980): 5-12, 40-44.

B219   Roberts, Ray A. "John Updike: A Bibliographical Checklist: Section B—Secondary Publications." *American Book Collector* 1, new series (Mar.-Apr. 1980): 39-47.

*B220   Stuttaford, Genevieve. "*John Updike and the Three Great Secret Things.*" *Publishers Weekly* 24 Apr. 1980: 37.

B221   Thomas, Heather. "Is Updike Up to His Literary Tricks?" *Reading* (Pa.) *Eagle* 31 Aug. 1980.

B222   Stuttaford, Genevieve. "Lectures on Literature." *Publishers Weekly* 12 Sept. 1980: 22.

B223   Blechner, Michael Harry. "Tristan in Letters: Malory, C. S. Lewis, Updike." *Tristania* 6 (Autumn 1980): 30-37.

B224   Merkin, Daphne. "Learning from Nabokov: *Lectures on Literature.*" *The New Leader* 63 (20 Oct. 1980): 13-14.

B225   LaSalle, Peter. "*John Updike and the Three Great Secret Things: Sex, Religion and Art.*" *America* 130 (1 Nov. 1980): 273. (Reviews *John Updike and the Three Great Secret Things: Sex, Religion and Art*, by George Hunt.)

*B226   Stewart, Anne. "Styron, Updike, Bacall and Mailer Join in a Romp at Roseland." *People* 10 Nov. 1980: 144.

B227   Bailey, Peter. "Notes on the Novel-as-Autobiography." *Genre* 14 (1981): 79-83.

B228   Galloway, David D. "The Absurd Man as Saint: The Novels of John Updike." *The Absurd Hero in American Fiction*. Austin: U of Tex. P, 2nd rev. ed.. 1981. 17-80.

B229   Greiner, Donald J. "John Updike." *Dictionary of Literary Biography Yearbook: 1980*. Detroit: Gale, 1981. 107-16.

B230   —. *The Other John Updike: Poems/ Short Stories/ Prose/ Play*. Athens: Ohio UP, 1981.

B231   Hallissy, Margaret. "George Hunt's *John Updike and the Three Great Secret Things: Sex, Religion, and Art.*" *Christianity and Literature* 30. 4 (1981): 99-101.

B232   Nadeau, Robert. "John Updike." *Readings from the New Book on Nature: Physics and Metaphysics in the Modern Novel.* Boston: U of Mass. P, 1981. 95-120.

B233   Stafford, William T. *Modern Fiction Studies* 27 (1981): 374-77. (Review of *John Updike: A Collection of Critical Essays,* by David Thorburn and Howard Eiland; *John Updike,* by Suzanne Henning Uphaus; and *John Updike and the Three Great Secret Things: Sex, Religion and Art,* by George Hunt.)

B234   Vaughan, Philip H. *John Updike's Images of America.* Reseda: Mojave, 1981.

B235   Waller, Gary F. "Jocoserious or Without Qualities? The (Hi)story of Recent American Literature: Thorburn and Eiland's *John Updike: A Collection of Critical Essays.*" *Canadian Review of American Studies* 12, iii (1981): 413-23.

*B236   Wentz, R. "George Hunt's *John Updike and the Three Great Secret Things.*" *Rocky Mountain Review of Language and Literature* 35, iv (1981): 312-13.

B237   McConnell, Frank. "John Updike and the Great Secret Things." *National Catholic Reporter* 5 Mar. 1981: 17.

B238   Hamilton, Alice and Kenneth Hamilton. "Labyrinthine Ways." *The Christian Century* 98 (8 Apr. 1981): 394-95. (Reviews *John Updike and the Three Great Secret Things* by George Hunt.)

B239   Kakutani, Michiko. "'Be More Like Graham Greene, Dear.'" *The New York Times Book Review* 16 Aug. 1981: 3.

B240   ———. "Turning Sex and Guilt into an American Epic." *Saturday Review* 253 (Oct. 1981): 14-15, 20-22. (Rpt. in Michiko Kakutani, *Poet at the Piano.* N.Y.: Times Books, 1988. 80-88.)

B241   Wolcott, James. "Running On Empty." *Esquire* 96 (Oct. 1981): 20, 22-23.

B242   Hunt, George. "Religious Themes in the Fiction of John Updike and John Cheever." *New Catholic World* 224 (Nov.-Dec. 1981): 248-51.

*B243   Bowman, Diane Kim. "Flying High: The American Icarus in Morrison, Roth and Updike." *Perspectives on Contemporary Literature* 8 (1982): 10-17.

B244   Eiland, H. "Updike's Womanly Man." *Centennial Review* 26 (1982): 312-23.

B245   Fogel, S. "Biopsy: Biography: Uphaus's *John Updike.*" *Canadian Review of American Studies* 13. 2 (1982): 267-73.

B246   Hallissy, Margaret. "Donald Greiner's *The Other John Updike.*" *Christianity and Literature* 32. i (1982): 71-72.

B247   Hansen, Klaus. P. "Psychologie und religiöse Typologie bei John Updike." *Amerika Studien* 27 (1982): 119-39. ("Psychology and Religious Typology in John Updike's Fiction.") See **B327**.

B248   Klinkowitz, Jerome. "Fiction: The 1950s to the Present." *American Literary Scholarship: An Annual/1979.* Ed. James Woodress. Durham: Duke UP, 1982. 34, 284, 289-91, and 470.

B249   Macnaughton, William R. *Critical Essays on John Updike.* Boston: Hall, 1982. (Includes: William R. Macnaughton, "Introduction: A Survey of John Updike Scholarship in English"; Whitney Balliet, "Writer's Writer"; Granville Hicks, "A Little Good in Evil"; Arthur Mizener, "Behind the Dazzle is a Knowing Eye"; Renata Adler, "Arcadia, Pa."; Jonathan Miller, "Off-Centaur"; Anthony Burgess, "Language, Myth and Mr. Updike"; Michael Novak, "Son of the Group"; Jonathan Raban, "Talking Head"; Charles Samuels, "Updike on the Present"; William T. Stafford, from "The 'Curious Greased Grace' of John Updike"; Tony Tanner, "The Sorrow of Some Central Hollowness"; D. Keith Mano, "Doughy Middleness"; Gilbert Sorrentino, "Never on Sunday"; Alfred Kazin, from "Alfred Kazin on Fiction"; Joyce Carol Oates, "*The Coup* by John Updike"; Paul Theroux, "A Marriage of Mixed Blessings"; Gerry Brenner, "*Rabbit, Run*: John Updike's Criticism of the 'Return to Nature'"; H. Peter, "John Updike's Metaphoric Novels"; Alice and Kenneth Hamilton, "Metamorphosis Through Art: John Updike's 'Bech: A Book'" [*sic.*]; Robert Detweiler, "Updike's *Couples*: Eros Demythologized"; Larry Taylor, "The Wide-Hipped Wife and the Painted Landscape: Pastoral Ideals in *Of The Farm*"; Clinton S. Burhans, Jr., "Things Falling Apart: Structure and Theme in *Rabbit, Run*"; Suzanne Henning Uphaus, "*The Centaur*: Updike's Mock-epic"; Victor Strandberg, "John Updike and the Changing of the Gods"; Bernard A. Schopen, "Faith, Morality, and the Novels of John Updike"; George W. Hunt, "Reality, Imagination, and Art: The Significance of Updike's 'Best' Story"; James M. Mellard, "The Novel as Lyric Elegy: The Mode of Updike's *The Centaur*"; George J. Searles, "*The Poorhouse Fair*: Updike's Thesis Statement"; Gordon E. Slethaug, "*Rabbit Redux*: 'Freedom is Made of Brambles'"; Kathleen Verduin, "Fatherly Presences: John Updike's Place in a Protestant Tradition"; Gay Waller, "Stylus Dei or the Open-Endedness of Debate?: Success and Failure in *A Month of Sundays*"; and Joyce Markle, "*The Coup*: Illusions and Insubstantial Impressions." The article by Brenner is rpt. from David Thorburn. *John Updike: A Collection of Critical Essays.* Ed. David Thorburn and Howard Eiland. Englewood Cliffs: Prentice, 1979. The essay by Mellard is rpt. in *Modern Critical Views: John Updike.* Ed. Harold Bloom. N.Y.: Chelsea House, 1987.)

B250 Macnaughton, William R. "Introduction: A Survey of John Updike Scholarship in English." *Critical Essays on John Updike*. Ed. William R. Macnaughton. Boston: Hall, 1982. 1-36.

B251 May John R. "George Hunt's *John Updike and the Three Great Secret Things*." *Horizons* 9 (1982): 408-09.

B252 Oriard, Michael. *Dreaming of Heroes: American Sport Fiction, 1868-1980*. Chicago: Nelson-Hall, 1982. 160-69.

B253 Klinkowitz, Jerome. "Fiction: The 1950s to the Present." *American Literary Scholarship: An Annual/1980*. Ed. J. Albert Robbins. Durham: Duke UP, 1982. 323-25, 542-43.

B254 Seed, D. "Donald Greiner's *The Other John Updike*." *Journal of American Studies* 16.2 (1982): 280-82.

B255 Tallent, Elizabeth. *Married Men and Magic Tricks: John Updike's Erotic Heroes*. Berkeley: Creative Arts, 1982.

B256 Verduin, Kathleen. "Fatherly Presences: John Updike's Place in a Protestant Tradition." *Critical Essays on John Updike*. Ed. William R. Macnaughton. Boston: Hall, 1982. 254-68.

B257 Wilhelm, Albert E. "The Search for Meaningful Work in John Updike's Fiction." *Perspectives on American Business*. Ed. Don Harkness. Tampa: American Studies, 1982. 27-33. (Error in MLA bibliography: "The Search for Meaning: Work in John Updike's Fiction.")

B258 Weixlmann, Joe. *American Short Fiction Criticism and Scholarship, 1959-1977: A Checklist*. Athens: Swallow P/Ohio UP, 1982. 571-76.

B259 "Attorney Loses Libel Suit Against *New Yorker*, Updike." *Reading* (Pa.) *Eagle* 18 Feb. 1982.

B260 Amend, Edward. "George Hunt's *John Updike and the Three Great Secret Things*." *Journal of the American Academy of Religion* 50.1 (Mar. 1982): 162-64.

B261 Balitas, Vincent. "*The Other John Updike* by Donald Greiner." *American Literature* 54 (Mar.1982): 144-45.

B262 Brown, Carl W., Jr. "Rabbit Won." *Reading* (Pa.) *Times* 13 Apr. 1982: 1, 8.

B263 Kihss, Peter. "Sessions, Sylvia Plath and Updike Are Among Pulitzer Prize Winners." *The New York Times* (13 Apr. 1982): A1, B4.

B264 "Publication Award Won by Updike." *Reading* (Pa.) *Times* 13 Apr. 1982: 1.

B265   "Updike Had Lost Hope for Pulitzer." *Reading* (Pa.) *Eagle* 13 Apr. 1982.

B266   "Albright to Confer Degrees." *Reading* (Pa.) *Times* 19 May 1982.

B267   Gilmartin, David. "'Berks Boy' Updike Receives Degree." *Reading* (Pa.) *Times* 24 May 1982.

B268   "Literary Soirée for John Updike." *Chicago* 31 (June 1982): 16.

B269   Atlas, James. "Languid, But Never Dull." *Atlantic* 250 (Oct. 1982): 103-04.

B270   Gray, Paul. "Perennial Promises Kept." *Time* 120 (18 Oct. 1982): 72-74, 79-81.

B271   Robinson, Donald. "1982's Top 25 Americans Over 50." *50 Plus* Dec. 1982: 26-30. (Page 30 pertains to Updike.)

B272   Stafford, William T. "John Updike." *Modern Fiction Studies* 27 (Wint. 1982): 742-43. (Reviews *The Other John Updike* by Donald Greiner, and *John Updike: A Comprehensive Bibliography* by Elizabeth Gearhart.)

B273   Raith, Mark Allan. "Literature...A Salute to Updike and a Farewell to Cheever." *Reading* (Pa.) *Eagle* 26 Dec. 1982: 21, 25.

B274   Appasamy, S. P. "The Novelist as Poet: John Updike." *The Laurel Bough: Essays Presented in Honour of Professor M. V. Rama Sarma.* Ed. G. Nageswara Rao. Bombay: Blackie, 1983. iv. 153-64.

B275   Au, Bobbye G. "Contemporary Novels: A Reflection of Contemporary Culture." In *Modern American Cultural Criticism.* Ed. Mark Johnston. Warrensburg: Central Mo. State U, 1983. 99-105. (Pages 102-03 refer to Updike.)

B276   Balbert, P. "Exuberances of Style in Pynchon and Updike: A Panoply of Metaphor." *Studies in the Novel* 15 (1983): 265-76.

*B277   Bandic, Milos I. "Naslage cudesa u stvarnosti pesnistva." *Knjizevnost* 38 (1983): 1785-95.

B278   Greiner, Donald, adv. ed. "John Updike." *Dictionary of Literary Biography: Ed. Mary Bruccolli. Documentary Series: An Illustrated Chronicle.* Volume 3. Detroit: Gale, 1983. 251-320.

B279   ---. "John Updike." *Dictionary of Literary Biography Yearbook: 1982.* Ed. Richard Ziegfeld. Detroit: Gale, 1983. 195-200.

B280   ---. "John Updike." *Dictionary of Literature: Documentary Series.* Ed. Mary Bruccoli. Detroit: Gale, 1983. 251-320.

B281 Halio, Jay L. "Contemplation, Fiction, and the Writer's Sensiblity." *Southern Review* 1983. 19, i: 203-18.

B282 Karl, Frederick R. *American Fictions 1940-1980.* N.Y.: Harper, 1983. 35-36, 169-172, 251-52, 259-61, 347-55.

B283 Klinkowitz, Jerome. "Fiction: The 1960s to the Present." *American Literary Scholarship: An Annual/1981.* Ed. James Woodress. Durham, N.C.: Duke UP, 1983. 39 and 288-89.

B284 Macnaughton, William R. *Studies in American Fiction* 11 (1983): 268-69. (Reviews *John Updike and the Three Great Secret Things: Sex, Religion and Art*, by George Hunt and *The Other John Updike* by Donald Greiner.)

B285 Robison, James C. "1969-1980: Experiment and Tradition." *The American Short Story, 1945-1980.* Boston: Twayne, 1983. 77-110. (Pages 106-108 pertain to Updike.)

B286 Smith, Kent D. *Faith: Reflections on Experience, Theology and Fiction.* Lanham, Md.: UP of America, 1983.

B287 Walkiewicz, E. P. "1957-1968: Toward Diversity of Forms." *The American Short Story, 1945-1980.* Ed. Gordon Weaver. Boston: Twayne, 1983. 35-75. (Pages 40-44 pertain to Updike.)

B288 Coale, Samuel C. "Marriage in Contemporary American Literature: The Mismatched Marriages of Manichean Minds." *Thought* 58 (March 1983): 111-20.

B289 "Updike Honored by Commonwealth." *Reading* (Pa.) *Eagle* 20 Apr. 1983.

B290 "Another Honor Is Bestowed on Updike." *Reading* (Pa.) *Times* 23 Apr. 1983.

B291 "John Updike Receives Pennsylvania Award." *Reading* (Pa.) *Eagle* 3 May 1983.

B292 "Happy Medium." *Reading* (Pa.) *Eagle* 4 May 1983.

B293 Ecenbarger, William. "Updike Is Home." *The Philadelphia Inquirer Magazine* 12 June 1983: 19-21, 24-25.

B294 "What Makes Rabbit Run? A Profile of John Updike." *People* 27 June 1983: 11.

B295 Koehler, Ray. "Sorry, Video Cassette Eschews 'Rabbit'." *Reading* (Pa.) *Times* 16 July 1983.

B296 S. U. C. *Vogue* 173 (Sept. 1983): 98.

B297   Greiner, Donald J. "Pynchon, Hawkes, and Updike: Readers and the Paradox of Accessibility." *South Carolina Review* 16 (Fall 1983): 45-51.

B298   Harris, Robert R. "Rabbit in the Rough." *The New York Times Book Review* 30 Oct. 1983: 43.

B299   Detweiler, Robert. *John Updike*. Rev. ed. Boston: Hall, 1984.

B300   Greiner, Donald J. *John Updike's Novels*. Athens: Ohio UP, 1984. (The chapter "*The Coup*" was rpt. in *Modern Critical Views: John Updike*. Ed., Harold Bloom. N.Y.: Chelsea House, 1987. 139-53.)

B301   Klinkowitz, Jerome. "Fiction: The 1960s to the Present." *American Literary Scholarship: An Annual/1982*. Ed. J. Albert Robbins. Durham: Duke UP, 1984. 281-82, 473, 488-89, 498.

B302   ---. *Literary Subversions: New American Fiction and the Practice of Criticism*. Carbondale: Southern Ill. UP, 1984. 59-69.

B303   Lewicki, Zbigniew. *The Bang and the Whimper*. Westport: Greenwood, 1984. 110-14.

B304   Moritz, Charles, ed. "John Updike." *Current Biographical Yearbook*. N.Y.: Wilson, 1984. 413-17.

*B305   Spector, Judith. "Taking Care of Mom: Erotic Degradation, Dalliances, and Dichotomies in the Works of Just About Everyone." *The Sphinx* 4 (1984): 184-201.

B306   Walker, Warren S. *Twentieth-Century Short Story Explication: Supplement II to Third Edition*. The Shoe String P, 1984. 282-84.

B307   Baker, John F. "NBCC Announces Award Winners." *Publishers Weekly* 225 (20 Jan. 1984): 29.

B308   ---. "NBCC Awards: All Present and Eloquent." *Publishers Weekly* 225 (17 Feb. 1984): 32.

*B309   Pétillon, Pierre-Yves. "Hors du terrier natal." *Critique: Revue Générale des Publications Françaises et Etrangéres* 40 (Mar. 1984): 214-23.

B310   "Another Award for Updike." *Publishers Weekly* 225 (23 Mar. 1984): 15.

B311   Means, Howard. "*Rabbit, Run*." *Washingtonian* May 1984: 104.

B312   Hardwick, Elizabeth. "Citizen Updike." *The New York Review of Books* 36 (18 May 1984): 3. (Rpt. from *Book Digest* Dec. 1981.)

B313   Johnson, Diane. "Warlock." *The New York Review of Books* 14 June 1984: 3.

B314 Boasberg, Leonard W. "Updike Discusses Women's Underwear, Draws Laughs." *Reading* (Pa.) *Eagle* 20 June 1984.

B315 Sternhell, Carol. "Bellow's Typewriters and Other Tics of the Trade." *The New York Times Book Review* 2 Sept. 1984: 1, 21-22. (Page 21 pertains to Updike.)

B316 Miller, Miriam Youngerman. "A Land Too Ripe for Enigma: John Updike as Regionalist." *Arizona Quarterly* 40 (Autumn 1984): 197-218.

B317 "John Updike." *Current Biography* Oct. 1984: 38.

B318 L'Heureux, John. "The Best American Short Stories 1984." *The New York Times Book Review* 7 Oct. 1984. Sun. ed.: 41.

B319 Allen, Bryce. "*The Best American Short Stories 1984.*" *Saturday Review* 10 (Dec. 1984): 83.

B320 McLean, Milly. "'Rabbit, Run' Author Slows Down." *Reading* (Pa.) *Eagle* 9 Dec. 1984: C-20-21.

B321 Adams, Timothy Dow. "Neither out Far nor in Deep: Religion and Suburbia in the Fiction of John Cheever, John Updike, and Walker Percy." In *Literature and the Visual Arts in Contemporary Society*. Ed. Suzanne Ferguson and Barbara Grosecloses. Columbus: Ohio State UP, 1985. 47-72.

B322 Bozeman, Pat. *John Updike: An Exhibition*. M. D. Anderson Library: U Park, Tex.: 1985.

B323 Coale, Samuel C. "The Beauty of Duality." In *Hawthorne's Shadow: American Romance from Melville to Mailer*. Lexington: Ky. UP, 1985. 123-46.

B324 Denisova, Tamara Naumovna. "The Problem of the Self in the Contemporary American Realistic Novel: The Self and Morality in the Postwar Novel." *Ekzistentsialism i sovremennyi amerikanskii roman* [*Existentialism and the Contemporary American Novel.*] Kiev. 1985.

B325 Greiner, Donald J. *Adultery in the American Novel: Updike, James, and Hawthorne*. Columbia: The USC P, 1985. 3-71, 97-131.

B326 Grobel, Lawrence. *Conversations with Capote*. N.Y.: New American Library, 1985. 36, 129, 141-42.

B327 Hansen, Klaus P. "Psychologie und religiöse Typologie bei John Updike." *Amerikastudien-American Studies* 27 (1985): 119-39. See **B247**.

B328 Klinkowitz, Jerome. "Fiction: The 1950s to the Present." *American Literary Scholarship: An Annual/1983.* Ed. Warren G. French. Durham: Duke UP, 1985. 301, 309, 314, and 505.

B329 Matthews, John T. "Intertextuality and Originality: Hawthorne, Faulkner, Updike." *Intertextuality in Faulkner.* Ed. Michel Gresset and Noel Polk. Jackson: U of Mississippi P, 1985. 144-57.

*B330 Patanjali, V. R. "John Updike's Fiction and His Themes." *The Literary Endeavour* 6 (1985): 114-19.

B331 Schlueter, Paul and June Schlueter. "John Updike." *Modern American Literature: A Library of Literary Criticism.* Volume V, Supplement to 4th Edition. N.Y.: Ungar, 1985. 504-09, 601.

B332 Searles, George J. *The Fiction of Philip Roth and John Updike.* Carbondale: Southern Ill. UP, 1985.

B333 Weber, Ronald. *Seeing Earth: Responses to Space Exploration.* Athens: Ohio UP, 1985. 26-27, 62-65, 72, 89-91, 93.

B334 Lehman, David. "A Silver Age of Short Stories." *Newsweek* 105 (14 Jan. 1985): 68. (Reviews *The Best American Short Stories: 1984*, ed. by Updike.)

B335 "K[utztown] U[niversity] Foundation Plans to Honor Berks Novelist." *Reading* (Pa.) *Eagle* 7 Mar. 1985.

B336 Hamilton, Kenneth. "John Updike's Novels." *The Christian Century* 102 (20 Mar. 1985): 302. (Reviews *John Updike's Novels* by Donald Greiner.)

B337 Wolcott, James. "A Scorecard for the All-American Literary All-Star Game." *Vanity Fair* June 1985: 14, 16.

B338 Stafford, William T. *Modern Fiction Studies* 31 (Summer 1985): 415-16. (Review of Robert Detweiler, *John Updike*; George Searles, *The Fiction of Philip Roth and John Updike*; and Donald Greiner, *John Updike's Novels.*)

B339 "Updike Tales to Be Subject of Program." *Reading* (Pa.) *Eagle* 7 Nov. 1985.

B340 Koehler, Ray. "A Journey to Updike Country." *Reading* (Pa.) *Times* 12 Nov. 1985.

B341 Morey, Ann-Janine. "Beyond Updike: Incarnated Love in the Novels of Mary Gordon." *The Christian Century* 102 (20 Nov. 1985): 1059-63. (Pages 1059-60 pertain to Updike.)

B342 Wright, Stuart. "John Updike's Contributions to *Chatterbox*." *Bulletin of Bibliography* 42 (Dec. 1985): 171-78.

B343	Bodmer, George R. "Sounding the Fourth Alarm: Identity and the Masculine Tradition in the Fiction of Cheever and Updike." In *Gender Studies: New Directions in Feminist Criticism*. Ed. Judith Spector. Bowling Green, Ohio: Popular, 1986. 148-61.
B344	Cosgrove, William. "Donald Greiner. *Adultery in the American Novel: Updike, James, and Hawthorne*." *South Carolina Review* 19 (1986): 88-90.
B345	Curley, Dorothy Nyren, Maurice Kramer, and Elaine Kramer. "John Updike." *A Library of Literary Criticism: Modern American Literature* Vol. III, Part 2. N.Y.: Ungar, 1986. 289-94, 455.
B346	Greiner, Donald J. "John Updike." *Contemporary Authors Bibliographical Series*. Vol. I. Ed. James J. Martine. Detroit: Gale, 1986. 347-82.
B347	Hart, James. D. "John Updike." *The Concise Oxford Companion to American Literature*. N.Y.: Oxford UP, 1986. 415-16.
B348	"John Updike." *The Reader's Advisor: A Layman's Guide to Literature*. N.Y.: R. R. Bowker, 1986. 13th Edition, Volume 1. 574-76.
B349	Klinkowitz, Jerome. "Fiction: The 1950s to the Present." *American Literary Scholarship: An Annual/1984*. Ed. J. Albert Robbins. Durham: Duke UP, 1986. 270, 311-12, 440-41.
*B350	Lawson, L. "*John Updike's Novels* by Donald Greiner." *South Atlantic Review* 51. 3 (1986): 108-11.
B351	Villaverde, Fernando. "'Imagination of State' Comes Alive at Writers' PEN." *The Miami Herald* 19 Jan. 1986: 7-C.
B352	Kinsella, Rebbie. "Pigeon Feathers and Witches." *Christianity Today* 30 (7 Mar. 1986): 60.
B353	Salgas, Jean-Pierre. "Hawthorne, Melville, Whitman et l'expérience américaine." *La Quinzaine Littéraire* 462 (May 1986): 11-12.
B354	Koehler, Ray. "Literary Giant Wipes out Seminar." *Reading* (Pa.) *Eagle* 5 June 1986.
B355	Harris, Charles B. "Updike and Roth: The Limits of Representationalism." *Contemporary Literature* 27 (Sum. 1986): 279-84.
B356	Winkler, Willi. "Eine amerikanische Zeitgeschichte: Uber John Updike." *Merkur* 40 (Aug. 1986): 689-93.
B357	Chesnick, Eugene W. "Individual Authors: Donald Greiner's *John Updike's Novels*." *Journal of Modern Literature* 13 (Nov. 1986): 546-47.

*B358 Wang, Changrong. "American Fiction of the 1960s and 1970s as a Laboratory of Language." *Waiguoyu* 6 (Nov. 1986): 59-63.

B359 Crews, Frederick. "Mr. Updike's Planet." *The New York Review of Books* 33 (4 Dec. 1986): 7-10, 12, 14.

B360 Aptly, Keith. "The Nine Lives of Literary Realism." *Contemporary American Fiction*. Ed. Malcolm Bradbury and Sigmund Ro. London: Arnold, 1987. 1-16.

B361 Bloom, Harold. "Introduction." *Modern Critical Views: John Updike*. N.Y.: Chelsea House, 1987. 1-8.

B362 Bloom, Harold. Modern *Critical Views: John Updike*. N.Y.: Chelsea House, 1987. (Includes: Harold Bloom, "Introduction"; John W. Aldridge, "The Private Vice of John Updike"; Richard H. Rupp, "John Updike; Style in Search of a Center"; David Lodge, "Post-Pill Paradise Lost: John Updike's *Couples*"; Tony Tanner, "A Compromised Environment"; Joyce Carol Oates, "Updike's American Comedies"; Mary Allen, "John Updike's Love of 'Dull Bovine Beauty'"; James M. Mellard, "The Novel as Lyric Elegy: The Mode of Updike's *The Centaur*"; Jane Barnes, "John Updike: A Literary Spider"; Cynthia Ozick, "Bech, Passing"; Donald J. Greiner, "*The Coup*"; Chronology; and Bibliography. Articles by Lodge and Oates were rpt. from *John Updike: A Collection of Critical Essays*. Ed. David Thorburn and Howard Eiland. Englewood Cliffs: Prentice, 1979. Allen's piece was rpt. from her *The Necessary Blankness: Women in Major American Fiction of the Nineteen Sixties*. Urbana: U of Illinois P, 1976. 97-132.)

B363 Campbell, Jeff H. *Updike's Novels: Thorns Spell a Word*. Wichita Falls: Midwestern State UP, 1987.

B364 Falsey, Elizabeth A. *The Art of Adding and the Art of Taking Away: Selections from John Updike's Manuscripts, an Exhibition at the Houghton Library*. Cambridge: Harvard College Library, 1987.

B365 Greiner, Donald J. and Elizabeth. A. Falsey. "John Updike." *First Printings of American Authors: Contributions Toward Descriptive Checklists*. Volume V. Ed. Philip B. Eppard. Detroit: Gale, 1987. 329-43.

B366 Klinkowitz, Jerome. "Fiction: The 1960s to the Present." *American Literary Scholarship: An Annual/1985*. Ed. J. Albert Robbins. Durham: Duke UP, 1987. 42, 155, 278, 279, 280, 282, 284, 287-88, 416, 419, 485, 492.

B367 Moramarco, Fred. "Speculations: Contemporary Poetry and Painting." *Mosaic* 20. 3 (1987): 23-36. (Concerns "Gradations of Black.")

General Commentary 161

B368 Patrick, D. L. Introductions by Lewis Leary, and Warren French. "John Updike." *Reference Guide to American Literature*. Chicago: St. James P, 1987. 547-49.

B369 Walker, Warren S. *Twentieth-Century Short Story Explication: Supplement III to Third Edition*. The Shoe String P, 1987. 393-94.

B370 Abbey, Edward. "Reading Updike." *Nation* 244 (28 Mar. 1987): 409-410. (Concerns *Roger's Version*.)

B371 Greiner, Donald J. "Updike on Hawthorne." *The Nathaniel Hawthorne Review* 13 (Spring 1987): 1-4.

B372 "Susquehanna Gives Updike Doctorate." *Reading* (Pa.) *Eagle* 17 May 1987: D-3.

B373 Leithauser, Brad. "Light Verse: Dead but Remarkably Robust." *The New York Times Book Review* 7 June 1987: 1, 26-27. (Page 26 concerns Updike.)

B374 Cheever, Benjamin. *The Letters of John Cheever*. N.Y.: Simon, 1988. 280, 285-87, 294-95, 298, 312, 321, 326-27, 354-55, 362, 363-64, 366-67, 372.

B375 Donaldson, Scott. *John Cheever: A Biography*. N.Y.: Random, 1988. 137, 156, 206, 213, 214-16, 222, 241-42, 252, 259-60, 266, 286, 288, 293, 300, 318-19, 322, 339, 341, 345, 357-58.

*B376 Eckley, Wilton. *From Mice to Rabbits*. Bled, Slovenia, Yugoslavia, 1988.

B377 Fishman, Ethan. *Natural Law and Right in Contemporary American Middle-Class Literature*. Ernest J. Yarnella and Lee Sigelman. N.Y.: Greenwood, 1988. 110-12.

B378 Hamilton, Ian. *In Search of J. D. Salinger*. N.Y.: Random, 1988. 181-82.

B379 Hansen, Klaus. "'Mimesis— You Can't Beat It': Die neuartige— Traditionalität des John Updike." In Gerhard Hoffmann, *Der zietgenössische amerikanische Roman*. Munchen: Fink, 1988, Volume 3, *Von der Modern zur Postmoderne*. 313-33.

B380 ---. "John Updike." *Der zietgenössische amerikanische Roman, von den Moderne zur Postmoderne*. Vol. 3. ed. Gerhard Hoffmann. Munchen: Fink, 1988. 313-33.

B381 Kahn, E. J., Jr. *Year of Change: More About The New Yorker and Me*. N.Y.: Viking, 1988. 76, 78, 96, 267.

B382 Johnson, Claudia D. "Hawthorne." *American Literary Scholarship: An Annual/1986*. Ed. David J. Nordloh. Durham: Duke UP, 1988. 36-37, 288, 291, 301, 404, 408, 422, and 443.

B383   Newman, Judie. *John Updike*. N.Y.: St. Martin's, 1988.

B384   Ristoff, Dilvo I. *Updike's America: The Presence of Contemporary American History in John Updike's Rabbit Trilogy*. N.Y.: Lang, 1988.

B385   Wood, Ralph C. *The Comedy of Redemption: Christian Faith and Comic Vision in Four American Novelists*. South Bend: U of Notre Dame P, 1988. 178-206.

B386   Lurie, Alison. "The Woman Who Rode Away." *The New York Review of Books* 35 (12 May 1988): 3-4.

B387   "Updike Receives Prestigious Prize." *Reading* (Pa.) *Eagle* 20 Nov. 1988: E-21.

B388   "Albright Program to Focus on Author Updike's Locales." *Reading* (Pa.) *Eagle* 27 Nov. 1988: A-18.

B389   Conn, Peter. *Literature in America: An Illustrated History*. N.Y.: Cambridge UP, 1989. 48b-8L.

B390   Greiner, Donald J. "John Updike." *Broadening Views, 1968-88: Concise Dictionary of American Literature Biography*. Detroit: Gale, 1989. 276-297.

B391   Klinkowitz, Jerome. "Fiction: The 1960s to the Present." Woodress, James. *American Literary Scholarship: An Annual/1987*. Ed. James Woodress. Durham: Duke UP, 1989. 33, 294, 341, 415, 428, 429, 467, 478, and 498.

B392   Leo, John. "John Updike." *Guide to American Poetry Explication*. Volume 2: *Modern and Contemporary*. Boston: Hall, 1989. 447-49. (Incorrectly lists "Pigeon Feathers" as a poem.)

B393   Luscher, Robert M. "*John Updike* by Judie Newman." *American Literature* 61 (1989): 325-27.

B394   Nabokov, Vladimir. Letter to William Maxwell. *Selected Letters 1940-1977*. Harcourt, 1989. 358. (Rpt. in *The John Updike Newsletter* No. 4 [Fall 1977]: [4].)

B395   ---. Letter to John Updike. *Selected Letters 1940- 1977*. Harcourt, 1989. 526.

*B396   Northouse, Cameron, ed. *John Updike: A Bibliography of Research and Criticism, 1970-1986, with a descriptive checklist of first printings of John Updike's works*. Dallas: Contemporary Research Associates, 1989. (The sole copy of this work is in the Library of Congress.)

*B397   Saueressig, Heinz. *Arzte und Arztliches: Essayistische Anregungen*. Sigmaringendorf: Regio Verlag Glock und Lutz, 1989.

*B398 Selby, Mabel M. Updike. *History of the John Updike Family*. Denver, Colo.: Sherry Redd-Kelly-Strobel, 1989.

B399 Walker, Warren S. *Twentieth-Century Short Story Explication: Supplement IV to Third Edition*. The Shoe String P, 1989. 281-82.

B400 Wear, Delese. "What Literature Says to Preservice Teachers and Teacher Educators." *Journal of Teacher Education* 40 (Jan. 1989): 51-55.

B401 Brofman, John. "Inside Updike." *Life* 12 (Mar. 1989): 10.

B402 Neary, John M. "'Ah, Runs': Updike, Rabbit, and Repetition." *Religion and Literature* 21 (Spring 1989): 89-110.

B403 Rohland, Pamela. "Classmates Fondly Recall 'The Sage of Plowville.'" *Reading* (Pa.) *Eagle* 16 Apr. 1989: E-1.

B404 ----. "Updike Remembered." *Reading* (Pa.) *Eagle* 16 Apr. 1989: E-1-2. (Photos)

B405 Fleischauer, John F. "John Updike's Prose Style: Definition at the Periphery of Meaning." *Critique* 30 (Sum. 1989): 277-90.

B406 Pinsker, Sanford. "General Studies: John Updike." *Journal of Modern Literature* 16 (Fall 1989): 220, 261, 415, 254-55.

B407 Brown, Clarence "Pen Pals." *The New Republic* 118 (2 Oct. 1989): 40-41. (Reprints "Still of Some Use" in *The Human Experience: Contemporary American and Soviet Fiction and Poetry*. Ed. The Soviet/American Joint Editorial Committe.)

B408 "Mother of Updike Dies at 85." *Reading* (Pa.) *Eagle* 12 Oct. 1989: 53.

B409 Koehler, Ray. "Stunning the Audience." *Reading* (Pa.) *Eagle* 15 Oct. 1989: A-9.

B410 Abrams, Mark. "'No One Can Escape the Predator.'" *Reading* (Pa.) *Eagle* 2 Nov. 1989: 9.

B411 ----. "'No One Can Escape the Predator.'" *Reading* (Pa.)*Eagle* 6 Nov. 1989: 9.

B412 "Updike Books Wonderful Gift." *Reading* (Pa.) *Eagle* 15 Nov. 1989: 4.

B413 Miller, Karen L. "Updike Reflects on 'Shillington Thoughts'/ His Mother's Death Leaves a Certain Sadness for Writer." *Reading* (Pa.) *Eagle* 10 Dec. 1989: E-1.

B414 Wood, Ralph C. "Karl Barth, John Updike and the Cheerful God." *Books and Religion* 16 (Wint. 1989): 5, 26-31.

B415 Yanofsky, Joe. "Smiles of a Lucky Man," Montreal *Gazette* 23 Dec. 1989: H-9.

B416 Klinkowitz, Jerome. "Fiction: The 1960s to the Present." *American Literary Scholarship: An Annual/1988*. Ed. J. Albert Robbins. Durham: Duke UP, 1990. 300-01, 471, 499, 515, 518, 539.

B417 Stout, Cushing. "In Hawthorne's Shadow: The Minister and the Women in Howells, Adams, Frederic, and Updike." In his *Making of an American Tradition*. New Brunswick, N.J.: Rutgers UP, 1990. 22-39.

B418 Weber, Bruce. "As Good a Writer's Mother as One Could Ask For." *The New York Times Book Review* 14 Jan. 1990: 11.

B419 Rudman, Mark. "An Erotics of Contemplation" *Art News* 89 (Feb. 1990): 104.

B420 Lasseter, Victor K. "*Updike's America: The Presence of Contemporary American History in John Updike's Rabbit Trilogy*." *American Literature* 62 (Mar. 1990): 153. (Reviews *Updike's America*, by Dilvo I. Ristoff.)

B421 "Updike autographs program of Shillington High School class of 1950 reunion." *Reading* (Pa.) *Eagle* 10 June 1990: 2.

*B422 Dodson, James. "18 Holes with...John Updike." *Golf Magazine* 32 (July 1990): 108-114.

*B423 Coates, Joseph. "Fall Harvest." *Chicago Tribune* 14 (15 July 1990): 14, 1:1.

B424 Seed, David. "John Updike." *Journal of American Studies* 24 (Aug. 1990): 288-89. (Reviews *John Updike*, by Judie Newman.)

B425 Gray, Paul. "Rabbit Stew." *Time* 136 (24 Aug. 1990): 13.

B426 Streitfeld, David. "Family Pictures." *Washington Post Book Week* 23 Sept. 1990: 15. (Review of *U and I*, by Nicholson Baker.)

*B427 Feeney, Mark. "John Updike." *Boston Globe* 21 Oct. 1990: B-22.

B428 "Another 'Rabbit' Movie Due?" *Reading* (Pa.) *Eagle* 24 Oct. 1990: 24.

B429 Trueheart, Charles. "Sex, God and John Updike." *Washington Post* 116 (28 Oct. 1990): F-1.

*B430 Gatlin, Josh. "Character Assassination." *Los Angeles Times* 4 Nov. 1990: E-1:2.

B431 Mabe, Chauncey. "Updike Up-close." *Miami* (Fla.) *Herald* 11 Nov. 1990: E-1, 6.

*B432   Italie, Hillel. "Updike Bids Farewell to the 'Rabbit.'" *Houston Post* 25 Nov. 1990: C-7.

B433   Astor, David. "Updike Is Honored by Cartoonists." *Editor & Publisher* 15 Dec. 1990: 36. (Updike receives the National Cartoonists Society's ACE Award for "Amateur Cartoonist Extraordinary.")

B434   Baker, Nicholson. *U and I*. N.Y.: Random House, 1991.

B435   Boyd, Brian. *Vladimir Nabokov: The American Years*. Princeton: Princeton UP, 1991. 477, 483, 485, 542, 557n, 567-68, 576, 608, 654, 662.

*B436   Brownstone, David M. and Irene M. Franck. *People in the News*. N.Y.: Macmillan, 1991. 3009-13.

B437   Cheever, John. *The Journals of John Cheever*. Ed. Robert Gottlieb. N.Y.: Knopf, 1991. 195-96, 247, 330, and 323-24.

B438   Neary, John M. *Something and Nothingness: The Fiction of John Updike and John Fowles*. Carbondale, Ill.: Southern Ill. UP, 1991. (Chapters 3, 5, and 6 concern Updike.)

B439   Klinkowitz, Jerome. "John Updike." *Academic American Encyclopedia*. Grolier: Danbury, Conn., 1991. 473.

B440   Rollyson, Carl. *The Lives of Norman Mailer*. N.Y.: Paragon, 1991. 326, 342.

*B441   Singh, Sukhbir. *The Survivor in Contemporary American Fiction: Saul Bellow, Bernard Malamud, John Updike, Kurt Vonnegut, Jr.* Delhi, India: B. R., 1991.

B442   "Updike and Caro Win Book Critics Award." *The New York Times* 17 Feb. 1991: Sec. 1: 44.

B443   "Updike Honored by Critics." *Reading* (Pa.) *Eagle* 17 Feb. 1991: A-9.

*B444   "National Book Critics Salute Best of '90." *Boston Globe* 18 Feb. 1991: 32.

B445   "Updike Right on Writing AND Reading." *Reading* (Pa.) *Eagle* 25 Feb. 1991: 8.

B446   Steinberg, Sybil. "Knopf Authors Win Two of Five National Book Critics Circle Awards." *Publishers Weekly* 238 (1 Mar. 1991): 20.

B447   De Bellis, Jack. "Updike: A Selected Checklist 1974-1990." *Modern Fiction Studies* 37 (Spring 1991): 129-56.

B448   Ra'ad, Basem. "Updike's New Versions of Myth in America." *Modern Fiction Studies* 37 (Spring 1991): 25-33.

*B449   Powers, Katherine A. "Literary Boston: Mind Benders." *Boston* 83 (Apr. 1991): 50-54.

*B450   Marshall, Steve. "Updike Snares Second Pulitzer." *USA Today* 119 (10 Apr. 1991): A-2.

B451   "Correction." *Washington Post* 114 (11 Apr. 1991): A-3.

B452   Kakutani, Michiko. "What John Updike Means to Him." *The New York Times* 140 (12 Apr. 1991): C-27. (Reviews *U and I*, by Nicholson Baker.)

B453   Farrell, Joseph N. "Insight Came to Updike the Outsider." *Reading* (Pa.) *Eagle* 13 Apr. 1991.

B454   Frumkes, Lewis Burke. "Mr. Updike, I'm Your Biggest Fan." *The New York Times* 14 Apr. 1991: 12. (Review of *U and I*, by Nicholson Baker.)

*B455   ——. "Nicholson Baker's *U and I*." *The New York Herald Tribune Book Review* 14 Apr. 1991: 12.

*B456   Taylor, Robert. "Nicholson Baker Writes about the Updike He Imagines." *Boston Globe* 17 Apr. 1991: 33. (Review of *U and I*, by Nicholson Baker.)

*B457   Wood, James. "You Don't Give No Lip to Big John." *Guardian* 18 Apr. 1991: 23. (Review of *U and I*, by Nicholson Baker.)

*B458   Kosman, Joshua. "Updike, from Memory." *San Francisco Chronicle* 28 Apr. 1991: Rev.: 5. (Review of *U and I*, by Nicholson Baker.)

*B459   Carroll, Jon. "A Riches of Embarrassment." *San Francisco Chronicle* 29 Apr. 1991: Sec. D-6. (Review of *U and I*, by Nicholson Baker.)

B460   Dirda, Michael. "Rabbit Pursuit: 'A Passion for Updike.'" *Washington Post Book Week* 114 (6 May 1991): B-3. (Review of *U and I*, by Nicholson Baker.)

*B461   Eder, Richard. "Psoriasis and All." *Los Angeles Times* 12 May 1991: BR: 2. (Review of *U and I*, by Nicholson Baker.)

B462   Cooper, Rand Richards. "Rabbit Loses the Race: John Updike's 'Small Answer of a Texture.'" *Commonweal* (17 May 1991): 315-21.

B463   Slater, Joyce. "Updike's Biggest Fan Puts Pen to His Affection." *Atlanta Journal Constitution* 19 May 1991: N-11. (Review of *U and I*, by Nicholson Baker.)

General Commentary 167

*B464 Slater, Joyce. "'Growing Up with John Updike, Sort Of.'" *Houston Post* 26 May 1991: C-6. (Review of *U and I*, by Nicholson Baker.)

B465 "America's Suburban Chronicler: John Updike." *Vis-a-Vis* (United Airlines in-flight magazine). June 1991: 26. (Photo of Updike by Yusaf Karsh.)

B466 Wilson, Mike. "Biographical Essay on Updike Effusive in Praise." *Reading* (Pa.) *Eagle* 2 June 1991: F-12. (Review of *U and I*, by Nicholson Baker.)

B467 Pinsker, Sanford. "William Faulkner and My Middle East Problem." *Virginia Quarterly Review* 67 (Sum. 1991): 397-415. (Pages 412-14 concern Updike.)

B468 Shult, Douglas. "Updike and I: The Story of a Novel Fixation." *Los Angeles Times* 28 June 1991, E-1. (Review of *U and I*, by Nicholson Baker.)

B469 Cheever, John. "Journals: From the Seventies and Early Eighties— II." *New Yorker* 67 (19 Aug. 1991): 27. (Rpt. in *The Journals of John Cheever*. N.Y.: Knopf, 1991. 323-24.)

B470 Wind, James P. "Clergy Lives: Portraits from Modern Fiction." *The Christian Century* 100 (4 Sept. 1991): 805-10.

*B471 Raymo, Chet. "The Psalmist and the Astronomer." *Boston Globe* 11 Nov. 1991: 28.

B472 Brown, Carl W., Jr. "Updike Pays Homage to Mom." *Reading* (Pa.) *Times* 4 Dec. 1991: B-1.

B473 ——. "Updike Reflects on Childhood in Ursinus Visit." *Reading* (Pa.) *Eagle* 4 Dec. 1991: A-1. (Updike's talk was entitled, "A Writing Mother and Son.")

B474 Strickland, Michael R. "Updike Reads his Works, Works of Fanciful Mother." *Allentown* (Pa.) *Morning Call* 5 Dec. 1991: B-12.

*B475 Lind, Angus. "One of the Best of Escape Clauses." *New Orleans Times-Picayune* 18 Dec. 1991: E-1. (Lind uses Updike's "Is Life Too Short for Golf?" to muse about golf.)

B476 Luscher, Robert M. *John Updike: A Study of the Short Fiction*. Boston: Hall, 1992.

B477 Schiff, James A. *Updike's Version: Rewriting The Scarlet Letter*. Columbia: U of Mo., 1992.

B478 McTavish, John. "John Updike and the Funny Theologian." *Theology Today* 48 (Jan. 1992): 413-25.

B479 Clausen, Jan. "Native Fathers." *Kenyon Review* 14 (Spring 1992): 44-55.

B480 Donohoe, Cathryn. "Updike Poetry Gives Folger Change of Pace." *Washington Post* 8 Apr. 1992: E-2. (Reviews Updike's reading at the Folger Shakespeare Library, 6 Apr. 1992.)

B481 Schneiderman, Leo. "Updike: Fiction and the Writer's Access to Contradictory Ego States." *American Journal of Psychoanalysis* 52 (June 1992): 149-59.

B482 Runyon, R. "English & American— *Something and Nothingness: The Fiction of John Updike and John Fowles by John Neary*." *Choice* 29 (July-Aug. 1992): 1679-80.

B483 "Music Professor, Updike Pair up for Composition." Albright (Pa.) *Reporter* 15 (Fall 1992): 5. (The poem "A Pear Like a Potato" set to music by Roy Hinkle, for chorus and orchestra. Premier: 6 Dec. 1992, at Albright (Pa.) College. 15 minutes.)

*B484 Shaughnessy, Dan. "Booking Round Trip to 1860." *Boston Globe* 29 Sept. 1992: 71.

B485 Winn, Marie. "Mr. Updike's Avian Error." *The Wall Street Journal* 9 Oct. 1992: B-12.

*B486 Hanson, Henry. "Back Talk." *Chicago* 41 (Nov. 1992): 204.

B487 Merrill, Robert. "*Something and Nothingness: The Fiction of John Updike and John Fowles* by John Neary." *American Literature* 64 (Wint. 1992): 844-45.

B488 Nyhan, David. "Updike at U Mass: Handle the World with Care." Boston *Globe*: 25 May 1993: OP-ED: 15.

B489 De Bellis, Jack. "'It Captivates': Updike Goes to the Movies: Part I." *Literature/Film Quarterly* Forthcoming.

B490 De Bellis, Jack. "'It Hypnotizes': Updike Goes to the Movies: Part II." *Literature/Film Quarterly* Forthcoming.

*B491 Greiner, Donald J. "Memory and Hope: Why John Updike Should Receive the Nobel Prize." *Kennesaw Review* 3 (1993) Forthcoming.

2. Criticism of Individual Works

The Carpentered Hen (1958):

B492   Bogan, Louise. "Books: Verse." *The New Yorker* 35 (18 Apr. 1959): 170. (Reprinted in *Dictionary of Literary Biography: Documentary Series: An Illustrated Chronicle*. Volume 3. Ed. Mary Bruccolli. Detroit: Gale, 1983. 256. The date is misidentified as 1958.)

B493   Busha, Virginia. "Poetry in the Classroom: 'Ex-Basketall Player.'" *English Journal* 59 (5 May 1970): 643-45.

B494   Bowles, Patrick. "Updike's 'Vacuum Cleaner.'" *Explicator* 37 (1978): i, 42-43.

B495   Manning, Margaret. "John Updike Redux." *Boston Sunday Globe* 21 Mar. 1982: A-19.

B496   Denman, Katherine L. "To Die at the Top: A Comparison of Housman and Updike." *English Journal* 74 (Feb. 1985): 74-75.

B497   Kopper, Edward A., Jr. "A Note on Updike's 'Ex-Basketball Player.'" *Notes on Contemporary Literature* 21 (Nov. 1991): 6.

The Poorhouse Fair (1959):

B498   Gilman, Richard. "A Last Assertion of Personal Being." *Commonweal* 69 (6 Feb. 1959): 499-500. (Rpt. in *Dictionary of Literary Biography: Documentary Series: An Illustrated Chronicle*. Volume 3. Ed. Mary Bruccolli. Detroit: Gale, 1983. 256-57, 259.)

B499   "Updike Gets National Award for 'Poor House Fair' [*sic*] Novel." *Reading* (Pa.) *Eagle* 18 Mar. 1960.

B500 Klausler, Alfred P. "Steel Wilderness." *The Christian Century* 77 (22 Feb. 1961): 245-46.

B501 Moraes, Dom. "Professional's Suite." *The Listener* 75 (3 Feb. 1966): 169-70.

B502 de Grummond, W. W. "Classical Influences in *The Poorhouse Fair*." *American Notes and Queries* 13 (1974): 21-23.

B503 Broyard, Anatole. "Twenty Eight Stories and Two Novels." *The New York Times Book Review* 17 Apr. 1977: 12.

B504 Searles, George J. "*The Poorhouse Fair*: Updike's Thesis Statement." In *Critical Essays on John Updike*. Ed. William R. Macnaughton. Boston: Hall, 1982. 231-36.

The Same Door (1959):

B505 "Collections of Short Stories." *The Times Weekly Review* 21 June 1962: 10.

B506 De Bellis, Jack. "The Group and John Updike." *Sewanee Review* 72 (July-Sept. 1964): 531-40.

B507 Hills, Penny Chapin and L. Rust Hills. *How We Live*. N.Y., 1968. 281-82. (Commentary on Updike and "Incest.")

B508 Friedman, Ruben. "An Interpretation of John Updike's Tomorrow and 'Tomorrow and So Forth.'" *English Journal* 61 (Nov. 1972): 1159-162.

*B509 Banks, Jeff R. "The Uses of Weather in 'Tomorrow and Tomorrow and So Forth.'" *Notes on Contemporary Literature* 3 (1973): 8-9.

B510 Nabokov, Vladimir. *Strong Opinions*. N.Y.: McGraw, 1973. 313.

B511 Griffith, Albert J. "Updike's Artist's Dilemma: 'Should Wizard Hit Mommy?'" *Modern Fiction Studies* 20 (Spring 1974): 111-115.

*B512 Herget, W. "John Updike: 'Tomorrow and Tomorrow and So Forth'." In *Die Amerikanische Short Story der Gegenwart*. Ed. P. Freese. Berlin: Schmit, 1976: 160.

*B513 Tanzoe, Kaneko. "Religious Themes in *The Poorhouse Fair*." *Kyushu American Literature* 20 (1979): 29-34.

B514 Wilhelm, Albert E. "Rebecca Cune: Updike's Wedge Between the Maples." *NMAL: Notes on Modern American Literature* 7 (Fall 1983): Item 9.

Criticism of Individual Works 171

B515 ___. "Three Versions of Updike's 'Snowing in Greenwich Village.'" *American Notes and Queries* 22 (1984): 80-82.

Rabbit, Run (1960):

B516 "New Novel by Berksman Wins Praise of Critics." *Reading* (Pa.) *Times* 8 Nov. 1960.

B517 "Run from Rabbit." *America* 104 (19 Nov. 1960): 257.

B518 Didion, Joan. "Into the Underbrush." *National Review* 10 (28 Jan. 1961): 54-56.

B519 Klausler, Alfred P. "Steel Wilderness." *The Christian Century* 77 (22 Feb. 1961): 245-46.

B520 Walcutt, Charles Child. "The Centripetal Action: John Updike's *The Centaur* and *Rabbit, Run* and Wright Morris's *One Day*." In *Man's Changing Mask: Modes and Methods of Characterization in Fiction*. Minneapolis: U M P, 1966. 326-32.

*B521 Standley, Fred. "*Rabbit, Run*: An Image of Life." *Midwest Quarterly* 8 (July 1967): 371-86.

B522 Brewer, Joseph E. "The Anti-Hero in Contemporary Literature." *Iowa English Bulletin: Yearbook* 12 (Fall 1967) 55-60. (Page 56 concerns Updike.)

B523 Alley, Alvin D. and Hugh Agee. "Existential Heroes: Frank Alpine and Rabbit Angstrom." *Ball State University Forum* 9 (1968): 3-5.

B524 Stubbs, John C. "The Search for Perfection in *Rabbit, Run*." *Critique* 10 (1968): 94-101.

B525 Byron, Stuart. "John Updike Barely Interested But Slavishly 'Faithful' to His 'Rabbit, Run'." *Variety* 20 Aug. 1969: 26.

B526 Suderman, Elmer F. "The Right Way and the Good Way in *Rabbit, Run*." *University Review* 26 (Oct. 1969): 13-21.

*B527 Camplin, Charles. "Rabbit, Run." *Los Angeles Times* 6 Dec. 1969: 36.

B528 Rotundo, Barbara. "*Rabbit, Run* and *A Tale of Peter Rabbit*." *Notes on Contemporary Literature* 1 (May 1971): 2-3.

B529 Iooss, Walter, Jr. "The Dawn of the Possible Dream." *Sports Illustrated* 36 (21 Feb. 1972): 38-45. (Photos accompany Rabbit's thoughts.)

B530   Burhans, Clinton S., Jr. "Things Falling Apart: Structure and Theme in *Rabbit, Run.*" *Studies in the Novel* 5 (1973): 336-51. (Rpt. in *Critical Essays on John Updike.* Ed. William R. Macnaughton. Boston: Hall, 1982. 148-62.)

B531   Beckoff, Samuel. *John Updike's Rabbit, Run and Rabbit Redux: A Critical Commentary.* N.Y.: Monarch Press, 1974.

B532   Burr, Richard W. *Puer Aeternus: An Examination of John Updike's Rabbit, Run.* Zurich: Juris Verlag, 1974.

B533   Waldmeir, Joseph. "It's the Going That's Important, Not the Getting There: Rabbit's Questing Non-Quest." *Modern Fiction Studies* 20 (Spring 1974): 13-27.

B534   Lawson, Lewis A. "Rabbit Angstrom as a Religious Sufferer." *Journal of the American Academy of Religion* 42 (June 1974): 232-46.

B535   Le Clair, Thomas. "Death and Black Humor." *Critique* 17. 1 (1975): 5-40.

*B536   Lubbers, Klaus. "John Updike: *Rabbit, Run.*" *Amerikanische Erzählliteratur 1950-1970.* Ed. Frieder Busch and Renate Schmidt-von Bardleben. Munich: 1975. 75-87.

B537   Wilhelm, Albert E. "The Clothing Motif in Updike's *Rabbit, Run.*" *South Atlantic Bulletin* 40 (1975): 87-89.

B538   Ellis, James. "Karl Barth and Socrates as Mouseketeers in *Rabbit, Run.*" *Notes on Contemporary Literature* 3 (Dec. 1977): 10-13.

B539   Borgman, Paul. "The Tragic Hero of Updike's *Rabbit, Run.*" *Renascence* 29 (Wint. 1977): 106-112.

B540   Ellis, James. "Plato's 'Allegory of the Cave' in *Rabbit, Run.*" *Notes on Modern American Literature* 2 (1978): item 15.

B541   McGuinness, Wayne D. "Salvation by Death in *Rabbit, Run.*" *Notes on Contemporary Literature* 8 (1978): 7-8.

*B542   Searles, George J. "'Rabbit, Gun': Linguistic Evidence of Harry Angstrom's Self Delusion." *Notes on Contemporary Literature* 8, iv (1978) 10-11.

B543   Seigel, Gary. "Rabbit Runs Down." *The Modern American Novel and the Movies.* Ed. Gerald Peary and Roger Shatzkin. N.Y.: Ungar, 1978. 247-55.

*B544   Terry, R. "Luckmann's 'Invisible Religion' and the Problem of Belief in Updike's Harry Angstrom." *Iliff Review* 33 (Mar. 1978): 39-46.

B545	Hogan, Robert E. "Catharism and John Updike's *Rabbit, Run*." *Renascence* 32 (1980): 229-39.
B546	Wilhelm, Albert E. "Updike's Revisions of *Rabbit, Run*." *Notes on Modern American Literature* 5 (Sum. 1981): item 15.
B547	Hallissy, Margaret. "Updike's *Rabbit, Run* and Pascal's *Pensées*." *Christianity and Literature* 30 (Wint. 1981): 25-32.
B548	Martin, John Stephen. "Rabbit's Faith: Grace and the Transformation of the Heart." *Pacific Coast Philology* 17 (1982): 103-11.
*B549	Wilhelm, Albert E. "Rabbit Restored: A Further Note on Updike's Revisions." *NMAL: Notes on Modern American Literature* 6 (Spring-Sum. 1982): item 7.
B550	Yost, Nicholas. "What John Updike Never Got to Say." *Reading* (Pa.) *Times* 31 May 1982.
B551	Morey-Gaines, Ann-Janine. "Embodiment and the American Imagination: A Preliminary Skirmish with Some Critical-Cultural Issues Raised by Religion and Sexuality in American Fiction." *Modern American Cultural Criticism*. Ed. Mark Johnson. Warrensburg: Central Mo. State UP, 1983. 39-45.
B552	Waldron, Randall H. "Rabbit Revised." *American Literature* 56 (1984): 51-67.
B553	Ecenbarger, William. "Finding Inspiration in Pennsylvania: Rabbit's Realm." *Travel Holiday* Aug. 1985: 20-25, 27.
B554	Siegle, Robert. *The Politics of Reflexivity*. Baltimore: Johns Hopkins UP, 1986. 150-56.
B555	Ahearn, Kerry. "Family and Adultery: Images and Ideas in Updike's Rabbit Novels." *Twentieth Century Literature* 34 (1988): 62-83.
B556	Armstrong, Peggy. "Updike's *Rabbit, Run*." *Explicator* 47 (1988): 46-47.
B557	Bodmer, George R. "Rabbit to Roger: Updike's Rockin' Version." *Journal of Popular Culture* 22 (1988): 111-17.
B558	Porter, Gilbert M. "From Babbitt to Rabbit: The American Materialist in Search of a Soul." *American Literature in Belgium*. Ed. Gilbert Debusscher and Marc Maufort. Amsterdam: Rodopi, 1988. 185-96.
B559	De Bellis, Jack. "The 'Extra Dimension': Character Names in Updike's 'Rabbit' Trilogy." *Names* 36 (Mar.-June 1988): 29-42.

B560 Armstrong, Peggy. "Updike's *Rabbit, Run.*" *Explicator* 47 (Fall 1988): 46-47.

B561 Horvath, Brooke. "The Failure of Erotic Questing in John Updike's Rabbit Novels." *Denver Quarterly* 23 (Fall 1988): 70-89.

B562 De Bellis, Jack. "Oedipal Angstrom." *Wascana Review* 24 (1989): 45-59.

B563 Mazurek, Raymond. "'Bringing the Corners Forward': Ideology and Representation in Updike's Rabbit Trilogy." *Politics and the Muse: Studies in the Politics of Recent American Literature.* Ed. Adam J. Sorkin. Bowling Green, Ohio: Bowling Green State U Popular P, 1989. 142-60.

B564 Neary, John M. "'Ah, Runs': Updike, Rabbit, and Repetition." *Religion and Literature* 21 (Spring 1989): 89-110.

B565 Wilson, Matthew. "The Rabbit Tetralogy: From Solitude to Society to Solitude Again." *Modern Fiction Studies* 37 (Spring 1991): 3-24.

B566 Wright, Derek. "Mapless Motion: Form and Space in Updike's *Rabbit, Run.*" *Modern Fiction Studies* 37 (Spring 1991): 35-44.

Pigeon Feathers (1962):

*B567 Leonard, John. "Pigeon Feathers." *New York* 21 (22 Feb. 1960): 66.

B568 Klausler, Alfred P. "Steel Wilderness." *The Christian Century* (22 Feb. 1961): 245-46.

*B569 Slavitt, D. R. *Pigeon Feathers. Book-of-the-Month Club News* Apr. 1962: 15.

B570 Bellow, Saul. *Recent American Fiction.* Washington: Library of Congress, 1965. 5-6.

B571 Hamilton, Alice. "Between Innocence and Experience: From Joyce to Updike." *Dalhousie Review* 49 (Spring 1969): 102-09.

B572 Reising, R. W. "Updike's 'A Sense of Shelter.'" *Studies in Short Fiction* 7 (Fall 1970): 651-52.

B573 Edwards, A. S. G. "Updike's 'A Sense of Shelter.'" *Studies in Short Fiction* 8 (Sum. 1971): 467-68.

B574 Sykes, Robert H. "A Commentary on Updike's 'Astronomer.'" *Studies in Short Fiction* 8 (Fall 1971): 575-79.

B575 Overmyer, Janet. "Courtly Love in the A & P." *Notes on Contemporary Literature* 2 (May 1972): 4-5.

B576	Porter, M. Gilbert. "John Updike's 'A & P': The Establishment and an Emersonian Cashier." *English Journal* 61 (Nov. 1972): 1155-58.
B577	Cochran, Robert W. "The Narrator Then and Now in Updike's FLIGHT." *Rendezvous* 10 (1975): 29-32.
B578	Crowley, Sue Mitchell. "The Rubble of Footnotes Bound Into Kierkegaard." *Journal of the American Academy of Religion* 45. 3 Supplement (1977): 1011-35.
B579	Hunt, George W. "Kierkegaardian Sensations into Real Fiction: John Updike's 'The Astronomer.'" *Christianity and Literature* 26 (1977): 3-17.
B580	Broyard, Anatole. "One Critic's Fiction." *The New York Times Book Review* 17 Apr. 1977: 12.
B581	Waxman, Robert E. "Invitations to Dread: John Updike's Metaphysical Quest." *Renascence* 29 (Sum. 1977): 201-10.
B582	Shurr, William H. "The Lutheran Experience in John Updike's 'Pigeon Feathers.'" *Studies in Short Fiction* 14 (Fall 1977): 329-35.
*B583	Diller, Hans-Jurgen. "John Updike: 'Dear Alexandros.'" *Anglistik & Englischunterricht* 18 (1982): 41-53.
B584	McFarland, Ronald E. "Updike and the Critics: Reflections on 'A & P.'" *Studies in Short Fiction* 20 (Spring-Sum. 1983): 95-100.
B585	Goss, Marjorie Hill. "Widening Perceptions in Updike's 'A & P.'" *Notes on Contemporary Literature* 14 (Nov. 1984): 8.
B586	Conn, Saundra M. "Do Not Go Gentle: Visions of Death and Immortality in John Updike's 'Pigeon Feathers' and 'Packed Dirt, Churchgoing, A Dying Cat, A Traded Car.'" *Publications of the Mississippi Philosophical Association* [n.v.] (1985): 29-31.
B587	Klinkowitz, Jerome. *Literary Subversions: New American Fiction and the Practice of Criticism.* Carbondale: Southern IL UP, 1985. 62-63.
B588	Emmett, Paul J. "A Slip That Shows: Updike's 'A & P.'" *Notes on Contemporary Literature* 15 (Mar. 1985): 9-11.
B589	Perry, Alice H. "The Dress Code in Updike's 'A & P.'" *Notes on Contemporary Literature* 16 (1986): 8-10.
B590	Shaw, Patrick W. "Checking Out Faith and Lust: Hawthorne's 'Young Goodman Brown' and Updike's 'A & P.'" *Studies in Short Fiction* 23 (1986): 321-23.

B591 Chanley, Steven M. "Quest for Order in 'Pigeon Feathers': Updike's Use of Christian Mythology." *Arizona Quarterly* 43 (Autumn 1987): 251-63.

B592 Partch, Ken. "The Updike Story, Redux. (John Updike's 'A & P'—Lust in the Aisles)." *Supermarket Business Magazine* 42 (Dec. 1987): 5.

B593 Searles, George J. "The Mouths of Babes: Childhood Epiphany in Roth's 'Conversion of the Jews' and Updike's 'PigeonFeathers.'" *Studies in Short Fiction* 24 (Wint. 1987): 59-62.

B594 Dessner, Lawrence Jay. "Irony and Innocence in John Updike's 'A & P.'" *Studies in Short Fiction* 25 (1988): 315-17.

B595 Martin, Dell. "Stories To Be Read Aloud." *English Journal* 78 (Feb. 1989): 88. (Considers "A & P.")

B596 Hurley, C. Harold. "Updike's 'A & P': An 'Initial' Response." *Notes on Contemporary Literature* 20 (May 1990): 12.

B597 Perisho, Steve. "Irony in John Updike's 'Pigeon Feathers.'" *Notes on Contemporary Literature* 21 (May 1991): 7-11.

Telephone Poles (1962):

B598 Matson, Elizabeth. "A Chinese Paradox but Not Much of One: John Updike in his Poetry." *Minnesota Review* 8 (1967): 157-67.

B599 Edward, R. "Close Reading and Teaching." *English Journal* 59 (Oct. 1970): 938-42.

B600 Kopper, Edward A., Jr. "A Note on Updike's 'Ex- Basketball Player.'" *Notes on Contemporary Literature* 21 (Nov. 1991): 6.

The Centaur (1963):

B601 "John Updike's *Centaur* Is Praised." *Reading* (Pa.)*Eagle* 20 Jan. 1963.

*B602 Elistratova, A. "Man Is a Tragic Animal: John Updike's Two Novels." *Inostrannaya Literature* 9.12 (Feb. 1963): 220-26.

B603 "Days of Mortals and Myths." *Philadelphia Sunday Bulletin* 3 Feb. 1963.

B604 Hyman, Stanley Edgar. "Chiron at Olinger High." *New Leader* 66 (4 Feb. 1963): 20. (Rpt. in his *Standards: A Chronicle of Books for Our Time.* N.Y.: Horizon Press, 1966: 128-32.)

B605 "Reading for Pleasure: Chiron in Pa." *Wall Street Journal* 4 Feb. 1963.

B606 La Course, Guerin. *Commonweal* 77 (8 Feb. 1963): 512-14.

B607 Gilman, Richard. "Fiction: John Updike." *New Republic* 148 (13 Apr. 1963): 25-27. (Rpt. in his *The Confusion of Realms*. N.Y.: Random House, 1970. 62-68.)

B608 Ward, J. A. "John Updike: *The Centaur*." *Critique* 6 (Fall 1963): 109-14.

B609 "New Fiction." *The Times Weekly Review* 10 Oct. 1963: 12.

B610 O'Connor, William Van. "John Updike and William Styron: The Burden of Talent." In *Contemporary American Novelists: Crosscurrents/Modern Critiques*. Ed. Harry T. Moore. Carbondale: Southern Ill. U P, 1964: 205-21. (Pages 205-14 concern *The Centaur*.)

B611 "National Book Awards Judges Announce Leading Contenders." *Library Journal* 89 (2 Feb. 1964): 820.

B612 "Leading Contenders for NBA Announced." *Publisher's Weekly* 185 (3 Feb. 1964): 66.

B613 "National Book Awards." *Library Journal* 89 (3 Mar. 1964): 1126.

B614 "Updike Wins Book Award for Distinguished Fiction."*Reading* (Pa.) *Eagle* 11 Mar. 1964.

B615 "Updike Wins Book Prize for *Centaur*." *Reading* (Pa.)*Times* 11 Mar. 1964.

B616 "Five Books Win National Book Awards." *Publisher's Weekly* 185 (16 Mar. 1964): 28.

B617 De Bellis, Jack. "The Group and John Updike." *Sewanee Review* 72 (July-Sept. 1964): 531-40.

B618 *Library Journal* 91 (15 Feb. 1965): 1058.

B619 Walcutt, Charles Child. "The Centripetal Action: John Updike's *The Centaur* and *Rabbit, Run* and Wright Morris's *One Day*." In *Man's Changing Mask: Modes and Methods of Characterization in Fiction*. Minneapolis: UMP, 1966. 326-32.

B620 Haas, Rudolf. "Griechischer Mythos im Modernen Roman: John Updikes *The Centaur*." *Lebende Antike: Symposion für Rudolf Suhnel*. Ed. Horst Meller and Hans-Joachim Zimmermann. Berlin: E Schmidt, 1967. 513-27.

B621 Alley, Alvin D. "*The Centaur*: Transcendental Imagination and Metaphoric Death." *English Journal* 56 (Oct. 1967): 982-85.

B622   Seelbach, Wilhelm. "Die antike Mythologie in John Updikes Roman *The Centaur*." *Arcadia* v.5 (1970): 176-94.

B623   White, John J. *Mythology in the Modern Novel: A Study of Prefigurative Techniques*. Princeton: PUP, 1971. 5, 53, 70, 87a, 113, 123, 133, 135.

B624   Myers, David. "The Questing Fear: Christian Allegory in John Updike's *The Centaur*." *Twentieth Century Literature* 17 (Apr. 1971): 73-82.

B625   Kort, Wesley A. "*The Centaur* and the Problem of Vocation." *Shirven Selves: Religious Problems in Recent American Fiction*. Philadelphia: Fortress, 1972. 64-89.

B626   Vargo, Edward P. "The Necessity of Myth in Updike's *The Centaur*." *PMLA* 88 (May 1973): 452-60. (Rpt. in *Rainstorms and Fire: Ritual in the Novels of John Updike*. Port Washington, N.Y.: Kennikat, 1973. 81-103.

B627   Vickery, John B. "*The Centaur*: Myth, History, and Narrative." *Modern Fiction Studies* 20 (Spring 1974): 29-43.

B628   LeClair, Thomas. "Death and Black Humor." *Critique* 17. 1 (1975): 5-40. (Pages 7-9 and 30 concern Updike.)

B629   Curtler, Betsy S. "Science, the Saving Grace of John Updike: *The Centaur* and *Couples*." *A Festschrift for Professor Marguerite Roberts, on the Occasion of Her Retirement from Westhampton College, University of Richmond, Virginia*. Ed. Frieda Penninger. Richmond: U of Richmond, 1976. 209-18.

B630   Uphaus, Suzanne Henning. "*The Centaur*: Updike's Mock Epic." *Journal of Narrative Technique* 7 (1977): 24-36. (Rpt. in *Critical Essays on John Updike*. Ed. William R. Macnaughton. Boston: Hall, 1982. 163-74.)

*B631   Stehlikova, Eva. "The Function of Classical Myths in John Updike's *The Centaur*." *Listy Filologicke* I (1978): 1-12.

B632   Strandberg, Victor. "John Updike and the Changing of the Gods." *Mosaic* 12 (1978): 157-75. (Rpt. in *Critical Essays on John Updike*. Ed. William R. Macnaughton. Boston: Hall, 1982. 175-94.)

B633   Trimmer, Joseph F. *The National Book Awards for Fiction: An Index to the First Twenty-five Years*. Boston: Hall, 1978. xvi, xxi, xxv, xxvii (n41, n50): 129-31, 141-42, 144, 149, 157, 159, 165-78, 200, 210, 221, 230, 241-43, 244, 245, 256-57, 272-73.

B634   Mellard, James M. "The Novel as Lyric Elegy: The Mode of Updike's *The Centaur*." *Texas Studies in Language and Literature* 21 (Spring 1979): 112-27. (Rev. in *Doing Tropology: Analysis of Narrative Discourse*, by James Mellard. Urbana: Ill.: U of Ill. P, 1987. Rpt. in *Critical Essays on John Updike*. Ed. William R. Macnaughton. Boston: Hall, 1982. 217-30;

and in *Modern Critical Views: John Updike.* Ed. Harold Bloom. N.Y.: Chelsea House, 1987. 97-110.)

B635 Hoag, Ronald. Wesley. "*The Centaur*: What Cures George Caldwell?" *Studies in American Fiction* 8.1 (1980): 88-98.

B636 Pincus, Cynthia, Leslie Elliott, and Trudy Schlachter. *Roots of Success.* Englewood Cliffs: Prentice, 1980: 66-67.

B637 Werner, Craig. "Homer's Joyce: John Updike, Ronald Sukenick, Robert Coover, Toni Morrison." In *Paradoxical Resolutions: American Fiction Since James Joyce.* U of Ill. P, 1982. 68-96. (Pages 70-75 concern *The Centaur*.)

B638 Vickery, John B. "Myth and Narrative: The Nature of the Tale and the Name of the Teller." *Myths and Texts: Strategies of Incorporation and Displacement.* Baton Rouge: UP, 1983. 149-65.

*B639 Patanjali, V. V. R. "John Updike's Fiction and His Themes." *The Literary Endeavour* 6 (1985): 114-19.

*B640 Funck, Susana. "The Self and Beyond: A Reading of *The Fixer*, *The Centaur*, and *Henderson the Rain King*." *Ilha do Desterro* 15-16 (1986): 166-82.

*B641 Zhorunuya, S. "Kentavr: Mif, netafora, real'nost.'" [*The Centaur*: Myth, Metaphor, Reality.] *Lit. Gruziya* 8 (1986): 192-95.

B642 Neary, John M. "*The Centaur*: John Updike and the Face of the Other." *Renascence* 38 (Sum. 1986): 228-44.

B643 Gabbard, Krin. "Updike, Shaffer, and the Centaurs." *Helios* 14 (Spring 1987): 47-58.

B644 Heuermann, Hartmut. "Von Tiermenschen und den Tucken der Padagogik: John Updike's *The Centaur*." *Mythos, Literatur, Gesellschaft. Mythokritische Analysen zur Geschichte des amerikanischen Romans.* Munchen: Fink, 1988. 354-64.

*B645 *Classical and Modern Literature* 10 (Fall 1989): 60.

Assorted Prose (1965):

B646 Grunwald, Henry Anatole. "Comment." In his *Salinger: A Critical and Personal Portrait.* N.Y.: Harper and Row, 1962: 53-56. (Retitles and comments on Udpike's review of *Franny and Zooey* rpt. from "Anxious Days for the Glass Family." *The New York Times Book Review* 17 Sept. 1961: 1, 52; retitled, "Is Cute the Word?"; rpt. in *Assorted Prose.* NY: Knopf, 1965. 234-39, retitled, "*Franny and Zooey.*")

B647	"*Assorted Prose.*" *Booklist* 61 (15 June 1965): 982.
B648	Galloway, David. D. "Belfast Blues." *Spectator* 216 (4 Feb. 1966): 142-43.
B649	"That Long Atlantic Crossing." *The Times Literary Supplement* 17 Feb. 1966: 124.
B650	Sullivan, Walter. "Updike, Spark and Others." *Sewanee Review* 74 (Sum. 1966): 709-16. (Pages 711-13 refer to Updike.)
B651	Harper, Howard M., Jr. "Trends in Recent American Fiction." *Contemporary Literature* 12 (Spring 1971): 204-29. (Pages 222-23 pertain to Updike.)
B652	Gediman, Helen March. "Reflections on Romanticism, Narcissism, and Creativity." *Journal of the American Psychoanalytic Association* 23 (1975): 407-23. (Comments on Updike's reviews of De Rougemont's *Love in the Western World* and *Love Declared*.)

A Child's Calendar (1965):

B653	*Library Journal* 91 (15 Feb. 1965): 1058.
B654	*Kirkus* 33 (1 Oct. 1965): 1038.
B655	*Bulletin of the Center for Children's Books* 19 (Feb. 1966): 107
*B656	*Hornbook Magazine* 65 (Nov. 1989): 805.
B657	Baumgold, Julie. "Children's Books: In 'Fruitcake Weather.'" *New York* 22 (18 Dec. 1989): 80.

Of the Farm (1965):

B658	"*Of the Farm.*" *Reading* (Pa.) *Eagle* 14 Nov. 1965.
B659	Beers, Paul B. "Reporter at Large." *The Harrisburg* (Pa.) *Evening News* 15 Nov. 1965.
B660	Cook, Roderick. "*Of the Farm.*" *Harper's* 232 (Jan. 1966): 100.
B661	*Choice* 2 (Feb. 1966): 862.
B662	Wright, Andrea. "The Question of Updike." *Kenyon Review* 25 (Mar. 1966): 268-276.
B663	"Mother's Boy." *The Times Literary Supplement* 14 Apr. 1966: 321.

B664	Davenport, John. "The Generation Between." *The Spectator* 216 (29 Apr. 1966): 537.
B665	Sullivan, Walter. "Updike, Spark and Others." *Sewanee Review* 74 (Sum. 1966): 709-16. (Pages 711-13 refer to Updike.)
B666	Sams, Henry W. "Updike to Win." *Journal of General Education* 18 (July 1966): 146-49.
B667	Taubman, Robert. "Updike." *New Statesman* 12 Aug. 1966: 233.
B668	Lurie, Alison. "Witches and Fairies: Fitzgerald to Updike." *The New York Review of Books* 17 (2 Dec. 1971): 6, 8-11. (Pages 10-11 pertain to *Of the Farm*.)
*B669	Feinberg, Susan. "Anaclitic Love in John Updike's Novel *Of The Farm*." *Journal of Evolutionary Psychology* 4 (1983): 163-68.

The Music School (1966):

*B670	*Kirkus* 34 (15 July 1966): 708.
B671	Cook, Roderick. *Harper's* 233 (Sept. 1966): 113.
B672	"*The Music School*." *Reading* (Pa.) *Eagle* 18 Sept. 1966.
B673	Kauffmann, Stanley. "Onward with Updike." *New Republic* 155 (24 Sept. 1966): 15-17.
B674	"John and Bruce." *Newsweek* 68 (Sept. 1966): 116.
B675	Morse, J. Mitchell. "Where Is Everybody?" *Hudson Review* 19 (Wint. 1966-67): 673-82. (Page 682 concerns Updike.)
B676	*Choice* 3 (Feb. 1967): 1130.
B677	Bergonzi, Bernard. "Updike, Dennis, and Others." *The New York Review of Books* 9 (9 Feb. 1967): 28-30.
B678	Gray, Simon. "Myth and Magic." *New Statesman* 71 (16 June 1967): 840.
B679	Price, R. G. G. "New Novels." *Punch* 252 (21 June 1967): 924.
B680	Braybrooke, Nevile. "New Novels: Meditations." *Spectator* 218 (23 June 1967): 744.
*B681	Bradbury, Malcolm. *Manchester Guardian* 96 (29 June 1967): 10.

B682	Haworth, J. D. S. "Fiction: Seekers and Lovers." *Listener* 77 (29 June 1967): 861.
B683	"Keeping It Short." *The Times Literary Supplement* 24 Aug. 1967: 757.
B684	*Publisher's Weekly* 190 (16 Oct. 1967): 59.
B685	Hartley, Lois. "*The Music School.*" *Studies in Short Fiction* 5 (1968): 91-92.
B686	Markle, Joyce B. "On John Updike and 'The Music School.'" *The American Short Story*. Ed. Calvin Skaggs. N.Y.: Dell, 1977. 389-93.
B687	Schmitt-von Muhlenfels, Franz. "'Four Sides of One Story': Tristan und Isolde bei John Updike." *Germanisch-Romanische Monatsschrift*, Neue Folge 27 (1977): 98-113.
B688	Hunt, George. "Reality, Imagination and Art: The Significance of Updike's 'Best Story.'" *Studies in Short Fiction* 16 (Sum. 1979): 219-29. (Rpt. in *Critical Essays on John Updike*. Ed. William R Macnaughton. Boston: Hall, 1982. 207-16.)
*B689	Sant'Anna, Norma. "Some Considerations on John Updike's 'Music School.'" *Estudios Anglo-Americanos* 3-4 (1979-1980): 200-05.
*B690	*Book World* 10 (12 Aug. 1980): 12.
B691	Blechner, Michael Harry. "Tristan in Letters: Malory, C. S. Lewis, Updike." *Tristania* 6 (Autumn 1980): 30-37.
B692	Tracy, Bruce H. "The Habit of Confession: Recovery of the Self in Updike's 'The Music School.'" *Studies in Short Fiction* 21 (Fall 1984): 339-55.
B693	Kleimen, Ed. "John Updike's 'Giving Blood': An Experiment in Genre." *Studies in Short Fiction* 29.2 (Spring 1992): 153-60.

Olinger Stories (1966):

B694	Klinkowitz, Jerome. "John Updike's America." *North American Review* 265 (Sept. 1980): 229-39. (Rpt. in Richard Kostelanetz, *American Writing Today*. U. S. International Communication Agency, 1982. 311-21.)
*B695	Luscher, Robert M. "John Updike's Olinger Stories: New Light Among the Shadows." *Journal of the Short Story in English* 11 (Autumn 1988): 99-117.

Couples (1968):

*B696	*Kirkus*. 36 (1 Feb. 1968): 143.
B697	*Publisher's Weekly* 193 (12 Feb. 1968): 70.
B698	"Updike on Sex." *Reading* (Pa.) *Eagle* 7 Mar. 1968.
B699	Cayton, Robert F. "Updike, John. *Couples*." *Library Journal* 93 (15 Mar. 1968): 1164.
B700	Fremont-Smith, Eliot. "The Evidence in Tarbox." *The New York Times* 25 Mar. 1968: 39.
B701	"View from the Catacombs." *Time* 91 (26 Mar. 1968):66-68, 73-75.
B702	Bradley, Van Allen. "Mr. Updike's Fakery." *Chicago Daily News Panorama* 30 Mar. 1968: 10.
B703	Trilling, Diana. "Updike's Yankee Traders." *Atlantic* 221 (Apr. 1968): 129-31.
B704	Maddocks, Melvin. "John Updike's Uptown Peyton Place." *Life* 64 (5 Apr. 1968): 8.
B705	Hicks, Granville. "God Has Gone, Sex Is Left." *Saturday Review* 51 (6 Apr. 1968): 21-22.
*B706	Kazin, Alfred. "Updike: Novelist of the New, Post-Pill America." *Chicago Tribune Book World* 7 Apr. 1968: 1, 3.
B707	Sheed, Wilfrid. "Play in Tarbox." *The New York Times Book Review* 7 Apr. 1968: 1, 30-33. (Rpt. as "John Updike: *Couples*." In his *The Morning After: Selected Essays and Reviews*. N.Y.: Farrar, 1971: 36-42.)
B708	Stern, Richard. "Men, Women and Lovestuff: All About it." *Chicago Sunday Sun-Times Book Week* 7 Apr. 1968: 1, 9.
B709	Sokolov, Raymond A. "Musical Beds." *Newsweek* 71 (8 Apr. 1968): 125-26.
B710	Gass, William H. "Cock-a-doodle-doo." *The New York Review of Books* 11 Apr. 1968: 3. (Rpt. in his *Fiction and the Figures of Life*. N.Y.: Knopf, 1971. 206-11.)
*B711	Archer, William H. "Couples." *Best Sellers* 28 (15 Apr. 1968): 32-33.
*B712	Kennedy, William. *National Observer* 7 (15 Apr. 1968): 19.
B713	Conroy, Frank. "Death and Games." *New York* (22 Apr. 1968): 55.

B714   Greenfeld, Josh. "A Romping Set in a Square New England Town." *Commonweal* 88 (26 Apr. 1968): 185-87.

B715   Thompson, John. "Updike's *Couples*." *Commentary* 45 (May 1968): 70-73.

B716   Murray, Michele. "*Couples* All Surface: 'Updike Has Narrowed His Vision to the Bed.'" *National Catholic Reporter* 1 May 1968: 11.

B717   Broyard, Anatole. "Updike's Twosomes." *The New Republic* 158 (4 May 1968): 28-30.

B718   Fuller, Edmund. "Case for Celibacy." *Wall Street Journal* 13 May 1968: 16.

B719   Yglesias, José. "Coupling and Uncoupling." *Nation* 206 (13 May 1968): 637-38.

B720   Hyman, Stanley E. "Couplings." *New Leader* 31 (20 May 1968): 20-21. (Rpt. in *The Critic's Credentials*. Ed. Phoebe Pettingell. N.Y.: Atheneum, 1978: 107-11.)

B721   Griffin, C. W., Jr. "Updike's Tarbox." *Reporter* 38 (30 May 1968): 43-44.

B722   Collier, Peter. "Surburban Surfeit." *Progressive* 32 (June 1968): 48.

B723   "*Couples*." *Booklist* 64 (1 June 1968): 1129.

B724   Hill, William B. "Couples." *America* 118 (8 June 1968): 757.

B725   "Notes on Current Books." *Virginia Quarterly Review* 44 (Sum. 1968): xcvi.

B726   Pritchard, William H. "Fiction Chronicle." *Hudson Review* 21 (Sum. 1968): 364-76. (Pages 375-76 concern Updike.)

B727   Novak, Michael. "Son of the Group." *Critic* 26 (June- July 1968): 72-74.

B728   Kazin, Alfred. "*Couples*." *Choice* 5 (July 1968): 628.

B729   Turner, Michael. "Worth Noting." *The Cresset* 31 (Sept. 1968): 19.

B730   "Updike: Endless Infidelity." *Philadelphia Inquirer* 7 Sept. 1968.

B731   Gordon, David J. "Some Recent Novels: Styles of Martyrdom." *Yale Review* 58 (Oct. 1968): 112-26. (Pages 117-19 refer to Updike.)

B732   Kort, Wesley. "Desperate Games." *The Christian Century* 85 (23 Oct. 1968): 1340-42.

B733   "Community Feeling." *The Times Literary Supplement* 7 Nov. 1968: 1245.

B734   Kermode, F. "Shuttlecock." *Listener* 80 (7 Nov. 1968): 619.

B735   Hope, Francis. "Screwing in Turn." *The New Statesman* 76 (8 Nov. 1968): 639-40.

B736   Tanner, Tony. "Hellow, Olleh." *Spectator* 221 (8 Nov. 1968) 658-659.

B737   Price, R. G. G. "New Novels." *Punch* 2551 (13 Nov. 1968): 710.

*B738 Flint, Joyce. "John Updike and Couples: The WASP's Dilemma." *Research Studies* 36 (Dec. 1968): 340-47.

B739   Cranston, Maurice. "Selected Books." *London Magazine* 8 (Feb. 1969): 94-96.

B740   Ditsky, John. "Roth, Updike and the High Expense of Spirit." *University of Windsor Review* 5 (Fall 1969): 111-120.

B741   Lodge, David. "Post-Pill Paradise Lost: John Updike's *Couples*." In his *The Novelist at the Cross-roads, and Other Essays on Fiction and Criticism*. Ithaca, N.Y.: Cornell UP, 1971. 237-44. (Rpt. in *John Updike: A Collection of Critical Essays*. Ed. David Thorburn and Howard Eiland. Englewood Cliffs: Prentice, 1979. 84-92; and in *Modern Critical Views: John Updike*. Ed. Harold Bloom. N.Y.: Chelsea House, 1987. 29-36.)

B742   Detweiler, Robert. "Updike's *Couples*: Eros Demythologized." *Twentieth Century Literature* 17 (Oct. 1971): 235-46.

B743   Sharrock, Roger. "Singles and Couples: Hemingway's *A Farewell to Arms* and Updike's *Couples*." *Ariel* 4 (1973): 21-43.

B744   Hills, Rust. "Fiction." *Esquire* 79 (Apr. 1973): 30, 34, 36, 38, 40.

B745   Backscheider, Paula and Nick. "Updike's *Couples*: Squeak in the Night." *Modern Fiction Studies* 20 (Spring 1974): 45-52.

B746   McKenzie, Alan T. "'A Craftsman's Intimate Satisfactions': The Parlor Games in *Couples*." *Modern Fiction Studies* 20 (Spring 1974): 53-58.

B747   "Getting a Fix on Fall Books." *The New York Times Book Review* 29 Aug. 1976: 7.

B748   Quinn, Sally. "Updike on Women, Marriage & Adultery." *Washington Post* 9 Dec. 1976: C-1.

B749   Plagman, Linda M. "*Eros* and *Agape*: The Opposition in Updike's *Couples*." *Renascence* 28 (Wint. 1976): 83-93.

B750   Wahl, William. "Updike's World and *Couples.*" *Essays in Honour of Professor Tyrus Hillway.* Ed. Erwin A. Sturzl. Salzburg: Salzburg Institut für Englische Sprache und Literatur, 1977. 256-95.

B751   Eiland, Howard. "Play in *Couples.*" *John Updike: A Collection of Critical Essays.* Ed. David Thorburn and Howard Eiland. Englewood Cliffs, N. J.: Prentice, 1979. 69-83.

B752   Nahal, Chaman. "Sexual Psychology in Contemporary American Fiction." *Contemporary American Life.* Ed. Jagdish N. Sharma and B. Ramesh Babu. New Delhi: Arnold-Heinemann, 1979. 134-47. (Pages 134-38 concern Updike.)

B753   Tanner, Tony. *Adultery in the Novel.* Baltimore: Johns Hopkins UP, 1979. 89.

B754   Long, Elizabeth. *The American Dream and the Popular American Novel.* Boston: Routledge, 1985. 108-09.

*B755   "*Couples* by John Updike." *American Libraries* 22 (Feb. 1991): 184.

Bottom's Dream (1969):

B756   Magid, Nora L. "Clear the Stage for a Repeat Performance." *The New York Times Book Review* 9 Nov. 1969: 2, 65.

B757   Heins, Paul. "John Updike, Adapter: *Bottom's Dream.*" *Horn Book* 45 (Dec. 1969): 667.

B758   Heyen, William. "Sensibilities." *Poetry* 115 (Mar. 1970): 428-29.

B759   McConnell, Lynda. "*Bottom's Dream.*" *Library Journal* 95 (15 Apr. 1970): 1643.

Midpoint and Other Poems (1969):

B760   Demos, John. "*Midpoint and Other Poems.*" *Library Journal* 94 (1 Apr. 1969): 1504.

B761   Adams, Phoebe-Lou. "Short Reviews: Books." *Atlantic* June 1969: 118.

B762   Gates, Anne. "John Updike— Wearing His Poet's Hat." *The Christian Science Monitor* 15 Aug. 1969: 9.

B763   "Answers to Questions Unasked." *The Times Literary Supplement* 29 Jan. 1970: 104.

Criticism of Individual Works

B764   Heyen, William. "Sensibilities." *Poetry* 115 (Mar. 1970): 426-29. (Pages 428-29 refer to Updike.)

B765   Brownjohn, Alan. "Dualities." *The New Statesman* 79 (6 Mar. 1970): 330-32. (Page 332 concerns Updike.)

B766   Fuller, John. "Innocents Abroad." *Listener* 84 (23 July 1970): 122.

B767   Sissman, L. E. "John Updike: Midpoint and After." *Atlantic* 226 (Aug. 1970): 102-104.

B768   Hamilton, Alice and Kenneth. "Theme and Techniques in John Updike's *Midpoint*." *Mosaic* 4.1 (Fall 1970): 79-106.

Bech: A Book (1970):

B769   "*Bech: A Book*." *Playboy* 17 (June 1970): 22-23.

B770   Nelson, Barbara. "*Bech: A Book*." *Library Journal* 95 (1 June 1970): 2183.

B771   Lehmann-Haupt, Christopher. "Updike: A Mensch." *The New York Times* 120 (11 June 1970): 43.

B772   Gallagher, Charles M. "Bech Called Funny, Sad, Lonely, Satirical—Good Updike." *Reading* (Pa.) *Eagle* 14 June 1970.

B773   Sokolov, Raymond A. "Gentile Parody." *Newsweek* 75 (15 June 1970): 106.

B774   Broyard, Anatole. "All the Way with Updike." *Life* 68 (19 June 1970): 12.

B775   Edwards, Thomas R. "*Bech: A Book*." *The New York Times Book Review* 21 June 1970: 1, 38.

B776   "The Lion That Squeaked." *Time* 95 (22 June 1970): 82-84.

B777   Gold, Ivan. "'You Really Gets.'" *Nation* 210 (29 June 1970): 791-92.

B778   Shickel, Richard. "*Bech: A Book*." *Harper's* 241 (July 1970): 102.

B779   Seelye, John. "Notable." *The New Republic* 163 (11 July 1970): 27.

*B780   Murray, John. "*Bech: A Book*." *Best Sellers* 30 (15 July 1970): 159-60.

*B781   Kramer, Hilton. "Portrait of the Artist as a Jewish Intellectual." *Chicago Tribune Book World* 19 July 1970: 3.

B782   Bolger, Eugenie. "The New Updike." *New Leader* 20 July 1970: 16-17.

B783   Sissman, L. E. "John Updike: Midpoint and After." *Atlantic* 226 (Aug. 1970): 102-04.

B784   Davenport, Guy. "On the Edge of Being." *National Review* 22 (25 Aug. 1970): 903-04.

B785   Donoghue, Denis. "Silken Mechanism." *Listener* 84 (15 Oct. 1970): 524-25.

B786   "On Not Rocking the Boat." *Times Literary Supplement* 16 Oct. 1970: 1183.

B787   Raban, Jonathan. "Talking Head." *New Statesman* 16 Oct. 1970: 494.

B788   Richardson, Jack. "Keeping Up with Updike." *The New York Review of Books* 15 (22 Oct. 1970): 46-48. (Rpt. in *John Updike: A Collection of Critical Essays*. Ed. David Thorburn and Howard Eiland. Englewood Cliffs: Prentice, 1979. 196-202.)

B789   Ozick, Cynthia. "Bech, Passing." *Commentary* Nov. 1970: 106-14. (Rpt. in Art and Ardor. N.Y.: Knopf, 1983. 114-29; and in Harold Bloom. *Modern Critical Views: John Updike*. N.Y.: Chelsea House, 1987. 127-38.)

B790   Richler, Mordecai. "Porky's Plaint." *London Magazine* 10 (Nov. 1970): 106-08.

B791   Algren, Nelson. "Bech: A Book." *Critic* 29 (Nov.-Dec. 1970): 84-86.

B792   Hamilton, Alice and Kenneth. "Metamorphosis Through Art: John Updike's *Bech: A Book*." *Queen's Quarterly* 77 (Wint. 1970): 624-36.

B793   Cowley, Malcolm. "Holding the Fort on Audubon Terrace." *Saturday Review* 54 (3 Apr. 1971): 17, 41-42.

B794   Townley, Rod. "Bech: A Book." *Studies in Short Fiction* 8 (Sum. 1971): 343-44.

B795   Perez-Minik, Domingo. "La Novela Extranjera en España: *El Libro de Bech*, de John Updike." *Insula* 26 (Oct. 1971): 6.

*B796   Theroux, Paul. "A Has-Been, 10 Years Later." *Chicago Tribune Book World* 14 Nov. 1971: 3, 10.

B797   Shanker, Israel. "The Old Manager at Home." *The New York Times Book Review* 9 Jan. 1972: 2.

B798   Lemeunier, Barbara Smith. "Henry Through the Looking-Glass: Eastern Europe and America in John Updike's *Bech: A Book*." Actes du Groupe de Recherche et Etudes Nord-Américaines. *L'Amérique et l'Europe:*

Réalites et représentations, Vol. 2. Ed. Serge Ricard. Aix-en-Provence: U de Provence, 1986. 131-45.

B799 Pinsker, Sanford. "John Updike and the Distractions of Henry Bech, Professional Writer and Amateur American Jew." *Modern Fiction Studies* 37 (Spring 1991): 97-111.

Rabbit Redux (1971):

B800 Raymont, Henry. "John Updike Completes a Sequel to *Rabbit, Run*." *The New York Times* 27 July 1971.

B801 "Presenting the Past." *New York* 13 Sept. 1971: 61.

B802 Allen, Bruce D. "Of a Linotype Operator at the Edge of Obsolescence." *Library Journal* 96 (1 Nov. 1971): 3640.

B803 Broyard, Anatole. "Updike Goes All Out At Last." *The New York Times* 121 (5 Nov. 1971): 40.

B804 Putney, Michael. "John Updike's 'Rabbit' Returns, Pale and Prepared to Grow Up." *The National Observer* 13 Nov. 1971.

B805 Leonard, John. "The Last Word: The Novel, Redux." *The New York Times Book Review* 14 Nov. 1971: 71. (Rpt. in *The New York Times Reviews John Updike, The Author and His Works*. N.Y. Fawcett, 1971. 15-17.)

B806 Locke, Richard. "Rabbit Returns: Updike Was Always There— It's Time We Noticed." *The New York Times Book Review* 14 Nov. 1971: 1-2, 12-16, 20-21. (Rpt. as *Rabbit Redux* in *The New York Times Reviews John Updike, The Author and His Works*. N.Y. Fawcett, 1971. 15-17.)

B807 Prescott, Peter. "Angstrom's Angst." *Newsweek* 78 (15 Nov. 1971): 124-25.

B808 Sheppard, R. Z. "Cabbage Moon." *Time* 96 (15 Nov. 1971): 89.

B809 Howes, Victor. "Rerun Rabbit Run." *Christian Science Monitor* 63 (18 Nov. 1971): 11.

*B810 "With Return of 'Rabbit,' Updike Among Top U. S. Writers, Says *Times*." *Ipswich Chronicle* 18 Nov. 1971: 8.

B811 Maddocks, Melvin. "The Old Cager, Still Running." *Life* 71 (19 Nov. 1971): 16.

B812 Samuels, Charles T. "Updike on the Present." *The New Republic* 165 (20 Nov. 1971): 29-30.

B813 Weber, Brom. "*Rabbit Redux.*" *Saturday Review* 54 (27 Nov. 1971): 54-55.

B814 "Seven Books of Special Significance Published in 1971." *The New York Times Book Review* 5 Dec. 1971: 2.

B815 Fuller, Edmund. "Return of Updike's Rabbit." *Wall Street Journal* 178 (6 Dec. 1971): 12.

*B816 Murray, Michele. "Rabbit Runs in Circles." *National Catholic Reporter* (10 Dec. 1971): 13.

*B817 Kennedy, Eileen. "*Rabbit Redux.*" *Best Sellers* 31 (15 Dec. 1971): 429-30.

B818 Ricks, Christopher. "Flopsy Bunny." *The New York Review of Books* 17 (16 Dec. 1971): 7-9.

B819 Davenport, Guy. "Even as the Heathen Rage." *National Review* 23 (31 Dec. 1971): 1473-1474.

B820 Suderman, Elmer. *Carleton Miscellany* 12 (Spring-Sum. 1972): 156-61.

B821 Epstein, Seymour. "The Emperor's Blue Jeans." *Denver Quarterly* 6, iv (1972): 89-95.

B822 Heidenry, John. "The Best American Novel in a Decade." *Commonweal* 95 (7 Jan. 1972): 332-33.

B823 Gill, Brendan. "A Special Case." *The New Yorker* 47 (8 Jan. 1972): 83-84.

B824 Oldsey, Bernard. "Rabbit Run to Earth." *Nation* 214 (10 Jan. 1972): 54, 56.

B825 "*Rabbit Redux.*" *Booklist* 68 (15 Jan. 1972): 414.

B826 Delrogh, Dennis. "Says the Rabbit, 'What's Updike?' Masterful Major Author." *Village Voice* 17 (27 Jan. 1972): 24-26.

B827 Edwards, Lee R. "Says the Rabbit, 'What's Updike?' As Pioneer, Most Wanting." *Village Voice* 17 (27 Jan. 1972): 24, 26.

B828 Lindroth, James R. "*Rabbit Redux.*" *America* 126 (29 Jan. 1972): 102-104.

B829 Wohlfert, Lee. "Rabbit Punch." *Women's Wear Daily* 18 Feb. 1972.

B830 Gordon, John. "Updike Redux." *Ramparts* 10 (Mar. 1972): 56-59.

*B831 Pochoda, Elizabeth. "Why Rabbit Thinks Vietnam Is Just a Head Fake." *Glamour* 67 (Mar. 1972): 6.

Criticism of Individual Works

B832 Gill, Brendan. "Notes on Current Books." *Virginia Quarterly Review* 48 (Spring 1972): lxviii.

B833 Lyons, Eugene. "John Updike: The Beginning and the End." *Critique* 14 (Spring 1972): 44-59.

B834 Mudrick, Marvin. "Fiction and Truth." *Hudson Review* 25 (Spring 1972): 142-56. (Pages 151-52 concern Updike.)

B835 Wyndham, Francis. "John Updike's Bulging Suitcases." *The Listener* 6 Apr. 1972: 454.

B836 Trevor, William. "All Right, Sort of." *New Statesman* 83 (7 Apr. 1972): 462-63.

B837 "Unsentimental Education." *Times Literary Supplement* 7 Apr. 1972: 385.

B838 Heidenry, John. "Back to Pennsylvania." *The Economist* 243 (8 Apr. 1972): 12.

B839 "Nicholas Richardson on John Updike." *Spectator* 228 (8 Apr. 1972): 553.

*B840 Symons, Julian. *London Sunday Times* 9 Apr. 1972: 40.

B841 Lodge, David. "The Lost American Dream." *Tablet* 15 Apr. 1972: 349-50.

B842 Hill, William B. "Fiction." *America* 126 (20 May 1972): 549-60. (Page 550 pertains to *Rabbit Redux*.)

B843 *Choice* 9 (June 1972): 510.

B844 Cooke, Michael. "Recent Fiction." *Yale Review* 61 (Sum. 1972): 599-609. (Pages 606-07 pertain to Updike.)

*845 Symons, Julian. *London Sunday Times* 9 Aug. 1972: 40.

B846 *Best Sellers* 32 (1 Dec. 1972): 423.

B847 Doherty, Paul C. "The Year's Best Buys in Paperbacks." *America* 127 (16 Dec. 1972): 526.

B848 Russell, Mariann. "White Man's Black Man: Three Views: *Mr. Sammler's Planet, Rabbit Redux, The Tenants*." *College Language Association Journal* 17 (1973): 93-100.

B849 O'Connell, Shawn. "Rabbits Remembered." *Massachusetts Review* 15 (Sum. 1974): 511-20.

B850 Falke, Wayne. "*Rabbit Redux*: Time/Order/God." *Modern Fiction Studies* 20 (Spring 1974): 59-75.

B851　　Horton, Andrew S. "Ken Kesey, John Updike and The Lone Ranger." *Journal of Popular Culture* 8 (Wint. 1974): 570-78. (Rpt. *Seasoned Authors for a New Season: The Search for Standards in Popular Writing*. Ed. Louis Filler. Bowling Green State UP, 1980. 83-90.)

B852　　Turner, Kermit S. "Rabbit Brought Nowhere: John Updike's *Rabbit Redux*." *South Carolina Review* 8 (1975): 35-42.

B853　　Vanderwerken, David L. "Rabbit 'Re-docks': Updike's Inner Space Odyssey." *College Literature* 2 (1975): 73-78.

B854　　Le Pellec, Yves. "Rabbit Underground." *Les Américainistes: New French Criticism on Modern American Fiction*. Ed. Ira D. Johnson and Christine Johnson, Port Washington: Kennikat, National University Publications, 1978. 94-109.

B855　　Waldmeir, J. J. "*Rabbit Redux* Reduced: Rededicated? Redeemed?" *Essays in Honor of Russell B. Nye*. East Lansing: Michigan State UP, 1978. 247-61.

B856　　Alter, Robert. "Updike, Malamud, and the Fire This Time." *Defense of the Imagination: Jewish Writers and Modern Historical Crisis*. Jewish Publication Society of America, 1978, 233-48. (Rpt. in *John Updike: A Collection of Critical Essays*. Eds. David Thorburn and Howard Eiland. Englewood Cliffs, N. J.: Prentice, 1979. 39-49.)

*B857　　Campbell, Jeff H. "Updike's Honky Apocalypse: *Rabbit Redux*." *New Mexico Humanities Review* May 1978: 53-60. (Rpt. in significantly different form in his *Updike's Novels: Thorns Spell a Word*. Wichita Falls: Midwestern State U P, 1987. 97-158.)

B858　　Held, George. "Men on the Moon: American Novelists Explore Lunar Space." *Michigan Quarterly Review* 18 (Spring 1979): 333-42. (Pages 333-41 pertain to Updike.)

B859　　Pritchard, William. "In Clover." *The New Republic* 185 (30 Sept. 1981): 30-32.

B860　　Slethaug, Gordon E. "*Rabbit Redux*: 'Freedom Is Made of Brambles.'" *Critical Essays on John Updike*. Ed. William R. Macnaughton. Boston: Hall, 1982. 237-53.

B861　　Berryman, Charles. "The Education of Harry Angstrom: Rabbit and the Moon." *Literary Review* 27 (Fall 1983): 117-26.

B862　　Khan, A. G. "Defiance and Acceptance: Two Modes of Cultural Response in Mailer's *American Dream* and *The Armies of the Night* and Updike's *Rabbit Redux*." *Indian Journal of American Studies* 14 (July 1984): 103-09.

Criticism of Individual Works 193

B863   Weber, Ronald. *Seeing Earth: Responses to Space Exploration.* Athens: U of Ohio P, 1985. 62-65, 89-91.

B864   Jackson, Edward M. "Rabbit Is Racist." *College Language Association Journal* 28 (June 1985): 444-451.

B865   De Bellis, Jack. "'The Awesome Power': John Updike's Use of Kubrick's '2001' in *Rabbit Redux.*" *Literature/Film Quarterly* 21.3 (1993): 209-217.

Museums and Women and Other Stories (1972):

B866   Hartman, Matthew. "*Museums and Women and Other Stories.*" *Library Journal* Aug. 1972: 2649.

B867   "Fact and Fiction." *New York* 11 Sept. 1972: 60.

B868   Breslin, John. *America* 127 (7 Oct. 1972): 265-268.

B869   Show, John. "Sliding Seaward." *Time* 100 (16 Oct. 1972): 91-92.

B870   Grumbach, Doris. "Suburban Middle Age." *New Republic* 167 (21 Oct. 1972): 30-31.

B871   Mano, Keith. "Every Inch an Updike." *Book World* 7 (22 Oct. 1972): 3.

B872   Tanner, Tony. "The Sorrow of Some Central Hollowness." *The New York Times Book Review* 22 Oct. 1972: 5, 24.

B873   Prescott, Peter S. "Following Through, Sadly." *Newsweek* 180 (23 Oct. 1972): 109, 112.

B874   Smith, Miles. "Updike's Style Criticized." *Reading* (Pa.) *Eagle* 5 Nov. 1972.

B875   Kennedy, Eileen. *Best Sellers* 32 (15 Nov. 1972): 392.

B876   Todd, Richard. "Updike and Barthelme: Disengagement." *Atlantic* 230 (Dec. 1972): 129-32. (Rpt. as "Disengagement in *Museums and Women.*" *John Updike: A Collection of Critical Essays.* Ed. David Thorburn and Howard Eiland. Englewood Cliffs, N. J.: Prentice, 1979. 207-11.)

B877   Wood, Michael. "Great American Fragments." *The New York Review of Books* 19 (14 Dec. 1972): 12-18. (Pages 14-17 pertain to Updike.)

B878   Rohrbach, Peter. "Paperbacks." *America* 127 (16 Dec. 1972): 535-36.

B879   *Choice* 9 (Jan. 1973): 451.

B880   Deemer, Charles. "Exploring Suburbia." *New Leader* 22 Jan. 1973: 18-19.

B881	Suderman, Elmer. "Alas-- Updike's Twice-Told Tales-- Poor Uric." *Carleton Miscellany* 13 (Spring 1973): 153.
B882	Mahon, Derek. "Pantsing." *Listener* 89 (26 Mar. 1973): 560.
B883	Phillips, Robert. *Commonweal* 98 (30 Mar. 1973): 92-93.
B884	Meyer, Arlin G. "Form, Fluidity, and Flexibility in Recent American Fiction." *The Cresset* 36 (Apr. 1973): 11-15. (Page 15 pertains to Updike.)
B885	Hope, Francis. "Too Much." *New Statesman* 86 (27 Apr. 1973): 626.
*B886	*Observer* (London) 29 Apr. 1973: 39.
B887	Dinnage, Rosemary. "At the Flashpoint." *Times Literary Supplement* 4 May 1973: 488. (Rpt. in *John Updike: A Collection of Critical Essays*. Ed. David Thorburn and Howard Eiland. Englewood Cliffs, N. J.: Prentice, 1979. 203-06.)
B888	Lipsius, Frank. *Books and Bookmen* 18 (Sept. 1973): 90-91.
B889	Hamilton, Alice and Kenneth. "John Updike's *Museums and Women and Other Stories*." *Thought* 49 (Mar. 1974): 56-71.
B890	Rosa, Alfred F. "The Psycholinguistics of Updike's 'Museums and Women.'" *Modern Fiction Studies* 20 (Spring 1974): 107-11.
B891	*The London Times* 2 Feb. 1975: 38e.
B892	Culbertson, Diana. "Updike's 'The Day of the Dying Rabbit.'" *Studies in American Fiction* 7 (1979): 95-99.
B893	*Book World* 27 Sept. 1981: 12.

Buchanan Dying (1974):

B894	Schlesinger, Arthur, Jr. "The Historical Mind and the Literary Imagination." *Atlantic* 233 (June 1974): 54-59. (Rpt. in *Dictionary of Literary Biography: Documentary Series: An Illustrated Chronicle*. Vol. 3. Ed. Mary Bruccolli. Detroit: Gale, 1983. 294-98.)
B895	"'Final Homage' Paid to His State." *Philadelphia Inquirer* 9 June 1974.
B896	Weintraub, Stanley. "Closet Drama." *The New Republic* 170 (22 June 1974): 26.
B897	Prescott, Peter S. "Immobile President." *Newsweek* 24 (June 1974): 82, 85-86.

Criticism of Individual Works 195

B898   Taylor, Robert. "Biographer, Subject Merge in Updike Book." *Boston Globe* 25 June 1974: 11.

B899   Putney, Michael. "Historian Updike Looks at...James Buchanan??" *National Observer* 6 July 1974: 17.

B900   "*Buchanan Dying*: A Play." *The New Yorker* 50 (8 July 1974): 80.

B901   Ehrenpreis, Irvin. "Buchanan Redux." *The New York Review of Books* 21 (8 Aug. 1974): 6, 8.

B902   Mano, D. Keith. "Doughy Middleness." *National Review* 26 (30 Aug. 1974): 987-88. (Rpt. in *Critical Essays on John Updike*. Ed. William R. Macnaughton. Boston: Hall, 1982. 74-76.)

B903   Straub, Peter. "Wise Women." *The New Statesman* 89 (10 Jan. 1975): 50.

B904   "F & M Featuring Updike Exhibit." *Reading* (Pa.) *Eagle* 6 Mar. 1976.

B905   Taylor, Sam. "Author John Updike Has Always Been Fascinated by Buchanan." *Lancaster* (Pa.) *New Era* 9 Mar. 1976.

B906   Fidler, John. "'Buchanan' Plays Well for Updike." *Reading* (Pa.) *Times* 30 Mar. 1976: 25, 27.

B907   "Updike Play Opens." *Reading* (Pa.) *Eagle* 30 Mar. 1976.

B908   Sullivan, Dan. "Updike Breathes Some Life into Buchanan." *Los Angeles Times* 27 Mar. 1977: 1, 54.

B909   "John Updike's *Buchanan Dying*: A Chamber Theatre Production." *Readers Theatre* 7 (Fall/Wint. 1979): 7, 8, 37.

A Month of Sundays (1975):

B910   Hartman, Matthew. "M&W&OS" *Library Journal* Aug. 1972: 2649.

B911   LeClair, Thomas. "Updike's Anti-Metafiction." *Fictional International* 4/5 (1975): 130-32.

B912   Bannon, Barbara A. *Publishers Weekly* 6 Jan. 1975: 52.

B913   Gray, Larry. *Library Journal* 1 Feb. 1975: 312.

*B914   *Book World* 16 Feb. 1975: 1.

B915   Gray, Paul. "Ring Around the Collar." *Time* 17 Feb. 1975: 82.

B916   Broyard, Anatole. "Some Unoriginal Sins." *The New York Times* 19 Feb. 1975: 33.

B917   Hall, Joan Joffe. "A Month of Sundays." *New Republic* 172 (22 Feb. 1975): 29-30.

B918   Stade, George. "The Resurrection of Reverend Marshfield." *The New York Times Book Review* 23 Feb. 1975: 4.

B919   Fuller, Edmund. "A Fallen Minister Searches His Soul." *Wall Street Journal* 25 Feb. 1975: 16.

B920   Edwards, Thomas R. "Busy Minister." *The New York Review of Books* 3 Mar. 1975: 18-19.

B921   Prescott, Peter S. "The Passionate Cleric." *Newsweek* 3 Mar. 1975: 72. (Rpt. in *Dictionary of Literary Biography: Documentary Series: An Illustrated Chronicle.* Volume 3. Ed. Mary Bruccolli. Detroit: Gale, 1983. 305-06.)

B922   DeMott, Benjamin. "Mod Masses, Empty Pews." *Saturday Review* 8 Mar. 1975: 20-21.

B923   Steiner, George. "Scarlet Letters." *The New Yorker* 51 (10 Mar. 1975): 116-18. (Rpt. in *John Updike: A Collection of Critical Essays.* Ed. David Thorburn and Howard Eiland. Englewood Cliffs, N.J.: Prentice, 1979. 93-98; and in *Dictionary of Literary Biography: Documentary Series: An Illustrated Chronicle.* Volume 3. Ed. Mary Bruccolli. Detroit: Gale, 1983. 299-302.)

B924   Iacobuzio, Ted. "Savor *A Month of Sundays.*" *Amherst Student Review* 17 Mar. 1975: 11.

B925   Hicks, Granville. "A Month of Sundays." *The American Way* Apr. 1975: 56-58.

B926   Hill, William B. "*A Month of Sundays.*" *America* 26 Apr. 1975: 320. (Rpt. in *Best Sellers 15 Mar. 1975: 559-60.)

B927   Larson, Janet Karsten. "A Man Out of the Cloth." *The Christian Century* 30 Apr. 1975: 445-47.

B928   *Critic* 33 (May/June 1975): 81.

B929   Morrissey, Daniel. "*A Month of Sundays.*" *Commonweal* 102 (6 June 1975): 187-188.

B930   De Feo, Ronald. "Sex, Sermons, and Style." *National Review* 27 (20 June 1975): 679.

Criticism of Individual Works

B931   Hunt, George. "John Updike's Sunday Sort of Book." *America* 132 (21 June 1975): 477-80.

B932   Gelfant, Blanche H. "Fiction Chronicle." *Hudson Review* 28 (Sum. 1975): 313.

B933   Sleeth, Ronald. "*A Month of Sundays*." *Perkins Journal* 28 (Sum. 1975): 41-42.

B934   Ackroyd, Peter. "Wittery." *The Spectator* 234 (28 June 1975): 781.

B935   Hepburn, Neil. "Ad Libidum." *The Listener* 3 July 1975: 30-31.

B936   Carey, John. "Desert Father." *New Statesman* 90 (4 July 1975): 21.

B937   Dinnage, Rosemary. "Lusting for God." *Times Literary Supplement* 4 July 1975: 713.

*B938   *Guardian Weekly* 5 July 1975: 21.

B939   Lipsius, Frank. "Yankee Saints and Sinners." *Books and Bookmen* 20 (Sept. 1975): 28.

B940   Baker, Carlos. "*A Month of Sundays*." *Theology Today* 32 (Oct. 1975): 335-36.

B941   Forbes, Cheryl. "John Updike: Words, Words." *Christianity Today* 20 (24 Oct. 1975): 16-18.

*B942   *Book World* 7 Mar. 1976: 7.

B943   Doherty, Gail and Paul. "Spring Paperback Parade." *America* 134 (20 Mar. 1976): 230.

B944   Galgan, Gerald J. "After Christianity, What?" *Commonweal* 103 (5 Nov. 1976): 723-25.

B945   Pinsker, S. "*A Month of Sundays*, by John Updike." *Studies in Short Fiction* 13 (Wint. 1976): 93-94.

B946   Sorrentino, Gilbert. "Never on Sunday." *Partisan Review* 43 (Wint. 1976): 119-21. (Rpt. in *Critical Essays on John Updike*. Ed. William R. Macnaughton. Boston: Hall, 1982. 77-79.)

B947   Thomas, Lloyd Spencer. "Scarlet Sundays: Updike vs. Hawthorne." *CEA Critic* 39. 3 (1977): 16-17.

B948   Uphaus, Suzanne Henning. "The Unified Vision of *A Month of Sundays*." *University of Windsor Review* 12 (Spring-Sum. 1977): 5-16.

B949   Hunt, George. "Updike's Omega-Shaped Shelter: Structure and Psyche in *A Month of Sundays*." *Critique* 19. 3 (1978): 47-60.

*B950   Kesterton, David B. "Updike and Hawthorne: Not So Strange Bedfellows." *Notes on Modern American Literature* 3 (1979): item 11.

B951   Detweiler, Robert. "Updike's *A Month of Sundays* and the Language of the Unconscious." *Journal of the American Academy of Religion* 47 (Dec. 1979): 611-25. (Rpt. in *Essays in Honour of Edwin Sturzl on his 60th Birthday*. Ed. James Hogg. Salzburg: FustfürEng.Spring & Lit, 1982. 76-100; and as a "short version" in Detweiler's *Story, Sign, and Self*. Philadelphia: Fortress, 1978. 154-64.)

B952   Abbott, H. Porter. "Diary Fiction." *Orbis Litterarum: International Review of Literary Studies* 37 (1982): 12-31. (Page 17 discusses *A Month of Sundays*.)

B953   Waller, Gary. "Stylus Dei or the Open-Endedness of Debate?: Success and Failure in *A Month of Sundays*." *Critical Essays on John Updike*. Ed. William R. Macnaughton. Boston: Hall, 1982. 269-80.

B954   Eiland, Howard. "Updike's Womanly Man." *Centennial Review* 26 (Fall 1982): 312-23.

B955   Matthews, John T. "The World as Scandal: Updike's *A Month of Sundays*." *Arizona Quarterly* 39 (1983): 351-380.

B956   Davies, Marie-Hélène. "Fools for Christ's Sake: A Study of Clerical Figures in De Vries, Updike and Buechner." *Thalia* 6. 1 (Spring–Sum. 1984): 60-72. (Pages 64-67 concern *A Month of Sundays*.)

B957   Crowley, Sue Mitchell. "John Updike and Kierkegaard's Negative Way: Irony and Indirect Communication in *A Month of Sundays*." *Soundings* 68 (Sum. 1985): 212-28.

B958   Greiner, Donald. "Body and Soul: John Updike and *The Scarlet Letter*." *Journal of Modern Literature* 15 (Spring 1989): 475-95.

B959   Schiff, James A. *Updike's Version: Rewriting The Scarlet Letter*. Columbia, Mo.: U Mo. P, 1992.

Picked-Up Pieces (1975):

B960   Ott, William A. *Library Journal* 1 Oct. 1975: 1828.

B961   Johnson, Albert H. *Publishers Weekly* 6 Oct. 1975: 84.

B962   Cole, William. "Open Mind, Full Book." *Saturday Review* 15 Nov. 1975: 28.

Criticism of Individual Works   199

B963   Graver, Lawrence. "Even the Footnotes Sparkle." *The New York Times Book Review* 30 Nov. 1975: 39. (Rpt. in *Dictionary of Literary Biography: Documentary Series: An Illustrated Chronicle.* Volume 3. Ed. Mary Bruccolli. Detroit: Gale, 1983. 302, 304-05.)

B964   Broyard, Anatole. "On a Spree with Updike." *The New York Times* 2 Dec. 1975: 37.

B965   *Progressive* 40 (Mar. 1976): 45.

B966   Amis, Martin. "Life Class." *New Statesman* 91 (19 Mar. 1976): 368.

B967   Russell, John. "Praising and Sharing." *Times Literary Supplement* (19 Mar. 1976): 309.

B968   *Observer* 21 Mar. 1976: 30.

Marry Me (1976):

*B969   *Book World* 29 Aug. 1976: M-1.

B970   Hendin, Josephine. "Updike as Matchmaker." *Nation* 223 (30 Oct. 1976): 437-39. (Rpt. in *John Updike: A Collection of Critical Essays*. Ed. David Thorburn and Howard Eiland. Englewood Cliffs, N. J.: Prentice, 1979. 99-106.)

B971   Howard, Maureen. "Jerry and Sally and Richard and Ruth." *The New York Times Book Review* 31 Oct. 1976: 2.

B972   Todd, Richard. "A Ladies' Man." *Atlantic* 238 (Nov. 1976): 115-16.

B973   Prescott, Peter S. "To Have and to Hold." *Newsweek* 8 Nov. 1976: 103.

B974   Lehmann-Haupt, Christopher. "When Couples Married." *The New York Times* 11 Nov. 1976: 39.

*B975   *Book World* 14 Nov. 1976: L-1.

B976   Foote, Timothy. "Uncouples." *Time* 15 Nov. 1976: 97.

B977   Davis, L. J. "Getting Too Full of Updike." *National Observer* 20 Nov. 1976: 25.

B978   Kazin, Alfred. "Alfred Kazin on Fiction." *The New Republic* 175 (27 Nov. 1976): 22-23. (Rpt. in *Critical Essays on John Updike*. Ed. William R. Macnaughton. Boston: Hall, 1982. 79-80.)

B979   Brophy, Brigid. "Love in the Garden State." *Harper's Magazine* 253 (Dec. 1976): 80-82.

B980   Kapp, Isa. "In and Out of Wedlock." *New Leader* 6 Dec. 1976: 6.

B981   Fuller, Edmund. "Updike at the Top of His Form." *Wall Street Journal* 7 Dec. 1976: 22.

*B982   *Book World* 12 Dec. 1976: H-1.

B983   Thomas, Phil. "Weak Spots Mar Updike's Novel." *Reading* (Pa.) *Eagle* 26 Dec. 1976.

*B984   McGill, Deborah. "Promises Made and Broken." Durham (N.C.) *Morning Herald* 2 Jan. 1977: 3-D.

B985   [Hunt, George W.] *America* 136 (8 Jan. 1977): 18-19. (No author given; author interpolated.)

B986   Miller, Karl. "Couples." *The New York Review of Books* 24 (3 Feb. 1977): 38-41. (Pages 38-39 pertain to Updike.)

B987   Kennedy, Eileen. *Choice* 13 (4 Feb. 1977): 1602.

B988   LeClair, Thomas. "Updike and Gardner: Down from the Heights." *Commonweal* 104 (4 Feb. 1977): 89-90.

B989   Irwin, Michael. *Virginia Quarterly Review* 53 (Spring 1977): 62, 64.

B990   Johnson, Greg. "Updike's Infidelities." *Southwest Review* 62 (Spring 1977): 207-08.

B991   Pritchard, William H. "Merely Fiction." *Hudson Review* 30 (Spring 1977): 147-60.

B992   Way, Brian. "The Case for the Defensive." *The New Review* 4 (Apr. 1977): 55-57.

B993   Hepburn, Neil. "Blank Looks." *Listener* 97 (21 Apr. 1977): 83-84.

B994   Irwin, Michael. "Jerry & Sally & Richard & Ruth." *Times Literary Supplement* 22 Apr. 1977: 477.

B995   Ackroyd, Peter. "Paradise Lost." *Spectator* 238 (23 Apr. 1977): 22.

B996   Bradbury, Malcolm. "Made in Heaven." *New Statesman* 93 (29 Apr. 1977): 568-69.

B997   Mount, Ferdinand. "The Novel of the Narcissus." *Encounter* 48 (June 1977) 51-65. (Page 54 concerns Updike.)

B998   *Booklist* 73 (1 June 1977): 1476.

B999   Thorburn, David. "Recent Novels: Realism Redux." *Yale Review* 66 (Sum. 1977): 584-85.

B1000   Sullivan, Walter. "The Insane and the Indifferent: Walker Percy and Others." *Sewanee Review* 86 (Wint. 1978): 153-59. (Pages 153-54 pertain to Updike.)

B1001   Cameron, Dee Birch. "The Unitarian Wife and the One-Eyed Man: Updike's *Marry Me* and 'Sunday Teasing.'" *Ball State University Forum* 21 (1980): 54-64.

B1002   Monnier-Brousse, Françoise. "Mort, amour et religion dans *Marry Me*." *Le Facteur religieux en Amérique du Nord*, Volume 2, *Les Etats-Unis*. Ed. Jean Béranger. Talence: Centre d'Etudes Canadiennes en Sciences Sociales, Université de Bordeaux III: 1981. 59-76.

B1003   Hallissy, Margaret. "Marriage, Morality and Maturity in Updike's *Marry Me*." *Renascence* 37 (1985): 96-106.

B1004   Leckie, Barbara. "'The Adulterous Society': John Updike's *Marry Me*." *Modern Fiction Studies* 37 (Spring 1991): 61-79.

*B1005 Magaw, Malcolm O. "From Vermeer to Bonnard: Updike's Interartistic mode in *Marry Me*." *Midwest Quarterly* 33 (Wint. 1992): 137-50.

Tossing and Turning (1977):

B1006   Vendler, Helen. "John Updike on Poetry." *The New York Times Book Review* 10 Apr. 1977: 3, 28. (Excerpted in *The John Updike Newsletter* 3 (1977): 2. See "Interviews.")

B1007   *Booklist* 73 (15 May 1977): 1398.

B1008   Juhasz, Suzanne. "Tossing and Turning." *Library Journal* 102 (1 June 1977): 1281.

B1009   *Choice* 14 (Oct. 1977): 1057.

B1010   Hodgart, Matthew. "Family Snapshots." *Times Literary Supplement* 13 Oct. 1978: 1158.

B1011   *Virginia Quarterly Review* 54 (Wint. 1978): 10.

B1012   "*Playboy*'s Annual Awards: Best Short Story: 'Killing.'" *Playboy* 30 (Jan. 1983): 192.

The Coup (1978):

B1013   Dalton, Elizabeth. "To Have and Have Not." *Partisan Review* 36 (Wint. 1969): 134-36.

B1014   Wiehe, Janet. *Library Journal* 103 (15 Oct. 1978): 2137.

B1015   Prescott, Peter S. *Newsweek* 92 (20 Nov. 1978): 125-125-E.

B1016   "*The Coup.*" *Playboy* 25 (Dec. 1978): 36.

B1017   Merkin, Daphne. "Updike in Africa." *New Leader* 4 Dec. 1978: 21-22.

B1018   Burgess, Anthony. "Lyric and Loving." *Inquiry* 2 (11 Dec. 1978): 12-14.

B1019   Siedenbaum, Art. *Los Angeles Times* 3 Dec. 1978.

B1020   Towers, Robert. "Updike in Africa." *The New York Times Book Review* 83 (10 Dec. 1978): 1, 55. (Rpt. in *John Updike: A Collection of Critical Essays*. Ed. David Thorburn and Howard Eiland. Englewood Cliffs, N.J.: Prentice, 1979. 157-61.)

B1021   Nordell, Roderick. *Christian Science Monitor* 13 Dec. 1978: 21.

B1022   Buckley, William F. Jr. "Jungle Music." *New York* 11 (18 Dec. 1978): 93.

B1023   Reid, Alastair. "Updike Country." *The New Yorker* 54 (18 Dec. 1978): 65-67.

B1024   Sheppard, R. Z. "White Mischief." *Time* 112 (18 Dec. 1978): 90-91.

B1025   Hayes, Harold. "Updike's African Dream." *Esquire* 90 (19 Dec. 1978): 27-29.

B1026   Thompson, John. "Updike le Noir." *The New York Review of Books* 25 (21 Dec. 1978): 3-4.

B1027   LaSalle, Peter. "More Than You Are Dreamt of in Your Philosophy." *America* 139 (23 Dec. 1978): 482.

B1028   McGill, Deborah. "Boy's Life." *Harper's* 258 (Jan. 1979): 87-89. (Rpt. in *John Updike: A Collection of Critical Essays*. Ed. David Thorburn and Howard Eiland. Englewood Cliffs, N.J.: Prentice, 1979. 162-66.)

B1029   Oates, Joyce Carol. "*The Coup* by John Updike." *The New Republic* 180 (6 Jan. 1979): 32-35. (Rpt. in *Critical Essays on John Updike*. Ed. William R. Macnaughton. Boston: Hall, 1982. 80-86; and in *Dictionary of Literary Biography: Documentary Series: An Illustrated Chronicle*. Volume 3. Ed. Mary Bruccolli. Detroit: Gale, 1983. 309, 311-13.)

B1030	Lyons, Gene. "Cultural Deformations." *Nation* 228 (3 Feb. 1979): 117.
B1031	Hill, Douglas. "Rabbit Angstrom, I presume?" *Books in Canada* Mar. 1979: 12-13.
B1032	Jones, D. A. N. "Kismet Kush." *The Listener* 101 (Mar. 1979): 390, 392.
B1033	Murray, James G. "*The Coup*." *Critic* 37 (1 Mar. 1979): 4.
*B1034	Collier, Peter. "Author's Choice." *Book-of-the-Month Club News* Spring 1979: 21.
B1035	Howard, Maureen. "New Books in Review: Eight Recent Novels." *Yale Review* 68 (Spring 1979): 436-37.
B1036	Kuball, David. "John Updike: *The Coup*." *Gramercy Review* 3 (Spring 1979): 57-59.
B1037	Sullivan, Walter. "Model Citizens and Marginal Cases Heroes of the Day." *Sewanee Review* 87 (Spring 1979): 343-44.
B1038	Lodge, David. "The King's Head." *New Statesman* 97 (23 Mar. 1979): 404-05.
B1039	Ableman, Paul. "Poetic Precision, Prose Breadth." *Spectator* 242 (24 Mar. 1979): 18.
B1040	Tomalin, Claire. "State of Africa." *Punch* 276 (28 Mar. 1979): 552-53.
B1041	Evanier, David. "An Affirmative Action." *National Review* 31 (13 Apr. 1979): 490-91.
B1042	Browne, Joseph. "The Coup." *America* 140 (5 May 1979): 379-80.
B1043	Flower, Dean. "Picking Up the Pieces." *Hudson Review* 32 (Sum. 1979): 292-307. (Pages 300-02 pertain to Updike.)
B1044	Paulin, Tom. "Operatic Surface, Deep Politics." *Encounter* 53 (Aug. 1979): 52-55.
*B1045	Broyard, Anatole. "Books of the Times." *The New York Times* 29 Nov. 1979: C-24.
B1046	Ryle, John. "Going with the Current." *Times Literary Supplement* 30 Nov. 1979: 77.
B1047	Markovitz, Irving Leonard. "John Updike's Africa." *Canadian Journal of African Studies* 14 (1980): 536-45.
B1048	Cooke, Judy. "Bull's Eye." *New Statesman* 99 (10 Oct. 1980): 22-23.

B1049   Lemeunier, Barbara. "A Fable for Modern Times: America and Africa in John Updike's *The Coup*." *Les Américaines et les autres*. Ed. Serge Ricard. Actes du Groupe de Recherche et d'Etudes Nord-Américaines, 1981. Aix-en-Provence: Publications U de Provence, 1982. 101-16.

B1050   Chukwu, Augustine. "The Dreamer as Leader: Ellellou in John Updike's *The Coup*." *Literary Half-Yearly* 23, I (1982): 61-69.

B1051   Markle, Joyce. "*The Coup*: Illusions and Insubstantial Impressions." *Critical Essays on John Updike*. Ed. William R. Macnaughton. Boston: Hall, 1982. 281-301.

B1052   *London Review of Books* 4 Feb. 1982: 19.

B1053   Last, Brian W. "Literary Reactions to Colonialism: A Comparative Study of Joyce Cary, Chinua Achebe and John Updike." *World Literature Written in English* 22 (Autumn 1983): 151-170.

*B1054   Moore, Jack B. "Africa Under Western Eyes: Updike's *The Coup* and Other Fantasies." *African Literature Today* 14 (1984): 60-67.

B1055   Lathrop, Kathleen. "*The Coup*: John Updike's Modernist Masterpiece." *Modern Fiction Studies* 31 (Sum. 1985): 249-62.

B1056   Greiner, Donald J. "*The Coup*." *Modern Critical Views: John Updike*. Ed. Harold Bloom. N.Y.: Chelsea House, 1987. 139-153. (Rpt. from *John Updike's Novels*. Athens: Ohio UP, 1984. 28-43.)

B1057   Schueller, Malini. "Containing the Third World: John Updike's *The Coup*." *Modern Fiction Studies* 37 (Spring 1991): 113-28.

Problems and Other Stories (1979):

B1058   Wiehe, Janet. "*Problems and Other Stories*." *Library Journal* 104 (Aug. 1979): 1592.

B1059   Romano, John. "Updike's People." *The New York Times Book Review* 28 Oct. 1979: 1, 44-45.

B1060   Clemons, Walter. "Chamber Music of Betrayals." *Newsweek* 94 (29 Oct. 1979): 99.

B1061   Loercher, Diana. *Christian Science Monthly* 17 (Nov. 1979): 17.

B1062   Broyard, Anatole. "*Problems and Other Stories*." *The New York Times Book Review* 2 Nov. 1979: 1.

B1063   Towers, Robert. "Cuisine Minceur: *Problems and Other Stories*." *The New York Review of Books* 8 Nov. 1979: 18-20.

B1064	*"Problems and Other Stories." Los Angeles Magazine* 25 (Feb. 1980): 223.
A1065	Evanier, David. "Wearing Down." *National Review* 32 (22 Feb. 1980): 231.
B1066	Hunt, George W. "The Problems of John Updike." *America* 142 (8 Mar. 1980): 187-88.
B1067	Murray, James G. *"Problems and Other Stories." Critic* 38 (11 Mar. 1980): 3-4.
B1068	*Virginia Quarterly Review* 56 (Spring 1980): 68.
B1069	Murtaugh, Daniel M. *"Problems and Other Stories." Commonweal* 107 (28 Mar. 1980): 189-90.
B1070	Walsh, William. "American Ambitions." *Books and Bookmen* 25 (May 1980): 38-39.
B1071	Dinnage, Rosemary. "John Updike: 'Problems.'" *The Times Literary Supplement* 23 May 1980: 575.
B1072	*Observer* 25 May 1980: 29.
B1073	Campbell, James. "Front Lawn." *New Statesman* 30 May 1980: 821-22.
B1074	Davies, Russell. "Modern Torments." *Listener* 103 (12 June 1980): 771-72.
B1075	Garrett, George. "Technics and Pyrotechnics." *Sewanee Review* 88 (Sum. 1980): 412-23.
B1076	Johnson, M. *World Literature Today* 54 (Sum. 1980): 440-41.
B1077	Pritchard, William. "Fictional Fixes." *Hudson Review* 33 (Sum. 1980): 257-270.
B1078	*Illustrated London News* 268 (July 1980): 69.
B1079	*Observer* 13 July 1980: 29.
B1080	Gu, Xuefan and Fu Shi. "Updike's Novelette 'Son', I: Translation and Background Information; II: Four Taboos on Translating Literary Works." *Waiguoyu* 3 (1983): 48-54.
B1081	Zhou, Guozhen and Maoru Qiu. "Updike's 'Son': An Analysis of Its Theme and Some Expressions." *Waiguoyu* 2 (Mar. 1983): 40-45. (In Japanese).

Too Far to Go (1979):

B1082   Cole, William. "Too Explicit." *Saturday Review* 4 (16 Apr. 1977): 50.

B1083   Broyard, Anatole. "Falling Into Love." *The New York Times* 17 Mar. 1979: 17.

B1084   Theroux, Paul. "A Marriage of Mixed Blessings." *The New York Times Book Review* 8 Apr. 1979: 7, 34. (Rpt. in *Critical Essays on John Updike*. Ed. William R. Macnaughton. Boston: Hall, 1982. 86-88.)

B1085   Jong, Erica. "*Too Far to Go*." *The New Republic* 181 (15 Sept. 1979): 36-37.

B1086   *National Forum* 60 (Sum. 1980): 46.

B1087   Barnes, Jane. "John Updike: A Literary Spider." *Virginia Quarterly Review* 57 (Wint. 1981): 79-98. (Rpt. in *Modern Critical Views: John Updike*. Ed. Harold Bloom. N.Y.: Chelsea House, 1987. 111-26.)

B1088   Wilhelm, Albert E. "Narrative Continuity in Updike's *Too Far to Go*." *Journal of the Short Story in English* 7 (Autumn 1986): 87-90.

B1089   ___. "The Trail-of-Bread-Crumbs Motif in Updike's Maples Stories." *Studies in Short Fiction* 25 (Wint. 1988): 71-73.

B1090   Mann, Susan Garland. "John Updike's *Too Far to Go*: The Maples Stories." *The Short Story Cycle*. N.Y.: Greenwood P, 1989. 173-83, 206-07.

Rabbit Is Rich (1981):

B1091   Le Pellec, Yves. "Rabbit Underground." *Les Américanistes: New French Criticism on Modern American Fiction*. Ed. Ira D. and Christiane Johnson. Port Washington, N.Y.: Kennikat National U Publications, 1978. 94-109.

B1092   Ehresmann, Julia M. *Booklist* 77 (1 June 1981): 1277.

B1093   Wiehe, Janet. *Library Journal* 106 (July 1981): 1445.

B1094   *Publishers Weekly* 14 Aug. 1981: 51.

B1095   Leonard, John. "Books of the Times." *The New York Times* 22 Sept. 1981: C-13.

B1096   [Bech, Henry] "Updike on Updike." *The New York Times Book Review* (27 Sept. 1981): 1, 34-35.

B1097   Sale, Roger. "Rabbit Returns." *The New York Times Book Review* (27 Sept. 1981): 1, 32-34.

Criticism of Individual Works

B1098   Prescott, Peter S. "Rabbit Rides Again." *Newsweek* 98 (28 Sept. 1981): 89-90.

B1099   Fremont-Smith, Eliot. "Rabbit Ruts." *Village Voice* 26 (30 Sept.-6 Oct. 1981): 35, 55. (Rpt. in *Dictionary of Literary Biography: Documentary Series: An Illustrated Chronicle*. Volume 3. Ed. Mary Bruccolli. Detroit: Gale, 1983. 315-20.)

B1100   Pritchard, William. "In Clover: *Rabbit Is Rich* by John Updike." *New Republic* 185 (30 Sept. 1981): 30-32.

B1101   Simon, John. "In Clover." *The New Republic* 185 (30 Sept. 1981): 30.

B1102   Bell, Pearl K. "Sequels." *Commentary* 72 (Oct. 1981): 72.

B1103   Edwards, Thomas R. "Updike's Rabbit Trilogy." *Atlantic* 248 (Oct. 1981): 94, 96, 100-01.

B1104   Ellison, James. "Rabbit Is Buying Krugerrands." *Psychology Today* 15 (Oct. 1981): 110-15.

B1105   Kakutani, Michiko. "Turning Sex and Guilt into an American Epic." *Saturday Review* 8 (Oct. 1981): 14-15, 20-22. (Rpt. in Michiko Kakutani, *Poet at the Piano*. N.Y.: Times Books, 1988. 80-88.)

B1106   Wolcott, James. "Running On Empty." *Esquire* 96 (Oct. 1981): 20, 22-23.

B1107   Gray, Paul. "A Crisis of Confidence." *Time* 5 Oct. 1981: 90-91.

B1108   Holleran, Andrew. "Rabbit Resplendent." *New York* 5 Oct. 1981: 64.

B1109   Clapperton, Jane. "Cosmo Reads the New Books." *Cosmopolitan* Nov. 1981: 28.

B1110   Croghan, L. A. "Wilson Library Reviews." *Wilson Library Bulletin* 56 (Nov. 1981): 224.

B1111   Evans, Nancy. "*Rabbit Is Rich*." *Glamour* Nov. 1981: 204.

B1112   Spitz, Bob. "*Rabbit Is Rich*." *Penthouse* 13 (Nov. 1981): 59.

B1113   Murtaugh, Dennis M. "At Home with Obsolescence." *Commonweal* 6 Nov. 1981: 624-25.

B1114   Lyons, Gene. "The Way We Are." *The Nation* 233 (7 Nov. 1981): 477-79.

B1115   Pritchett, V. S. "Updike." *The New Yorker* 9 Nov. 1981: 201-06.

B1116   Mallon, Thomas. "Rabbit, Jog." *National Review* 33 (13 Nov. 1981): 1356, 1358.

B1117   Kazin, Alfred. "Easy Come, Easy Go." *The New York Review of Books* 28 (19 Nov. 1981): 3.

B1118   Hunt, George W. "Updike's Rabbit Returns." *America* 145 (21 Nov. 1981): 321-22.

B1119   Harris, Robert R. "The 20 Best Books of 1981." *Saturday Review* 8 (Dec. 1981): 77.

B1120   Woodward, Kenneth. "Books: Critics' Christmas Choices." *Commonweal* 4 Dec. 1981: 694.

B1121   "Editor's Choice." *The New York Times Book Review* 6 Dec. 1981: 14.

B1122   Broyard, Anatole. "Ordinary People." *The New York Times Book Review* 86 (13 Dec. 1981): 43.

B1123   Lekachman, Robert. "The Year in Books." *The Nation* 26 Dec. 1981: 712.

B1124   Pochoda, Elizabeth. "The Year in Books." *The Nation* 26 Dec. 1981: 89.

B1125   Patterson, Jack. "The Christmas Books to Give and Receive." *Business Week* 28 Dec. 1981: 11.

B1126   Wolmuth, Roger. "John Updike's Fictional Hero Comes Back Fat, Rich and Ready for the '80s." *People* 28 Dec. 1981: 36-37.

B1127   "*Playboy's* Annual Awards: Best Major Work: *Rabbit Is Rich.*" *Playboy* 29 (Jan. 1982): 198.

B1128   Cooke, Judy. "Rabbit Is Rich." *New Statesman* 15 Jan. 1982: 19.

B1129   Rumens, Carol. "The Tackier Textures of Success." *Times Literary Supplement* 15 Jan. 1982: 48.

B1130   Wood, Ralph. "John Updike's Rabbit Saga." *The Christian Century* 99 (20 Jan. 1982): 50-54.

B1131   "Rabbit Is Rich." *The Progressive* 46 (Feb. 1982): 63.

B1132   Taubman, Robert. "Nobody Is God." *London Review of Books* 4 (4 Feb. 1982): 19-20.

B1133   McDowell, Edwin. "Middle-Aged Domesticity." *The New York Times Book Review* 87 (28 Feb. 1982): 34. (Includes an excerpt from Updike's Circle Critics Award acceptance speech for *Rabbit Is Rich*.)

B1134	Jacobs, Rita D. "*Rabbit Is Rich.*" *World Literature Today* 56 (Spring 1982): 340.
B1135	Lively, Penelope. "Recent Fiction." *Encounter* 58 (Apr. 1982): 74-81. (Pages 75-76 pertain to *Rabbit Is Rich*.)
B1136	"Updike's 'Rabbit' Wins Anew." *Reading* (Pa.) *Eagle* 20 Apr. 1982.
B1137	"Updike Wins 2nd Award for Same Rabbit Novel." *Reading* (Pa.) *Times* 20 Apr. 1982.
B1138	"*Rabbit Is Rich* Wins American Book Award." *Publishers Weekly* 30 Apr. 1982: 18.
B1139	Wolfe, Peter. "Small Pocket of Middle-Aged Peace." *Prairie Schooner* 56 (Fall 1982): 86-88.
B1140	Pawley, Daniel W. "Updike's Rich Rabbit: Suffocating in Sin." *Christianity Today* 26 (12 Nov. 1982) 100-01.
B1141	Halio, Jay. L. "Contemplation, Fiction, and the Writer's Sensiblity." *Southern Review* 19 (Jan. 1983): 203-18.
B1142	Campbell, Jeff H. "Light on Your Fur: Regeneration in Updike's *Rabbit Is Rich.*" *Lamar Journal of the Humanities* 10 (Spring 1984): 7-13.
B1143	Koehler, Ray. "*Rabbit Is Rich* and So's Updike." *Reading* (Pa.) *Times* 13 Aug. 1985.
B1144	Ancona, Francesco Aristide. *Writing the Absence of the Father: Undoing Oedipal Structures in the Contemporary American Novel.* Lanham: UP of America, 1986. 81-91.
B1145	Amis, Martin. "John Updike: Rabbitland and Bechville." *The Moronic Inferno and Other Visits to America.* N.Y.: Viking, 1987. 155-59.
B1146	Gullette, Margaret. "John Updike: Rabbit Angstrom Grows Up." In *Safe at Last in the Middle Years.* Berkeley: U of Calif. P, 1988. 59-84.
B1147	Porter, M. Gilbert. "From Babbitt to Rabbit: The American Materialist in Search of a Soul." In Gilbert Debusscher and Marc Maufort, *American Literature in Belgium.* Amsterdam: Rodopi, 1988. 185-96.
B1148	Lasseter, Victor K. "*Rabbit Is Rich* as a Naturalistic Novel." *American Literature* 61 (Oct. 1989): 429-45.
*B1149	Powers, Katherine A. "Mind Benders: Out of Step." *Boston* 83 (Apr. 1991): 50-52.

Bech Is Back (1982):

B1150   Atlas, James. "*Bech Is Back*." *Atlantic* 250 (Oct. 1982): 103.

B1151   Marcus, Greil. "Caveat Emptor. *Bech Is Back*." *California* 7 (Oct. 1982): 124.

B1152   Wiehe, Janet. "*Bech Is Back*." *Library Journal* 1 Oct. 1982: 1897.

B1153   Gray, Paul. "Perennial Promises Kept." *Time* 120 (18 Oct. 1982): 72-74, 79-81.

B1154   Clapperton, Jane. "Cosmo Reads the New Books." *Cosmopolitan* Nov. 1982: 66.

B1155   Medwick, Cathleen. "John Updike's Notorious Alter Ego." *Vogue* Nov. 1982: 60.

B1156   "*Bech Is Back*." *Business Week* 1 Nov. 1982: 15.

B1157   Sigal, Clancy. "Return of the Kvetch." *New York* 1 Nov. 1982: 70.

B1158   Rubins, Josh. "Jew D'Esprit." *The New York Review of Books* 29 (18 Nov. 1982): 17-19.

B1159   "*Bech Is Back*." *The New Yorker* 58 (29 Nov. 1982): 174.

B1160   Williamson, Bruce. "*Bech Is Back*." *Playboy* 29 (Dec. 1982): 34.

B1161   Lynn, Kenneth S. "Bunny Stuff." *National Review* 34 (10 Dec. 1982): 1558.

B1162   Kapp, Isa. "Updike in a Foreign Country." *New Leader* 85 (13 Dec. 1982): 5-7.

B1163   Howard, Jane. "*Bech Is Back*." *Mademoiselle* Jan. 1983: 26, 30.

B1164   Gilbert, Harriett. "Making It." *New Statesman* 105 (21 Jan. 1983): 26.

B1165   Amis, Martin. "John Updike: Rabbitland and Bechville." *The Moronic Inferno and Other Visits to America*. N.Y.: Viking, 1987. 155-59.

Hugging the Shore (1983):

B1166   S. V. C. "Updike Redux: Grace Notes." *Vogue* Sept. 1983: 98.

B1167   Wolcott, James. "The Price of Finesse." *Harper's* 267 (Sept. 1983): 63-66.

Criticism of Individual Works 211

B1168   Donoghue, Denis. "The Zeal of a Man of Letters." *The New York Times Book Review* 18 Sept. 1983: 1, 30-31.

B1169   Lehman, David. "Charting a Literary Course." *Newsweek* 19 Sept. 1983: 78.

B1170   Wilson, Victor. "John Updike Unveils Opinions on Authors in his New Collection." *Reading* (Pa.) *Eagle* 25 Sept. 1983.

B1171   "*Hugging the Shore: Essays and Criticism.*" *Playboy* 30 (Oct. 1983): 27.

B1172   Koenig, Rhoda. "*Hugging the Shore.*" *New York* 3 Oct. 1983: 69-71.

B1173   Spencer, Scott. "Updike Delux." *Esquire* Nov. 1983: 197-98.

B1174   Mysak, Joe. "Gossip of a Higher Sort." *National Review* 35 (11 Nov. 1983): 1426.

B1175   Simon, John. "Plying a Periplus." *The New Republic* 189 (21 Nov. 1983): 34-37.

B1176   Schwartz, Sanford. "Top of the Class." *The New York Review of Books* 30 (24 Nov. 1983): 26-30, 35.

B1177   Stuttaford, Genevieve. *Commonweal* 2 Dec. 1983: 663.

B1178   "Editor's Choice: The Best Books of 1983." *The New York Times Book Review* 4 Dec. 1983: 74.

B1179   Hunt, George. "*Hugging the Shore.*" *America* 151 (31 Dec. 1983): 437.

B1180   Blades, John. "Updike Adds Critics Award." *Reading* (Pa.) *Eagle* 10 Jan. 1984.

B1181   Montrose, David. "Non-Slip Polish." *New Statesman* 20 Jan. 1984: 23-24.

B1182   Clapp, Rodney. "The Generous Critic: John Updike." *Christianity Today* 28 (2 Mar. 1984): 87-88.

B1183   Riggan, William. "Shallow Drafts: John Updike's *Hugging the Shore.*" *World Literature Today* 58 (Sum. 1984): 380-83.

B1184   Oster, Daniel. "Exotique et Opaque Updike." *La Quinzaine Littéraire* 462 (1-15 mai 1986): 10.

The Witches of Eastwick (1984):

B1185   Gray, Paul. "Fruits of Blossoming Selfhood." *Time* 123 (7 May 1984): 113.

B1186   Prescott, Peter S. "Updike's Three Weird Sisters." *Newsweek* 103 (7 May 1984): 92.

B1187   Atwood, Margaret. "Wondering What It's Like to Be a Woman." *The New York Times Book Review* 13 May 1984: 1, 40.

B1188   Stevens, Andrea. "A Triple Spell." *The New York Times Book Review* 13 May 1984: 40.

B1189   Koenig, Rhoda. "That Old White Magic." *New York* 14 May 1984: 76-77.

*B1190 "Mocking Feminism." *Glamour* June 1984: 118.

B1191   Rinzler, Carol E. *Cosmopolitan* June 1984: 54.

B1192   Corwin, Phillip. "Oh, What the Hex." *Commonweal* 111 (1 June 1984): 340-41.

B1193   Goodwin, Gail. "Wicked Witches of the North." *The New Republic* 190 (4 June 1984): 28-29.

B1194   Johnson, Diane. "Warlock." *The New York Review of Books* 31 (14 June 1984): 3-4.

B1195   Pollitt, Katha. "Bitches and Witches." *Nation* 239 (23 June 1984): 773-75.

B1196   "The Witches of Eastwick." *The New Yorker* 25 June 1984: 107.

B1197   Thomas, Phil. "John Updike Brews Up Some Ole Black Magic in Spell-binding *The Witches of Eastwick*." *Reading* (Pa.) *Eagle* 8 July 1984.

B1198   Wood, Ralph C. "Updike: Evil as Sexual Society." *The Christian Century* 101 (25 July 1984): 715-17.

B1199   Breed, Donald D. "John Updike's Eastwick: Is It Really Wickford?" *Providence* (R. I.) *Sunday Journal* 29 July 1984: E-O1.

B1200   Adams, Phoebe-Lou. "*The Witches of Eastwick*." *Atlantic* 254 (Aug. 1984): 112.

B1201   Raine, Craig." Sisters with the Devil in Them." *Times Literary Supplement* 28 Sept. 1984: 1084.

B1202   Bloom, Alice. "Recent Fiction II." *Hudson Review* 37 (Wint. 1984-85): 624-26.

B1203   Verduin, Kathleen. "Sex, Nature, and Dualism in *The Witches of Eastwick*." *Modern Language Quarterly* 46 (Sept. 1985): 293-315.

Criticism of Individual Works 213

B1204 Slavitt, David R. "Smoke and Mirrors, Or Making an Elephant Appear: Strategies in the Novels of Updike and Heller." *Michigan Quarterly Review* 24 (Wint. 1985): 134-39.

B1205 Berryman, Charles. "Updike and Contemporary Witchcraft." *South Atlantic Quarterly* 85 (1986): 1-9.

B1206 Kinsella, Rebbie. "Pigeon Feathers and Witches." *Christianity Today* 30 (7 Mar. 1986): 60.

B1207 Oster, Daniel. "Exotique et Opaque Updike." *La Quinzaine Littéraire* 462 (1-15 mai 1986): 10.

B1208 Welch, James M. "Bewitched and Bewildered over 'Eastwick.'" *Literature/Film Quarterly* 15. 3 (1987): 152-54.

B1209 Sillitoe, Alan. *The New Statesman* 114 (25 Sept. 1987): 31.

B1210 Greiner, Donald J. "Updike's Witches." In *Selected Essays: International Conference on Wit and Humor, 1986*. Ed. Dorothy M. Joiner. West Georgia College International Conference, 1988. 20-25.

B1211 Campbell, Jeff H. "Sit Down Cher, Michelle, and Susan: Or, Will the Real Witches of Eastwick Please Stand Up." *Conference of College Teachers of English Studies* 53 (Sept. 1988): 74-82.

Facing Nature (1985):

B1212 Thomas, Heather. "A Metaphysical Poet for the Modern Age." *Reading* (Pa.) *Eagle* 31 Mar. 1985: B-B-B-18, 19.

*B1213 Grove, Lee. "Facing Nature." *Boston Magazine* (Boston) June 1985: 84.

B1214 Lehman, David. "Footnotes." *Newsweek* 106 (26 Aug. 1985): 67.

B1215 Wood, Ralph C. "*Facing Nature*." *The Christian Century* 103 (19 Feb. 1986): 180-81.

B1216 "*Facing Nature*." *Poetry* 148 (Mar. 1986): 297-98.

B1217 Forbes, Peter. "Master of Mimesis." *Poetry Review* June 1987: 22-23.

B1218 Moramarco, Fred. "Speculations: Contemporary Poetry and Painting." *Mosaic* 20. 3 (Sum. 1987): 23-36. (Comments on "Gradations of Black," pages 27-30.)

Roger's Version (1986):

B1219   Steinberg, Sybil. "Fiction: *Roger's Version*." *Publishers Weekly* 230 (18 July 1986): 79-80.

B1220   Gray, Paul. "Theology and the Computer." *Time* 128 (25 Aug. 1986): 67.

B1221   Lodge, David. "Chasing After God and Sex." *The New York Times Book Review* 31 Aug. 1986: 1, 15.

B1222   Lehman, David. "Back to the Steamy Suburbs." *Newsweek* 8 (Sept. 1986): 64.

B1223   Bemrose, John. "God, Sex and Software." *Macleans* 99 (22 Sept. 1986): 54-55.

B1224   Kramer, Hilton. "A High-Tech Shrine to Sex and Society." *Wall Street Journal* 24 Sept. 1986: 30.

B1225   Eder, Richard. "Brilliancies of Updike Book Can Make Darkness Palatable." *Allentown* (Pa.) *Morning Call* 28 Sept. 1986: F-1, 2.

B1226   Robertson, William. "'Roger's Version' A Deserving Novel." *Reading* (Pa.) *Eagle* 28 Sept. 1986.

B1227   Sanoff, Alvin P. "Writers 'Are Really Servants of Reality.'" *U. S. News and World Report* 101 (20 Oct. 1986): 67-68. (Sanoff interviews Updike.)

B1228   "Briefly Noted." *The New Yorker* 62 (10 Nov. 1986): 144.

B1229   Morey, Ann-Janine. "Updike's Sexual Language for God." *The Christian Century* 103 (19 Nov. 1986): 1036-37.

B1230   Crews, Frederick. "Mr. Updike's Planet." *The New York Review of Books* 33 (4 Dec. 1986): 7-10, 12, 14.

B1231   Enright, D. J. "Love Bytes." *The New Republic* 196 (2 Feb. 1987): 41-42.

B1232   Pritchard, William H. and George Hunsinger. "Updike's Version." *The New York Review of Books* 34 (12 Feb. 1987): 41.

B1233   Mehl, Duane. "The Downward Trajectory of John Updike." *National Review* 39 (13 Feb. 1987): 53-54, 56.

B1234   Weiss, Eric A. "John Updike's Version of Computing." *Abacus* 4 (Spring 1987): 45-48.

B1235   Abbey, Edward. "Reading Updike." *Nation.* 244 (28 Mar. 1987): 409-410.

B1236   "*Roger's Version* by John Updike." *Radio-Electronics* 58 (May 1987): 137.

Criticism of Individual Works 215

B1237   Forbes, Peter. "Master of Mimesis." *Poetry Review* June 1987: 22-23.

B1238   Mutter, John. *Publishers Weekly* 233 (24 July 1987): 183.

B1239   Greiner, Donald J. "Body and Soul: John Updike and *The Scarlet Letter*." *Journal of Modern Literature* 15 (Spring 1989): 475-95.

B1240   Wilson, Raymond III. "*Roger's Version*: Updike's Negative-Solid Model of *The Scarlet Letter*." *Modern Fiction Studies* 35 (Sum. 1989): 241-50.

B1241   Wood, Ralph C. "Karl Barth, John Updike and the Cheerful God." *Books and Religion* Wint. 1989: 5, 26-31.

B1242   Duvall, John N. "The Pleasure of Textual/Sexual Wrestling: Pornography and Heresy in *Roger's Version*." *Modern Fiction Studies* 37 (Spring 1991): 81-95.

B1243   Wind, James P. "Clergy Lives: Portraits from Modern Fiction." *The Christian Century* 108 (4 Sept. 1991): 805-10. (Pages 809-10 concern *Roger's Version*.)

Trust Me (1987):

B1244   Suderman, Elmer. "Art as a Way of Knowing." *Discourse* 12 (1969): 3-14. (Pages 10-14 pertain to "Unstuck.")

B1245   "*Playboy*'s Annual Awards: Best Short Story: 'Killing.'" *Playboy* 30 (Jan. 1983): 192.

B1246   Steinberg, Sybil. *Publishers Weekly* 231 (13 Mar. 1987): 73.

B1247   Lehmann-Haupt, Christopher. "Books of the Times." *The New York Times* 136 (20 Apr. 1987): C-17.

B1248   Kennedy, Eugene. "Exploring the Abyss of Aging with Updike." *Chicago Sun-Times* 26 Apr. 1987: 13.

B1249   Robinson, Marilynne. "At Play in the Backyard of the Psyche." *The New York Times Book Review* 92 (26 Apr. 1987): 1, 44-45.

B1250   Koenig, Rhoda. *New York* 20 (4 May 1987): 120.

B1251   Sheppard, R. Z. "Punch Lines." *Time* 4 May 1987: 104.

B1252   Crane, Hugh M. *Library Journal* 112 (15 May 1987): 99-100.

B1253   Dooley, Susan. "Updike's Stories of Shriveled Souls." The Cleveland Plain Dealer 17 May 1987: H-10.

B1254   Brookhiser, Richard. "Northeast News: White-Bread Slices of Life." *The Wall Street Journal* 18 May 1987: 25.

B1255   Lehmann, David. "Betraying Your Loved Ones." *Newsweek* 109 (18 May 1987): 82.

B1256   Rohland, Pamela. "Updike: Trusting in Suburbia Too Much?" *Reading* (Pa.) *Eagle* 7 June 1987: E20.

B1257   Blue, Adrianne. "The Compassionate Wasp." *The New Statesman* 14 (18 Sept. 1987): 27-28.

B1258   Wood, Michael. "Hiding the Harm Away." *Times Literary Supplement* 9-15 Oct. 1987: 1106.

B1259   Koenig, Rhoda. *New York* 20 (21-27 Dec. 1987): 125-26.

B1260   Lesser, Wendy. "Serious Comedy." *Hudson Review* 40 (Wint. 1988): 661-68. (Pages 662-63 concern *Trust Me*.)

B1261   Suderman, Elmer. "Art as a Way of Knowing." *Discourse* 12 (Wint. 1989): 3-14.

S. (1988):

B1262   Steinberg, Sybil. *Publishers Weekly* 233 (22 Jan. 1988): 102-03.

B1263   Gray, Paul. "Karma in the Sunbelt." *Time* 131 (29 Feb. 1988): 98.

*B1264 Bernikow, Louise. "Books." *Cosmopolitan* 204 (Mar. 1988): 51.

B1265   Medwick, Cathleen. "The Scarlet Letter." *Vogue* 178 (Mar. 1988): 316, 320.

B1266   Rothstein, Mervyn. "In *S.* Updike Tries Woman's Viewpoint." *The New York Times* 137 (2 Mar. 1988): C-21.

B1267   Lehmann-Haupt, Christopher. "In John Updike's Latest, The Woman Called 'S.'" *The New York Times* 137 (7 Mar. 1988): C-16.

B1268   Koenig, Rhoda. "The Story of S." [sic] *New York* 21 (7 Mar. 1988): 64.

B1269   Broyard, Anatole. "Letters from the Ashram." *The New York Times Book Review* 13 Mar. 1988: 7.

B1270   Hobhouse, Janet. "The Salvation Letters." *Newsweek* 14 Mar. 1988: 58.

B1271   Podhoretz, Norman. "Updike and Roth: Serious at Last." *The Washington Post* 111 (15 Mar. 1988): A-23.

B1272	McCullough, David Willis. "S." *Book-of-the-Month Club News* Spring, 1988: 2, 4.
B1273	Sokolov, Raymond. "Mom's Troubles at an Ashram." *The Wall Street Journal* 29 Mar. 1988: 28.
*B1274	Abeel, Erica. "Books." *New Woman* 18 (Apr. 1988): 24.
B1275	Adams, Phoebe-Lou. "S." *Atlantic* 261 (Apr. 1988): 78.
B1276	Rohland, Pamela. "Does Updike's Book *S.* Stand for Snore?" *Reading* (Pa.) *Eagle* 3 Apr. 1988: E-13.
B1277	Fisher, Ann H. *Library Journal* 113 (15 Apr. 1988): 97.
B1278	Davis, Hope Hale. "Distaff Doormat." *New Leader* 18 Apr. 1988: 20-21.
B1279	Hitchens, Christopher. "The Karmic Polymorphous Perverse." *Times Literary Supplement* No. 4438 (22-28 Apr. 1988): 453.
B1280	Brookner, Anita. "Getting Rid of the Garbage." *Spectator* 260 (30 Apr. 1988): 35-36.
*B1281	Disch, Thomas M. "Books." *Playboy* 35 (May 1988): 28.
B1282	Hochschild, Adam. "When Worlds Divide." *Mother Jones* 13 (May 1988): 49.
B1283	Kakutani, Michiko. "Updike's Struggle to Portray Women." *The New York Times* 137 (5 May 1988): C-29.
B1284	Bendictus, David. "Going West." *Punch* 294 (6 May 1988): 50-51.
B1285	Lurie, Alison. "The Woman Who Rode Away." *The New York Review of Books* 35 (12 May 1988): 3-4.
B1286	Lipsky, David. "*S.*-Trogen." *National Review* 40 (13 May 1988): 58-59.
B1287	"Briefly Noted." *The New Yorker* 64 (16 May 1988): 64.
B1288	Searles, George J. "S." *The Christian Century* 105 (18 May 1988): 508-10.
B1289	Gilman, Richard. "The Witches of Updike." *The New Republic* 198 (20 June 1988): 39-41.
B1290	Prose, Francine. "Men Who Read Women's Minds." *Savvy* Aug. 1988: 18-20.
B1291	Iannone, Carol. "Adultery, from Hawthorne to Updike." *Commentary* 85 (Oct. 1988): 55-59.

B1292   Bluestein, Gene. *The Progressive* 52 (Nov. 1988): 42-43.

B1293   Leonard, John. "Bad-Boy Books." *Ms. Magazine* 17 (Jan.-Feb. 1989): 124.

B1294   Milton, Edith. "The Year in Fiction: 1988." *The Massachusetts Review* 30 (Spring 1989): 106-07.

*B1295   *Washington Post Book World* 19 (5 Nov. 1989): 16.

B1296   Gessert, George. "Updike's Passage to India." *Northwest Review* 28 (1990): 136-41.

B1297   Leavis, L. R. and J. M. Blom. "I: New Writing: Novels and Short Stories." *English Studies* 71 (1990): 136.

B1298   Goldman, Marion S. *Society* 27 (Sept.-Oct. 1990): 94-96.

Just Looking (1989):

B1299   Wolfe, Peter. *Saturday Review* 4 (Nov. 1976): 41.

B1300   [Wade, Rosalind ?]. "Quarterly Fiction Review." *Contemporary Review* 231 (1977): 45-48. (Page 46 pertains to Updike, who is misnamed "Updyke.")

B1301   Stuttaford, Genevieve. *Publishers Weekly* 236 (25 Aug. 1989): 53.

B1302   Skeats, Terry. *Library Journal* 114 (1 Oct. 1989): 94.

*B1303   Hoover, Paul. "Artful Insights." *Chicago Tribune* 8 Oct. 1989: Sec. 14: 6.

B1304   Lehmann-Haupt, Christopher. "A Man of Letters and the Pull of Visual Arts." *The New York Times* 138 (9 Oct. 1989): C-18.

B1305   Taylor, Robert. "Updike, Ashbery: Two Ways of Seeing." *Boston Globe* 11 Oct. 1989: 76.

B1306   Danto, Arthur C. "What MOMA Done Tole Him." *The New York Times Book Review* 15 Oct. 1989: 12.

*B1307   Hulbert, Dan. "Updike Essays Capture Art's Nuances." *Atlanta Constitution* 24 Oct. 1989. G-3.

B1308   Solomon, Deborah. "Reader, Run." *The New Criterion* 8 (Nov. 1989): 70-73.

B1309   Kramer, Hilton. "Every Picture Tells a Story." *Washington Post Book Week* 26 Nov. 1989: 9.

*B1310   *Guardian Weekly* 141 (17 Dec. 1989): 20.

*B1311   Baker, Kenneth. "Three Writers with Keen Eyes for Art." *San Francisco Chronicle* 24 Dec. 1989. Rev.: 14.

B1312   "Just Looking." *The New Yorker* 65 (8 Jan. 1990): 100.

B1313   Raine, Craig. "Updike's Innocence." *London Review of Books* 12 (25 Jan. 1990): 12.

B1314   Rudman, Mark. "An Erotics of Contemplation." *Art News* 89 (Feb. 1990): 104.

B1315   Donnelly, Jerome. "*Just Looking.*" *America* 162 (24 Feb. 1990): 179-80, 182.

B1316   Wollheim, Richard. "Objects of Love." *Times Literary Supplement* 25 May 1990: 553.

B1317   Welish, Marjorie. "Writers on Art—Reported Sightings: Art Chronicles." *Partisan Review* 58 (Fall 1991): 742-45.

Self-Consciousness (1989):

B1318   Stuttaford, Genevieve. *Publishers Weekly* 235 (27 Jan. 1989): 458.

B1319   Budd, John. *Library Journal* 114 (15 Feb. 1989): 159.

B1320   Donaldson, Scott. "Uniquely Updike." *Chicago Tribune* 26 Feb. 1989: 14: 1.

B1321   Brofman, John. "Inside Updike." *Life* 12 (Mar. 1989): 10.

B1322   Gazzaniga, Marin; Cathleen Medwick; and Katha Pollitt. "Book Notes: American Pie." *Vogue* 179 (Mar. 1989): 334.

*B1323   Hitchens, Christopher. "Shelf Life." *Interview* 19 (Mar. 1989): 108.

B1324   Donoghue, Denis. "'I Have Preened, I Have Lived.'" *The New York Times Book Review* 138 (5 Mar. 1989): 7.

*B1325   Feeney, Mark. "Updike: A Self-Portrait of the Artist." *Boston Globe* 5 Mar. 1989: B-16.

*B1326   Walters, Colin. "John Updike: Candor, Family Relations and Life's Early Evening." *Washington Times* 6 Mar. 1989: E-8.

B1327   Lehmann-Haupt, Christopher. "Why Updike Writes and What He Writes About." *The New York Times* 138 (9 Mar. 1989): C-5.

B1328	Pritchard, William H. "Updike's Perceptive *Self Consciousness.*" *USA Today* 10 Mar. 1989: D-5.
*B1329	Eder, Richard. "Nothing to Declare." *Los Angeles Times Book Review* 12 Mar. 1989: BR: 3.
*B1330	Hawley, John C. "Inside Out and Upside Down." *San Francisco Chronicle* 12 Mar. 1989. Rev.: 6.
*B1331	Johnson, Greg. "Updike Pens Own 'Self-Consciousness.'" *Atlanta Journal Constitution* 12 Mar. 1989. M-8.
B1332	Gray, Paul. "A Burden of Answered Prayers." *Time* 133 (13 Mar. 1989): 77-78.
B1333	Koenig, Rhoda. "The Watchful I." *New York* 22 (13 Mar. 1989): 66.
B1334	Prescott, Peter S. "Advertisements for Himself: Updike's Lessons as a Boy and His Life as a Man." *Newsweek* 13 Mar. 1989: 71.
*B1335	Higgins, George V. "Beating the Pillager to the Punch." *Houston Post* 19 Mar. 1989. E-6.
B1336	Higgins, George V. "The Man Who Made Rabbit Run." *Washington Post Book World* 112 (19 Mar. 1989): 3.
B1337	Adams, Phoebe-Lou. "Self-Consciousness." *Atlantic* 263 (Apr. 1989): 100.
B1338	Diehl, Digby. "Books." *Playboy* 36 (Apr. 1989): 26-27.
B1339	"Noted with Pleasure." *The New York Times Book Review* 2 Apr. 1989: 43. (Reprints a paragraph from *Self-Consciousness.*)
*B1340	Olson, Clarence E. "Shy Boy Beneath the Gloss." *St. Louis Post-Dispatch* 9 Apr. 1989. E-5.
*B1341	Berkov, Walter. "Getting Under the Skin of Updike." *Detroit News* 16 Apr. 1989. E-2.
B1342	Rohland, Pamela. "Updike's Memoirs Leave Room for Sequels." *Reading* (Pa.) *Eagle* 16 Apr. 1989: E-2.
B1343	Bawer, Bruce. "A Wordsmith's 'Careful' Life." *The Wall Street Journal* 17 Apr. 1989: A-10.
B1344	Italie, Hillel. "Writer John Updike Remembers the Little Things, Glosses Over Honors." Rochester (N.Y.) *Sunday Democrat and Chronicle* 23 Apr. 1989: 4-D.

B1345 MacCurtain, Austin. "In Search of a Blessing." *Times Literary Supplement* 5 May 1989: 479.

*B1346 MacWilliam, Candia. "Honky America." *Guardian Weekly* 12 May 1989: 31.

B1347 Wood, Michael. "Out of Harm's Way." *New Statesman and Society* 2 (12 May 1989): 34.

B1348 Brookner, Anita. "Books: Happy Child Father to a Happy Man." *Spectator* 262 (13 May 1989): 37-38.

B1349 "The Loathly Glass." *Economist* 311 (13 May 1989): 98, 100.

B1350 Wood, Ralph C. "Updike's Song of Himself." *The Christian Century* 106 (17 May 1989): 526-28.

B1351 Hardwick, Elizabeth. "Citizen Updike." *The New York Review of Books* 36 (18 May 1989): 3, 4, 6, 8.

B1352 Vigilante, Richard. "The Observer Observed." *National Review* 41 (19 May 1989): 51-52, 54-55.

B1353 Denby, David. "A Life of Sundays." *New Republic* 200 (22 May 1989): 29-33.

B1354 Wollheim, Richard. *Times Literary Supplement* 25-31 May 1990: 553.

B1355 Teleky, Richard. "Skin-Deep Reflections." *Macleans* 102 (29 May 1989): 60.

B1356 Barnes, Fred. "*Self-Consciousness*: Memoirs." *American Spectator* 22 (June 1989): 51.

B1357 Kellman, Steven G. "Memoirs: *Self-Consciousness*." *USA Today* 118 (July 1989): 95-96.

B1358 Inglis, Fred. "On Being a Dud." *Nation* 249 (10 July 1989): 59-61.

*B1359 Taylor, Charles. "Only Skin-Deep." *Saturday Night* 104 (Aug. 1989): 51-52.

B1360 Baumann, Paul. "Beckoned by the Mother Tongue." *Commonweal* 116 (11 Aug. 1989): 438-39.

*B1361 Wilson, Robert. "Memoirs Make a Mark." *USA Today* 29 Dec. 1989: D-4.

B1362 "*Self-Consciousness*." *Booklist* 86 (15 Jan. 1990): 982.

*B1363   Petersen, Clarence. "*Self-Consciousness.*" *Chicago Tribune Books* 1 July 1990: 14: 4.

B1364   Anker, Roy M. "Under the Skin." *The Reformed Journal* July-Aug. 1990: 22-26.

B1365   Berman, Paul. "John Updike's Transparent Eyeball." *Dissent* 37 (Wint. 1990): 114-17.

B1366   Bailey, Peter J. "'Why Not Tell the Truth?': The Autobiographies of Three Fiction Writers." *Critique* 32 (Sum. 1991): 211-23.

Rabbit at Rest (1990):

B1367   "Updike to Bring Back Rabbit." *Reading* (Pa.) *Eagle* 8 May 1988: E-18.

B1368   Steinberg, Sybil. "Rabbit at Rest." *Publishers Weekly* 237 (10 Aug. 1990): 433.

B1369   Gray, Paul. "Rabbit Stew." *Time* 136 (13 Aug. 1990): 13.

B1370   Birkerts, Sven. "The Inner Rabbit." *Chicago Tribune Books* 20 (30 Sept. 1990): 1, 4.

B1371   "*Rabbit at Rest.*" *Kenyon Review* 58 (15 Aug. 1990): 1128.

B1372   Hooper, Brad. "*Rabbit at Rest.*" *Booklist* 87 (1 Sept. 1990): 5.

B1373   Dunne, Elizabeth. "Elegant Variations." *Sewanee Review* 98 (Fall 1990): cvii-cviii.

B1374   Caldwell, Gail. "Updike: 'Rabbit' Has His Final Say, But the Writer Has More to Tell." *Boston Globe* 25 Sept. 1990: 61.

B1375   Kakutani, Michiko. "Just 30 Years Later, Updike Has a Quartet." *The New York Times* 139 (25 Sept. 1990): C-13, 17.

B1376   Wilson, Robert. "'Rabbit' Takes Leap into the Hereafter." *USA Today* 28 Sept. 1990: D-1.

B1377   Feeney, Mark. "Updike's Rabbit Makes His Final Run." *Boston Globe* 30 Sept. 1990: B-43, 45-46.

B1378   Oates, Joyce Carol. "So Young!" *The New York Times Book Review* 30 Sept. 1990: 1, 43.

*B1379   Olson, Clarence E. "Updike's Rabbit Angstrom Runs a Final Lap." *St. Louis Post-Dispatch* 30 Sept. 1990: 5-1.

Criticism of Individual Works 223

B1380   Raban, Jonathan. "Rabbit's Last Run." *Washington Post* 30 Sept. 1990: 1, 15.

B1381   Kaplan, James. "Requiem for Rabbit." *Vanity Fair* 53 (Oct. 1990): 112, 114, 116, 122.

B1382   "*Rabbit at Rest.*" *Cosmopolitan* 209 (Oct. 1990): 56.

B1383   Koenig, Rhoda. "Rabbit Is Good." *New York* 23 (1 Oct. 1990): 65-66.

B1384   Prescott, Peter S. "Read All About It: *Rabbit at Rest.*" *Newsweek* 116 (1 Oct. 1990): 66.

B1385   Rungren, Lawrence. "*Rabbit at Rest.*" *Library Journal* 115 (1 Oct. 1990): 118.

*B1386   Delbanco, Nicholas. "*Rabbit at Rest.*" *Detroit News and Free Press* 7 Oct. 1990: Q-8.

*B1387   Eder, Richard. "Rabbit Runs Down." *Los Angeles Times* 7 Oct. 1990: BR: 3.

*B1388   Gerber, Eric. "Rabbit's Reckoning." *Houston Post* 7 Oct. 1990: C-6.

B1389   Skenazy, Paul. "Rabbit Elbows Through the '80s." *San Francisco Chronicle* 7 Oct. 1990: Rev.:1.

B1390   Hart, Jeffrey. "'Rabbit' Hops into Oblivion with Tale Between Legs." *Washington Times* 8 Oct. 1990: F-1.

B1391   Roback, Diane and Richard Donahue. "Seven Times Eight." *Publishers Weekly* 237 (12 Oct. 1990): 64.

B1392   "God Bless America." *Economist* 317 (13 Oct. 1990): 93.

B1393   Gray, Paul. "*Rabbit at Rest.*" *Time* 136 (15 Oct. 1990): 84.

B1394   Rifkind, Donna. "The End of the Line for Rabbit Angstrom." *Wall Street Journal* 15 Oct. 1990: A-14.

*B1395   *Observer* 21 Oct. 1990: 36.

*B1396   Sleeth, Peter. "'Rabbit' Finale Isn't 'Depressed.'" *Denver Post* 21 Oct. 1990: D-8.

*B1397   Coughlin, Ruth Pollack. "The Trouble with Harry." *Detroit News* 22 Oct. 1990: F-1.

B1398   "*Rabbit at Rest.*" *The New Yorker* 66 (22 Oct. 1990): 143.

B1399   Wills, Gary. "Long-Distance Runner." *The New York Review of Books* 25 Oct. 1990: 11-14.

*B1400 Wood, James. "The Beast in the American Ice Cream Parlour." *Guardian* 25 Oct. 1990: 23.

B1401   Quinn, Anthony. "Fifty Five and Fading." *New Statesman* 3 (26 Oct. 1990): 33.

B1402   Trueheart, Charles. "Sex, God and John Updike." *Washington Post* 116 (26 Oct. 1990): F-1.

B1403   Brookner, Anita. "Ending the Heartache." *Spectator* 265 (27 Oct. 1990): 28-29.

B1404   *Sunday Times Books* 28 Oct. 1990: 8: 5.

B1405   Will, George. "Rabbit Is Mortal, But Is the U.S.?" *Washington Post* 113 (28 Oct. 1990): C-7.

B1406   "Rabbit Depressing." *Reading* (Pa.) *Eagle* 30 Oct. 1990: 6.

B1407   *Modern Maturity* 33 (Oct.-Nov. 1990): 22.

*B1408 Abeel, Erica. "*Rabbit at Rest.*" *New Woman* 20 (Nov. 1990): 34.

B1409   Kirn, Walter. "Rabbit's Run." *Gentlemen's Quarterly* 60 (Nov. 1990): 166, 172, 174.

*B1410 Mallon, Thomas. "Books: *Rabbit at Rest.*" *American Spectator* 23 (Nov. 1990): 42-43.

B1411   Menand, Louis. "Rabbit Is Dead." *Esquire* 114 (Nov. 1990): 93, 97.

B1412   Solomon, Andy. "A Swan Song for Rabbit." *Applause* 16 (Nov. 1990): 53, 57.

B1413   Donahue, Deirdre. "Why Updike's 'Rabbit' Keeps Winning the Race." *USA Today* 2 Nov. 1990: D-4.

B1414   Staples, Brent. "Why So Hard on Rabbit?" *The New York Times* 140 (5 Nov. 1990): A-20.

B1415   Getlin, Josh. "Laying a 'Rabbit' to Rest." *Allentown* (Pa.) *Morning Call* 9 Nov. 1990: D-9.

*B1416 Ahearn, Barry. "Rabbit in Retirement." *New Orleans Times-Picayune* 11 Nov. 1990: E-6.

B1417	Christian, Ed. "Reading at Rest?" *The Reading* (Pa.) *Eagle* 11 Nov. 1990: F-1, 2.
B1418	Italie, Hillel. "Last Rabbit Not Easy To Write." *The Reading* (Pa.) *Eagle* 11 Nov. 1990: F-2.
B1419	Ritts, Morton. "Sick at Heart." *Macleans* 103 (19 Nov. 1990): 71.
B1420	Williamson, Chilton. Jr. "Harry's End." *National Review* 42 (19 Nov. 1990): 51-53.
B1421	Wood, Ralph C. "Rabbit Runs Down." *The Christian Century* 107 (21 Nov. 1990): 1099-101.
*B1422	O'Briant, Don. "Updike in Autumn." *Atlanta Constitution* 24 Nov. 1990: N: 1.
B1423	"Editors' Choice: The Best Books of 1990." *The New York Times Book Review* 2 Dec. 1990: 7: 3.
B1424	Disch, Thomas M. "Rabbit's Run." *Nation* 251 (3 Dec. 1990): 688, 690, 692, 694.
B1425	Lee, Hermione. "The Trouble with Harry." *New Republic* 203 (24 Dec. 1990): 34-37.
*B1426	O'Briant, Don. "Class of '90: The Famous and the Forgotten." *Atlanta Constitution* 30 Dec. 1990: K-9.
B1427	Gray, Paul. "*Rabbit at Rest*." *Time* 136 (31 Dec. 1990): 55.
B1428	Kellman, Steven G. "Books— *Rabbit at Rest*." *USA Today* 119 (Jan. 1991): 96.
*B1429	Blades, John. "Critics Honor Updike for 4th 'Rabbit' Novel." *Chicago Tribune* 17 Feb. 1991: 1, 5.
*B1430	Suderman, E. "English and American: *Rabbit at Rest*." *Choice* 28 (Mar. 1991): 1138.
B1431	Steinberg, Sybil. "Knopf Authors Win Two of Five National Book Critics Circle Awards." *Publisher's Weekly* 238 (1 Mar. 1991): 20.
B1432	Baker, Russell. "'Play It Sam— Fast!'" *The New York Times* 5 Mar. 1991: A-21.
B1433	Warrior, Robert Allen. "Sacred Hoopsters in America's Heart." *Christianity and Crisis* 51 (18 Mar. 1991): 94-96.

B1434	Olster, Stacey. "Rabbit Rerun: Updike's Replay of Popular Culture in *Rabbit at Rest.*" *Modern Fiction Studies* 37 (Spring 1991): 45-59.
*B1435	Caldwell, Gail. "'Rabbit' Wins Again." *Boston Globe* 10 Apr. 1991: 1.
B1436	Hevesi, Dennis. "Pulitzer Prizes in Letters Go to Updike and Simon." *The New York Times* 140 (10 Apr. 1991): A-21.
B1437	"'Rabbit' Wins Updike 2nd Pulitzer." *Reading* (Pa.) *Eagle* 10 Apr. 1991: 1.
B1438	"Winners of the 1991 Pulitzer Prizes in the Arts and Journalism." *The New York Times* 10 Apr. 1991. A-20.
*B1439	Ricci, James. "Kidnap Updike's Pulitzer Until Rabbit Is Ransomed." *Detroit News and Free Press* 14 Apr. 1991. H-1.
B1440	"Updike Lets Rabbit Ride Out in Style." *Reading* (Pa.) *Eagle* 14 Apr. 1991: A-8.
B1441	"Updike to Bring Back Rabbit." *Reading* (Pa.)*Eagle* 8 May 1991: E-18.
B1442	Cooper, Rand Richards. "Rabbit Loses the Race: John Updike's 'Small Answer of a Texture.'" *Commonweal* 118 (17 May 1991): 315-23. (Also reviews *Rabbit, Run; Rabbit Redux; Rabbit Is Rich*; and *Self-Consciousness.*)
B1443	Flower, Dean. "*Rabbit at Rest.*" *Hudson Review* 44 (Sum. 1991): 320-21.
B1444	Javer, Ron. "Rabbit Ran." *Philadelphia* 82 (Aug. 1991): 8. (Considers *Rabbit, Run; Rabbit Redux;* and *Rabbit Is Rich.*)
B1445	Welish, Marjorie. "Writers on Art." *Partisan Review* 58 (Fall 1991): 742-45.
*B1446	Petersen, Clarence. "Paperbacks." *Chicago Tribune* 20 Oct. 1991: 14: 8.
B1447	Shapiro, Susan. "Paperbacks." *Washington Times* 3 Nov. 1991: B-8.
B1448	Manley, Will. "The Manley Arts." *Booklist* 89 (1 Sept. 1992): 9.

Odd Jobs (1991):

B1449	Kuczkowski, Richard. "*Odd Jobs.*" *Library Journal* 116 (1 Sept. 1991): 192.
B1450	Searles, George. "Angst Up to the End." *The New Leader* 73 (1 Oct. 1990): 21. (Concerns *Rabbit at Rest.*)

Criticism of Individual Works   227

B1451   Kakutani, Michiko. "The Magic Act of a Novelist." *The New York Times* 66 (25 Oct. 1991): C-29.

*B1452   Rose, Phyllis. "America's Jack of All Bookish Trades." *Boston Globe* 27 Oct. 1991: A-15.

B1453   Skenazy, Paul. "Odds and Ends of John Updike." *San Francisco Chronicle* 27 Oct. 1991: Rev-4.

B1454   Bering-Jensen, Helle. "From Updike: Machine Dreams of Diversity and Depth." *Washington Times* 3 Nov. 1991: B-8.

B1455   Koenig, Rhoda. "Swell's Lettres." *New York* 24 (4 Nov. 1991): 130-31.

B1456   Coates, Joseph. "Cultivating the Field of Literature." *Chicago Tribune* 7 Nov. 1991: 5-3.

B1457   Amis, Martin. "Magnanimous in a Big Way." *The New York Times Book Review* 10 Nov. 1991: 7:12.

*B1458   "Non-Fiction Digest: *Odd Jobs*." *Atlanta Journal Constitution* 10 Nov. 1991: N-9.

*B1459   Barron, John. "Master Mind." *Detroit News* 13 Nov. 1991: D-3.

B1460   Donoghue, Denis. "The Words, Some Odd, of Updike." *Houston Post* 17 Nov. 1991: C-4.

B1461   Donoghue, Denis. "John Updike on the Books of the '80s." *Washington Post Book Week* 17 Nov. 1991: 5.

*B1462   Lannon, Linnea. "Updike's Weighty Collection Shows Off New Tool, Old Spirit." *Detroit News and Free Press* 17 Nov. 1991: H-9.

B1463   Bawer, Bruce. "He's Still Giving Praise." *Wall Street Journal* 21 Nov. 1991: A-12.

*B1464   Diehl, Digby. "Books: *Odd Jobs*." *Playboy* 38 (Dec. 1991): 46.

*B1465   Olson, Clarence E. "Updike Recycled: New Collection Includes a Bit for Almost Everyone." *St Louis Post-Dispatch* 22 Dec. 1991. C-5.

B1466   Dyer, Geoff. "No Problem." *New Statesman and Society* 5 (17 Jan. 1992): 45-46.

*B1467   Hamilton, Ian. "Genial Learning Offered with Shy Generosity." *Guardian* 23 Jan. 1992: 23.

*B1468   Bigsby, Christopher. "Sugar and Spice Rabbit— *Odd Jobs* by John Updike." *The Times Educational Supplement* No. 3943 (24 Jan. 1992): 28.

B1469 Wood, James. "The Professional Image: *Odd Jobs.*" *The Times Literary Supplement* No. 4634 (24 Jan. 1992): 21.

B1470 "A Master of Craft: *Odd Jobs.*" *Economist* 322 (1 Feb. 1992): 100.

B1471 Searles, George J. "*Odd Jobs.*" *The Christian Century* 109 (5 Feb. 1992): 164-165.

B1472 Trevor, William. "Discourse Most Eloquent Musing: *Odd Jobs.*" *Spectator* 268 (8 Feb. 1992): 29-30.

B1473 Kenner, Hugh. "Jobs Well Done: *Odd Jobs.*" *National Review* 44 (17 Feb. 1992): 52-54.

*B1474 O'Briant, Don. "Sex, Politics a Potent Mix for Updike, Others This Fall." *Atlanta Constitution* 30 Aug. 1992: K-16.

Memories of the Ford Administration (1992):

B1475 Steinberg, Sybil. "*Memories of the Ford Administration.*" *Publishers Weekly* 239 (17 Aug. 1992): 485.

B1476 Hooper, Brad. "*Memories of the Ford Administration.*" *Booklist* 89 (1 Sept. 1992): 5.

B1477 Koenig, Rhoda. "Books: *Memories of the Ford Administration.*" *New York* 25 (14 Sept. 1992): 108-115.

*B1478 Diehl, Digby. "*Memories of the Ford Administration.*" *Modern Maturity* 35 (Oct. 1992): 20.

B1479 Michaud, Charles. "*Memories of the Ford Administration.*" *Library Journal* 117 (1 Oct. 1992): 121.

*B1480 Olson, Clarence E. "Modern Lust, Historic Love: Hard Lessons from Updike." *St. Louis Post-Dispatch* 18 Oct. 1992: C-5.

B1481 Lehmann-Haupt, Christopher. "A Heroic Then, a Realistic Now." *The New York Times* 22 Oct. 1992: C-25.

B1482 Hoagland, Edward. "Updike's Nimble Time Travels." *USA Today* 23 Oct. 1992: D-4.

B1483 Griffith, Benjamin. "'Sex Still Had a Good Name.'" *Atlanta Journal Constitution* 25 Oct. 1992: N-8.

B1484 Lescaze, Lee. "Musings on a Much-Mocked President." *Wall Street Journal* 28 Oct. 1992: A-16.

*B1485	Solomon, Andy. "Presidential Timbre: Updike's Resonating Prose Gives Shape to Some Capital Ideas." *Detroit News* 28 Oct. 1992: C-3.
*B1486	Davis, Ruth. "John Updike; Replacing Rabbit." *M* 10 (Nov. 1992): 88-89.
B1487	Bawer, Bruce. "Academic Obsessions and Political Passions." *Washington Post Book World* 1 Nov. 1992: 1, 9.
B1488	Eder, Richard. "Updike at Rest." *Los Angeles Times* 1 Nov. 1992: BR-3.
*B1489	Gerber, Eric. "Updike Tinkers with Old Ideas for *Memories*." *Houston Post* 1 Nov. 1992: C-4.
B1490	Johnson, Charles. "The Virgin President." *The New York Times Book Review* 1 Nov. 1992: 11.
B1491	von Hoffman, Nicholas. "The Epochs of Updike." *Chicago Tribune* 1 Nov. 1992: 14: 1.
B1492	McNamee, Thomas. "John Updike, Playing Around." *The Philadelphia Inquirer* 8 Nov. 1992. H-1, 4.
*B1493	Walters, Colin. "Updike's Probing *Memories*." *Washington Times* 8 Nov. 1992: B-6.
B1494	Gates, David. "Now, Old Buck Redux." *Newsweek* 9 Nov. 1992: 68.
B1495	Gray, Paul. "Gerald Ford Redux." *Time* 140 (9 Nov. 1992): 80-81.
B1496	"*Memories of the Ford Administration*." *The New Yorker* 68 (23 Nov. 1992): 145.
B1497	Rubin, Merle. "Updike's Vintage *Memories*." *The Christian Science Monitor* 81 (27 Nov. 1992): 13: 3.
B1498	Kazin, Alfred. "The Middle Way." *The New York Review of Books* 17 Dec. 1992: 45-46.

3. Other Media

Updike Works Read on Audio or Video Tape by Others:

*B1499   "The Music School." *American Short Story Series*. Deerfield, Il.: Learning in Focus, 1976. Three video cassettes.

*B1500   "More Stately Mansions." *The Esquire Collection of Great Fiction*. N.Y.: Esquire Audio, 1985. (Included in 6 sound cassettes.)

*B1501   "Poker Night." *Contemporary Esquire Stories*, Volume 1. Albuquerque, N.M.: Newman Communications, 1986. Two sound cassettes.

B1502   *Assorted Prose*. Books on Tape.

B1503   *Bech: A Book*. Books on Tape.

B1504   *The Centaur*. Books on Tape.

B1505   *The Coup*. Books on Tape.

B1506   *Couples*. Books on Tape.

B1507   "Responding Records Sequence." Lexington, Mass.: Ginn, 1973. Two sound discs, 102 minutes, 33 1/3rpm, mono. (Includes "We Only Came to Sleep," "Exposure" and "Thoughts While Driving Home.")

*B1508   *Selected Shorts* from Symphony Space, Vol IV. Old Greenwich, Conn: Listening Library, 1991. "Hub Fans Bid Kid Adieu." Read by Jonathan Hadary.

B1509   *Hugging the Shore*. Books on Tape.

B1510   *Marry Me*. Books on Tape.

B1511	*A Month of Sundays.* Books on Tape.
B1512	*Of the Farm.* Books on Tape.
B1513	*Picked-Up Pieces.* Books on Tape.
B1514	*The Poorhouse Fair.* Books on Tape.
B1515	*Rabbit at Rest.* Books on Tape.
B1516	*Rabbit Is Rich.* Books on Tape.
B1517	*Rabbit Redux.* Books on Tape.
B1518	*Rabbit, Run.* Books on Tape.
B1519	*Roger's Version.* Books on Tape.
B1520	*S.* Read by Kathryn Walker. Audio Prose Library, Inc.
B1521	*The Witches of Eastwick.* Books on Tape.

Updike Works Made into Films or Videos:

B1522	*Rabbit, Run.* Directed by Jack Smight. With James Caan, Anjanette Comer, Jack Albertson, Arthur Hill and Carrie Snodgrass. Warner Bros.-Seven Arts, 1970.
B1523	"The Music School." Deerfield, Ill.: Coronet/MTI Film & Video, 1976. One videocassette, VHS, 69 minutes, 1/2 inch. (On the same tape: Richard Wright, "Almos' a Man." Also issued with two other cassettes featuring Ernest Hemingway's "Soldier's Home," F. Scott Fitzgerald's "Bernice Bobs Her Hair," and Willa Cather's "Paul's Case.")
B1524	*Too Far to Go.* Directed by Fielder Cook. With Blythe Danner, Michael Moriarity and Kathryn Walker. MTV. 1979. (Adapted for televison on Mar. 12, 1979, as a 2-hour dramatic special; later released as a commercial film.)
B1525	"The Music School." Chicago: Perspective Films. One videocassette, VHS, 30 minutes, 1/2 inch. 1982.
B1526	"The Roommates." American Playhouse. Based on "The Christian Roommates," from *The Music School.* (N.Y.: Knopf, 1968.) Directed by Nell Cox. Screenplay by Morton Miller. Starring Barry Miller and Lance Guest. 27 Jan. 1984.

B1527   *The Witches of Eastwick*. Directed by George Miller. Screenplay by Michael Cristofer. Starring Jack Nicholson, Cher, Michelle Pfeiffer, Susan Sarandon and Veronica Cartwright. Warner Bros. 1987.

B1528   "Pigeon Feathers." American Playhouse. Robert Geller, Executive Producer. Sharon Miller Director. Public Broadcasting System. Feb. 17, 1988.

Reviews of Audio Tapes, Videos, and Films:

B1529   O'Connor, John J. "TV: Drama of Updike's Sad Couple." *The New York Times* (12 Mar. 1979): C-16.

B1530   "Too Far to Go". *Playboy* Apr. 1979: 48 (Reviews the two-hour television special aired Mar. 12, later released as a film.)

B1531   Fultz, Norma J. *Rabbit, Run* phonotape review. *Library Journal* 106 (1 Sept. 1981): 1615.

B1532   Ansen, David. "Too Far to Go." *Newsweek* 99 (10 May 1982): 81.

*B1533 Crist, Judith. "Too Far to Go." *50 Plus* 22 June 1982: 58.

B1534   "Too Far to Go." *Playboy* 29 (Aug. 1982): 32.

B1535   "'Witches' Protest Filming of Updike Novel." *Reading* (Pa.) *Eagle* 6 June 1986.

B1536   Hatza, George. "'Witches' Conjures Up the Devil in Nicholson." *The Reading* (Pa.) *Eagle* 14 June 1987: D-2.

B1537   Kael, Pauline. "The Witches of Eastwick." *The New Yorker* 63 (29 June 1987): 72.

B1538   Kauffmann, Stanley. "The Witches of Eastwick." *The New Republic* 197 (13 July 1987): 26.

B1539   Postman, Andrew. "In Their Own Voices: How Authors Are Making the Transition from Page to Tape." *Publishers Weekly* 232 (6 Nov. 1987): 33-35.

B1540   *Publishers Weekly* 232 (6 Nov. 1987): 29-30. (Review of stories from *Trust Me*.)

B1541   *Publishers Weekly* 232 (6 Nov. 1987): 42. (Audio tape review of *Roger's Version*.)

B1542   Goodman, Walter. *The New York Times* 137 (17 Feb. 1988): 27.

B1543   "Pigeon Feathers." *Variety* 330 (24 Feb. 1988): 500-01.

B1544   *Library Journal* 115 (1 Oct. 1990): 118.

B1545   Leader, Zachary. *Times Literary Supplement* 26 Oct. 1990: 1145-46.

B1546   Zinsser, John. "Rabbit at Rest." *Publishers Weekly* 237 (2 Nov. 1990): 50.

B1547   Carty, Brad. "Video Shopper— Understanding John Updike's Fiction. Presented by Donald Greiner." *Wilson Library Bulletin* 65 (Jan. 1991): 77-79, 139-40.

B1548   McCray, Nancy. *Booklist* 87 (15 Jan. 1991): 1079. (Review of Updike reading *Rabbit at Rest*.)

B1549   Cheuse, Alan. "Reviews on Tape— *Rabbit at Rest* written and read by John Updike." *Forbes* 18 Mar. 1991: 24-27.

B1550   Hiett, John. "Audio Reviews: *Rabbit at Rest*." *Library Journal* 116 (15 Apr. 1991): 139.

B1551   Ezell, Johanna. "Audio Reviews: The Prose and Poetry of John Updike read by John Updike." *Library Journal* 116 (July 1991): 157.

B1552   Stuttaford, Genevieve."*Odd Jobs: Essays and Criticism*." *Publishers Weekly* 238 (20 Sept. 1991): 115.

*B1553 Seaman, Donna. "*Odd Jobs*." *Booklist* 88 (1 Oct. 1991): 202.

Film Strip:

*B1554 "The Music School." Chicago: Coronet Instructional Media, 1978. Two rolls (97 frames, 107 frames) 35mm and 2 cassettes (22 minutes), with program guide and 4 worksheet masters.

Video Lecture:

*B1555 Freeman, L. "John Updike's Unhooked Pilgrim." *Minister's Taped Digest*. Waco, Tex.: Minister's Taped Digest. One cassette. 1970.

*B1556 Beyerhaus, Peter. "The Holy Spirit in Biblical Exegesis: An Address." St. Louis, Mo.: Concordia Publication House. One sound cassette. 1972.

*B1557 Geller, Robert. "From Words to Films: Opportunities and Challenges." Instant Replay. One cassette, 2-track mono, 80 minutes. 1975. (Concerns the translation of "The Music School" into film.)

*B1558   "Great American Writers/Two as Reported in the *The New York Times*." Sanford, North Carolina: Microfilming corporation of America. 40 microfiches with program guide. 1981.

*B1559   Kazin, Alfred. ["The American Procession."] One sound tape reel. 10 minutes, 3/4 ips, mono. 1984.

*B1560   "Beautiful Machine: Rivers in American Literature." Research Triangle Park, North Carolina: National Humanities Center. On one side of one sound disc, 33 1/3, 12 inch. 1985. (Comments on Updike's reviews in *Hugging the Shore*.)

*B1561   Greiner, Donald J. "Understanding John Updike's Fiction." "Emminent Scholar/Teachers Series." Detroit: Omnigraphics. 40 minute video cassette. 1990.

Radio Reviews:

B1562   De Bellis, Jack. "All the Way Where? Updike's *Rabbit, Run*." KPFK, Los Angeles. Pacifica Foundation. Forty minutes. 12 June, 1963.

B1563   Solomon, Andy. "*Memories of the Ford Administration*." National Public Radio. 23 Nov. 1992.

Photographs of Updike:

B1564   Krementz, Jill. *The Writer's Image*. Boston: Godine, 1980. (Contains four photographs of Updike on unnumbered pages.)

B1565   Karsh, Yusaf. In "America's Suburban Chronicler: John Updike." *Vis-à-Vis* (United Airlines in-flight magazine). June 1991: 26.

Updike Works Set to Music:

B1566   Vaughan, Rodger. "Three Songs for Soprano and Tuba." S.1.: s.n., 1968. (The poems are: "The Clan," "Lament for Cocoa," and "Recital.")

*B1567   Miller, Lewis M. "In Updike Land: Four Settings of Poems by John Updike: For Mixed Chorus and Piano." 1989. (Poems are: "The Cars in Caracas," "Recital," "Insomnia the Gem of the Ocean," and "Some Frenchmen." They were composed for the Fort Hays State University Chamber Choir, Dr. David Rasmussen, Director.)

*B1568   "A Pear Like a Potato." By Roy Hinkle. For Chorus and Orchestra. Premier: Dec. 6, 1992, at Albright (Pa.) College. 15 minutes. (See also **A215**.)

4. Dissertations and Theses

Dissertations:

*B1569 Galloway. David D. "The Absurd Hero in Contemporary American Fiction: The Works of John Updike, William Styron, Saul Bellow, and J. D. Salinger." *DA* 23 (1963): 356A-75A.

B1570 Harper, Howard Morrall, Jr. "Concepts of Human Destiny in Five American Novelists: Bellow, Salinger, Mailer, Baldwin, Updike." Pennsylvania State U *DA* 25 (1965): 6625A.

*B1571 Falke, Wayne Clinton. "The Novel of Disentanglement: A Thematic Study of Lewis's *Babbitt*, Bromfield's *Mr. Smith* and Updike's *Rabbit, Run*." U of Mich. *DA* 1967: 28/01A.

*B1572 Vargo, Edward. "The Middleness of Man: Ritual in the Novels of John Updike." *DA* 1968.

*B1573 Flint, Joyce M. "In Search of Meaning: Bernard Malamud, Norman Mailer, John Updike." *DAI* 30 (1969): 3006A.

*B1574 Nadon, Robert Joseph. "Urban Values in Recent American Fiction: A Study of The City in the Fiction of Saul Bellow, John Updike, Philip Roth, Bernard Malamud, and Norman Mailer." *DAI* 30 (1969): 2543A.

*B1575 Plourde, Ferdinand J., Jr. "Time Present and Time Past: Autobiography as a Narrative of Duration." *DAI* 30 (1969): 334A-35A.

*B1576 Taylor, Larry. "Pastoral and Anti-Pastoral Patterns in John Updike's Fiction." *DAI* 29 (1969): 3622A-23A.

*B1577 Flint, Joyce Marlene. "In Search of Meaning: Bernard Malamud, Norman Mailer, John Updike." 1969. Wash. State U.

*B1578   Goss, James. "The Assembling of the Meaning of God in the Short Stories of Flannery O'Connor, Bernard Malamud and John Updike." 1970. *DAI* (1970): 31/12 A: 6700. Claremont Graduate School.

*B1579   Nelson, Doris L. "The Contemporary American Family Novel: A Study in Metaphor." *DAI* 31 (1970): 2229A.

*B1580   Wyatt, Bryant Nelson. "Supernaturalism in John Updike's Fiction." *DAI* 31/09A (1970): 4802. U of Va.

*B1581   Markle, Joyce. "Fighters and Lovers: Theme in the First Five Novels of John Updike." *DAI* 32 (1971): 975A.

*B1582   Carlson, Constance. "Heroines in Certain American Novels." *DAI* 32 (1972): 5175A.

*B1583   Knoke, Paul D. "The Allegorical Mode in the Contemporary Novel of Romance." *DAI* 32 (1972): 2695A.

*B1584   Pomeroy, Charles W. "Soviet Russian Criticism 1960-1969 of Seven Twentieth Century American Novelists." *DAI* 32 (1972): 449A.

*B1585   Scafella, Frank. "Patterns of Sacralization: Mark Twain, Faulkner, Hemingway, and Updike." *DAI* 32 (1972) U of Chicago.

*B1586   Strassberg, Mildred P. "Religious Commitment in Recent American Fiction: Flannery O'Connor, Bernard Malamud, John Updike." *DAI* 32 (1972): 6457A.

*B1587   Taylor, Cheet H. "The Aware Man: Studies in Self-Awareness in the Contemporary Novel." *DAI* 32 (1972): 5246A.

*B1588   Borgman, Paul. "The Symbolic City and Christian Existentialism in Fiction by Flannery O'Connor, Walker Percy, and John Updike." *DAI* 1973.

*B1589   Drier, James Sigurd. "Religious Elements of a Portion of John Updike's Fiction." *DAI* 34/09A (1973): 6094. Brown U.

*B1590   Larsen, Richard Bruce. "The Short Stories of John Updike." *DAI* 34 (1973): 2634A.

*B1591   Lewis, Robert W. "Sport and the Fiction of John Updike and Philip Roth." *DAI* 34/11A (1973): 7028. Ohio State U.

*B1592   Swanson, Trevor. "A Transformational-Generative Approach to Style in John Updike's Novels." *DAI* 34/09A (1973): 5999. Southern Ill. U at Carbondale.

*B1593 Bowker, Larsen. "The Pursuit of Permanence: A Study of the Thematic Structure of John Updike's Novels." *DAI* 35/05A 1974. 2980A. U of R.I.

*B1594 Foltz, David Allen. "Beyond Alienation in Four Contemporary American Novels." *DAI* 1974. U of Ariz.

*B1595 McCoy, Charles Robert. "Moral Ambiguity in John Updike's Short Stories." *DAI* 35/09A (1974): 6147. U So. Calif.

*B1596 Fritz, Donald Eric. "Phenomenological Criticism: An Analysis and an Application to the Fiction of John Updike." *DAI* 36/10A (1975): 6655. U of Mo.

*B1597 Ready, Richard Michael. "'Not Only'— An Examination of Abstraction in the Writings of John Updike, With Particular Emphasis on the Olinger Narratives." *DAI* 36/11A (1975): 7415. U of Minn.

*B1598 Plagman, Linda Marie. "The Modern Pilgrims: Marriage and the Self in the World of John Updike." *DAI* 36 (1975): 325A-326A.

*B1599 Wright, Ona. "Though Much Has Changed, Much Endures: Concepts of the Epic Hero in Selected Modern American Novels." *DAI* 35 (1975): 6738A-6739A.

*B1600 Hunt, Rev. George W. "John Updike: The Dialectical Vision— The Influence of Kierkegaard and Barth." *DAI* 36 (1976): 6674A.

*B1601 Schopen, Bernard A. "The Aesthetics of Ambiguity: The Novels of John Updike." *DAI* 36 (1976): 7415A.

*B1602 Uphaus, Suzanne Henning. "Mode and Meaning in the Novels of John Updike." *DAI* 37/05A (1976): 2882. U of Wash.

*B1603 Hill, Steele Waychoff. "Structural Unity in the Novels of John Updike." U of Md., 1977.

*B1604 Neal, William Ray. "The Theology of Karl Barth as an Interpretative Key to the Fiction of John Updike." *DAI* 38/03A (1977): 1382. U of Miss.

*B1605 Pally, Erwin. "From Realism to Romance in Six Novels by Bellow, Updike and Malamud." *DAI* 38/01A. (1977): 266. U of Mass.

*B1606 Waxman, Robert Ernest. "Updike, Gass, and Vonnegut: 'Studies in Contemporary American Fiction.'" *DAI* 38/07A (1977): 4173. Yale.

*B1607 Wright, Barbara Ann. "Perceptions and Reflections: The Short Story Art of John Updike." 1977. *DAI* 38/02A. (1977): 794. U of Rochester.

*B1608   Bodmer, George Ray. "The Right Life: The Problem of Existence in John Updike's Fiction." *DAI* 39/09A. (1978): Ind. U

B1609   Cox, David Michael. "An Examination of Thematic and Structural Connections Between John Updike's Rabbit Novels." *DAI* 39/09A. (1978): Ohio U.

*B1610   Nesset, Michael Paul. "John Updike and Andrew Wyeth: The Nostalgic Mode in Contemporary American Art." 1978. U of Minn.

*B1611   Schopen, Bernard Anthony. "The Aesthetics of Ambiguity: The Novels of John Updike." 1978. U of Nev. See **B1601**.

*B1612   Hull, James Horace. "*Ceremonies of Farewell: The Continuity of John Updike's Protagonist*." *DAI* 40 (1979): 5865.

*B1613   Searles, George John. "The Fiction of Philip Roth and John Updike." *DAI* 39/10A (1979): 361. SUNY Binghamton.

*B1614   Swick, Marly A. "Romantic Ministers and Phallic Knights: A Study of *A Month of Sundays*, *Lancelot* and *Falconer*." 1979. American U.

*B1615   Vik, Susan Frances. "A Study of Sexuality in Selected American Novels Since 1945." *DAI* 41/08A.(1979): 3586. U of R.I.

*B1616   Deen, Carol Ann Stanley. "Women in the novels of John Updike: A Critical Study." *DAI* 41 (1980): 1593. Tex. A & M.

*B1617   Sahlin, Nicki. "Manners in the Contemporary American Novel: Studies in Cheever, John Updike and Joan Didion." *DAI* 41/12A (1980): 5102. Brown U.

*B1618   Silver, Mark A. "Sports and Literature: A Rationale and Guide for the Use of American Sports Literature in the Teaching of a College Undergraduate General Education Course in Fiction." *DAI* 42/02A. (1980): 645. U of Md., College Park.

*B1619   Verduin, Kathleen. "Religious and Sexual Love in American Protestant Literature: Puritan Patterns in Hawthorne and John Updike." *DAI* 41/03A (1980): 1059. Ind. U.

*B1620   Wright, Barbara. "The Short Story: Writer's Control/Reader's Response." *DAI* 41/02A (1980): 660. Columbia U.

*B1621   Denby, Priscilla Lee. "The Self Discovered: The Car in American Folklore and Literature." *DAI* 42/08A (1981): 3703. Ind. U.

*B1622   Nickens, Susan Jean. "A Right Relation: John Updike's Norm of Marital Commitment." *DAI* 43/01A (1981): 169. U of Md., College Park.

*B1623	Perunilam, Thomas Varkey. "Elements of Contemporary American Culture as Reflected in Selected Works of American Literature, 1960-1974." *DAI* 43/04A. (1981) Rutgers, New Brunswick.
*B1624	Riley, Kathryn Louise. "The Use of Suburbia as a Setting in the Fiction of O'Hara, John Cheever, and John Updike." *DAI* 42/09A (1981): 4002. U of Md., College Park.
*B1625	Alderman, Timothy C. "The Integrated Short Story Collection as a Genre (Barth, Fowles, Updike)." *DAI* 43/08A. (1982): 2649. Purdue U.
*B1626	Friedman, Ruben. "Short Stories in Preservice Teacher Education." *DAI* 43/02A (1982): 423. Columbia Teachers College.
*B1627	Lanchester, Duane Preston. "A Critical Exploration of John Updike as American Theologian." *DAI* 1982. San Francisco Theological Seminary.
*B1628	Lathrop, Kathleen Lee. "Updike on America: The Expanding Vision of Updike in His Post-Olinger Novels." *DAI* 43/11A (1982): 3597. NYU.
*B1629	Lindholm, Karl Lambert. "Anticlimax: The Sporting Hero in Modern American Literature." *DAI* 43/05A (1982): 2013. Case Western Reserve U.
*B1630	Nerney, Brian James. "Katharine S. White, 'New Yorker' Editor: Her Influence on the 'New Yorker' and on American Literature." *DAI* 43/11A. (1982): 3637. U of Minn.
*B1631	Paravisini, Lizabeth. "The Novel as Parody of Popular Narrative Forms in the United States and Latin America: 1963-1980." *DAI* 43/07A (1982): 2342. NYU.
*B1632	Edgerton, Larry. "Transcending the Cliché: Transformed Conventions in Postwar American Novels." *DAI* 44/05A. (1983): 1453. U of Wis., Madison.
*B1633	Luscher, Robert Michael. "American Regional Short Story Sequences." *DAI* 45/11A (1984): 3350. Duke U
*B1634	Whitesides, Mary Parr. "Marriage in the American Novel from 1882 to 1982." *DAI* 45/09A (1984): 2878. U So. Calif.
*B1635	Ryan, Francis Joseph. "Lasch and the Portrayal of Narcissistic Personality in Adolescent Fiction (Salinger, Golding, Knowles, Updike)." *DAI* 46/03A (1985): 645. Temple U.
*B1636	Ripley, Jonathan Grant. "The Treatment of Burial Rituals in the Modern American Novel." *DAI* 46/09A (1985): 2694. Saint John's U.

*B1637   Shostak, Debra B. "Survivors: Perspectives on Transformative Violence in Contemporary American Narrative (1970's, Fiction, Autobiography)." *DAI* 46/10A. (1985): 3036. U of Wis., Madison.

*B1638   Horvath, Brooke Kenton. "Dropping Out: Spiritual Crisis and Countercultural Attitudes in Four American Novelists of the 1960's (Updike, Percy, Brautigan, Pynchon)." *DAI* 47/06A (1986): 2157. Purdue U.

*B1639   Keever, J. Robert. "Discerning Theological Dimensions in the Fiction of Updike." 1986. San Francisco Theological Seminary.

*B1640   Hartman, Susan Beth. "The Role of the Berks County Setting in the Novels of John Updike." *DAI* 48/08A (1987): 2062. U of Pittsburgh.

*B1641   Rose, Irene Kathryn. "Testing Coalition Theory in 'The Great Gatsby' and the 'Rabbit' Trilogy." *DAI* 47/07A. (1986): 2757. U of Okla.

*B1642   Smith, Peter Andrew. "Entropy in American Fiction (Poe, Hawthorne, Melville, Faulkner, Hemingway." *DAI* 48/06A (1987): 1456. Notre Dame.

*B1643   Ebert, Teresa Lynn. "Patriarchy, Ideology, Subjectivity: Towards a Theory of Feminist Critical Cultural Studies." *DAI* 50/01A (1988): 138. U of Mich.

*B1644   Plath, James Walter. "The Painterly Aspects of John Updike's Fiction." *DAI* 49/08A. (1988): 2221. U of Wis., Milwaukee.

*B1645   Powers, Meredith. "The Chthonic Heroine: Revision and Reemergence of the Archetype." *DAI* 50/04A (1988): 943. U of R.I.

*B1646   Thomas, Jim. "A Changing American Family: Cheever, Gardner, Irving, Updike." *DAI* 1988: 258. U of Mo., Columbia.

*B1647   Price, Andrew Jude. "The Entropic Imagination in Twentieth-Century American Fiction: A Case for Don DeLillo." *DAI* 49/05A (1988): 1143. U of Notre Dame.

*B1648   Buchanan, Mark Aldham. "Intact and Infrangible as Metal, and Like Metal Dead: Patterns of Faith and Forgetfulness in Three John Updike Novels with Special Reference to Nathaniel Hawthorne's 'The Scarlet Letter.'" (1989) MCS Regent College.

*B1649   Horner, Carl Stuart. "The Boy Inside the American Businessman: Corporate Darwinism in Twentieth Century American Literature (Salinger, Vonnegut, Miller, Heller, Updike)." *DAI* 50/08A (1989): 2485. Fla. State U.

*B1650   Gruesser, John Cullen. "White on Black: Non-Black Literature About Africa Since 1945." *DAI* 50/09A (1989): 2892. U of Wis., Madison.

*B1651   Ristoff, Dilvo I. "Updike's America: The Presence of Contemporary American History in John Updike's Rabbit Novels." *DAI* 49/07A (1989): 1804.

*B1652   Fuoroli, Caryn. "The Paradox of Language and Form of Contemporary Fiction." *DAI* 41/12A (1990): 5096. Brown U.

*B1653   Sethuraman, Ramchandran. "The Contours of Desire: Obsessional and Hysterical Discourse Structures in Updike, Cheever and Lurie." 1990. U of Fla.

*B1654   Singh, Sukhbir. "The Survivor in Contemporary American Fiction: Saul Bellow, Bernard Malamud, John Updike, Kurt Vonnegut, Jr." Delhi, India: B. R. Pub. Corp, 1991.

Master's and Honor's Theses:

*B1655   Roberts, Joe Donald. "A Critical Examination of the Prose Works of John Updike." 1964. U of Okla.

*B1656   Wagner, Don Henry. "The Use of Sexuality in the Fiction of John Updike." 1965. U of Notre Dame.

*B1657   Avery, William Scott. "An Analysis of *Harper's* Magazine: A Report on John Updike." 1966. Boston U.

*B1658   Walker, Claudine Dianne. "Structural Unity in John Updike's *The Centaur*." 1966 U of Fla.

*B1659   Kelley, Wnifred Peabody. "A Consideration of the Portrayal of the Anti-Hero in Selected Fiction of John Updike." 1967. U of R.I.

*B1660   Kutz, Anna W. "A Comparison of Major Concerns of John Updike and John Milton: Does Updike Give Evidence of Puritanism?" 1967. Notre Dame.

*B1661   Peters, Edmund Richard. "Art, Music, and Literature in John Updike's Fiction." 1968. Fla. State U.

*B1662   Warner, Margo Larson. "Landscapes Without a Country: the Novels of John Updike." 1968. Moorhead State U.

*B1663   Bates, Marvin Randolph. "The Fiction of John Updike: A Romantic Quest for Spiritual Permanence." 1969. Tulane U.

*B1664 Deen, Carol Ann Stanley. "The Women Characters in the Novels of John Updike." 1969. Tex. A & M U.

*B1665 Hecht, Carole Lynn. "Rabbit Angstrom's Spiritual Homelessness." 1969. U of N.C., Chapel Hill.

*B1666 Kuhl, St. Paul, Sister. "The Initiation Theme in the Writings of Ernest Hemingway, William Faulkner, and John Updike." 1969. Nazareth College of Rochester.

*B1667 Lindler, Barbara Anne. "The Sense of Alienation and the Search for Meaning in the Works of John Updike." Master's thesis. 1969. Winthrop College.

*B1668 Lucas, Patricia E. "The Social Quest in John Updike's Major Fiction." 1969. U of Nebr., Omaha.

*B1669 Mozolak, Harvey S. "Man in Relationship: A Comparative Study of Martin Luther's Theology of Man and Man as Presented in John Updike's *Rabbit, Run* and *Couples*." 1969. Concordia Theological Seminary, Springfield, Ill.

*B1670 Owens, Phillip Lamar. "The Oedipal Conflict in the Novels of John Updike." 1969. U of N.C., Chapel Hill.

*B1671 Petrarca, Anthony J. "An Analysis of John Updike's *Rabbit, Run* in the Context of Social Criticism." 1969. Indiana U of Pa.

*B1672 Quillen, Frank W. "The Influence of Neo-orthodoxy in the Fiction of John Updike." 1969. East Tenn. State U.

*B1673 Shenstone, Susan Louise Burgess. "Karl Barth and the Novels of John Updike: Updike's Novels as Christian Testimony." 1969. George Washington U.

*B1674 Verduin, Kathleen. "The Sense of Mortality in the Fiction of John Updike." 1969. George Washington U.

*B1675 Gardner, Jeanne Elizabeth. "The Search for Goodness in the Fiction of John Updike." 1970. Northeast Mo. State College.

*B1676 Jennings, Ben Hill. "The Religious Themes in John Updike's *Couples*." 1970. U of N.C., Chapel Hill.

*B1677 Smallwood, Patricia R. "John Updike and the Critics: An Interpretation and Evaluation of the Criticism of John Updike's Work." 1970. Southwest Tex. State U.

*B1678 Conte, Donald James. "The Search for Identity Through Time-Consciousness in John Updike's Fiction." 1971. Indiana U of Pa..

*B1679	Goldstein, Mona. "A High, Blank, Reflecting Wall of Glass: The Novels of John Updike." 1971. Washington U.
*B1680	Schiller, Robert Evett. "The Quest for Freedom in the Novels of John Updike." 1971. U of Miss.
*B1681	Thommen, Paula Marie. "The Evolution of an Author: A Stylistic Analysis of Selected Novels by John Updike." 1971. Montclair State College.
B1682	Hartsoe, Judith S. "The Medieval Fantasy of Courtly Love in Iris Murdoch's *A Severed Head* and John Updike's *Couples*." 1972. Indiana U of Pa.
*B1683	Johnson, Randell Gaw. "John Updike's Use of Allusions and Symbols in *Rabbit, Run* and *Rabbit Redux* to Reveal Ethical Views and Different Attitudes toward Religion." 1972. Tenn. Tech. U.
*B1684	Matheny, Fredrick Ross. "The American Everyman: A Study of the Athlete in *Rabbit, Run*, *The Great Gatsby*, and *Death of a Salesman*." 1972.
*B1685	Schuszler, Cornelius L. "*Rabbit, Run*: A Reconsideration." 1972. U of N.C., Chapel Hill.
*B1686	Schenck, Janice. "John Updike: The Author's View." 1973. Montclair State College.
*B1687	Tondora, Nancy E. "An Examination of the Theme of Man's Search for a Meaningful Contemporary Religion in John Updike's Fiction." 1973. Indiana U of Pa.
B1688	Egge, Marion F. "A Membrane of Consciousness: John Updike and Point of View." 1974. Lehigh U.
*B1689	Jo Ashley. "Ceremony and the Search for Meaning in the Fiction of John Updike." 1975. Central Conn.
*B1690	Heneghan, Gail Lorraine. "Rabbit Grows Up: The Adamic Theme in *Rabbit Redux*." 1975. Tenn. Technological U.
*B1691	Gordon, Jeffrey W. "The Theme of Adultery in the Fiction of John Updike." 1976. U of N.C., Chapel Hill.
*B1692	Gilchriest, William E. "An Analysis of the Man-Woman Relationships in John Updike's *Rabbit, Run* and *Rabbit Redux*." 1977. Lamar U.
*B1693	Ridgeway, Patricia Moore. "Father and Son in the Fiction of John Updike." 1977. Winthrop College.

*B1694 Wayland, Elisabeth R. "John Updike's Philosophy as Revealed in His Poem 'MidPoint.'"1978. Shippensburg State College.

*B1695 Ducote, D'Ann. "The Quest Theme in John Updike's Early Novels." 1980. West Tex. State U.

*B1696 McClain, Susanna Alice. "Sexual Love in John Updike's *Rabbit, Run, Couples*, and *A Month of Sundays*." 1980. Abilene Christian U.

*B1697 Afshar, Carolyn Anne McKinney. "Early and Late Patterns of the Search Motif Contrasted in John Updike's Fiction: *Rabbit, Run* and *The Coup*." 1981. Ga. Southern College.

*B1698 Botvinick, Risa D. "The Resolution of Guilt in the Novels of John Updike." 1981. N.C. State U.

*B1699 Crowell, Carol Ann. "The Authentic Man: A Sartrean Analysis of *Dangling Man* and *Rabbit, Run*." 1982. Western Carolina U.

*B1700 Kohli, Mary Ann. "Updike's Pilgrims: Marriage in Twentieth-Century America." 1982. USC.

*B1701 Hyman, Lisa Diane. "The Use of Language in John Updike's Short Stories." 1983. USC.

*B1702 Kopelowitz, Lynn Wolf. "Circles of Paradise and Inferno: The Women in John Updike's 'Rabbit' Trilogy." 1984. Fla. Atlantic U.

*B1703 Upshaw, Kathryn Jane. "John Updike and Norman Mailer." 1984. U of N.C., Greensboro.

*B1704 Ward, Susan D. "Sin and Grace as Praxis: An Analysis of Life and Death in the Trilogy of John Updike." 1984. Graduate Theological Union.

*B1705 Wilson, Carol Brasington. "John Updike's Harry 'Rabbit' Angstrom as American Adam." 1984. U of Southern Calif.

*B1706 Hendey, Sara Louise. "Didion and Updike: Images of the American Woman and the Sixties." 1985. Mount Holyoke College.

*B1707 Nelson, Margaret Lorraine. "John Updike's Rabbit Trilogy: From Running to Jogging: Motions of Grace in Harry Angstrom." 1985. Central Washington U.

*B1708 Szpila, Joseph B. "Religion and Myth in the Early Novels of John Updike." 1985. R.I. College.

*B1709 Atwater, Allison Elizabeth. "Space in John Updike's Rabbit Trilogy: A Search for Balance." 1986. Northeast Mo. State U.

Dissertations and Theses

*B1710   Austenfeld, Thomas Carl. "Beyond Nostalgia: Childhood and Remembrance in John Updike's Fiction." 1986. U of Va.

*B1711   Alexander, Robert Allen. "The Fear of Death in the Short Fiction of John Updike." 1987. U of N.C., Chapel Hill.

*B1712   Cunningham, Nancy Ashworth. "John Updike, in the Tradition of American Classic Literature." 1987. U of San Diego.

*B1713   Gamble, Sharon. "Romance of the Quotidian: Realistic Style and Romantic Ideas in John Updike's Short Fiction." 1987. Butler U.

*B1714   Steel, Diana Staynskas Moran. "An Archetypal Approach to John Updike's Rabbit Trilogy." 1987. Cleveland State U.

*B1715   Steinley, Nan. "Music School: A Dance with John Updike's Poetry." 1987. S. Dak. State U.

*B1716   Gray, Nancy L. "Of All Men the Most Miserable: A Study of Two Ministers in the Works of John Updike." 1988. U of N.C. at Chapel Hill.

*B1717   Holley, H. "Hawthorne's Hester Prynne, Updike's Sarah Worth, and the 'Three Great Secret Things.'" 1989. U of Southern Calif.

*B1718   Sheppard, Barbara Dillard. "Arendt and Updike: Philosopher and Novelist on the Human Condition." 1989. Emory.

*B1719   Thrasher, D. G. "The Mirrors of Self: Female Characters Used as Metaphor for the Great Mother in *Lolita*, *Herzog*, and *Rabbit, Run*." 1989. Calif. State U, Bakersfield.

*B1720   Van Wyk, S. Elizabeth. "The Search for Faith in John Updike's Fiction." Honor's thesis. 1989. U of Wis., Milwaukee.

*B1721   Fox, Matthew Graham. "The Life and Death of a Modern American Rabbit: A Reading of John Updike's Rabbit Tetralogy." B. A. Honors. 1992 Duke U.

*B1722   Zervanos, James T. "Rabbit Angstrom and the Changing of the American Man." B. A. Honors. 1992. Bucknell U.

5. Parodies and Caricatures

Parodies:

B1723   Hatcher, Randall. "Of the Breezeway." *Snooze*. Ed. Alfred Gingold and John Buskin. NY: Workman, 1986. 54.

B1724   *Medigate* (Harvard) Sum. 1991: 22. (Parody of *Rabbit, Run*.)

Caricatures:

B1725   Levine, David. Caricature. In Jack Richardson, "Keeping Up with Updike." *The New York Review of Books* 15 (22 Oct. 1970): 46-48. (The same caricature is used in "Long-Distance Runner." *The New York Review of Books* 30 [25 Oct. 1990]: 11.)

B1726   Caricature. In "The Signet Society Medal for Achievement in the Arts Awarded to John Updike, Class of 1954 [on Mar. 20, 1971]." *The John Updike Newsletter* No. 8 (Fall 1978): [p. 4].

B1727   Roth, Arnold. Caricature. In "Henry Bech Redux." *The New York Review of Books* 14 Nov. 1971: 3.

B1728   Levine, David. Caricature. In Christopher Ricks, "Flopsy Bunny." *The New York Review of Books* 17 (16 Dec. 1971): 7-9.

B1729   Caricature. In James Wolcott, "Running On Empty." *Esquire* 96 (Oct. 1981): 20, 22-23. (Updike is shown as Hamlet confronting Yorick's skull.)

B1730   Caricature. In Paul Gray, "Perennial Promises Kept." *Time* 120 (18 Oct. 1982): 72-74, 79-81. (Henry Bech cover portrait.)

B1731 Banfield, Elliot. Caricature. In Robert R. Harris, "Rabbit in the Rough." *The New York Times Book Review* 30 Oct. 1983: 43.

B1732 Levine, David. Caricature. In Elizabeth Hardwick, "Citizen Updike." *The New York Review of Books* 36 (18 May 1984): 3. (Rpt. from *Book Digest* Dec. 1981.)

B1733 ---. Caricature. In Diane Johnson. "Warlock." *The New York Review of Books* 14 June 1984: 3.

B1734 ---. Caricature. In Frederick Crews. "Mr. Updike's Planet." *The New York Review of Books* 33 (4 Dec. 1986): 7-10, 12, 14.

B1735 Palmer, Kate S. Caricature. In Donald J. Greiner, "Updike on Hawthorne." *The Nathaniel Hawthorne Review* 13 (Spring 1987): 1-4.

B1736 Caricature. Accompanies *S.* publicity, 1988. (Artist not given.)

B1737 Levine, David. Caricature. In Alison Lurie, "The Woman Who Rode Away." *The New York Review of Books* 35 (12 May 1988): 3-4.

B1738 Caricature. *The New Republic* 20 June 1988: 40.

B1739 Caricature. *National Review* 19 May 1989: 52. (Artist's name not legible. "Merka?")

B1740 Lawrence, Vint. Caricature. *The New Republic* 20 May 1989.

B1741 Caricature. In Paul Gray, "Rabbit Stew." *Time* 136 (13 Aug. 1990): 13.

B1742 Caricature. In Jonathan Raban, "Rabbit's Last Run." *Washington Post* 30 Sept. 1990: 1. (Artist unidentified.)

B1743 Fasch. Caricature. "The Inner Rabbit." *Chicago Tribune Books* 30 Sept. 1990: 1.

B1744 Caricature. In Walter Kirn, "Rabbit's Run." *Gentlemen's Quarterly* 60 (Nov. 1990): 166. (Unsigned caricature.)

B1745 Caricature. In Thomas Mallon, "*Rabbit at Rest.*" *American Spectator* 23 (Nov. 1990): 42. (Unsigned.)

B1746 Caricature. In Rand Richards Cooper, "Rabbit Loses the Race: John Updike's 'Small Answer of a Texture.'" *Commonweal* (17 May 1991): 315. (Unsigned.)

B1747 Klinge, Mama. Caricature. In James Thompson, "Mr. Nice Guy." *The World & I* 1 Mar. 1992: 319.

B1748 Levine, David. In Alfred Kazin. "The Middle Way." *The New York Review of Books* 39 (17 Dec. 1992): 45.

Appendix I
Translations of Updike's Work

Books:

The Poorhouse Fair (1959):

*1		French: *Jour de fête à l'hospice*. Trans. Alain Delahaye. Paris: Julliard, 1979.
*2		German: *Das Fest am Abend*. Translator not given. Hamburg: Rowohlt, 1973.
3		Greek: *To Pazapi Sto Asglo*. Athens: Ekloseis Kastanioth, 1989.
*4		Hungarian: *Szegényházi Vásár*. Trans. Goncz Arpad. Budapest: Szepirodalmi Könyvkiadö, 1983.
*5		Italian: *Festa all'ospizio e altri racconti*. Trans. Bruno Oddera. Milan: Mondadori, 1961.
*6		Japanese: *Poorhouse Fair*. Trans. Hirano Yukio. Tokyo: Gene shuppansha, 1969.
*7		Japanese: *Rofuin no Matsuri*. Trans. Hiran Yuihito. Tokyo Taiyosha, 1970.
*8		Japanese: *Pua Hausu-Fea*. Trans. Suyama Shizuo. Tokyo: Shinchosha, 1971.
*9		Polish: *Jarmark Domu Ubogich*. Krakow: Wydownichtwo Literackie, 1981.
*10		Portuguese: *A Fiera*. Trans. Fiama Hasse Pais Brandao and Walter J. Hossman. Lisbon: Portugalia Editora, 1961, 1969.

*11	Serbo-Croatian: *Sajam u Ubozinci*. Trans. Gordana Popovic-Vujicic. Zagreb: August Cesarec, 1979.
*12	Spanish: *La Feria Del Asilo*. Trans. Patricia Scantlebury. Santiago: Zigzag, 1969.
*13	Spanish: *La Feria Del Asilo*. Trans. Enrique Hegewicz. Barcelona: Bruguera, 1980.
*14	Swedish: *Basar i Fattighuset*. Trans. Gottfried Grafstrom. Stockholm: Bonnier, 1962.

The Same Door (1959):

*15	Czechoslovakian: *Z Drava Tesany Vtak*. Trans. Ivan Mojik. Bratislava: Slov. spis, 1968.
*16	Danish: *I Morgen og i Morgen og sa Videre*. Trans. Elsa Gress Wright. Copenhagen: Gyldendals Bekkasinboger, 1965.
17	German: *Gesammelte Erzählungen*. Trans. Maria Carlsson, Susana Rudemacher and Herman Stiehl. Reinbach bei Hamburg: Rowohlt, 1971. (Includes *Pigeon Feathers*.)
18	German: *Glücklicher war ich nie*. Trans. Maria Carlsson. Frankfurt am Main: S. Fisher Verlag, 1966. (Includes *Pigeon Feathers*.)
*19	Japanese: *Onaji Hitotsu no doa*. Trans. Takeda Katsuhiko. Tokyo: Kadokawa shoten, 1970.
*20	Spanish: *La Misma Puerta*. Trans. Carmen Cienfuegos. Santiago: Zig-Zag, 1970.

Rabbit, Run (1960):

*21	Czechoslovakian: *Kraliku, Utikej!* Translator not given. Prague: Odeon, 1980.
*22	Danish: *Hare Hop*. Trans. Elsa Gress Wright. Copenhagen: Gyldendal, 1963.
*23	Danish: *Hare Hop*. Trans. Elsa Gress Wright. Copenhagen: Gyldendals Bogklub, 1971.
*24	Dutch: *Hazehart*. Translator not given. Bussum: Uitgeverij Villa, 1960.
*25	Dutch: *Hazehart*. Trans. R. Germeraad. Amsterdam: Meulenhoff, 1971.

*26   Finnish: *Juokse, Janis*. Trans. Oiva Oksanen. Helsinki: Otava, 1963.

27   Finnish: *Juokse, Janis*. Trans. Oiva Oksanen. Helsinki: Otava, 1992.

*28   French: *Coeur de Lièvre*. Trans. Jean Rosenthal. Paris: Editions du Seuil, 1962. Reprinted, 1983.

*29   German: *Hasenherz*. Trans. Maria Carlsson. Frankfurt am Main: Fischer Bucherie, 1962, 1967. Also published: Berlin: Ferlag Volk und Welt, 1978.

30   German: *Hasenherz*. Trans. Maria Carlsson. Reinbek bei Hamburg: Rowohlt Verlag GmbH, Fibel zur Jahrhundert-Edition, 1990. (With a small handbook and slipcase.)

*31   Hebrew: *Ruts Shafan*. Trans. Devorah Shtaynhart. Tel Aviv: Mifalim Universitaiyim le Hostaah la or, 1977.

*32   Hungarian: *Nyúlcipó*. Trans. Adam Rez. Budapest: Európa Könyvkiadö, 1968, 1970.

33   Italian: *Corri, Coniglio*. Trans. Bruno Oddera. Milan: Mondadori, 1961, 1974, 1979.

*34   Japanese: *Hashire Usagi*. Trans. Yokichi Miyamoto. Tokyo: Hakusuisha, 1964, 1975.

35   Latvian: *Trusi, Bedz!* Trans. Valdis Brauns. Riga: Liesma, 1983. (Published with *Precesimies!*)

*36   Norwegian: *Hare, Hopp*. Trans. Colbjorn Helander. Oslo: Gyldendal Norsk Forlag, 1960, 1962.

*37   Polish: *Uciekaj, Kroliku*. Trans. Ariadna Demkoswka-Bohdziewicz. Warszawa: Pantwowy Intytut Wydawn, 1988.

38   Portuguese: *Corre Coelho*. Trans. Fiama Hassa Pais Brandao. Lisboa: Europa-America, 1965.

39   Portuguese: *Coelho, Corre*. Trans. Paulo Henriques Britto. Lisboa: Companhia Das Letras, 1992.

*40   Russian: *Krolik, Begi*. Translator not given. Moscow: Khudozhestvennaia Literatura, 1979.

*41   Russian: *Krolik, Begi*. Translator not given. Moscow: Fizkultura i sport, 1991.

*42   Spanish: *Corre, Conejo*. Trans. Baldomero Porta. Barcelona: Seix Barral, 1965, 1970.

*43 Spanish: *Corre, Conejo.* Trans. Enrique Hegewicz. Barcelona: Editorial Bruguera, 1979.

*44 Spanish: *Corre, Conejo.* Trans. Jorid Fibla. Barcelona: Tusquets, 1990.

*45 Swedish: *Haren Springer.* Trans. Gottfried Grafstrom. Stockholm: Boforlaget Alduro Bonniers, 1961, 1965.

Pigeon Feathers and Other Stories (1962):

*46 French: *Les Plumes du Pigeon: Nouvelles.* Trans. J. Rosenthal. Paris: Editions du Seuil, 1964.

47 German: *Gesammelte Erzählungen.* Trans. Maria Carlsson, Susana Rudemacher and Herman Stiehl. Reinbach bei Hamburg: Rowohlt, 1971. (Includes *The Same Door.*)

48 German: *Glücklicher war ich nie.* Trans. Maria Carlsson. Frankfurt am Main: S. Fisher Verlag, 1966. (Includes *The Same Door.*)

*49 Italian: *Nella Fattoria e altre storie.* Trans. Luigi Brioschi and Bruno Oddera. Milan: Mondadori, 1970, 1992. Introduction by Vincenzo Mantovani. Milan: Mandadori, 1992. ("Introduction," v-xv. Also includes *Of the Farm.*)

*50 Japanese: *Hato no Hane.* Trans. Terakado Yasuhiko. Tokyo: Hakusuisha, 1968, 1986.

*51 Spanish: *Plumas de Paloma y Otros Relatos.* Trans. José Ma Valverde. Barcelona: Seix Barral, 1967.

*52 Swedish: *Basar i fattighuset.* Stockholm: Oversattning Cai Melin, Forum, 1962. (See *14 above.)

*53 Yugoslavian: *Golubije Perje* Trans. Vera Ilic. (Pripovetke). Beograd: Nolit, 1966.

The Centaur (1963):

*54 Bulgarian: *Kentavarat.* Trans. Krastan Djankov. Sofija: Narjultura, 1967.

*55 Czechoslovakian: *Kentaur.* Trans. Igor Hajek. Praja: Cs. spisovatel, 1967.

*56 Czechoslovakian: *Kentaur.* Trans. Jozef Kot. Bratislava: Tatran, 1967.

*57 Dutch: *Mijn Vader, de Centaur.* Trans. Frans Bijlsma. Amsterdam: Meulenhoff, 1963, 1965.

*58	Esthonian: *Kentaur*. Trans. E. Soosaar. Tallinn: Eesti raamat, 1968.
*59	French: *Le Centaure*. Trans. L. Casseau. Paris: Editions du Seuil, 1965.
*60	German: *Der Zentaur*. Trans. Maria Carlsson. Frankfurt: Fischer, 1966, 1979.
*61	German: *Der Zentaur*. Trans. Maria Carlsson. Berlin: Volk und Welt, 1972.
*62	Italian: *Il Centauro*. Trans. Bruno Oddera. Milan: Mondadori, 1964.
*63	Japanese: *Centaur*. (*Ararashii seai no bungaku, 51*) Trans. Terakado Yasuhiko and Komiya Teruo. Tokyo: Hakusuisha, 1968.
*64	Latvian: *Kentaurs*. Trans. Rute Runcis. Riga: Liesma, 1969.
*65	Lithuanian: *Kentauras*. Trans. L. Vanagiene. Vilnjus: 'aga, 1967.
*66	Norwegian: *Kentauren*. Trans. Magli Elster. Oslo: Pax, 1966.
*67	Portuguese: *O Centauro*. Trans. Carmen Gonzalez. Lisboa: Europa-America, 1967.
*68	Rumanian: *Centaurui*. Trans. Sorin Alexandrescu. Bucuresti: Editura pentru Literatura Universala, 1968.
*69	Russian: *Kentavr*. Trans. V. Hinkis. Moskva: Progress, 1966.
*70	Russian: *Kentavr*. Trans. A. Zvereva. Moskva: Raduga, 1984.
*71	Serbo-Croatian: *Kentaur*. Trans. Milknko Popovic. Zagreb: Zora, 1968.
*72	Spanish: *El Centauro*. Translator not given. Buenos Aires: Emece, 1979.
*73	Spanish: *El Centauro*. Trans. Mario Bertorelli. Barcelona: Seix y Barral, 1968.
*74	Spanish: *El Centauro*. Trans. Enrique Hegewicz. Barcelona: Bruguera, 1980.
75	Spanish: *El Centauro*. Trans. Enrique Murillo. Barcelona: Tusquets, 1991.
*76	Swedish: *Kentauren*. Trans. Pelle Fritz-Crone. Stockholm. Bonnier, 1963.
*77	Yugoslavian: *Kentaur*. Trans. Melenk Popovic. Zagreb: Zora, 1968.

Assorted Prose (1965):

78   German: *Gesammelte Erzählungen*. Trans. Maria Carlsson and others. Hamburg: Rowohlt, 1971.

Of the Farm (1965):

*79   Czechoslovakian: *O Farme*. Trans. Igor Hajek, 1968. Introduction by Updike. (Reprinted in *Picked-Up Pieces*. NY: Knopf, 1975. 82-83. See **A719**.)

*80   Czechoslovakian: *O Farme*. Translator not given. Prague: Cekoslovensky Spisovatel, 1973.

*81   Dutch: *Terug en Verder*. Trans. Frans Bijlsma. Amsterdam: Meulenhoff, 1967.

*82   French: *La Ferme*. Trans. Raphael Noris. Paris: Editions du Seuil, 1968, 1974.

*83   French: *La Ferme*. Trans. Raphael Noris. Lausanne: La Guilde du Livre, 1970.

*84   German: *Auf der Farm*. Trans. Fritz Lorch. Frankfurt: Fischer, 1969.

*85   German: *Auf der Farm*. Translator not given. Berlin: Volk und Welt, 1973. (East German edition of the previous work.)

*86   Hungarian: *Szegényházi Vásár*. Translator not given. Budapest: Európa, 1975.

87   Italian: *Nella Fattoria e altre storie*. Trans. Luigi Brioschi and Bruno Oddera. Introduction by Vincenzo Mantovani. Milan: Mondadori, 1970, 1992. ("Introduzione," pp. v-xv. Includes stories from *Pigeon Feathers*, *49.)

*88   Japanese: *Nojo*. Trans. Kono Ichiro. Tokyo: Kawa shobo shinsha, 1969.

89   Polish: *Farma*. Trans. Maria Skinbniewska. Wwa: Czytelnik, 1967.

*90   Spanish: *En Torno a la Granja*. Trans. Carlos Mellizo. Madrid: Novelas y Cuentos, 1967.

91   Spanish: *De la Finca*. Trans. Josep M. Fulquet.[sic] Barcelona: Ediciones Proa, 1987.

*92   Swedish: *Fran Garden*. Trans. Pelle Fritz-Crone. Stockholm: Bonnier, 1970.

The Music School (1966):

*93	Danish: *Musikskolen*. Trans. Harry Mortensen. Kovenhavn: Gyldendal, 1968.
*94	French: *Les Quatre Faces d'une Histoire: Nouvelles*. Trans. Adriana R. Salem and Patrick Reumaux. Paris: Editions du Seuil, 1971.
*95	Japanese: *Myujikku Sukuru*. Trans. Suyama Shizuo. Tokyo: Shinchosha, 1970, 1974.
*96	Polish: *Szkola Muzyczna*. Trans. Henryk Krzeckowski. Warsaw: Panstwowy Instyut Wydawn, 1969.
*97	Portuguese: *Escola de Musica*. Trans. Daniel Goncalves. Porto: Civilizacao, 1969.

Couples (1968):

98	Czechoslovakian: *Dvojice*. Trans. Dusan Slobodnik. Bratislava: Vydavatelstvo Slovensky Spisovatel, 1991.
*99	Danish: *Hver ta'r sin*. Trans. Knud Sogaard. Kovenhavn: Gylendalis Bogklub, 1969.
*100	Dutch: *Paren*. Amsterdam: Meulenhoff, 1969.
*101	Finnish: *Parit*. Trans. Heimo Pihlajamaa. Helsinki: Otava (1-2 ed.), 1969.
*102	French: *Couples*. Trans. Ann-Marie Soulac. Paris: Gallimard, 1969.
*103	German: *Ehepaare*. Translator not given. Gutersloh: Bertelsmann, 1968.
*104	German: *Ehepaare*. Trans. Maria Carlsson. Hamburg: Rowohlt (4. Aufl), 1969, 1970. Berlin: Dt. Buch- Gemeinschaft; Gutersloh: Bertelsmann; Stuttgart: Europ. Buch-u-Phonoklub, 1971. Berlin: Verlag Volk und Welt, 1969, 1983.
*105	Greek: *Ta Zeugaria: Mythistorema*. Trans. Maro Loizou. [Greece]: Maiandros, 1972.
106	Hungarian: *Parok*. Trans. Julia Debreczeni. [Budapest]: Victoria, 1990.
*107	Italian: *Coppie*. Trans. Attilio Veraldi. Milan: Feltrinelli, 1969, 1971.
*108	Japanese: *Kappuruzu Miyamoto Yokichi Yaku*. Translator not given. Tokyo: Shinchosha, 1970, 1975, 1978.
*109	Norwegian: *Par*. Trans. Helge Simonsen. Oslo: Gyldendal, 1969.

*110   Portuguese: *Casais Trocados*. Trans. Pinheiro de Lemos. Rio de Janeiro. Distr. Record, 1969.

*111   Portuguese: *Casais Trocados*. Translator not given. Sao Paulo: Circulo do Libro, 1973.

*112   Portuguese: *Casais Trocados*. Trans. Pinheiro de Lemos. Sao Paulo: Abril Cultural, 1982.

*113   Serbocroatian: *Parovi*. Translator not given. Belgrad: Prosveta, 1968, 1979.

*114   Slavic: *Parovi*. Trans. Dzon Apdajk. Belgrad: Prosveta, 1977.

*115   Slovenian: *Zakonski Pari*. Trans. Mira Miheliceva. Ljubjana: Cankarjeva Zalozba, 1971.

*116   Spanish: *Parejas*. Translator not given. Madrid: Jucar, 1974, 1976, 1977.

*117   Swedish: *Par om Par*. Trans. Else Lundgren. Stockholm: Bonnier, 1969.

Bech: A Book (1970):

*118   Danish: *Bech, en Bog*. Trans. Kurt Freutzfeld. Kobenhavn: Gyldendal, 1971.

*119   Dutch: *Bech: een Boek*. Trans. Else Hoog. Amsterdam: Meulenhoff, 1971.

120   French: *Bech Voyage*. Trans. Georges Magnane. Paris: Gallimard, 1972, 1985.

*121   Italian: *Bech, lo Scrittore alla Moda*. Trans. Attilio Veraldi. Milan: Feltrinelli, 1971.

*122   Norwegian: *Bech, en Bok*. Translator not given. Oslo: Gyldendal Norsk, 1971.

*123   Spanish: *El Libro de Bech*. Trans. Andres Bosch. Barcelona: Noguer, 1971.

*124   Swedish: *Boken om Bech*. Translator not given. Halmstad, Sweden: Forum, 1971.

Rabbit Redux (1971):

*125   Danish: *Rabbit Igen*. Trans. Mógens Boisen. Haslev, Denmark: Gyldendal, 1972.

Appendix I: Translations of Updike's Work

*126	Dutch: *Rabbit Redux*. Trans. Dolf Koning. Amsterdam: Meulenhoff, 1973.
127	Croatian. *Rabbit Se Vraca*. Trans. Breda Varl. Croatia, Yugoslavia: Maribor, 1975.
128	French: *Rabbit Rattrapé*. Trans. Georges Magnane. Paris: Gallimard, 1973.
*129	German: *Unter dem Astronautenmond*. Trans. Kai Molvig. Zurich: Buchclub Ex Libris, 1973, 1985.
130	Italian: *Il Ritorno di Coniglio*. Trans. Attilio Veraldi. Milan: Feltrinelli, 1971.
*131	Italian: *Torna, Coniglio*. Trans. Attilio Veraldi. Milan: Club degli autori, 1972.
*132	Norwegian: *Hare Hvorhen?* Trans. Olav Angell. Oslo: Glydendal Norsk Forlag, 1972.
133	Portuguese: *Coelho em Crise*. Lisboa: Companhia Das Letras, 1992.
*134	Spanish: *El Regreso de Conejo*. Trans. A. Bosch. Barcelona: Noguer, 1973.
135	Spanish: *El Regreso de Conejo*. Trans. Iris Menéndez. Barcelona: Tusquets, 1993.
*136	Swedish: *Haren aterstalld*. Stockholm: Oversattning Cai Melin, Forum, 1972.

Seventy Poems (1972):

*137	Serbo-Croatian: *Sedamdeset Pjesama*. Trans. Jadranka Slokovic-Glumac. Zagreb: Prosvjeta, 1981.

Museums and Women (1972):

*138	Danish: *Marchen gennem Boston og Andre Noveller*. Translator not given. [Denmark]: Gyldendal, 1974.
*139	French: *Des Musées et des femmes, et Autres Nouvelles*. Trans. Georges Magnane. Paris: Gallimard, 1975.
*140	Italian: *Donne e Musei*. Trans. E. Capriolo. Milan: Feltrinelli, 1974.
*141	Polish: *Muzea i Kobiety Oraz Inne Opowiadania*. Trans. Maria Skibniewska. Warsaw: Panstwowy Instytut Wydawniczy, 1978.

*142   Rumanian: *Muzee si Femei*. Trans. Radu Lupan. Bucharest: Editura Univers, 1980.

*143   Spanish: *Museos y Mujeres*. Translator not given. Barcelona: Noguer, 1974.

*144   Swedish: *Aktenskap och Karlek*. Trans. Kurt Kreutzfeld. Vanersborg: Forum, 1973.

A Month of Sundays (1975):

*145   French: *Un Mois de Dimanches*. Paris: Gallimard, 1979.

*146   German: *Der Sonntagsmonat*. Trans. Kurt Heinrich 6ansen. Rheinbek bei Hamburg: Rowohlt, 1976, 1981.

147   Italian: *Un Mese di Domeniche*. Trans. Attilio Veraldi. Milan: Rizzoli, 1976, 1980.

148   Italian: *Un Mese di Domeniche*. Trans. Attilio Veraldi. Bergamo: Euroclub, 1979.

*149   Italian: *Un Mese di Domeniche*. Trans. Attilio Veraldi. Milan Club Italiano dei Lettori, 1979.

*150   Portuguese: *Un Mes so de Domingos*. Trans. Luzia Machado da Costa. Sao Paulo: Circulo do Livro, 1979.

*151   Spanish: *Un Mes de Domingos*. Trans. Marta Pessarrodona. Barcelona: Noguer, 1977.

Picked-Up Pieces (1975):

152   French: *La Vie Littéraire*. Trans. Jean Malignon. Paris: Gallimard, 1979.

Marry Me (1976):

*153   Bulgarian: *Ozheni Se Za Men*. Trans. Belin Tonchev. Sofia: Narodna Kultura, 1979.

154   Czechoslovakian: *Chces si me Vzit?* Trans. Luba and Rudolf Pellarovi. Afterword by Miroslav Jindra, 293-298. Prague: Mlada Fronta, 1983.

*155   Danish: *Til Kaerligheden os Skiller*. [Denmark]: Glyndendals Bogklub, 1976, 1977.

*156   Dutch: *Trouw met Mij*. Amsterdam: Meulenhoff, 1978.

*157   Finnish: *Kunnes Rakkaus Meidat Erottaa*. Trans. Elina Hytonen. Helsingissa: Otava, 1976, 1981.

158   French: *Epouse-moi*. Trans. Maurice Rambaud, 1978. Paris: Gallimard, 1978.

*159   German: *Heirate Mich!* Trans. Angela Praesent. Reinbek bei Hamburg: Rowohlt, 1978, 1982. Also published: Berlin: Verlag Volk und Welt.

*160   Hebrew: *Hinasi Li*. Trans. Ofirah Rahat. Tel Aviv: Zemorah, Bitan, Modan, 1979.

*161   Hugarian: *Gyere Hozzam Felesegul*. Trans. Goncz Arpad. Budapest: Europa, 1981.

162   Italian: *Sposami*. Trans. Ettore Capriolo. Milan: Rizzoli, 1977, 1980.

*163   Italian: *Sposami*. Trans. Ettore Capriolo. Milan: Euroclub, 1978.

164   Latvian: *Trusi, Bedz!* Trans. Anna Bauga and Inese Veide. Riga: Liesma, 1983.

*165   Norwegian: *Gift deg Med Meg*. Trans. Leo Strom. Oslo: Glyndendal Norsk Forlag, 1976, 1977.

166   Polish: *Wyjdz za Mnie: Apowiesc Romantyczna*. Trans. Cecylia Wojewoda. Warsaw: Panstwowy Instytut Wydawniczy, 1983, 1992.

*167   Swedish: *Gift dig med mig*. Trans. Kerestin Apell. Stockholm: Forum, 1976, 1977.

The Coup (1978):

*168   Dutch: *De Coup*. Trans. Aad Nuis. Amsterdam: Meulenhoff, 1981.

*169   Finnish: *Mina Olen Eversti Ellellou*. Trans. Jukka Kemppinen. Helsingissa: Otava, 1978, 1980.

170   French: *Le Putsch*. Trans. Maurice Rambaud. France: Gallimard, 1980. Includes an Acknowledgement, "Remerciements," 9-10.

171   French: *Le Putsch*. Trans. Maurice Rambaud. France: Gallimard, 1980. Includes an Acknowledgement "Remerciements," 7-8. (Paperback printing.)

*172   French: *Le Putsch*. Trans. Maurice Rambaud. Paris: Gallimard, 1984.

*173   German: *Der Coup*. Trans. Jurgen Abel. Berlin: Deutsche Buch-Gemeinschaft, 1981.

*174   Hebrew: *Ha-Hafekhah*. Trans. Aharon Amir. Tel Aviv: Zemorah, Bitan, Modan, 1980.

*175   Italian: *Il Colpo di Stato*. Trans. Pier Francesco Paolini. Milan: Rizzoli, 1980. Also published: Milan: Club Italiano dei Lettori, 1980, 1981.

*176   Italian: *Il Colpo di Stato*. Trans. Pier Francesco Paolini. Milan: Club Italiano dei Lettori, 1980, 1981.

*177   Japanese: 1981. (Only information available.)

*178   Norwegian: *Kuppet*. Trans. Leif Toklum. Oslo: Gyldendal Norsk Forlag, 1978, 1979

179   Portuguese (Brazil): *O Golpe*. Trans. Donaldson M. Garschagen. Rio de Janeiro: Nova Fronteira, 1978, 1979.

*180   Spanish: *Golpe de Estado*. Trans. Rolando Costa Picazo. Barcelona: Bruguera, 1979.

*181   Spanish: *El Golpe*. Trans. Rolando Costa Picazo. Buenos Aires: Emece Editores, 1980.

*182   Swedish: *Cuppen*. Trans. Hans-Jacob Nilsson. Sweden: Forum, 1979.

Too Far to Go (1979):

*183   Dutch: *Een Huweljik in Afleveringen: Hat Verhaal van de Maples*. Trans. Willem van Toorn and Jan and Tineke Donkers. Amsterdam: Meulenhoff, 1981.

184   French: *Trop Loin: (Les Maple)* Trans. Suzanne Mayoux and Georges Magnane. Paris: Gallimard, 1986.

185   German: *Der weite Weg zu Zweit: Szenen einer Liebe*. Trans. Maria Carlsson, Inge Friederich, Karin Polz, Susanna Rademacher and Herman Stiehl. Reinbek bei Hamburg: Rowohlt, 1982.

*186   German: *Der weite Weg zu Zweit: Szenen einer Liebe*. Trans. Maria Carlsson, Inge Friederich, Karin Polz, Susanna Rademacher and Herman Stiehl. Reinbek bei Hamburg: Rowohlt Taschenbuch Verlag GmbH, 1982.

187   Hebrew: *Derekh rabah mi-day: Sipure ha-zug Maypl*. Trans. Meir Wieseltier. Tel-Aviv, Israel: Zmora, 1984.

*188   Japanese. *Too Far to Go*. Japan: Shinchoska, 1990.

*189	Spanish: *Demasiado Lejos*. Translator not given. Buenos Aires: Emece Editores, 1980.
*190	Spanish: *Donde Termina el Camino*. Trans. Jesus Zulaika. Barcelona: Bruera, 1982.

Problems (1979):

*191	French: *La Concubine de Saint Augustin et Autres Nouvelles*. Trans. Georges Magnane. Paris: Gallimard, 1981. (Includes an "Author's Note.")
192	German: *Wie man Amerika gleichzeitig liebt und verlasst*. Trans. Uwe Friesel, Monica Michieli, Dieter E. Zimmer. Berlin: Rowohlt: 1989. (Selections)

Rabbit Is Rich (1981):

*193	Chinese: *T'u Tzu Fa Ts'ai Liao*. Translator not given. Tapei: Crown, 1982.
194	Czechoslovakian: *Kralik, Je Bohaty*. Trans. Antonin Pridal. Prague: Soudoba Svetova Proza Odenon, 1990.
195	Finnish: *Autokauppiaan Unelmat*. Translated with an introduction by Jukka Kemppinen. Parvaa: Werner Soderstrom Osakeyhtio, 1981, 1983.
196	French: *Rabbit Est Riche*. Trans. Maurice Rambaud. Paris: Gallimard, 1981, 1983. (A segment of the novel, Trans. Maurice Rambaud, appeared as "Il Court, Il Court." *Nouvelle Revue Française* [July-Aug. 1983] N366: 13-22.)
*197	German: *Bessere Verhältnisse*. Trans. Barbara Henninges. Berlin: Verlag Volk und Welt, 1983, 1984. Also published by Mohndruckand Rowohlt in these years.
*198	German: *Bessere Verhältnisse*. Translator not given. Frankfurt am Main: Buchergilde Gutenberg, 1983, 1985.
*199	Hungarian: *Nyúlháj: Regeny* Trans. Goncz Arpad. Budapest: Európa Könyvkiadó, 1984.
200	Italian: *Sei Ricco, Coniglio*. Trans. Stefania Bertola. Milan: Rizzoli, 1983, 1984.
*201	Korean: *Takki nun pujada*. Trans. An Chong-Hya. Seoul: Chu-u, 1981.
*202	Portuguese: *O Coelho Esta Rico*. Trans. Sonia Regis. Rio de Janeiro: Nova Fronteira, 1981.

203 Portuguese: *Coelho Cresce*. Lisboa: Companhia Das Letras, 1992. Trans. Sergio Flaksman.

*204 Serbocroatian: *Zeka je Bogat*. Trans. Aleksandar Sasa Petrovic. Belgrad: Prosveta, 1981, 1983.

*205 Spanish: *Conejo es Rico*. Trans. Jaime Zulaika. Barcelona: Editorial Argos Vergara, 1982.

*206 Swedish: *Haren ar rik*. Trans. Hans-Jacob Nilsson. [Sweden]: Forum, 1981, 1982.

Bech Is Back (1982):

207 French: *Bech est de Retour*. Trans. Maurice Rambaud. Paris: Gallimard, 1984.

*208 Spanish: *Más Bech*. Trans. Jaime Zulaika. Barcelona: Editorial Argos Vergara.

*209 Swedish: *Bech ar tillbaka*. Stockholm: Oversattning Cai Melin, Forum, 1984.

Hugging thè Shore (1983):

210 French: *Navigation Litteraire*. Trans. Daria Olivier. Paris: Gallimard, 1986.

The Witches of Eastwick (1984):

*211 Dutch: *De witte wijven van Eastwick*. Holland: Agathon, 1986.

212 French: *Les Sorcières d'Eastwick*. Trans. Maurice Rambaud. Paris: Gallimard, 1986.

213 German: *Die Hexen von Eastwick*. Trans. Maria Carlsson, Uwe Friesel and Monica Michieli. Reinbek bei Hamburg: Rowohlt, 1985.

214 Hebrew: *HaMechashfot MaEastwick*. Trans. Amir Oren. Tel-Aviv, Israel: Zmora-Bitan, 1990.

215 Italian: *Le Streghe di Eastwick*. Trans. Stefania Bertola. Milan: Rizzoli, 1986.

*216 Italian: *Le Streghe di Eastwick*. Trans. Stefania Bertola. Milan: Club degli Editori, 1986.

Appendix I: Translations of Updike's Work

*217   Japanese. *The Witches of Eastwick*. Japan: Shinchoska, 1991.

218   Portuguese: *As Bruxas de Eastwick*. Trans. Luzia Maria Martins. Lisboa: Gradiva, 1987.

*219   Spanish: *Las Brujas de Eastwick*. Trans. José Ferrer. Esplugues de Liobregat Barcelona: Plaza & Janes, 1990.

*220   Swedish: *Haxorna i Eastwick*. Stockholm: Oversattning Cai Melin, Forum, 1985.

Facing Nature (1985):

221   French: *La Condition Naturelle*. "Préface à l'Edition Française" in French by Updike. Trans. Alain Suied. Paris: Gallimard, 1988. See **267**.

Roger's Version (1986):

222   French: *Ce que pensait Roger*. Paris: Gallimard, 1988. Trans. Maurice Rambaud.

223   German: *Das Gottesprogramm*. Trans. Thomas Piltz. Reinbek bei Hamburg: Rowohlt, 1988.

224   German: *Das Gottesprogramm*. Trans. Thomas Piltz. Reinbek bei Hamburg: Rowohlt, 1989. (Printed in Berlin for the German Democratic Republic, East Germany.)

225   German: *Das Gottesprogramm*. Trans. Thomas Piltz. Reinbek bei Hamburg: Rowohlt Taschenbuch Verlag GmbH, 1990.

226   Italian: *La Versione di Roger*. Trans. Stefania Bertola. Milan: Rizzoli, 1988.

*227   Korean: *Ivu ui Tosi*. Seoul Tukpyolsi: Chanyewon, 1987.

*228   Spanish: *La Versión de Roger*. Trans. Jose Ferrer. Barcelona: Plaza and Janes, 1988.

*229   Swedish: *Rogers Version*. Stockholm: Oversattning Cai Melin, Forum, 1987.

Trust Me (1987):

*230   Dutch: *Vertrouw op mij*. Holland; Agathon, 1988.

231	French: *Confiance, confiance...nouvelles.* Trans. Maurice Rambaud. Paris: Gallimard, 1989.
232	German: *Spring doch!.* Trans. Uwe Friesel and Hannelore Gauster. Reinbek bei Hamburg: Rowohlt, 1990.
*233	German: *Spring doch!.* Trans. Uwe Friesel and Hannelore Gauster. Wiener Verlag, Himberg bei Wien: Druck und Bindung, 1990.
234	German: *Spring doch!.* Trans. Uwe Friesel and Hannelore Gauster. Reinbek bei Hamburg: Rowohlt Taschenbuch, 1992.
235	Italian: *Fidati di Me.* Trans. Andrea Terzi. Milan: Rizzoli, 1991.
*236	Portugese: *Uma Questao de Confianca.* Trans. Daniel Goncalves. Lisbon: Difel, 1988.
237	Portuguese: *Confie em Mim.* Trans. Aulyde Soares Rodrigues. Rio de Janeiro: Rocco, 1988.
238	Japanese: *Trust Me.* Trans. Kohji Numasawa. The English Agency, Ltd.: 1993.
*239	Spanish: *Fídame.* Trans. Jesus Zulaika. Barcelona: Bruera, 1988.
240	Swedish: *Lita pa mig.* Stockholm: Oversattning Cai Melin, Forum, 1988.

S. (1988):

241	Dutch: *S.* Trans. C. A. G, van den Broek. Netherlands: Agathon, 1988.
242	German: *S.* Trans. Heidrun Adler. Reinbek bei Hamburg: Rowohlt, 1992.
243	French: *S.* Trans. Maurice Rambaud.Paris: Gallimard, 1991.
244	Italian: *S.* Translator not given. Milan: Rizzoli, 1990.
245	Portuguese: *S.* Trans. Fernanda Pinto Rodrigues. Lisbon: Livros do Brazil, 1991.
246	Spanish: *S.* Trans. Ana M. Lafuente.Barcelona: Plaza & Janes, 1988.
247	Swedish: *S.* Stockholm: Oversattning Cai Melin, Forum, 1989.

Appendix I: Translations of Updike's Work 269

Self-Consciousness (1989):

248   Spanish: *A Conciencia: Memorias*. Trans. Manuel Saenz de Heredia. Barcelona: Tusquets, 1990.

249   Swedish. *Sjalvmedvetande*. Trans. Jan Wahlen. Boras: Forum, 1990.

Rabbit at Rest (1990):

250   Dutch: *Rabbit Rust*. Trans. R. P. Meijer en Gija Schoor. Holland: Agathon, 1990.

251   Hungarian: *Nyúlszív*. Trans. Gy. Horváth László. Budapest: Európa Könyvkiadó, 1992.

252   Portuguese: *Coelho Cai*. Trans. Paulo Henriques Britto. Lisboa: Companhia Das Letras, 1992.

253   Spanish: *Conejo En Paz*. Trans. Iris Menendez. Barcelona: Tusquets, 1992.

Short Works in Translation:

"Tomorrow and Tomorrow, Etc.":

*254   Russian: "Zavtra, zavtra, zavtra." Trans. V. Zhilvis. *Nedelya* 15 Sept. 1968, no. 38: 16-17. (As "Tomorrow, Tomorrow, Tomorrow.")

"Should Wizard Hit Mommy?":

255   Russian: "Udarit li volshebnik mamu?" Trans. M. Grinberg. *Nedelya* 26 Jan-1 Feb 1964, no. 5: 16-17. (As "Will the Magician Strike Mother?")

*256   Russian: "Dolzhen li mudrets pobit' mamochku?" Trans. Yu. Raiskii and F. Solomatin. *Znamiya*, 1967, no. 5: 150-155. (As "Must The Man Beat His Mother?")

"Die Neuen Heiligen":

*257   German: *Die Neuen Heiligen, Übertragen von Uwe Johnson zum Jahreswechsel*. 1969-1970. Biberach an der Riss: Dr. Karl Thomae GmbH Chemischpharmzaeutische Fabrik. [1970]. (Holograph poem by Updike with German translation by Uwe Johnson.)

"Lucid Eye in Silver Town":

*258   Czechslovakian: *Milenci a Manzele*. Trans. Antonin Pridal. Prague: Odeon, 1984. Pravda. 21 June, 1964.

259   Russian: "Sorinka v glazu." Trans. N. Kurdimov. *Pravda* 21 June 1964, no. 4: 4. (As "Speck in the Eye.")

*260   Russian: "Chistyi vzglyad v serbryanom gorode." Trans. I. Yakushkina. *Nedelya*, 19-25 June 1966, no. 26: 16-17. (Abridged version of "A Clear View in Silver City.")

"The Cars in Caracas":

261   Spanish: "Los Carros en Caracas." In *Tossing and Turning*. NY: Knopf, 1977. 43.

"Farewell to the Middle Class":
*262   Japanese: "Farewell to the Middle Class." *Suntory Fiction Essays*. Tokyo: Suntory, 1974. (This item may be Updike's joke on bibliographers, for he claims the essay was hitherto published only in Japanese for a series of commercials advertising Suntory Whiskey. See *Picked-Up Pieces*. New York: Knopf, 1975. 13.)

"Correspondence":

263   Russian: "Perespiska." Trans. G. Sokol. *Znamiya*, 1964, no. 4: 129-134.

Story titled "It's Closing Down Around Him":

*264   Russian: "Smykaetsya nokrug nego." Trans. Yu. Raiskii and F. Solomatin. *Sel'skaya molodezh*, 1967, no. 6: 29-31.

265   French: *La Condition Naturelle*. "Préface à l'Edition Française." By Updike. Trans. Alain Suied. Paris: Gallimard, 1988.

Appendix II
Periodicals in Which Updike Has Published

American Heritage A429, A1149
American Poetry Review A556, A561, A625-A626
American Scholar, The A215, A483, A493, A512, A528, A531, A543, A563, A903
American Studies International A771
Antaeus A565
Applause Magazine A1206
Architectural Digest A411, A824, A856, A873,
Arion A698
Art and Antiques A854, A868, A870, A879, A882, A890, A1144, A1208
Atlantic A328, A346, A374, A379, A398, A426, A491, A510, A538, A551, A582, A608, A741, A923
Audience A333, A365, A747-A748

Bennington Review A542, A585
Beverly, Mass. *Times* A502
Bits A530, A539, A544, A555
Blue Cloud Quarterly, The A66
Bookends: Journal of the Friends of the Reading-Berks Public Libraries A884
Book Digest A380
Boston *Globe* A847, A869, A871, A1251
Boston Review A855, A859
Boston University Journal, The A525, A536, A553-A554
Bulletin of Bibliography, The "Foreword" to this book

Canto A1183
Cencrastus A1194
Christian Century, The A465
Colony Newsletter A794
Commonweal A501, A508, A712, A1244
Cosmopolitan A395, A829
Critic, The A521

Eastern Review A377, A786, A789, A1202

Episcopal Life A1218
Esquire A232, A314, A330, A342, A360, A362, A385, A394, A423, A746, A797, A812, A814, A844, A893
Et cetera A603

Family Circle A41
Forbes A305, A894
Ford Times A750

Golf Digest A891
Golf Magazine A557, A788
Granta A413, A610, A828, A834
Guardian A878, A1211

Harper's A54, A154, A307, A313, A331, A338, A474, A514, A529, A559, A819-A820, A855, A859
Harvard Crimson A1167
Harvard Lampoon A432-A449, A639
Harvard Magazine A1171
Hayden's Ferry Review A1204
Holiday A1282
Horizon A938

Idol, The A1166, A1312
Inquiry Magazine A1180
Ipswich Chronicle, The A1245

Jerusalem Post A1179
John Updike Newsletter, The A22, A34, A50, A104, A112, A129, A459, A518, A532, A540-A541, A544, A548, A552, A555-A556, A774, A1176, A1178, A1253-A1255, A1304, A1316
Lear's A865
Life A611, A877, A914, A1160, A1280-A1281
Light A624
Listener, The A727, A729, A1163
Los Angeles Times A1315

Magazine Littéraire A1196
Michigan Quarterly Review A574-A575, A584, A849, A876
Milwaukee Journal A1209
Mirabella A888-A889, A892
Modern Fiction Studies A1314

Nathaniel Hawthorne Review, The A1200
National Review, The A774
New Republic, The A153, A475, A479-A481, A484-A485, A487-A488, A490, A492, A498-A500, A519, A522, A527, A548, A558, A562, A566, B570, A589, A607, A627, A690, A765, A810-A811, A830, A851, A857, A862, A872, A895, A900, A904, A1112, A1146
New Statesman A926

Appendix II: Periodicals in Which Updike Has Published 273

New York A418
New York Arts Journal A1178
New York Quarterly, The A95, A516
New York Review of Books, The A157, A166, A773, A787, A825, A832, A852-A853, A1028, A1123, A1128, A1131, A1133, A1137, A1155
New York Times, The A754, A782, A1205, A1221
New York Times Book Review, The A414-A415, A549, A552, A586, A677, A753, A783, A795, A804, A841, A875, A902, A946, A995, A1013, A1024, A1041, A1069, A1082, A1095, A1110, A1127, A1134, A1161, A1165, A1175-A1176, A1186, A1192, A1199, A1201, A1207, A1304, B107, B1096
New York Times Sunday Magazine A341-342, A1181
New Yorker, The A34, A55, A115, A121, A124, A138, A144, A149, A151, A156, A168, A181, A201, A220, A228-229, A231, A234, A252, A278-285, A287-298, A300-301, A303-306, A308-309, A311-312, A315-316, A318-27, A329, A332, A334, A336-337, A339-41, A343, A345, A353-354, A356-A359, A361, A363-A364, A366, A368-A369, A372, A377-378, A381-A382, A384, A386-A387, A389, A391, A397, A401-403, A405-A409, A412, A416, A419, A421-422, A424-A425, A427-A428, A450-457, A459-460, A463-464, A466-A471, A473, A476-A478, A482, A486, A489, A494, A497, A503, A507, A511, A513, A515, A517-A518, A520, A524, A526, A533, A537, A545, A550, A560, A567-A568, A573, A576-A578, A583, A588, A590, A593, A601-A602, A609, A614-A615, A620, A628, A632-A633, A638, A640-A676, A678-A684, A686-A689, A691-A697, A699-A703, A706-A711, A713, A715-A718, A721-A723, A728, A731-A737, A742, A744, A749, A763, A770, A781, A790, A792-A793, A802-A803, A813, A821, A823, A827, A839-A840, A842-A843, A850, A860-A861, A896-A899, A901, A905-A913, A915-A922, A924-A925, A927-A937, A939-A945, A947-A994, A996-A1001, A1003-1012, A1014-1023, A1025-A1027, A1029-A1040, A1042-A1058, A1060-A1068, A1070-A1081, A1083-A1094, A1096-A1109, A1111, A1113-A1122, A1124-A1126, A1129-A1130, A1132, A1135-A1136, A1138-A1143, A1145, A1147-A1148, A1150-1154, A1156-A1158, A1303, A1307-A1308
Nouvelle Revue Française A172, A388

Observer Magazine, The A623
Omni A390
Ontario Review A373, A399, A535, A547, A572, A591-A592, A594, A604-A606, A612-A613, A616-A617, A621-A622, A634, A636-A637

Parabola: The Magazine of Myth & Tradition A569
Parents' Magazine A281
Paris Review, The A534, A600, A619, A1162, A1297
People A1193
Philip Morris Magazine A874
Pieces A376
Playboy A31, A95, A344, A348, A350, A355, A367, A371, A375, A380, A383, A393, A404, A417, A420, A516, A725, A796, A1283
Popular Mechanics A863
Poetry A629-A631
Poets & Writers Magazine A838, A1215
Proceedings of the American Academy and Institute of Arts and Letters A166, A778, A1002

Quinzaine Littéraire, La A1198

Reader's Digest publications A281
Reading (Pa.) *Eagle* A1203, A1212
Réalités A791

Salmagundi A1188
Saturday Evening Post A299
Saturday Review A458, A496, A504-A506, A509, A1187
Scandinavian Review A999
Scientific American A50, A495
Scop, The A1159
Southwest Review A1185
Special Report A410
Sports Illustrated A745

Texas Arts Journal A273
Theology Today A1252
Transatlantic Review A129, A181, A302, A310, A335, A347, A472, A523, A532, A730, A767
Tri-Quarterly A738
TV Guide A831
Twentieth Century Studies A1164

United Church Herald, The A465
Ursinus Bulletin A887, A1301

Vanity Fair A396, A1197, A1210
Vogue A392, A822, A1163, A1195, A1216

Wall Street Journal, The A864, A1217
World Tennis A800
Writer's Digest A1177

Yankee A400

Index

"A & P," A291
A & P. Lust in the Aisles, A217, B575, B576, B584-B596 passim
"A group of young men and women....," A710
"A L'Ecole Berlitz," A499
"A United Press dispatch....," A721
"A vacationing correspondent....," A736
Abbess of Crewe, The: A Modern Morality Tale, review of, A958
Abbey, Edward, B370, B1235
Abbott, H. Porter, B952
Abe, Kobo, A1016
Abeel, Erica, B1274, B1408
Abish, Walter, A960
Ableman, Paul, B1039
About Fiction, review of, A961
Abrahams, William, A300, A307, A315, A346, A381, A403
Abrams, Mark, B410
"Absurd Hero in Contemporary American Fiction, The; The Works of John Updike, William Styron, Saul Bellow, and J. D. Salinger," B1569
"Absurd Man as Saint, The: The Novel of John Updike," B138, B228
"Academic Obsessions and Political Passions," B1487
"Academy," A636
"Academy Elects Updike," B163
Acastos, review of, A1097
"Acceptance of Alienation: John Updike and James Purdy," B29
"Acceptance of the American Book Award for Fiction, An," A805

"Acceptance of the National Book Critics Circle Award for Fiction, An," A801
Accidental Tourist, The, review of, A1078
"Accuracy," A756
"Ace in the Hole," A278
Achebe, Chinua, A1105
Ackroyd, Peter, A1071, B934, B995
"Act of Seeing, An: Looking Back Through the Window of His Magazine Covers to Norman Rockwell's Silver Age," A879
"Ad Libidum," B935
Ada, review of, A922
Adams, Alice, A416, A1068
Adams, Mildred, B17
Adams, Phoebe-Lou, B761, B1200, B1275, B1337
Adams, Timothy Dow, B321
"Addendum: Excerpts from the Symposium, 'Reality and the Novel in Africa and America'," A752
Adelman, Irving, B110
"Adequate Wiring," A644
Adler, Renata, B249
"'Adulterous Society, The': John Updike's *Marry Me*," B1004
"Adultery, from Hawthorne to Updike," B1291
Adultery in the American Novel: Updike, James, and Hawthorne, B325
Adultery in the Novel, B753
"Advancing Over Water," A996
Adventures of a Photographer in La Plata, The, review of, A1124
Adventures of Mao on the Long March, The, review of, A935

"Advertisements for Himself: Updike's Lessons as a Boy and His Life as a Man," B1334
"Aerie," A577
"Aesthetics of Ambiguity, The: The Novels of John Updike," B1601, B1611
"Affirmative Action, An," B1041
"Africa Under Western Eyes: Updike's *The Coup* and Other Fantasies," B1054
"African Accents," A985
African Calliope: A Journey to the Sudan, review of, A1018
Afshar, Carolyn Anne McKinney, B1697
"After Christianity, What?," B944
Afterlife, The, A229
"Afterlife, The," A402
Afternoon of a Writer, The, review of, A1122
"Afterword"
    in *Expelled*, A835
    in *First Picture Book, The: Everyday Things for Babies*, A1144
    in *Memoirs of Hecate County*, A784
    in *West of the Rockies*, A931
"Agatha Christie and Beatrix Potter," A26
Agatha Moudio's Son, review of, A948
Agee, Hugh, B523
Ageyev, M., A1084
"Agony of Rabbit Angstrom, The: The Search for a Secure Self," B152
"'Ah, Runs': Updike, Rabbit, and Repetition," B402, B564
Ahearn, Barry, B1416
Ahearn, Kerry, B555
"Air Show," A52
"Airmail Interview," A1159
"Airport," A591
Aksyonov, Vassily, A1072
Alan, Peter, A543
"Alas--Updike's Twice-Told Tales--Poor Uric," B881
Albert Pinkham Ryder, review of, A1133
"Albertine Disparue," A920
"Albright Program to Focus on Author Updike's Locales," B388
"Albright to Confer Degrees," B266
Alderman, Timothy C., B1625
Aldridge, John, B35, B86, B362
Aleshkovsky, Yuz, A1084
Alexander, Robert Allen, B1711
"Alfred Kazin on Fiction," B978
Algren, Nelson, B791
Alice in Bed, review of, A1056
"Alive and Free from Employment," A955

All Fires the Fire and Other Stories, review of, A949
"All Right, Sort of," B836
"All the Way Where? Updike's *Rabbit, Run*," B1562
"All the Way with Updike," B774
"All the While," A131
"Allegorical Mode in the Contemporary Novel of Romance, The," B1583
Allen, Bruce D., B802
Allen, Bryce, B319
Allen, Mary, B157, B362
Allende, Isabel, A1099
Alley, Alvin D., B523, B621
"Alligators," A281
"All's Well in Skyscraper National Park," A979
"Alone but not Aloof," A966
Alone Together, review of, A1093
Alphabetical Africa, review of, A960
Alter, Robert, B165, B202, B856
Amadi, Elechi, A948
Amend, Edward, B260
"America and I Sat Down Together," translation of, A1282
"American Ambitions," B1070
American and British Literature 1945-1975; An Annotated Bibliography of Contemporary Scholarship, B215
"American Arts Academy in Annual Honors to 63," B205
"American Authors Assess Hollywood," B185
"American Children," A246
American Dream and the Popular American Novel, The, B754
"American Everyman, The: A Study of the Athlete in *Rabbit, Run*, *The Great Gatsby*, and *Death of a Salesman*," B1684
"American Fiction of the 1960s and 1970s as a Laboratory of Language," B358
American Fictions 1940-1980, B282
"American in London, An," A727
American Literature in the Twentieth Century, B30
American Novel, The: A Checklist of Criticism of Novels Written Since 1789. Volume II: Criticism Written 1960-1968, B79
American Novel and Reflections on the European Novel, The, review of, A1130
"American Procession, The," B1559
"American Regional Short Story Experience," B1633
American Short Fiction Criticism and Scholarship, 1959-1977: A Checklist, B258

Index

American Writers Since 1900, B217
"Americans watching television.....," A732
America's 85 Greatest Living Authors Present This Is My Best in the Third Quarter of the Century, letter in, A1246
"America's Jack of All Bookish Trades," B1452
"America's Suburban Chronicler: John Updike," B465, B1565
"amerikanische Zeitgeschichte, Eine: Über John Updike," B356
Amherst College Library, collection at, A1263
Amis, Kingsley, A1012
Amis, Martin, A1148, A1203, B966, B1145, B1165, B1457
"Amish, The," A458
"Amoeba, The," A485
"Amor Vincit omnia ad Nauseum (After Awakening from *Bruno's Dream*, by Iris Murdoch, and Falling Into the Nursery)," A728
"Anaclitic Love in John Updike's Novel *Of the Farm*," B669
"Analysis of Harper's Magazine, An: A Report on John Updike," B1657
"Analysis of John Updike's *Rabbit, Run* in the Context of Social Criticism, An," B1671
"Analysis of the Man-Woman Relationship in John Updike's *Rabbit, Run* and *Rabbit Redux*, An," B1692
Anatomy Lesson, The, review of, A1057
"Ancient Optics," A627
Ancona, Francesco Aristide, B1144
Angels, The, A36
"Angels, The," A489
"Angstrom's Angst," B807
"Angst up to the End," B1450
Anker, Roy M., B1364
Annotated Bibliography of John Updike Criticism, 1967-1973, and a Checklist of His Works, The, B150
"Another Award for Updike," B310
"Another Honor is Bestowed on Updike," B290
Another Life, review of, A1072
"Another Rabbit Movie Due?," B428
Ansen, David, B1532
"Answers to Questions Unasked," B763
Anthills of the Savannah, review of, A1105
"Anticlimax: The Sporting Hero in Modern American Literature," B1629
"Antigua," A486

"Anti-Hero in Contemporary Literature, The," B50, B522
"Anti-Hero of Updike, Bellow and Malamud, The," B112
"antike Mythologie in John Updike's Roman *The Centaur*, Die," B622
"Anxious Days for the Glass Family," A902
Apell, Alfred, Jr., A738
"Aperto e Chiuso," A420
Apocrypha, The, review of, A1097
Apollinaire, Guillaume, A1064
Appasamy, S. P., B274
"Appendix A," A57
"Appendix B," A57
"Apple's Fresh Weight, The," A246
Appointment in Samarra
  "Introduction" to, A845
  review of, A851
"Appreciation of Women, An," A829
Approximation, review of, A1020
Aptly, Keith, B360
Arabesques, review of, A1109
Arabia: A Journey Through the Labyrinth, review of, A1018
"Arcadia, Pa.," A249
Archer, William H., B711
"Archetypal Approach to John Updike's Rabbit Trilogy, An," B1714
"Arendt and Updike: Philosopher and Novelist on the Human Condition," B1718
"*Arion* Questionnaire, An: 'The Classics and the Man of Letters'," A698
"Armful of Field Flowers, An," A1026
Armstrong, Peggy, B556, B560
Arnason, David E., B98
Arnavon, Cyrille, B39
Arndt, Walter, A1110
"Around the Mall and Beyond," B171
Arrowroot, review of, A1047
"Art, Music, and Literature in John Updike's Fiction," B1661
Art and Act, review of, A982
"Art and Artillery," A1064
"Art as a Way of Knowing," B1244, B1261
Art of Adding and the Art of Taking Away, The, A1257, A1265, A1272, B364
Art of Albert Pinkham Ryder, The, review of, A1133
"Art of Fiction XLIII, The: John Updike," A1162
Art of Mickey Mouse, The, "Introduction" to, A882
"Artful Insights," B1303

Artful Life, An: A Biography of D. H. Kahnweiler, review of, A1142
Artful Partners: Bernard Berenson and Joseph Duveen, review of, A1095
Articles, A639-A899
"Artist and His Audience, The," A825
Artze und Artzliches: Essayistische Anregungen, B397
"As Good a Writer's Mother as One Could Ask For," B418
"As Others See Us," A1060
As They Were, review of, A1045
"As we read....," A735
Ashley, Jo, B1689
"Askew Halo for John Updike, An," B86
"Assassination, The," A696, A697
Assault, The, review of, A1081
Asselineau, Roger, B207
"Assembling of the Meaning of God in the Short Stories of Flannery O'Connor, Bernard Malamud and John Updike, The," B1578
Assorted Prose, A18-A20, A27, A37, A49, A140
 criticism of, B646-B652
 on audio tape, B1502
"*Assorted Prose*," B647
Assouline, Pierre, A1142
Astor, David, B433
Astragal, review of, A920
"Astronomer, The," B579
"Astronomer", B574
Asvarishch, Boris I., A1137
"At a Bar in Charlotte Amalie," A297
"At Home With Obsolescence," B1113
"At Play in the Backyard of the Psyche," B1249
At Swim-Two-Birds, review of, A964
"At the End of the Rainbow," A637
"At the Flashpoint," B887
"At the Flashpoint: *Museums and Women*," B202
"At the Hairy Edge of the Possible," A1141
"At War with my Skin," A827
"Atlantises," A369
Atlas, James, A1181, B196, B269
"Attorney Loses Libel Suit Against *New Yorker*, Updike," B259
Atwater, Allison Elizabeth, B1709
Atwood, Margaret, A1085, B1187
Au, Bobbye G., B275
"Auction," A666
"Audio Reviews: *Rabbit at Rest*," B1550

"Audio Reviews: The Prose and Poetry of John Updike read by John Updike," B1551
Audio tapes, B1499-B1521, B1529-B1553
"Augustine's Concubine," A349
Austenfeld, Thomas Carl, B1710
"Australia and Canada," A350
"Authentic Man, The: A Sartrean Analysis of *Dangling Man* and *Rabbit, Run*," B1699
"Author as Librarian, The," A790, A906
"Author John Updike Has Always Been Fascinated by Buchanan," B905
"Author's Choice," B1034
"Author's Residences: After Visiting Hartford," A529
"Autobiographical Note," A776
Autograph, A1273
"Average Egyptian Faces Death," A492
Avery, William Scott, B1657
"Aware Man, The: Studies in Self-Awareness in the Contemporary Novel," B1587
"'Awesome Power, The': John Updike's Use of Kubrick's '2001' in *Rabbit Redux*," B865
Awoonor, Kofi, A932
Ayrton, Michael, A942
"Ayrton Fecti," A942
"Azores," A474

"B. W. W.," A26
Babbitt, review of, A1158
Babu, B. Ramesh, B752
"Baby's First Step," A427
"Back From Vacation," A629
"Back in the U. S. S. R.," A1072
"Back Talk," B486
"Back to Nature," A1096
"Back to Pennsylvania," B838
"Back to the Classics," A1097
"Back to the Steamy Suburbs," B1222
Backscheider, Nick, B144, B745
Backscheider, Paula, B144, B745
"Bad Neighbors," A1077
Bad News, review of, A929
"Bad-Boy Books," B1293
Bagguley, John, A714
"Baggy Monsters," A1058
Bailey, Peter, B227, B1366
Baker, Carlos, A1032, B940
Baker, John F., B307
Baker, Keith H., A1261
Baker, Kenneth, B1311
Baker, Nicholson, A1140, B426, B434, B452, B454-B461, B463, B464, B466

Baker, Robert A., A463
Baker, Russell, A474, A513, B1432
Baker's Dozen, A: Being a Selection of Books and Manuscripts by One English and Thirteen American Authors from the Library of Keith H. Baker of Oshkosh, Wisconsin, A1262
Balbert, P., B276
Baldeshwiler, Eileen, B69
Balitas, Vincent, B261
"Ballad About Nuggets," translation of, A1280
"Ballade for Subway Sitters," A446
Balliet, Whitney, B249
Baltasar and Blimunda, review of, A1103
"Baluchitherium, The," A329
"Band and the Whimper, The," B303
Bandic, Milos I., B277
Banfield, Elliot, B1731
"Bankrupt Man, The," A161, A167, A360
Banks, Jeff R., B509
Bannon, Barbara A., B912
Barber, Noel, A952
Bark Tree, The, review of, A929
Barnes, Fred, B1356
Barnes, Jane, B362, B1087
Barnes, Julian, A1075, A1135
Barnet, Sylvan, A291, A452
Barrenechea, Ana Maria, A906
Barron, John, B1459
Barth, Karl, A901, A1252
Barthelme, Donald, A1129
Barthes, Roland, A967, A978, A1023
"Baseball," A1274
"Baseball, that national....," A693
Bates, Marvin Randolph, B1663
Bath After Sailing, A38
Baumann, Paul, B1360
Baumgold, Julie, B657
Bawer, Bruce, B1343, B1463, B1487
Baybrooke, Nevile, B680
Baym, Nina, A283, A353, A540
"Be More Like Graham Greene, Dear," B239
"Bear Who Hated Life, The," A1017
"Beast in the American Ice Cream Parlour, The," B1400
"Beating the Pillager to the Punch," B1335
Beattie, Ann, A402, A980, A1076
"Beattieniks," A1076
Beatty, Richmond Croom, A300
"Beautiful Husbands," A404
"Beautiful Machine: Rivers in American Literature," B1560
"Beauty of Duality, The," B323

Bebey, Francis, A948
Bech: A Book, A57-A61, A67, A75, A155, A199, A200, B86-87, B107, B202, B249
  criticism of, B769-B799
  on audio tape, B1503
Bech: A Book, B769, B770, B778
"Bech: A Book," B775, B780, B791, B794
Bech, Henry, A1165, A1186, B107, B1096
"Bech, Passing," B362, B789
"Bech Called Funny, Sad, Lonely, Satirical—Good Updike," B772
"Bech Enters Heaven," A57
"Bech in Czech," A405
"Bech in Romania," A306
Bech Is Back, A179, A180, A194-A196
  criticism of, B1150-B1165
"*Bech Is Back*," B1150, B1152, B1156, B1159, B1160, B1163, B1164
"Bech Meets Me: *The New York Times Book Review* Persuades Henry Bech, Literary Man for All Thin Seasons, To Conduct an Interview," A1165
"Bech Panics," A57
"Bech Swings?," A324
  worksheets for, A1256
"Bech Takes Pot Luck," A315
"Bech Third-Worlds It," A355
"Bech Wed," A179
Beckett, Samuel, A964, A1117
Beckoff, Samuel, B531
  letter to, A1247
"Beckoned by the Mother Tongue," B1360
"Beer Can," A699
Beers, Paul B., B659
"Before the Sky Collapses," A956
Beginning Place, The, review of, A1021
"Behind the Dazzle is a Knowing Eye," B249
"Behold Gombrowicz," A915
"Being on TV is Like Being Alive, Only More So," A831
Being There, review of, A929
Belfant, Blanche H., B932
"Belfast Blues," B648
"Believers," A338
Bell, Pearl K., B1102
Bellman, Samuel Irving, B122
Bellow, Saul, A760, A965, A1039, A1116, B570
"Bellow's Typewriters and Other Tics of the Trade," B315
Beloved, The, A181
"Beloved, The," A347
Bely, Andrei, A998
Bemrose, John, B1223

Bend in the River, A, review of, A1006, A1009
Bendictus, David, B1284
"Bendix," A26
Benitez-Rojo, Antonio, A1139
Bentley, Robert H., A671
Beranger, Jean, B1002
Bergonzi, Bernard, B677
Bering-Jensen, Helle, B1454
Berkov, Walter, B1341
"Berks Boy Updike Receives Degree," B267
Berlin, Isaiah, A978
Berman, Morton, A291, A452
Berman, Paul, B1365
Bernanos, Georges, A913
Bernard Berenson: The Making of a Legend, review of, A1095
Bernard Shaw: Collected Letters, Vol. 1: 1855-1898, The Search for Love, review of, A1114
Bernard Shaw: Collected Letters, Vol. 2, 1926-1950, review of, A1114
Bernhard, Thomas, A1070, A1120
Bernikow, Louise, B1264
Bernstein, Burton, A365
Berryman, Charles, B861, B1205
"Best American Novel in a Decade, The," B822
"Best American Short Stories 1984, The," B318
Best American Short Stories 1984, The, B319
"Introduction" to, A816
"Bestiary," A26
"Betraying Your Loved Ones," B1255
"Better Than Nature," A1133
Between Fantoine and Agapa, review of, A1055
"Between Innocence and Experience: From Joyce to Updike," B571
"Between Pinget's Ears," A1055
"Bewitched and Bewildered over 'Eastwick'," B1208
Beyerhaus, Peter, B1556
"Beyond Alienation in Four Contemporary American Novels," B1594
"Beyond Nostalgia: Childhood and Remembrance in John Updike's Fiction," B1710
"Beyond Survival: Leisure Stalemate and Redemption and the Later Fiction of John Updike and Walker Percy," B175
"Beyond Updike: Incarnated Love in the Novels of Mary Gordon," B341

Bibliographical Introduction to Seventy-Five Modern American Authors, A, B160
Bibliography, B56, B79, B98, B105, B110, B143, B144, B150, B160, B180, B212, B215, B218, B219, B258, B272, B322, B342, B346, B364, B365, B396, B447
"Bicycle Chain, A," A511
Bigsby, Christopher, B1468
"Bindweed," A620
"Biographer, Subject Merge in Updike Book," B898
"Biographical Essay on Updike Effusive in Praise," B466
Biography, B1-B5, B9, B22, B23, B26, B27, B36, B47, B51, B58, B60, B62, B71, B91, B92, B119, B155, B163, B164, B172, B174, B205, B229, B259, B262-B268, B289-B291, B294, B304, B315, B317, B320, B335, B340, B354, B372, B387, B388, B390, B398, B403, B404, B408, B409, B413, B418, B421, B431, B442-B445, B453, B472, B473, B553
Bioy Casares, Adolfo, A1088, A1124
"Bird Census," A658
Birkerts, Sven, B1370
"Bitches and Witches," B1195
Bitov, Andrei, A1108
"Bitter Life, A," A26
Bjorksten, Ingmar, B199
"Black Suicide," A741
Blades, John, B1180, B1429
Blaise, Bharati Mukherjee, A1188
Blanchot, Maurice, A1037
"Blank Looks," B993
Blechner, Michael Harry, B223, B691
"Blessed Man of Boston, The, My Grandmother's Thimble, and Fanning Island," A294
"Blessing, The," A26, A1256
Blindness, review of, A1003
"Bliss Blanc," A530
Blom, J. M., B1297
Bloom, Alice, B1202
Bloom, Harold, B156, B249, B300, B361, B362, B634, B741, B789, B1056, B1B087
Bloom, Lynn Z., A124, A681, A827
Blue, Adrianne, B1257
Blue Highways: A Journey Into America, review of, A1051
"Blue Nights and Happy Days," A796
Bluestein, Gene, B1292
Blythe, Ronald, A1019, A1061
Boasberg, Leonard W., B314
Bodmer, George R., B343, B557, B1608

Index 283

"Body and Soul: John Updike and *The Scarlet Letter*," B958, B1239
Bogan, Louise, B492
"Boil," A539
Bolger, Eugenie, B782
Böll, Heinrich, A1043
"Bombs Made out of Leftovers," A929
"Book Notes: American Pie," B1322
Book of Laughter and Forgetting, The, review of, A1024
Book repositories, A1260-1268
"Book That I'm Writing, The," A1192
"Bookbuilder," A837
"Booking Round Trip to 1860," B484
"Bookish Boy, A," A877
Books, A1-A271
"Books," B1264, B1274, B1281, B1338
"Books: Critics' Christmas Choices," B1120
"Books: Happy Child Father to a Happy Man," B1348
"Books: *Memories of the Ford Administration*," B1477
"Books: *Odd Jobs*," B1464
"Books: *Rabbit at Rest*," B1410
"Books: Verse," B492
"Books of the Times," B1045, B1095, B1247
Books on tape, B1499-B1521
"Books That Gave Me Pleasure," A804
"Books That Made Writers," A783
"Books—*Rabbit at Rest*," B1428
Borges: A Reader, review of, A1042
Borges, Jorge Luis, A906, A1074, A1284
Borges the Labyrinth Maker, review of, A906
"Borges Warmed Over," A1042
Borgman, Paul, B175, B539, B1588
"Boston Red Sox, The," A847
Boswell, Laird of Auchinleck, 1778-1782, review of, A992
"*Bottom's Dream*," B759
Bottom's Dream, A50
  criticism of, B756-B759
Botvinick, Risa D., B1698
Bound to Violence, review of, A932
Bowers, Fredson, A787
Bowker, Larsen, B1593
Bowles, Patrick, B494
Bowman, Diane Kim, B243
"Boy Inside the American Businessman, The: Corporate Darwinism in Twentieth Century American Literature (Salinger, Vonnegut, Miller, Heller, Updike)," B1649
Boyd, Brian, B435
Boyd, William, A1145

Boyers, Robert, A1188
"Boy's Life," B202, B1028
Bozeman, Pat, B322
Bradbury, Malcolm, B360, B681, B996
Bradley, Ed Sculley, A300
Bradley, Van Allen, B702
Brawer, Roberta, A1141
Brazzaville Beach, review of, A1145
Brecht, Bertolt, A1010
Brecht's Dicta: Diaries, 1920-1922, review of, A1010
Breed, Donald D., B1199
Brennan, Maeve, A923
Brenner, Gerry, B249
Breslin, John, B868
Brewer, Joseph E., B50, B522
Bridge of Beyond, The, review of, A954
"Briefly Noted," B1228, B1287
"Brilliancies of Updike Book Can Make Darkness Palatable," B1225
"'Bring the Corners Forward': Ideology and Representation in Updike's Rabbit Trilogy," B563
Brittin, Norman A., A284, A450
Britton, Burt, A1299
"Broad Spectrum of Writers Attacks Obscenity Ruling," A754
Brodin, Pierre, B16
Brodsky, Joseph, A1150
Brofman, John, B401, B1321
Brookhiser, Richard, B1254
Brookner, Anita, A1116, B1280, B1348, B1403
Brooks, Louise, A1045
Brophy, Brigid, B979
Brother Grasshopper, A252
"Brother Grasshopper," A407
Broun, Elizabeth, A1133
Brown, Carl W., Jr., B261, B472
Brown, Clarence, B407
"Brown Chest, The," A426
Browne, Joseph, B1042
Brownjohn, Alan, B765
Brownstone, David M., B436
Broyard, Anatole, B503, B580, B717, B774, B803, B916, B964, B1045, B1062, B1083, B1122, B1269
Bruccoli, Mary, A719, A755, A756, A759, A1161, A1163, A1165, A1176, A1256, A1300, A1306, B278, B280, B492, B498, B894, B921, B923, B963, B1029, B1099
Bruccoli, Matthew J., A1000
Bruckner, D. J. R., A1134
Bruning, Eberhard, B53

"Bruno Schulz, Hidden Genius," A1013
"Bryant Park," A678
Buchanan, Mark Aldham, B1648
Buchanan Dying, A123
   criticism of, B894-B909
"*Buchanan Dying*: A Play," B900
"'Buchanan' Plays Well for Updike," B906
"Buchanan Redux," B901
Buckley, William F., Jr., B197, B1022
Budd, John, B1319
"Building Decor," A642
Bulgarian language, translations from, A1276-A1279
"Bulgarian Poetess, The," A300
"Bull in the Typography Shop, A," A1134
Bullette, Margaret, B1146
"Bull's Eye," B1048
"Bunny Stuff," B1161
Burchard, Rachael C., B94, B105, B122
"Burden of Answered Prayers, A," B1332
Burgess, Anthony, B37, B249, B1018
   reply to, A1244
Burgin, Richard, A1178
"Burglar Alarm, The," A839
Burhans, Clinton S., Jr., B249, B530
Burnett, David, A282, A292
Burnett, Whit, A293, A1246
"Burning Trash," A633
Burnley, Judith, A306, A311, A312
Burns, Stanley B., A1149
Burr, Richard W., B532
Burroughs, William S., A1022
"Burroughs e Updyke," B11
Burto, William, A291, A452
Busch, Eberhard, A1005
Busch, Frieder, B536
Busha, Virginia, B493
"Business Acquaintances," A500
Buskin, John, B1723
"Busy Minister," B920
By the Evidence, review of, A960
Byrne, Evelyn B., A739
Byron, Stuart, B525

"Cabbage Moon," B808
Cabrera Infante, G., A933
Calderone, Mary Steichen, A1144
"Calder's Hands," A33
Caldwell, Gail, B1374, B1435
"Calendar," A26
"Caligula's Dream," A26
Calisher, Hortense, A377
"Call Him Mister," A444
Callaway, John, A1229

Calvino, Italo, A959, A984, A1027, A1033, A1067, A1079, A1113
Cameron, Dee Birch, B1001
Campbell, James, B1073
Campbell, Jeff H., A1174, B189, B363, B857, B1142, B1211
Camplin, Charles, B527
Camus, Albert, A939
"Can a Nice Novelist Finish First," A1160
"Can Updike Win a Nobel?," B170
"Cancelled," A672
Cantwell, Mary, A1195
"Capacity," A26
Capek, Karel, A1069
Capp, Al, A880
"Card Tricks," A984
Carey, John, B936
Caricatures, B1725-B1748
Carlisle, Olga, A1281
Carlson, Constance, B1582
Carnival: Entertainments and Posthumous Tales, review of, A991
"Carol Sing, The," A326
Carpentered Hen, The
   criticism of, B492-B497
   "Foreword" to, A798
Carpentered Hen and Other Tame Creatures, The, A26, A182
Carrère, Emmanuel, A1106
Carroll, Jon, B459
"Carros En Caracas, Los," A131
"Cars in Caracas, The," A515, B1567
Carter-Danforth Family Papers, A1260
Cartoons, A1312-A1317
Carty, Brad, B1547
"Case for Celibacy," B718
"Case for the Defensive, The," B992
"Case of Melancholia, A," A246, A861
"Case of Overestimation, A," A246
"Case of Solicitude, A," A246
Caskey, Jefferson D., B54
Caspar David Friedrich and the Subject of Landscape, review of, A1137
Cassill (editor), A389
Castle of Crossed Destinies, The, review of, A984
"Catharism and John Updike's *Rabbit, Run*," B545
"Caveat Emptor *Bech Is Back*," B1151
Cavett, Dick, A1222-1224, A1227, A1228, A1242
Cayton, Robert F., B699
Celebrity drowning in cement at Grauman's Chinese Theater (cartoon), A1315

Céline, review of, A977
"Cemeteries," A730
"Cemetery of Whales," translation of, A1282
Centaur, The, A8, A12, A28, A76-77, A197, A1320, B76, B144, B202, B249
    criticism of, B601-B645
    on audio tape, B1504
"*Centaur, The*, and the Problem of Vocation," B625
"*Centaur, The*: Epic Paean and Pastoral Lament," B202
"*Centaur, The*: John Updike and the Face of the Other," B642
"*Centaur, The*: Myth, History and Narrative," B144, B627
"*Centaur, The*: Transcendental Imagination and Metaphoric Death," B621
"*Centaur, The*: Updike's Mock Epic," B630
"*Centaur, The*: Updike's Mock-epic," B249
"*Centaur, The*: What Cures George Caldwell?," B635
"Central Park," A648
"Central Park...," A688
"Centripetal Action, The: John Updike's *The Centaur* and *Rabbit, Run* and Wright Morris's *One Day*," B521, B619
"Ceremonies of Farewell: The Continuity of John Updike," B1612
"Ceremony and the Search for Meaning in the Fiction of John Updike," B1689
Chain of Chance, review of, A1004
"Chamber Music of Betrayals," B1060
"Changing American Family, A: Cheever, Gardner, Irving, Updike," B1646
Chanley, Steven M., B591
Chapin, Henry B., A124, A457, A681
Chapin, Penny (Penny Chapin Hills), A280, A290, A301, B507
"Character Assassination," B430
Characters and Their Landscapes, review of, A1061
"Characters Narrowed as 'Rabbit, Run' Unreels," B90
"Charleston," A613
Charters, Ann, A285, A288, A353, A809, A813, A1052
"Charting a Literary Course', B1169
"Chasing After God and Sex," B1221
Chaste Planet, The, A156
    "Foreword" to, A785
"Chaste Planet, The," A763
"Chat with John Updike, A," A1177
Chatwin, Bruce, A1050

"Checking Out Faith and Lust: Hawthorne's 'Young Goodman Brown' and Updike's 'A & P'," B590
"Cheerful Alphabet of Pleasant Objects, A," A26
Cheever, Benjamin, B374
Cheever, John, A835, A1040, B437, B469
"Cheever's Triumph," B173
Chekhov: A Spirit Set Free, review of, A1111
Chesnick, Eugene W., B357
Cheuse, Alan, B1549
"Child Bride, The," A161, A167
"Child Within, The," A246
Children of the Arbat, review of, A1108
"Children's Books: In 'Fruitcake Weather'," B657
Child's Calendar, A, A21
    criticism of, B653-B657
Chilly Scenes of Winter, review of, A980
Chine, Cathleen, A1056
"Chinese Disharmonies," A1115
"Chinese Paradox, But Not Much of One, A: John Updike in His Poetry," B43, B598
Chinese Shadows, review of, A990
"Chiron at Olinger High," B604
"Chloe's Poem," A52
Christian, Ed, B1417
Christian, R. F., A1090
"Christian Roommates, The," on videotape, B1526
"Christmas Books to Give and Receive, The," B1125
Christy, George, A1190
Chronicle in Stone, review of, A1103
"Chronicles and Processions," A1103
"Chronology," B202
"Chthonic Heroine, The: Revision and Reemergence of the Archetype," B1645
Chukwu, Augustine, B1050
Cimatti, Pietro, B11
Cioran, E. M., A962
"Circles of Paradise and Inferno: The Women in John Updike's 'Rabbit' Trilogy," B1702
"Citation Composed for the Awarding of the 1968 National Book Award for Fiction to *The Eighth Day*, by Thornton Wilder," A757
Cities of Salt, review of, A1109
"Citizen Updike," B312, B1351, B1732
"City, The," A381
"City Frieze, A," A246
"Clan, The," A26, B1566

Clandestine in Chile: The Adventures of Miguel Littin, review of, A1099
Clapp, Rodney, B1182
Clapperton, Jane, B1109, B1154
"Class of '90: The Famous and the Forgotten," B1426
"Classical Influences in *The Poorhouse Fair*," B502
"Classics of Realism, The," A903
"Classmates Fondly Recall 'The Sage of Plowville'," B403
Clausen, Jan, B479
Clayton (editor), A353
"Clear the Stage for a Repeat Performance," B756
Clemons, Walter, B173, B1060
Cleopatra; Histories, Dreams and Distortions, review of, A1127
"Clergy Lives: Portraits from Modern Fiction," B470, B1243
Clocks of Columbus, The: The Literary Career of James Thurber, B113
"Close Reading and Teaching," B599
"Closet Drama," B896
"Clothing Motif in Updike's *Rabbit, Run*, The," B537
"Cloud of Witnesses, A," A1019
"Cloud Shadows," A26, A182
Coale, Samuel C., B288, B323
Coates, Joseph, B423, B1456
Cochran, Robert W., B577
"Cock-a-doodle-doo," B710
"Code, The," A572
"Coffee Table Books for High Coffee Tables," A946
Cohend, Sarah, B187
"Cohn's Doom," A1046
Cole, William, A503, A538, B962, B1082
Collected Poems, A26
 cartoon for, A1317
 interview about, A1243
Collected Poems, 1953-1993, A271
Collected Stories, review of, A1073
"Collections of Short Stories," B505
Collier, John, A944
Collier, Peter, B722, B1034
Comedy of Redemption, The: Christian Faith and Comic Vision in Four American Novelists, B385
"Commencement: Pingree School," A519
Comment, on John Gardner's *On Moral Fiction*, A775
"Comment," B646
"Comment on 'Seagulls'," A806

"Commentary on Updike's 'Astronomer', The," B574
"Commercial," A337
"Community Feeling," B733
"Comp. Religion," A26
"Comparison of Major Concerns of John Updike and John Milton, A: Does Updike Give Evidence of Puritanism?," B1660
"Compassionate Wasp, The," B1257
Complete Book of Covers from the New Yorker 1925-1989, The, "Foreword" to, A858
Complete Collected Essays, review of, A1151
"*Complete Collected Essays* by V. S. Pritchett," A1151
Complete Lyrics of Cole Porter, The, "Foreword" to, "807
"Compromised Environment, A," B99, B362
"Conception and Reproduction by the Amalgamated Fools of 1951, Inc.," A430
"Concepts of Human Destiny in Five American Novelists: Bellow, Salinger, Mailer, Baldwin, Updike," B1570
Concrete, review of, A1070
"Condo Moon," A602
Confessions of a Wild Bore, A201
"Confessions of a Wild Bore," A676
"Conjunction," A406
Conn, Peter, B389
Conn, Saundra M., B586
Conroy, Frank, B713
"Consideration of the Portrayal of the Anti-Hero in Selected Fiction of John Updike, A," B1659
"Constellation of Events, A," A397
"Containing the Third World: John Updike's *The Coup*," B1057
Conte, Donald James, B1678
"Contemplation, Fiction, and the Writer's Sensibility," B281, B1141
"Contemporary American Family Novel, The: A Study in Metaphor," B1579
Contemporary Novel, The: A Checklist of Critical Literature on the British and American Novel Since 1945, B110
"Contemporary Novels: A Reflection of Contemporary Culture," B275
"Contemporary Writers in Christian Perspective," B42
"Contours of Desire, The: Obsessional and Hysterical Discourse Structures in Updike, Cheever and Lurie," B1653
Conversation with John Updike, A, A1166

Index

"Conversation with John Updike, A," A1178, A1183, A1226
  cartoon for, A1312
"Conversational Highlights," A1236
Conversations with Capote, B326
"Convincing," A656
Cook, David M., A291
Cook, Roderick, B660, B671
Cooke, Judy, B1048, B1128
Cooke, Michael, B844
Cooper, Barbara Eck, B215
Cooper, Rand Richards, B462, B1442, B1746
Corn, Alfred, A881
"Corner," A316
"Correction," B451
Corregidora, review of, A963
Cortázar, Julio, A949
Corwin, Philip, B1192
Cosgrove, William, B344
"Cosmic Gall," A26, A463
"Cosmo Reads the New Books," B1109, B1154
Costantini, Humberto, A1088
Coughlin, Ruth Pollack, B1397
"Counsellor, The," A161, A167
Counterlife, The, review of, A1094
Coup, The, A132-A137, A141-A143, B249, B1697
  criticism of, B1013-B1057
  on audio tape, B1505
  work sheets for, A1253, A1255, A1256
"Coup, The," B1042
"*Coup, The*," B1016, B1033, B1056
"*Coup, The*, by John Updike," B249, B1029
"*Coup, The*; Chronology; and Bibliography," B362
"*Coup, The*: Illusions and Insubstantial Impressions," B249, B1051
"*Coup, The*: John Updike's Modernist Masterpiece," B1055
Couples, A39-A42, A51, A62, A165, A183, A1323, A1326, A1336, B76, B81, B144, B202, B249, B1676, B1682, B1696
  criticism of, B696-B755
  jacket design of, A1288
  on audio tape, B1506
  work sheets for, A1256
"Couples," B723, B728
"Couples," B724, B986
"'Couples'," B711
Couples: A Short Story, A113
"*Couples* All Surface: 'Updike Has Narrowed His Vision to the Bed'," B716
"*Couples* by John Updike," B755

"Coupling and Uncoupling," B719
"Couplings," B720
"Courtly Love in the A&P," B575
Cousins, James Gould, A919
Cousins, Norman, B193
Cowley, Malcolm, B793
Cox, David Michael, B1609
"Crab Crack," A559
"'Craftsman's Intimate Satisfactions, A': The Parlor Games in *Couples*," B144, B746
Crane, Hugh M., B1252
Crane, Milton, A299
Cranston, Maurice, B739
Creative Explosion, The: An Inquiry Into the Origins of Art and Religion, review of, A1048
Crews, Frederick, B359, B1230, B1734
"Crisis of Confidence, A," B1107
Crist, Judith, B1533
"Critical Examination of the Prose Works of John Updike, A," B1655
"Critical Exploration of John Updike as American Theologian, A," B1627
"Criticism of John Updike: A Selected Checklist," B143, B144, B150
"Critic's Choice, 1970," B93
"Critics Honor Updike for 4th 'Rabbit' Novel," B1429
Croghan, L. A., B1110
Crowell, Carol Ann, B1699
Crowley, Sue Mitchell, B578, B957
"Crunch of Happiness, The," A934
"Crush vs. Whip," A669
"Cuckoo and the Rooster, The," A1007
Culbertson, Diana, B892
"Cultivating the Field of Literature," B1456
Cultural Deformations," B1030
"Cultural Situation of the American Writer, The," A771
Cunningham, Nancy Ashworth, B1712
Cunts (Upon Receiving the Swingers Life Club Membership Solicitation), A97
"Cunts: Upon Receiving the Swingers Life Club Membership Solicitation," A516
Curfew, review of, A1105
"Curious Greased Grace of John Updike, Some of his Critics, and the American tradition," B115
"'Curious Greased Grace' of John Updike, The," B249
Curley, Dorothy Nyren, B345
Curtler, Betsy, S., B629
Cyril Connolly: Journal and Memoir, review of, A1066

"Czarist Shadows, Soviet Lilacs," A998
"Czech Angels," A1024

Dalton, Elizabeth, B1013
Dance of the Solids, The, A52
"Dance of the Solids, The," A495
Dance the Eagle to Sleep, review of, A928
Danto, Arthur C., B1306
Dark, Larry, A867
"Dark Smile, Devilish Saints," A1022
"Daughter, Last Glimpses of," A343
Davenport, Guy, B784, B819
Davenport, John, B664
Davie, Donald, A1041
Davies, Marie-Hélène, B956
Davies, Russell, B1074
Davis, Hope Hale, B1278
Davis, L. J., B977
Davis, Linda H., A1098
Davis, Ruth, B1486
Davison, Peter, A995
"Dawn of Art, The," A1048
"Dawn of the Possible Dream," A745
"Dawn of the Possible Dream, The," B529
"Day of the Dying Rabbit," A318, B892
"Days of Mortals and Myths," B603
De Bellis, Jack, A1270, B447, B489, B506, B559, B562, B617, B865, B1562
De Carlo, Andrea, A1138
de Civrieux, Marc, A1031
De Feo, Ronald, B930
de Grummond, W. W., B502
De Lillo, Don, A994
"Deacon, The," A323
Dean's December, The, review of, A1039
"Dear Alexandros," B583
"Death and Black Humor," B535, B628
"Death and Games," B713
Death of a Beekeeper, The, review of, A1037
"Death of God in American Literature, The," B57
Death Sentence, review of, A1037
"Death's Heads," A905
"Deaths of Distant Friends," A384
Debusscher, Gilbert, B558, B1147
December, A43
"Décor," A483
Deemer, Charles, B880
Deen, Carol Ann Stanley, B1616, B1664
"Deep Time and Computer Time," A1100
Defense, The, review of, A904
"Defiance and Acceptance: Two Modes of Cultural Response in Mailer's *American*

Dream and *The Armies of the Night* and Updike's *Rabbit Redux*," B862
"Deities and Beasts," A26
"Déjà, Indeed," A595
Delbanco, Nicholas, B1386
Deliverance to the Captives, review of, A901
Delrogh, Dennis, B826
Demos, John, B760
DeMott, Benjamin, A333, B922
"Den Otillfredsställde Amerikanen," B19
Denby, David, B1353
Denby, Priscilla Lee, B1621
Denisova, Tamara Naumovna, B324
Denman, Katherine L., B496
Desauliniers, Louise, A349
"Descent of Mr. Aldez, The," A26
"Desert Father," B936
"Désespoir de John Updike, Le," B76
"Desperate Faith," B61
"Desperate Games," B732
Dessner, Lawrence Jay, B594
Detweiler, Robert, B14, B95, B109, B111, B202, B208, B249, B299, B742, B951
"Deus Dixit," A342
"Devil's Advocate," B137
"Diary Fiction," B952
"Dick Cavett Show, The," A1222-1224, A1227, A1228, A1242
Dickstein, Morris, B166
Dictionary of Literary Biography
  drawing in, A1306
  self-portrait in, A1300
Didion, Joan, B518
"Didion and Updike: Images of the American Woman and the Sixties," B1706
"Died 30 B.C. Still Going Strong," A1127
Diehl, Digby, B1338, B1464, B1478
"Different One, The," A275
"Differnt Ending, A," A579
"Dilemma in the Delta," A26, A182
"Dilemma of Ipswich, The," A750
Dillard, Annie, A1122
Diller, Hans-Jurge, B583
Dimitrova, Blaga, A1276-A1278
Dinesen, Isak, A991
Dinnage, Rosemary, B202, B887, B937, B1071
Dinner at the Homesick Restaurant, review of, A1040
"Dinosaur Egg," A667
Dirda, Michael, B460
"Disaffection in Deutsch," A1020
"Discerning Theological Dimensions in the Fiction of John Updike," B1639
Disch, Thomas M., B1281, B1424

"Discontent in Deutsch," A988
"Discourse Most Eloquent Musing: *Odd Jobs*," B1472
Discourse on Thinking, review of, A909
Discovery of America, The, review of, A1155
"Disengagement in *Museums and Women*," B202
Dissertations and theses, B1569-B1722
"Distaff Doormat," B1278
Ditsky, John, B740
Divine Right's Trip, review of, A937
"Divorcing: A Fragment," A370
"Do Not Go Gentle: Visions of Death and Immortality in John Updike's 'Pigeon Feathers' and 'Packed Dirt, Churchgoing, A Dying Cat, A Traded Car'," B586
"Doctor's Son, The," A1000
"Doctor's Wife, The," A289
Dodson, James, B422
"Does Updike's Book *S.* Stand for Snore?," B1276
Dogeaters, review of, A1138
"Dog's Death," A540
Dog's Death, A22
Doherty, Gail, B943
Doherty, Paul, B847, B943
Dolan, Paul J., A288
"Domestic Life in America," A363
Donahue, Deidre, B1413
Donahue, Richard, B1391
Donald, Miles, B178
"Donald Greiner, *Adultery in the American Novel: Updike, James, and Hawthorne*," B344
"Donald Greiner's *The Other John Updike*," B246, B254
Donaldson, Scott, B375, B1320
Doner, Dean, B202
Donnelly, Jerome, B1315
Donoghue, Denis, B785, B1168, B1324, B1460, B1461
Donohoe, Cathryn, B480
Donoso, José, A1105
Doody, Terrence, B204
Dooley, Susan, B1253
"Doomsday, Mass.," A683
"Doris Day: A Sentimental Journey," A1275
Doris Day: Her Own Story, review of, A969
Dorothy Parker: What Fresh Hell Is This?, review of, A1104
Dostoevski, Fyodor, A941
Double Yoke, review of, A1062
Doubly Gifted, "Foreword" to, A832

Doubly Gifted: The Author as Visual Artist, A1309
"Doubt and Difficulty in Leningrad and Moscow," A1108
"Doubt and Faith of John Updike, The," B31
Doughty, Charles M., A1018
"Doughy Middleness," B249, B902
"Downward Trajectory of John Updike, The," B1233
Doyle, Paul A., B25
Drabble, Margaret, A968, A1101
"Drabbling in the Mud," A968
Dragons of Eden, The: Speculations on the Evolution of Human Intelligence, review of, A987
"Draping Radiance with a Worn Veil," A965
Drawings, A1303-A1311
"Dream and Reality," A537
"Dream Objects," A494
"Dreamer as Leader, The: Ellellou in John Updike's *The Coup*," B1050
Dreaming of Heroes: American Sport Fiction, 1868-1980, B252
Dreamtigers, review of, A906
"Dress Code in Updike's 'A & P', The," B589
Drier, James Sigurd, B1589
Driscoll, Edward A., Jr., B23
"Dropping Out: Spiritual Crisis and Countercultural Attitudes in Four American Novelists of the 1960s (Updike, Percy, Brautigan, Pynchon)," B1638
"Dualities," B765
Dubus, Andre, A1070
Ducote, D'Ann, B1695
"Due Respect," A26
"Duet, with Muffled Brake Drums," A26
Duffy, Martha, B104
Dunne, Elizabeth, B1373
"During Menstruation," A131
"During the Jurassic," A302, A390
"Dutch Cleanser," A131, A534
"Dutchmen and Turks," A1081
Duvall, John N., B1242
Dworkin, Rita, B110
Dyer, Geoff, B1466

"Earlier Day, An," A1025
"Early and Late Patterns of the Search Motif Contrasted in John Updike's Fiction: *Rabbit Run* and *The Coup*," B1697
Earthly Possessions, review of, A986
Earthworm, A144
"Earthworm," A26, A468

Eastern Review, interview in, A1202
"Easthampton-Boston By Air," A561
Easton, Elizabeth Wynne, A1128
"Easy Come, Easy Go," B1117
Ebert, P. K., A457, A460
Ebert, Teresa Lynn, B1643
Ecenbarger, William, B293, B553
Eckley, Wilton, B376
"Eclatement du mythe, L'," B106
"Eclipse," A706
Eco, Umberto, A1058, A1087, A1124
"Ecolalia," A1087
Eder, Richard, B461, B1329, B1387, B1488
Edgerton, Larry, B1632
"Editor's Choice," B1121
"Editor's Choice: The Best Books of 1983," B1178
"Editor's Choice: The Best Books of 1990," B1423
Edler, Richard, B1225
"Edmund Wilson and the Landscape of Literature," A814
"Education of Harry Angstrom: The Rabbit and the Moon," B861
Edward, R., B599
Edwards, A. S. G., B573
Edwards, Lee R., B827
Edwards, Thomas R., B775, B920, B1103
"Egg Race, The," A364
Egge, Marion, F., B1688
Ego and Art in Walt Whitman, A157
Ehrenpreis, Irvin, B901
Ehresmann, Julia M., B1092
Ehrlich, Richard A., A461
Ehrlich, William, A461
Eight O'Clock, review of, A1154
"18 Holes with...John Updike," B422
Eiland, Howard, B156, B202, B233, B244, B249, B362, B741, B751, B856, B876, B887, B923, B954, B970, B1020, B1028
"Eisenhower's Eloquence," A687
Elder, John, A686, A706
"Elderly Sex," A630
"Elegant Variations," B1373
"Elements of Contemporary American Culture as Reflected in Selected Works of American Literature, 1960-1974," B1623
Elements of John Updike, The, B80, B102, B105
"*Elements of John Updike, The*: Another Appraisal," B95, B109
"Eliot Without Words," A1071
Elistratova, A., B602
Elkin, Stanley, A371

Elliott, Leslie, B636
Ellis, James, B538, B540
Ellison, James, B1104
Ellmann, Richard, A970
"Embodiment and the American Imagination: A Preliminary Skirmish with Some Critical-Cultural Issues Raised by Religion and Sexuality in American Fiction," B551
Emecheta, Buchi, A1009, A1062
"Emergency," A641
Emersonianism, A202
"Emersonianism," A821
Emmett, Paul J., B588
Emperor, The: Downfall of an Autocrat, review of, A1053
"Emperor's Blue Jeans, The," B821
"Empire's End," A1053
Enchanter, The, review of, A1092
Enchi, Fumiko, A1060
"Encounter Left Out of *Rabbit Redux*, An," A376
"End of the Line for Rabbit Angstrom, The," B1394
"Endearing Truth, The," A895
"Ending the Heartache," B1403
Endo, Shusaku, A1016
"Energy: A Villanelle," A550
"Engadine...," A675
"English and American: *Rabbit at Rest*," B1430
"English & American--*Something and Nothingness: The Fiction of John Updike and John Fowles by John Neary*," B482
"English Train Compartment," A26
"Enormous Package," A277
Enright, D. J., B33, B1231
"Entropic Imagination in Twentieth-Century American Fiction, The: A Case for Don Delillo," B1647
"Entropy in American Fiction (Poe, Hawthorne, Melville, Faulkner, Hemingway)," B1642
"Epochs of Updike, The," B1491
Epstein, Seymour, B821
Erofeev, Benedict, A1049
"*Eros* and *Agape*: The Opposition in Updike's *Couples*," B749
"Eros Rampant," A313
Erotic Art of the East, review of, A946
Erotic Art of the West, review of, A946
"Erotic Epigrams," A26
"Erotics of Contemplation, An," B419, B1314

"Escritor John Updike, El ¿Cuento o Novela?," B17
"Ethiopia," A345, A520
"Eva and Eleanor and Everywoman," A976
Evanier, David, B1041, B1065
Evans, Nancy, B1111
Eva's Man, review of, A976
"Even as the Heathen Rage," B819
"Even Egrets Err," A26
"Even the Footnotes Sparkle," B963
"Evening with John Updike, An," A1188
"Every Inch an Updike," B871
"Every Picture Tells a Story," B1309
"Everybody's Castle," B194
"Evidence in Tarbox, The," B700
"Evolution Be Praised," A1080
"Evolution of an Author, The: A Stylistic Analysis of Selected Novels by John Updike," B1681
Evolution of Useful Things, The, review of, A1156
Evtushenko, Evgenil (Yevtushenko,Yvgeny/Yevgen A1072, A1280-A1283
Ewert, William B., A168, A793
"Examination of the Theme of Man's Search for a Meaningful Contemporary Religion in John Updike's Fiction, An," B1687
"Examination of Thematic and Structural Connections Between John Updike's Rabbit Novels, An," B1609
"Ex-Basketball Player," A26, A460, B600
Excellent Women, review of, A1004
Exercises in Style, review of, A1030
Exhibits, A1269-A1272
"Exhuberances of Style in Pynchon and Updike: A Panoply of Metaphor," B276
"Exile on Main Street," A1158
"Exile's Impressions, An," A856
"Existential Heroes: Frank Alpine and Rabbit Angstrom," B523
"Existentialism," B28
"Exotique et Opaque Updike," B1184, B1207
"Expeditions to Gilead and Seegard," A1085
Expelled, "Afterword" in, A835
"Exploring the Abyss of Aging with Updike," B1248
"Exposé," A471
"Exposure," A26
  sound discs of, B1507
"'Extra Dimension,' The: Character Names in Updike's 'Rabbit' Trilogy," B559
"Eye on Book," B146
Ezell, Johanna, B1551

"F & M Featuring Updike Exhibit," B904
"Fable for Modern Times, A: America and Africa in John Updike's *The Coup*," B1049
Fabrications, review of, A942
"Facing Death," A1149
Facing Nature, A213, A218
  criticism of, B1212-B1218
"Facing Nature," B1213
"*Facing Nature*," B1215, B1216
"Fact and Fiction," B867
"Fading of the Fad, The," A639
Fagunwa, D. O., A1062
"Failure of Erotic Questing in John Updike's Rabbit Novels, The," B561
"Faint, The," A367
"Fairy Godfathers, The," A361
"Faith, Morality, and the Novels of John Updike," B198, B249
Faith: Reflections on Experience, Theology and Fiction, B286
Falke, Wayne, B144, B850, B1571
"Fall," A625
"Fall Harvest," B423
"Fallen Minister Searches His Soul, A," B919
"Falling Asleep up North," A422
"Falling Into Love," B1083
Falsey, Elizabeth A., A836, A1257, A1265, A1272, B364, B365
"Family and Adultery: Images and Ideas in Updike's Rabbit Novels," B555
"Family Meadow," A301
"Family Pictures," B426
"Family Quarrels in *Of the Farm*,2914,32 B202
"Family Snapshots," B1010
"Family Ways," A971
Fancy Foods/Open All Night, review of, A1067
"Fancy-Forger Takes the Lectern, The," A1035
Far Cry from Kensington, A, review of, A1107
"Farewell to the Shopping District of Antibes," A470
"Farfetched," A1138
Farney, Dennis, A1217
Farrell, James T., B48
Farrell, Joseph N., B453
"Farrell's Caddie," A421
Fasch, caricature by, B1743
"Fast Art: The Sweatless Creations of Andy Warhol," A862
"Fate of the Traditional Novel, The," B178

"Father and Son in the Fiction of John Updike," B1693
"Fatherly Presences: John Updike's Place in a Protestant Tradition," B249, B256
"Fear of Death in the Short Fiction of John Updike, The," B1711
Fear of Flying, review of, A947
"Feast of Reason, A," A1011
"February 22," A26
Feeney, Mark, B427, B1325, B1377
Feinberg, Susan, B669
"Fellatio," A52
"Female Body, The," A876
"Female Pilgrims," A1045
Ferdydurke, review of, A915
Ferguson, Suzanne, B321
"Fever," A26
"Fiabe Italiane," A1027
Ficowski, Jerzy, A1110
"Fiction," B135, B744, B842
"Fiction: 1930 to the Present," B44
"Fiction: John Updike," B607
"Fiction: *Roger's Version*," B1219
"Fiction: Seekers and Lovers," B682
"Fiction: The 1930s to the Present," B55, B82, B148, B168
"Fiction: The 1950s to the Present," B159, B183, B200, B211, B248, B253, B328, B349
"Fiction: The 1960s to the Present," B283, B301, B366, B391, B416
"Fiction and Truth", B834
"Fiction Chronicle," B726, B932
"Fiction of John Updike, The," B25
"Fiction of John Updike, The: A Romantic Quest for Spiritual Permanence," B1663
Fiction of Philip Roth and John Updike, The, B332
"Fiction of Philip Roth and John Updike, The," B1613
"Fictional Fixes," B1077
"Fictional Houses," A824
Fidler, John, B906
Fiedler, Leslie, B78
"Field's Luminous Folk," A246
"1587, A Year of No Significance," A1034
"Fifty Five and Fading," B1401
"Fighters and Lovers: Theme in the First Five Novels of John Updike," B1581
Fighters and Lovers: Theme in the Novels of John Updike, B129
Filler, Louis, B851
"Film Aids Our Economy," B72
"Film Company to Start Shooting 'Rabbit, Run' in Berks," B65
Films and videos, B428, B489, B490, B1522-B1561, B1529-B1553
"'Final Homage.' Paid to His State," B895
Finch, Robert, A686, A706
"Finding Inspiration in Pennsylvania: Rabbit's Realm," B553
Findlay, William, A1194
"Fine-Tuning a Collection," A1201
Finkelstein, Sidney, B29, B112
Fire Within, The, review of, A905
"Fireworks," A478
"First Impressions, Lasting Effects," A1059
"First Lunar Invitational, The," A742
First Person: Conversations on Writers and Writing, A1166
First Picture Book, The: Everyday Things for Babies, review of, A1144
"First Things First," A1144
"First Wives and Trolley Cars," A386
"Fish Story," A1001
Fisher, Ann H., B1277
Fisher, M. F. K., A1045
Fisher, Richard E., B13
"Fisherman and His Wife, A Tale from the Brothers Grimm, The Libretto of a Children's Opera, The," A273
Fishman, Ethan, B377
Fitzgerald, F. Scott, A1122
"Five Books Win National Book Awards," B616
"Five Days in Finland at the Age of Fifty-Five," A843
Five Poems, A158
 cover design of, A1291
 drawing for, A1305
"Flaming Chalice, The," A1125
Flamingo's Smile, The: Reflections in Natural History, review of, A1080
"Flann Again," A974
Flaubert's Parrot, review of, A1075
"Fleckings, The," A562
Fleischauer, John F., B405
"Flight," A285, B577
Flight of Icarus, review of, A949
Flint, Joyce M., B738, B1573, B1577
Flirt, A99
"Flirt," A26
"Flopsy Bunny," B108, B818, B1728
Flounder, The, review of, A1001
Flower, Dean, B1043, B1443
"Flurry," A622
Flute-Player, The, review of, A1036

Index 293

"Fly," A618
"Flying High: The American Icarus in Morrison, Roth and Updike," B243
Fogel, S., B245
Foley, Martha, A282, A292, A341, A354
"Following Through, Sadly," B873
Foltz, David Allen, B1594
Food, A267
"Fools for Christ's Sake: A Study of Clerical Figures in De Vries, Updike and Buechner," B956
"Fool's Gold," A925
Foote, Timothy, B976
"Footnotes," B1214
Forbes, Cheryl, B941
Forbes, Peter, B1217, B1237
Forest of a Thousand Daemons, review of, A1062
"Foreword"
   to *The Carpentered Hen*, A798
   to *The Chaste Planet*, A785
   to *The Complete Book of Covers from the New Yorker 1925-1989*, A858
   to *The Complete Lyrics of Cole Porter*, A807
   to *Doubly Gifted*, A832
   to *Franz Kafka: The Complete Stories of Franz Kafka*, A1052
   to *Great New England Churches: 65 Houses of Worship That Changed our Lives*, A799
   to *Hugging the Shore*, A808
   to *Jester's Dozen*, A815
   to *My Well-Balanced Life on a Wooden Leg*, A880
   to *Picked-Up Pieces*, A758
   to *The Poorhouse Fair*, A25, A704, A1256
   to *Rabbit Run* (5th edition, revised), A704
   to *The Harvard Lampoon Centennial Celebration, 1876-1973*, A751
   to *Too Far to Go: The Maples Stories*, A777
"Foreword: The Ant and the So-Called Grasshopper," A866
"Foreword for Young Readers," A685
"Fork, The," A907
"Form, Fluidity, and Flexibility in Recent American Fiction," B884
"Formal Vision," A888
Forstner, Lorne, A686
Forty Stories, A230
Foucault's Pendulum, review of, A1124
Foulke, Robert Bud, A1188

"Four New Poems, translation of", A1283
"Four Sides of One Story," B687
"'Four Sides of One Story': Tristan und Isolde bei John Updike," B687
"Fourth of July, The," A874
Fox, Matthew Graham, B1721
Franck, Irene M., B436
Frank, Joseph, A706
Franz Kafka: The Complete *Stories of Franz Kafka*, "Foreword" to, A1052
Frederic Goudy, review of, A1134
"Free Bee-hours," A695
Freeman, L., B1555
Freese, P., B512
Fremont-Smith, Eliot, B700, B1099
French, Warren G., B328
"Fresh from the Forties," A1030
Friedman, Ruben, B508, B1626
Fripp, Bill, B194
"Fritillary, The," A26
Fritz, Donald Eric, B1596
"From Above," A592
"From Babbitt to Rabbit: The American Materialist in Search of a Soul," B558, B1147
"From Dyna Domes to Turkey-Pressing," A937
"From Fumie to Sony," A1016
"From Guidelines to Censorship? One Writer's Testimony," A774
From Mice to Rabbits, B376
"From Realism to Romance in Six Novels by Bellow, Updike and Malamud," B1605
From The Diary of a Snail, review of, A945
From the Journal of a Leper, A138
"From the Journal of a Leper," A358
"From Updike: Machine Dreams of Diversity and Depth," B1454
"From Vermeer to Bonnard: Updike's Interartistic Mode in *Marry Me*," B1005
"From Words to Films: Opportunities and Challenges," B1557
"Front Lawn," B1073
"Frost," A612
Fruchter, Norman, A928
"Fruits of Blossoming Selfhood," B1185
Frumkes, Lewis Burke, B454
Fuchs, Daniel, A931
Fuentes, Carlos, A1083
Full Forty Years Have Flown, No Less..., A253
Fuller, Edmund, B718, B815, B919, B981
Fuller, John, B766
Fultz, Norma J., B1531
Funck, Sistine, B640

"Function of Classical Myth in John Updike's *The Centaur*, The," B631
Funny Dirty Little War, A, review of, A1088
Fuoroli, Caryn, B1652
"Furniture, The," A576
"Future of the Novel, The," A759

Gabbard, Krin, B643
Gado, Frank, A1166, A1312
"Gaiety in the Galleries," A982
Galgan, Gerald J., B944
Gallagher, Charles M., B90, B772
Gallego, Candido Pérez, B125
Galloway, David D., B138, B228, B648, B1569
Gamble, Sharno, B1713
Gambler, The, review of, A941
García Márquez, Gabriel, A933, A1073, A1088, A1099
Garden of Eden, The, review of, A1086
Gardener's Year, The, review of, A1069
Gardner, Jeanne Elizabeth, B1675
Gardner, John, A775, B179
Gardner, Peter, B176
Garrett, George, B1075
Gasca, Eduardo, B63
Gass, William H., B710
Gates, Anne, B762
Gates, David, B1494
Gates of Eden, B166
Gates of Horn, The: A Study of Five French Realists, review of, A903
"Gathering of the Poets of Faith," A1041
Gatlin, Josh, B430
Gay, Peter, A982
Gazzaniga, Marin, B1322
Gearhart, Elizabeth, B180, B272
Gediman, Helen, B147, B652
Gelb, Arthur, A571
Geller, Evelyn, B9
Geller, Robert, B1557
"General Studies: John Updike," B406
"Generation Between, The," B664
"Generic College," A616
"Generous Critic, The: John Updike," B1182
Genet, Jean, A916
"Genial Learning Offered with Shy Generosity," B1467
"Genius without a Cause," A1066
"Gentile Parody," B773
"George Hunt's *John Updike and the Three Great Secret Things*," B236, B251, B260
"George Hunt's *John Updike and the Three Great Secret Things: Sex, Religion, and Art*," B231
"Gerald Ford Redux," B1495
Gerber, Eric, B1388, B1489
Geronimo Rex, review of, A937
Gerstenberger, Donna, B79
Gessert, George, B1296
"Gesturing," A371
Getlin, Josh, B1415
"Getting a Fix on Fall Books," B747
"Getting Into the Set," A396
Getting Older, A219
"Getting Rid of the Garbage," B1280
Getting the Words Out, A234
"Getting the Words Out," A834
"Getting Too Full of Updike," B977
"Getting Under the Skin of Updike," B1341
Giacomo Joyce, review of, A918
"Giant Who Isn't There, The," A990
Gibson, Charles, A1241
"Gift from the City, A," A282
Gilbert, Harriett, B1164
Gilchreist, William E., B1692
Gill, Brendan, B823, B832
Gilman, Richard, B202, B498, B607, B1289
Gilmartin, David, B267
Gindin, James, B96
Gingher, Robert S., B141, B144
Gingold, Alfred, B1723
"Giving Blood," A296, B693
"Glad Rags," A899
"Glance," A651
"Glasnost, Home, and Conquistadores," A1139
"Glasses," A26
Glatzer, Nahum N., A813, A1038
Glory, review of, A934
"God, Sex and Software," B1223
"God Bless America," B1392
"God Has Gone, Sex Is Left," B705
"God Speaks," A342
God's Grace, review of, A1046
Going After Cacciato, review of, A994
"Going Barefoot," A789
"Going West," B1284
"Going with the Current," B1046
Gold, Ivan, B777
Gold in the Kingdom, review of, A936
"Golden Age of the 30-second Spot, The," A820
Golden Droplet, The, review of, A1118
Goldman, Marion S., B1298
Goldstein, Moona, B1679

Index 295

"Golf," A753
"Golf Course Owner, The," A161, A167, A373
"Golf Dreams," A781
"Golfers," A527
Gombrowicz, Witold, A915
"Good, Bad and Beyond--It's Where You Stand at the Time," A871
Good Apprentice, The, review of, A1085
"Good Morning America" interviews, A1241, A1243
Good Place, A: Being a Personal Account of Ipswich, Massachusetts written on the occasion of its Seventeenth-Century Day, 1972, by a Resident, John Updike, A85
"Goodbye, Goteborg," A593
Goodman, Walter, B1542
Goodwin, Gail, B1193
"Goody Sergeant; The Powerful Katrinka; K. S. W.," A1098
Gordon, Alice, A454, A874
Gordon, David J., B731
Gordon, Jeffrey, W., B1691
Gordon, John, B830
Gordon, Peter, A314
"Gospel According to Saint Matthew, The," A881
Goss, James, B1578
Goss, Marjorie Hill, B585
"Gossip of a Higher Sort," B1174
Gottesman, Ronald, A283, A353, A540
Gottlieb, Robert, A1146, B437
Gould, Stephen Jay, A1080, A1100
"Grabbing Dilemmas: John Updike Talks about God, Love, and the American Identity," A1163
"Gradations of Black," A573, B1218
"Grandma Moses," A684
"Grandmaster Nabokov," A904
"Granite," A615
Graphic arts, A1285-A1317
Grass, Günther, A945, A1001, A1033, A1043
Gratton, Margaret, B75
Graver, Lawrence, B963
Gray, Larry, B913
Gray, Nancy L., B1716
Gray, Paul, B270, B425, B915, B1107, B1153, B1185, B1220, B1263, B1332, B1369, B1393, B1427, B1495, B1730, B1741
Gray, Simon, B678
"Great American Fragments," B877
"Great American Writers/Two as Reported in the *New York Times*," B1558

Great New England Churches: 65 Houses of Worship That Changed our Lives, "Foreword" to, A799
"Great Paraguayan Novel and Other Hardships, The," A1088
Great Ponds, The, review of, A948
"Great Scarf of Birds, The," A26
Great Tom: Notes Towards the Definition of T. S. Eliot, review of, A951
"Green," A640
Green, Henry, A772, A1003
"Green Green," A1003
"Green Grow the Yesses, O!," A660
Greenfeld, Josh, B714
Greiner, Donald J., A1200, A1259, B209, B229, B261, B272, B278, B284, B297, B300, B325, B336, B346, B350, B362, B365, B371, B390, B491, B958, B1056, B1210, B1239, B1561, B1735
Grekova, I., A1072
Gresset, Michel, B329
"Griechischer Mythos im Modernen Roman: John Updike's *The Centaur*," B620
Griffin, C. W., Jr., B721
Griffith, Albert J., B144, B511
Griffith, Benjamin, B1483
Grobel, Lawrence, B326
Grosecloses, Barbara, B321
Gross, John, A360
Gross, Terry, A1206
"Group and John Updike, The," B506, B617
Grove, Lee, B1213
"Grove Is My Press, and Avant My Garde," A916
"Growing Up with John Updike, Sort Of," B464
Gruesser, John Cullen, B1650
Grumbach, Doris, B870
Grunwald, Henry, A902, B646
Gu, Xuefan, B1080
"Guilt-Gems," A366
Gumble, Bryant, A1240
"Gun Shop, The," A339
Gustafsson, Lars, A1037, A1060
Guth, Dorothy Lobrano, A981

Haas, Rudolf, B620
"Habit of Confession, The: Recovery of the Self in Updike's 'The Music School'," B692
Hadary, Jonathan, B1508
Hagedorn, Jessica, A1138
Hagstrom, Jack W. C., Collection, of books and manuscripts, A1263

Hainsworth, J. D., B46
Hajek, Igor, A719
Half of Man Is Woman, review of, A1115
Halio, Jay L., B281, B1141
Hall, Joan Joffe, B917
Hallissy, Margaret, B231, B246, B547, B1003
Hamilton, Alice, B42, B80, B102, B105, B123, B136, B158, B238, B249, B571, B768, B792, B889
Hamilton, Ian, B378, B1467
Hamilton, Kenneth, B42, B80, B102, B105, B123, B136, B158, B238, B249, B336, B768, B792, B889
Hamsun, Knut, A917, A921, A930, A972, A999
"Hand of Saint Saens, The," A791
Handke, Peter, A988, A1122
Handmaid's Tale, The, review of, A1085
Handyman, The, review of, A1077
Hannah, Barry, A937
Hansen, Klaus, B247, B327, B379
Hanson, Henry, B486
"Happiest I've Been, The," A283
Happy Death, A, review of, A939
"Happy Medium," B292
"Happy Moments at the Mailbox," B176
"Happy on Nono Despite Odosha," A1031
Hardwick, Elizabeth, B312, B1351, B1732
Harkness, Don, B257
Harmon, William, A458, A466, A467, A1261
Harper, Howard M., B167, B651, B1570
Harris, Charles B., B355
Harris, Robert R., B298, B1119, B1731
Harrison, Gilbert, A900, A904
"Harry's End," B1420
Hart, James D., B347
Hart, Jeffrey, B1390
Hartley, Lois, B685
Hartman, Matthew, B866, B910
Hartman, Susan Beth, B1640
Hartsoe, Judith S., B1682
Hartwell, David G., A1125
Hartwell, Patrick, A671
"Harv is Plowing Now," B127
Harvard Lampoon Centennial Celebration, 1876-1973, The
    cartoons in, A1313
    "Foreword" to, A751
    self-portrait in, A1298
Harvard University, collection at, A1265
"Has Anyone Seen Michelangelo, Seen His Marvelous Frescoes the Way We Can Here?," A892
"Has John Updike Anything to Say?," B141

"Has Updike Anything to Say?," B144
"Has-Been, 10 Years Later, A," B796
Haslip, Joan, A952
Hatcher, Randall, B1723
Hatza, George, B1536
Hawley, John C., B1330
Haworth, J. D. S., B682
"Hawthorne," B382
"Hawthorne, Melville, Whitman et l'expérience américaine," A1198, B353
Hawthorne's Creed, A166
"Hawthorne's Hester Prynne. Updike's Sarah Worth, and 'the Three Great Secret Things'," B1717
"Hawthorne's Religious Language," A778, A1002, A1028
Hayes, Harold, B1025
"Head of a Girl, at the Met," A213
Headbirths; or The Germans Are Dying Out, review of, A1043
"Heading for Nandi," A524
"Hear the Roaring of the Buds," A1069
Heart Prepared, The: Grace and Conversion in Puritan Spiritual Life, review of, A912
"Heartless Man, The," A1114
"Heaven of an Old Home, The," A983
"Heavily Hyped Helga," A246
Hecht, Carole Lynn, B1665
Heffernan, William A., A291
Heidegger, Martin, A909
Heidenry, John, B822, B838
Heins, Paul, B757
Held, George, B858
Hello, Darkness: The Collected Poems of L. E. Sissman, review of, A995
"Hellow, Olleh," B736
Helterman, Jeffrey, B184
"Hem Battles the Pack; Wins, Loses," A1032
Hemingway, Ernest, A926, A1032, A1086
Hemingway's Selected Letters 1917-1961, review of, A1032
Hendey, Sara Louise, B1706
Hendin, Josephine, B181, B202, B970
Hendrick, George, B79
Hendrikson, Paul, B154
Heneghan, Gail Lorraine, B1690
"Henry Bech Redux," A1165, B107, B1727
"Henry Through the Looking-Glass: Eastern Europe and America in John Updike's *Bech: A Book*," B798
Hepburn, Neil, B935, B993
"Here Come the Maples," A359
"Here I Am," A860
Herget, W., B512

Heroes and Anti-Heroes, "Introduction" to, A883
"Heroic Then, a Realistic Now, A," B1481
Heroines in Certain American Novels, B1582
"He's Still Giving Praise," B1463
Heuermann, Hartmut, B644
Hevesi, Dennis, B1436
Heyen, William, B758, B764
Hicks, Granville, B249, B705, B925 "John Updike," B81
"Hiding the Harm Away," B1258
Hiett, John, B1550
Higgins, George V., B1335, B1336
Higgs, Robert J., A278, A456
"High, Blank, Reflecting Wall of Glass, A: The Novels of John Updike," B1679
"High-Hearts, The," A26
"High-Tech Shrine to Sex and Society, A," B1224
Hill, Douglas, B1031
Hill, John S., B74, B102
Hill, Steele Waychoff, B1603
Hill, William B., B724, B842, B926
"Hill of Life, The," cartoon for, A1317
"Hillies, The," A321
Hills, L. Rust, A280, A290, A301, A385, A755, A1170, B135, B507, B744
Hills, Penny Chapin, A280, A290, A301, B507
Hinkle, Roy, A220, A588, B483, B1568
"His Mother Inside Him," A425
"Historian Updike Looks at ... James Buchanan?," B899
"Historical Mind and the Literary Imagination, The," B894
History of the John Updike Family, B398
Hitchens, Christopher, B1279, B1323
Hjerter, Kathleen, A832, A1309
Hoag, Ronald Wesley, B635
Hoagland, Edward, A1018, A1096, B1482
Hobhouse, Janet, B1270
Hochschild, Adam, B1282
Hodgart, Matthew, B1010
Hodgins, Frank, A291
"Hoeing," A26
Hoeper, Jeffrey D., A291, A460, A554
Hoffmann, Gerhard, B379, B380
Hogan, Robert E., B545
"Holding the Fort on Audubon Terrace," B793
Holland, Laurence B., A283, A353, A540
Holleran, Andrew, B1108
Holley, H., B1717
Holmes, Charles S., B113

Holroyd, Michael, A1114
"Holy Land, The," A375
"Holy Spirit in Biblical Exegesis, The: An Address," B1556
"Home Movies," A484
Homer, William Innes, A1133
"Homer's Joyce: John Updike, Ronald Sukenick, Robert Coover, Toni Morrison," B637
"Honky America," B1346
Hooper, Brad, B1372, B1476
Hoover, Paul, B1303
Hope, Francis, B735, B885
Hoping for a Hoopoe, A1
Horner, Carl Stuart, B1649
"Hors du terrier natal," B309
Horton, Andrew S., B851
Horvath, Brooke, B561, B1638
"Hostile Haircuts," A896
Hotchner, A. E., A969
Houghton Library, collection at, A1265
"House Growing, The," A518
  work sheets for, A1254
House on the Embankment, The, review of, A1072
"Houses of Ipswich, The," A873
"How Hollywood Influenced Me," A1190
How I Changed My Mind, review of, A911
"How the Other Half Lives," A1049
"How to Be Uncle Sam," A26
"How to Milk a Millionaire," A1095
"How to Watch a Crew Race," A433
How We Live, B507
Howard, Jane, A1160, B1163
Howard, Maureen, B971, B1035
Howells, W. D., A1123
"Howells as Anti-Novelist," A842
Howells as Anti-Novelist, A231
Howes, Victor, B809
Huang, Ray, A1034
Hub Fans Bid Kid Adieu, A124
  "Preface" to, A768
"Hub Fans Bid Kid Adieu," A681
  on audio tape, B1508
Hugging the Shore, A167, B1560
  criticism of, B1166-B1184
  "Foreword" to, A808
  on audio tape, B1509
"*Hugging the Shore*," B1172, B1173, B1179, B1181
Hugging the Shore: Essays and Criticism, A203, A204
"*Hugging the Shore: Essays and Criticism*," B1171

Hughes-Hallet, Lucy, A1127
Hulbert, Dan, B1307
Hull, James Horace, B1612
"Human Capacities," A989
"Human Experience, The: Contemporary American and Soviet Fiction and Poetry," B407
"Humanities Course," A26, A453
Humboldt's Gift, review of, A965
Hunger, review of, A917
Hunsinger, George, B1232
Hunt, George W., A1247-A1249, B182, B210, B225, B233, B238, B242, B249, B284, B579, B688, B931, B949, B985, B1066, B1118, B1179, B1600
Hurley, C. Harold, B596
Hyman, Lisa Diane, B1701
Hyman, Stanley E., B604, B720
"Hymn to These Newly Abbreviated States," A596
"Hymn to Tilth," A1069

I Am a Cat, review of, A1047
"I Am Dying, Egypt, Dying," A317
"I have Preened, I have Lived," B1324
"I Like to Sing Also," A447
"I Missed His Book, But I Read His Name," A26, A467
I the Supreme, review of, A1088
"I Was a Teen-Age Library User," A884
"I Will Not Let Thee Go, Except Thou Bless Me," A319
Iacobuzio, Ted, B924
Iannone, Carol, B1291
"Idyll," A26
"If at First You Do Succeed, Try, Try, Again," A928
If on a Winter Night a Traveler, review of, A1033
"Il Court, Il Court," A172, A388
Illustrations, A1285-A1294
"Image of Precarious Life, An," B202
"Imaginable Conference, An," A26
"'Imagination of State' Comes Alive at Writers' PEN," B351
"Imagining Things," A1021
"Immobile President," B897
"Importance of Fiction, The," A826
Impossible H. L. Mencken, The: A Selection of His Best Newspaper Stories, review of, A1147
Impressions, A214
"In a Steelworker's Home," translation of, A1282

"In and Out of Wedlock," B980
"In Borges' Wake" ("In Borges's Wake"), A1124
"In Clover," B859, B1101
"In Clover: *Rabbit is Rich* by John Updike," B1100
"In Dispraise of the Powers That Be," A1105
"In Extremis," A52
"In Hawthorne's Shadow: The Minister and the Women in Howells, Adams, Frederic, and Updike," B417
"In John Updike's Latest, The Woman Called '*S.*'," B1267
"In Memoriam," A26, A182
In Memoriam Felis Felis, A244
"In Praise of the Blind, Black God," A939
In Praise of the Stepmother, review of, A1132
"In Praise of $(C_{10}H_9O_5)x$," A26
"In Print: John Updike," B10
"In *S.* Updike Tries the Woman's Viewpoint," A1205
"In *S.* Updike Tries Woman's Viewpoint," B1266
"In Search of a Blessing," B1345
In Search of J. D. Salinger, B378
In Search of Love and Beauty, review of, A1056
"In Search of Meaning: Bernard Malamud, Norman Mailer, John Updike," B1573, B1577
In the Fog of the Season's End, review of, A948
"In the Tub," A131
"In Their Own Voices: How Authors Are Making the Transition from Page to Tape," B1539
"In These Books Lived Great Friends of My Childhood: A Symposium," A677
"In Updike Land: Four Settings of Poems by John Updike: For Mixed Chorus and Piano," B1567
"Inadequate American, The: John Updike's Fiction," B33
"Incest," A280, B507
"Incontri Americani," B97
"Indestructible Elena," A1036
Index to American Periodical Verse, B101, B116
Index to Poetry in Popular Periodicals, 1960-1964, B54
"India Going On," A1044
Indian, The, A66
Indian Summer
"Introduction" to, A1123

Index 299

review of, A1123
"Indianapolis," A617
"Indifference," A919
"Individual Authors: Donald Greiner's *John Updike's Novels*," B357
"Industrious Drifter in Room Two," A1171
"Infante Terrible," A933
"Influence of Neo-orthodoxy in the Fiction of John Updike, The," B1672
Inglis, Fred, B1358
"Initiation Theme in the Writings of Ernest Hemingway, William Faulkner, and John Updike, The," B1666
"Inner Rabbit, The," B1370, B1743
"Innerlichkeit und Eigentümlichkeit," A1137
Innocent Bystander: The Scene from the 70's, "Introduction" to, A761
"Innocents Abroad," B766
Inquisitor, The, review of, A916
"Insane and the Indifferent, The: Walker Percy and Others," B1000
"Inside Out and Upside Down," B1330
"Inside Updike," B401, B1321
"Insight Came to Updike the Outsider," B453
"Insomnia the Gem of the Ocean," A513, B1567
"Inspired Marketeer," A1142
"'Intact and Infrangible as Metal, and Like Metal Dead': Patterns of Faith and Forgetfulness in Three John Updike Novels with Special Reference to Nathaniel Hawthorne's 'The Scarlet Letter'," B1648
"Integrated Short Story Collection as a Genre (Barth, Fowels, Updike), The," B1625
"Interesting Emendation in the Text of *Mr. Sammler's Planet*, by Saul Bellow," A760
"Interpretation of John Updike's Tomorrow and Tomorrow and So Forth," B508
"Intertexuality and Originality: Hawthorne, Faulkner, Updike," B329
"Interview about *Rabbit at Rest*," A1240
"Interview about *S.*," A1237
"Interview with John Updike," A1194
"Interview with John Updike, An," A1204, A1214
"Interview with John Updike Conducted by Jeff Campbell, Georgetown, Massachusetts, 9 Aug. 1976," A1174
Interviews, A1159-A1243
Intimate Interiors of Edouard Vuillard, review of, A1128
"Into the Underbrush," B518
"Introduction"
to *Appointment in Samarra*, A845
to *The Art of Mickey Mouse*, A882
to *The Best American Short Stories 1984*, A816
to *Heroes and Anti-Heroes*, A883
to *Indian Summer*, A1123
to *Innocent Bystander: The Scene from the 70's*, A761
to "Leaves," A755
to *Lectures on Literature*, A788, A1256
to *Loving, Living, Party Going: Three Novels by Henry Green*, A772
to *Mirror After Mirror. Reflections on Woman*, A764
to *Modern Critical Views: John Updike*, B361
to *Of the Farm*, Czech edition, A719
to *Pens and Needles: Literary Caricatures*, A726
to *The Poorhouse Fair*, A766, A817
to *Sanatorium Under the Sign of the Hourglass*, A779
to *Sounding in Satanism*, A743, B137
to *Talk from the Fifties*, A780
to *Writers at Work: The Paris Review Interviews, Seventh Series*, A833, A846
"Introduction: A Survey of John Updike Scholarship in English," B249, B250
"Introduction: 'Alive in a Place and Time'," B202, B203
Introduction to A Science of Mythology, review of, A1011
"INVALID.KEYSTROKE," A564
Invasion of the Book Envelopes, A168
"Invasion of the Book Envelopes," A793
Invention of Morel and Other Stories, The, review of, A1088
"Invention of the Horse Collar, The," A335
Invisible Cities, review of, A959
"Invitations to Dread: John Updike's Metaphysical Quest," B581
"Inward and Onward," A950
Inward Turn of Narrative, The, review of, A950
Iooss, Walter, Jr., B529
Iowa, A159
"Ipswich Brings Past to Life," B124
"Ipswich Play Penned by Updike," B73
"Irony and Innocence in John Updike's 'A & P.,'" B594
"Irony in John Updike's 'Pigeon Feathers'," B597
Irwin, Michael, B989, B994
"Is Art Worth It?" A246

"Is Art Worth It? Renoir at the Mercy of the Megashow," A830
"Is Life Too Short for Golf?" A891, B475
"Is There Life After Golf?" A749, A936
"Is Updike Up to His Literary Tricks?" B221
Isenberg, Barbara, B206
Island of Crimea, The, review of, A1072
"Island Sun," A571
Islands in the Stream, review of, A926
Issacs, Neil D., A278, A456
"'It Captivates': Updike Goes to the Movies: Part I," B489
"'It Hypnotizes': Updike Goes to the Movies: Part II," B490
Italian Folk Tales, review of, A1027
Italie, Hillel, A1212, B432, B1344, B1418
"Italo Calvino," A828
"It's the Going That's Important, Not the Getting There: Rabbit's Questing Non-Quest," B144, B533

Jackson, Edward M., B864
Jacobs, Rita, D., B1134
"Jake and Lolly Opt Out," A1012
Jake's Thing, review of, A1012
Janeczko, Paul, A22, A464, A469, A540, A806
Jarry, Alfred, A905, A989
Javer, Ron, B1444
Jelleman, Roderick, B42
Jennings, Ben Hill, A291, B1676
"Jerry & Sally & Richard & Ruth," B994
"Jerry and Sally and Richard and Ruth," B971
Jester's Dozen, A205
    drawings for, A1310
    "Foreword" to, A815
"Jesus on Honshu," A334
"Jew D'Esprit," B1158
Jhabvala, Ruth Prawer, A1056
"Jobs Well Done: *Odd Jobs,*" B1473
"John and Bruce," B674
"John Callaway Interviews John Updike," A1229
John Cheever: A Biography, B375
"John H. Updike," B3
"John Marquand," A680
"John McEnroe," A800
"John Updike," B317, B348
"John Updike," (Brodin), B16
"John Updike," (Curley et al), B345
John Updike (Detweiler), B111, B299
"John Updike," (Feeney), B427
"John Updike," (Gado), A1166
"John Updike," (Greiner), B209, B229, B278, B346, B365, B390
"John Updike," (Gross), A1206
"John Updike," (Hainsworth), B46
"John Updike," (Hart), B347
"John Updike," (Hoffman), B380
"John Updike," (Klinkowitz), B184, B439
"John Updike," (Leo), B392
"John Updike," (Moritz), B36, B304
"John Updike," (Nadeau), B232
John Updike (Newman), B383, B424
"John Updike," (Nyren and Kramer), B161
"John Updike," (Patrick), B368
"John Updike," (Samuels), B139
John Updike (Samuels), B64
"John Updike," (Schlueter), B331
"John Updike," (Stafford), B272
John Updike (Stafford), B233
John Updike (Uphaus), B216
"John Updike," (Wakeman), B153
"John Updike," (Ziegfeld), B279, B280
"John Updike: A Bibliographical Checklist: Section A--Primary Publications," B218
"John Updike: A Bibliographical Checklist: Section B--Secondary Publications," B219
John Updike: A Bibliography, B56
John Updike: A Bibliography of Research and Criticism, 1970-1986, B396
"John Updike, A Collection," A1271
John Updike: A Collection of Critical Essays, B156, B202, B233, B235
John Updike: A Comprehensive Bibliography, B98, B272
John Updike: A Comprehensive Bibliography with Selected Annotations, B180
"*John Updike: A Comprehensive Bibliography with Selected Annotations* by E. Gearhart," B212
John Updike: A Critical Essay, B42
"John Updike: A Literary Spider," B362, B1087
John Updike: A Study of the Short Fiction, B476
"John Updike, Adapter: *Bottom's Dream,*" B757
John Updike: An Annotated Checklist, B105
John Updike: An Exhibition, A1264, B322
"John Updike: Between Heaven and Earth," B149
"John Updike," B424
"John Updike: 'Dear Alexandros'," B583
"John Updike: From Blocks to Books," A855
"John Updike: From *Rabbit, Run* to *Marry Me,*" B169

"John Updike, in the Tradition of American Classic Literature," B1712
"John Updike/ 1981 Medalist," A794
"John Updike: Midpoint and After," B767, B783
"John Updike, Playing Around," B1492
"John Updike: 'Problems'," B1071
"John Updike: *Rabbit, Run*," B536
"John Updike: Rabbit Angstrom Grows Up," B1146
"John Updike: Rabbitland and Bechville," B1145, B1165
"John Updike: Replacing Rabbit," B1486
"John Updike: Style in Search of a Center," B52, B362
"John Updike: The Author's View," B1686
"John Updike: The Beginning and the End," B114, B833
"John Updike: *The Centaur*," B608
"John Updike: *The Coup*," B1036
"John Updike: The Dialectical Vision—The Influence of Kierkegaard and Barth," B1600
"John Updike: The Intrinsic Problem of Human Existence," B167
"John Updike: The Psychological Novel in Search of Structure," B49
"John Updike: The Story as Lyrical Meditation," B127
"John Updike: Theme and Form in the Garden of Epiphanies," B13
"John Updike: 'Tomorrow and tomorrow and So Forth'," B512
"John Updike: Verfall eines Realisten," B85
"John Updike: What Makes Rabbit Run?" A1231
"John Updike: Words, Words," B941
John Updike: Yea Sayings, B94, B105, B122
"John Updike and Andrew Wyeth: The Nostalgic Mode in Contemporary American Art," B1610
"John Updike and Couples: The WASP's Dilemma," B738
"John Updike and Kierkegaard's Negative Way: Irony and Indirect Communication in *A Month of Sundays*," B957
"John Updike and Norman Mailer," B1703
"John Updike and the Changing of the Gods," B249, B632
"John Updike and the Critics: An Interpretation and Evaluation of the Criticism of John Updike's Work," B1677

"John Updike and the Distractions of Henry Bech, Professional Writer and Amateur American Jew," B799
"John Updike and the Funny Theologian," A1252, B478
"John Updike and the Great Secret Things," B237
"John Updike and the Higher Theology," B86
"John Updike and the Indictment of Culture-Protestantism," B14
"John Updike and the Parabolic Nature of the World," B133
"*John Updike and the Three Great Secret Things*," B220
John Updike and the Three Great Secret Things: Sex, Religion, and Art, A1247-A1249, B210, B225, B233, B236, B238, B251, B260, B284
"John Updike and William Styron: The Burden of Talent," B610
"John Updike Barely Interested But Slavishly 'Faithful' to His 'Rabbit, Run'," B525
"John Updike Breaks Out of Suburbia," A1181, B196
"John Updike Brews Up Some Ole Black Magic in Spell-binding *The Witches of Eastwick*," B1197
"*John Updike* by Judie Newman," B393
"John Updike, Candor, Family Relations and Life's Early Evening," B1326
"John Updike Comments on His Work and the Role of the Novelist Today," A1219
"John Updike Completes a Sequel to *Rabbit, Run*," B800
"John Updike Completes a Sequel to 'Rabbit, Run'," A1221
"John Updike in Conversation," A1232
"John Updike on Franz Kafka and *The Metamorphosis*," A1052
"John Updike on Poetry," A1176, B1006
"John Updike on the Books of the '80s," B1461
"John Updike Raps Schools," B164
"John Updike Reappointed to Library," B155
"John Updike Receives Pennsylvania Award," B291
"John Updike Redux," B495
"John Updike Reminisces in 'Olinger'," B62
"John Updike since *Midpoint*," B213
"John Updike Talks to Eric Rhode About the Shapes and Subjects of His Fiction," A1163

"John Updike Unveils Opinions on Authors in his New Collection," B1170
"John Updike's 'A & P': The Establishment and an Emersonian Cashier," B576
"John Updike's Africa," B214, B1047
"John Updike's America," B694
"John Updike's *Buchanan Dying*: A Chamber Theater Production," B909
"John Updike's Bulging Suitcases," B835
"John Updike's *Centaur* is Praised, B601
"John Updike's Contribution to *Chatterbox*," B342
"John Updike's Eastwick: Is it Really Wickford?" B1199
"John Updike's Fiction," B12
"John Updike's Fiction: Cross and Grace in *Beruf*," B83
"John Updike's Fiction and His Themes," B330, B639
"John Updike's Fictional Hero Comes Back Fat, Rich and Ready for the '80s," B1126
"John Updike's First Film," B88
"John Updike's 'Giving Blood': An Experiment in Genre," B693
"John Updike's Harry 'Rabbit' Angstrom as American Adam," B1705
John Updike's Images of America, B234
"John Updike's Literary Apprenticeship on *The Harvard Lampoon*," A1314
"John Updike's Literary Apprenticeship on *The National Lampoon*," B142, B144
"John Updike's Love of 'Dull Bovine Beauty'," B157, B362
"John Updike's Metaphoric Novels," B66, B249
"John Updike's *Museums and Women and Other Stories*," B889
"John Updike's Notorious Alter Ego," B1155
"John Updike's Novels," B336
John Updike's Novels, B300
John Updike's Novels: Thorns Spell a Word, A1174
"*John Updike's Novels* by Donald Greiner," B350
"John Updike's Olinger Stories: New Light Among the Shadows," B695
"John Updike's Philosophy as Revealed in his Poem Midpoint," B1694
"John Updike's Prescription for Survival," B123
"John Updike's Prose Style: Definition at the Periphery of Meaning," B405
John Updike's Rabbit, Run and Rabbit Redux: A Critical Commentary, B531

"John Updike's 'Rabbit' Returns, Pale and Prepared to Grow Up," B804
"John Updike's Rabbit Saga," B1130
"John Updike's Rabbit Trilogy: From Running to Jogging: Motions of Grace in Harry Angstrom," B1707
"John Updike's Sermons," B208
"John Updike's Sunday Sort of Book," B931
"John Updike's Theological World," B177
"John Updike's *Too Far To Go*: The Maples Stories," B1090
"John Updike's Transparent Eyeball," B1365
"John Updike's Unhooked Pilgrim," B1555
"John Updike's Uptown Peyton Place," B704
"John Updike's Use of Allusions and Symbols in *Rabbit, Run* and *Rabbit Redux* to Reveal Ethical Views and Different Attitudes toward Religion," B1683
"John Updike's Version of Computing," B1234
"John Updike--Wearing His Poet's Hat," B762
Johnson, Albert H., B961
Johnson, Charles, B1490
Johnson, Christine, B854, B1091
Johnson, Claudia D., B382
Johnson, Diane, B313, B1194, B1733
Johnson, Greg, B990, B1331
Johnson, Ira D., B854, B1091
Johnson, M., B1076
Johnson, Mark, B551
Johnson, Randell Gaw, B1683
Johnson, Robert K., B177, B188
Johnson, Uwe, A913
Johnston, Mark, A291, B275
Joiner, Dorothy M., B1210
Joke, The, review of, A1049
"Jolly Greene Giant, The," A521
Jones, D. A. N., B1032
Jones, Gayl, A963, A976
"Jones Boys, The," A1050
Jong, Erica, A947, B1085
"Jong Love," A947
"Jorge Luis Borges," A790
"Journals: From the Seventies and Early Eighties--II.," B469
Journals of John Cheever, The, B437
  review of, A1146
"Journey to the Dead, The," A408
"Journey to Updike Country, A," B340
"Journeyers," A1018
Joyce, James, A918
Joys of Motherhood, The, review of, A1009

Juhasz, Suzanne, B1008
"July," A628
"Jungle Music," B1022
"Just 30 Years Later, Updike Has a Quartet," B1375
Just Looking, A245-A248, A254
   criticism of, B1299-B1317
   drawings for, A1311
"*Just Looking*," B1312, B1315
Justus, James H., B82, B148, B159, B168, B183, B200, B211

Kabakov, Alexander, A1139
Kadare, Ismail, A1103
Kael, Pauline, B1537
Kafka, Franz, A996, A1038
"Kafka's Short Stories," A813, A1052
Kahler, Erich, A950
Kahn, A. G., B862
Kahn, E. J., Jr., B381
Kakutani, Michiko, A1187, B239, B240, B452, B1105, B1283, B1375, B1451
Kalstone, David, A283, A353, A540
Kangaroo, review of, A1084
Kanreki: A Tribute to Allen Ginsberg. Part 2, A1250
Kaplan, James, A1210, B1381
Kaplan, Martin, A272, A275, A276, A430-A432, A434, A437, A443, A639, A751, A1169, A1258, A1298, A1312
Kapp, Isa, B980, B1162
Kappler, Frank, B28
Kapuscinski, Ryszard, A1053
Karaangov, Peter, A1279
Karl, Frederick, R., B282
Karl Barth: His Life from Letters and Autobiographical Texts, review of, A1005
"Karl Barth, John Updike and the Cheerful God," B414, B1241
"Karl Barth and Socrates as Mouseketeers in *Rabbit, Run*," B538
"Karl Barth and the Novels of John Updike: Updike's Novels as Christian Testimony," B1673
Karlinsky, Simon, A1007
"Karma in the Sunbelt," B1263
"Karmic Polymorphous Perverse, The," B1279
Karsh, Yusaf, B465, B1565
"Katharine S. White. 'New Yorker' Editor: Her Influence on the 'New Yorker' and on American Literature," B1630
Kattan, Naim, B106
Kauffmann, Stanley, B673, B1538

Kazin, Alfred, B128, B249, B706, B728, B978, B1117, B1498, B1559, B1748
Keating, Helane Levine, A288
"Keeping It Short," B683
"Keeping Up with Updike," B89, B788, B1725
"Keeping Up with Updike: *Bech: A Book*," B202
Keever, J. Robert, B1639
Kelley, Winifred Peabody, B1659
Kellman, Steven G., B1357, B1428
Kemal, Yashar, A1081
"Ken Kesey, John Updike, and The Lone Ranger," B851
Kenison, Katrina, A416
Kennedy, Eileen, B817, B875, B987
Kennedy, Eugene, B1248
Kennedy, William, B712
Kennedy, X. J., A290
Kenner, Hugh, B1473
"Kenneths," A26
"Kentavr: Mif, netafora, real'nost'," B641
Kermode, F., B734
Kesterton, David B., B950
Key, The, review of, A1139
"Kidnap Updike's Pulitzer Until Rabbit is Ransomed," B1439
Kiely, Benedict, A1077
Kierkegaard, Søren, A907
"Kierkegaardian Sensations into Real Fiction" John Updike's 'The Astronomer'," B579
Kihss, Peter, B262
"Killing," A383, B1012, B1245
Killinger, John, B57
Kimball, Robert, A807
King, The, review of, A1129
"King's Head, The," B1038
Kinsella, Rebbie, B352, B1206
Kirkland, James W., A460
Kirkpatrick, D. L., B217
Kirn, Walter, B1409, B1744
"Kismet Kush," B1032
Kitaj, R. B., A244
Kjima, Nobuo, A82
Klausler, Alfred P., B500, B519, B568
Kleimen, Ed, B693
Klima, Ivan, A1143
"Klimt and Schiele Confront the Cunt," A600
Klinge, Mama, B1747
Klinkowitz, Jerome, B184, B212, B248, B253, B283, B301, B328, B349, B366, B391, B416, B439, B587, B694
Knoke, Paul D., B1583

"Knopf Authors Win Two of Five National Book Critics Circle Awards," B446, B1431
Knudson, R. R., A457, A460
Koehler, Ray, B295, B340, B354, B409, B1143
Koenig, Rhoda, B1172, B1189, B1250, B1259, B1268, B1333, B1383, B1455, B1477
Koerner, Joseph Leo, A1137
Kohli, Mary Ann, B1700
Konwicki, Tadeusz, A1049, A1060
Kopelowitz, Lynn Wolf, B1702
Kopper, Edward A., Jr., B497, B600
Kort, Wesley, B83, B625, B732
Kosinski, Jerzy, A929
Kosman, Joshua, B458
Kostelanetz, Richard, B694
Kramer, Elaine, B161, B345
Kramer, Hilton, B781, B1224, B1309
Kramer, Maurice, B161, B345
Krementz, Jill, B1564
Kronenberger, Louis, A740
Kuball, David, B1036
Kuhl, St. Paul, Sister, B1666
Kundera, Milan, A1024, A1049
Kunkel, Francis L., B149
Kunze, Reiner, A988
Kutz, Anna W., B1660
"K[utztown] U[niversity] Foundation Plans to Honor Berks Novelist," B335

"L. A.," A567
La Course, Guerin, B606
La Guma, Alex, A948
La Rochelle, Pierre Drieu, A905
"Labyrinth, The," translation of, A1284
"Labyrinthine Ways," B238
"Ladies' Man, A," B972
"Lament for Cocoa," B1566
"Lamplight," A475
Lanchester, Duane Preston, B1627
"Land Too Ripe for Enigma, A: John Updike as Regionalist," B316
"Landscapes Without a Country, The Novels of John Updike," B1662
"Language, Myth, and Mr. Updike," B37, B249
  letter on, A1244
"Languid, But Never Dull," B269
Lannon, Linnea, B1462
Lanzinger, Klaus, B208
Larsen, Richard B., B127, B1590
Larson, Janet Karsten, B927
LaSalle, Peter, B225, B1027

"Lasch and the Portrayal of Narcissistic Personality in Adolescent Fiction (Salinger, Golding, Knowles, Updike)," B1635
"Last Blague." A1129
Lasseter, Victor K., B420, B1148
Last, Brian W., B1053
"Last Assertion of Personal Being, A," B498
Last Call, review of, A1119
"Last Call," A1119
"Last of Barthes, The," A1023
"Last Rabbit Not Easy to Write," A1212, B1418
"Last Word, The: The Novel, Redux," B805
Last Years, The: Journals, 1853-1855, review of, A907
"Lasting Impressions," A797
"Late January," A131
Latecomers, review of, A1116
Lathrop, Kathleen, B1055, B1628
"Latin Strategies," A1083
"Laughter from the Yokels," A1147
Laurence, Dan H., A1114
Lawrence, Vint, B1740
Lawson, Lewis A., B350, B534
"Layers of Ambiguity," A994
"Laying a 'Rabbit' to Rest," B1415
Layman, Richard, B184
Le Clair, Thomas, B535
Le Pellec, Yves, B854, B1091
Le Vot, André, B34, B77
Leader, Zachary, B1545
"Leading Contenders for NBA Announced," B612
"Leaf Season," A403
Leaky, Louis S. B., A960
"Learn a Trade," A382
Least Heat Moon, William, A1051
"Leaves," "Introduction" to, A755
"Leaving Church Early," A535
"Leaving Home," A1078
Leavis, L. R., B1297
Leavis, Q. D., A1130
Leckie, Barbara, B1004
LeClair, Thomas, B628, B911, B988
"Lectures on Literature," B222, B224
Lectures on Literature, "Introduction" to, A787, A1256
Lectures on Russian Literature by Vladimir Nabokov, review of, A1035
Lee, Hermione, B1425
LeGuin, Ursula K., A1021
Lehman, David, B334, B1169, B1214, B1222, B1255

Lehmann-Haupt, Christopher, B771, B974, B1247, B1267, B1304, B1327, B1481
Leithauser, Brad, B373
Lekachman, Robert, B1123
Lem, Stanislaw, A1004
"Lem and Pym," A1004
Lemeunier, Barbara, B798, B1049
"Lens Factory, The," A413, A610
Leo, John, B392
Leonard, John, B567, B805, B1095, B1293
Leopardvackning: Tio Forfattare och dan utsatta borgerligheten, B199
Lepper, Gary M., B160
Lescaze, Lee, B1484
Lesser, Wendy, B1260
"Letter from Anguilla," A723
  drawing for, A1303
"Letter Slot," A182
"Letter to John Updike," B395
Letters, A1244-A1259
Letters and Drawings of Bruno Schulz, review of, A1110
Letters from Colette, review of, A1026
"Letters from the Ashram," B1269
Letters of E. B. White, B162
  review of, A981
Letters of Gustave Flaubert, The, review of, A1017
Letters of John Cheever, The, B374
Letters of Karl Barth and Carl Buchmayer, The, review of, A1054
Letters to Friends, Family, and Editors, review of, A996
Letters to Ottla and the Family, review of, A1038
Levin, Gerald, A294, A706
Levin, Harry, A903
Levine, David, A726, B1725, B1728, B1732, B1737, B1748
Lévi-Strauss, Claude, A1011
Levy, Walter, A288
Lewicki, Zbigniew, B303
Lewis, Robert W., B1591
Lewis, Sinclair, A1158
Leys, Simon, A990
L'Heureux, John, B318
Libera Me Domine, The, review of, A1014
"Life and Death of a Modern American Rabbit, The: A Reading of John Updike's Rabbit Tetralogy," B1721
"Life Class," B966
"Life Interrupts Me Occasionally," A1199
Life of Ivy Compton-Burnett, The, review of, A943

"Life of Sundays. A," B1353
"Lifeguard," A290, B127
"Light on Your Fur: Regeneration in Updike's *Rabbit Is Rich*," B1142
"Light Switches," A619
"Light Verse: Dead but Remarkably Robust," B373
Lightman, Alan, A1141
Lilly Library, collection at, A1262
Lind, Angus, B475
"Linda Grace Hoyer Updike Papers Collection, The," A1266
Lindholm, Karl Lambert, B1629
Lindler, Barbara Anne, B1667
Lindroth, James R., B828
"Lines," A440
"Lines on the Passing of the *Jackolantern*," A442
Lingeman, Richard, A1136, B191
"Lingual Jingle, or Don, Don, The Criterion," A437
"Lion That Squeaked, The," B776
Lipsius, Frank, B888, B939
Lipsky, David, B1286
"Literally Personal," A1213
"Literary Boston: Mind Benders," B448
"Literary Dublin," A624
"Literary Giant Wipes out Seminar," B354
"Literary Note," B48
"Literary Reactions to Colonialism: A Comparative Study of Joyce Cary, Chinua Achebe and John Updike," B1053
"Literary Soirée for John Updike," B268
Literary Subversions: New American Fiction and the Practice of Criticism, B302, B587
Literatura de la tierra baldía; John Updike, B63
Literature: Art and Artifact, A291
Literature in America: An Illustrated History, B389
"Literature...A Salute to Updike and a Farewell to Cheever," B273
"Little Good in Evil, A," B249
Little Hotel, The, review of, A963
"Little Lightnings," A246
"Little Phone Magic, A," A392
"Little Poems," A26, A182
Lively, Penelope, B1135
Lives of Norman Mailer, The, B440
Lives of the Cell, The: Notes of a Biology Watcher, review of, A953
"Living Death," A1073
"Living with a Wife," A549
"Loathly Glass, The," B1349

"Local View, The," A1061
Locke, Richard, B202, B806
"Locked in a Star," B104
Lodgebloom, David, B202, B362, B741, B841, B1038, B1221
Loercher, Diana, B1061
Logu, Pietro, B18
Loitering with Intent, review of, A1030
Lolly Willowes; or, The Loving Huntsman, review of, A1012
Loneliness of the Long-Distance Runner, review of, A900
"Loneliness of the Long-Distance Runner, The," A900
Long, E. Hudson, A300
Long, Elizabeth, B754
Long and Reluctant Stasis of Wan-Li, The, review of, A1034
Long Goodbye, The, review of, A998
Long Night of Francisco Sanctis, The, review of, A1088
"Long Shadow," A569
"Long Way Home, A," A1051
"Long-Distance Runner," B1399, B1725
Long-Winded Lady, The: Notes from The New Yorker, review of, A923
Look at the Harlequins!, review of, A957
"Loosened Roots," A986
"Lord John: Publishing on the Press of Immortality," B206
Lord John Signatures, A1273
Loss of El Dorado, The, review of, A925
"Lost American Dream, The," B841
"Louise in the New World, Alice on the Magic Molehill," A1056
"Love: First Lessons," A181, A332, A507
Love Always, review of, A1076
Love and Garbage, review of, A1143
"Love as a Standoff," A921
"Love Bytes," B1231
"Love in the Garden State," B979
"Love Song, for a Moog Synthesizer," A357
"Love Sonnet," A52
Lovelorn Astronomer, The, A139
"Lovely Troubled Daughters of Our Old Crowd, The," A378
"Lovely Way Through Life, A: An Interview with John Updike," A1185
Loving, Living, Party Going; Three Novels by Henry Green, "Introduction" to, A772
"Loving the Sox," A847
Lowrey, Burling, A671
Lubbers, Klaus, B536
Lucas, Patricia E., B1668

Luce, Robert B., A681, A690
"Lucid Eye in Silver Town, The," A299
"Luckmann's 'Invisible Religion' and the Problem of Belief in Updike's Harry Angstrom," B544
Lulu in Hollywood, review of, A1045
Lurie, Alison, B386, B668, B1285, B1737
Luscher, Robert M., B393, B476, B695, B1633
"Lusting for God," B937
"Lutheran Experience in John Updike's 'Pigeon Feathers', The," B582
Lynn, Kenneth S., B1161
Lyons, Eugene, B114, B833
Lyons, Gene, B1030, B1114
"Lyric Short Story, The: The Sketch of History," B69

M. D. Anderson Library, collection at, A1264
Mabe, Chauncey, B431
"Macbech," A179
McCaffrey, Anne, A495
McCarthy, Patrick, A977
McClain, Susanne Alice, B1696
McCombe, Leonard, A868
McConnell, Frank, B237
McConnell, Lynda, B759
McCoy, Charles Robert, B1595
McCoy, Robert, A1314, B142, B144
McCray, Nancy, B1548
McCullough, David, A1182, A1184, B146, B1272
McCullough's Brief Lives: Selected 'Eye on Books' Interviews, A1182
MacCurtain, Austin, B1345
MacDonald, Craig, A1177
Macdonald, Dwight, A671
McDowell, Edwin, A1201, B1133
McEnroe, John, A800
McFarland, Ronald E., B584
McGahern, John, A1015
McGill, Deborah, B202, B984, B1028
McGuinness, Wayne D., B541
McKenzie, Alan T., B144, B746
McKowen, Clark, A8, A288
McLean, Milly, B320
McNally, T. M., A1204
McNamee, Thomas, B1492
Macnaughton, William R., B198, B249, B250, B256, B284, B504, B530, B630, B632, B634, B688, B860, B902, B946, B978, B1051, B1084
McTavish, John, A1252, B478
MacWilliam, Candia, B1346

Maddocks, Melvin, B704, B811
"Made in Heaven," A398, B996
Magaw, Malcolm O., B1005
Magazine Littéraire, interview in, A1196
Magazine notes, B6
"Magic Act of a Novelist, The," B1451
Magic Flute, The, A4, A13
Magid, Nora L., B756
"Magnanimous in a Big Way," B1457
Mahon, Derek, B882
"Mailman, The," A161, A167
Main Street, review of, A1158
Maison de Rendez-Vouz, La, review of, A916
"Making It," B1164
"Making the Spiritual Connection," A865
Malamud, Bernard, A1046
Malgudi Days, review of, A1044
Mallon, Thomas, A1207, B1116, B1410, B1745
"Man and Daughter in the Cold," A312
"Man in Relationship: A Comparative Study of Martin Luther's Theology of Man and Man as Presented in John Updike's *Rabbit, Run* and *Couples*," B1669
"Man is a Tragic Animal: John Updike's Two Novels," B602
"Man of Letters and the Pull of Visual Arts, A," B1304
"Man of Secrets," A1152
"Man Out of the Cloth, A," B927
"Man Who Became a Soprano, The," A409
"Man Who loved Extinct Mammals," A354
"Man Who Made Rabbit Run, The," B1336
"Mandarins," A1150
Manea, Norman, A1154
Manley, Will, B1448
"Manley Arts, The," B1448
Mann, Susan Garland, B1090
"Manners in the Contemporary American Novel: Studies in John Cheever, John Updike and Joan Didion," B1617
Manning, Margaret, B495
Mano, Keith, B249, B871, B902
Manuscripts, A1260-1268
"Many Bens," A850
"Maples in a Spruce Forest," A26
"Mapless Motion: Form and Space in Updike's *Rabbit, Run*," B566
"March," A451
"March: A Birthday Poem," A26
"Marching Through a Novel," A506
"Marching Through Boston," A303
Marcovaldo; or the Seasons in the City, review of, A1067

Marcus, Greil, B1151
Markle, Joyce, B129, B202, B249, B686, B1051, B1581
Markovitz, Irving, B214, B1047
"Marriage, Morality and Maturity in Updike's *Marry Me*," B1003
"Marriage Counsel," A26
"Marriage in Contemporary American Literature: The Mismatched Marriages of Manichean Minds," B288
"Marriage in the American Novel from 1882-1982," B1634
"Marriage of Mixed Blessings, A," B249, B1084
Married Men and Magic Tricks: John Updike's Erotic Heroes, B255
Marry Me, B169, B202
   criticism of, B969-B1005
   on audio tape, B1510
Marry Me: A Romance, A114-A117, A125, A126
Marshall, Steve, B449
Martin, Dell, B595
Martin, John Stephen, B548
Martine, James J., B346
Mary, review of, A927
Mary Washington College, exhibits at, A1269
Masks, review of, A1060
"Mass. Mental Health," A546
"Master Mind," B1459
"Master of Craft, A: *Odd Jobs*," B1470
"Master of Mimesis," B1217, B1237
"Materialist Look at Eros, A," A1132
Matheny, Fredrick Ross, B1684
Mating, review of, A1145
Matson, Elizabeth, B43, B598
Matson, Katinka, A1022
Matthews, John T., B329, B955
Matthews, T. S., A951
Maufort, Marc, B558, B1147
Maxwell, William, letter to, B394
May, John R., B251
Mazurek, Raymond, B563
Meade, Marion, A1104
Means, Howard, B311
"Medieval Fantasy of Courtly Love in Iris Murdoch's *A Severed Head* and John Updike *Couples*," B1682
Medigate, B1724
"Meditation on a News Item," A26
Medwick, Cathleen, B1155, B1265, B1322
Meeting at Telgte, The, review of, A1033
"Megalotopia and the Wasp Backlash: The Fiction of Mailer and Updike," B96

Mehl, Duane, B1233
"Melancholy of Storm Windows, The," A536, A553
Mellard, James M., B249, B362, B634
Meller, Horst, B620
Mellow, James R., A1152
"Melting," A523
Melville, Robert, A946
"Melville's Withdrawal," A803
"Membrane of Consciousness, A: John Updike and Point of View," B1688
"Memoirs Make a Mark," B1361
Memoirs of Hecate County, "Afterword" in, A784
"Memories of Anguilla," A488
Memories of the Ford Administration, A268, A269
  criticism of, B1475-B1498,
"*Memories of the Ford Administration*," B1475, 1476, B1478, B1496, B1563, B1579
"Memory and Hope: Why John Updike Should Receive the Novel Prize," B491
"Memory in *Pigeon Feathers*," B202
Memory Palace of Matteo Ricci, The, review of, A1074
"Memory Palaces," A1074
"Men, Women and Lovestuff. All About it," B708
"Men on the Moon: American Novelists Explore Lunar Space," B858
"Men Who Read Women's Minds," B1290
"Menagerie at Versailles in 1775, The," A26
Menand, Louis, B1411
Mercier and Camier, review of, A964
Meredith, William, A1276-1279
"Merely Fiction," B991
Merkin, Daphne, B224, B1017
Merrill, Judith, A302
Merrill, Robert, B487
Mesher, David R., B201
"Messed-Up Life, A ," A951
"Metamorphosis Through Art: John Updike's *Bech: A Book*," B792
"Metamorphosis Through Art: John Updike's 'Bech: A Book'," B249
"Metaphysical Poet for the Modern Age, A," B1212
"Metro Gate," A670
"Metropolis, Village, and Suburbia: The Short Fiction of Manners," B151
"Metropolises of the Mind," A959
Meyer, Albert R., A886
Meyer, Arlin G., B105, B143, B144, B150, B883

Meyer, Nicholas, B185
Meyer, Susan E., A1059
Michaud, Charles, B1479
"Michel Tournier," A1118
"Middle Way, The," B1498, B1748
"Middle-Aged Domesticity," B1133
"Middleness of Man, The: Ritual in the Novels of John Updike," B1572
Midpoint and Other Poems, A53-A55, A63
  criticism of, B760-B768
  jacket design of, A1287
"*Midpoint and Other Poems*," B760
"Milady Reflects," A131
"Mild Complaint, A," A802
Miller, Edwin Haviland, A1152
Miller, Jonathan, B249
Miller, Karen L., B413
Miller, Karl, B986
Miller, Lewis M., B1567
Miller, Miriam Youngerman, B316
Miller, Perry, A720
Miller, Roger, A1209
Milton, Edith, B1294
"Milton Adapts Genesis: Collier Adapts Milton," A944
Milton's Paradise Lost: Screenplay for Cinema of the Mind, review of, A944
"Mime," A526
"Mimesis--You Can't Beat It: Die neuartige Traditionalität des John Updike," B379
"Mind Benders: Out of Step," B1149
Ming Dynasty in Decline, The, review of, A1034
Minor Apocalypse, A, review of, A1060
"Minority Report," A52
Minutes of the Last Meeting, A78
"Minutes of the Last Meeting," A365
Miracle of the Rose, The, review of, A916
Mirror After Mirror. Reflections on Woman, "Introduction" to, A764
"Mirrors of Self, The: Female Characters Used as Metaphor for the Great Mother in *Lolita*, *Herzog*, and *Rabbit, Run*," B1719
"Mischievous Monet, A," A246
Miss Herbert, review of, A976
"Miss Moore at Assembly," A52
"Mr. High-Mind," A26, A182
"Mr. Nice Guy," B1747
Mr. Palomar, review of, A1079
"Mr. Updike, I'm Your Biggest Fan," B454
"Mr. Updike's Avian Error," B485
"Mr. Updike's Fakery," B702
"Mr. Updike's Planet," B359, B1230, B1734

Index 309

"Mrs. Wesley R. Updike Sees Son Become Novelist of High Stature," B7
Mitchell, Sidney H., library of, A1269
"Mites," A601
Mitgang, Herbert, A1199
Miura, Kiyohiro, A82
"Mixed Reports from the Interior," A1009
Mizener, Arthur, B202, B249
"Mobile of Birds," A26
"Mocking Feminism," B1190
"Mod Masses, Empty Pews," B922
"Mode and Meaning in the Novels of John Updike," B1602
"Model Citizens and Marginal Cases Heroes of the Day," B1037
"Moderate, The," A26
"Modern Americans-I," A435
"Modern Art," A700
"Modern Art: Always Offensive to Orthodoxy," A864
Modern Critical Views: John Updike, B 741
Modern Fiction Studies, B144, B233, B338
"Modern Lust, Historic Love: Hard Lessons from Updike," B1480
"Modern Pilgrims, The: Marriage and the Self in the World of John Updike," B1598
"Modern Torments," B1074
"Modernist, Postmodernist, What Will They Think of Next?" A1067
"Modest Mound of Bones, A," A26
"Modigliani's Death Mask," A26
Moenegal, Emir, A1042
Moment of True Feeling, A, review of, A988
"Mom's Troubles at an Ashram," B1273
Mon, review of, A1047
"Monet Isn't Everything: An Orgy of Impressionism in Boston," A872
"Monk Manque, A," A962
Monnier-Brousse, Françoise, B1002
"Monologue of a Broadway Actress," translation of, A1282
"Monologue of a Polar Fox on an Alaska Fur Farm," translation of, A1282
"Monologue of an American Poet," translation of, A1282
"Montes Veneris," A638
Month of Sundays, A, A100-A104, A118, A119, A184, B202, B249, B1696
criticism of, B910-B959
on audio tape, B1511
"Month of Sundays, A," A348, B917, B925
"*Month of Sundays, A*," B926, B929, B933, B940
"*Month of Sundays, A*, by John Updike," B945

"*Month of Sundays, A*: Scarlet Letters," B202
Montrose, David, B1181
Moons of Jupiter, The, A215
"Moons of Jupiter, The," A563
Moore, Harry T., B610
Moore, Jack B., B1054
Moraes, Dom, B501
"Moral Ambiguity in John Updike's Short Stories," B1595
"Morality Play," A674
Moramarco, Fred, B367, B1218
Morand, Paul, A1067
Moravia, Alberto, A960
More Stately Mansions, A232
woodcut in, A1302
"More Stately Mansions," A385
on audio tape, B1500
"More Than You Are Dreamt of in Your Philosophy," B1027
Morey-Gaines, Ann-Janine, B314, B551, B1229
Morgan, Berry, A910
Morgan, Bill, A1250
Morgan, Darla J., A1191
Morgan, Fred, A291, A460
Morgan, Roy J., B91
Morgan's Passing, review of, A1021
Moritz, Charles, B36, B304
Morning, Noon and Night, review of, A919
"Morocco," A374
Morra-Yoe, Janet, A882
Morris, Margery, A291
Morris, Wright, A961
Morrissey, Daniel, B929
Morse, J. Mitchell, B675
"Mort, amour et religion dans *Marry Me*," B1002
"Mortal Games," A949
Mortimer, Penelope, A1077
Moscow Circles, review of, A1049
"Mosquito," A26
"Most Original Book The," A1024
"Most Unforgettable Character I've Met," A822
"Mostly Glass," A691
"Mother of Updike Dies at 85," B408
"Mother Shows Writing Runs in the Family," B8
"Mother's Boy," B663
"Motlier Than Ever" A957
"Motley But True", A957
Mouchette, review of, A913
Mount, Ferdinand, B997
"Mountain Impasse," A26

"Mouse Trappings," A623
"Mouths of Babes, The: Childhood Epiphany in Roth's 'Conversion of the Jews' and Updike's 'Pigeon Feathers'," B593
"Movie House," A26
Movies and videos, B428, B489, B490, B1522-B1561, B1529-B1553
"Moving Along," A246
Mozolak, Harvey S., B1669
Mphahlele, Ezekiel, A932
Mudrick, Marvin, B834
Mulisch, Harry, A1081, A1119
"Munich," A589
Munif, Abdelrahman, A1109
Muradian, Thaddeus, B32
Murdoch, Iris, A728, A958, A1029, A1058, A1085, A1097
Murphy, Francis, A283, A353, A540
Murphy, Michael, A936
Murphy, Richard W., B10
Murray, James G., B1033, B1067
Murray, John, B780
Murray, Michele, B87, B716, B816
Murtaugh, Daniel M., B1069
Murtaugh, Dennis M., B1113
Museums and Women, A105, A169, B144, B202
   cover photograph of, A1295
"Museums and Women," A309
Museums and Women and Other Stories, A79-A80, A84, A85, A185
   criticism of, B866-B893
"*Museums and Women and Other Stories*," B866
Music, works used in, A220, A588, B483, B1566-B1568
"Music Professor, Updike Pair up for Composition," B483
"Music School: A Dance with John Updike's Poetry," B1715
Music School, The, A29-A33, A64, A88, A160, B202
   criticism of, B670-B693
"*Music School, The*," B672, B685
"Music School, The," B1557
   on audio tape, B1499
   on film strip, B1554
   on videotape, B1523, B1525
"*Music School, The*: A Place of Resonance," B202
"Musical Beds," B709
"Musings on a Much-Mocked President," B1484
Mustache, The, review of, A1106

Mutrux, Robert, A799
Mutter, John, B1238
"M&W&OS," B910
"My Children at the Dump at Ipswich," A472
My Days, review of, A955
"'My Mind Was Without a Shadow'," A917
My Travel Diary, review of, A924
My Well-Balanced Life on a Wooden Leg, "Foreword" to, A880
Myers, David, B624
Myrin Library, collection at, A1266
Mysack, Joe, B1174
Mysteries, review of, A930
"Mystery of Mickey Mouse, The," A890
"Myth and Magic," B678
"Myth and Narrative, The Nature of the Tale and the Name of the Teller," B638
Myth Makers, The, review of, A1008
"Mythic Dimensions in Updike's Fiction," B136
Mythology in the Modern Novel: A Study of Prefigurative Techniques, B623

Nabokov, Vladimir, A787, A904, A914, A922, A927, A934, A940, A957, A973, A1035, A1092, A1121, A1256, B130, B394, B510
"Nabokov's Look Back: A National Loss," A914
Nabokov-Wilson Letters, The: Correspondence Between Vladimir Nabokov and Edmund Wilson, 1940-1971, review of, A1007
Nadeau, Robert, B232
Nadon, Robert Joseph, B1574
Nageswara, G., B274
Nagler, Michael, A353
Nahal, Chaman, B752
Naipaul, Shiva, A1009
Naipaul, V. S., A925, A1006, A1009
"Naked Ape, The," A490
"Nakedness," A346
Name of the Rose, The, review of, A1058
Naomi, review of, A1079
Narayan, R. K., A955, A975, A1044
"Narrativa di John Updike, La," B18
"Narrative Continuity in Updike's *Too Far To Go*," B1088
"Narrator Then and Now in Updike's FLIGHT, The," B577
"Naslage cudesa u stvarnosti pesnistva," B277
Nathaniel Hawthorne in His Times, review of, A1152
"National Book Awards," B20, B24, B613

Index 311

National Book Awards for Fiction, The: An Index to the First Twenty-Five Years, B633
"National Book Awards Judges Announce Leading Contenders," B21, B611
"National Book Critics Salute Best of '90," B444
"Native Fathers," B479
Natural Law and Right in Contemporary American Middle-Class Literature, B377
Nature's Diary, review of, A1089
"NBCC Announces Award Winners," B307
"NBCC Awards: All Present and Eloquent," B308
Neal, William Ray, B1604
Neary, John M., B402, B438, B564, B642
"Necessity of Myth in Updike's *The Centaur*, The," B626
"Neither out Far nor in Deep: Religion and Suburbia in the Fiction of John Cheever, John Updike, and Walker Percy," B321
Nelson, Barbara, B770
Nelson, Doris L., B1579
Nelson, Margaret Lorraine, B1707
Nelson, Victoria, A1110
Nemioanu, Virgil, B140
"Neoteny," A634
Nerney, Brian James, B1630
Nesset, Michael Paul, B1610
Nesvisky, Matthew, A1179
"Neuen Heiligen, Die," A26, A56
"Nevada," A344
"Never on Sunday," B249, B946
"New Books in Review: Eight Recent Novels," B1035
New Critical Essays, review of, A1023
"New Fiction," B609
New Gods, The, review of, A962
"New Meliorism, A," A953
"New Novel by Berksman Wins Praise of Critics," B516
"New Novels," B679, B737
"New Novels: Meditations," B680
New Oxford Book of Christian Verse, The, review of, A1041
"New Updike, The," B782
"I: New Writing: Novels and Short Stories," B1297
"New York Elegy," translation of, A1282
New York Times Book Review, interview in, A1175
New Yorker, The
  as clipping repository, A1268
"Notes and Comment" column, A640-A744 passim, A841

"Newlyweds, The," A26
Newman, Charles, A738
Newman, Judie, B383, B424
"News from the Underworld," A528
"Newsmakers," B70, B103
"Nice Tries," A1116
"Nicholas Richardson on John Updike," B120, B839
Nichols, Lewis, A1161
"Nicholson Baker Writes about the Updike He Imagines," B456
"Nicholson Baker's *U and I*," B455
Nickens, Susan Jean, B1622
"Night Flight, Over Ocean," A131
"Night Table Reading: Who Reads What Between the Sheets," A1197
Nightmare of Reason, The: A Life of Franz Kafka, review of, A1063
Nims, John Frederick, A450
"Nine Lives of Literary Realism, The," B360
"1957-1968: Toward Diversity of Forms," B287
"1960-1980: Experiment and Tradition," B285
"No Dearth of Death," A1037
"No Dodo," A657
No Man's Land, review of, A1120
"No More Mr. Knightleys," A1068
"No One Can Escape the Predator," B410, B411
"No Problem," B1466
No Return, review of, A1139
"No Use Talking," A690
"Nobody Gets Away with Everything," A1148
"Nobody Is God," B1132
"Non-Fiction Digest: *Odd Jobs*," B1458
"Non-Slip Polish," B1181
"Non-Traditional Novelist, The," A1220
Nordell, Roderick, B1021
Nordloh, David J., B382
Norman, Gurney, A937
North of South: An African Journey, review of, A1009
"Northeast News: White-Bread Slices of Life," B1254
Northouse, Cameron, B396
"'Not Only'--An Examination of Abstraction in the Writings of John Updike, With Particular Emphasis on the Olinger Narratives," B1597
"Not Quite Adult," A1136
"Note," in *Three Texts from Early Ipswich*, A720
"Note on Character in *The Centaur*, A," B202

"Note on Updike's 'Ex-Basketball Player', A," B497, B600
"Note to the Previous Tenants," A522
"Noted with Pleasure," B1339
"Notes and Comment" (*New Yorker* column), A640-A744 passim, A841
"Notes on Current Books," B725, B832
"Notes on People," B190
"Notes on the Novel-as-Autobiography," B227
Nothing Happens in Carmincross, review of, A1077
"Nothing is Easy," A1038
"Nothing to Declare," B1329
Novak, Michael, B202, B249, B727
"Novel as Lyric Elegy, The: The Mode of Updike's *The Centaur*," B249, B362, B634
"Novel as Parody of Popular Narrative Forms in the United States and Latin America, The: 1963-1980," B1631
"Novel of Disentanglement, The: A Thematic Study of Lewis's *Babbitt*, Bromfield's *Mr. Smith* and Updike's *Rabbit, Run*," B1571
"Novel of the Narcissus, The," B997
Novel with Cocaine, review of, A1084
"Novela Extranjera en España, La: *El Libro de Bech*, de John Updike," B795
"Novelist as Poet, The: John Updike," B274
"Novelist Updike Sees a Nation Frustrated by its Own Dreams," A1217
"Novelistica de John Updike, La," B125
"Nuda Natens," A52
Nunley, Jan, A1218
Nuns and Soldiers, review of, A1029
Nyham, David, B488
Nyren, Dorothy, B161

"Oasis," A673
Oates, Joyce Carol, A809, A876, A1102, B156, B202, B249, B362, B1029, B1378
"Obfuscating Coverage," A679
"Objects of Love," B1316
O'Briant, Don, B1422, B1426, B1474
O'Brien, Flann, A974
O'Brien, Tim, A994
"Observer Observed, The," B1352
Ockenga, Starr, A764
O'Connell, Shawn, B849
O'Connor, John J., B1529
O'Connor, William Van, B610
Odd Jobs, criticism of, B1449-B1474
"*Odd Jobs*," B1449, B1471
on audio tape, B1553

Odd Jobs: Essays and Criticism, A264, A265, A270
"Preface" to, A885
"*Odd Jobs: Essays and Criticism*," B1552
Oddly Lovely Day Alone, An, A145
"Odds and Ends of John Updike," B1453
"Ode, An," A26
"Ode II.ii: Horace," A26
"Ode to Crystallization," A583
"Ode to Entropy," A584
"Ode to Evaporation," A578
"Ode to Growth," A574
"Ode to Healing," A575
"Ode to Rot," A582
"Oedipal Angstrom," B562
"Oedipal Conflict in the Novels of John Updike, The," B1670
"Of a Linotype Operator at the Edge of Obsolescence," B802
"Of All Men the Most Miserable: A Study of Two Ministers in the Works of John Updike," B1716
"Of Beauty and Consternation," A981
"Of Heresy and Loot," A980
Of Love and Shadows, review of, A1099
"Of Sickened Times," A1154
"Of the Breezeway," B1723
Of the Farm, A23, A34, A44, A89, A90, A106, A235, B76, B202, B249
criticism of, B658-B669
Czech edition, "Introduction" to, A719
on audio tape, B1512
"*Of the Farm*," B658, B660
"Off-Centaur," B249
Ogle, Jane, A1168
"Oh, What the Hex," B1192
Oh What a Paradise It Seems, review of, A1040
O'Hara, John, A845, A851, A1000
"Ohio," A543
"Old and Precious," A661
"Old Cager, Still Running, The," B811
"Old Fashioned Lightning Rod," A26
Old Gringo, The, review of, A1083
"Old Manager at Home, The," B797
"Old Tobacconist, The," A461
"Old World Wickedness," A1092
"Old-Fashioned Novel, An," A1015
Oldsey, Bernard, B824
Olinger Stories, criticism of, B694, B695
Olivas, Michael A., B105, B143, B144, B150
Olson, Clarence E., B1340, B1379, B1465, B1480
Olster, Stacey, B1434

Index 313

"On a Spree with Updike," B964
"On an Island," A504
"On Being a Dud," B1358
On Clowns: The Dictator and the Artist, review of, A1154
"On Creativity," A725
"On Hawthorne's Mind," A1002, A1028
"On John Updike and 'The Music School'," B686
On Meeting Authors, A45
On Moral Fiction, comment on, A775
"On Moral Fiction," B179
"On Not Rocking the Boat," B786
"On One's Own Oeuvre," A1189
"On Such a Beautiful Green Little Place," A1040
On the Black Hill, review of, A1050
On the Boundary, review of, A908
"On the Edge of Being," B784
"On the Inclusion of Miniature Dinosaurs in Breakfast Cereal Boxes," A52
On the Move, A236
"On the Recently Minted Hundred-Cent Piece," A603
"On the Sidewalk (After Reading, at Long Last, *On the Road*, by Jack Kerouac)," A671
"One Big Interview," A1162, A1172
"One Critic's Fiction," B580
"102 Vie for 10 National Book Awards," B118
One Hundred Years of Solitude, review of, A933
"One More Interview," A387
"One of My Generation," A320
"One of the Best of Escape Clauses," B475
"One Small Shelf for Literature," A1207
"$1,250 for the Updike," B191
"One's Neighbors's Wife," A161, A167
"One-Year-Old, The," A26, A182
Only Problem, The, review of, A1065
"Only Skin-Deep," B1359
O'Nolan, Brian, A964
Onward and Upward: A Biography of Katharine S. White, review of, A1098
"Onward with Updike," B673
"Open Letter to Voyager 2, The," A611
"Open Mind, Full Book," B962
"Operatic Surface, Deep Politics," B1044
Operation Shylock: A Confession, review of, A1157
"Ordinary People," B1122
Oriard, Michael, B252

"Origin of Laughter (After Desmond Morris), The," A491
"'Original Ending' of *Self-Consciousness*, The," A867
Origins: The Lives and Worlds of Modern Cosmologists, review of, A1141
"Orphaned Swimming Pool, The," A325
"Orthodontia," A607
Oster, Daniel, B1184, B1207
"Other, The," A389
Other Inquisitions, review of, A906
Other John Updike, The, B246, B254, B261, B272, B284
"*Other John Updike, The*, by Donald Greiner," B261
Other John Updike, The: Poems/Short Stories/Prose/Play, B230
Other People's Worlds, review of, A1029
"Other Side of the Street, The," A424
"Other Woman, The," A401
Ott, William A., B960
Ouologuem, Yambo, A932
"Our Own Baedeker," A649, A664
Ousmane, Sembene, A985
"Out of Harm's Way," B1347
"Out of the Glum Continent," A932
"Outdoor Art," A652
"Outdoor Vermeer, An," A246
"Overheard in Widener," A436
Overmyer, Janet, B575
Owens, Philip Lamar, B1670
"Oxford, Thirty Years After," A590
Ozick, Cynthia, B362, B789

"Packed Dirt, Churchgoing, A Dying Cat, A Traded Car," A293, B586
letter on, A1246
Paglia, Camille, A1153
"Pain," (Dimitrova), translation of, A1276
"Pain," (Updike), A570
Painter of Signs, The, A975
"Painterly Aspects of John Updike's Fiction, The," B1644
Paintings, A1301
"Pair of Parrots, A," A1075
"Pal, The," A161, A167
"Pale Bliss," A131
Pally, Erwin, B1605
Palmer, Kate S., B1735
Pamuk, Orhan, A1143
"Pantsing," B882
"Papa's Sad Testament," A926
"Paperbacks," B878, B1446, B1447
"Parade, The," A399

"Paradise Lost," B995
"Paradox of Language and Form of Contemporary Fiction, The," B1652
Paravisini, Lizabeth, B1631
Park, Edwards, B171
Parker, Hershel, A283, A353, A540
Parodies, B1723, B1724
Parrot's Perch, review of, A1075
"Part of the Process," A410
Partch, Ken, B592
"Party Knee," A26
Passacaglia, review of, A1014
"Passion of Graham Greene, The," A1131
"Passionate Cleric, The," B921
"Pastoral," A580
"Pastoral and Anti-Pastoral Patterns in John Updike's Fiction," B1576
Pastoral and Anti-Pastoral Patterns in John Updike's Fiction, B100, B105, B122
Patanjali, V. V. R., B330, B639
"Patriarchy, Ideology, Subjectivity: Towards a Theory of Feminist Cultural Studies," B1643
Patrick, D. L., B368
Patriotism, Inc., and Other Tales, review of, A935
"Patterns of Sacralization: Mark Twain, Faulkner, Hemingway, and Updike," B1585
Patterson, Jack, B1125
Pauck, Marion, A1005
Pauck, Wilhelm, A1005
Paul Tillich: His Life and Thought, Volume I: Life, review of, A1005
Pauley, Jane, A1237
Paulin, Tom, B1044
Pawel, Ernest, A1063
Pawley, Daniel W., B1140
"Pe' Pourrie, Un," A1006, A1009
Pear Like a Potato, A, A220, B483
"Pear Like a Potato, A," A588, B1568
Peary, Gerald, B186, B543
Peden, William, B151
Pencil, The, review of, A1126
"Pendulum," A182
Penninger, Frieda, B629
"Pen Pals," B407
Pens and Needles: Literary Caricatures, "Introduction" to, A726
"Penumbrae," A560
Penzler, Otto M., A739
"People Books & Book People," A1184
People in the News, B436
"People One Knows," A767

People One Knows:Interview with Insufficiently Famous Americans, A161, A167
"Perceptions and Reflections: The Short Story Art of John Updike," B1607
"Perennial Promises Kept," B270, B1153, B1730
Perez-Minik, Domingo, B795
"Perfection Wasted," A614
Perfume: The Story of a Murderer, review of, A1092
Perisho, Steve, B597
Perkins, George, A300
Perosa, Sergio, B97
Perry, Alice H., B589
"Personal History: A Soft Spring Night in Shillington," A823
    drawing for, A1307
"Personal History: At War with my Skin," A827
    drawing for, A1308
"Personally Speaking," A1216
Perunilam, Thomas Varkey, B1623
Petals of Blood, review of, A1009
Peter, H., B249
Peters, Edmund Richard, B1661
Petersburg, review of, A998
Petersen, Clarence, B1363, B1446
Petillon, Pierre-Yves, B76, B309
Petit, Norman, A912
"Petit Monde de John Updike, Le," B77
Petrarca, Anthony J., B1671
Petroski, Henry, A1126, A1156
Petter [sic], Henri, B66
Pettingell, Phoebe, B720
Pfeiffer, John E, A1048
"Phantom Life," A931
Phelps, Robert, A1026
"Phenomena," A517
"Phenomenonological Criticism: An Analysis and an Application to the Fiction of John Updike," B1596
Phi Beta Kappa Poem, Harvard, 1973, A91
Phillips, Robert, B883
"Philological," A26
Philosopher's Pupil, The, review of, A1058
Photographs
    by Updike, A1295, A1296
    of Updike, B1564, B1565
"Physiologist's Holiday," A662
Picked-Up Pieces, A107-A110, A120
    criticism of, B960-B968
    "Foreword" to, A758
    on audio tape, B1513

Pickering, James H., A291, A353, A460, A554
"Picking Up the Pieces," B1043
Piercy, Marge, A928
Pierrot Mon Ami, review of, A1106
Pigeon, The, review of, A1106
Pigeon Feathers, A5, A9, A24, A90, A146, A1323, A1326, B202
   criticism on, B567-B597
"Pigeon Feathers," A292, B567, B1543
   on videotape, B1528
Pigeon Feathers and Other Stories, A69, A170, B76
"Pigeon Feathers and Witches," B352, B1206
"Pilgrim's Progress," A1155
Pincus, Cynthia, B636
"Pinget," A1014
Pinget, Robert, A916, A1014, A1056, A1097
Pinsker, Sanford, B406, B467, B799, B945
Pinter, Harold, A993
"Pinter's Unproduced Proust Printed," A993
Plagman, Linda M., B749, B1598
"Planting a Mail Box," A26
"Plastic Menagerie, The," A272
Plath, James Walter, B1644
"Plato's 'Allegory of the Cave' in *Rabbit, Run*," B540
"Play in *Couples*," B202, B751
"Play in Tarbox," B707
"Play It Sam--Fast!" B1432
"*Playboy*'s Annual Awards: Best Major Work: *Rabbit Is Rich*," B1127
"*Playboy*'s Annual Awards: Best Short Story: 'Killing'," B1012, B1245
"Player Piano," A26, A182, A450
Players, review of, A994
"Playing with Dynamite," A428
Plays, A272-A274
"Pleasure of Textual/Sexual Wrestling, The: Pornography and Heresy in *Roger's Version*," B1242
Pleasure of the Text, The, review of, A967
Plimpton, George, A124, A305, A681, A833, A846, A1297
Plourde, Ferdinand, J., Jr., B1575
"Plow Cemetery," A565
"Plumbing," A327
"Plying a Periplus," B1175
Pochoda, Elizabeth, B831, B1124
Podhoretz, Norman, B1271
"Poem for a Far Land," A480
Poems, A430-A638
Poet Assassinated, The, review of, A1064
"Poetess," A26

"Poetic Precision, Prose Breadth," B1039
"Poetry from Downtroddendom," A900
"Poetry in the Classroom: 'Ex-Basketball Player'," B493
"Poetry Poorly Served," A869, A1251
"Poetry's Nouvelle Cuisine," A586
Poets and Writers, interview in, A1215
Poirier, Richard, A289, A300
"Poisoned in Nassau," A525
"Poker Night," A394
   on audio tape, B1501
"Polina and Aleksei and Anna and Losnitsky," A941
Polish Complex, The, review of, A1049
"Politics of Art, The," B192
Politics of Reflexivity, The, B554
Polk, Noel, B329
Pollitt, Katha, B1195, B1322
Pomeroy, Charles W., B1584
"Pompeii," A52
"Pooem," A26
"Poor Chap...," A431
Poorhouse Fair, The, A2, A14, A25, A46, A127, A206, A207, B81, B202, B249
   criticism of, B498-B504
   "Foreword" to, A704, A1256
   "Introduction" to, A766, A817
   on audio tape, B1514
   work sheets for, A1256, A1259
"*Poorhouse Fair, The*: A Fragile Vision of Specialness," B202
"*Poorhouse Fair, The*: Updike's Thesis Statement," B249, B504
"Pop Smash, Out of Echo Chamber," A26
"Pop/Mom/Moon," A328
"Popular Revivals, 1956," A26
"Population of Argentina, The," A26, A182
"Porky's Plaint," B790
Pornografia, review of, A915
Pornographer, The, review of, A1015
Port of Saints, review of, A1022
Porte, Joel, A202, A821
Porter, Gilbert, B558, B576, B1147
"Portrait of the Artist as a Jewish Intellectual," B781
"Postal Complaints," A655, A665
"Postcards from Soviet Cities: Moscow, Kiev, Leningrad, Yerevan," A482
"Post-Impressionist Wives," A496
Postman, Andrew, B1539
"Post-Pill Paradise Lost: *Couples*," B202, B362
"Post-Pill Paradise Lost: John Updike's *Couples*," B741
Pottle, Frederick A., A992

"Povestiri de John Updike," B140
Powers, Katherine A., B448, B1149
Powers, Meredith, B1645
"Praising and Sharing," B967
"Precise Language," A712, A1244
"Pre-Expulsion Yellow," A647
"Preface"
  to *Hub Fans Bid Kid Adieu*, A768
  to *Odd Jobs: Essays and Criticism*, A885
"Préface à l'Edition Française," *La Condition Naturelle (Facing Nature)*, A848
"Preface to a Partial Catalogue of My Own Leavings," A836
Prescott, Peter S., B807, B873, B897, B921, B973, B1015, B1098, B1186, B1334, B1384
"Presenting the Past," B801
"Presidential Timbre" Updike's Resonating Prose Gives Shape to Some Capital Ideas," B1485
Price, Andrew Jude, B1647
Price, Martin, B202
Price, R. G. G., B679, B737
"Price of Finesse, The," B1167
"Primal Modern, A," A972
Primitive Erotic Art, review of, A946
Prishvin, Mikhail, A1089
"Prishvin's Nature," A1089
Pritchard, William H., A283, A353, A540, B726, B859, B991, B1077, B1100, B1232, B1328
Pritchett, V. S., A1008, A1111, A1151, B1115
"Private Vice of John Updike, The," B35, B362
"Pro, The," A305
"Problem of the Self in the Contemporary American Realistic Novel, The: The Self and Morality in the Postwar Novel," B324
"Problems," A356
Problems and Other Stories, A147, A148, A162, A171
  criticism of, B1058-B1081
  jacket design of, A1290
"*Problems and Other Stories*," B1058, B1062-B1064, B1067, B1069
"Problems of John Updike, The," B1066
"Process and the Lock, The," A1063
"Professional Image, The: *Odd Jobs*," B1469
"Professional Observers: Cozzens to Updike," B128
"Professional Viewpoint, The," A1164
"Professional's Suite," B501
"Professor Harlow Shapley Warbles the Praises of Natural Sciences 115," A438

"Professor Nabokov," A787
"Profile of a Literary Hustler," B87
"Prolegomena to the Study of Fictional *Dreck*," B187
"Promises Made and Broken," B984
"Promising," A901
Prose, Francine, B1290
Proud Happiness: Details of a Sunset and Other Stories, review of, A973
Proust Screenplay, The, review of, A993
Pryce-Jones, David, A1066
"Psalmist and the Astronomer, The," B471
"Psoriasis and All," B461
"Psycholinguistics of Updike's 'Museums and Women', The," B144, B890
"Psychologie und religiose Typologie bei John Updike," B247, B327
"Publication Award Won by Updike," B264
"Publius Vergilius Maro, The Madison Avenue Hick," A26
Puer Aeternus: An Examination of John Updike's Rabbit, Run, B532
Puig, Manuel, A1148
"Pulitzer Prizes in Letters Go to Updike and Simon," B1436
"Punch Lines," B1251
Pursuit, review of, A910
"Pursuit of Permanence, The: A Study of the Thematic Structure of John Updike's Novels," B1593
Pushkin House, review of, A1108
"Pussy," A131
Putney, Michael, B804, B899
"Put-Ons and Take-Offs: Contemporary Furniture that Parodies or Pays Homage to the Classics," A870
"Pygmalion," A379
Pym, Barbara, A1004
"Pynchon, Hawkes, and Updike: Readers and the Paradox of Accessibility," B297

Qiu, Maoru, B1081
"Quarterly Fiction Review," B1300
Quartet in Autumn, review of, A1004
"Queen's Jewels," A415
Queneau, Raymond, A929, A949, A989, A1030, A1036, A1106
Quennell, Peter, A1066
Query, A98
"Quest for Belief: Theme in the Novels of John Updike," B74
"Quest for Freedom in the Novels of John Updike, The," B1680

"Quest for Order in 'Pigeon Feathers': Updike's Use of Christian Mythology," B591
"Quest Theme in John Updike's Early Novels, The," B1695
"Questing Fear, The: Christian Allegory in John Updike's *The Centaur*," B624
Question of Hu, The, review of, A1115
"Question of Updike, The," B662
"Questions Concerning Giacomo," A918
Quillen, Frank W., B1672
"Quilt," A182
Quinn, Anthony, B1401
Quinn, Edward, A288
Quinn, Sally, B748

Ra'ad, Basem, B448
Raban, Jonathan, A1018, B249, B787, B1380, B1742
"'Rabbit, Gun': Linguistic Evidence of Harry Angstrom's Self Delusion," B542
"Rabbit, Jog," B1116
Rabbit, Run, A3, A6, A15, A25, A65, A74, A82, A94, A128, A189, A260, A1221, B71, B76, B169, B249, B1571, B1669, B1671, B1683-B1685, B1692, B1696, B1697, B1699, B1719
  criticism of, B516-B566, B1442, B1444
  film of, B65, B67, B68, B72, B88, B90
  "Foreword" to, A704
  jacket design of, A1285
  on audio tape, B1518, B1531
  on film, B1522
  work sheets for, A1256
"*Rabbit, Run*," B311
"Rabbit, Run," B527
"*Rabbit, Run*: A Reconsideration," B1685
"*Rabbit, Run*: An Image of Life," B521
"*Rabbit, Run*: John Updike's Criticism of the 'Return to Nature'," B249
"*Rabbit, Run* and *A Tale of Peter Rabbit*," B528
"'Rabbit, Run' Auditions to Begin Here," B67
"'Rabbit, Run' Author Blending of Parents, Says *Eagle* Writer after Meeting Updikes," B71
"'Rabbit, Run' Author Slows Down," B320
"'Rabbit, Run' Role Runs Into a Warren," B68
"Rabbit Angstrom, I presume?" B1031
"Rabbit Angstrom and the Changing of the American Man," B1722

"Rabbit Angstrom as a Religious Sufferer," B534
"Rabbit Angstrom's Spiritual Homelessness," B1665
"Rabbit Angstrom's Unseen World," B202
Rabbit at Rest, A255-A259, A1210-A1212, A1335
  criticism of, B1367-B1448
  excerpt from, A418
  interview about, A1239, A1244
  jacket design of, A1294
  on audio tape, B1515, B1548-B1550
"Rabbit at Rest," A417, B1368, B1393, B1745, B1546
"*Rabbit at Rest*," B1371, B1372, B1382, B1385, B1386, B1398, B1408, B1427, B1443
"Rabbit Brought Nowhere: John Updike's *Rabbit Redux*," B852
"Rabbit Depressing," B1406
"Rabbit Elbows Through the '80s," B1389
"'Rabbit' Finale Isn't 'Depressed'," B1396
"Rabbit Grows Up: The Adamic Theme in *Rabbit Redux*," B1690
"'Rabbit' Hops into Oblivion with Tale Between Legs," B1390
"Rabbit in Retirement," B1416
"Rabbit in the Rough," B298, B1731
"Rabbit is Buying Krugerrands," B1104
"Rabbit is Dead," B1411
"Rabbit is Good," B1383
"Rabbit is Mortal, But is the U.S.?" B1405
"Rabbit is Racist," B864
Rabbit Is Rich, A172-A176, A186-A188, A260, B1111, B1112
  criticism of, B1091-B1149, B1442, B1444
  jacket design of, A1292
  on audio tape, B1516
  work sheets for, A1256
"Rabbit Is Rich," A380, B1128, B1131
"*Rabbit Is Rich*," B1134
"*Rabbit Is Rich* and So's Updike," B1143
"*Rabbit Is Rich* as a Naturalistic Novel," B1148
"*Rabbit is Rich* Wins American Book Award," B1138
"Rabbit Loses the Race: John Updike's 'Small Answer of a Texture'," B462, B1442, B1746
Rabbit Omnibus, A, A260
"Rabbit Punch," B829
"Rabbit Pursuit: A Passion for Updike," B460
"Rabbit Ran," B1444
"Rabbit 'Re-docks': Updike's Inner Space Odyssey," B853

Rabbit Redux, A70-A73, A79, A91, A176, A177, A260, A1221, B144, B189, B249, B1683, B1690, B1692
    criticism of, B800-B865, B1442, B1444
    jacket design of, A1289
    on audio tape, B1517
    work sheets for, A1256
"Rabbit Redux," B813, B817, B825
"Rabbit Redux," B828
"*Rabbit Redux*: 'Freedom is Made of Brambles'," B249, B860
"*Rabbit Redux*; Time/Order/God," B144, B850
"*Rabbit Redux* Reduced: Rededicated? Redeemed?" B855
"Rabbit Rerun: Updike's Replay of Popular Culture in *Rabbit at Rest*," B1434
"Rabbit Resplendent," B1108
"Rabbit Restored: A Further Note on Updike's Revisions," B549
"Rabbit Returns," B1097
"Rabbit Returns: Updike Was Always There-- It's Time We Noticed," B806
"Rabbit Revised," B552
"Rabbit Rides Again," B1098
"Rabbit Run to Earth," B824
"Rabbit Runs Down," B186, B543, B1387, B1421
"Rabbit Runs in Circles," B816
"Rabbit Ruts," B1099
"Rabbit Stew," B425, B1369, B1741
"'Rabbit' Takes Leap into the Hereafter," B1376
"Rabbit Tetralogy, The: From Solitude to Society to Solitude Again," B565
"Rabbit to Roger: Updike's Rockin' Version," B557
"Rabbit Underground," B854, B1091
"'Rabbit' Wins Again," B1435
"'Rabbit' Wins Updike 2nd Pulitzer," B1437
"Rabbit Won," B262
"Rabbit's Evening Out," A330
"Rabbit's Faith: Grace and the Transformation of the Heart," B548
"Rabbit's Last Run," B1380, B1742
"Rabbit's Progress," B202
"Rabbit's Reckoning," B1388
"Rabbits Remembered," B849
"Rabbit's Run," B1409, B1424, B1744
"Rack of Paperbacks, A," A26
Radiant Way, The, review of, A1101
Radio reviews, B1562, B1563
Raine, Craig, B1201, B1313
Raining at Magens Bay, A129

"Raining at Magens Bay," A532
Rainstorms and Fire, B131
Raith, Mark Allan, B273
"Raman and Daisy and Olivia and the Nawab," A975
Rambaud, Maurice, A388
Rasmussen, David, B1567
"Rational Faith," A1054
"Rats," A538
Ravenel, Shannon, A371, A384, A402, A816
Rawson, Philip, A946
Raymo, Chet, B471
Raymont, Henry, A1221, B118, B800
"Read All About It: *Rabbit at Rest*," B1384
"Reader, Run," B1308
Reader's Advisor, The: A Layman's Guide to Literature, B348
"Readers and Writers," A1033
"Reading at Rest?" B1417
"Reading for Pleasure: Chiron in Pa.," B605
Reading Public Library, as book repository, A1267
"Reading Updike," B370, B1235
Ready, Richard Michael, B1597
Real Life of Alejandro Mayta, The, review of, A1083
"Reality, Imagination, and Art: The Significance of Updike's 'Best Story'," B249, B688
Realms of Gold, The, review of, A968
"Rebecca Cune: Updike's Wedge Between the Maples," B514
Reber, Carole, B71
Recent American Fiction, B570
"Recent Fiction," B844, B1135
"Recent Fiction II," B1202
"Recent Novels: Realism Redux," B999
Recent Poems, A261
Recent Poems 1986-1990, A249
"Recital," A26, A466, B1566, B1567
"Recitative for Punished Products," A26
"Reconsideration," A765
"Reconsideration: *Appointment in Samarra*: O'Hara's Messy Masterpiece," A851
"Recruiting Raw Nerves," A1157
"Red-Herring Theory: Part 2," A352
"Red-Herring Theory, The," A351
Reed, Joseph W., A992
Reed, Virginia, B7
"Reel," A26
"Reflections on Romanticism, Narcissism, and Creativity," B147, B652
Regan, Robert A., B144, B145
"Regionalistische Literatuur," B41

Index

Reid, Alastair, A1042, B1023
Reilly, Charlie, A1180, A1183
Reindeer Moon, review of, A1096
Reising, R. W., B572
"Religion and Myth in the Early Novels of John Updike," B1708
"Religious and Sexual Love in American Protestant Literature: Puritan Patterns in Hawthorne and John Updike," B1619
"Religious Commitment in Recent American Fiction: Flannery O'Connor, Bernard Malamud, John Updike," B1586
"Religious Elements of a Portion of John Updike's Fiction," B1589
"Religious Themes in John Updike's *Couples*, The" B1676
"Religious Themes in the Fiction of John Updike and John Cheever," B242
"Religious Themes in *The Poorhouse Fair*," B51
"Reluctant Butterfly: The Fierce Development of Edgar Degas," A857, A1112
"Remarks on the Occasion of E. B. White's Receiving the 1971 National Medal for Literature on December 2, 1971," A762
"Remembering Mr. Shawn," A898
"Remembrance of Things Past," A938
"Reminiscence," A1169
"Report of Health," A497
"Reporter At Large," B659
Repp, John, A371
"Requiem for Rabbit," A1210, B1381
"Rereading 'Indian Summer'," A1123
"Rerun Rabbit, Run," B809
"Resemblances," A659
"Resisting the Big Guys," A1099
"Resolution of Guilt in the Novels of John Updike, The," B1698
"Responding Records Sequence," sound discs of, B1507
"Restaurant for Two," translation of, A1281
"Resurrection of Reverend Marshfield, The," B918
"Return of the Kvetch," B1157
"Return of Updike's Rabbit," B815
"Revenge Symposium, The," A812
"Reverie," A445
Reviews, by Updike, A900-A1158
"Reviews on Tape--*Rabbit at Rest* written and read by John Updike," B1549
Rewald, Sabine, A1137
Rhode, Eric, A1163, A1164
Rhys, Jean, A1022

Ricard, Serge, B798, B1049
Ricci, James, B1439
"Rich in Russia," A322
Richardson, Jack, B89, B202, B788, B1725
Richardson, Nicholas, B120
"Riches of Embarrassment, A," B459
Richler, Mordecai, B790
Ricks, Christopher, B108, B818, B1728
"Ride," A340
Ridgeway, Patricia Moore, B1693
Rifkin, Jeremy, A1100
Rifkind, Donna, B1394
Riggan, William, B1183
"Right Life, The: The Problem of Existence in John Updike's Fiction," B1608
"Right Relation, A.: John Updike's Norm of Marital Commitment," B1622
"Right Way and the Good Way in *Rabbit, Run*, The," B526
Riley, Kathryn Louise, B1624
Ring, The, A16
"Ring Around the Collar," B915
Rinzler, Carol E., B1191
Rio, Michel, A1075
"Rio De Janeiro," A632
Ripley, Jonathan Grant, B1636
Ristoff, Dilvo I., B384, B420, B1651
Ritts, Morton, B1419
Ro, Sigmund, B360
Roa Bastos, Augusto, A1088
"Road, The," translation of, A1277
Roback, Diane, B1391
Robbe-Grillet, Alain, A916
Robbins, J. Albert, B183, B211, B253, B301, B349, B366, B416
Roberts, Joe Donald, B1655
Roberts, Ray A., B218, B219
Robertson, William, B1226
Robinson, Donald, B271
Robinson, Marilynne, B1249
Robison, James C., B285
"Rockefeller Center Ho!" A646
"Rockettes, The," A568
Rodgers, Marion Elizabeth, A1147
Roger's Version, A221-A226
  criticism of, B370, B1219-B1243
  on audio tape, B1519, B1541
"*Roger's Version*: Updike's Negative-Solid Model of *The Scarlet Letter*," B1240
"'Roger's Version' A Deserving Novel," B1226
"*Roger's Version* by John Updike," B1236
Rohland, Pamela, B403, B1256, B1276, B1342
Rohrbach, Peter, B878

"Roland Barthes," A967
"Role of the Berks County Setting in the Novels of John Updike, The," B1640
Rollyson, Carol, B440
"Roman Portrait Busts," A479
"Romance of the Quotidian: Realistic Style and Romantic Ideas in John Updike's Short Fiction," B1713
Romano, John, B1059
"Romans de John Updike, Les," B39
"Romantic Ministers and Phallic Knights: A Study of *A Month of Sundays*, *Lancelot* and *Falconer*," B1614
Romantic Vision of Caspar David Friedrich, The: Paintings and Drawings from the USSR, review of, A1137
"Romp with Job, A," A1065
"Romping Set in a Square New England Town, A," B714
"Room 28," A26, A182
"Roommate, The," interview following, A1233
"Roommates, The," on videotape, B1526
Roots of Success, B636
Rosa, Alfred F., B144, B890
Rose, Irene Kathryn, B1641
Rose, Phyllis, B1452
Rosenblum, Robert, A1137
Rosenthal, A. M., A571
Roth, Arnold, B1727
Roth, Gerhard, A1020
Roth, Philip, A1057, A1094, A1157
"Roth, Updike and the High Expense of Spirit," B740
Rothstein, Mervyn, B1266
Rotkirch, Kristina, B19
Rotundo, Barbara, B528
"Rubble of Footnotes Bound Into Kierkegaard, The," B578
"Rubble of Ruined Temples," A502
Rubin, Merle, B1497
Rubins, Josh, A1171, B1158
Rudman, Mark, B419, B1314
Rumens, Carol, B1129
"Rumor, The," A423
"Run from Rabbit," B517
Runaway, The, review of, A920
Rungren, Lawrence, B1385
"Running Mate, The," A161, A167, A362
"Running on Empty," B241, B1106, B1729
Runyon, R., B482
Rupp, Richard H., B52, B362
Rush, Norman, A1145
Russell, John, B967

Russell, Mariann, B848
"Russian Delinquents," A1084
Russian language, translations from, A1280-A1283
Russian Women: Two Stories, review of, A1072
Ryan, Francis Joseph, B1635
Rybakov, Anatoli, A1108
Ryle, John, B1046

S., A237-A242, A250, B1736
   criticism of, B1262-B1298
   jacket design of, A1293
   on audio tape, B1520
"*S.*," B1272, B1275, B1288
S. U. C., B296
S. V. C., B1166
"S.-Trogen," B1286
Sacred and Profane Love Machine, The, review of, A958
"Sacred Hoopsters in America's Heart," B1433
"Sacred Places," A863
"Saddled with the World," A999
Sade/Fourier/Loyola, review of, A978
"Safe in the Bosom of Ursinus," A887
Safety Net, The, review of, A1043
Sagan, Carl, A987
Sagan, Francoise, A954
"Saganland and the Back of Beyond," A954
Sahli, Nicki, B1617
"Said Yonkers to Gloversville," A654
"Saint of the Mundane," A995
"Saints Nouveaux, Les," A26
Sakharov, Elena Bonner, A1093
Sale, Roger, B1097
Salem Is My Dwelling Place: A Life of Nathaniel Hawthorne, review of, A1152
Salgas, Jean-Pierre, A1198, B353
"Salvation by Death in *Rabbit, Run*," B541
"Salvation Letters, The," B1270
Same Door, The, A7, A17, A47, A178, B202
   criticism of, B505-B515
"*Same Door, The*: Unexpected Gifts," B202
Sams, Henry W., B40, B666
Samuels, Charles T., A1162, B64, B139, B202, B249, B812
Samuels, Ernest, A1095
Samuels, Jayne Newcomer, A1095
Sanatorium Under the Sign of the Hourglass, "Introduction" to, A779
"Sand Dollar," A510
Sanders, F. David, A460
"Sandstone Farmhouse, A," A416

Sanitorium Under the Sign of the Hourglass, review of, A1013
Sanoff, Alvin P., B1227
Sant'Anna, Norma, B689
Saramago, José, A1103
Sarazin, Albertine, A920
"Satan's Work and Silted Cisterns," A1109
"Satire without Serifs," A935
Saueressig, Heinz, B397
"Savor *A Month of Sundays,*" B924
"Says the Rabbit, 'What's Updike?' As Pioneer, Most Wanting," B827
"Says the Rabbit, 'What's Updike?' Masterful Major Author," B826
Scafella, Frank, B1585
"Scandal of *Ulysses,* The: An Exchange," letter on, A853
"Scarlet Letter, The," B1265
"Scarlet Letters," B923
"Scarlet Sundays: Updike vs. Hawthorne," B947
Scars of the Soul, review of, A954
Scenic, A121
"Scenic," A26, A459
Schadlich, Jans Joachim, A1020
Schiff, James A., A1214, B477, B959
Schiller, Robert Evett, B1680
Schlachter, Trudy, B636
Schlesinger, Arthur, Jr., B894
Schlueter, June, B331
Schlueter, Paul, B331
Schmidt-von Bardleben, Renate, B536
Schmitt-von Muhlenfels, Franz, B687
Schneck, Janice, B1686
Schneiderman, Leo, B481
Schopen, Bernard A., B198, B249, B1601, B1611
Schueller, Malini, B1057
Schulz, Bruno, A779, A1013
"Schulz's Charred Scraps," A1110
Schuszler, Cornelius L., B1685
Schwartz, Sanford, B1176
Schwarz-Bart, Simone, A954
"Science, the Saving Grace of John Updike: *The Centaur* and *Couples,*" B629
"Science takes away....," A692
"Scorecard for the All-American Literary All-Star Game, A," B337
"Screwing in Turn," B735
"Sea Knell," A476
Sea of Lentils, review of, A1139
Sea-Crossed Fisherman, The, review of, A1081
"Seagulls," A26, A469
  comment on, A806

"Seal in Nature," A52
Seaman, Donna, B1553
"Search for Faith in John Updike's Fiction, The," B1720
"Search for Goodness in the Fiction of John Updike, The," B1675
"Search for Identity Through Time-Consciousness in John Updike's Fiction, The," B1678
"Search for Meaningful Work in John Updike's Fiction, The," B257
"Search for Perfection in *Rabbit, Run,* The," B524
Searching for Caleb, review of, A971
Searles, George J., B249, B332, B504, B542, B593, B1288, B1450, B1471, B1613
"Sea's Green Sameness, The," A286
Secret History of the Lord of Musashi, The, review of, A1047
Secret Rendezvous, review of, A1016
Seed, David, B254, B424
Seeing Earth: Responses to Space Exploration, B333, B863
"Seeking Connections in an Insecure Country," A1101
Seelbach, Wilhelm, B622
Seelye, John, B779
"Seeresses," A980
Seib, Philip, A1185
Seigel, Gary, B186, B543
Selby, Mable M. Updike, B398
"Selda, Lilia, Ursa, Great Gram, and Other Ladies in Distress," A963
"Selected Books," B739
Selected Essays of Cyril Connolly, The, review of, A1066
Selected Letters, 1940-1977, review of, A1121
Selected Letters of James Joyce, review of, A970
Selected Letters of John O'Hara, review of, A1000
Selected Works (Jarry), review of, A905
"Self and Beyond, The: A Reading of *The Fixer, The Centaur,* and *Henderson the Rain King,*" B640
Self-Consciousness, A251, A262, A263, A1334
  criticism of, B1318-B1366, B1442
"Self-Consciousness," B1337
"*Self-Consciousness,*" B1357, B1362, B1363
"*Self-Consciousness: Memoirs,*" B1356
"Self-Discovered, The: The Car in American Folklore and Literature," B1621
Self-Portrait: Book People Picture Themselves, A1299
Self-portraits, A1297-A1300

"Self-Service," A551
"Sense of Alienation and the Search for Meaning in the Works of John Updike, The," B1667
"Sense of Mortality in the Fiction of John Updike, The," B1674
Sense of Shelter, A, A163
"Sense of Shelter, A," A287, B572, B573
"Sensibilities," B758, B764
"Sensualist, The," A26
"Separating," A353
"Sequels," B1102
"Sere Life, A; or Sprigge's Ivy," A943
"Serious Comedy," B1260
"Sessions, Sylvia Plath and Updike are Among Pulitzer Prize Winners," B263
Sethuraman, Ramchandran, B1653
"Seven Books of Special Significance Published in 1971," B814
"*Seven Gothic Tales*: The Divine Swank of Isak Dinesen," A1082
Seven Gothic Tales a New Introduction by John Updike, A227
"Seven New Ways of Looking at the Moon," A131
Seven Nights, review of, A1074
Seven Rivers West, review of, A1096
"Seven Stanzas at Easter," A26, A465
"Seven Times Eight," B1391
Seventy Poems, A66, A83
Sex, Art, and American Culture, review of, A1153
"Sex, God and John Updike," B429, B1402
"Sex, Nature, and Dualism in *The Witches of Eastwick*," B1203
"Sex, Politics a Potent Mix for Updike, Others This Fall," B1474
"Sex, Sermons, and Style," B930
"Sex Still Had a Good Name," B1483
"Sexual Love in John Updike's *Rabbit, Run, Couples*, and *A Month of Sundays*," B1696
"Sexual Psychology in Contemporary American Fiction," B752
"Shades of Black," A948
"Shallow Drafts: John Updike's *Hugging the Shore*," B1183
Shammas, Anton, A1109
Shanker, Israel, B797
Shapiro, Susan, B1447
Sharma, Jagdish N., B752
Sharrock, Roger, A284, B743
Shattuck, Roger, A905
Shatzkin, Roger, B186, B543
Shaughnessy, Dan, B484

"Shaving Mirror," A542
Shaw, Patrick W., B590
Sheed, F. J., A743
Sheed, Wilfrid, B707
"Sheherazade," A991
"Shelf Life," B1323
Shenstone, Susan Louise Burgess, B1673
Sheppard, Barbara Dillard, B1718
Sheppard, R. Z., B808, B1024, B1251
"She's Got Personality," A1153
Shi, Fu, B1080
Shickel, Richard, B778
"Shillington," A26
Shining Note, The, A981
"Shipbored," A26
"Short and Scary Walk with Andrew Jackson, A," A267, A429
"Short Days, The," A26
"Short Easter," A412
Short fiction, A275-A429
"Short Life, A," A910
Short Lives, review of, A1022
"Short Reviews: Books," B761
"Short Stories in Preservice Teacher Education," B1626
Short Stories of F. Scott Fitzgerald, The, review of, A1122
"Short Stories of John Updike, The," B1590
"Short Story, The: Writer's Control/Reader's Response," B1620
Shostak, Debra A., B1637
"Should Wizard Hit Mommy?" A284, B144, B511
Show, John, B869
"Shrine and Sanctuary: *Of the Farm*," B202
Shulman, Max, A277, A435, A444, A447
Shult, Douglas, B468
Shurr, William H., B582
"Shuttlecock," B734
"Shy Boy Beneath the Gloss," B1340
"Sick at Heart," B1419
Siedenbaum, Art, B1019
Siegle, Robert, B554
Sigal, Clancy, B1157
"Signet Society Medal for Achievement in the Arts Awarded to John Updike, Class of 1954, The," B195, B1726
Signore, The: Shogun of the Warring States, review of, A1138
Silence, review of, A1016
"Silken Mechanism," B785
Sillitoe, Alan, A900, B1209
Silver, Mark A., B1618
"Silver Age of Short Stories, A," B334

Index 323

Simon, John, B1101, B1175
Simon, Peter, A789
"Simple-Minded Jim," A970
Simpson, Colin, A1095
"Sin and Grace as Praxis: An Analysis of Life and Death in the Trilogy of John Updike," B1704
"Sin City, D. C.," A131
Singh, Sukhbir, B441, B1654
Single File, review of, A928
"Singles and Couples: Hemingway's *A Farewell to Arms* and Updike's *Couples*," B743
"Sinister Sex, The," A1086
Sissman, L. E., A761, B767, B783
"Sisters with the Devil in Them," B1201
"Sit Down Cher, Michelle, and Susan: Or, Will the Real Witches of Eastwick Please Stand Up," B1211
Six Fragments, review of, A1113
"Six persons....," A689
Six Poems, A95
Sixteen Sonnets, A149
Sixty Photographs to Celebrate the Sixtieth Anniversary of Alfred Knopf, Publisher, A111
Skaggs, Calvin, B686
Skeats, Terry, B1302
Skenazy, Paul, B1389, B1453
"Skin-Deep Reflections," B1355
"Skyey Developments," A498
"Skylark Story," A276
Slapstick, or Lonesome No More!, review of, A979
Slater, Joyce, B463, B464
Slavitt, David R., B569, B1204
Sleeping Beauty: Memorial Photography in America, review of, A1149
"Sleeping with You," A585
"Sleepless in Scarsdale," A554
Sleeth, Peter, B1396
Sleeth, Ronald, B933
Slethaug, Gordon E., B249, B860
"Sliding Seaward," B869
"Slip that Shows, A: Updike's 'A & P'," B588
"Slippage," A391
"Slump, The," A314
"Small Cheer from the Old Sod," A964
Small City People, A190
"Small Packages," A1106
"Small Pockets of Middle-Aged Peace," B1139
Smallwood, Patricia R., B1677
Smile, Please, review of, A1022

"Smiles of a Lucky Man," B415
Smith, Kent D., B286
Smith, Miles, B874
Smith, Peter Andrew, B1642
Smith, Ronald Gregor, A907
"Smog," translation of, A1282
"Smoke and Mirrors, Or Making an Elephant Appear: Strategies in the Novels of Updike and Heller," B1204
"Snail on the Stump," A945
"Snapshots," A26
"1982's Top 25 Americans Over 50," B271
"Snowdrops 1987," A594
"Snowing in Greenwich Village," A279, B515
Snyder, Randall, A215
"So Young!" B1378
"Social Quest in John Updike's Major Fiction, The," B1668
Soft Spring Night in Shillington, A, A228
"Soft Spring Night in Shillington, A," A823
Sokoloff, B. A., B98
Sokolov, Raymond A., B709, B773, B1273
"Solitaire," A336, A597
"Solitary Pond, The," A131
Solomon, Andy, B1412, B1485, B1563
Solomon, Barbara H., A288, A377
Solomon, Deborah, B1308
"Some Considerations on John Updike's 'Music School'," B689
"Some Frenchmen," A473, B1567
"Some months ago Mr. Kingsley....," A733
"Some Recent Novels: Styles of Martyrdom," B731
"Some Rectangles of Blue," A246
"Some Unoriginal Sins," B916
Somer, John, B215
Something and Nothingness: The Fiction of John Updike and John Fowles, B438
"*Something and Nothingness: The Fiction of John Updike and John Fowles* by John Neary," B487
"Something Missing," A246
"Something Substantial and Useful About It," A1126
Something to Preserve, photography in, A1296
"Sometime Sportsman Greets the Spring, The," A587
Sommers, Jack, A1219
"Son," A341, B1080, B1081
"Son of the Group," B249, B727
"Song of Paternal Care, A," A26
"Song of the Open Fireplace," A26
"Sonic Boom," A26
"Sonnet to Human Grandeur," A598

"Sons of Slaves," A952
Sontag, Susan, A890
"Søren Kierkegaard," A740
Soriano, Osvaldo, A1088
Sorrentino, Gilbert, B249, B946
"Sorrow of Some Central Hollowness, The," B249, B872
"Sorry, Video Cassette Eschews 'Rabbit'," B295
"Sort of Intimate Whirlwind, A," A1128
Soseki, Natsume, A1047
"Sounding the Fourth Alarm: Identity and the Masculine Tradition in the Fiction of Cheever and Updike," B343
Soundings in Satanism, "Introduction" to, A743, B137
"South of the Alps," A501
Souvenirs and Prophecies: The Young Wallace Stevens, review of, A983
"Soviet Russian Criticism 1960-1969 of Seven Twentieth Century American Novelists," B1584
"Space in John Updike's Rabbit Trilogy: A Search for Balance," B1709
Spanish language, translations from, A1284
"Spanish Sonnets," A545
Spark, Muriel, A958, A980, A1030, A1065, A1107
Sparke, William, A8, A288
"'Spat' An Architectural Fiction," A411
"Spatial Remarks," A663
Speak, Memory, review of, A914
"Special Case, A," B823
"Special Message for the First Edition from John Updike, A," A818
"'Special Message' to Purchasers of the Franklin Library limited edition, in 1977, of *Rabbit, Run*, A," A769
Spector, Judith, B305, B343
"Speculations: Contemporary Poetry and Painting," B367, B1218
"Speech on Spool," A643
Spence, Jonathan D., A1074, A1115
Spencer, Scott, B1173
Spender, Stephen, A966
"Spent Arrows and First Buddings," A1047
Spike, Paul, A929
Spitz, Bob, B1112, B1134
"Sport and the Fiction of John Updike and Philip Roth," B1591
"Sports and Literature: A Rationale and Guide for the Use of American Sports Literature in the Teaching of a College Undergraduate General Education Course in Fiction," B1618
Sprigge, Elizabeth, A943
"Spring Paperback Parade," B943
"Spring Rain," A686
Spring Trio, A191
"Squeeze Is On, The," A1043
"Squirrels Mating," A608
Sragow, Michael, A1167
Stade, George, B918
Stafford, William T., B44, B55, B115, B144, B233, B249, B272, B338
"Stalled Starters," A980
Standley, Fred, B521
Staples, Brent, B1414
Staring at the Sun, A1135
"State of Africa," B1040
"State of Ecstacy, A," A1208
"State of Ecstacy, A: The Erotics of a Chance Moment, Snapped and Seen," A868
"States of Mind," A1079
Stead, Christina, A963, A976
Steegmuller, Francis, A1017
Steel, Diana Staynskas Moran, B1714
"Steel Wilderness," B500, B520, B568
Stehlikova, Eva, B631
Steichen, Edward, A1144
Steinberg, Saul, A1155
Steinberg, Sybil, B446, B1219, B1246, B1262, B1368, B1431, B1475
Steiner, Dorothea, B169
Steiner, George, B202, B923
Steinley, Nan, B1715
Stern, Richard, B708
Sternhell, Carol, B315
Stevens, Andrea, B1188
Stevens, Holly, A983
Stevick, Philip, B187
Stewart, Anne, B226
Still life, in *Ursinus Bulletin*, A1301
"Still of Some Use," A377
"Still Staring," A1135
Stirrings Still, review of, A1117
"Stolen Apples," translation of, A1283
Stone, Allan, A285, A292
Stone, Sue Smart, A292, S285
Stories and Plays, review of, A974
Stories from Museums and Women, A84
"Stories to Be Read Aloud," B595
"Story Examines Updike's Career," B58
Story of a Shipwrecked Sailor, review of, A1088
"Story of My Life, The," A26
"Story of S. [sic]," B1268

Storyteller, The, review of, A1122
Stout, Cushing, B417
Stover, Dean, A1204
Strandberg, Victor, B249, B632
"Strange Case of Dr. Destouches and M. Céline, The," A977
Strassberg, Mildred P., B1586
Straub, Peter, B903
Straumann, Heinrich, B30
Streitfeld, David, B426
Strickland, Michael R., B474
Strong Opinions, B130, B510
"Structural Unity in John Updike's *The Centaur,*" B1658
Structural Unity in the Novels of John Updike, B1603
Stubbs, John C., B524
Studies in American Fiction II, B284
"Studies in Post-Hitlerian Self-Condemnation in Austria and Germany." A1120
"Study of Sexuality in Selected American Novels Since 1945, A," B1615
"Stunning the Audience," B409
"Stunt Flier, The," A26
Sturzl, Erwin A., B169, B750
Stuttaford, Genevieve, B220, B222, B1177, B1301, B1318, B1552
Styles of Bloom, A192
"Stylus Dei or the Open-Endedness of Debate?: Success and Failure in *A Month of Sundays,*" B249, B953
"Styron, Updike, Bacall and Mailer Join in a Romp at Roseland," B226
"Sublimating," A331
"Suburban Madrigal," A26
"Suburban Middle Age," B870
"Suburban Surfeit," B722
"Subway Love," A487
Suderman, Elmer, B121, B526, B820, B881, B1244, B1261, B1430
"Sugar and Spice Rabbit--*Odd Jobs* by John Updike," B1468
Suied, Alain, A848
Sullivan, Dan, B908
Sullivan, Nancy S., A300
Sullivan, Walter, B650, B665, B1000, B1037
Sultan, The: The Life of Abdul Hamid II, review of, A952
Sultans, The, review of, A952
"Summer: West Side," A26
"Summer Reader, The," A441
Summons to Memphis, A, review of, A1091
"Summonses, Indictments, Extenuating Circumstances," A1091

"Sunday," A512
Sunday in Boston, A112
Sunday of Life, The, review of, A989
"Sunday Rain," A505
"Sunflower," A26, A455
"Sunglasses," A26, A454
"Sunshine on Sandstone," A481
Superior Women, review of, A1068
Supermale, The, review of, A989
Superman, A122
"Superman," A26, A456
"Supernaturalism in John Updike's Fiction," B1580
Survivor in Contemporary American Fiction, The: Saul Bellow, Bernard Malamud, John Updike, Kurt Vonnegut, Jr., B441, B1654
"Survivors: Perspectives on Transformative Violence in Contemporary American Narrative (1970s, Fiction, Autobiography)," B1637
Süskind, Patrick, A1092, A1106
"Susquehanna Gives Updike Doctorate," B372
"Sustaining Stream, The," B15
"Suzie Creamcheese Speaks," A969
"Swan Song for Rabbit, A," B1412
Swanson, Trevor, B1592
Swanson, William, A353
Swauger, Craig, A291
"Swell's Letters," B1455
Swick, Marly A., B1614
"Swifts and Stuffers," A645
Sykes, Robert H., B574
"Symbolic City and Christian Existentialism in Fiction by Flannery O'Connor, Walker Percy, and John Updike, The," B1588
Symons, Julian, B840
"Symposium on Contemporary American Fiction: 34 Authors Comment on Their Craft and on the Contemporary Literary Scene," A849
S/Z, review of, A967
Szpila, Joseph B., B1708

"T. S. Eliot," A707
T. S. Eliot: A Life, review of, A1071
"Tackier Textures of Success, The," B1129
Taggert, Edward A., B8
Takeover, The, review of, A980
"Taking Care of Mom: Erotic Degradation, Dalliances, and Dichotomies in the Works of Just About Everyone," B305
Talk from the Fifties, A150

"Introduction" to, A780
"Talk of a Sad Town," A923
"Talk of a Tired Town," A923
"Talk with John Updike," A1161
"Talking Head," B249, B787
"Talking with John Updike," A1180
Tallent, Elizabeth, B255
Tanizaki, Junichiro, A1047, A1079, A1139
Tankel, Sylvia, A288
Tanner, Tony, B99, B249, B362, B736, B753, B872
Tanzoe, Kaneko, B513
"Tao in the Yankee Stadium Bleachers," A26, A182, A457
Tapes, audio, B1499-B1521
"Tarbox Police," A746
"Taste," A556
"Taste of Metal, The," A308
Taubman, Robert, B667, B1132
"Tax-Free Encounter," A26
Taylor, C. Clarke, B56
Taylor, Charles, B1359
Taylor, Cheet H., B1587
Taylor, Larry E., B100, B105, B122, B202, B249, B1576
Taylor, Peter, A1091
Taylor, Robert, B456, B898, B1305
Taylor, Sam, B905
Taylor, Simon Watson, A905
"Technics and Pyrotechnics," B1075
Teleky, Richard, B1355
Telephone Poles
    criticism of, B598-B600
    jacket design of, A1286
"Telephone Poles," A26, A464
Telephone Poles and Other Poems, A10, A11, A26, A1320
Television appearances, A1219-A1243, A1274, 1275
"Tendenzen der Personlichkeitgestaltung im amerikanischen egenwartsroman," B53
Tennis Players, The, review of, A1060
Terry, R., B544
"Testing Coalition Theory in 'The Great Gatsby' and the 'Rabbit' Trilogy," B1641
"Texts and Men," A978
Thanatopses, A266
"That Long Atlantic Crossing," B649
That Mighty Sculptor, Time, review of, A1150
"That Old White Magic," B1189
That Voice, review of, A1056
"The fine hairs...," A722
"The obituaries of Judy Garland....," A731
Theft, A, review of, A1116

"Theme and Techniques in John Updike's *Midpoint*," B768
"Theme of Adultery in the Fiction of John Updike, The," B1691
Theodore Dreiser: An American Journey, review of, A1136
"Theology and the Computer," B1220
"Theology of John Updike, The," B105
"Theology of Karl Barth as an Interpretative Key to the Fiction of John Updike, The," B1604
"There are years....," A713
Theroux, Paul, B249, B796, B1084
Theses and dissertations, B1569-B1722
"Thin Air," A621
"Things, Things," A1156
"Things Falling Apart: Structure and Theme in *Rabbit, Run*," B249, B530
Thiong'o, Ngugi Wa, A1009
"13 Ways of Looking at the Masters," A557, A788
Thirties, The, review of, A1025
"Thirty Wise Men: Eleven Literary Lights Reveal Their Modern Magi," A844
"Thirty-four Years Late, Twice," A1030
This Earth, My Brother..., review of, A932
"This Fair Land....," A737
"This Isn't a Chain I'm Smoking," A443
Thomas, D. M., A1036
Thomas, Elizabeth Marshall, A1096
Thomas, Heather, B221, B1212
Thomas, Jim, B1646
Thomas, Lewis, A953
Thomas, Lloyd Spencer, B947
Thomas, Phil, B983, B1197
Thommen, Paula Marie, B1681
Thompson, James, B1747
Thompson, John, B715, B1026
Thorburn, David, B156, B202, B203, B233, B249, B362, B741, B751, B856, B876, B887, B923, B970, B999, B1020, B1028
"Thorburn and Eiland's *John Updike: A Collection of Critical Essays*," B235, B741
"Though Much Has Changed, Much Endures: Concepts of the Epic Hero in Selected Modern American Novels," B1599
"Thoughts of Faith Infuse Prolific Updike's Novels," A1218
"Thoughts While Driving Home," A26
    sound discs of, B1507
Thrasher, D. G., B1719
"3 A. M.," A26
"Three Documents," A694

Three Illuminations in the Life of an American Author, A151
"Three Illuminations in the Life of an American Author," A368
"Three Men on the Moon: Friedman, Updike, Bellow and Apollo Eleven," B201
"Three Songs for Soprano and Tuba," B1566
"Three Tales from Nigeria," A1062
Three Texts from Early Ipswich, "Note" in, A720
Three Texts from Early Ipswich: A Pageant, A48
"Three texts from Early Ipswich: A Pageant," A747
Three Trapped Tigers, review of, A933
"Three Versions of Updike's 'Snowing in Greenwich Village'," B515
"Three Writers with Keen Eyes for Art," B1311
"Through a Continent, Darkly," A960
"Through the Mid-Life Crisis with James Boswell, Esq.," A992
"Tick," A581
Tillich, Paul, A908, A924
"Time Present and Time Past: Autobiography as a Narrative of Duration," B1575
Time Wars: The Primary Conflict in Human History, review of, A1100
Time's Arrow, review of, A1148
Time's Arrow, Time's Cycle: Myth and Metaphor in the Discovery of Geological Time, review of, A1100
"Time's Fool," A26
"Timestyle," A434
"To a Box Turtle," A609
"To a Former Mistress, Now Dead," A631
"To a Waterbed," A514
"To an Usherette," A26
"To Crystallization," A583
"To Die at the Top: A Comparison of Housman and Updike," B496
"To Ed Sissman," A547
"To Evaporation," S578
"To Have and Have Not," B1013
"To Have and to Hold," B973
"To the Tram Halt Together," A1005
Today Show interviews, A1237, A1240
"Today's Youth Looks at AAK," A705
Todd, Albert C., A1282
Todd, John, A686
Todd, Richard, B126, B202, B876, B972
Toebasch, Wim, B41
Tolstoy, Leo, A1090

Tolstoy's Diaries, review of, A1090
Tomalin, Claire, A1234, B1040
"Tome-Thoughts, from the Times," A26
"Tomorrow and tomorrow and So Forth," B508, B509, B512
Tondora, Nancy E., B1687
"Too Explicit," B1082
Too Far To Go
 criticism of, B1082-B1090
 on videotape, B1524
"*Too Far to Go*," B1085, B1534
"Too Far to Go," B1530, B1532, B1533
Too Far To Go: The Maples Stories, A193
Too Far to Go: The Maples Stories, A152
 "Foreword" to, A777
"Too Much," B885
"Toothache Man," A26
"Top of the Class," B1176
"Topnotch Witcheries," A958
"Toppling Towers Seen by a Whirling Soul," A1039
"Topsfield Fair," A493
Tossing and Turning, A54, A130, A131
 criticism of, B1006-B1012
"Tossing and Turning," B1008
"Tote That Quill," A997
Tothstein, Mervyn, A1205
"Touch of Spring," A131
Tournier, Michel, A1118
Towers, Robert, B202, B1020, B1063
Townley, Rod, B794
Trachtenberg, Alan, A333
Tracy, Bruce H., B692
"Tragic Hero of Updike's *Rabbit, Run*, The," B539
"Trail-of-Bread-Crumbs Motif in Updike's Maples Stories, The," B1089
Transcendental Constant in American Literature, The, B207
"Transcending the Cliché: Transformed Conventions in Postwar American Novels," B1632
"Transformational-Generative Approach to Style in John Updike's Novels, A," B1592
Translations, by Updike, A1276-A1284
"Translucing of Hugh Person, The," A940
Transparent Things, review of, A940
"Travel Tips," A544
"Traveling Alone," translation of, A1278
Travels in Arabia Deserta, review of, A1018
Travels in Hyperreality, review of, A1087
Treasury of Great Children's Book Illustrators, A, review of, A1059

"Treatment of Burial Rituals in the Modern American Novel, The," B1636
Tree, Christina, B124
"Trees Eat Sunshine," A26
"Trends in Recent American Fiction," B651
Trevor, William, A1029, B836, B1472
"Tribute," A738
Trifonov, Yuri, A998, A1072
Trilling, Diana, B703
Trimmer, Joseph F., A291, B633
"Triple Spell, A," B1188
"Tristan and Iseult," A419
"Tristan in Letters: Malory, C. S. Lewis, Updike," B223, B691
"Tritylodonts," A653
"Tropical Beetles," A26
Tropical Night Falling, review of, A1148
"Trouble with Harry, The," B1397, B1425
Trueheart, Charles, B429, B1402
Trust Me, A233, A243, A1333
   criticism of, B1244-B1261
   on audio tape, B1540
"Trust Me," A372
"Tsokadze O Altitudo," A26
Tsuji, Kuno, A1138
"Tulsa," A604
"Tune, in American Type," A26
"Tuning out the Inner Critic," A841
Turner, Kermit S., B852
Turner, Michael, B729
"Turning Sex and Guilt Into an American Epic," A1187, B240, B1105
Tuten, Frederic, A935
Tutuola, Amos, A1062
"TV: Drama of Updike's Sad Couple," B1529
"Twelve Terrors of Christmas, The," A897
Twentieth-Century Short Story Explication: Interpretations, 1900- 1966 of Short Fiction Since 1800, B45
Twentieth-Century Short Story Explication: Supplement I to Second Edition, 1967-1969, B84
Twentieth-Century Short Story Explication: Supplement II to Second Edition, B132
Twentieth-Century Short Story Explication: Supplement II to Third Edition, B306
Twentieth-Century Short Story Explication: Supplement III to Third Edition, B370
Twentieth-Century Short Story Explication: Supplement IV to Third Edition, B399
"20 Best Books of 1981, The," B1119
"Twenty Eight Stories and Two Novels," B503
"Twin Beds in Rome," A298
"Twisted Apples," A819
"Two Exhibitions in the Library of Mary Washington College," A1269
"Two Heroes," A682
"Two Hoppers on Display at the National Gallery," A566, A810
"Two Late Arrivals, Featuring Resilient Females," A1030, A1036
"Two Limericks After Lear," A599
"Two Points on a Descending Curve," A913
Two Sonnets Whose Titles Came to Me Simultaneously, A198
Two Views, review of, A913
Tyler, Anne, A384, A971, A986, A1021, A1040, A1078
"Typical Optical," A552
   cartoon for, A1316
   drawing for, A1304

U and I, B426, B434, B452, B454-B461, B463, B464, B466
   review of, A1140
"Ugly Duckling, The," A1090
"Umbrella," A182
Umphlett, Wiley Lee, B152
"Uncouples," B976
"Under the Microscope," A310
"Under the Skin," B1364
"Under the Sunlamp," A131
"Understanding John Updike's Fiction," B1561
"Undertaker, The," A161, A167
"Ungreat Lives," A1070
"Unified Vision of *A Month of Sundays*, A," B948
"Uniquely Updike," B1320
"Unitarian Wife and the One-Eyed Man, The: Updike's *Marry Me* and 'Sunday Teasing'," B1001
University of North Carolina at Chapel Hill, manuscripts at, A1261
University of Texas, collection at, A1264
"Unsentimental Education," B837
"Unstuck," A295, B1244
"Untitled," A635
Untitled poems, A439, A448, A449
Untitled reply, to "Which book or books were your favorites or influenced you most as a teenager and why?" A739
Untitled statement, A714
"Updike," (Pritchett), B1115
"Updike," (Taubman), B667
"Updike: A Mensch," B771

Index 329

"Updike: A Selected Checklist 1974-1990," B447
"Updike: A Self-Portrait of the Artist," B1325
"Updike, Ashbery: Two Ways of Seeing," B1305
"Updike Delux," B1173
"Updike, Dennis, and Others," B677
"Updike: Endless Infidelity," B730
"Updike: Evil as Sexual Society," B1198
"Updike: Fiction and the Writer's Access to Contradictory Ego States," B481
"Updike, from Memory," B458
"Updike, Gass, and Vonnegut: 'Studies in Contemporary American Fiction'," B1606
"Updike, John. *Couples*," B699
"Updike: Life Under a Microscope," A1203
"Updike, Malamud, and the Fire This Time," B165, B202, B856
"Updike: No Encore Merited," B47
"Updike: Novelist of the New, Post-Pill America," B706
"Updike: 'Rabbit' Has His Final Say, but the Writer Has More to Tell," B1374
"Updike, Shaffer, and the Centaurs," B643
"Updike, Spark and Others," B650, B665
"Updike: Story to Novel," B102
"Updike: Trusting in Suburbia Too Much?" B1256
"Updike Adds Critics Award," B1180
"Updike and Barthelme: Disengagement," B126, B876
"Updike and Caro Win Book Critics Award," B441
"Updike and Contemporary Witchcraft," B1205
"Updike and Gardner: Down from the Heights," B988
"Updike and Hawthorne: Not so Strange Bedfellows," B950
"Updike and I: The Story of a Novel Fixation," B468
"Updike and Roth: Serious at Last," B1271
"Updike and Roth: The Limits of Representationalism," B355
"Updike and the Critics: Reflections on 'A & P'," B584
"Updike as Matchmaker," B970
"Updike as Matchmaker: *Marry Me*," B202
"Updike at Rest," B1488
"Updike at the Top of His Form," B981
"Updike at UMASS: Handle the World with Care," B488
"Updike Attends Shillington Class Reunion," B5

"Updike Autographs Program of Shillington High School Class of 1950 Reunion," B421
"Updike Bids Farewell to the 'Rabbit'," B432
"Updike Books Wonderful Gift," B412
"Updike Breathes Some Life into Buchanan," B908
"Updike Country," B1023
"Updike Discusses Reading," B174
"Updike Discusses Women's Underwear, Draws Laughs," B314
"Updike Elected to Institute," B22
"Updike Essays Capture Art's Nuances," B1307
"Updike 'Flatly Denies' That Tarbox is Ipswich," A1245
"Updike FourFiveSix, 'Just Like That': An Essay Review," B144
"Updike Gets National Award for 'Poor House Fair'[sic] Novel" , B499
"Updike Goes All Out At Last," B803
"Updike Had Lost Hope for Pulitzer," B265
"Updike Honored by Commonwealth," B289
"Updike Honored by Critics," B443
"Updike in a Foreign Country," B1162
"Updike in Africa," B202, B1017, B1020
"Updike in Autumn," B1422
"Updike Involved in Suit," B172
"Updike is Home," B293
"Updike Is Honored by Cartoonists," B433
"Updike is Uneasy About Literary Prizes," B23
"Updike Lauds National Medalist E. B. White," B117
"Updike le Noir," B1026
"Updike Lets Rabbit Ride Out in Style," B1440
"Updike Named to Head Board of Lampoon," B1
"Updike Named to Post," B119
"Updike on America: The Expanding Vision of John Updike in His Post-Olinger Novels," B1628
"Updike on Hawthorne," A1200, B371, B1735
"Updike on Sex," B698
"Updike on the Present," B249, B812
"Updike on Updike," A795, A1186, B1096
"Updike on Women, Marriage, & Adultery," B748
"Updike Pays Homage to Mom," B472
"Updike Pens Own 'Self-Consciousness'," B1331
"Updike Play Opens," B907

"Updike Poète, ou le Mythe d'Antée," B34
"Updike Poetry Gives Folger Change of Pace," B480
"Updike Reads his Works, Works of Fanciful Mother," B474
"Updike Receives Prestigious Prize," B387
"Updike Recycled: New Collection Includes a Bit for Almost Everyone," B1465
"Updike Redux," B830
"Updike Redux: Grace Notes," B1166
"Updike Reflects on Childhood in Ursinus Visit," B473
"Updike Reflects on 'Shillington Thoughts'/His Mother's Death Leaves a Certain Sadness for Writer," B413
"Updike Remembered," B404
"Updike Report, The," A782
"Updike Right on Writing AND Reading," B445
"Updike Run: At 42 Still Making 'Em Look Easy," B154
"Updike Says This Year's Will Be the Last Rabbit Tale—but No Promises," A1209
"Updike Snares Second Pulitzer," B450
"Updike Story, Redux, The," B592
"Updike Tales to Be Subject of Program," B339
"Updike Talks of his Work, and Film," B92
"Updike Talks Reluctantly," B91
"Updike Tinkers with Old Ideas for Memories," B1489
"Updike to Bring Back Rabbit," B1367, B1441
"Updike to Receive Degree from Ursinus," B26
"Updike to Receive Honorary Degree," B27
"Updike to Receive Literary Degree," B51
"Updike to Win," B40, B666
"Updike Up-close," B431
"Updike Visits School," B60
"Updike Wins Book Award for Distinguished Fiction," B614
"Updike Wins Book Prize for *Centaur*," B615
"Updike Wins Fellowship at Oxford," B4
"Updike Wins 2nd Award for Same Rabbit Novel," B1137
"Updike-Pennington," B2
"Updike's 'A & P': An 'Initial' Response," B596
"Updike's *A Month of Sundays* and the Language of the Unconscious," B951
"Updike's 'A Sense of Shelter'," B572, B573
"Updike's African Dream," B1025

Updike's America: The Presence of Contemporary American History in John Updike's Rabbit Novels, B1651
Updike's America: The Presence of Contemporary American History in John Updike's Rabbit Triolgy, B384, B420
"Updike's American Comedies," B156, B202, B362
"Updike's Anti-Metafiction," B911
"Updike's Artist's Dilemma: 'Should Wizard Hit Mommy?'" B144, B511
"Updike's Couples," B715
"Updike's *Couples*: Eros Demythologized," B249, B742
"Updike's *Couples*: Squeak in the Night," B144, B745
"Updike's Honky Apocalypse: *Rabbit Redux*," B189, B857
"Updike's Idea of Reification," B204
"Updike's Infidelities," B990
"Updike's Innocence," B1313
"Updike's Memoirs Leave Room For Sequels," B1342
"Updike's New Versions of Myth in America," B448
"Updike's Nimble Time Travels," B1482
"Updike's Novelette 'Son', I: Translation and Background Information; II: Four Taboos on Translating Literary Works," B1080
Updike's Novels: Thorns Spell a Word, B363
"Updike's Omega-Shaped Shelter: Structure and Psyche in *A Month of Sundays*," B949
"Updike's Passage to India," B1296
"Updike's People," B1059
"Updike's Perceptive *Self-Consciousness*," B1328
"Updike's Pilgrims: Marriage in Twentieth-Century America," B1700
"Updike's Pilgrims in a World of Nothingness," B182
"Updike's Probing *Memories*," B1493
"Updike's *Rabbit, Run*," B556, B560
"Updike's *Rabbit, Run* and Pascal's *Pensées*," B547
"Updike's Rabbit Angstrom Runs a Final Lap," B1379
"Updike's Rabbit Makes His Final Run," B1377
"Updike's Rabbit Returns," B1118
"Updike's Rabbit Trilogy," B1103
"Updike's 'Rabbit' Wins Anew," B1136
"Updike's Revisions of *Rabbit, Run*," B546
"Updike's Rich Rabbit: Suffocating in Sin," B1140

Index 331

"Updike's Search for Liturgy," B202
"Updike's Sermons," B208
"Updike's Sexual Language for God," B1229
"Updike's 'Son': An Analysis of Its Theme and Some Expressions," B1081
"Updike's Song of Himself," B1350
"Updike's Stories of Shriveled Souls," B1253
"Updike's Struggle to Portray Women," B1283
"Updike's Style Criticized," B874
"Updike's Symbol of the Center," B144, B145
"Updike's Tarbox," B721
"Updike's 'The Day of the Dying Rabbit'," B892
"Updike's Three Weird Sisters," B1186
"Updike's Twosomes," B717
"Updike's Ups and Downs," B33
"Updike's Vacuum Cleaner," B494
"Updike's Version," B1232
Updike's Version: Rewriting The Scarlet Letter, B477, B959
"Updike's Vintage *Memories*," B1497
"Updikes Visit Black Africa, Strangers in a Strange Land," B134
"Updike's Weighty Collection Shows Off New Tool, Old Spirit," B1462
"Updike's Witches," B1210
"Updike's Witchy Women," A1195
"Updike's Womanly Man," B244, B954
"Updike's World and *Couples*," B750
"Updike's Yankee Traders," B703
Uphaus, Suzanne Henning, B216, B233, B249, B630, B948, B1602
"Uphaus's *John Updike*," B245
"Upon Learning that a Town Exists in Virginia Called Upperville," A26
"Upon Learning that a Bird Exists Called the Turnstone," A26
"Upon Shaving off One's Beard," A503
"Upon the Last Day of His Forty-Eighth Year," A558
"Upon the Last Day of His Forty-Ninth Year," A213
"Upright Carpentry," A668
Upshaw, Kathryn Jane, B1703
"Urban Values in Recent American Fiction: A Study of The City in the Fiction of Saul Bellow, John Updike, Philip Roth, Bernard Malamud, and Norman Mailer," B1574
Ursinus Bulletin, still life in, A1301
Ursinus College, collection at, A1266
"Use of Language in John Updike's Short Stories, The," B1701

"Use of Rhythm in Three Novels by John Updike, The," B75
"Use of Sexuality in the Fiction of John Updike, The," B1656
"Use of Suburbia as a Setting in the Fiction of John O'Hara, John Cheever, and John Updike," B1624
"Uses of Weather in 'Tomorrow and Tomorrow and So Forth'," B509

"V. B. Nimble, V. B. Quick," A26
"Vacuum Cleaner," A26, A182
"Vagueness on Wheels, Dust on a Skirt," A1143
"Validation of Religious Faith in the Writings of John Updike, The," B158
"Van Loves Ada, Ada Loves Van," A922
van Ostaijen, Paul, A935
Van Wyk, S. Elizabeth, B1720
Vanderwerken, David L., B853
Vargas Llosa, Mario, A1083, A1099, A1122, A1132
Vargo, Edward P., B131, B202, B626, B1572
Vaughn, Philip H., B234
Vaughn, Rodger, B1566
Vendler, Helen, A1176, B1006
"Venezuela for Visitors," A792
"Venus and Others," A876
Verburg, Carol J., A378
Verduin, Kathleen, B249, B256, B1203, B1619, B1674
"Vermont," A26
Verse, A26, A35
"Vibration," A26
Vickery, John B., B144, B627, B638
Vico and Herder, review of, A978
Victoria, review of, A921
"Video," A605
"Video Shopper—Understanding John Updike's Fiction Presented by Donald Greiner," B1547
Videos and films, B428, B489, B490, B1522-B1561, B1529-B1553
"View from the Catacombs," B59, B701
View in Winter, The, review of, A1019
"Views," A729
Vigilante, Richard, B1352
Vik, Susan Frances, B1615
Villas Boas, Claudio, A956
Villas Boas, Orlando, A956
Villaverde, Fernando, B351
Vincent, Theophilus, A752
Vinson, James, B217
"Violence at the Windows," A246

Virga, Vincent, A454, A874
"Virgin President, The," B1490
"Virgins' Ornament, The," A414
"Virtues of Playing Cricket on the Village Green, The," A1130
"Vision, A," A541
"Visionary of Drohobycz, The," A1110
Visions of Mackenzie King, The, A153
"Visions of MacKenzie King, The," A548
"Visiting the Land of the Free," A1093
Visual arts, A1285-A1317
"Visual Poetry," A1270
"Vital Push, The," A246
"Vladimir Nabokov," A770
Vladimir Nabokov: The American Years, B435
"V.N. Again and Again." A1121
Voice Through a Cloud, A, review of, A910
Voices from the Moon, review of, A1070
"Voices in the Biltmore," A650
von Hoffman, Nicholas, B1491
"Von Tiermenschen und den Tucken der Padagogik: John Updike's *The Centaur*," B644
Vonnegut, Kurt, A979
Vormweg, Heinrich, B85
"Vow," A477
"Voznesensky Met," A717
Vulnerable People: A View of American Fiction Since 1945, B181

W. H. Auden--A Tribute, review of, A966
Wade, Rosalind[?], B1300
Wagner, Don Henry, B1656
Wahl, William, B750
Wain, John, A765
"Wait, The," A115, A311
Waite, Robert, B134
Waiting for the End, B78
"Waiting Rooms: I. Boston Lying-In; II. Mass. Mental Health," A213
Wakeman, John, B153
Walcutt, Charles Child, B521, B619
Waldmeir, Joseph, B144, B533, B855
Waldron, Randall H., B552
Walker, Claudine Dianne, B1658
Walker, Warren S., B45, B84, B132, B306, B369, B399
Walkiewicz, E. P., B287
Wallace, Robert, A267, A545, A550-A552, A555, A564, A568, A579-A581, A586, A587, A595-A597, A599
Waller, Gary, B235, B249, B953
Waller, Sydney, A314
"Wallet, The," A400

Walser, Martin, A1120
Walsh, John F., B170
Walsh, William, B1070
"Walt Whitman: Ego and Art," A773
"Walter Biggs," work sheets for, A1256
Walters, Colin, B1326, B1493
Wanderer, The, review of, A972
Wanderers, The, A932
Wang, Changrong, B358
War, Susan D., B1704
Ward, J. A., B12, B607
"Warlock," B313, B1194, B1733
Warm Wine, A96
Warner, Margo Larson, B1662
Warner, Sylvia Townsend, A1012
Warrior, Robert Allen, B1433
"Was B. B. a Crook?" A1095
"Wash," A26
"Washington: Tourist View," A606
"Waspshot Chronicle, The," A1146
"Watchful I, The," B1333
Watermark, review of, A1150
Watkins, Stanley, J., B62
Watunna: An Orinoco Creation Cycle, review of, A1031
Waxman, Robert E., B581, B1606
Way, Brian, B992
"Way We Are, The," B1114
Wayland, Elisabeth R., B1694
We Always Treat Women Too Well, review of, A1030, A1036
"We are in receipt....," A702
"We confess ourself....," A708
"We discover that the question....," A716
"We found ....," A744
"We have found new life....," A715
"We have had occasion....," A711
"We live in the midst of flux....," A734
"We looked forward....," A703
"We Only Came to Sleep," sound discs of, B1507
"We used to think....," A718
"Weak Spots mar Updike's Novel," B983
Wear, Delese, B400
"Wearing Down," B1065
Weaver, Gordon, B287
Weber, Brom, B813
Weber, Bruce, B418
Weber, Ronald, B333, B863
Weinman, Paul, A314
Weintraub, Stanley B896
Weiser, Irwin, B101, B116
Weiss, Eric A., B1234
Weixlmann, Joe, B258

Welch, Denton, A910
Welch, J. M., B1208
"Welcome to New York's Most Endearing Small Museum," A889
Welish, Marjorie, B1317, B1445
Wentz, R., B236
Werner, Craig, B637
West, William W., A287
West of the Rockies
  "Afterword" in, A931
  review of, A931
"What John Updike Means to Him," B452
"What John Updike Never Got to Say," B550
"What Literature Says to Preservice Teachers and Teacher Educators," B400
"What Makes Rabbit Run? A Profile of John Updike," A1193, A1231, B294
"What MOMA Done Tole Him," B1306
"What MOMA Done Tole Me," A854
"What You Deserve Is What You Get," A1102
"When American and Soviet Writers Meet," B193
"When Couples Married," B974
"When Everybody (Everyone) Was Pregnant," A333
When I Whistle, review of, A1016
"When Worlds Divide," B1282
"Whenever we return....," A701
"Where Is Everybody," B675
"Where is the Space to Chase Rainbows?" A894
"Where Money and Energy Gather: A Writer's View of a Computer Laboratory," A886
Which Tribe Do You Belong To? review of, A960
"While Awaiting Service in a Shoe Store," A432
White, E. B., A762, B162
White, Edward M., A827
White, John J., B623
White Castle, The, review of, A1143
"White Dwarf," A26
"White Man's Black Man: Three Views," B848
"White Mischief," B1024
"White on Black: Non-Black Literature About Africa Since 1945," B1650
"White on White," A179
Whitesides, Mary Parr, B1634
Whitman, Walt, A773
"Whitman's Egotheism," A157, A773

Who Killed Palomino Molero? review of, A1099
"Who Wants to Know?" A987
"Why is it, we asked ourself....," A709
"Why Not Tell the Truth?" B1366
"Why Rabbit Finally Ran to Ground," A878, A1211
"Why Rabbit Had to Go," A875
"Why Rabbit Thinks Vietnam Is Just a Head Fake," B831
"Why Robert Frost Should Receive the Nobel Prize," A748
"Why So Hard on Rabbit?" B1414
"Why the Telephone Wires Dip and the Poles Are Cracked and Crooked," A26, A462
"Why Updike Writes and What He Writes About," B1327
"Why Updike's 'Rabbit' Keeps Winning the Race," B1413
"Why Write?" A809
"Wicked Witches of the North," B1193
"Wide-Hipped Wife and the Painted Landscape, The: Pastoral Ideals in *Of the Farm*," B249
"Widening Perceptions in Updike's 'A & P'," B585
"Widow, The," A161, A167
Wiehe, Janet, B1014, B1058, B1093, B1152
Wieniewska, Ceilina, A779
"Wife-wooing," A288, B127
Wild Berries A1072
Wilhelm, Albert E., B257, B514, B537, B546, B549, B1088, B1089
Will, George, B1405
"William Faulkner and My Middle East Problem," B467
Williamson, Bruce, B1160
Williamson, Chilton, Jr., B1420
Wills, Gary, B1399
Wilson, Carl Brasington, B1705
Wilson, Edmund, A784, A1025
Wilson, Matthew, B565
Wilson, Mike, B466
Wilson, Raymond, III, B1240
Wilson, Robert, B1361, B1376
Wilson, Victor, B1170
"Wilson Library Reviews," B1110
"Wind," A508
Wind, James P., B470, B1243
Wind Spirit, Giles & Jeanne, The, review of, A1118
Winkler, Willi, B3556
Winn, Marie, B485

"Winners of the 1991 Pulitzer Prizes in the Arts and Journalism," B1438
Winston, Lara, A1038
Winston, Richard, A1038
"Winter," translation of, A1279
"Winter Ocean," A26
Winterreise, review of, A1020
"'Wisdom' of John Updike, The," B188
"Wise Women," B903
"Witches and Fairies: Fitzgerald to Updike," B668
"'Witches' Conjures Up the Devil in Nicholson," B1536
Witches of Eastwick, The, A208-A212, A216
   criticism of, B1185-B1211
   on audio tape, B1520
   on film, B1527, B1237, B1538
"Witches of Eastwick, The," A393, A395, A818, B1196, B1289
"*Witches of Eastwick, The*," B1200
"Witches' Protest Filming of Updike Novel," B1535
Witch-Herbalist of the Remote Town, The, review of, A1062
"With Return of 'Rabbit,' Updike Among Top U. S. Writers, says *Times*," B810
"Witnesses, The," A304
"Witold Who?" A915
"Wittery," B934
Wittgenstein's Nephew, review of, A1120
"Witty Dotty," A1104
"WLB Biography: John Updike," B9
Wohlfert, Lee, A1173, B829
Wolcott, James, B241, B337, B1106, B1167, B1729
Wolfe, Peter, B1139, B1299
Wolff, Geoffrey, B93
Wollheim, Richard, B1316, B1354
Wolmuth, Roger, B1126
"Woman Who Rode Away, The," B386, B1285, B1737
"Woman's Continent, A," A1145
Women at the Pump, The, review of, A999
"Women Characters in the Novels of John Updike, The," B1664
Women in the Novels of John Updike: A Critical Study, B1616
"Women We Love: Dolly Parton," A893
Wonderful Years, The, review of, A988
"Wondering What It's Like to Be A Woman," B1187
Wood, James, B457, B1400, B1469
Wood, Michael, B877, B1258, B1347

Wood, Ralph C., B385, B414, B1130, B1198, B1215, B1241, B1350, B1421
Woodcut, A1302
"Wooden Darning Egg, A," A26
Woodress, James, B44, B55, B82, B148, B159, B168, B200, B248, B283, B391
Woodward, Kenneth, B1120
Woolf, Cecil, A714
"Words, Some Odd, of Updike, The," B1460
"Wordsmith's 'Careful Life', A," B1343
"Working Outdoors in Winter," A626
"Working Space," A246
"World as Scandal, The: Updike's *A Month of Sundays*," B955
"World of Fairfield Porter, The: Nice People, Nice Places, Pleasantly Redolent of Affection and Money," A811
"World of Updike, The," B32
World Treasury of Science Fiction, The, review of, A1125
"Worldly Monk's Song," A555
"Worlds and Worlds," A1029
"Worth Noting," B729
"Wrestling to Be Born," A1094
Wright, Andrea, B662
Wright, Barbara, B1607, B1620
Wright, Derek, B566
Wright, Ona, B1599
Wright, Stuart, B342
"Wright on Writing," A961
"Writer John Updike Remembers the Little Things, Glosses Over Honors," B1344
"Writer Lectures, The," A852
"Writer-Consciousness," A1122
"Writers and Artists," A246
"Writers 'Are Really Servants of Reality'," B1227
"Writers as Progenitors and Offspring," A838
Writers at Work, self-portrait in, A1297
Writers at Work: The Paris Review Interviews, Seventh Series, "Introduction" to, A833, A846
"Writer's Blocks, A," A859
"Writers I Have Met," A724
"Writers in Conversation," A1234
"Writers on Art," B1445
"Writers on Art—Reported Sightings: Art Chronicles," B1317
"Writer's Writer," B249
Writing Life, The, review of, A1122
Writing the Absence of the Father: Undoing Oedipal Structures in the Contemporary American Novel, B1144
Wyatt, Bryant, B49, B1580

Wyndham, Francis, B835

Xala, review of, A985
Xianliang, Zhang, A1115
Xingu: The Indians, Their Myths, review of, A956

"Yahweh Over Dionysus, in Disputed Decision," A1057
"Yankee Saints and Sinners," B939
Yanofsky, Joe, B415
Yates, Norris W., B31
"*Yea Sayings* and *Pastoral and Anti-Pastoral* in the Fiction of John Updike," B122
"Year in Books, The," B1123, B1124
"Year in Fiction, The: 1988," B1294
Year of Change: More About The New Yorker and Me, B381
"Year's Best Buys in Paperbacks, The," B847
Years of American Illustration, review of, A997
Yevtushenko, Yvgeny/Yevgeny (Evtushenko, Evgenil), A1280-A1283
Yglesias, José, B719
Yoe, Craig, A882
Yost, Nicholas, B550
"You Don't Give No Lip to Big John," B457
You Must Remember This, review of, A1102
"'You Really Gets,'" B777
"You Who Swim," A531
Young, Diana, A291
"Young Matrons Dancing," A509
"Your Lover Just Called," A307
"Your Lover Just Called: A Playlet," A274
Your Lover Just Called: Stories of Joan and Richard Maple, A154, A164
Yourcenar, Marguerite, A1150
"Youth's Progress," A26, A452
Yucatan, review of, A1138

Zaffiro, Vincent, B68
"Zeal of a Man of Letters, The," B1168
Zervanos, James T., B1722
Zhorunuya, S., B641
Zhou, Guozhen, B1081
Ziegfeld, Richard, B279
Zimmerman, Hans-Joachim, B620
Zinsser, John, B1546
Zissa, Robert F., B174
Zuckerman, Jerome, B61
Zulaf, Sandor, B101, B116
"Zulus Live in Land without a Square," A26
Zwick, Edward, A487
Zylstra, S. A., B133

About the Compiler

JACK DE BELLIS is professor of English at Lehigh University, where he specializes in American Literature. In addition to his book *Sidney Lanier* (1969), his articles have appeared in *Modern Fiction Studies, Film/Literature Quarterly,* and *The Journal of Modern Literature.* He also wrote the entry on Henry Timrod for *Fifty Southern Writers Before 1900: A Bio-Bibliographical Sourcebook* (Greenwood Press, 1987).

ISBN 0-313-28861-5

HARDCOVER BAR CODE